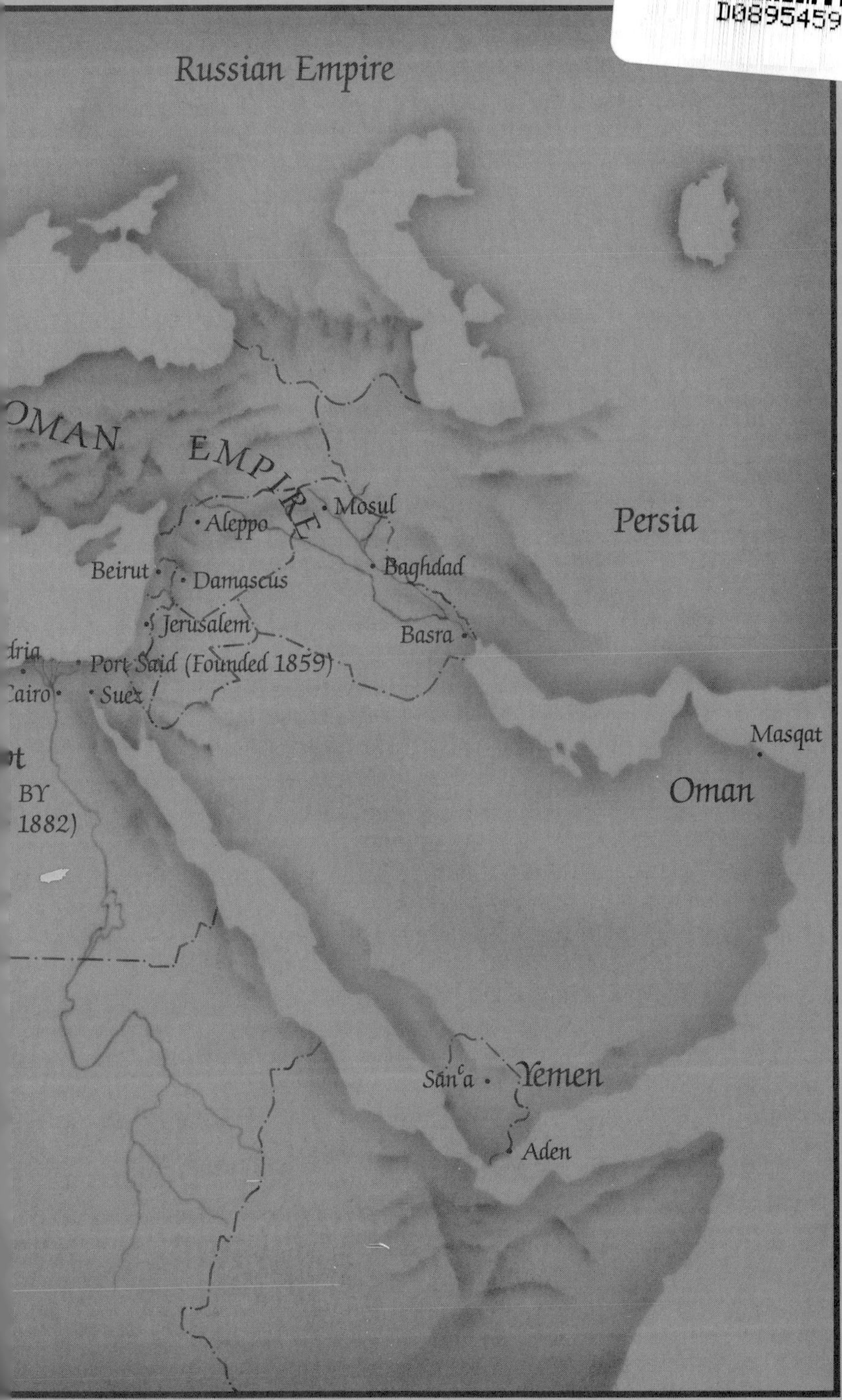
Russian Empire
OMAN
EMPIRE
Mosul
Aleppo
Persia
Beirut
Damascus
Baghdad
Jerusalem
Basra
dria
Port Said (Founded 1859)
Cairo
Suez
Masqat
ot
BY
1882)
Oman
San'a
Yemen
Aden

THE JEWS OF ARAB LANDS IN MODERN TIMES

THE JEWS OF ARAB LANDS IN MODERN TIMES

NORMAN A. STILLMAN

Philadelphia • New York *5751–1991*

THE JEWISH PUBLICATION SOCIETY

Manufactured in the United States of America

Library of Congress Cataloging-in-Publication Data
Stillman, Norman A., 1945–
The Jews of Arab lands in modern times / Norman A. Stillman.
p. cm.
Includes bibliographical references (p.) and index.
ISBN 0–8276–0370–3
1. Jews—Arab countries—History—19th century—Sources.
2. Jews—Arab countries—History—20th century—Sources.
3. Zionism—Arab countries—History—Sources.
4. Antisemitism—Arab countries—History—Sources.
5. Arab countries—Ethnic relations—Sources.
6. Jewish–Arab relations—Sources. I. Title.
DS135.A68S75 1991 305.8'92'40174927—dc20 90-5341
CIP

Designed by Adrianne Onderdonk Dudden
Endpaper maps by Larry Ward

The author wishes to thank the following publishers and/or authors for permission to quote from the sources listed:

By permission of the University of Texas Press and Professor Renzo de Felice, for *Jews in an Arab Land: Libya, 1835–1970,* by Renzo de Felice, translated by Judith Roumani © 1985; Mr. Naim Kattan for *Farewell Babylon,* by Naim Kattan ©, translated by Sheila Fischman; Eyre Methuen Ltd. for *Baghdad: The City of Peace,* by Richard Coke (Thorton Butterworth Publishers, 1927); Simon & Schuster for *Behind the Silken Curtain: A Personal Account of Anglo-American Diplomacy in Palestine and the Middle East,* by Bartley C. Crum © 1947.

To my beloved parents

MELVIN STILLMAN

of blessed memory

and

JOYCE GIDDEN STILLMAN

who not only gave me life,

but taught me how to live it

CONTENTS

LIST OF ILLUSTRATIONS

Rabbi Raphael Aaron Ben Simeon, the modernist *Ḥākhām Bāshī* of Cairo (1891–1920) and a leading Sephardi legal authority

Interior of the Eliyahu Hannabi Synagogue, looking toward the ark. The building was inaugurated in 1850 and enlarged considerably in 1865

Gallicized Jewish children in front of the synagogue in Orléansville, Algeria, late nineteenth or early twentieth century

Alumnae of the Alliance Girls' School in Tetouan, Morocco, ca. 1925

Jewish junk dealers, Morocco, early Protectorate period

Jewish seller of rolls, Morocco, early Protectorate period

following p. 420

Jacob Cattaoui Bey (1801–1883), patriarch of a dynasty of Egyptian Jewish bankers, courtiers, and communal leaders

Joseph Aslan Cattaoui Pasha (1861–1942), member of the committee that drafted Egypt's first constitution, minister of finance in 1924, and minister of communications in 1925

Sir Sassoon Heskel (1860–1932), first finance minister of Iraq and the only Jew ever to serve in an Iraqi cabinet

Jewish banker and communal leader, Halfallah Nahum, conversing with Mussolini during the latter's visit to Tripoli in 1926

Jews of the Ḥāra of Tripoli, lined up to give Mussolini a festive welcome (1937)

Portrait of an Egyptian Jewish girl, dressed for a modernist religious initiation ceremony (confirmation), Alexandria, 1927

Jewish girls' basketball team, Cairo, 1930s or 1940s

Partisans for Elie Samama, candidate for president of the Jewish Communal Council of Tunis, rally outside the polling station in the courtyard of the Alliance Israélite Universelle School, 1934

One of the buildings of the Jewish Community School of Alexandria, twentieth century

Letter to Theodor Herzl, from the Ahavat Ṣiyyon Society of Safi, Morocco, 1903

Rabbi Jacob Boccara of Tunis (standing center), with the North African delegates to the Tenth Zionist Congress, Basel, Switzerland, August 1911

Rabbi Joseph Brami, Zionist and modernist educator, with his Hebrew students, La Goulette, Tunisia, 1922

Albert Mosseri (1867–1933), founder of the pro-Zionist Egyptian Jewish newspaper, *Israël*

Front page of the Iraqi Jewish newspaper, *al-Miṣbāḥ* (June 15, 1926)

Members of Snunit, the senior girls group of Hashomer Hatzair, Tunis, 1931

The first senior group of the socialist Zionist Hashomer Hatzair, Tunis, 1930

following p. 510

Allied Jewish servicemen at an Oneg Shabbat sponsored by the Jewish community of Cairo during World War II

The Chief Rabbi of Tripoli, bestowing a blessing upon Brigadier Lush, the first British military governor, and the officers of the Palestinian Brigade in the main synagogue, Tripoli, 1943

Welcoming the British forces at the entrance of the Ḥara of Tripoli, 1943

José Aboulker, leader of the uprising that paralyzed communications and captured strategic points in Algiers on the eve of the Allied landing, November 7–8, 1942

Members of the Resistance group led by José Aboulker receiving the Cross of Liberation in Algiers, 1947

Libyan Jewish survivors of Nazi concentration camps in Europe, on their way home via Italy

Maḥane Ge'ūla (Camp Redemption) for Yemenite Jews on their way to Israel; Hashid, Aden Protectorate, late 1940s

Yemenite Jews on their way to Israel in Operation "On Wings of Eagles," 1948–1949

Wealthy Jewish merchant Shafīq ᶜAdes, accused of having supplied scrap metal to Israel, being led to his trial in Basra, Iraq, summer 1948

Crowds of Jews outside the Masᶜuda Shem Tov Synagogue in Baghdad, waiting to register for ᶜaliya to Israel, 1950

General Muḥammad Najīb, just two months after coming to power, making an unprecedented appearance for an Egyptian head of state at Cairo's Great Synagogue on Yom Kippur, 1952

PREFACE

Barely a generation ago, there were over 800,000 Jews living in the Arab world. Some of the Jewish communities in this region were large and important. Many had their roots in antiquity, going back before the great Islamic conquests of the seventh century, before most of what today are called the Arab countries had any Arabs. Today only a small, vestigial, and for the most part moribund remnant of perhaps 16,000 souls is left behind. There is no reason to expect this demographic trend to go anywhere but down.

The near extinction of Arabic-speaking Jewry was not due to annihilation as with Europe's Jews in the Holocaust—although the Jews of a number of Arab countries did not emerge totally unscathed either physically or psychologically from Nazi and Fascist anti-Semitism during World War II—but rather, it was due to mass migration. This was one of those migratory movements that have been so important in Jewish history overall, and particularly in the past one hundred years. The departure of the overwhelming majority of Jews from their age-old Arab homelands was also part and parcel of a wider phenomenon of massive shifts or transfers of populations that followed in the wake of major political and social upheavals in the twentieth century.

The reasons for the departure of Jews from the Arab lands, as with all migrations, were a result of forces of both push and pull. These forces were set in motion by political, religious, and socioeconomic factors. The great majority of Arabic-speaking Jewry emigrated to the new state of Israel between 1949 and 1967. They and their children now make up over half the population there and are now beginning to put their own distinctive imprint on Israel's evolving society. After Israel, the most important center for Middle Eastern and North African Jewish immigration is France. Half of Maghrebi Jews and nearly all of Algerian Jews migrated there. They too now constitute a majority among the Jews in their adopted home and have totally transformed and revived French Jewry. Considerable concentrations of Jews from Arab and Islamic countries are also to be found in Canada, the United States, Mexico, Venezuela, and Brazil.

Many historians and writers have seen the founding of the State of Israel and the Arab-Israeli conflict as the primary forces of push and pull that impelled the Jews to leave the Arab countries. This, however, is a gross oversimplification. As it shall become clear throughout the course of this book, the establishment of a Jewish homeland in Palestine and the Arab-Israeli conflict were only the final manifestations of a complex variety of processes, some subtle and some not, that were at work transforming both the Jews of the Middle East and North Africa (along with Jews elsewhere) and their Arab neighbors over the past century and a half. These processes that led to the dissolution of most of the Jewish communities in the Arab world can conveniently be subsumed under the generalized rubric of modernization. Modernization and the far-reaching transformations associated with it comprise what has been dubbed "the master theme of contemporary social science."[1]

It is a popular intellectual exercise to debate just when did modern times begin within one particular society or another, or in this part of the world or that. While I am fully aware how arbitrary and artificially neat are most historical lines of demarcation, I have chosen to begin this account of Arabic-speaking Jewry's encounter with modernity at the beginning of the nineteenth century when Europe began its inexorable intrusion into the Middle East and North Africa which were the very heartlands of the traditional Islamic world. The increasing European economic, cultural, and political encroachments upon the Muslim society were generally welcomed by the native Jewish and Christian minorities, whereas they were deeply resented and frequently opposed by most of the majority population. For many Jews and Christians of the Islamic world, modern education with its strong component of western languages and cultural values, ties to the ascendant European economic interests in their countries, and ultimately a strong identification with European colonial or imperial regimes meant a way out of, or at least an improvement of their own traditional subordinate status.

[1] See Calvin Goldscheider and Alan S. Zuckerman, *The Transformation of the Jews* (Chicago and London, 1984), p. 4.

In addition to more general Western influences, the Jews of Arab lands also experienced a renewed sense of identification and solidarity with the wider Jewish world through the educational and welfare efforts of organizations like the Alliance Israélite Universelle, through contacts with the Zionist movement, and through a growing awareness from both the Jewish and the general press of currents affecting their coreligionists abroad. The rise of Arab nationalism with its strong Pan-Arab and Pan-Islamic overtones and a widespread disillusionment with Europe caused by anti-Semitism and the betrayal of the minorities by the colonial powers only served to heighten Jewish self-awareness in the twentieth century.

The rapid collapse and dissolution of the Jewish communities of the Arab world were the denouement of the Jews' and the Arabs' encounter with modern times. It was an encounter that had been going on for more than a century and a half when the end came. The mass exodus of most Jews from the Arab countries also marked the end of a history that extended back more than a millennium. This previous thirteen-hundred-year history was the subject of my earlier book *The Jews of Arab Lands: A History and Source Book*.[2]

This book takes up the history of the Jews of Arab lands where its predecessor left off. Like the earlier book, it consists of two parts. Part One consists of seven chapters that offer a survey of Jewish social history in the Arab world from the beginning of the nineteenth century until 1967, by which time most Jews had left the Arab world. Part Two is a mirror image of the first. It is divided into seven sections corresponding to the chapters in Part One. It contains a rich and varied collection of documents that provide detailed flesh tones to the general portrait presented in the first part of the book. These sources represent both published and unpublished materials translated from Arabic, Hebrew, and European languages. Most of the translations are my own, although in several cases I have included the translations of others. There is also material from English-language sources. In these documents we hear the voices of Jews, Arabs, and outside observers, and the reader is given the opportunity see and to interpret for himself the raw materials from which history is written. In order to assist the reader, most of the sources have been well annotated with footnotes. The subject matter and historical context of the source material are referred to throughout the text and footnotes in Part One which represents, of course, my own interpretative vision.

[2] (Philadelphia, 1979).

This book covers a far shorter span of time than its predecessor, and yet it is longer. I must also confess that I found it more difficult to write, and although I had already begun the research for it while completing the first book, nearly a decade would pass before I would finish the second. First, there was much more material to contend with. (After all, there were no newspapers in premodern times, and considerably less documentary sources have survived from past centuries.) Second, the events of the recent history of the Jews of Arab lands arouse considerable passion and are frequently distorted by partisans of one side or the other of the Middle East conflict. I therefore felt an even greater need than usual for careful and dispassionate reflections in trying to form my own interpretations.

No less than its predecessor, this book could not have been researched or written without the generous support, abundant good will, and continuous encouragement of numerous individuals and institutions. It is my pleasant duty to acknowledge their assistance.

Initial funding for research during my sabbatical in 1982–1983 came from the Anti-Defamation League of B'nai B'rith, the International Sephardic Education Foundation, and the Shiloah Institute of Tel Aviv University. A research assistant for a survey of the Arabic press was provided me through a grant from the Bronfman Foundation. Grants from the SUNY Foundation, the Memorial Foundation for Jewish culture, and the American Philosophical Society all facilitated my research in archives and libraries in the United States and abroad over the years.

A grant from the Eugene R. Warner Fund of the Anti-Defamation League of B'nai B'rith and another from the Lucius N. Littauer Foundation, supplemented by a Title F Leave from my university, allowed me to dedicate eight months to writing in 1987. Another sabbatical the following year gave me the opportunity to complete the final chapters and revisions.

Every historian is greatly dependent upon archives and libraries. Many anonymous members of the staffs of the Public Records Office in London and the National Archives in Washington, D.C., were extremely helpful to me. While working at the Public Records office, I was assisted by my wife and colleague, Yedida. Our colleague Dr. David Patterson of the Center for Jewish Studies at Oxford, our friend Mr. Adam Raphael, and the Reverend and Mrs. Samuel Venitt were all helpful during our stay in Britain.

My work at the Central Zionist Archives in Jerusalem was facilitated by its director, Dr. Heiman. I am particularly indebted for the guidance I received there from Mr. Yoram Majorek, who is a veritable walking catalogue. Dr. David Harman of the Joint Distribution Committee in Jerusalem granted me free access to the JDC Archives as well as generous photocopying privileges. My colleague Dr. Irene Grumach-Shirun stood surety for me with the Jewish National and University Library while I worked there. Mr. Robert Attal, the Librarian of the Ben-Zvi Institute, was always most helpful to me while working there.

In Paris, I was shown every courtesy by M. Georges Weill, the Chief Curator and Archivist, and by Mme. Yvonne Levyne, the Librarian, of the Archives et Bibliothèque de l'Alliance Israélite Universelle. I also benefitted from various forms of assistance that were rendered me by Professor Gérard Nahon of the CNRS, Professor Haïm Zafrani of the Université de Paris—Vincennes, Mr. Steven Uran of the CNRS, and my good friends the Belhassen family.

Mrs. Fannie Zelcer of the American Jewish Archives, Cincinnati, kindly found and expedited my receipt of important unpublished materials. The adjoining Klau Library permitted me to borrow rare items from its rich collection for lengthy periods of time.

Ms. Carol Clemente and the staff of the State University of New York at Binghamton Interlibrary Loan Office cheerfully provided me with their invaluable services, processing countless requests for books, periodicals, and microfilmed documents from all over the world.

Thanks are also due to the many colleagues who kindly obtained books, photocopies of periodicals and documents, and other materials to which I did not have immediate access. These include Professors Aron Rodrigue, Michel Abitbol, Steven Katz, Gary Rendsburg, Bernard Lewis, Don Peretz, Drs. Zvi Yehuda, Itshaq Avrahami, Michael Laskier, Richard Ayoun, Jan Gunneweg, Ms. Lois Gottesman, Ms. Hadassah Wartman, and Mr. Jonathan Benros.

Several of my graduate students provided various forms of assistance. In particular, I would like to single out Mrs. Susan O. Savitch, who proofread an earlier draft and helped to prepare the index of archival sources.

I benefited enormously from discussions or correspondence with many colleagues who helped me give form to my thoughts, made helpful suggestions, and responded to my queries. Among them are many of my colleagues already acknowledge above. In addition, I wish to thank Professor Sasson Somekh, Professor Joseph Chetrit, Dr. Menahem Ben-Sasson, Dr. Avraham Haim, Dr. Daniel Schroeter, and Mr. Zvi Zohar. As always, my colleague at Binghamton, Professor Samuel Morell, was a most knowledgeable and ready source of rabbinic references.

I am indebted to a number of individuals for their good offices. Mr. Herbert Neuman was my first liaison with the Littauer Foundation. Professor Ittamar Rabinovitch acted in a similar capacity with the Bronfman Foundation. Dr. Jack Kantrowitz paved the way for my smooth reception at the Alliance Israélite Archives. Professor Shimon Shamir arranged for my being a guest of the Israel Research Center in Egypt. The late Theodore Freedman took a continual interest in my research both for this book and its predecessor, and it was he who helped to obtain the grant from the Warner Fund.

Mrs. Phyllis Antos, Mrs. Lois Orzel, and Mrs. Elizabeth Regan of the University Manuscript Center of the State University of New York at Binghamton worked tirelessly and with unceasing good nature to put my manuscript onto diskettes and to take it through the numerous revisions.

It is with particular pleasure that I take this opportunity to acknowledge the longstanding support of the Jewish Publication Society. Our association on this project goes back to 1976, at which time already two books on the Jews of Arab lands were envisaged—one for the medieval and early modern periods and one for modern times.

As always, I conclude my acknowledgments with yet another inadequate attempt to thank my beloved wife and colleague, Yedida, who has—I am convinced—taught me more about the culture, language, and spirit of the Jews of Arab lands than has anyone or anything else. I believe that Rabbi Akiba's words to his students about his own wife recorded in the Talmud (Ketubbot 63a) apply most aptly to my case—"mine and yours are hers."

Norman A. Stillman
Binghamton, N.Y.

NOTE ON STYLE

Foreign terms are always explained or translated at their first occurrence and are italicized throughout. The transcription of Arabic words follows the system employed by the *Encyclopaedia of Islam,* new edition, with the usual exception made by most English-speaking Arabists of *j* for *dj* and *q* for *ḳ*. Place names are given in their familiar English forms without diacritical marks.

Hebrew words have been transcribed according to a simple, standardized system that is on the whole compatible with the Arabic transcription. Common biblical Hebrew names are rendered in the accepted English forms.

Total consistency seemed impossible in the case of Ottoman Turkish words and names. In general, purely Turkish words appear in the orthography adopted by the Republic of Turkey, whereas proper names and some common terms appear in their Arabic form. There is also some inconsistency in the rendering of Jewish family names of Arabic derivation. In those cases where the family had adopted a standard Europeanized form for rendering the name in Latin characters, I have followed that spelling (for example, Cattaoui for Qaṭṭāwī).

Most of the documents in Part Two are unabridged. In those instances where minor deletions have been made, I have indicated the ellipses with the usual system of points. A full line of points indicates a major deletion; however, deletions at the end of paragraphs have not been indicated. Parentheses are usually used for interpolations, which I have made for clarification of the reading, although they may also indicate parenthetical remarks in the texts themselves. In several instances, I have made slight revisions in the punctuation and spelling within a document in order to bring these into line with standard usage. Most of the archaisms of spelling, punctuation, and style have been left untouched so as not to detract from the period flavor.

The few abbreviations used in the text are mostly self-evident. For readers not familiar with Hebrew or Arabic, the abbreviation "b." between two personal names indicates "son of" or "daughter of." The unabbreviated forms (Ibn, Ben, Bint, Bat) are used when the first name is omitted or where it has become part of a modern family name.

N. A. S.

PART ONE

HISTORY

1

THE NINETEENTH CENTURY AND THE IMPACT OF THE WEST

On July 30, 1798, Napoleon Bonaparte landed on the coast of Egypt at the head of more than 30,000 French troops. Suddenly and rudely, the physical penetration of the Middle East by Europe had begun. The path to direct European intervention had been paved by two centuries of expanding European commercial interests that extended from the Levant to India and by concessions of extraterritorial rights for foreign nationals and their protégés in the Ottoman Empire under agreements known as capitulations (from their arrangement into *capitula*, or headings). The French attempt to extend the conquest into Palestine and Syria in 1799 failed, in no small measure because of the intervention of another European power, France's rival, England. The occupation of Egypt by Napoleon's Armée d'Orient lasted only three years and had little immediate effect on the existing social framework of the country or of the larger region. Brief though it may have been, however, the occupation heralded increasing European political, economic, and ultimately social and cultural influence during the nineteenth century. The impact of European hegemony was to prove one of the prime causes for change in Middle Eastern society, which was in a state of general stagnation and decay at the time of the French invasion. The effects of this hegemony were profound—indeed overwhelming—and their consequences are still being felt today.

For all intents and purposes, the impact of an ascendant Europe upon the Middle East and North Africa, with all of its ramifications, is synonymous with the process that commands so much attention in contemporary social scientific literature and theory—modernization. All the peoples in the Muslim world would be affected and transformed by it, and the non-Muslim minorities would be among the first, although this certainly must not have seemed obvious when French rule in Egypt ended in 1801.

At the time of the French invasion, the Arab world was a traditional Muslim society. Morocco in the west was under the sway of the Sharifan sultan. All the lands from Algeria to the borders of Persia were under the actual or nominal rule of the Ottoman sultan. These were Islamic states. Islam was not merely the dominant faith in these lands; it constituted their legal and social framework. The native non-Muslim minorities (Jews only in Morocco, Algeria, Tunisia, Libya, and Yemen and both Christians and Jews almost everywhere else) were *ahl al-dhimma* (People of the Pact), or protégés of the Islamic community. As dhimmīs, the non-Muslim subjects of the two sultans and of the various semiautonomous viceroys and regional rulers enjoyed a status that, on the one hand, combined a position of defined inferiority with certain legal and social disabilities and, on the other hand, guaranteed their lives, their property, and the right to worship as they chose (within certain discreet limits).

The traditional Islamic social framework permitted non-Muslims a considerable measure of economic opportunity. Most important, it accorded a great deal of internal communal autonomy to the various religious minorities. The system, which had developed over twelve centuries of Islamic rule, was by no means uniform throughout time and place. Many local variations had always existed with regard to both details and strictness of application. During periods of economic, social, and political stability, such as the Islamic High Middle Ages (ca. 800–1250) and the Ottoman revival of the sixteenth century, the system tended to be more liberal. By the same token, in times of stress or decadence, the harsher and more restrictive elements of the system came to the fore.[1] The seventeenth, eighteenth, and early nineteenth centuries were such times.

As the nineteenth century began, the vast majority of Middle Eastern and North African Jewry, like the vast majority of the general populace, was poor.[2] In addition to their poverty, however, the Jews had to bear the burden of social isolation, inferiority, and general opprobrium. Over the preceding four centuries, they had become

[1] For a survey of Jewish life in the Arab world from the beginning of the Islamic Middle Ages to the dawn of modern times, see Norman A. Stillman, *The Jews of Arab Lands: A History and Source Book* (Philadelphia, 1979), pp. 22–107.

[2] This remained true well into the twentieth century. As late as 1910, 60 percent of the Jews of Baghdad were estimated as poor and another 5 percent as "beggars." See the memorandum from the Baghdad British Consulate in Elie Kedourie, *Arabic Political Memoirs and Other Studies* (London, 1974), p. 267.

increasingly confined into overcrowded ghettolike quarters, which were called by a variety of names throughout the Muslim world (for example, *Mellāḥ, Ḥārat al-Yahūd,* and *Maḥallat al-Yahūd*). European travelers of the eighteenth and nineteenth centuries were unanimous in their reports of the overall debasement of the Jews living in the Islamic lands. The Italian Jewish poet and traveler Samuel Romanelli, who spent four years among his coreligionists in Morocco in the late eighteenth century, described them as "oppressed, miserable creatures, having neither the mouth to answer an Arab, nor the cheek to raise their head."[3] And the Englishman Edward William Lane, who lived in Cairo during the 1820s and 1830s and was a keen and sympathetic observer of native life, depicted the Jews of Egypt as being "held in the utmost contempt and abhorrence by Muslims in general."[4] He also noted that the condition of the Jewish lower class was wretched and that many in this group depended on alms.[5]

Not all Jews lived in poverty, of course. There had always been a very small prosperous minority whose wealth and connections frequently—but by no means always—protected it from the more inconvenient implications of its dhimmī-hood. These non-Muslims predominated in some of those professions considered reprehensible by the Islamic faith, such as goldsmithing and silversmithing, money lending, tax farming, and collecting customs duties.

Some of the dhimmī elite also acted as intermediaries between European commercial interests and the local population. Since the sixteenth century, European trading companies had conducted much of their business in the Levant with the help of local Christian and Jewish agents. In Morocco and Algeria, the so-called court Jews were in fact primarily business agents of the sultan and the dey with European connections.[6] This state of affairs was perfectly in keeping

[3] Samuel Romanelli, *Travail in an Arab Land,* ed. and trans. Yedida K. Stillman and Norman A. Stillman (Tuscaloosa and London, 1989), p. 47.

[4] Edward William Lane, *The Manners and Customs of the Modern Egyptians* (reprint ed., London, 1908), p. 267. The passage is also reprinted in Stillman, *Jews of Arab Lands,* p. 325.

[5] Lane, *Modern Egyptians,* p. 561; and Stillman, *Jews of Arab Lands,* p. 327.

[6] The court Jews described by Romanelli, *Travail in an Arab Land,* pp. 78–86 and passim, were all merchants of this sort. Some Jews even bore the title "the Sultan's merchants" (*tujjār al-sulṭān*). See Michel Abitbol, "Une élite économique juive au Maroc pré-colonial: les tujjar al-sultan," in *Judaïsme d'Afrique du Nord aux XIXe–XXe siècles,* ed. M. Abitbol (Jerusalem, 1980), pp. 25–34 [Heb.]; and Norman A. Stillman and Yedida K. Stillman, "The Jewish Courtier Class in Eighteenth-Century Morocco as Seen Through the Eyes of Samuel Romanelli," in *The Islamic World, Classical and Medieval, Ottoman and Modern—Essays in Honor of Bernard*

with current Islamic sentiment that dhimmīs were eminently suited to the disagreeable though necessary task of having extended intercourse with foreign infidels. Furthermore, dhimmīs were more likely to know and more willing to learn foreign languages at this time than were Muslims. The Sephardi upper class from Tangier to Istanbul knew Spanish. The Grana, or Livornese Jews of Tunisia and Algeria, spoke Italian. Iraqi Jewish merchants who did business in India knew English. The European consulates generally employed non-Muslim dragomans and often non-Muslim personal servants as well. For example, in a typical list from the early nineteenth century of native employees in the service of the British consulate in Baghdad and of the British firms there, of forty-six employees, there were twenty-eight Christians, fourteen Jews, and only four Muslims.[7] Throughout the Maghreb, native consular agents, vice consuls, and honorary consuls were invariably Jews.[8] In Aleppo, a family of Livornese Jews, the Picciottos, had almost a monopoly on consular offices from the end of the eighteenth and through much of the nineteenth century.[9] Thus, even as the century of European interest in the Islamic world was beginning, there were already significant ties with at least some elements of the native Christian and Jewish communities.

In addition to these commercial ties, a strong feeling of sympathy was held among nineteenth-century Europeans, particularly for the lot of Christians, but also for that of the Jews, who lived under "the terrible Turk." The European powers openly espoused the cause of the non-Muslim subjects of the Ottoman Empire during the nineteenth century. Their sincere moral sentiments complemented their imperialistic designs; indeed, they were inextricably joined. From the European point of view, religious tolerance in the Islamic world was

---

Lewis, ed. C. E Bosworth et al. (Princeton, N.J., 1988), pp. 845–54. For Algerian examples, see Morton Rosenstock, "The House of Bacri and Busnach; A Chapter from Algeria's Commercial History," *JSS* 14 (1952): 343–64.

[7] See Public Records Office (London) FO 195/204, f. 223a–b, published in Stillman, *Jews of Arab Lands,* pp. 375–76.

[8] As of 1770, all consular representatives of the European nations were Jews. See Romanelli, *Travail in an Arab Land,* pp. 19 and 157, n. 5. See also Isaac D. Abbou, *Musulmans andalous et judéo-espagnols* (Casablanca, 1953), pp. 410–11. For a Jew as Austrian consular representative in Tripoli, Libya, see Stillman, *Jews of Arab Lands,* p. 409.

[9] See Walter P. Zenner, "Jews in Late Ottoman Syria: External Relations," in *Jewish Societies in the Middle East: Community, Culture, and Authority,* ed. Shlomo Deshen and Walter P. Zenner (Lanham, Maryland, 1982), pp. 163–64; and also Hayyim J. Cohen, "Picciotto," *EJ* 13:498.

one of the necessary first steps toward progress in the region.[10] The fact that at first the European powers were interested almost exclusively in the lot of the local Christians is immaterial as far as the Jews were concerned. Their legal status as dhimmīs was one and the same. Any amelioration, therefore, in the legal position of Ottoman Christians was shared by Jews of the empire as well.

Even before the nineteenth century, certain European powers had taken a special interest in certain religious groups. For centuries France had been the recognized protector of Latin Christians in the Levant. Russia obtained a similar status vis-à-vis the Eastern Orthodox churches as of 1774. No country, however, paid much notice to the Jews at first. This, of course, was natural. Prior to the French Revolution, no European nation had yet extended full civil emancipation to its own Jews, much less cared about the lot of Jews in faraway and exotic lands.

During his brief and disastrous campaign in Palestine, Napoleon had issued a proclamation on April 19, 1799, in which he invited all the Jews of Asia and Africa—under his banner, naturally—to reestablish their ancestral commonwealth in Jerusalem.[11] Napoleon cared nothing for the Jews. The proclamation was merely a propaganda gesture with no results in any case. But it was the first instance in which a European power took some sort of official action on behalf of Middle Eastern Jewry.

In the 1830s, England began to take a protective interest in the welfare of Ottoman Jews as a group and particularly the Jews of Palestine. In 1838, the first British consulate was established in Jerusalem. In his charge to William Young, the newly appointed consul, Foreign Secretary Lord Palmerston wrote: "[I]t will be a part of your duty as British Vice Consul at Jerusalem to afford Protection to the Jews generally."[12]

This curious concern for Jewish welfare was due in part to English liberal sentiments and in part to the fact that England was a

[10] For an interesting and succinct analysis of European thinking on this subject, see Norman Daniel, *Islam Europe and Empire* (Edinburgh, 1966), pp. 338–47.

[11] Concerning this curious and little-known episode, see Barbara W. Tuchman, *Bible and Sword: England and Palestine from the Bronze Age to Balfour* (New York, 1956), pp. 162–67.

[12] PRO (London) FO 78/368 (No. 2), dated January 31, 1839, published in Albert M. Hyamson, *The British Consulate in Jerusalem in Relation to the Jews of Palestine, 1838–1914,* vol. 1 (London, 1939), p. 2, No. 2. The memo is actually from John Bidwell, Palmerston's private secretary, but was drafted upon the latter's instructions and initialed by him.

latecomer to the religious protection game, and most of the other religious minorities already had protectors. (Protestantism was a recent arrival in the Middle East, and the number of native Protestants was small.) This solicitude for the Jews must also be understood in the light of deep evangelical, messianic convictions that were current in Great Britain at this time. The London Society for Promoting Christianity among the Jews was turning to the Middle East at this time, and Palmerston's stepson-in-law and confidant in spiritual matters, Lord Ashley (later Lord Shaftesbury), was a devoted supporter of the society.[13]

Jews and cases pertaining to Jewish welfare appear frequently in the British consular correspondence from Palestine, Syria, and Iraq from the 1840s on.

The first formal move toward improving the status of non-Muslim subjects of the Ottoman Empire occurred in 1839, not through European intervention, but rather through European inspiration in the initiative of the reform-minded Turkish foreign minister Muṣṭafā Rashīd Pasha. Imbued with European notions, Rashīd got the boy sultan ᶜAbd al-Majīd I to issue the Khaṭṭ-i Sharīf of Gülhane, an edict enumerating reforms that affected the individual subjects of the empire. In tones reminiscent of the French Declaration of the Rights of Man, the Khaṭṭ-i Sharīf, on paper at least, extended civil equality to non-Muslims.

Although the Khaṭṭ-i Sharīf sprang from sincere reformist circles within the Ottoman Empire, it was in part calculated to obtain European, and in particular British, support in a time of crisis when the sultan was threatened by the successes of his rebellious, modernist viceroy in Egypt, Muḥammad ᶜAlī.[14] It did in fact meet with the approval of Britain and the other powers that had been lobbying for reform through their ambassadors at the Sublime Porte. It also was to provide a good justification for their intervention in the decades that followed its promulgation, since it took some forty years to implement the reforms promised in the Khaṭṭ-i Sharīf in Turkey itself, whereas in the Arab provinces of the Ottoman Empire, whose governors were often corrupt, semifeudal lords, the decree was on the whole ignored.

The sultan had to reiterate and expand the promised reforms of the Khaṭṭ-i Sharīf in a new proclamation, the Khaṭṭ-i Humayun, on

[13] See Tuchman, *Bible and Sword,* pp. 113–33.

[14] Concerning the circumstances surrounding the edict's promulgation, see Roderic H. Davison, *Reform in the Ottoman Empire, 1856–1876* (Princeton, N.J., 1963),

February 18, 1856.[15] This new decree had been worked out by the ambassadors of England, France, and Austria, Turkey's allies against Russia in the Crimean War, which was just ending after three long years of belligerency. The Khaṭṭ-i Humayun was the Ottoman Empire's entrance ticket to the European Concert of Powers and was supposedly a guarantee of continuing Western recognition of Ottoman territorial integrity.

The Khaṭṭ-i Humayun went much further than the Khaṭṭ-i Sharīf in stipulating the rights of non-Muslims in the empire. The traditional poll tax, or *jizya,* which had symbolized the dhimmīs' humble, subject status since the earliest days of Islam, was now rescinded.[16] The fiscal change was, however, cosmetic in a sense, since the *jizya* was replaced with a new levy, the *bedel-i askeri,* or military substitution tax, which exempted non-Muslims from military service, for which they had become technically liable with the granting of civil equality. This destigmatized tax was entirely suitable to most non-Muslims, who had no desire to enter the army.[17]

Another symbolic mark of the non-Muslims' improved status was the banning from official use of derogatory terms, such as *raᶜāya* (grazing cattle), when referring to non-Muslims.[18]

The Khaṭṭ-i Humayun may have eliminated the decidedly inferior classification of dhimmī with its civil disabilities, but it did not erase the legal and social differentiation of Ottoman subjects according to ethnoreligious communities. Confessional particularism was maintained and codified by the recognition of the *millets,* or religious

---

pp. 38–39; and Bernard Lewis, *The Emergence of Modern Turkey* (London, 1968), pp. 106–7. The official French text of the Khaṭṭ-i Sharīf is given in E. Engelhardt, *La Turquie et le Tanzimat ou histoire des réformes dans l'Empire Ottoman depuis 1826 jusqu'à nos jours,* vol. 1 (Paris, 1882), pp. 257–61.

[15] Complete French text in ibid., pp. 263–70. An abridged English translation is given in Stillman, *Jews of Arab Lands,* pp. 357–60.

[16] Concerning the history and significance of the *jizya* as a fact of dhimmī life in the Islamic world, see Stillman, *Jews of Arab Lands,* p. 464, s.v. *"jizya."*

[17] For a few isolated instances of Jews serving in the army at this time, see Zenner, "Jews in Late Ottoman Syria: External Relations," p. 168; also Hayyim J. Cohen, *The Jews of the Middle East, 1860–1972* (New York and Jerusalem, 1973), p. 14. The highly arabicized Christians of Syria took exception to paying the new tax, seeing it as the *jizya* by another name. See Moshe Maᶜoz, *Ottoman Reform in Syria and Palestine, 1840–1861: The Impact of the Tanzimat on Politics and Society* (Oxford, 1968), p. 204.

[18] The term *raᶜāya* was not originally derogatory and referred to all subjects, both Muslim and non-Muslim, who were metaphorically the ruler's "flock." However, by the nineteenth century it had become the common appellation for the dhimmī populace.

communities, as fundamental corporate entities in society. The important difference now was that, from the standpoint of civil law, these entities were all equal. This difference did not sit well with traditional-minded Muslims, who lamented that Islam was no longer the ruling millet (*milleti hakime*).[19] But the traditionalists were not the policymakers, nor would they be again until very recently.

The improvement in the civil status of Ottoman Jews and Christians who were affected by the reform decrees did not entice those who had obtained foreign nationality or protection to give up these privileges. It was still far better for non-Muslims to be totally outside the Ottoman legal system. They paid lower tariffs and customs duties on their goods and avoided some taxes to which ordinary subjects of the sultan were liable.[20]

The most far-reaching consequences of the Khaṭṭ-i Humayun came not in the arena of civil rights, but in the very structure of the *millets*.[21] In keeping with the general reforming spirit in Ottoman ruling circles, there was a call for the constitutional reorganization of each *millet* with lay and religious governing bodies on a national and provincial basis. As so often was the case with Ottoman decrees, this reorganization was done at first in Istanbul and the territories closest to it and only later and more imperfectly in the Arab provinces.

For Ottoman Jews, religious leadership was vested in the *ḥākhām bāshī,* or chief rabbi. This office was created in late 1836 or early 1837, first for Istanbul and later for provincial capitals and other major towns. The first *ḥākhām bāshī* of Jerusalem, for example, was appointed in 1841, and the first *ḥākhām bāshī* of Baghdad received his *berat* (patent of office) eight years later. Originally, the *ḥākhām bāshī* in Istanbul was recognized by the Turkish authorities as both the chief religious authority (*rav ha-kōlēl*) and temporal chief (*shaykh zamānī*). However, the Organizational Regulations of the Rabbinate

[19] See, for example, the sentiments recorded by Jevdet Pasha in his *Tezakir* translated in Stillman, *Jews of Arab Lands,* p. 361.

[20] Charles Issawi, "The Transformation of the Economic Position of the *Millets* in the Nineteenth Century," in *Christians and Jews in the Ottoman Empire: The Functioning of a Plural Society,* vol. 1, ed. B. Braude and B. Lewis (New York and London, 1982), p. 273.

[21] The centralized *millet* system has been projected back to earlier Ottoman times by Hamilton A. R. Gibb and Harold Bowen, *Islamic Society and the West* (London, 1966), vol. 1, pt. 2, pp. 206–60, passim. This view has been persuasively revised by Benjamin Braude, "Foundation Myths of the *Millet* System," in *Christians and Jews in the Ottoman Empire: The Functioning of a Plural Society, Vol. I* (New York and London, 1982), pp. 69–88.

(*haham hane nizam namesi*), enacted in 1865, emphasized primarily the religious aspects of the post.[22] The appointment of chief rabbis bureaucratized the official rabbinate in the empire and frequently put into office reform-minded men who had close ties with the Turkish authorities. This sometimes led to friction with the local communities.[23]

The lay governance of individual Jewish communities was vested in a committee of notables (Ar. *majlis jismānī;* Heb. *vaᶜad gashmī*), which included both rabbis and laity, with the latter in the majority. In Baghdad, for example, nine laymen and three rabbis were on the committee as of 1879.[24] The wealthy elite dominated the committee. In some communities, such as Baghdad, Aleppo, and Cairo, many of the committee members belonged to families that held a near monopoly on positions of communal leadership for generations.[25] Although socially conservative and paternalistic insofar as their respective communities were concerned, this oligarchic elite contained men who had Western connections, who knew at least one European language, and who believed in some degree of modern education. A number of them, it shall be seen, acted as agents in the modernization of the Jewish communities.

Once again, it should be emphasized that the changes that occurred in the civil status and in the communal organization of Ottoman Jewry in the wake of the Khaṭṭ-i Sharīf and Khaṭṭ-i Humayun were merely an incidental part of a wider process of reform known as the Tanzimat, which was set in motion by internal and external forces that had little or no interest in the Jews per se. Furthermore, the changes that the reforms were supposed to bring about did not touch all Jewish communities equally. In those provinces where Ottoman control was nominal or tenuous the effects varied greatly. In Yemen,

[22] Concerning the development of the Ottoman chief rabbinate between 1836 and 1865, see H. Z. [J. W.] Hirschberg, "The Oriental Jewish Communities," in *Religion in the Middle East: Three Religions in Concord and Conflict,* vol. 1, ed. A. J. Arberry (Cambridge, 1969), pp. 196–202.

[23] See, for example, Zenner, "Jews in Late Ottoman Syria: External Relations," p. 167; and H. Z. [J. W.] Hirschberg, *A History of the Jews in North Africa,* vol. 2 (Leiden, 1981), p. 183. See also Part Two, pp. 231–235.

[24] Abraham Ben-Jacob, *A History of the Jews in Iraq: From the End of the Gaonic Period to the Present Time,* 2nd rev. ed. (Jerusalem, 1979), p. 268 [Heb.].

[25] Ibid.; also Walter P. Zenner, "Jews in Late Ottoman Syria: Community, Family and Religion," in *Jewish Societies in the Middle East: Community, Culture and Authority,* ed. Shlomo Deshen and Walter P. Zenner (Lanham, Maryland, 1982), p. 190; and Jacob M. Landau, *Jews in Nineteenth-Century Egypt* (New York and London, 1969), p. 53.

for example, where the Jews were the only element in the population not hostile to the Ottomans, there was only a partial application of the reforms, and that was only in cities under direct Ottoman control. A *ḥākhām bāshī* was appointed in Sanᶜa, and several degrading practices that were unique to Shiᶜite Yemen were rescinded. But most of the improvements were short-lived. The Turkish *wālī* (governor) simply did not wish to stir up the Muslim majority by ameliorating the lot of the Jews.[26] The province was too isolated physically and socially from outside influences for the implementation of reforms.

In Tunisia, which was an autonomous tributary state of the Ottoman Empire, the local ruler, Muḥammad Beg, promulgated his own reform decree, the ᶜAhd al-Amān (Covenant of Security) in September 1857, little more than a year after the Khaṭṭ-i Humayun was issued. The ᶜAhd al-Amān reflected the spirit of the Ottoman Tanzimat decrees. Like the Khaṭṭ-i Humayun, it was issued under pressure from the European powers. This pressure had reached considerable intensity in 1857, after the execution of a Tunisian Jew, Batto Sfez, for blasphemy against Islam.[27]

The ᶜAhd al-Amān was a *qānūn asāsī* (fundamental law) that in contemporary Ottoman usage expressed the European notion of "constitution." Unlike the Turkish Tanzimat decrees, it did not spell out a reorganization or restructuring of the social units in the state along constitutional lines. It proclaimed, among other things, the equality of Tunisian Jews and Muslims before the law and guaranteed their persons, property, and honor. It abolished corvée labor, which had been particularly burdensome to the Jews. It opened employment in the state bureaucracy to all Tunisians irrespective of their religion. Like the Khaṭṭ-i Humayun, it made all citizens liable to military service, but as in Turkey and its Levantine provinces, this was not carried out. In fact, in another clause, the Jews of Tunisia are still

[26] See Yehuda Nini, *Yemen and Zion: The Jews of Yemen, 1800–1914* (Jerusalem, 1982), pp. 69–90 [Heb.]; also Yosef Tobi, *The Jews of Yemen in the 19th Century* (Tel Aviv, 1976), pp. 72–103 [Heb.].

[27] The Batto Sfez affair, which became an international cause célèbre, is discussed at length by André Raymond, "La France, la Grande-Bretagne et le problème de la réforme à Tunis," in *Etudes Maghrébines: Mélanges Charles-André Julien* (Paris, 1964), pp. 137–64. See also David Cazès, *Essai sur l'histoire des Israélites de Tunisie: depuis les temps les plus reculés jusqu'à l'établissement du protectorat de la France en Tunisie* (Paris, 1889), pp. 150–51; Hirschberg, *The Jews in North Africa,* vol. 2, p. 150; André N. Chouraqui, *Between East and West: A History of the Jews of North Africa* (New York, 1973), pp. 159–60. Concerning other such cases and the whole problem of Jewish vulnerability to such accusations, see Stillman, *Jews of Arab Lands,* pp. 103–4, 385–87.

recognized as dhimmīs, which justified taxes being imposed on them as a group. Thus, the ᶜAhd al-Amān did not abolish discriminatory taxation, although it did promise a progressive lightening of the tax burden.[28]

With the exception of some random phrases on the natural rights of the individual, the language of the ᶜAhd al-Amān was more traditionally Islamic than that of the Khaṭṭ-i Humayun. "Politically conscious Tunisians"—to use L. Carl Brown's phrase—were wary of and resistant to the Ottoman reforms.[29] Although based on an outline drafted by the British and French consuls in Tunis, the text of the ᶜAhd al-Amān was formulated by the beg's secretary, Aḥmad b. Abī Ḍiyāf, the famous chronicler, in a way that was meant to be more acceptable to the country's Muslims. Despite this caution, the traditional Muslim majority considered the decree an attack on Islamic primacy imposed by hostile outside forces that aimed to undermine the very nature of its society.

Popular sentiment led to a rebellion in Tunisia, and in 1864, Muḥammad al-Ṣādiq Beg revoked the ᶜAhd al-Amān and the other reform decrees that had followed it. In spite of this, many outward improvements in the condition of Tunisian Jewry remained intact. The traditional discriminatory dress code (*ghiyār*) was not reimposed,[30] nor was corvée labor. Economic inequalities with regard to tariffs were not reinstituted.[31] The overall impact of the setback in civil rights was further alleviated by the ready availability of foreign protection for Tunisian Jews as the rival European powers—England, France, and Italy—vied with each other to come to the assistance of

[28] The full Arabic text of the ᶜAhd al-Amān is given in Aḥmad b. Abi 'l-Ḍiyāf, *Itḥāf Ahl al-Zamān bi-Akhbār Mulūk Tūnis wa-ᶜAhd al-Amān,* vol. 4 (Tunis, 1963), pp. 240–44. The full French translation is to be found in Elie Fitoussi and Aristide Benazet, *L'état tunisien et le Protectorat français: histoire et organisation (1525 à 1931),* vol. 1 (Paris, 1931), Annexes, Doc. 1, pp. III–IX. For excerpts in English, see Part Two, pp. 183–185.

[29] L. Carl Brown, *The Tunisia of Ahmad Bey, 1837–1855* (Princeton, N.J., 1974), p. 239.

[30] Concerning the traditional Islamic requirement for dhimmīs to wear distinguishing clothing and its varied applications, see Stillman, *Jews of Arab Lands,* pp. 65, 77, 83–84, 92, 157–58, 251, 264, 273. In Tunisia, one of the distinctive Jewish badges had been a black cap. However, the German traveler Heinrich von Maltzan reports that during his second visit to Tunis in 1868, he noticed that many Jews had adopted the red fez of the Muslims. See Hirschberg, *The Jews in North Africa,* vol. 2, p. 116.

[31] On discriminatory tariffs for non-Muslim businessmen, see Stillman, *Jews of Arab Lands,* pp. 27, 34, 43–44, 73, 264, 296.

local Jews and at the same time gain greater influence in Tunisian internal affairs.[32]

In Morocco, which had the largest Jewish population in the entire Arab world, the spirit of civil reform made no headway with the Sharifan sultan or his officials.[33] It should be recalled that throughout the later Middle Ages and early modern times, Morocco and Yemen were by far the harshest Arab countries in their treatment of Jews, who were their only dhimmīs. The highly ritualized degradation of Moroccan Jews included compulsory ghettoization in most towns, having to wear black garments, walking barefoot through the streets of the imperial cities and before mosques everywhere, being pressed frequently into onerous corvée labor even on holidays and sabbaths, being pelted with pebbles by children, and suffering other public humiliations.[34]

Lobbying by British Jewish subjects of Moroccan origin in Gibraltar and perhaps by Jews living in the Moroccan coastal towns who had commercial contacts with Europe led to the mission of Sir Moses Montefiore in late 1863. Sir Moses, with the full backing of the British government, approached Sultan Muḥammad IV with a petition that the sultan guarantee the safety and tranquillity of his Jewish subjects. The memorandum did not mention emancipation but did allude to Tanzimat reforms by noting Ottoman firmans issued on behalf of Jews during Sir Moses' missions to the Sublime Porte in 1840 and 1863. The Sharifan historian al-Nāṣirī, who reflects official Moroccan thinking at that period, writes that what the Jews were really seeking was "emancipation" like the Jews of the Ottoman Empire.[35] The word used by al-Nāṣirī for "emancipation" is *ḥurriyya,*

[32] See Jacques Chalom, *Les Israélites de la Tunisie: leur condition civile et politique* (Paris, 1908), p. 29; Hirschberg, *The Jews in North Africa,* vol. 2, pp. 114–15; Chouraqui, *Between East and West,* p. 164. Cazès, *L'histoire des Israélites de Tunisie,* p. 158, notes that Jews were now less exposed to the arbitrary abuse of government power than were Arabs because they could count on the foreign consuls to advocate their case. However, this was the case in the major towns. It was probably less true in the interior.

[33] They were, however, open to some Tanzimat reforms with respect to the military and other areas of administration. See Muḥammad al-Manūnī, *Maẓāhir Yaqẓa al-Maghrib al-Ḥadīth,* vol. 1 (Rabat, 1973).

[34] See Stillman, *Jews of Arab Lands,* pp. 83–87; 304–5, 308–17. For a dramatic description of Jews being dragged away from Sabbath services for corvée labor, see Romanelli, *Travail in an Arab Land,* p. 62.

[35] Al-Nāṣirī writes that the Jews "wished for emancipation similar to that of Egypt and countries like it," but what he means is the Ottoman Levant. See the passage from his *Kitāb al-Istiqṣā',* translated in Stillman, *Jews of Arab Lands,* pp. 371–73.

which had the double connotation in Morocco at that time of "liberty" and "libertinism." The sultan had no intention of granting anything of the sort. For the sake of diplomacy, he issued a *dahir* (royal decree) on February 5, 1864, which stated his intention to protect his Jewish subjects from injustice and oppression in accordance with Islamic law. No change was made in the civil status of the Jews. Even this token gesture was considered too much of a concession by most Moroccans. According to al-Nāṣirī, the Jews now "became arrogant and reckless, and they wanted to have special rights under the law—especially the Jews of the ports."[36] Soon after Montefiore's departure, Muḥammad IV issued a second decree that clarified his original *dahir* to the point of nullifying it. There would be no major change in the legal status of Moroccan Jews or in their internal communal organization until the French takeover of Morocco half a century later.

Of all the Jews in the Arab world during the nineteenth century, none were more affected by the impact of Europe and none underwent more profound transformations than the Jews of Morocco's eastern neighbor, Algeria.

At the beginning of the French conquest in 1830, the Jews were regarded as natives, albeit friendly ones. Their traditional corporate status and internal communal autonomy were officially recognized and reinforced. The French military authorities reconfirmed Jacob Bacri as *muqaddam* (*mekdam* or *mokdam* in the French transcriptions), or "head of the Jewish nation." He was charged with overseeing and directing Jewish affairs in Algiers.[37] The French also gave full judicial recognition to the *bēt dīn,* or rabbinic court, with regard to internal Jewish matters. The edict of the French commander and chief regulatory local justice stated: "All cases among Jews, whether civil or criminal, will be brought before a tribunal composed of three rabbis who will pronounce judgment with supreme authority and without appeal, according to the terms and following the procedures of Jewish law."[38] Within less than a year, the French authorities began to whittle away Jewish autonomy. The office of the head of the Jewish nation was replaced in 1836 by that of a Jewish adjutant to the mayor in each main town. The Jewish courts by this time had been reduced

[36] Ibid., p. 372.

[37] Concerning the man and the office, see Hirschberg, *The Jews in North Africa,* vol. 2, pp. 44–45, 50; also Simon Schwarzfuchs, *Les Juifs d'Algérie et la France (1830–1855)* (Jerusalem, 1981), pp. 15, 30; Michel Ansky, *Les Juifs d'Algérie du Décret Crémieux à la libération* (Paris, 1950), pp. 27–28.

[38] Quoted in Schwarzfuchs, *Les Juifs d'Algérie et la France,* p. 32.

to dealing primarily with matters of marriage and divorce. Even this limited competence was removed in 1841. Henceforth, the French courts would hear all cases involving Jews, including cases of personal status, marriage, and divorce. The only legal role left to duly recognized rabbinical authorities was that of an expert witness who could be asked to give an advisory opinion to the civil courts in cases involving Jews.[39] Traditional Jewish judicial autonomy was no more.

The communal structure of Algerian Jewry was totally reorganized by administrative fiat in 1845. On November 9, 1845, an ordinance was published creating consistories for Algeria on the French model.[40] The Consistoire Général in France and French Jewish colonists in Algeria had been lobbying for this for more than a decade.[41] Algerian Jewry was organized into three consistories—a central consistory in Algiers and provincial consistories in Oran and Constantine. Each consistory would be composed of a chief rabbi, who was appointed and paid by the state, and of lay members (four in Algiers, three in each of the others). The president of each consistory would always be a layman. The chief rabbis and most of the lay leaders were to be French, not Algerian, in order to weaken the traditionalist majority, whom the European Jews considered superstitious and primitive, and to hasten the assimilation of French culture and values. The "civilizing" role of the consistories was clearly spelled out in the definition of its functions:

1. To maintain order in the synagogues; to see that no assemblies for prayer or religious purposes are held without express authorization; to appoint clergy in the temples and other religious functionaries, particularly ritual slaughterers.
2. To see that families send their children to nurseries and schools.
3. To encourage Jews to exercise useful professions, more particularly agricultural work.

[39] Schwarzfuchs, *Les Juifs d'Algérie et la France,* pp. 31–34; and Ansky, *Les Juifs d'Algérie,* pp. 28-29.

[40] For a brief history and description of the French consistorial system, see Moshé Catane and Isaac Levitats, "Consistory," *EJ* 5: 907–12.

[41] These lobbying efforts are described in detail by Zosa Szajkowski, "The Struggle for Jewish Emancipation in Algeria after the French Occupation," *Historia Judaica* 18, pt. 1 (April 1956): 27–40; also by Morton Rosenstock, "The Establishment of the Consistorial System in Algeria," *JSS* 18, no. 1 (January 1956): 41–54; and by Simon Schwarzfuchs, "Colonialisme français et colonialisme juif," in *Judaïsme d'Afrique du Nord aux XIXe–XXe siècles,* ed. Michel Abitbol (Jerusalem, 1980), pp. 37–48. See also idem, *Les Juifs d'Algérie et la France,* passim. The consistories

4. To oversee the use of funds designated for synagogue, charitable institution and school expenses . . . and all other expenses of a similar nature.[42]

In addition to his obvious religious and ceremonial duties, the chief rabbi, who was a civil servant, was supposed "to inculcate unconditional obedience to the laws, loyalty to France, and the obligation to defend it."[43]

Through the combined efforts of "French and Jewish colonialism" (to use Simon Schwarzfuchs's phrase), the communal structure and governance of Algerian Jewry were transformed more radically than any other Jewish community in the Arab world. The changes went far beyond those of the Tanzimat. Constitutionally, Algerian Jewry had been recast into a mirror image of the Jewish community of France. The reforming efforts of Chief Rabbi Michel Weill and his colleagues did not always go unopposed by the traditionalists, but there was little that the traditionalists could do since the consistories were state institutions.[44] When the Algerian consistories were placed under the authority of the Central Consistory in Paris in 1862, Algerian Jewry became an official branch of French Jewry.

The Jews of Algeria were still not French citizens, but "natives" (*indigènes*) under the rule of French law. The final step toward total emancipation was not far away. On October 24, 1870, the provisional government of the Third Republic, meeting in Tours, issued a decree granting French citizenship to the Jews of Algeria. The document became known as the Crémieux Decree, after Isaac Adolphe Crémieux, the minister of justice and French Jewish leader who was the moving force behind the declaration.[45] By the single stroke of a pen, some 30,000 Jews living in the three northern departments of Algeria (although not the Jews in the Saharan south) had become citizens of

---

were not actually put into operation until 1847 in Algiers and Oran and 1849 in Constantine.

[42] Schwarzfuchs, *Les Juifs d'Algérie et la France,* p. 50. The full text of the royal ordinance establishing the consistories can be found in ibid., Appendices I–II, pp. 373–91.

[43] Ibid.

[44] Concerning these conflicts, see Szajkowski, "Jewish Emancipation in Algeria," pp. 37–39; Rosenstock, "The Establishment of the Consistorial System in Algeria," p. 50; and Richard Ayoun and Bernard Cohen, *Les Juifs d'Algérie: deux mille ans d'histoire* (Paris, 1982), pp. 126–27. See also Hirschberg, *The Jews in North Africa,* vol. 2, pp. 52–55.

[45] For the immediate steps leading up to the decree, see Ansky, *Les Juifs d'Algérie,* pp. 32–40. The text of the decree is in ibid., p. 38.

a democratic Western European state and were no longer considered—and most no longer considered themselves—Jews of an Arab land.

The various changes in the civil status and community structure of the Jews living in the Arab world during the nineteenth century were accompanied by socioeconomic and cultural transformations as well. These internal metamorphoses, like the more external political ones, differed greatly in their degree of intensity from one country and one region to another—and even in a single place from one stratum of Jewish society to another. Once again, as in the case of political reform, the impact of European forces and influences was crucial, although not exclusive.

No native group benefited more from Europe's intrusion into the Middle East than did the non-Muslim minorities. They were quick to see that increased European influence and penetration meant a weakening of the traditional Islamic norms of society that had defined their social and political status for more than a millennium. Although the great majority of Muslims had a deeply ingrained wariness and even hostility toward the ever-intrusive "Franks" (as Europeans were still called) and the modernizing efforts of the *mutafarnajūn* (those who act like Franks), the non-Muslim minorities were inclined to view the process of modernization as a means for their own betterment. Jews and Christians accepted the trappings of westernization earlier and with greater ease than did most Muslims. This early receptivity to aspects of Western culture on the part of Jews and Christians seems to be in accord with Toffler's observation that "minorities experiment; while majorities cling to the forms of the past."[46]

As noted, the dhimmīs had acted for centuries as intermediaries between the dominant Islamic society and European consular and mercantile interests since they were more likely to already know a European language than were Muslims. They were also more willing to learn foreign tongues. As the nineteenth century progressed, many Arabic-speaking Jews and Christians began to consider a knowledge of Western languages as a requisite entry ticket into the modern world with all the benefits it might confer. They were assisted in their quest to acquire foreign languages by the growing number of Western religious and cultural missionaries who flocked to the Middle East and North Africa during the nineteenth century. Indeed, the Jews and Christians received a great deal more than a linguistic education from those zealous do-gooders, who were imbued with the ideals of

[46] Alvin Toffler, *Future Shock* (New York, 1971), p. 221.

bringing progress and enlightenment (and in the case of religious missionaries, salvation) to the downtrodden and benighted minorities.

Foreign language instruction—modern education of any kind, for that matter—was unavailable in the traditional Jewish schools of the Arab world. The *kenīs, ṣlā, kuttāb,* and *maᶜalma,* as these Jewish elementary schools were variously called, offered a minimal religious education by rote comparable to that of the traditional Ashkenazi *ḥeder.* Higher education in the yeshiva was limited to a very few students and was completely traditional in its curriculum.[47]

Christian missionaries were the earliest disseminators of modern education among the Christians and Jews of the Arab world. Most Jews avoided them at first because of communal opposition. In 1846, the rabbis of Baghdad, for example, issued a proclamation of *ḥerem* (the Jewish equivalent of excommunication) against any member of the community studying English with Anglican missionaries.[48] In 1853, the rabbis of Jerusalem employed guards with whips to prevent Jewish women from attending Miss Cooper's School of Industry, a charitable institution offering both instruction and employment in needlework.[49]

[47] For descriptions of traditional Jewish education, see for Yemen: S. D. Goitein, "The Social Structure of Jewish Education in Yemen," in *Jewish Societies in the Middle East,* ed. S. Deshen and W. Zenner (Lanham, Maryland, 1982), pp. 211–33; and Cohen, *The Jews of the Middle East,* pp. 147–52. For Iraq, see: Cohen, *The Jews of the Middle East,* pp. 113–16; and Nissim Rejwan, *The Jews of Iraq: 3000 Years of History and Culture* (London, 1985), pp. 178, 188–89. For Syria, see: Zenner, "Jews in Late Ottoman Syria: Community, Family and Religion," pp. 191–92; Wolf Schur, "Mikhtevē Massāᶜ: Massāᶜ Mi-Yam el Yam," *Magid-Mischne 1,* no. 7 (1879): 28; and Joseph A. D. Sutton, *Magic Carpet: Aleppo-in-Flatbush: The Story of a Unique Ethnic Jewish Community* (New York, 1979), pp. 218–22. For Egypt, see: Landau, *Jews in Nineteenth-Century Egypt,* p. 73; and Maurice Fargeon, *Les Juifs en Egypte depuis les origines jusqu'à ce jour* (Cairo, 1938), pp. 258–59. For Libya, see: Renzo de Felice, *Jews in an Arab Land: Libya, 1835–1970,* trans. Judith Roumani (Austin, 1985), p. 301, n. 15. For Tunisia, see: Robert Attal and Claude Sittbon (eds.), *Regards sur les Juifs de Tunisie* (Paris, 1979), pp. 88–93. For Morocco, see: Haïm Zafrani, *Mille ans de vie juive au Maroc: Histoire et culture, religion et magie* (Paris, 1983), pp. 59–76. The only detailed study of traditional Jewish education in an Arab country is Haïm Zafrani, *Pédagogie juive en Terre d'Islam: l'enseignement traditionnel de l'Hébreu et du Judaïsme au Maroc* (Paris, 1969).

[48] For the text of the proclamation and accompanying correspondence from the British Consulate in Baghdad on this matter, see Stillman, *Jews of Arab Lands,* pp. 377–83.

[49] James Finn, *Stirring Times, or Records from Jerusalem Consular Chronicles of 1853 to 1856,* vol. 2 (London, 1878), pp. 72–73.

By mid-century, missionary schools began to attract more Jews in Syria and Egypt, the two Arab countries besides Algeria in which European influences were strongest at the time. Their primary Jewish clientele were the children of the wealthy mercantile elite. The numbers, however, were still relatively small. For example, in 1863, twenty-three Jewish girls were enrolled in the British Syrian Mission School in Damascus.[50] Twenty Jewish boys attended the Collège des Frères in Alexandria, and five attended the Collège des Frères in Cairo in 1857.[51]

The number of Jewish pupils in missionary institutions increased during the second half of the nineteenth century, especially in the more cosmopolitan coastal cities of the Levant. The Scottish Church maintained no less than three schools for Jews in Beirut, although many of the pupils were non-Jews as well.[52] By the early 1890s, there were 750 Jewish pupils in various Christian schools in Alexandria and 400 in the English missionary school in Tunis.[53] The German traveler Ernst von Hesse-Wartegg, who visited Tunis in the 1880s, assumed that the parents of the Jewish children in the missionary school believed "that the Christian doctrines will not make any deep impression, but the secular instruction only will be listened to."[54]

In the overwhelming majority of instances, this confidence in the inefficacy of Christian propaganda to win over Jewish students proved to be justified. All of the sources—Jewish and missionary alike—attest to the general failure of proselytizing efforts.[55] This resistance was probably due to the strong ties of familial loyalty and the well-defined ethnic and communal nature of religious identity in Middle Eastern and North African society even after the Tanzimat decrees and, indeed, through the first half of the twentieth century up to the period

[50] Reverend W. T. Gidney, *The History of the London Society for Promoting Christianity amongst the Jews from 1809–1908* (London, 1980), p. 380.

[51] Landau, *Jews in Nineteenth-Century Egypt,* p. 83.

[52] See Ellen Clare Miller, *Eastern Sketches: Notes of Scenery, Schools, and Tent Life in Syria and Palestine* (reprint ed., New York, 1977), p. 32; Cohen, *The Jews of the Middle East,* p. 136.

[53] Landau, *Jews in Nineteenth-Century Egypt,* p. 84; Chevallier de Hesse-Wartegg, *Tunis: The Land and the People,* 2nd ed. (London, 1899), p. 128, reprinted in Stillman, *Jews of Arab Lands,* pp. 421–22.

[54] Hesse-Wartegg, Tunis, p. 128; Stillman, *Jews of Arab Lands,* p. 422.

[55] See, for example, Ludwig August Frankl, *The Jews in the East,* vol. 1, trans. the Rev. P. Beaton (reprint ed., Westport, Conn., 1975), pp. 222, 299; Julius Richter, *A History of Protestant Missions in the Near East* (reprint ed., New York, 1970), pp. 394–99; A. L. Tibawi, *American Interests in Syria, 1800–1901: A Study of Educational, Literary and Religious Work* (Oxford, 1966), pp. 38, 102, 224. The missionaries were

of the great exodus. One notable exception occurred in Egypt in 1914, when twenty-two boys then enrolled or recently graduated from Catholic institutions in Cairo and Alexandria secretly converted to Christianity. The incident scandalized the Jewish community and galvanized it into action. Through legal, political, and familial pressures, most of the young people were brought back into the fold. Several of them signed affadavits that they had been temporarily deranged.[56] This case was clearly extraordinary, as was the case of Félix Nataf, a gallicized Tunisian Jew who worked for the French colonial administration in Morocco and converted to Catholicism in 1945.[57]

Upper-class Jewish families in Egypt and Lebanon in particular continued to send their children to missionary and European secular schools, which in the case of French schools meant Sabbath desecration, despite the vigorous protests of rabbis and communal activists.[58] In Egypt, there was a clear element of snobbery in this. The Egyptian Jewish elite considered non-Jewish schools to be superior to most Jewish educational institutions (some of which even bore their names). Some parents had to send their children to Christian schools because there were not enough places in the Jewish ones. Still another factor was that in many places, even after the establishment of modern Jewish schools, such as those of the Alliance Israélite Universelle, there were not always opportunities for secondary education.

There were few indigenous attempts to establish modern Jewish religious schools, such as the community Talmud Torahs founded in

---

more successful in winning converts from among the members of the Eastern Rite churches.

[56]The affair is extensively documented in the Alliance Israélite Universelle Archives (Paris), AIU Egypte I.C.15, excerpts from which are translated in Part Two, pp. 245–249. Echoes of this affair spilled over into the general press of the period. See, for example, N. Cardozo, "A propos de conversions: A qui la faute?" *La Bourse Egyptienne* (May 10, 1914), "Tribune Libre" column; and Elie Antébi, "A propos des Conversions," *La Bourse Egyptienne* (May 11–22, 1914), "Tribune Libre" column. See also the documents translated in Part Two, p. 249.

[57]Nataf discusses his conversion in his autobiography *Juif maghrébin: Une vie au Maghreb (racontée à ma fille)* (Paris, 1975), pp. 133–48.

[58]See, for example, Israel Moses Ḥazzan, *She'erīt ha-Naḥala: Vikkū'aḥ Shō'ēl u-Mēshīv* (Alexandria, 1862), p. 40, where Ḥazzan, who was chief rabbi of Alexandria, approves of Jews learning foreign languages, but preferably not from Gentile teachers, and certainly not from priests or missionaries. See also A. Mosseri, "Conservons notre patrimoine: Intolérance: Parents juifs ouvrez vos yeux," *Israël* (September 7, 1924): 1; ibid. (May 28, 1925): 1; ibid. (October 16, 1925): 1. Christian mission schools in Algeria were also "frequented by the children of prominent Jews" (Chouraqui, *Between East and West,* p. 208).

Alexandria during the 1850s and 1860s; or Ḥakham Zaki Cohen's boarding school in Beirut, Tiferet Yisra'el, which operated from the 1870s to 1904; or Mori Yiḥye Qafiḥ's Dar Daᶜ school in Sanᶜa, which was open only between 1909 and 1913.[59] Most Jews in the Muslim world perceived modern education, like modernity itself, as something to be acquired from its genuine Western source. Hence, it was the schools founded by their enlightened and emancipated European brethren that provided the largest number of Middle Eastern and North African Jews with their primary introduction to modern Western education and—for better or for worse—Western cultural norms and values.

The earliest efforts were sporadic and often acts of individual philanthropists. Adolphe Crémieux was shocked by the backward state of Jewish education in Egypt during his mission there with Sir Moses Montefiore in 1840 on behalf of the Jews accused in the Damascus Blood Libel. He established a boys' and girls' school in Cairo and, shortly thereafter, another two in Alexandria. Money for the schools was collected in both Egypt and France, including a generous grant from the Rothschilds. Despite initial success, however, these four institutions closed down within two years after opening.[60]

European Jews had a long tradition of endowing schools and other institutions in the Holy Land and particularly in Jerusalem, but these schools were, as a rule, of the traditional sort. The Bavarian rabbi Joseph Schwartz, himself the head of a yeshiva in mid-nineteenth-century Jerusalem, mentions no less than twenty-seven major schools of this kind in the Holy City.[61] The French Rothschilds tried to establish modern schools and hospitals in Jaffa and Jerusalem in

[59] Concerning the Alexandrian Talmud Torahs, see Landau, *Jews in Nineteenth-Century Egypt,* pp. 74–76; and Fargeon, *Les Juifs en Egypte,* pp. 258–59. For Tiferet Yisra'el, see Cohen, *The Jews of the Middle East,* pp. 135–36; and Sydney Montagu Samuel, *Jewish Life in the East* (London, 1881), pp. 161–63. For the Dar Daᶜ school, see Aharon Ṣadoq, "R. Yiḥye Qāfiḥ—Teqūfātō ū-Mifᶜālō," in *Shevūt Tēmān,* ed. Yisra'el Yeshayahu and Aharon Ṣadoq (Tel Aviv, 5705/1944–45), pp. 170–71; Ḥayyim Sharᶜabi, "Perāqīm mi-Pārāshat ᶜDōr Dēᶜā' be-Tēmān," in ibid., pp. 200–1; and Yomtob Sémach, *Une mission de l'Alliance au Yémen* (Paris, 1910), pp. 54–57. Actually, the Sanᶜa school was opened by the Turkish government at Rabbi Qafiḥ's request.

[60] Landau, *Jews in Nineteenth-Century Egypt,* pp. 73–74. The curriculum set by Crémieux included Jewish studies, Hebrew, Arabic, French, and mathematics for boys and handicrafts and some academic subjects for girls.

[61] Joseph Schwarz, *Descriptive Geography and Brief Historical Sketch of Palestine,* trans. Isaac Leeser (Philadelphia, 1850), p. 276; also included in Stillman, *Jews of Arab Lands,* pp. 330–31.

1854 through their emissary Albert Cohn. The Jerusalem school did not succeed because of rabbinical opposition. More successful was the Laemel School, founded in Jerusalem in 1856 by Ludwig Frankl on behalf of a philanthropic Austrian Jewess, Elisa Laemel Herz. The school offered both secular and religious education, including German language instruction. The ultra-orthodox Ashkenazi community of the Holy City regarded the school as no less sacrilegious than those operated by non-Jews and showed the extent of its hostility by issuing a ban of excommunication against Frankl. The school flourished nevertheless.[62]

The sporadic efforts of individual European Jews at establishing modern schools for their brethren in the Middle East and North Africa during the first sixty years of the nineteenth century were replaced in the last four decades of the century by more programmatic group endeavors. The most notable educational undertaking was spearheaded by the Alliance Israélite Universelle.

The Alliance Israélite Universelle was founded in Paris in 1860 by a group of liberal French Jews that included Adolphe Crémieux. The Alliance was the first modern Jewish organization to operate internationally. Among its primary goals stated in the first article of its statutes were "working everywhere for the emancipation and moral progress of Jews" and "lending effective assistance to those who suffer because of their being Jews."[63] One way of achieving Jewish emancipation was believed to be through education—"l'émancipation par l'instruction," in the words of Narcisse Leven, a founder and longtime president of the Alliance.[64]

Although the Alliance operated in Christian lands as well, its major educational activities were focused in the Muslim world. Its first school, founded in Tetouan, Morocco, in 1862, was the model for the wide-ranging network of schools that followed. The curriculum combined religious and secular studies. Alliance schools were strongly imbued with the French spirit of the *mission civilisatrice,* and naturally, the French language was given primacy of place. Hebrew and

[62] Concerning the establishment of the Laemel School and the difficulties encountered, see Frankl, *The Jews in the East,* vol. 2, pp. 56–58, 68–69, 92–97, 105–7, 113–14. Concerning the activities of Albert Cohn, see ibid., pp. 69–72; and Finn, *Stirring Times,* vol. 2, pp. 79–80.

[63] André N. Chouraqui, *Cent ans d'histoire: l'Alliance Israélite Universelle et la renaissance juive contemporain (1860–1960)* (Paris, 1965), pp. 412, 415. See also Georges Ollivier, *L'Alliance Israélite Universelle, 1860–1960* (Paris, 1959), pp. 14–20.

[64] Narcisse Leven, *Cinquante ans d'histoire: l'Alliance Israélite Universelle (1860–1910),* vol. 2 (Paris, 1920), pp. 7–8.

at least one other language (Arabic, Turkish, Spanish, or English) were also taught.[65]

The Tetouan school was followed by a school for boys in nearby Tangier in 1864. That same year, Damascus and Baghdad got their first schools. In 1865, a school for girls was started in Tangier. Two years later, the Jerusalem school opened its doors to students. In 1870, the Mikveh Israel Agricultural School was established outside of Jaffa under the direction of Charles Netter, another founder and officer of the Alliance. The school had been conceived by Netter during his first visit to Palestine in 1868. He envisioned it as a model of an entire network of such institutions that would help to make Oriental Jewry productive.[66] However, the only other such school in the Arab world was the Ferme-Ecole in Djedeïda, Tunisia, which was founded in 1895.[67]

More and more schools continued to appear throughout the Maghreb and the Levant. In 1878, an Alliance school was opened in Tunis. A school for girls was set up in Beirut that same year and

[65] A number of significant studies dealing with the Alliance's activities in the Arab and the wider Muslim world have appeared in recent years. The most detailed picture of Alliance educational programs and curricula may be found in Paul Silberman, "An Investigation into the Schools of the Alliance Israélite Universelle: 1862–1940" (Ph.D. diss., New York University, 1973); and Michael M. Laskier, *The Alliance Israélite Universelle and the Jewish Communities of Morocco: 1862–1962* (Albany, N.Y., 1983). See also Aron Rodrigue, "French Jews, Turkish Jews: The Alliance Israélite Universelle in Turkey, 1860–1914" (Ph.D. diss., Harvard University, 1985); Joan Gardner Roland, "The Alliance Israélite Universelle and French Policy in North Africa: 1860–1918" (Ph.D. diss., Columbia University, 1969); and Eliahou Cohen, "L'influence intellectuelle et sociale des écoles de l'Alliance Israélite Universelle sur les Israélites du Proche-Orient" (thèse pour le doctorat d'université, Université de Paris, 1962). See also the important collection of studies in Simon Schwarzfuchs (ed.), *"L'Alliance" dans les communautés du bassin méditerranéen à la fin du 19ème siècle et son influence sur la situation sociale et culturelle. Actes du deuxième Congrès international de recherche du patrimoine des Juifs Sepharades et d'Orient 1985* (Jerusalem, 1987).

[66] Ephraim Orni, "Mikveh Israel," *EJ* 11: 1544–45; Israel Klausner, "Netter, Charles," *EJ* 12: 1001–2; Georges Weill, "Charles Netter ou les oranges de Jaffa," *Les Nouveaux Cahiers* 21 (1970): 2–36.

[67] See S. Avigdor, *Le mouvement agricole juif: ferme-école de Djédéïda* (Algiers, 1902); "Ferme-Ecole de Djedeïda," *BAIU,* 2e ser., 2 (1895): 112. There were discussions throughout the last three decades of the nineteenth century about opening an experimental farm school near Tangier, but nothing ever came of them. See Laskier, *The Alliance Israélite Universelle and the Jewish Communities of Morocco,* pp. 128–29. A training farm was opened in Turkey in the late 1880s, which became the Or Yehudah Agricultural School in 1900. See Rodrigue, "French Jews, Turkish Jews," pp. 272–75.

another for boys the following year. The Jewish community of Cairo got its Alliance school in 1896. It was so successful that an additional building was required after one year, at which time two more schools were opened in Alexandria.[68]

Until the end of World War I, most of the Alliance institutions were six- or seven-year elementary schools to which some advanced courses were added. The only secondary institutions in the Arab world were the agricultural schools and the highly successful vocational school founded in Jerusalem in 1882. Already in 1867, however, the Alliance opened its teachers' college, the Ecole Normale Israélite Orientale, in Paris. It sent some of its most promising graduates there, creating a native teaching staff at a very early stage for its growing network of schools.[69]

At the turn of the century, 100 Alliance schools were located in most of the major towns and cities that had Jewish communities, from Morocco to Persia, with approximately 26,000 pupils enrolled. The number of graduates and other students who had spent some time in the Alliance schools was already several times that number. The Alliance educational network, which in addition to the schools had established vocational apprenticeship programs in many places, produced cadres of Western-educated and skilled Oriental Jews who now possessed a distinct advantage of opportunity over the largely uneducated Muslim masses as their region was drawn ineluctably into the modern world economic system. Together with the rapidly evolving native Christians who benefited from missionary schools, they came to have a new and unparalleled mobility and achieved a place in the economic life of Muslim world that was far out of proportion to their numbers or their social status in the general population. Non-Muslims also came to have a disproportionate role in the newly developing liberal professions for which a modern education was essential.[70] They also acted as agents of modernity, and in this respect, they continued in their accustomed role as intermediaries, albeit on a scale that had no precedent in recent centuries.

[68] Landau, *Jews in Nineteenth-Century Egypt,* pp. 86–88.

[69] For a good brief description of the founding, development, and program of the Ecole Normale, see Laskier, *The Alliance Israélite Universelle and the Jewish Communities of Morocco,* pp. 109–12. See also Chouraqui, *Cent ans d'histoire,* pp. 177–85. See also Elie Kedourie's personal tribute to the quality of the teachers produced by the Ecole Normale in his *Arabic Political Memoirs and Other Studies* (London, 1974), pp. 78–79.

[70] For a seminal study on this subject, see Charles Issawi, "The Transformation of the Economic Position of the *Millets,*" pp. 261–85.

The political, educational, and economic emancipation of Middle Eastern and North African Jewry during the nineteenth century under the impact of growing Western influences was, as we have seen, by no means an even, synchronized process. In Algeria, the process was almost complete at century's end. In the Ottoman provinces of the Middle East, it was partial, in Sharifan Morocco embryonic and limited, and in Yemen almost imperceptible. Moreover, there was a price to be paid for entry into the modern world. The transition was not without dislocations and traumas, both within the Jewish communities of the Arab world themselves and in their relations with the dominant society around them.

2

SOCIAL TRANSFORMATIONS

Despite the definite parallels between the emergence of Arabic-speaking Jewry and European Jewry into modern times, there are also significant differences. For the European Jews, coming out of the ghetto had as its concomitant a widespread abandoning of traditional corporate autonomy and of a life governed by *halākha* (Jewish law). It also marked an end to the spiritual and social isolation of Jews from their Gentile surroundings and their entry into the general life of society, in not a few instances to the point of total assimilation. Emancipation provided for many European Jews a substitution for, or at least a diversion from, their age-old messianic hope, which was now sublimated into social, economic, and political aspirations.[1]

The case of Algerian Jewry offers the closest parallel to the European model of Jewish modernization. This is understandable since Algeria was a European enclave on Arab soil.

As noted in the preceding chapter, Algerian Jewry gained total civil equality with the Crémieux Decree of 1870. In only forty years from the time of the French invasion, the Jews of Algeria went from being dhimmīs in a preindustrial, traditional Islamic society to being citizens of a modern, secular European state. They also went from being politically powerless subjects to being a potentially significant

[1] There is considerable literature—and scholarly debate—on the transition of European Jewry from medieval to modern times. A few noteworthy examples are Azriel Shochat, *Beginnings of the Haskalah among German Jewry* (Jerusalem, 1960) [Heb.]; Jacob Katz, *Out of the Ghetto: The Social Background of Jewish Emancipation, 1770–1870* (New York, 1978); Calvin Goldscheider and Alan S. Zuckerman, *The Transformation of the Jews* (Chicago and London, 1984); and for a succinct summary of the main lines of scholarly debate, Michael A. Meyer, "Where Does the Modern Period of Jewish History Begin?" *Judaism* 24, no. 3 (Summer 1975): 329–38.

swing vote in urban politics.[2] Their indigenous communal institutions were radically altered by the dominant French Jewish elite to mirror those of metropolitan France.

Even before the promulgation of the Crémieux Decree, cultural assimilation was proceeding rapidly. After 1870, Jewish schools all but disappeared in Algeria as the new Jewish citizens went to state and private French schools. Jewish education was so thoroughly neglected that by the beginning of the twentieth century the Alliance Israélite Universelle, which had not felt the need to establish any schools in Algeria previously, opened large schools in Algiers (1900) and Constantine (1902) and organized courses in religious education throughout the country.[3] By this time also, most Jewish men and many Jewish women had adopted European attire—an important symbolic statement of cultural identification.[4] The Jews' native Judeo-Arabic dialect was disappearing in favor of French. As the pioneer linguist Marcel Cohen noted early in this century, in a typical family of three generations:

> [T]he grandparents speak Arabic between themselves and with their children; they know little or no French; the parents, the middle generation, are truly bilingual; they use Arabic frequently, which was their home language, alongside French which they learned at school; but the language of their household, which they teach their children is only French, and frequently the children are, as a result, unable to converse with their grandparents.[5]

Naturally, this picture varied according to socioeconomic circumstances and geography.[6] The city of Constantine in the interior remained a bastion of traditionalism up to World War II, and some of

[2] Claude Martin, *Les Israélites algériens de 1830 à 1902* (Paris, 1936), p. 193. Martin is perhaps exaggerating somewhat when he dubs the Jews "the arbitors of the political situation." See Richard Ayoun and Bernard Cohen, *Les Juifs d'Algérie: deux mille ans d'histoire* (Paris, 1982), pp. 144–46; and André N. Chouraqui, *Between East and West: A History of the Jews of North Africa* (New York, 1973), p. 151.

[3] Nahum Slouschz, *Travels in North Africa* (Philadelphia, 1927), p. 321; Ayoun and Cohen, *Les Juifs d'Algérie,* p. 141; Chouraqui, *Between East and West,* pp. 205–7. There was, however, some resistance to the Alliance's tutelage. See Joan Gardner Roland, "The Alliance Israélite Universelle and French Policy in North Africa: 1860–1918" (Ph.D. diss., Columbia University, 1969), p. 272.

[4] See, for example, the observations of Yedida K. Stillman, "Libās," EI^2 5: 740; and also Elizabeth D. Friedman, "The Jews of Batna, Algeria: A Study of Identity and Colonialism" (Ph.D. diss., City University of New York, 1977), pp. 127–28.

[5] Marcel Cohen, *Le parler arabe des Juifs d'Alger* (Paris, 1912), p. 10.

[6] Ibid., p. 11; and also Friedman, "The Jews of Batna," pp. 124–25.

the oasis communities of the Mzab region in the Sahara were almost untouched by assimilation.[7]

This is not to say that the Algerian Jews accepted the systematic dismantling of their traditional culture without resistance. There were protests against the consistories and the imposition of foreign rabbis for several decades. As late as 1873 there were numerous cases of native rabbis performing religious wedding ceremonies for couples who had not first obtained the civil marriage required by French law.[8] The forces of resistance among the defenders of tradition within Algerian Jewry gave way in a relatively short period. By the beginning of the twentieth century, Algerian Jews came to see themselves as French, not as *indigènes* (natives). Elements of Algerian Jewish tradition still existed in family life, in religious practices, and in cuisine.[9] But these were vestigial remnants. The image that they held of themselves and that they consciously tried to project to Muslims and Christians was French. As shall be seen later, this presumption was to be fiercely challenged, first and foremost by the Christian colonists, but also by Muslims.

The sociological transformation of Algerian Jewry in the nineteenth and early twentieth centuries was the most radical and far-reaching experienced by any Jewish community in the Arabic-speaking world. It was imposed by the state (and in this respect resembles European Jewish emancipation) in partnership with the leadership of the Jews of France. In the rest of the Arab world the situation was different. Emancipation in the Ottoman style impinged upon civil

[7] For a fictionalized autobiographical account of traditional Jewish life in Constantine, see Camille El-Baz, *Sarah, ou moeurs et coutumes juives de Constantine (Algérie)* (Nice, 1971). For an ethnographic portrait of a Mzabi Jewish community at the end of the colonial period, see Lloyd Cabot Briggs and Norina Lami Guède, *No More For Ever: A Saharan Jewish Town,* Papers of the Peabody Museum of Archaeology and Ethnology, Harvard University, vol. 55, no. 1 (Cambridge, Mass., 1964). See also Pessah Shinar, "Réflexions sur la symbiose judéo-ibadite en Afrique du Nord," in *Communautés juives des marges sahariennes du Maghreb,* ed. Michel Abitbol (Jerusalem, 1982), pp. 81–114, and other studies in the same volume.

[8] Friedman, "The Jews of Batna," pp. 34–35; Robert Attal, "Le Consistoire de France et les Juifs d'Algérie: Lettre pastorale du Rabbin Isidor (1873)," *Michael* 5 (1978): 9–16; Elijah Bekhor Ḥazzan, *Zikhrōn Yerūshālayim* (Livorno, 1874), pp. 80–84; and Isaac Uhry, *Recueil des lois, décrets, ordonnances avis du conseil d'état, arrètés, règlements et circulaires concernant les Israélites (1850–1903),* 3rd ed. (Bordeaux, 1903), pp. 67–68, 223–24. See also the document translated in Part Two, pp. 187–189.

[9] Friedman, "The Jews of Batna," pp. 109–66. For continuity and change in cuisine, see Joëlle Bahloul, *Le culte de la Table Dressée: Rites et traditions de la table juive algérienne (Paris, 1983).*

status and communal organization and was not evenly applied in any case. It did not, as has been discussed, undo the traditional ethnoreligious corporate communities but recognized them as basic units of society, while at the same time encouraging and strengthening secularizing forces within them. Furthermore, the Ottoman state did not take an active role in reshaping the cultural and educational life of the non-Muslim communities. Indeed, it took no role at all until very late in the reform period, when it was already too late. Despite these important differences in the modernization process experienced by Algerian Jews as opposed to other Arabic-speaking Jews, there are elements and tendencies that they shared in common. The parallels are strongest in Tunisia and Morocco, which came under French colonial rule in 1883 and 1912, respectively. But the shared features are no less striking among Middle Eastern Jewries as well.

Under the influence of the Alliance Israélite Universelle schools, French became the prestige language of the greater part of Oriental Jewry by the eve of World War I. Only in the isolated Yemen did French make no inroads at all. In Libya, the role of French as the medium of modern Jewish cultural expression was always secondary. Almost everywhere else, however, it came to have a priority of place.

At first, Middle Eastern Jews wanted their children to acquire foreign languages for their usefulness in dealing with Europeans. The motive was primarily economic, not cultural. Some communities debated what was the most worthwhile language or languages.[10] In Alexandria, which was a heterogeneous, polyglot community, Italian was the lingua franca for Jews during most of the nineteenth century. It was the principal language of instruction in the Jewish communal schools, in which French, Arabic, and Hebrew were also taught, and it was the language in which the statutes of the community were drafted in 1872.[11] Italian was also the primary European language in

[10] See, for example, Jacob M. Landau, "'Language Competition' in Jewish Education in Modern Egypt," in *Bar-Ilan: Annual of Bar-Ilan University. Studies in Judaica and the Humanities,* vol. 4–5 (Ramat Gan and Jerusalem, 1967), pp. 220–33 [Heb.]; also Israel Moses Ḥazzan, *She'ērīt ha-Naḥala: Vikkū'aḥ. Shō'ēl ū-Mēshīv* (Alexandria, 1862), pp. 30–49; and Mordechai ha-Cohen, *Higgīd Mordekhay: Qōrōt Lūv Vīhūdēhā, Yishūvēhem u-Minhagēhem,* ed. Harvey Goldberg (Jerusalem, 1978), p. 236, and Yehuda Kahalon, "ha-Ma'avāq ᶜal Demūtāh hā-Rūḥānīt shel hā-ᶜēda ha-Yehūdīt be-Lūv be-Mē'a ha-19," in *Zakhor le-Abraham: Mélanges Abraham Elmaleh,* ed. H. Z. [J. W.] Hirschberg (Jerusalem, 1972), pp. 86–87.

[11] Jacob M. Landau, *Jews in Nineteenth-Century Egypt* (New York and London, 1969), pp. 75–76. The text of the communal statutes are translated in Part Two pp. 190–196.

Tripoli, Libya, at the time because of the presence of a strong Livornese community and because of extensive trade relations with Italy. It was natural, therefore, that the first modern Jewish school founded there in 1876 by members of the community conducted classes in Italian.[12] Spanish, which had been a widely used language of Jewish high culture around the Mediterranean since the arrival of the Sephardim, held its own in northern Morocco, where the Alliance had to employ it as the language of instruction in its first school.[13] Nevertheless, French rapidly gained ascendancy almost everywhere as the Alliance network expanded to be the sole provider of Jewish education on a mass scale.

There was never really a question during this period of making Arabic or Turkish the official language of education in the modern Jewish schools even before the arrival of the Alliance. Sir Moses Montefiore had urged the Ottoman Jewish leaders to introduce Turkish in the community schools, and in 1840, the *ḥākhām bāshī* of Istanbul, Moses Fresco, issued a proclamation requesting Jewish schools to engage teachers of Turkish—a request that was totally ignored.[14] The Alliance schools introduced a few weekly hours of Turkish in the 1890s when the Ottoman government finally required it, but this appears to have been minimal. Even at the time of the Young Turks' enforced Turkification policy, the director of the Alliance School for Boys in Baghdad, who himself strongly supported the teaching of Turkish, complained about the lack of interest for the language among his students.[15] Both in Turkey and in the Arab provinces, there was simply no feeling of identification with Turkish as a national language, much less a language of modern culture, among Jews. According to Marcel Franco, a Jew in Istanbul writing at the end of the nineteenth century, of the more than 300,000 Jews in the Ottoman Empire at the time (most of whom lived in the Arab provinces), approximately 80,000 to 100,000 men and women could both express themselves and reason in French, whereas only about 1,000 had an equivalent command of Turkish.[16]

[12] Renzo de Felice, *Jews in an Arab Land: Libya, 1835–1970,* trans. Judith Roumani (Austin, 1985), p. 11; H. Z. [J. W.] Hirschberg, *A History of the Jews in North Africa,* vol. 2 (Leiden, 1981), p. 183.

[13] Michael M. Laskier, *The Alliance Israélite Universelle and the Jewish Communities of Morocco: 1862–1962* (Albany, N.Y., 1983), p. 101.

[14] Aron Rodrigue, "French Jews, Turkish Jews: The Alliance Israélite Universelle in Turkey, 1860–1914" (Ph.D. diss., Harvard University, 1985), p. 16.

[15] AIU (Paris) France XII.F.22. Annual Report of Y. Albala (October 11, 1909).

[16] Marcel Franco, *Essai sur l'histoire des Israélites de l'Empire Ottoman depuis les origines jusqu'à nos jours* (Paris, 1897), p. 249.

The position of Arabic among the Jews was considerably more complicated than that of Turkish. The overwhelming majority of Jews from Morocco to Iraq had been native speakers of Arabic since the Middle Ages. With the exception of Algerian Jewry and the small, highly Europeanized elite in the main towns and cities around the Mediterranean, they remained Arabic-speaking until the dissolution of their communities in the mid-twentieth century, even after adopting French as their language of modern culture.

The Arabic they spoke was their own communal variety, which, depending on the community, might differ moderately or substantially from the variety of Arabic spoken by the Muslim majority.[17] The Jews wrote their Judeo-Arabic in Hebrew characters, a common hallmark of Jewish languages throughout the Diaspora. This use of their own alphabet was not a mere mechanical difference, since in Islamic and Jewish culture, script had religious sanctity and was intimately linked to communal identity.[18] The strong admixture of Hebrew and the Aramaic (another common feature of Jewish languages) and other linguistic elements, such as Old Spanish in the Maghreb and other places with a significant Sephardi element, indicates that the Jews drew upon quite different cultural models than did their Arab neighbors. Even during the height of the medieval Arab-Jewish cultural symbiosis in Islamic Spain, Jews were not imbued with the ideal of *al-ᶜarabiyya* (Arabic as the language of revelations and divine perfection).

There had always been Jews who could read Arabic script, but they were few since there was little need for it outside of the small circle of Jewish employees in the government bureaucracy and certain merchants. For daily intercourse with Muslims, the spoken vernaculars were sufficient, with the Jews speaking an approximation of the Muslim dialect with non-Jews or both sides speaking some sort of intermediate register. In general, however, the Jews of the Arab world did not identify with Classical Arabic, the only recognized written form of the language in Arab culture. They did not partake in the

[17] For a more detailed discussion of this phenomenon with specific examples, see Haim Blanc, *Communal Dialects in Baghdad,* Harvard Middle East Monograph Series, vol. 10 (Cambridge, Mass., 1964), pp. 12–16, passim; Norman A. Stillman, *The Language and Culture of the Jews of Sefrou, Morocco: An Ethnolinguistic Study,* Journal of Semitic Studies Monograph Series, no. 11 (Manchester, 1988), pp. 3–11, 31–61, passim.

[18] The parallel cases of Serbian and Croatian and of Hindi and Urdu are cogent examples.

late nineteenth-century revival (*Nahḍa*) of the Arabic literary language in which the Syrian Christians, by contrast, played so prominent a role. Jacob Ṣanūᶜ (Sanua), the Jewish pioneer of modern Egyptian Arabic theater and political journalism, was a unique phenomenon in the second half of the nineteenth century.[19] A comparatively small number of Jews followed his lead into Arabic belles lettres and journalism in the twentieth century, but they were still the exception and not the rule.

Arabic education for Jews varied considerably during this period. Many of the Alliance and other modern schools taught some Arabic. On the whole, instruction was better in the Levant, where a modicum of Arabic literacy was more useful, than in the Maghreb. The first Alliance schools in northern Morocco taught no Arabic at all. The language was taught at the initiative of the local school director in the interior city of Fez in 1888 "to a selected number of youths whose parents were favorably disposed to the idea."[20] Arabic was added to the curriculum of the Alliance school in Tangier in 1892 and in Casablanca in 1900, again at the initiative of the local directors, but there was little interest among the Moroccan Jews themselves, who saw a greater advantage for their children in the study of French and other European languages.[21] As a result, Arabic literacy was a low priority among Moroccan Jews. By contrast, in Iraq, at the opposite end of the Arab world where the European physical presence and cultural influences were still minimal, much greater stress was placed upon Arabic instruction.[22]

This noticeable lack of enthusiasm for Arabic education among most Jews of Arab lands had as its corollary a widespread lack of interest in the intellectual and political currents that were just beginning to develop among educated Arabs at the time, particularly in

[19] The two principal studies on Ṣanūᶜ's career are Irene L. Gendzier, *The Practical Visions of Yaᶜqub Sanuᶜ*, Harvard Middle Eastern Monograph Series, vol. 15 (Cambridge, Mass., 1966); and Jacob M. Landau, "Abu Naḍḍara, An Egyptian Jewish Nationalist," *JJS* 3 (1952): 30–44. See also Shmuel Moreh, "Yaᶜqūb Ṣanūᶜ: His Religious Identity and Work in the Theater and Journalism, According to the Family Archive," in *The Jews of Egypt: A Mediterranean Society in Modern Times,* ed. Shimon Shamir (Boulder, Colo., and London, 1987), pp. 111–29.

[20] Laskier, *The Alliance Israélite Universelle and the Jewish Communities of Morocco,* p. 103.

[21] Ibid., pp. 103–4.

[22] The Viennese Orientalist Jacob Obermeyer describes a young Jewish businessman who had graduated from the Alliance school in Baghdad as able to "speak and write excellent French and English, he also reads Classical Arabic and handles a not insignificant knowledge in Hebrew literature which he had acquired from his father

Syria and Egypt, the cradles of modern Arab cultural and political revival. Only a small number of Jews (most of whom have remained nameless) were involved in the nascent nationalist movement in Egypt. Here again, the enigmatic and highly individualistic Jacob Ṣanūᶜ stands out as a singular exception.[23]

Some contemporary historians have blamed the Alliance for having alienated large numbers of Middle Eastern and North African Jews from their surrounding cultural environment and creating secularized, half-westernized, deracinated individuals. Hayyim J. Cohen asserts that the Alliance graduates "left school without a command of, and at times barely able to speak, the language of the country where they lived."[24] H. Z. Hirschberg refers to their "pseudo-European superiority" and dismisses them as "the type of Levantine Jew lacking a spiritual homeland."[25]

These charges are not entirely just. The Jews of the Arab world were hardly passive participants in the modernizing process. For better or for worse, they had seen their fortunes tied to the rising star of European political, economic, and cultural power in their region long before the coming of the Alliance Israélite Universelle with its mission to "regenerate" (a key notion in Alliance philosophy) less fortunate Jewries. The Alliance was initially welcomed by most sectors of the Jewish community, including many religious leaders. Where the Alliance ran into opposition, it was often due to the impolitic or overzealous behavior of a particular school director. This, for example, was the case in Tetouan in 1874, when the school director, M. Gogman, belittled the local chief rabbi, or in Baghdad in 1884–1885, when the new director, Isaac Luria, abruptly deemphasized the religious component of the school's program and had the students' side

---

the Rabbi, Ḥākhām Abdallah." Jacob Obermeyer, *Modernes Judentum im Morgen- und Abendland* (Vienna and Leipzig, 1908), p. 4. See also the observations of a British journalist who visited Baghdad in 1878, quoted in Elie Kedourie, *Arabic Political Memoirs and Other Studies* (London, 1974), p. 264.

[23] Gendzier, *The Practical Visions of Yaᶜqub Sanuᶜ*, pp. 42, 55, passim. Contrariwise, see Landau, "Abu Naḍḍara," p. 30, who states that the Young Egypt Movement (Miṣr al-Fatāt) "seems to have had a particular attraction for a substantial number of young Jews." Just how *substantial* this number actually was is questionable.

[24] Hayyim J. Cohen, *The Jews of the Middle East: 1860–1972* (New York and Jerusalem, 1973), p. 106. This charge was also leveled against the Alliance by its opponents at the time. See the remarks cited in Zosa Szajkowski, "The Schools of the Alliance Israélite Universelle," *Historia Judaica* 22, pt. 1 (April 1960): 10.

[25] H. Z. [J. W.] Hirschberg, "The Oriental Jewish Communities," in *Religion in the Middle East: Three Religions in Concord and Conflict,* ed. A. J. Arberry, vol. 1 (Cambridge, 1969), p. 220.

curls (*pē'ōt*) shorn.[26] Despite these occasional instances of friction, many religious parents, among them leading rabbis, continued to send their children to Alliance schools. The *ḥākhām bāshī* of Alexandria, Elijah Bekhor Ḥazzan, sent his own son to the Alliance school and took him out only with great regret in 1904 because the boy had been beaten on several occasions by the schoolmaster.[27] (He put his son, by the way, into a non-Jewish European school.)

The Alliance schools may have created a certain degree of *crise d'identité* for many of its graduates, but certainly this was far less than that engendered in Jewish students by non-Jewish schools. It was also less radical than the internal conflicts of faith and culture experienced by many Arabic-speaking Christians of the Eastern Rite churches who attended Protestant missionary schools.[28] The Alliance schools furthered the secularizing tendencies within the Oriental Jewish communities, but they did not create them ex nihilo. The Tanzimat reforms, the protégé elite, and the rise of a new Jewish middle class linked to European economic and political interests had all fostered secularity. Nor were the schools the only media of Western secular ideas and new world outlooks. The Hebrew newspapers of the *Haskāla* (the European Jewish Enlightenment), such as *ha-Melīṣ, ha-Ṣefīra, ha-Yehūdī, ha-Levanōn,* and *ha-Maggīd,* were to be found in the towns and cities of the Arab world from Morocco to Iraq. Through these journals, Oriental Jews became aware of all the currents sweeping the Jewish world in their day, including religious reform, Hebrew language revival, Zionism, as well as more general issues not specifically pertaining to Jews.[29] Even before the newspapers, Hebrew books from Europe had been flowing into the Arab world. According to the Comte de Gobineau, most books from European presses that came into the Middle East from the mid-eighteenth

[26] Laskier, *The Alliance Israélite Universelle and the Jewish Communities of Morocco,* pp. 81–82; and Abraham Ben-Jacob, *A History of the Jews in Iraq: From the End of the Gaonic Period to the Present Time,* 2nd rev. ed. (Jerusalem, 1979), p. 290 [Heb.].

[27] See the letter from Rabbi Ḥazzan to the president of the Alliance in Paris which is translated in Part Two, pp. 241–242.

[28] "My soul was rent in twain," writes a Lebanese Christian of his own crisis of conscience while attending a missionary school. "Sentimentally I was still Greek Orthodox; intellectually I had leaned perceptibly toward Protestantism." See Abraham Mitrie Rihbany, *A Far Journey* (Boston and New York, 1914), pp. 128–40 (quotation is from p. 138).

[29] Concerning the Hebrew press in Morocco, see Joseph Chetrit, "Mūdāᶜūt Ḥadasha le-Anōmāliyūt ūle-Lāshōn—Niṣṣānēhā shel Tenūᶜat Haskāla ᶜIvrīt be-Marōqō be-Sōf ha-Mē'a ha-19," *Mi-Qedem umi-Yam* 2 (1986): 129–68; also Part Two,

to mid-nineteenth centuries were in Hebrew.[30] Gobineau relates his own amazement upon meeting a Jew in Persia who was familiar with the philosophy of Spinoza and wished to know specifics about the thought of Kant.[31] An East European Jewish traveler, Zvi Halevi Brecher, recounts his delight at finding a large collection of *Haskāla* books in the home of a Jew in Mogador during his visit there in 1890. He also mentions that this Moroccan *maskīl* (enlightened person) was a subscriber to the Warsaw Hebrew newspaper *ha-Ṣefīra.*[32]

As modern education and more generalized Western influences spread among the Jews of the Arab world, there was a gradual decline in the strictness of religious observances and in Jewish learning among the laity. This occurred first in Egypt and Algeria in the late nineteenth century. More acculturated individuals became less careful of the Jewish dietary laws, of keeping the minor fasts, of violating the Sabbath, and of not wearing garments made from the prohibited mixture of linen and wool (*shaᶜaṭnēz*).[33] The rabbinical literature of the period complains of laxer standards of decorum in the synagogue, and the lowering of inhibitions in public conduct with mixed dancing *à la européene* and frequenting bars. The rabbis also mention some weak-

---

pp. 312–313. For Egypt, see Zvi Zohar, *Halākha ū-Mōdernīzaṣiyya: Darkhē Heᶜanūt Ḥakhemē Miṣrayim le-Etgarē ha-Mōdernīzaṣiyya, 1822–1882* (Jerusalem, 1982), pp. 178, 183. For Iraq, see Obermeyer, *Modernes Judentum im Morgen- und Abendland,* pp. 43–44.

[30] Cited in Kedourie, *Arabic Political Memoirs and Other Studies,* p. 264. Of course, many of these books were standard devotional texts and not necessarily *Haskāla* works. Furthermore, some of the Jewish scholars and poets of the Arabic-speaking world had their own compositions printed on the Hebrew presses of Amsterdam, Venice, and, especially, Livorno. See Attilio Milano and the Editors, "Leghorn (Livorno)," *EJ* 10: 1572–73; and the Editors, "Printing, Hebrew," EJ 13: 1112. Hebrew books printed in Europe even made their way into the interior of Yemen, where they were recopied by hand. See, for example, Norman Golb, *Spertus College of Judaica Yemenite Manuscripts: An Illustrated Catalogue* (Chicago, 1972), pp. 14, nos. C9 and C10; 16, nos. C12 and C16.

[31] Kedourie, *Arabic Political Memoirs and Other Studies,* p. 264.

[32] Chetrit, "Mūdāᶜūt Ḥadasha le-Anōmāliyūt ūle-Lāshōn," pp. 134, 156–57, n. 38.

[33] Concerning transgressions of *kashrūt,* see Elijah Ḥazzan, Zikhrōn Yerūshālayim, p. 87; idem, *Nevē Shālōm* (Alexandria, 1893/94), pp. 32a–b, paras. 10 and 11. On neglect of minor fasts, see Ḥazzan, *Nevē Shālōm,* p. 24a. On Sabbath violations, see David Sulayman Sassoon, *Massaᶜ Bavel* (Jerusalem, 1954/55), pp. 107, 188; Walter P. Zenner, "Jews in Late Ottoman Syria: Community, Family and Religion," in *Jewish Societies in the Middle East: Community, Culture and Authority,* ed. Shlomo Deshen and Walter P. Zenner (Lanham, Maryland, 1982), pp. 191, 200, 201. On the wearing of *shaᶜaṭnēz,* see Raphael Aaron b. Simeon, *Nehar Miṣrayim* (Alexandria, 1907/08), pp. 126b–128a; also Zohar, *Halākha ū-Mōdernīzaṣiyya,* pp. 73–75.

ening in the discipline of the patriarchal family.[34] Cases are reported of daughters refusing to accept arranged marriages.[35] A more serious indication of the stresses on the traditional social fabric of the community was the rise of Jewish prostitution in Algeria, Egypt, Syria, and even the more conservative Yemen during the late nineteenth and early twentieth centuries.[36] Prostitution would also increase among Moroccan Jews later, after the establishment of the French protectorate.[37]

Another indication that some bonds of traditional Oriental Jewish society were loosening during this period is seen in the heightened physical mobility of the educated young people coming out of the Alliance and other modern schools throughout the second half of the nineteenth century and the early years of the twentieth century. There was considerable movement in all directions at this time. Jews emigrated from areas of lesser economic opportunity, such as Syria and

[34] On decorum in the synagogue, see Ḥazzan, *Nevē Shālōm,* pp. 8b, para. 20, 9a–b, para. 27; Raphael Aaron b. Simeon, *Ūmi-Ṣūr Devash* (Jerusalem, 1913/14), p. 7c; also Zohar, *Halākha ū-Mōdernīzaṣiyya,* pp. 98–99; and Landau, *Jews in Nineteenth-Century Egypt,* p. 104. On mixed dancing, see: Elijah Ḥazzan, *Taᶜalūmōt Lēv,* vol. 3 (Alexandria, 1902/03), p. 58c; Zohar, *Halākha ū-Mōdernīzaṣiyya,* pp. 81–83; also Friedman, "The Jews of Batna," p. 41. On frequenting bars and cabarets, see Zenner, "Jews in Late Ottoman Syria: Community, Family and Religion," p. 200; Elijah Ḥazzan, *Taᶜalūmōt Lēv,* vol. 2 (Livorno, 1892/93), p. 37d; and Zohar, *Halākha ū-Mōdernīzaṣiyya,* pp. 83–86.

[35] Isaac Abulafia, *Penē Yiṣḥāq,* vol. 1 (Aleppo, 1870/71), "Even ha-ᶜEzer," Sec. 17, pp. 100–16; also Zvi Zohar, "Halakhic Responses of Syrian and Egyptian Rabbinical Authorities to Social and Technological Change," in *Studies in Contemporary Judaism,* vol. 2, ed. Peter Y. Medding (Bloomington, 1986), pp. 33–38.

[36] Although the extent of Jewish prostitution was wildly exaggerated by the anti-Semites, there was a problem, particularly in Algiers, where in 1842, 37 of the city's 446 registered prostitutes were Jewish (8 percent). See Simon Schwarzfuchs, *Les Juifs d'Algérie et la France (1830–1855)* (Jerusalem, 1981), p. 101. For Egypt, see Ben Simeon, *Nehar Miṣrayim,* pp. 12a, 100a; also Zohar, *Halākha ū-Mōdernīzaṣiyya,* pp. 84–88, where other sources are cited. For Syria, see Abraham Elmaleh, *ha-Yehūdīm be-Dammeseq ū-Maṣṣāvām ha-Kalkalī veha- Tarbūtī* (Jaffa, 1912), pp. 27–28; Cohen, *The Jews of the Middle East,* pp. 158–59; also the report translated in Part Two, p. 267. For Yemen, see Yehuda Nini, *Yemen and Zion: The Jews of Yemen, 1800–1914* (Jerusalem, 1982), pp. 20, 83, 94, 111 [Heb.]; Yosef Tobi, *The Jews of Yemen in the 19th Century* (Tel Aviv, 1976), pp. 111, 160 [Heb.].

[37] Chouraqui, *Between East and West,* p. 240, notes that although Jews were only about 2 percent of Casablanca's registered prostitutes during this period, "a considerable number of underpaid working girls turned to so-called 'clandestine' prostitution to supplement their pay and support their families." The rise of prostitution in a society experiencing some of the strains of social dislocation is not overly surprising. Cf. the situation on New York's Lower East Side in the 1890s as described by Irving Howe, *The World of Our Fathers* (New York and London, 1976), pp. 96–98.

Morocco, to developing zones within the Arab world such as Algeria and Egypt. The Jewish population of Egypt in particular was multiplied several times over by immigration during the second half of the nineteenth century. The number of Jews in Egypt was augmented even more dramatically during the early years of the twentieth century. From 1897 to 1907, the number of Jews in Egypt grew by over 53 percent, from 25,200 to 38,635, and in the decade that followed, it increased by an additional 54 percent to 59,581.[38] Of course, the newcomers included many Eastern European and Turkish Jews as well as Jews from Syria, Iraq, Yemen, and the Maghreb. "Egypt had the reputation then of Pactolus," writes one Jewish immigrant whose family arrived in Alexandria early in this century.[39] In his annual report for 1920, the director of the Alliance Boys School in Damascus writes that there were more Damascene Alliance alumni in Cairo than in Damascus itself.[40]

There was also significant emigration of young Jews from the Arab world to countries totally outside the region—to Europe, India, the Far East, and the Americas. During the 1880s, it was estimated that 95 percent of the boys coming out of the Alliance schools in Tetouan immigrated to South America.[41] Most Jewish settlers in Belém and other northern Brazilian towns were from Morocco. Moroccans constituted the majority of Jewish immigrants in Venezuela around the turn of the century.[42] At about the same time on the other side of the world, the overwhelming majority of India's 18,000 Jews were immigrants from Iraq or their descendants.[43] Most of the 175 Jewish families in Shanghai at this time were also Iraqi.[44] Manchester, England, attracted Jewish settlers from North Africa, Egypt, Syria, and Iraq, most of whom were engaged in the booming cotton trade,

[38] Landau, *Jews in Nineteenth-Century Egypt,* p. 6, table. See also Cohen, *The Jews of the Middle East,* p. 70.

[39] Elie Politi, *L'Egypte de 1914 à Suez* (Paris, 1965), p. 33. Politi's family emigrated from Turkey.

[40] AIU (Paris) France XIII.F.24.

[41] Laskier, *The Alliance Israélite Universelle and the Jewish Communities of Morocco,* pp. 136–37, 146, n. 167.

[42] Robert Ricard, "Notes sur l'émigration des Israélites marocains en Amérique espagnole et au Brésil," *Revue Africaine* 88 (1944): 83–88; Shlomo Erel, "Brazil," *EJ* 4: 1328; idem, "Venezuela," *EJ* 16: 91. See also Sarah Leibovici, *Chronique des Juifs de Tétouan (1860–1896)* (Paris, 1984), pp. 184, 289–96.

[43] Abraham Ben-Jacob, *Babylonian Jewry in Diaspora* (Jerusalem, 1985), p. 27 [Heb.].

[44] P. G. Möllendorf, "Die Juden in China," *MGWJ* 39 (1895): 3; also Ben-Jacob, *Babylonian Jewry in Diaspora,* p. 430 [Heb.].

during the last thirty years of the nineteenth century and into the twentieth century.[45] By 1903, New York City had about 100 Syrian Jews, mostly from Aleppo. Their number was increased considerably by the arrival of more young Syrian Jews fleeing compulsory military service after the Young Turk Revolution of 1908.[46]

The most unusual migratory movement of Jews from any Arab land at this time was the exodus from Yemen, the country least affected by the modernizing forces at work elsewhere. From 1881 to 1914, some 3,000 (or between 5 and 10 percent depending on the estimate) Yemenite Jews, immigrated to Palestine, impelled primarily by a wave of messianic fervor as well as by the harsh and unstable conditions of Jewish life in Yemen.[47] During this same period some Yemenite Jewish emigrants settled in Egypt. Many of them had also been heading for Palestine but were unable to complete the journey because they were destitute.[48]

The steady flow of emigration throughout the late nineteenth and early twentieth centuries, which in proportion to the overall Jewish population was relatively modest, skimmed off a considerable number of the educated, energetic, and potentially highly productive young people from countries like Morocco and Syria. On the other hand, it prevented the growth of many educated but unemployed Jews in those countries whose economies were still unable to absorb all of them. (This in fact was a problem in parts of Turkey.[49]) Those young people who went to Egypt contributed to the expansion of that country's economy, whereas those who remained in their homeland became the nucleus of a small, but growing bourgeoisie that became a force for modernization within their respective communities.

[45] Bill Williams, *The Making of Manchester Jewry, 1740–1875* (Manchester and New York, 1976), pp. 319–24; Albert M. Hyamson, *The Sephardim of England: A History of the Spanish and Portuguese Jewish Community, 1492–1951* (London, 1951), pp. 358–60; Ben-Jacob, *Babylonian Jewry in Diaspora,* pp. 314–17 [Heb.]; Joseph A. D. Sutton, *Magic Carpet: Aleppo-in-Flatbush: The Story of a Unique Ethnic Jewish Community* (New York, 1979), pp. 5–6.

[46] Sutton, *Magic Carpet,* pp. 6–7.

[47] See Nitza Druyan, *Without a Magic Carpet: Yemenite Settlement in Eretz Israel (1881–1914)* (Jerusalem, 1981) [Heb.]; and Nini, *Yemen and Zion,* pp. 179–287 [Heb.].

[48] Landau, *Jews in Nineteenth-Century Egypt,* pp. 36–38, 68, 317; Gudrun Krämer, *Minderheit, Millet, Nation? Die Juden in Ägypten 1914–1952.* Studien zum Minderheitenproblem im Islam, 7 (Wiesbaden, 1982), pp. 25–30, 37–38. See also AIU Archives (Paris) Egypte I.D.3. Most of the file marked "Politique Extérieur" consists of letters dealing with the plight of Yemenite Jewish refugees in Egypt around 1905.

[49] Rodrigue, "French Jews, Turkish Jews," pp. 275–93.

Demographic shifts were also taking place at this time within the Jewries of individual Arab countries. Jews, as well as others, were beginning to move from the countryside and smaller towns to major cities, especially to new developing economic centers. Thus, for example, Jews from small communities in southern Iraq flocked to the port of Basra, which was benefiting from the thriving India trade during the late nineteenth and early twentieth centuries. The city's Jewish population, which comprised only about forty or fifty families during the second third of the nineteenth century, had swelled to some 4,000 to 5,000 individuals by just before World War I.[50]

Jews from the inland towns of Syria streamed steadily into Beirut, which had had only a small Jewish community of some 500 souls in 1856. Their number had doubled by 1880 and tripled by 1889. On the eve of World War I, the Jewish population of Beirut was estimated at around 5,000.[51] In Egypt, too, Jews steadily abandoned the countryside for Cairo, Alexandria, and the new towns in the Canal Zone. The Jewish communities of both Cairo and Alexandria quadrupled in the twenty-five years between 1882 and 1907, while at the same time the number of Jews in towns like al-Mahalla al-Kubra, Kafr al-Zayyat, Miyyet Ghamr, and Zifta declined. The Jewish community of Damietta, which had been a relatively large one in the early nineteenth century, actually dwindled to extinction.[52]

Algerian Jewry also witnessed an impressive degree of urban growth at this time. The Jewish population of Algiers doubled during the last two decades of the nineteenth century from 5,372 to 10,822, while that of Oran trebled from 3,549 to 10,651.[53] In neighboring

[50] Cohen, *The Jews of the Middle East,* p. 73. At the beginning of the twentieth century, the Jewish population of Basra was estimated at approximately 1,500. See the table of population figures for thirty-five Iraqi Jewish communities in *BAIU* 29, 2e série (1904): 166–67.

[51] Ludwig August Frankl, *The Jews in the East,* vol. 1, trans. the Rev. P. Beaton (reprint ed., Westport, Conn., 1975), p. 222; Simon Marcus, "Beirut," *EJ* 4:403; Cohen, *The Jews of the Middle East,* p. 79.

[52] Landau, *Jews in Nineteenth-Century Egypt,* pp. 29–50; Cohen, *The Jews of the Middle East,* p. 70; Krämer, *Minderheit, Millet, Nation?,* pp. 117–18; Maurice Fargeon, *Les Juifs en Egypte depuis les origines jusqu'à ce jour* (Cairo, 1938), pp. 305–7. This was a period of great urban population growth throughout most of the towns of Lower Egypt. In Cairo and Alexandria, the increase in the Jewish population was far in excess of that of the population as a whole. See Gabriel Baer, "Urbanization in Egypt, 1820–1907," in *Beginnings of Modernization in the Middle East: The Nineteenth-Century,* ed. W. R. Polk and R. L. Chambers (Chicago, 1968), pp. 156–57, Table 1.

[53] See the detailed table "Algérie—Movement de la Population" in Maurice Eisenbeth, *Les Juifs d'Afrique du Nord: Démographie et Onomastique* (Algiers, 1936), p. 14.

Morocco, however, rural Jews began pouring into the urban centers only in the wake of the expansion that followed the French occupation in 1912. Only in isolated and primitive Yemen was there no appreciable shift of the rural Jewish population toward the cities in either the nineteenth or the twentieth century. In fact, the vast majority of Yemenite Jewry—about 80 percent—remained scattered throughout the country in over 1,200 villages and towns, most of which had very small Jewish communities.[54]

Arabic-speaking Jewry went through this initial phase of its emergence into modern times with far more equilibrium than European Jewish society had been able to maintain when it came out of the ghetto. With the exception of Algeria, most North African and Middle Eastern Jewish communities were plagued far less by religious, social, and intergenerational tensions of the kind that tore the social fabric of Western Jewries apart.

As mentioned, some of the bonds of tradition were weakening within urban Jewish society. However, they were not cast off altogether. There are a number of reasons for this. First, Islamic society in which Jews lived was still highly traditional and continued to be divided along ethnoreligious lines. Jews might become westernized in dress, in education, and even in some of their tastes and habits, but with the exception of Algerian Jewry and some highly acculturated individuals elsewhere, few could pretend that they were truly French, British, or Italian as the case might be. The best they could do was to become foreign protégés. Most of them were first and foremost Jews both in their own eyes and in the eyes of others. As the anthropologist Lawrence Rosen observed with regard to Jews in twentieth-century Morocco:

> [T]he relative Europeanization of the city's Jews only served to underline their social separateness from the Muslim community. For all the apparent

[54] Nini, *Yemen and Zion,* pp. 21–25 [Heb.]; S. D. Goitein, "The Social Structure of Jewish Education in Yemen," in *Jewish Societies in the Middle East: Community, Culture and Authority,* ed. Shlomo Deshen and Walter P. Zenner (Lanham, 1982), pp. 211–12; Cohen, *The Jews of the Middle East,* pp. 83–84. The one exception to this general picture in Yemen was in the British-held territory of Aden on the coast, where the exponential growth of the Jewish urban population throughout the second half of the nineteenth century was along the lines as in the developing regions discussed previously. See Yomtob Sémach, *Une mission de l'Alliance au Yémen* (Paris, n.d.), p. 6; also Cohen, *The Jews of the Middle East,* pp. 82–83. Most of this influx of Jews came from the Yemenite interior. See Nini, *Yemen and Zion,* p. 186 [Heb.]; and Jacob Safir, *Iben Safir,* vol. 2 (Mainz, 1874), p. 1 (translated in Stillman, *Jews of Arab Lands,* p. 349).

change of some members of the Jewish community, the fact that they continued to adhere closely to their religious and traditional practices made it all the more obvious to the Muslims that their neighbors would always remain *yîhûd* (Jews): they could no more become *nâsârâ* (a word that means both Christian and European) than they could alter their membership in the human species.[55]

Another factor that established relative continuity and stability within Jewish society was that many youngsters who went to Alliance and other modern schools had first received the rudiments of a traditional religious education in the Oriental variant of the *ḥeder.* Even the Alliance schools originally offered some of the basic elements of a fairly traditional Jewish education alongside its modern curriculum, employing local rabbis. This practice continued in many Alliance schools well into the twentieth century.[56] Nor was it uncommon for pupils attending Alliance schools to also study in traditional religious schools later in the day.

A further factor that helped to prevent destabilizing conflicts within much of Oriental Jewish society was the important element of the Mediterranean honor/shame syndrome. (The more serious examples of social breakdown mentioned previously were still found only on the fringes of society.) The combination of respect for parents and social norms in public on the part of the younger generation and the general flexibility of the older generation to look the other way in matters of neglected religious observances as long as face was

[55] Lawrence Rosen, "Muslim-Jewish Relations in a Moroccan City," *IJMES* 3, no. 4 (October 1972): 445. That Jews maintained their essential identity despite outward changes is expressed by the North African saying: "The Jew is a Jew, even after forty generations" *(al-yahūdī yahūdī wa-law ʿalā arbaʿīn ʿurq).* See Mohammed Ben Cheneb, *Proverbes arabes de l'Algérie et du Maghreb,* vol. 3 (Paris, 1907), p. 63, no. 2062. See also Norman A. Stillman, "Muslims and Jews in Morocco: Perceptions, Images, Stereotypes," *Proceedings of the Seminar on Muslim-Jewish Relations in North Africa* (New York, 1975), pp. 13–14, passim.

[56] There was, in fact, a commission that was sent to investigate, among other things, the Hebrew and religious education provided by Alliance schools in the Levant and to look into charges that it "weakened the Jewish sentiment of the children." The commission found that most rabbis interviewed did not fault the religious instruction given in Alliance schools and that, in those places where nonobservance of Jewish religious practices was widespread, this was due to "the contagion of the movement of emancipation and progress, the spirit of the times . . . and the pressure of economic conditions." See Lucien Lazare, "L'Alliance Israélite Universelle en Palestine à l'époque de la révolution des [Jeune Turcs] et sa mission en Orient du 29 octobre 1908 au 19 janvier 1909," *REJ* 138 (1979): 307–35. (The quotation from the commission's report is from pp. 321–22.)

maintained lessened the possibilities for serious intergenerational tensions.[57]

Yet another mitigating factor that contributed to preventing the kinds of all-out rebellion against traditional Judaism that became so widespread in Europe as a result of emancipation was the generally nonconfrontational attitude of the religious leadership to the changes that were taking place. Although most rabbis in the Arab world lamented the decline in observance that frequently accompanied increasing westernization, especially in those areas with a strong European presence such as Egypt, the French Maghreb, and later Syria and Lebanon, they frequently showed a realistic and even tolerant attitude.

Many leading rabbis realized that modernity was not a temporary phenomenon that had merely to be waited out. They also understood that it brought with it an unprecedented measure of freedom of choice to the individual.[58] As Rabbi Raphael Aaron Ben Simeon, the *ḥākhām bāshī* of Cairo and a leading Sephardi legal authority in the late nineteenth and early twentieth centuries writes in one of his responsa:

> It was unheard of in any previous time that the governing authorities would loosen restraints so that an individual would be free in his religion and belief to the point that no one can say to him, "What doest thou?" No one has the authority to chastise a person who commits a religious transgression, even if it is committed in public. This is the result of the freedom and liberty prevailing in the land.[59]

He goes on to state, however, that this does not mean that rabbis do not have an important role in the new order of things. But they must be aware that in working for the spiritual good of the community, they cannot overreact to all of the changes that were taking place with ever-stricter and unrealistic demands.[60]

[57] See, for example, David Yellin's observations concerning the young Jews of Izmir and their elders in late nineteenth-century Turkey cited by Cohen, *The Jews of the Middle East,* pp. 166–67.

[58] Raphael Aaron Ben Simeon, *Nehar Miṣrayim* (Alexandria, 1907/08), p. 100a: "It is not in our power to eradicate [objectionable practices] because of the prevailing freedom and liberty (*ha-ḥofesh veha-derōr*)." Compare this with Berger's definition of modernization as "a shift from giveness to choice on the level of meaning" in Peter L. Berger, *Pyramids of Sacrifice* (New York, 1976), p. 186.

[59] Raphael Aaron Ben Simeon, *Ūmi-Ṣūr Devash* (Jerusalem, 1911/12), p. 111b.

[60] Ibid.: "It is incumbent upon the spiritual leader who is concerned for his religious faith and genuinely loves his coreligionists to strive for their welfare and preserve their maintenance of purity however he can without pulling the cord of strictness to its limit."

Ben Simeon's colleague in Alexandria, Rabbi Elijah Ḥazzan, had a similar practical attitude to many of the changes that came with increasing modernization and westernization. In his own responsa, Rabbi Ḥazzan argues that if Jewish religious authorities were to forbid every innovation that has appeared in the Gentile world, they might well be forbidding even some permissible things. Besides, he adds, "[T]he present age is not prepared for the addition of new prohibitions not instituted by the early sages."[61] In other words, rather than taking the position of the rejectionist Orthodox camp of Central and Eastern European Jewish authorities that "whatever is new is forbidden by the Torah in every instance,"[62] the chief rabbis of Egypt at the turn of the century and some of their colleagues in the Maghrebi Jewish centers followed a more pragmatic and conciliatory approach that was in keeping with Sephardi Jewry's historically greater openness to general culture beyond the proverbial "four cubits of Jewish law." Also in contradistinction to most of their European counterparts, the leading rabbis in Egypt and North Africa supported the nascent Zionist movement, which will be discussed in greater detail in Chapter 4.

There are various reasons for the greater receptivity to modernity of many Jewish religious leaders of the Arabic-speaking world than that shown by their confreres among Ashkenazi Jewry. There was, as noted, the traditional Sephardi openness to general cultural trends. Second, there was no Middle Eastern Reform Judaism for the rabbis to contend with, and thus their reactions in the face of modernization were not those of negating all innovation and change out of hand.[63]

[61] Ḥazzan, *Taᶜalūmōt Lēv,* vol. 3, p. 59a–b.

[62] This dictum, which comes originally from the Mishna (ᶜOrlah 3:9), was popularized as a rallying cry for the opponents of modernity by Rabbi Moses Sofer (d. 1839). See Moshe Samet, "Moses Sofer," *EJ* 15: 77–79. There were, of course, some Middle Eastern rabbis who were bitterly opposed to any reforms or compromises with modernity, as, for example, the dayyānīm (judges of the Jewish court) of Tripoli. See Yehuda Kahalon, "Ha-Ma'avāq ᶜal Demūtāh hā-Rūḥānīt shel ha-ᶜĒda ha-Yehūdīt be-Lūv ba-Mē'a ha-19 ūvā-ᶜĀsōr hā-Rishōn shel ha-Mē'a ha-ᶜEsrīm," *Zakhor le-Abraham: Mélanges Abraham Elmaleh à l'occasion du cinquième anniversaire de sa mort (21 Adar II 5727),* ed. H. Z. Hirschberg (Jerusalem, 1972), p. 88. On the island of Jerba in Tunisia, the rabbinical leadership also vigorously opposed—and was singularly successful in its opposition to—the incursions of modernity. See Abraham L. Udovitch and Lucette Valensi, *The Last Arab Jews: The Communities of Jerba, Tunisia,* Social Orders, 1 (Chur, London, Paris, and New York, 1984), pp. 20–21, 86–89.

[63] This point has been vigorously argued by Zohar, *Halākha ū-Mōdernīzaṣiyya,* pp. 156–70. Yehuda Nini has offered another argument to explain the different reactions of Oriental and Ashkenazi Jewish religious authorities, namely, that the

Furthermore, for the Jews of the Islamic world, the West—or more precisely the Western powers and their emancipated Jewries—had for some time represented a benevolent force to which the Jewish communities of North Africa and the Levant had been turning for assistance and protection. The increasing European economic, cultural, and political encroachments upon the Islamic world were perceived by the native Jewish and Christian minorities as effecting positive change. For this last reason, the Oriental rabbis also took such a different stance from that taken by Muslim religious leaders at that time, who, on the whole, regarded the penetration of modern Western civilization as an inimical threat to the Islamic community. Even the Islamic religious reformers who appeared in the late nineteenth and early twentieth centuries, such as Jamāl al-Dīn al-Afghānī, Muḥammad ᶜAbduh, and Rashīd Riḍā, saw the utilitarian elements of modernity primarily in terms of strengthening Islam in its struggle against the West.[64]

Thus, at the very time that Jews and Christians in most parts of the Islamic world were experiencing a growing sense of liberation from the restrictions and disabilities of the past, coupled with expanding horizons of opportunity, the Muslim majority—with the exception of the small modernizing elite—was feeling itself increasingly on the defensive, with its traditions, its social order, and its very independence in danger. The very same forces that represented benevolence to most Jews and Christians were perceived by most Muslims as quite the opposite. The budding optimism of the minorities stood in marked constrast to the dismay and pessimism of the majority. The forces of modernization had the effect of widening the gap that already existed in Islamic society between believer and unbeliever.

The intercommunal tensions that were fostered by this polarity of outlooks and interests on the parts of Muslims and non-Muslims

---

former enjoyed greater actual authority than the latter. See his *Mi-Mizraḥ ūmi-Yam: Yehūdē Miṣrayim, Ḥayyē Yōm-Yōm ve-Hishtaqfūtām be-Sifrūt ha-Shūt, 5642–5674* (Tel Aviv, 1979/80), pp. 20–25. Zohar, *Halākha ū-Mōdernīzaṣiyya,* pp. 149–53, rejects this with cogent replies. However, Nini's argument cannot be dismissed entirely.

[64] See, for example, Bernard Lewis, *The Middle East and the West* (New York, 1966), pp. 101–5. This ambivalent attitude toward the technology and skills of the West was also felt by many Muslims who had themselves received a modern education. Hodgson perceptively notes the "inner psychological gulf" that this caused and the self-mistrust at "having gone over, in practice, to the enemy without even the reward of being able to beat him at his own game." See Marshall G. S. Hodgson, *The Venture of Islam: Conscience and History in a World Civilization. Vol. 3: The Gunpowder Empires and Modern Times* (Chicago, 1974), p. 238.

erupted on numerous occasions into violence, especially in those Arab provinces of the Ottoman Empire where the forces of modernization were still relatively weak and Islamic conservatism strong, such as Iraq, Syria, and Libya, and in Sharifan Morocco. In Baghdad, Mosul, and many other parts of Iraq, there were both small-and large-scale anti-Christian and anti-Jewish riots during the late nineteenth and early twentieth centuries. The mere rumor of one was enough to throw the local non-Muslim communities into a panic.[65] In Syria, where the hostility between ethnic and religious groups ran deep, the large and conspicuous Christian community bore the brunt of Muslim animus, which reached its peak in the massacre of some 5,000 Damascene Christians in 1860.[66]

During the last four decades of the nineteenth century and the early years of the twentieth century, letters from all over the Middle East and North Africa complaining of injustices or abuses either against individual Jews or against Jews as a group streamed into the headquarters of the Alliance Israélite Universelle and the Board of Deputies of British Jews.[67] In more than a few instances the "pogroms" described by members of the local Jewish communities or by Alliance teachers in the field were not strictly anti-Jewish, but part of a general lawlessness of the period in which weak groups—and in particular non-Muslims—were especially vulnerable targets. There are many more instances, however, in which violence against Jewish life and property was a result of the tensions exacerbated by the forces of change that were affecting (albeit in different ways) both Muslims and non-Muslims in the Arab world.

[65] See, for example, Public Records Office (London) FO 195/624, excerpt published in Stillman, *Jews of Arab Lands,* p. 388.

[66] For the events leading up to this incident, see Moshe Maᶜoz, *Ottoman Reform in Syria and Palestine, 1840–1861: The Impact of the Tanzimat on Politics and Society* (Oxford, 1968), pp. 226–40. For an assessment by the British consul in Damascus of some of the specific causes of Muslim resentment, see FO 78/1520, Consul Brant to Ambassador Bulwer in Constantinople (August 30, 1860), published in Bat Ye'or, *The Dhimmi: Jews and Christians under Islam* (Rutherford, Madison, and Teaneck, N.J. 1985), pp. 272–74, no. 48.

[67] For some examples of such letters in translation, see AIU Archives (Paris) Tunisie I.C.3 (letters of October 28, 1864, and February 14, 1869) translated in Stillman, *Jews of Arab Lands,* pp. 410–12. Many still unpublished pleas for help can be found in the Alliance Archives. See, for example, the files Algérie II.C.10; Irak I.C.1, 2, 3, 5, and 7; Liban I.C.1 and 3; Lybie I.C.1, 14, 16, and 20; Maroc II.C.9, III.C.10, and IV.C.11; Syrie I.B.1–8.

3

BETWEEN NATIONALISM AND COLONIALISM IN THE AFTERMATH OF THE FIRST WORLD WAR

The First World War destroyed the old order not only in Europe, but in the Arab lands of North Africa and western Asia as well. In Europe, the collapse of the Hapsburg, Hohenzollern, and Romanov empires gave birth to a multitude of newly independent states in accordance with the popular Wilsonian doctrine of self-determination. In the Arab world, however, the collapse of the Ottoman Empire was followed by almost total European colonial domination. From Morocco to Iraq and along the coastline of the Arabian Peninsula, all of the Arab lands found themselves under either direct European rule or some form of protectorate status with only the trappings of an indigenous government. Quite understandably, Muslims, on the one hand, and Jews, on the other, viewed this new state of affairs from quite opposite perspectives. (The Christians of the Arab world, for their part, were torn in both directions.) As discussed in the preceding chapter, this polarity of attitude vis-à-vis the encroachments of European political, military, and economic power—and no less important, Western civilization—was already well established during the second half of the nineteenth century.

Outright foreign rule over the various Arab territories had begun seventy-five years before the fateful shots were fired at Sarajevo. Great Britain had captured Aden in 1839, and France established itself in Algeria a year later. French troops occupied Tunisia in 1881 and made it a protectorate in 1883. The British took de facto control of Egypt in 1882, although it was not until the outbreak of World War I that they declared it a protectorate. Italy invaded Libya in 1911, and France and Spain occupied Morocco in 1912. The Great War only confirmed these takeovers and completed the process by wresting the remaining Arab provinces in the eastern Mediterranean away from the Ottomans so that they might be carved up by the English and French victors.

There was little love lost at the passing of the Ottoman Empire among any inhabitants of the Arab world. The attempts of the Young Turks to create a feeling of nationhood throughout the heterogeneous empire had produced quite contrary effects. The initial enthusiasm of the non-Muslims at the restoration of the short-lived constitution of 1876 was quickly dampened by two sobering factors: the seething hostility of the Muslim Arab majority and the loss of the non-Muslims' traditional exemption from military service. Throughout the Arab provinces—in Tripoli, Syria, and Iraq—the notion of equality with Jews and Christians embodied in the Young Turk slogan of Liberty, Equality, and Justice was greeted with shock and dismay by all but the small westernizing elite.[1] It seriously compromised the Islamic legitimacy of Ottoman rule in the eyes of many Arabs. Violence against Jews in Baghdad, and against Christians in Mosul and Beirut and the threat of violence against Christians in Aleppo and Damascus disabused the minorities of any illusions they may have held regarding equality in these provinces.[2]

With the outbreak of the First World War, there was little pro-Ottoman sentiment, much less patriotism, among any inhabitants of

[1]See, for example, Public Records Office (London) FO 195/2271, letter of Justin Alvarez, consul in Tripoli (September 30, 1908): "The idea of the judicial and political equality of Moslems and non-Moslems which is the most remarkable feature in the Ottoman Constitution is especially distasteful to them [i.e., the Arabs]." See also Elie Kedourie, *Arabic Political Memoirs and Other Studies* (London, 1974), pp. 124–61; and Gertrude Lowthian Bell, *Amurath to Amurath* (London, 1911), pp. 7–8, 20, 250–51; and Part Two, p. 227.

[2]Concerning the attack against Jews in Baghdad on October 14, 1908, see Kedourie, *Arabic Political Memoirs and Other Studies,* pp. 140–42; also Yūsuf Rizq Allāh Ghanīma, *Nuzhat al-Mushtāq fī-Ta'rīkh Yahūd al-Irāq* (Baghdad, 1924), pp. 179–80. For instances of violence or the threat thereof in the other cities, see Kedourie, *Arabic Political Memoirs and Other Studies,* pp. 142–44, 148–49; also Bell, *Amurath to Amurath,* pp. 250–51; and Part Two, p. 227. There were some attacks against Jewish settlements in Palestine at this time (but there were also attacks by Muslim peasants against the property of some large Arab landholders). See Neville J. Mandel, *The Arabs and Zionism before World War I* (Berkeley and Los Angeles, 1976), pp. 66–69. Accusations against Jews of blaspheming Islam surface again at this time and in Basra reach epidemic proportions. See the correspondence from the Jewish community of Basra to the *ḥākhām bāshī* in Constantinople (June 2, and October 22, 1909) in AIU Archives (Paris) Irak I.C.5; also ibid. I.C.8, letter of Maurice Sidi, director of the Mosul Boys School to Alliance headquarters (November 13, 1908) about a charge of blasphemy against the Jewish director of the Ottoman Imperial Bank in Mosul.

the Arab provinces—Muslims, Christians, or Jews. Jews and Christians showed scant enthusiasm for military service even before the war since most of the native recruits, hapless Arab peasants who were none too enthusiastic themselves, were "poorly nourished, poorly billeted, and poorly dressed."[3] Gertrude Bell, who was traveling through Syria and Iraq shortly after the Young Turk coup, reports with a combination of surprise and admiration that about 100 young Baghdadi Jews had applied for admission to officers' training school.[4] But this was clearly exceptional. As noted in the preceding chapter, Jewish emigration from Syria and other Ottoman territories increased markedly at this time. Shortly after the outbreak of the war, many Jews began to flee from northern and central Iraq to Basra in the British-held south to avoid conscription.[5] Still, hundreds—perhaps several thousand—Jews from Iraq and Syria were drafted into the Ottoman army and sent off to distant fronts such as the Caucasus.[6]

With the exception of Algerian Jewry, which was eager to prove its French patriotism in spite of, and to no small extent in response to, the rampant anti-Semitism of the European colonists, most Jews in the Arab territories dominated by European imperial powers stayed out of the military during the First World War; 1,361 Algerian Jews are known to have died fighting for France.[7] The French, however, were disappointed that the Jews in their Tunisian protectorate did not sign up for military service in droves, as they had expected. The Tunisian Jews, who unlike their Algerian coreligionists were not French citizens and held a rather inferior legal and social status, felt

[3] AIU Archives (Paris) France XII.F.22. Report of M. Albala, director of the Baghdad Boys School, to the Alliance Central Committee (October 11, 1909).

[4] Bell, *Amurath to Amurath,* p. 187. She goes on to note: "The Christians showed no similar desire to take up the duties of the soldier."

[5] Hayyim J. Cohen, *The Jews of the Middle East, 1860–1972* (New York and Jerusalem, 1973), pp. 24–25; Abraham Ben-Jacob, *A History of the Jews in Iraq: From the End of the Gaonic Period to the Present Time,* 2nd rev. ed. (Jerusalem, 1979), p. 149 [Heb.].

[6] Cohen, *The Jews of the Middle East,* pp. 24–25; Ezra Laniado, *The Jews of Mosul: From Samarian Exile (Galuth) to "Operation Ezra and Nehemia"* (Tirat Carmel, 1981), pp. 92–96 [Heb.]; AIU Archives (Paris) Syrie XI.E.94, undated letter from Moussa H. Totah, president of the Jewish Communal Council of Damascus on the state of Syrian Jewry at the end of the war.

[7] Michel Ansky, *Les Juifs d'Algérie du Décret Crémieux à la libération* (Paris, 1950), p. 65. Many Algerians distinguished themselves for bravery, winning more than a thousand decorations and a similar number of citations. See ibid., pp. 65–66; also André N. Chouraqui, *Between East and West: A History of the Jews of North Africa* (New York, 1973), p. 153.

little inclination to fight for their colonial masters, especially in view of the pervasive anti-Semitism of both French officials and colonists in Tunisia.[8] Anti-Jewish feeling erupted into violence from August 20 to 22, 1917, when native troops attached to the French army went on a rampage in Tunis, attacking Jews and pillaging their shops. The rioting spread to Bizerte, Sfax, Sousse, Qayrawan, Gabes, and Mahdia before order was restored.[9]

One hundred fifty Egyptian Jews, including two members of the elite Rolo family, volunteered for the Zion Mule Corps, which was organized in 1915 by Joseph Trumpeldor and other refugees from Palestine who were in Alexandria. The unit fought in Gallipoli and later became the nucleus of the Jewish Legion. However, considering that Egyptian Jewry well exceeded 50,000 souls at this time, the number of Jews in arms was, to say the least, insignificant.[10]

[8] See the brief report by M. Rodrigue in Tunis to Alliance headquarters in Paris (June 23, 1916), entitled "Les Juifs de Tunis pendant la guerre," and the very lengthy report of C. Ouziel in Tunis (1917), entitled "Les Juifs tunisiens et la guerre," both in AIU Archives (Paris) Tunisie II.C.5. Ouziel outlines many of the Jewish grievances against the protectorate and lists examples of official anti-Semitism, including the rebuffs suffered by some of the young Tunisian Jews who had tried to volunteer early in the war. See also Ouziel's letter of February 17, 1915, in ibid., which discussed the problem of French anti-Semitism. Career opportunities in the French colonial administration were almost entirely closed to Jews at this time, and even the best Jewish students could have little hope for obtaining a government academic scholarship. See Elie Cohen-Hadria, "Les milieux juifs de Tunisie avant 1914 vus par un témoin," *Le Mouvement Social* 60 (July–September 1967): 102–3. Some 200 Tunisian Jews served in the French army despite everything. See Daniel Goldstein, *Libération ou annexion: aux chemins croisés de l'histoire tunisienne (1914–1922)* (Tunis, 1978), p. 366, n. 8; Chouraqui, *Between East and West,* p. 169; and also the document translated in Part Two, p. 253.

As to the status of Jews in Tunisia, which was still in accordance with Islamic law even after the establishment of the protectorate, see Jacques Chalom, *Les Israélites de la Tunisie: Leur condition civile & politique* (Paris, 1908), pp. 123–29, 140–47, 193–94. Jews outside the major cities were still required to pay the *majba,* the Tunisian equivalent of the *jizya* (canonical poll tax for *dhimmīs*). See ibid., p. 193; also AIU Archives (Paris) Tunisie II.C.5, series of letters dated May 30–June 23, 1902, concerning Jews imprisoned for failure to pay the *majba* to the Tunisian Muslim authorities.

[9] AIU Archives (Paris) Tunisie II.C.5, letters of C. Ouziel, dated August 24, 31, and September 16, 1917. The riots originally began after an altercation between Muslim soldiers on leave and either some Jewish military police or some pimps. See Daniel Goldstein, *Libération ou annexion,* p. 360. The Muslim population was seething during 1917 owing to the hardships caused by the war and the large number of native young men conscripted into the army. See ibid., pp. 124–25, 162–71.

[10] Maurice Fargeon, *Les Juifs en Egypte depuis les origines jusqu'à ce jour* (Cairo, 1938), pp. 177–78.

War's end saw very different situations obtaining in the various Jewish communities across the Arab world. The large Jewish population of French North Africa, which comprised over half of Arabic-speaking Jewry, came through the war years not only intact, but on the whole better off than it had been before. The Jews of Morocco in particular enjoyed far greater security and opportunity than they had in the violent and chaotic days that preceded the establishment of the protectorate. The Jewish middle class began to expand despite the reluctance of French officials to accord it too many benefits, too quickly, so as not to upset radically the existing social order.[11]

Egyptian Jewry also came through the war relatively unscathed. The haute and moyenne Jewish bourgeoisie, which constituted a significant portion of the Jews in Egypt, prospered, as did other Egyptians of that class, by supplying the demands created by the large British military force stationed there and by the lack of competition from abroad. However, the lower rungs of Jewish society, like the Egyptian masses, suffered from the inflation of the period and from the decline in employment at the end of the war.[12]

The Jews in the Italian colony of Libya fared less well than their coreligionists in Egypt and the French Maghreb. A widespread Arab revolt against the Italians broke out in 1914 even before Italy entered the war on the Allied side the following year. The Jewish communities of Tripolitania were the most seriously affected by the uprising. Trade throughout Libya was at a standstill until after 1917. Some 2,000 Jews from the smaller towns and villages had been displaced by the hostilities, and lives were lost as well as property.[13]

[11] Even a decade after the armistice, a French official could write, "We cannot let the former [the Jews] take an economic and social importance in the country to the detriment of their former masters." He realized, however, that the evolution of Moroccan Jewry was proceeding apace, namely: "Sooner or later there will be a rupture in the equilibrium between the economic and social situation of the Jew and the Muslim which we would like to delay." See Roger Gaudefroy-Demombynes, *L'oeuvre française en matière d'enseignement au Maroc* (Paris, 1928), p. 208.

[12] See Gudrun Krämer, *Minderheit, Millet, Nation? Die Juden in Ägypten 1914–1952.* Studien zum Minderheitenproblem im Islam, 7 (Wiesbaden, 1982), pp. 105, 241.

[13] Renzo de Felice, *Jews in an Arab Land: Libya, 1835–1970,* trans. Judith Roumani (Austin, 1985), pp. 53–54. On the demographic consequences resulting from this period of upheaval, see Harvey Goldberg et al., "Social and Demographic Aspects of the Jewish Community in Tripoli during the Colonial Period," *Judaïsme d'Afrique du Nord aux XIXe-XXe siècles,* ed. M. Abitbol (Jerusalem, 1980), pp. 71–73; also Harvey Goldberg, "Ecologic and Demographic Aspects of Rural Tripolitanian Jewry: 1853–1949," *IJMES* 2:3 (July 1971): 254–58.

It was, however, the Jews of northern Iraq and Greater Syria who had suffered the most physically and financially toward the war's end. In addition to suffering from the general deprivation caused by the war in their region, they were the targets for special exactions by the Turkish authorities.[14] The sorry state in which the Jewish communities of Syria and northern Iraq were languishing at this time is summed up by the pathetic, if somewhat hyperbolic, remarks of the president of the Jewish Communal Council of Damascus:

Poverty reigns and has been transformed into indigence, unhappily, as a consequence of the World War, from which our city has suffered, and in particular, our Community. Damascus which was the general headquarters of the 4th Army suffered enormously from all points of view. We are deeply saddened to inform you that all the youth from the age of 18 to 25[15] was taken into military service to lands far away from Syria. . . . A very large part of these people have succumbed and many others are till now prisoners leaving behind widows and orphans in the public charge.[16]

Iraqi Jewry recovered from the wartime hardships much more quickly under British occupation than did the Jews of Greater Syria, which was divided into three rival, occupied zones with the French on the Lebanese coast, the British in Palestine and Transjordan, and most of Syria proper under the administrative control of the Amir Fayṣal and his forces. Iraqi Jews, who had dominated the commercial life of the country prior to the war, were not long in regaining their preeminence in this domain as the economy and the physical infrastructure of the country were revived and expanded.[17] Syria, by contrast, continued in a state of administrative chaos during the years immediately following the war with little chance for economic development, since as Elie Kedourie had observed, "Most of the local notables were incompetent or corrupt; the men from the Hedjaz from Feisal down, had been accustomed only to the control of insanitary little desert towns and squalid villages."[18] Under these circumstances,

[14] Ben-Jacob, *A History of the Jews in Iraq,* pp. 148–49 [Heb.]; Laniado, *The Jews of Mosul,* pp. 95–96 [Heb.]; Ghanīma, *Nuzhat al-Mushtāq,* pp. 181–82; also Part Two, pp. 254–255.

[15] The letter has 52 written, but this must be a slip of the pen.

[16] AIU Archives (Paris) Syrie XI.E.94 (undated, probably 1918).

[17] See Part Two, pp. 261–262. See also Richard Coke, *The Heart of the Middle East* (New York, 1926), pp. 171–73, 203. When the British first occupied Basra in 1915, they apparently showed a marked preference for employing native Christians rather than Jews, whom they suspected of being pro-Turkish at first. This soon changed, however. See AIU Archives (Paris) Irak I.C.5, letter of M. Ittah (Basra), May 6, 1915, and the report of A. Zilberstein (Basra), August 28, 1915.

[18] Elie Kedourie, *England and the Middle East: The Destruction of the Ottoman Empire, 1914–1921* (London, 1956), p. 158.

Syrian Jewry remained dependent for the next few years upon the charitable relief sent by Jews in America, Egypt, France, and neighboring Palestine.[19]

The First World War had aroused a great deal of national and ethnic expectations in the Muslim world just as it had in Europe. The burning question facing the Jews of Arab lands in the years immediately following the war was one of direction, of individual and group orientation. The Jews found themselves torn among the conflicting forces of Zionism, Arab nationalism, and European colonialism, while they were also being pulled by apolitical economic aspirations. The struggles for communal leadership that can be observed in so many major urban Jewish communities at this time from Morocco to Iraq were no longer merely of the traditionalist-versus-modernist sort that had predominated in the prewar period (although this split was still very real and very much in evidence). Rather, these contests for control of rabbinical and lay councils or specific communal offices, more often than not, revolved around the question—with which of the aforementioned forces, if any, was the Jewish community to identify itself.

With the notable exception of Egypt, nowhere did Jews, as a group or even in significant numbers as individuals, identify with the nationalist movements in the Arab world because of these movements' strong Pan-Arab or Pan-Islamic coloring, which held little attraction for those who had traditionally been the humblest of the *ahl al-dhimma*. Only in Egypt, with its more westernized, liberal political tradition and its prevailing cosmopolitan atmosphere, did Jews become at all active and visible in political life. The secularly oriented nationalist party, Saᶜd Zaghlūl's Wafd, attracted a number of Jews to its ranks—men like Vita Sonsino, David Hazan, and the lawyers Félix Benzakein and Léon Castro. Castro was a close friend and adviser of Zaghlūl Pasha and his principal spokesman in French. In 1921, Castro was in charge of the party's propaganda campaign in Europe, and the following year, he founded and edited the Wafd's French-language daily *La Liberté*.[20]

[19] See the lengthy and detailed report translated in Part Two, pp. 263–271.

[20] See Maurice Mizrahi, *L'Egypte et ses Juifs: Le temps révolu (XIXe et XXe siècle)* (Geneva, 1977), pp. 41–42; and Krämer, *Minderheit, Millet, Nation?*, pp. 257–58. Castro's ardent nationalist editorials made him extremely unpopular with the British. See Public Records Office (London) FO 371/13150, report by Lord Lloyd, the British high commissioner to Sir Austen Chamberlain (June 25, 1928), in which he refers to "the notorious Léon Castro."

Jews could be found throughout the spectrum of Egyptian public life. Members of the Jewish elite with close ties to the monarchy regularly served in Parliament for the Ittiḥād party. Joseph Aslan Cattaoui, for example, was a member of the Legislative Assembly during the protectorate years. Between 1921 and 1923, he was a member of the commission that drafted the new Egyptian constitution. He was later elected to Parliament and served in the government of Zīwar Pasha, as minister of finance in 1924, and as minister of communications in 1925. Although he was the only Jew to have ever achieved cabinet rank, others achieved high positions in various ministries.[21] On the other side of the political spectrum, a number of Jews played a prominent role in the early Egyptian socialist movement, one of whose founders was Joseph Rosenthal, an Ashkenazi born in Beirut.[22]

The political identification of Egyptian Jewry with its country must be seen in its proper perspective. Although Jews were to be found in Egyptian political life, only about one third of the country's Jewish residents (21,944 of 63,550) were actually Egyptian citizens according to the census of 1927. Over a fifth held foreign passports, and nearly half (45 percent) were listed as "others," which included many stateless persons.[23] It would seem that relatively few of these stateless or foreign Jews tried to seek Egyptian citizenship under the Nationality Law of 1929 until almost a decade after its promulgation, when the government's Egyptianization program began to favor its own nationals and to put the squeeze on the foreigners' dominant position in the economy. By this time, however, it had become considerably more difficult in practice for non-Muslims to become citizens, despite the relatively liberal provisions of the law.[24]

[21] See Mizrahi, *L'Egypte et ses Juifs,* pp. 67–68; also Lois Gottesman, "Israel in Egypt: The Jewish Community of Egypt, 1922–1957" (unpublished master's thesis, Princeton University, 1982), pp. 27–28.

[22] See Public Records Office (London) FO 141/779/9065, file entitled "Cairo 1919–1921: Bolshevism," and also FO 371/7745, which contains a detailed police report on Rosenthal (who is also mentioned in the preceding file), dated November 16, 1922. For a broad survey of Jews and the Egyptian left, see Krämer, *Minderheit, Millet, Nation?,* pp. 334–53. Krämer rightly points out that the prominence of Jewish activists in the movement had the effect of branding the Jewish minority as a group with strong leftist leanings (ibid., pp. 334–35).

[23] See Krämer, *Minderheit, Millet, Nation?,* pp. 77–78 and the first table on p. 79. Gottesman, "Israel in Egypt," p. 40, interprets the census data somewhat differently, apparently viewing the "others" as primarily foreign nationals.

[24] See Shimon Shamir, "The Evolution of the Egyptian Nationality Laws and Their Application to the Jews in the Monarchy Period," in *The Jews of Egypt: A*

In the conquered eastern Ottoman Arab provinces, the political attitudes and aspirations of the local Jews, who unlike their brethren in Egypt comprised an almost totally indigenous element in the population, were quite different. In Syria and Iraq, the non-Muslim minorities welcomed the arrival of the European victors for obvious reasons. Already, in 1918, only a week after the armistice went into effect, the Jewish community of Baghdad, speaking on behalf of Iraqi Jewry, presented a petition to the civil commissioner of Baghdad requesting to become British subjects and opposing the promotion of any native (that is, Arab) government, which, as the document diplomatically put it, though "excellent in principle," would in reality be "hardly recommendable."[25]

Twice again, in 1919 and 1920, the Jews of Iraq appealed to Sir Percy Cox, the British high commissioner, to not allow an Arab government to come to power or at least to grant British citizenship to the Jewish community en masse. They argued that a native government could not avoid being prejudicial with respect to the non-Muslim minorities. Furthermore, they argued that "the British had no right to force them" as former Ottoman subjects to take on a new Iraqi citizenship against their will.[26] The Jews, of course, had no say in the matter. As one Englishman at the time noted with self-serving optimism, the Jews "were eventually appeased by the personal assurance that ample guarantees would be afforded against any form of local tyranny."[27] The value of such guarantees would soon be woefully apparent.

The Jews and the Christians, who had made similar representations to the British authorities, were given further assurances by the Amir Fayṣal, who was Great Britain's leading candidate for the Iraqi throne after he had been driven out of Syria by the French. The new

---

Mediterranean Society in Modern Times, ed. Shimon Shamir (Boulder, Colo., and London, 1987), pp. 33–67; Krämer, *Minderheit, Millet, Nation?,* pp. 78, 80; Gottesman, "Israel in Egypt," pp. 40–41. Gottesman emphasizes the bureaucratic difficulties and complications of obtaining citizenship under the Nationality Law, whereas Krämer only grants that this was the case after 1937.

[25] The full text of the petition is included in Part Two, pp. 256–258.

[26] Richard Coke, *The Heart of the Middle East,* pp. 220–21. See also Elie Kedourie, *The Chatham House Version and Other Middle-Eastern Studies* (New York and Washington, D. C., 1970), pp. 300–301.

[27] Coke, *The Heart of the Middle East,* p. 221. Coke did go on to concede: "It was, however, significant that the opposition of the Jews to the local application of 'self-determination' had to be met by a process of personal and moral persuasion, and *that there was in fact no logical argument to be urged against the position which they had taken up*" [my emphasis]. For a devastating critique of what Coke euphemistically refers to as "self-determination," see Kedourie, *England and the Middle East,* pp. 175–213.

monarch-to-be made numerous speeches, including one before the Jewish community leaders assembled in the house of the chief rabbi of Baghdad on July 18, 1921, one month before his coronation, in which he emphasized the equality of all Iraqis irrespective of religious confession.[28]

King Fayṣal continued to maintain cordial personal relations with individual members of the Jewish elite throughout his twelve-year reign, perhaps as Sylvia Haim has suggested because he himself was an outsider.[29] Fayṣal appointed as his first finance minister Sir Sassoon Heskel, the only Jew ever to hold cabinet rank in Iraq. Because of their generally superior educational qualifications, Jews and Christians could be found in many civil service positions during the first decade of the kingdom while it was still under British mandate. However, as early as 1921, the strong Arab nationalist element objected to the employment of foreigners and non-Muslims. This opposition intensified after Iraq gained full independence in 1932 and became even stronger after the death of Fayṣal the following year.

The Iraqi Jewish community as a whole remained studiously uninvolved in its country's political life. Most of the politicians and the people surrounding the king were strident Pan-Arab nationalists. In this atmosphere, there was really no place for Jews in the political parties.[30] And although the 1924 constitution, which was drafted mainly by British civil servants, guaranteed the equality of all Iraqis "before the law, whatever differences may exist in language, race or creed," it also declared Iraq to be an Islamic state, and following Ottoman models, it recognized the Jewish and Christian minorities as distinct entities with their own communal councils. The Electoral Law further emphasized their otherness by reserving eight seats in the Parliament for Jewish and Christian representatives.[31] What may

[28] See Philip Willard Ireland, *ʿIraq: A Study in Political Development* (London, 1937), pp. 329, 466; Sylvia G. Haim, "Aspects of Jewish Life in Baghdad under the Monarchy," *MES* 12, no. 2 (May 1976): 191; and Ghanīma, *Nuzhat al-Mushtāq,* p. 187. According to Ghanīma, after the speech the Jews brought out a Torah scroll in a golden case, which Fayṣal kissed in a gesture of respect.

[29] Haim, "Aspects of Jewish Life in Baghdad," p. 191.

[30] For the political atmosphere in Iraq at this time, see Reeva S. Simon, *Iraq between the Two World Wars: The Creation and Implementation of a Nationalist Ideology* (New York, 1986), pp. 45–57, passim; also Kedourie, *Arabic Political Memoirs and Other Studies,* pp. 46–47; and idem, *The Chatham House Version and Other Middle-Eastern Studies,* pp. 236–82.

[31] See the synopsis of the Organic Law (the Iraqi Constitution), Articles 2, 6, 78, and 80 in Ireland, *ʿIraq: A Study in Political Development,* pp. 382–86. For the Electoral Law, Article 6, see ibid., p. 389. The special minority representatives were

have seemed at first to be a guarantee of minority rights contributed in effect to the further isolation of Jews and Christians in a state that emphasized its Islamic Arab character with militant chauvinism.

The systematic massacre by the Iraqi army of the entire male population (some 400 men) of the Assyrian Christian village of Simel near Mosul served as a chilling warning to all minorities that the country's Arab nationalist policies would brook no opposition.[32] Similarly, the widespread anti-British sentiment among Muslim Iraqis, the increasingly vocal identification of Iraq with the Palestine Arab cause, and the barely veiled threats against the "abnormal signs and suspicious movements" among Iraqi Jews in the Arabic press[33] convinced most Jews that an apolitical profile safely on the sidelines of public life was their only prudent course. By the time the British mandate over the kingdom of Iraq ended in 1932, there simply was no viable place for either Jews or Christians in Iraqi politics.

Like the Jews of Iraq, the Jews of Syria entertained no enthusiasm for an independent Arab state. However, unlike their Iraqi brethren, they constituted an insignificant element in the general population numerically—approximately 3,500 Jews in Greater Lebanon and 10,600 in Syria proper out of a combined total population of some 2 million.[34] No less important, they were an insignificant economic element as well. Unlike the various and far more numerous Christian sects, they had no political pretensions.

The Jewries of the Syrian interior, which for all intents and purposes were the communities of Damascus, Aleppo, and Qamishli,

---

to be apportioned according to provinces, as follows: two Jews and one Christian (Baghdad), one Jew and two Christians (Mosul), one Jew and one Christian (Basra).

[32] See Lt.-Col. R. S. Stafford, *The Tragedy of the Assyrians* (London, 1935); Yusuf Malek, *The British Betrayal of the Assyrians* (Chicago, 1935); Simon, *Iraq between the Two World Wars,* pp. 119–23. For an Iraqi nationalist version of the incident, see Khaldun S. Husry, "The Assyrian Affair of 1933," *IJMES* 5, nos. 2–3 (April and June 1974): 161–76, 344–60. The noted British Arabist H.A.R. Gibb viewed the massacre of the Assyrians "however morally inexcusable," as "in effect a violent assertion that in an Arab Muslim State non-Arab and non-Muslim minorities have rights only in so far as they recognise that fundamental fact." See his review of Stafford, *The Tragedy of the Assyrians,* in *International Affairs* 15 (1936): 474–75.

[33] See the article translated in Part Two, pp. 345–347.

[34] These figures are based on the "highly imperfect" French census of 1922 and are somewhat low. However, the general proportion of Jews to the rest of the population is more or less correct. See Stephen Hemsley Longrigg, *Syria and Lebanon under French Mandate* (London, New York, and Toronto, 1958), pp. 127, n. 3, 128, no. 2. Five years after the 1922 rough census, "the most reliable statistics put the number of Jews in Syria (including Lebanon) at 18,950." See H. Kohn, "The Jews

found themselves at war's end not only under an Arab administration, but at the very nerve center of Arab nationalism. They had no part in the National Congress, which convened for the first time in Damascus on June 20, 1919, and claimed to be the official representative body for all of Syria, including the French-held coast and British-held Palestine.[35] Indeed, they were in no position to engage in any sort of active role in Syrian political life. They therefore turned their attention to internal communal affairs while maintaining discreet contacts with the authorities as required. They certainly welcomed the French takeover in 1920, as did the Maronites, the Greek Catholics, and some (but by no means all) of the other Christian groups. Many Jews had received some French education at the Alliance, lay, or mission schools. Like the Maronites of Lebanon, they viewed a French mandatory government as the best assurance of "freedom from Sunni domination."[36]

In accordance with France's colonial policy of *diviser pour regner,* which favored minorities and encouraged their participation in French-orchestrated public affairs, Syrian Jews were appointed to a few civil service positions and were given representation on the municipal and administrative state councils of Aleppo and Damascus. Their numbers were still too small to allow them representation on the fifteen-man Federal Council of Syria. Emboldened, however, by the mandatory government's pro-minority policy, the Jewish leadership of Aleppo actively campaigned for and won a seat that was to be reserved for a Jewish delegate to the Federal Council.[37] The precedent of reserving a seat for a Jewish representative was maintained in the parliament elected under the new constitution in 1932.[38]

Even under French tutelage, Syrian Jews could hardly be considered active participants in public life. There were the one or two notables on the representative bodies established by the French, but

---

in Syria," *The New Judaea* 3, no. 20 (June 17, 1927): 333. Kohn allows, however, that this figure "may be slightly overstated."

[35] Concerning the National Congress and its activities, see Philippe David, *Un gouvernement arabe à Damas: le congrès syrien* (Paris, 1923). Although Jews were not represented at the Congress, and none in the British or French zones had taken part in the elections, the Congress declared itself in a motion presented to the King-Crane Commission to be "armed with mandates and full powers by the Muslim, Christian, and Jewish inhabitants of our various districts." See ibid, p. 66.

[36] Longrigg, *Syria and Lebanon,* p. 144.

[37] "Informations 6. Etat d'Alep. Les israélites et le conseil fédéral," *Paix et Droit* 3, no. 10 (December 1923): 9; also J. Farhi, "Aperçu, général sur la communauté de Damas," *Hamenora* 2, nos. 7–8 (July–August 1924): 226.

[38] Longrigg, *Syria and Lebanon,* p. 190, n. 4.

these were institutions of extremely circumscribed authority, on which, in any case, the Jews formed the smallest and weakest of minorities. They could not afford to offend anyone—not the French, who were for the time being their protectors, or the much more numerous Christians, who for years had demonstrated great antipathy and hostility toward them, and not least the nationalists, who constituted the overwhelming majority of the population. As Syrian politics became increasingly vociferous and violent in the 1930s, and as Syria, like Iraq, became a leading center of anti-Zionist agitation, Jews became even less inclined to become involved in the country's affairs, whose course they were utterly powerless to affect.

North African Jewry was not more attracted to Arab nationalism, which was still a relatively weak and unorganized force in the postwar Maghreb, than were the Jews of the Middle Eastern countries. Their political outlook and aspirations, however, were quite different, as was their general situation.

First, the Jews of North Africa constituted a much more significant demographic element than did their Middle Eastern brethren in both absolute and proportional terms. There were more Jews in Morocco and Algeria alone than in all of the Middle Eastern Arab countries put together. Jews formed between 2.5 and 3 percent of the overall population in each of the Maghrebi states and considerably higher percentages (10 to 40 percent) in the principal towns and cities.[39]

Second, the North African states were outright colonial entities. They were geographically much closer to the ruling powers of France, Italy, and Spain. They had large numbers of European settlers who not only dominated the political and economic life, but whose foreign culture was given undisputed preeminence over native culture. The colonial powers had made no commitments of the kind that the British had with the Hashemite sharifs of Mecca, and they were under no mandatory obligation to prepare the territories for eventual independence. Colonial rule gave every appearance of permanence. After all, France in 1930 was celebrating its centenary in Algeria. The following year marked the fiftieth anniversary of its presence in Tunisia.

Even after World War I, Tunisian and Moroccan Jews were still technically dhimmīs, protected subjects of the Muslim rulers—the

[39] See the detailed tables of population statistics in Maurice Eisenbeth, *Les Juifs d'Afrique du Nord: démographie et onomastique,* (Algiers, 1936), pp. 13–66; and André Chouraqui, *Histoire des Juifs en Afrique du Nord* (Paris, 1985), pp. 531–81.

bey of Tunisia and the sultan of Morocco. French policy in both protectorates was to maintain the traditional social balance (*équilibre social*) as far as possible. This policy was a cause of considerable frustration not only to the small, highly gallicized urban Jewish elite, but also to the upwardly mobile middle classes, who were eager to extricate themselves from the jurisdiction of Muslim courts in civil matters and to leave their overcrowded, unsanitary quarters—the Tunisian *ḥāra* and the Moroccan *mellāḥ*.

The Tunisian Jews and their liberal French allies had been lobbying for an improved legal status or, at least, for some mechanism by which individual Jews might obtain French citizenship. For the first three decades of the protectorate, no Tunisian Jews had been able to acquire French nationality. However, a series of decrees issued in 1910, 1921, and 1923 improved the opportunities for Muslim and Jewish subjects of the bey to become naturalized citizens of France. It was the Jews primarily who availed themselves of the new laws. Between 1910 and 1923, only 299 Jews became French citizens. During the following decade, however, 6,460 Jews—over 10 percent of Tunisian Jewry—acquired certificates of naturalization.[40]

Moroccan Jewry was several times larger than Tunisian Jewry. But it had been under French rule for a considerably shorter period. It had been penetrated far less extensively by the modernizing forces of westernization and possessed a smaller gallicized elite. (As late as 1936, the French authorities estimated that only about 20,000 Jews, or 12.5 percent of the Jewish population in the protectorate, spoke French.[41]) The campaign for obtaining French citizenship was conducted primarily at first by the Alliance teachers in the country, rather than by the native Jewish leadership, although it was taken up by the Alliance alumni and other Francophiles. The French authorities, for their part, adamantly refused to make any concessions on the issue of Jewish naturalization on either the individual or group level. They wished to avoid any backlash among the European settlers of the sort

[40] Chouraqui, *Between East and West,* pp. 168–69; H. Z. [J. W.] Hirschberg, *A History of the Jews in North Africa*, vol. 2 (Leiden, 1981), p. 134; Goldstein, *Libération ou annexion,* pp. 482–86. Both the actual number and percentage of Jews who were naturalized were in fact higher, since all dependents of an individual also became French citizens. By the time Tunisia achieved independence in 1956, approximately one third (35,000) of the Jews living in Tunisia held French citizenship.

[41] Michael M. Laskier, *The Alliance Israélite Universelle and the Jewish Communities of Morocco: 1862–1962* (Albany, N.Y., 1983), p. 169. This figure was challenged by Yomtob Sémach, the Alliance's delegate to Morocco, as representing only half the actual number. See Y. D. Sémach, "Le recensement de 1936 au Maroc," *Paix et Droit* 19, no. 6 (June 1939): 8–10.

experienced in Algeria. They also wished to avoid offending the Muslim population and the nascent nationalist movement that was beginning to stir in the early 1930s.[42] Furthermore, impediments of international law stood in the way of any naturalization of Moroccan Jews. The Convention of Madrid in 1880 had made it almost impossible for a native Moroccan to hold foreign citizenship while living on Moroccan soil. The principle of perpetual allegiance to the sultan by his subjects was upheld by the Treaty of Algeciras in 1906 and by the sharifan *dahir* (decree) of November 8, 1921.[43] Thus, the French officials could argue that even if they wished to do so, they were unable to accord Moroccan Jews French citizenship either en masse, as they had done with the Jews of Algeria, or on an individual basis as in Tunisia. With the exception of a few individuals who were able to prove Algerian descent, the overwhelming majority of Moroccan Jews remained subjects of the sultan throughout the protectorate era. Nevertheless, most of them—and not just the French educated among them—considered France to be their *patrie adoptée.*

With the exception of the International Zone of Tangier where Jews could and did take part in the Legislative Assembly of the municipality, Moroccan Jews were for all intents and purposes excluded from the political life of the protectorate. There was not a single Jewish representative in either the French or the Moroccan Section of the Government Council from its founding in 1919 until 1947, when a series of reforms instituted by the Residency provided for the election of six Jewish delegates to the Moroccan Section. One delegate each was to be chosen by the communal committees of Casablanca, Fez, Marrakesh, Meknes, Oujda, and Rabat. Thus, the vote was not only indirect, but many Moroccan Jews were still not represented. It should be noted that the Government Council had no real political power in any case. Its function was primarily consultative in budgetary matters. However, the exclusion of the Jews even from such a token institution of governance throughout most of the protectorate period was indicative of their total lack of any political standing and their near powerlessness as a group in Moroccan society.[44]

[42] Laskier, *The Alliance Israélite Universelle and the Jewish Communities of Morocco,* pp. 163–71; idem, "Yōm Ṭōv Dāvīd Ṣemaḥ vīhūdē Marōqō: 1913–1940 (Nittū'aḥ ve-tīᶜud)," *Mi-Qedem ūmi-Yam* 2 (1986): 170–71, 174–79; Chouraqui, *Between East and West,* pp. 176–79. See also Part Two, p. 302.

[43] See André Chouraqui, *La condition juridique de l'Israélite marocain* (Paris, 1950), pp. 59–76; for the texts of the pertinent documents, see ibid., pp. 225–27.

[44] Ibid., pp. 111–13; idem, *Between East and West,* p. 179; and Laskier, *The Alliance Israélite Universelle and the Jewish Communities of Morocco,* p. 177; and

In contradistinction to Moroccan Jewry, the Jews of Tunisia did have some political representation in their country. The Grand Council of the Regency, which was established in 1922, enjoyed a greater measure of actual authority than did the Moroccan Government Council. The Jews were one of the five native electoral groups that directly or indirectly could choose delegates to the Tunisian Section (the French Section, of course, was dominant) of the Grand Council. One of the twenty-six seats in the Tunisian Section was reserved for a Jewish representative elected by the Jewish notables, who in turn had been elected by the Jewish community of Tunis.[45] Jews who had acquired French citizenship could vote directly as individuals (and not as members of the Jewish community) for the French Section. Native Jews were also represented on municipal councils and in the national and regional chambers of commerce in Tunisia.[46]

Though certainly limited, the participation of Jews in the officially sanctioned political life of Tunisia during the two decades following World War I was clearly far greater than that of their fellow Jews in Morocco.

Algerian Jews had been French citizens for two generations by the time World War I drew to a close. Their political aspirations, therefore, were necessarily quite different from those of Moroccan and Tunisian Jewry. Their goal was not to achieve citizenship, but rather to gain full acceptance as Frenchmen in Algerian society. To emphasize their Frenchness, and since the official Jewish organization, the Consistory, was forbidden by law from engaging in political activities, a group of young Algerian Jewish intellectuals founded an organization with the nondescript name of the Algerian Jewish Committee for Social Studies (usually called by the shorter and less Jewish appellation of the Algerian Committee for Social Studies, or CESA, according to its French acronym). The committee, headed by Dr. Henri Aboulker, a war hero and scion of one of the leading families of the Algerian Jewish elite, acted as a kind of antidefamation league. Its

---

Graham H. Stuart, *The International City of Tangier,* 2nd ed. (Stanford, Calif., 1955), pp. 113–14, 208, 222, 237. See also Part Two, pp. 300–301.

[45] Elie Fitoussi and Aristide Benazet, *L'état tunisien et le Protectorat français: histoire et organisation (1525 à 1931),* vol. 1 (Paris, 1931), pp. 234–55 (pp. 237–38, n. 2, deals specifically with the Jewish seat and the mechanism for electing a delegate to it). Concerning the highly circumscribed powers of the Grand Council, see Goldstein, *Libération ou annexion,* pp. 444–56.

[46] Chouraqui, *Between East and West,* p. 172.

stated goal was "to be on the alert that the free exercise of the Jews' rights as citizens not be violated or ignored."[47]

The CESA was in effect a lobby that worked through the French political process to achieve fuller social and civil rights for Algerian Jews, not as Jews, but as Frenchmen. One of its original aims, for example, was to remove the barrier preventing Jews from being accepted into membership in the Algerian General Association of Students. The committee also acted as a public relations organization and published the *Gold Book of Algerian Jewry* (*Le Livre d'Or des Israélites Algériens*), which listed all of the Jews who received honors and citations during the war, as well as those killed in action. The book was distributed to military and public figures both in Algeria and in France.

During the immediate postwar years, most of the stated goals of the committee were achieved, and the organization gradually became inactive. However, with the virulent recrudescence of anti-Semitism in the 1930s, CESA was revived in February 1937 and became the premier political organ and voice of Algerian Jewry.[48]

Libya was the Maghrebi country with the smallest Jewish population and was the least conscious politically during this period. There was in Libya a small Europeanized elite, some of whose members already possessed Italian citizenship or some other foreign nationality. This group constituted not only the most enthusiastic supporters of Italian colonial rule, but also the strongest advocates of cultural assimilation. Another small minority of Libyan Jews, who were also members of the educated elite, were adherents of Zionism, not the secular variety that was predominant in Europe and Palestine, but a Zionism that emphasized traditional spiritual and cultural values. This group was directly opposed to the Italianizers' assimilationist tendencies.[49]

The apolitical majority of Libyan Jews was concerned only with eking out a livelihood and preserving its traditional way of life against the encroachments of the colonial government and its Italianized Jewish allies. Continuous attempts by the authorities to coerce Jews to desecrate the Sabbath by requiring attendance in school or shops to remain open on Saturdays, as well as other ill-conceived policies,

[47] Ansky, *Les Juifs d'Algérie*, p. 77.

[48] Ibid., pp. 77–80; and Michel Abitbol, *Les Juifs d'Afrique du Nord sous Vichy* (Paris, 1983), pp. 29–31, 151–53.

[49] De Felice, *Jews in an Arab Land*, pp. 80–116.

alienated most Jews.[50] For the Libyan Jewish masses, Italy simply was not the "adopted fatherland" in the way that France was for so many Jews in the rest of the Maghreb. On the other hand, until the implementation of Fascist racial laws in the late 1930s and early 1940s, most of Libyan Jewry certainly appreciated Italian colonial rule, autocratic and high-handed as it was, as being far preferable to Muslim Arab alternatives. Like the great majority of Jews in the Maghreb and Mashreq (the Arab East), they were singularly unattracted by Arab national aspirations, which were intimately and inextricably interwined with Islamic sentiments.

During the period between the two world wars, Arab national consciousness was rising. But so too was a Jewish self-awareness that transcended local and regional particularism and that would even transcend the allure of "superior" European cultures when those cultures failed them. Increasingly, as the Jews of Arab lands sought to orient themselves amid the new social, economic, and political realities that emerged during these years, they found themselves affected, either directly or indirectly, by the Zionist movement—directly in its appeals to their own minds and hearts and indirectly in its effect on their Arab neighbors, whose own attitudes toward them were gradually being shaped by the growing conflict between Arabs and Jews in Palestine.

[50] Ibid., pp. 117–67. See also Harvey Goldberg, "The Jewish Community of Tripoli in Relation to Italian Jewry and Italians in Tripoli," *Les relations intercommunautaires juives en Méditerranée Occidentale, XIIIe-XXe siècles,* ed. J.-L. Miège (Paris, 1984), pp. 79–89.

4

ZIONISM AND THE JEWS OF ARAB LANDS

The Jews of the Arab world shared in the same messianic hope of redemption as did Jews everywhere throughout the history of the Diaspora. The last great outburst of millennial hysteria in the Jewish world had begun in the Levant with the appearance of the false redeemer Sabbatay Ṣevi in the second half of the eighteenth century. Kabbalistic mysticism with its strong apocalyptic overtones continued to permeate Middle Eastern and North African piety even after the Sabbatian debacle.[1] Moreover, Oriental Jews generally maintained very strong, direct ties with the land of Israel to a much greater extent than did their brethren in Europe. This was due to the greater physical propinquity of most of Oriental Jewry to the Holy Land and the fact that, until the colonial era, the vast majority of Oriental Jews lived in the Ottoman Empire, of which Palestine was a part. Many Jewish communities in the Muslim world had a long-standing practice of supporting institutions in the four holy cities of Jerusalem, Hebron, Safed, and Tiberias. The rabbinical emissaries (Heb. *shelūḥē de-rabbānān*), who frequently made the rounds of Middle Eastern and North African communities to collect contributions, were in fact important media of communication between Palestine and its Yishuv (the Palestinian Jewish community) and these scattered Jewries.[2]

[1] The comprehensive work on Sabbatianism and its impact on both Oriental and European Jewry is Gershom G. Scholem, *Sabbetai Ṣevi: The Mystical Messiah (1626–1676)* (Princeton, 1973). For a brief sketch of Kabbalistic elements in Oriental Judaism, see Raphael Patai, *The Seed of Abraham: Jews and Arabs in Contact and Conflict* (Salt Lake City, 1986), pp. 207–20.

[2] A great deal has been written in recent years on the multifaceted bonds that tied Middle Eastern and North African Jews (particularly the latter) to the land of Israel. See, for example, Shalom Bar-Asher and Aaron Maman, eds., *Yehūdē Ṣefōn*

During the nineteenth century, word of Sir Moses Montefiore's philanthropic reclamation and building projects in Palestine reached Jews in Arab lands via the Hebrew journals. These endeavors, too, received financial support. They offered a new and more modern object of charitable giving and served as an intermediary stage between the traditional religious philanthropies and the soon-to-be-established Zionist funds.

Among the Jews of the Islamic world, there was a tradition of ᶜaliya (emigration to Palestine) going back to the Middle Ages. The Maghrebi Jews, in particular, came to constitute large, distinguishable communities in Jerusalem, Haifa, and Jaffa. The revival of these towns in modern times was due in no small measure to the influx of North African Jewish settlers in the early and mid-nineteenth century.[3] Until the late nineteenth century, however, ᶜaliya for Oriental Jews was mainly a personal matter of piety for individuals, not a group concern. The first modern instance of Arabic-speaking Jews migrating to Palestine en masse involved the Yemenites, who, as mentioned in Chapter 2, began pouring into the country in 1881, fleeing the harsh conditions under which they lived in Yemen and gripped by a wave of messianic enthusiasm.

The combination of individuals and groups of Oriental Jewish settlers in the Holy Land constituted substantial numbers in the Yishuv up to the end of World War I.[4] Unlike most traditional Ashkenazi *ᶜōlīm* prior to the modern Zionist pioneering that began during

---

Afrīqa ve-Ereṣ Yisrā'ēl me-ᶜAliyat R. Ḥayyīm b. ᶜAṭṭar ᶜad Yāmēnū (1741–1981): Ṣiyyōnūt, ᶜAliya, ve-Hityashshevūt (Jerusalem, 1981). See also *Peᶜamim* 24 (1985), in which four articles are devoted to this topic. On rabbinical emissaries and Oriental Jewry, see the important study of Avraham Yaari, *Shelūḥē Ereṣ Yisrā'ēl: Tōledōt he-Shelīḥūt mēhā-Āreṣ la-Gōla mē-Ḥurbān Bayit Shēnī ᶜad ha-Mē'ā ha-Teshaᶜ ᶜEsreh* (Jerusalem, 1950/51). Of course, the emissaries went to Europe and, from the eighteenth century onward, to the New World as well.

[3] See Nahum Slouschz, "La colonie des Maghrabim en Palestine, ses origines et son état actuel," *AM* 2 (1904): 229–57; idem, "Les Maghrabim à Jérusalem," *RMM* 6 (1908): 676–78; Zev Vilnay, "ha-Yehūdīm ha-Maᶜarāviyyīm ke-Ḥalūṣē ha-Yishūv bā-Āreṣ," in *Yehūdē Ṣefōn Afrīqa ve-Ereṣ Yisrā'ēl,* ed. Shalom Bar-Asher and Aharon Maman (Jerusalem, 1981), pp. 83–90; Jacob Barnai, "hā-ᶜĒda ha-Maᶜarāvīt bīrūshālāyīm ba-Mē'a ha-19," in ibid., pp. 91–102; and Henry Toledano, "Yahadūt Mārōqō ve-Yishūv Ereṣ Yisrā'ēl: Tōledōt hā-ᶜAliyyōt ha-Shōnōt shel Yehūdē Mārōqō mēha-Mē'a ha-Shēsh ᶜEsreh ve-ᶜad Rēshīt ha-Mē'a hā-ᶜEsrīm," in *Hāgūt ᶜIvrīt be-Arṣōt hā-Islām,* ed. Menahem Zohori et al. (Jerusalem, 1981), pp. 229–52.

[4] Jews from North Africa were the founders of the modern Jewish communities in Haifa and Jaffa. In Haifa, they and their descendants constituted a majority of the Jewish population until the early twentieth century. In Jerusalem, where nearly half the Jewish community was Sephardi or Oriental, there were an estimated 2,000

the last two decades of the nineteenth century, the Sephardi and Oriental Jews who settled in Palestine were, on the whole, actually occupied in earning livelihoods through commerce, handicraft, and manual labor and were not engaged exclusively in prayer, study, and living off the *ḥaluqqa*, the dole funded by charitable contributions of Diaspora Jewry. The significance of the 10,000 to 20,000 Jews who came from Arab countries to Palestine during the nineteenth and early twentieth centuries should not be exaggerated. With the exception of the Yemenites, they were after all a minute fraction of the Jewish populations of the countries from which they came. On the other hand, their importance should not be underestimated or ignored. For they were not only the precursors of later mass immigration, but they also represented sentiments and impulses that were more widespread among their communities of origin than their own actual numbers might seem to suggest.

EGYPT

There is some evidence that at least a few pre-Herzlian Zionists were among the Eastern European Jews who settled in Egypt during the latter decades of the nineteenth century. Their activities, if any, were extremely limited and probably never went beyond their own small circle without exerting any influence at all upon the other elements of the Egyptian Jewish population.[5]

The earliest apostle of Zionism to actively propagandize for the Zionist cause in Arab countries was a young Turkish Jew named Joseph Marco Barukh.[6] He was a romantic and a tragic figure. Born in Constantinople in 1872, he died by his own hand in Florence in 1899 at the age of twenty-seven. He had studied in several European universities and was originally involved with radical student groups, which resulted in his being under police surveillance for much of his

Maghrebi Jews alone on the eve of World War I. There were more than 4,000 Yemenite Jews in Palestine at the time as well. See Abraham J. Brawer, "Israel, State of: Jewish Communities," *EJ* 9: 495–505; Alex Carmel, "Haifa," *EJ* 7: 1137; Hayyim J. Cohen, "Zionism in North African and Asian Countries," *EJ* 16: 1127, Table 2.

[5] See Zvi Yehuda, "Rēshītāh shel ha-Peʿīlūt ha-Ṣiyyōnīt be-Miṣrayim—Agūdat 'Bar Kōkhvā' (1897–1904)," *Sefunot,* n.s. 1 (1980): 312, n. 1*, and the sources cited there.

[6] See Jacob Weinschal, *Markō Barūkh: Nevī Milḥemet ha-Shiḥrūr* (Jerusalem, 1980). Although rather romanticized, this biography offers the most detailed picture of Barukh's life and is based upon his papers in the Central Zionist Archives.

brief adult life. His involvement with Jewish nationalism began when he joined the Zionist student association Kadimah in Vienna in 1893.

The following year, Barukh was in Algeria, where he tried to propagate Jewish nationalism among the rapidly assimilating Algerian Jews and edited a short-lived journal called *Le Juge*. He encountered the opposition not only of Jewish communal leaders, but also of the French authorities who suspected him of being an anarchist. He was forced to leave Algeria in 1895. Although he did not seem to leave behind any sort of organized movement in Algeria, he may have succeeded in raising the consciousness of some local Jews to the Zionist idea. Two years after Barukh's departure, an Algerian Jew was attending the First Zionist Congress in Basle. That same year, a Jewish youth organization in Constantine sent a strong letter of support to Theodor Herzl, and by 1900, there was a Zionist organization in Constantine.[7]

After a year of Zionist proselytizing in Bulgaria, where he founded a number of Zionist cells and another journal, Barukh went to Egypt. He arrived in Suez City in July 1896, and after several weeks in Port Said and Alexandria, he wound up in Cairo. There, he began haranguing Jewish audiences at every possible opportunity in Italian, Ladino, Arabic, and German. The vagabond agitator made almost no headway with the Sephardi community, which dubbed him "loco" (crazy), but he enjoyed a certain measure of success among the Ashkenazim, who employed him in their community's religious school. Together with Jacques Harmalin and Joseph Leibovitch, two local businessmen, he founded a Zionist circle that several months later became the Bar Kokhba Society with thirty founding members.[8]

[7] For Barukh's activities in Algeria, see Weinschal, *Markō Barūkh,* p. 19. Herzl twice refers to him as "the anarchist" in his diaries and also as "this obvious madman." See *The Complete Diaries of Theodor Herzl,* ed. Raphael Patai and trans. Harry Zohn (New York and London, 1960), vol. 2, p. 652, and vol. 3, pp. 875–76. Actually, two Algerian Jews were at the first Zionist Congress: M. E. Attali, representing Constantine, and Dr. E. Valensin, representing Montpellier in France. See *Protokoll des I. Zionistenkongresses in Basel vom 29. bis 31. August 1897.* Neu Herausgegeben. (Prague, 1911), pp. 219, 221. For the letter to Herzl from the young people's association in Constantine, see CZA (Jerusalem) Z 1/279 (September 12, 1897). Partially translated in Michel Abitbol, "Zionist Activity in the Maghreb," *The Jerusalem Quarterly* 21 (Fall 1981): 62. The head of the Zionist organization in Constantine in 1900 was Dr. Valensin, who had attended the First Zionist Congress representing Montpellier. See CZA (Jerusalem) Z 1/313 (August 12, 1900) and also Abitbol, "Zionist Activity in the Maghreb," p. 67.

[8] Yehuda, "Rēshītāh shel ha-Peʿīlūt ha-Ṣiyyōnīt be-Miṣrayim," pp. 314–16.

Until the turn of the century, most of the people who joined Bar Kokhba were Ashkenazim. As the officers of the society explained in a report sent to the Central Zionist Office in Vienna in 1900: "In general, Zionism is well known and accepted by the Ashkenazi colony. A vague idea of our movement flutters among the native Jews, not only in Cairo, but in all of Egypt."[9]

However, the authors of the report went on to say that they believed it would not be difficult to win over the non-Ashkenazi Egyptian Jews once sufficient propaganda material was available in the locally understood languages (Arabic, Italian, French, and Spanish). And indeed, by 1901, when membership had risen to 160, nearly half were Arabic or Ladino speakers. The following year the number of members more than doubled again, and by this time the society boasted a large library and reading room, a clubhouse containing a public cafe, and a school that had opened in 1900 with 100 students and now had nearly 300, many of whom were from the non-Ashkenazi Jewish communities.[10]

Zionist associations began forming in other Egyptian cities. In Alexandria, Charles Bogdadly, the son of a Levantine Jewish banker, founded a group in 1898. By 1904, there were two Zionist organizations, both led mainly by members of the Alexandrian Sephardi elite. Other Zionist associations had been established by this time in Port Said, Suez, Tanta, and Mansura. In addition to these organized groups, individuals purchased shekels, which were required for membership in the World Zionist Organization, in al-Mahalla al-Kubra, and in Damanhur.[11] A plethora of small, independent, and often short-lived Zionist groups sprang up in Cairo and Alexandria during the first decade of the twentieth century. Several Zionist or pro-Zionist periodicals in various languages, such as *Le Messager Sioniste* (French) and *Miṣraim* (Judeo-Arabic and Arabic), appeared in Egypt at this time. Again, most of these publications were of short duration. Some groups and individual activists also began publishing articles

[9] CZA (Jerusalem) Z 1/308.1582, from Jacques Galitzenstein and Aaron Kreutchmar (June 13, 1900). An extract from the French text of this report is included in Jacob M. Landau, *Jews in Nineteenth-Century Egypt* (New York and London, 1969), pp. 275–77.

[10] Yehuda, "Rēshītāh shel ha-Peʿīlūt ha-Ṣiyyōnīt be-Miṣrayim," pp. 328–30; Landau, *Jews in Nineteenth-Century Egypt,* pp. 81–82, 290–92.

[11] On the Zionist organizations and activities outside Cairo, see Yehuda, "Rēshītāh shel ha-Peʿīlūt ha-Ṣiyyōnīt be-Miṣrayim," pp. 332–40; and Landau, *Jews in Nineteenth-Century Egypt,* pp. 121–23.

and letters to the editor on Zionism in the Egyptian Arabic and foreign-language press.[12]

Throughout the first two decades of its existence, the Zionist movement in Egypt was decidedly more successful in attracting Ashkenazim than the indigenous Jewish masses. Part of the problem seems to have been due to a chronic shortage of propaganda materials in the necessary languages. Letters from the local associations to Zionist headquarters in Europe continually emphasize this fact. The Sephardi grandee families of Egypt, and especially in Cairo, posed an even more difficult problem. According to one Zionist leader, himself a native Jew, these men could be won over solely through direct personal persuasion (*la propagande de personne à personne*).[13] However, the only member of one of these ruling families to be converted to the Jewish national cause in the early years was Jack Mosseri. Other members of his family followed after him later, among them his cousin Albert Mosseri, who in 1920 founded and edited *Israël*, the pro-Zionist weekly, which for twenty years was Egypt's leading Jewish newspaper, read by Jews in other Arab countries as well.

Egyptian Zionism was plagued by a lack of unity throughout this early period despite the modest successes of its cultural and fund-raising programs (for example, over 800 Jews bought shekels in 1913).[14] It was not until after the outbreak of World War I, when more than 11,000 Jewish refugees arrived from Palestine, many of whom were *ḥalūṣīm* (Zionist pioneers), that a genuine federation of Egyptian Zionist organizations was finally established. The Palestinians made a highly favorable impression on the Egyptian Jews and probably did more to awaken large numbers of them to Zionism than many of the previous efforts of the local Zionist groups.[15]

[12] On the numerous Zionist organizations, see Zvi Yehuda, "ha-Irgūnīm ha-Ṣiyyōniyyīm be-Miṣrayim (1904–1917)," *Shevet ve-ᶜAm,* 2nd ser., 3 (April 1978): 147–96; Landau, *Jews in Nineteenth-Century Egypt,* pp. 120–24. On the early Egyptian Zionist journals, see Landau, *Jews in Nineteenth-Century Egypt,* pp. 102–3, 119–20. For numerous clippings and summaries of articles and letters by Zionists in such Egyptian papers as *Les Pyramides, Le Progrès Egyptien,* and *al-Muqaṭṭam,* see CZA (Jerusalem) Z 1/313 and Z 3/752.

[13] CZA (Jerusalem) Z 3/752, letter from Samuel Hassamsony, Cairo, to Central Zionist Office, Berlin (June 10, 1912). See also his many other letters and reports in this same file.

[14] CZA (Jerusalem) F 21/1 (May 24, 1913).

[15] See Gudrun Krämer, *Minderheit, Millet, Nation? Die Juden in Ägypten 1914–1952.* Studien zum Minderheitenproblem im Islam, 7 (Wiesbaden, 1982), pp. 353–59; Landau, *Jews in Nineteenth-Century Egypt,* pp. 123–24; and Yehuda, "ha-Irgūnīm ha-Ṣiyyōniyyīm be-Miṣrayim," pp. 184–95.

Modern Zionist stirrings also began in the Maghreb as the official movement was just coming into existence in Europe. As noted, Marco Barukh had been active in Algeria the year before he came to Egypt, though it is not known what, if anything, he accomplished during his sojourn there.

The first locus of Zionist activity was in Constantine, which had the most traditional and least assimilationist Jewish community of all the major cities of Algeria. In a letter sent to Theodor Herzl in the wake of the First Zionist Congress, the Jewish Youth Association of Constantine wrote that his undertaking "to realize the Zionist idea . . . has aroused an enormous response in Constantine."[16] The enormity of the response seems to have been the hyperbole of youthful enthusiasm more than anything else, for the actual number of Algerian Zionists remained insignificant until after the establishment of the State of Israel. As late as 1919, fewer than 400 Algerian members were registered with the French Zionist Federation.[17]

Algerian Jewry had set upon a course of radical assimilation and identified itself totally with France prior to the rise of Zionism. The virulent anti-Semitism of the *pieds noirs* (European colonists), which had reached a feverish and violent pitch the very year that the First Zionist Congress was held, and the hostility of the Muslim population stiffened the resolve of Algerian Jews to assert their Frenchness rather than to turn to the Jewish nationalist solution. The overwhelming majority of Algeria's Jews remained almost impervious to Zionism even as an object of philanthropy.[18]

The encounter between the Jewries of Morocco and Tunisia and modern Zionism was totally different from the Algerian case. The Jews of these two Maghrebi states were still deeply rooted in their

[16] CZA (Jerusalem) Z 1/279. Letter dated September 9, 1897.

[17] Fédération Sioniste de France, *Rapport Général, Année 1918–1919,* pp. 8–9, cited in Doris Bensimon-Donath, *Immigrants d'Afrique du Nord en Israël: évolution et adaptation* (Paris, 1970), p. 77. Zionist groups in five communities are listed: Algiers (30 members), Ferryville (21), Mostaganem (30), Tlemcen (129), and Medea (179). However, these figures may not be entirely accurate. Ferryville was in Tunisia, not Algeria. Nor is any mention made of Constantine, the original center of Algerian Zionism, or of Bordj Bou Arredidj, which had a Zionist group at the end of World War I (see G. Hirschler, "North Africa, Zionism in," *EZI* 2: 848). However, these numbers are a fair approximation of the proportions of Algerian affiliation with the Zionist movement.

[18] See the statistics cited by Bensimon-Donath, *Immigrants d'Afrique du Nord en Israël,* pp. 77–78 and 556, Annex 2.

tradition. Word of the Zionist movement's birth in Europe fueled the cherished hopes for national redemption that were an integral part of their religious conviction. Indeed, for more than half a century, there was a definite religious coloring to both Tunisian and Moroccan Zionism, all the way up to the mass exodus of the Jews from these countries after the establishment of the State of Israel.[19]

A group in Tunis calling itself "Zionist Youth" sent its greetings to the First Zionist Congress in 1897. The following year, greetings arrived at the Second Congress from "Tunisian Zionists" and from "the Zionist Group" of Mogador, Morocco. Nothing is known about these early groups except that they sent annual messages of support to the early congresses.[20]

The first two formally organized Zionist associations appeared independently of one another at about the same time in Morocco in 1900 in Mogador and Tetouan. Both of these coastal towns were in direct contact with Europe. As already mentioned in Chapter 2, the *Haskāla* had made inroads in Mogador during the latter decades of the nineteenth century, and some Jews there received Hebrew newspapers and books from Europe, which must have been the first source of information on the Jewish national revival.

The impetus for concerted Zionist activity apparently came with the arrival of Moses Logasy, a former resident of Mogador, who had become a merchant in Manchester. He returned to his native town at the turn of the century to sell shares in the Jewish Colonial Trust, apparently with the support of the local Alliance school director (an unusual circumstance, to be sure, since the Alliance Israélite Universelle was already at this early date rather cool toward the Zionist movement). Intensive propagandizing and public gatherings succeeded in winning broad support for Zionism in the community and resulted in the establishment of the Shaᶜarē Ṣiyyōn Society, presided over by leading merchants David Bohbot and Samuel Bendahan

[19] There have been several important recent studies on the historical development of Zionism in Morocco and Tunisia. Most noteworthy is Zvi Yehuda, *Organized Zionism in Morocco: 1900–1948,* 2 vols. (unpublished doctoral dissertation, Hebrew University, 1981) [Heb. with Engl. summary]. Less comprehensive but also valuable are Elie Benarroch, *La France et le sionisme au Maroc, 1897–1956* (thèse de 3e Cycle, l'Université de Provence, 1984); Shlomo Barad, *Le Mouvement sioniste en Tunisie* (Tel Aviv, 1980) [Heb. with Fr. introduction]; and al-Hādī al-Taymūmī (Hedi Timoumi), *al-Nashāṭ al-Ṣahyūnī bi-Tūnis bayn 1897 & 1948* (Tunis, 1982).

[20] See *Protokoll des I. Zionistenkongresses,* p. 257; *Stenographisches Protokoll der Verhandlungen des II. Zionisten-Congresses* (Vienna, 1898), pp. 465, 468; and *Stenographisches Protokoll der Verhandlungen des V. Zionisten-Congresses* (Vienna,

and by the community's spiritual leader Rabbi Jacob Ifargan. Within six months, the society had sold over 200 shekels and had collected 600 pesetas, which entitled it to send two representatives to the Fifth Zionist Congress.[21] However, like all of the early Moroccan and Tunisian Zionist associations, it did not take advantage of this privilege or participate in any way in the political and organizational life of the World Zionist Organization. For the early Maghrebi Zionists, the World Zionist Organization was, in the words of Zvi Yehuda, "fulfilling its God-sent mission and as such, was not to be questioned or criticized." This reverent messianic attitude resulted in "an unlimited faith in the WZO and its leadership, to the extent that they were completely uninterested in obtaining representation in the WZO's institutions."[22] It was not until after World War II that Moroccan Zionists considered it necessary that they be represented at the congresses. Tunisian Jewry, on the other hand, began sending delegates as of the Tenth Congress in 1911.[23]

One of the initiators of the short-lived Shivat Ṣiyyōn Society in Tetouan was a Russian-born physician, Dr. J. Berliawsky, who was probably familiar with Jewish nationalism before coming to Morocco. Like many of these early groups for whom Zionism also represented a cultural revival, the Shivat Ṣiyyōn Society established a Hebrew library.[24]

1901), pp. 465, 468. (The protocols of the Third and Fourth Congresses do not contain an appendix listing greetings.)

[21] See CZA (Jerusalem) Z 1/313 (October 4, 1900); Z 1/321 (May 1, 1901), translated in Part Two, p. 311; Z 1/336 (August 1, 1901). See also Yehuda, *Organized Zionism in Morocco,* vol. 1, pp. 73–74 [Heb.]; Abitbol, "Zionist Activity in the Maghreb," p. 63.

[22] Zvi Yehuda, "The Place of Aliyah in Moroccan Jewry's Conception of Zionism," *Studies in Zionism* 6, no. 2 (1985): 200. This subject is taken up in much greater detail by Yehuda in his dissertation, *Organized Zionism in Morocco,* vol. 1, pp. 38–83 [Heb.].

[23] Yehuda, "The Place of Aliyah in Moroccan Jewry's Conception of Zionism," p. 200, n. 5; and *Stenographisches Protokoll der Verhandlungen des X. Zionisten-Kongresses* (Berlin and Leipzig, 1911), p. 3, which lists Jacob Boccara as representing Tunis. Morocco was represented at the Sixteenth Zionist Congress in London in 1929 by Polish-born Jonathan Thursz. He continued to represent Morocco at subsequent congresses until World War II. Concerning him, see Yehuda, *Organized Zionism in Morocco,* vol. 1, pp. 116–120 [Heb.].

See also Thursz's address to the Congress concerning Moroccan Jewry in *Protokoll der Verhandlungen des XVI. Zionistenkongresses* (London, 1929), pp. 229–30.

[24] CZA (Jerusalem) Z 1/313, letter from Berliawsky in Hebrew (September 11, 1900), and another in Spanish from Leon Jalfon, president of the society (September 28, 1900).

Other Zionist groups soon followed. The Ahavat Ṣiyyōn Society was founded in Safi, another coastal town, in 1903. In a letter to Theodor Herzl, who is addressed as God's chosen president, the officers of the association, Me'ir Barchéchath (Bar Sheshet) and Jacob Murciano, explain that they first learned about Zionism from the Hebrew press. Although deeply inspired by what they had read, they found it insufficient and now wanted to know in detail the specific tenets and goals of the movement. Their queries reveal a probing curiosity and an insightful awareness unmatched by these other early groups. In addition to the general request for literature, they specifically requested a copy of Herzl's *The Jewish State* in Hebrew (as well as a portrait of him to grace their meeting hall).[25]

It took several more years before awareness of Zionism spread to the principal towns of the Moroccan interior and much longer until it reached the many isolated smaller communities. This lag behind the coastal towns was due to the generally poor communications and chaotic conditions prevailing in Morocco during that period.

Late in 1908, the Ḥibbat Ṣiyyōn Society was founded in Fez by twenty leading rabbis and notables, among them R. Moses Ibn Danan, R. Ḥayyim David Serrero, R. Saul Ibn Danan, R. Abner Serfaty, Solomon Bensimhon, and Ḥayyim Delmar.[26] The fact that the society's first letters were sent to Israel Zangwill, the head of the Jewish Territorial Organization in London, who had broken with the World Zionist Organization over the Uganda issue in 1905, only shows how hazy indeed was the Fasi Jews' knowledge of the Zionist movement. Once they were set straight, however, they began to perform the basic Zionist duties of selling shekels and shares in the Jewish Colonial Trust. In the autumn of 1909, the Ḥibbat Ṣiyyōn Society expanded to the neighboring towns of Meknes and Sefrou, where again the membership comprised members of the rabbinical and mercantile elite.[27]

The Jews of Fez directed their messianic hopes for redemption toward the Zionist movement with an even greater immediacy than

[25] CZA (Jerusalem) Z 1/343. Translated in Part Two, pp. 312–313.

[26] CZA (Jerusalem) Z 2/309, letter from the society to Israel Zangwill, London (undated). The names of the founding members are also given by Yehuda, *Organized Zionism in Morocco,* vol. 2, p. 267, n. 32. Biographical information on a number of these rabbis who were among the leading scholars of Moroccan Jewry can be found in Joseph Ben Nāyīm, *Malkhē Rabbānān* (Jerusalem, 1931), s.v.; and in David Ovadia, *Fās ve-Ḥakhāmēhā* (Jerusalem, 1978/79), pp. 249–367.

[27] CZA (Jerusalem) Z 2/309 and Z 2/511; also Yehuda, *Organized Zionism in Morocco,* vol. 1, pp. 80–81 [Heb.].

their coreligionists along the coast. Fasi Jewry was plagued not only by widespread poverty, but also by the oppressive atmosphere of Morocco's premier Islamic center. In their original letter to Zangwill, the founders of the Ḥibbat Ṣiyyōn Society clearly state that they were putting themselves under the aegis of the World Zionist Organization (which they mistakenly call the Ḥōvevē Ṣiyyōn Society) because they had heard that: "its desired goal is to gather the exiled to go to Zion, where each man will dwell under his vine and fig tree. The crown will be restored, and the banner of the Jews will be raised."[28]

It soon became apparent to the leaders of Ḥibbat Ṣiyyōn, however, that the Zionist Organization was in no position to take the Jewish community of Fez under its wing in any meaningful sense, and their hopes were profoundly disappointed. Herzl's successor, David Wolffsohn, who had no understanding of the social and political realities in Morocco, was unwilling to accede to the Fasi Zionists' request that he use his influence to place the Ḥibbat Ṣiyyōn Society under the protection of a consul of one of the European powers. As a result, they terminated their society's association with the World Zionist Organization and, at the urging of the local Alliance school director, Amram Elmaleh, who had been working behind the scenes to woo the Alliance alumni away from Zionism, turned instead to the Alliance Israélite Universelle as its patron.[29] The opposition of the Alliance and its representatives was to come increasingly into the open in the decades that followed—not only in Morocco, but also throughout North Africa and the Middle East.

After the initial burst of enthusiasm, organized Zionist activity in Morocco lost much of its momentum. Propaganda and the sale of shekels were still carried on by individuals, and the original sentiments remained strong among the rabbis, the traditional masses, and a select number of the Alliance-educated elite. It was the elite who began to reorganize the Moroccan Zionist movement after World War I despite Alliance opposition and the formidable obstacles placed in their way by the French colonial authorities who were wary of foreign organizations and any activities that they perceived as political. Furthermore, after the Balfour Declaration and the establishment of a British mandate over Palestine, the French viewed Zionism as an ally of their British imperial rivals.

[28] CZA (Jerusalem) Z 2/309.

[29] With the change of allegiance came both a change of name (to Alliance Israélite Marocaine) and, no less symbolic, a change of language (from Hebrew to French) in the society's correspondence. See Yehuda, *Organized Zionism in Morocco,* vol. 1, p. 82; vol. 2, pp. 270–72, nn. 48–50 [Heb.]; and Michael M. Laskier, *The*

Zionist activity in Tunisia began at about the same time as it did in Morocco, with groups springing up in various towns. As in Morocco, too, the local religious leaders played a prominent role in the movement from the start. The first Zionist association in Sousse, for example, was founded at the turn of the century by the local rabbi, Abraham Uzan, and in Beja, the Benē Ṣiyyōn Society was founded by the rabbi there, Hai Haggege, in 1913. The first Tunisian delegate to a Zionist congress was Rabbi Jacob Boccara in 1910. He assisted the lawyer Alfred Valensi in founding the first major Zionist organization in Tunis, the Agūdat Ṣiyyōn, that same year. And with another group of lawyers and leading citizens, he founded and was an officer of the Yōshevet Ṣiyyōn Society in 1914, the same year, by the way, that he was chosen chief rabbi of the Grana, or Livornese community.[30]

Like their coreligionists in Morocco and Libya, Tunisian Jews perceived Zionism as a thoroughly natural expression of Judaism. There was simply no parallel to the anti-Zionism of much of Europe's Orthodox and Reform leadership. As A. Torczyner, an emissary of the World Zionist Organization, wrote after visiting the country:

> Opposition, especially of the sort we find here in Europe is non-existent. The God-fearing regard our movement with warmth and reverence. When I addressed Agudat Zion in Tunis, among the audience were truly religious old people and members of the rabbinical court of justice. The Chief Rabbi, who is sick, apologized for his having withdrawn from the organization. It was the same in Sfax.[31]

Zionism spread more rapidly and more thoroughly throughout the general Jewish population in Tunisia than it had in Morocco as a result of the smaller geographic and demographic size of Tunisia, as well as the superior conditions prevailing in Tunisia for the dissemination of information. Tunisia had been under French rule for more than a generation when organized Zionism really began to make headway. There was also a more sophisticated understanding of Zionism in Tunisia where the modern Jewish elite was proportionately larger and better educated than its counterpart in Morocco. For

---

Alliance Israélite Universelle and the Jewish Communities of Morocco, 1862–1962 (Albany, N.Y., 1983), pp. 198–99.

[30] For the Zionist organization in Sousse, see CZA (Jerusalem) Z 1/321; for Beja, see Barad, *Le Mouvement sioniste en Tunisie,* p. 12; concerning Rabbi Boccara, see *Stenographisches Protokoll der Verhandlungen des X. Zionisten-Kongresses,* p. 3, and Barad, *Le Mouvement sioniste en Tunisie,* pp. 11–12.

[31] CZA (Jerusalem) Z 3/751, letter to Nahum Sokolow (September 26, 1913), quoted in Abitbol, "Zionist Activity in the Maghreb," p. 65.

example, Alfred Valensi, the founder of Agūdat Ṣiyyōn and the first president of the Tunisian Zionist federation in 1920, had been trained for the bar in France. There, he met Max Nordau, who introduced him to political Zionism. Valensi understood perfectly well the secular aspect of modern Zionism, as he showed in a trenchant defense of the movement and its goals that he published in the review *La Société Nouvelle* in 1911 as a response to the criticisms of the French social reformer Alfred Naquet.[32]

Information about Zionism and news of the movement reached more Jews, more rapidly, in Tunisia because of a flourishing native Jewish press. Several Jewish newspapers and journals in either Judeo-Arabic or French were published in Tunisia from the late nineteenth century on. Many of these were relatively short-lived, such as *El-Akhbar* (Ar. *al-Akhbār*), which ran for only a year (1908). Others, such as *al-Ṣabāḥ* (1904–1919) and *l'Egalité* (1912–1932), enjoyed considerable runs. The earliest paper to style itself as a Zionist organ was the Judeo-Arabic monthly *La Voix de Ṣiyyōn* (*Qōl Ṣiyyōn*), which was launched in 1913 by Joseph Brami, a young rabbi and an educator of the modern type. The paper was published for two years. The next Zionist paper to appear was *La Voix d'Israël,* which began publication in 1919 and continued until 1925. Another Zionist journal at this time was the bimonthly *La Voix Juive* (1920–1924), devoted to "Jewish information and education."[33]

In neither Algeria nor Morocco, each with its larger Jewish populations, was there ever anything approaching the number of Jewish,

[32] Alfred Valensi, "Sionisme et Socialisme: Reponse à M. Alfred Naquet," *La Société Nouvelle* (January 1911): 1–8. Valensi concludes his essay with the statement that Zionism is "an eminently secular, democratic, and popular movement which seeks by pacific means . . . to create a society which will come closer than any other modern society to the ideal of justice which, foreseen by the Hebrew prophets, was given a scientific formulation by the Jew Karl Marx. It is the duty of every liberal and just spirit to be in favor of such a movement's efforts" (Ibid., p. 8). The article is also reprinted in Barad, *Le Mouvement sioniste en Tunisie,* Annexe No. 2, pp. 70–77.

[33] Concerning these and other journals of the period, see Robert Attal, *Périodiques juifs d'Afrique du Nord* (Jerusalem, 1980), pp. 12–44; and Barad, *Le Mouvement sioniste en Tunisie,* pp. 12, 20–22. For correspondence between Joseph Brami and the Central Zionist Office concerning *La Voix de Sion,* see CZA (Jerusalem) Z 3/751. Laskier downplays the importance of the Zionist press in Tunisia. This, I believe, is a misassessment, since even the non-Zionist Jewish press gave considerable coverage to Zionist news. See Michael M. Laskier, "The Evolution of Zionist Activity in the Jewish Communities of Morocco, Tunisia and Algeria: 1897–1947," *Studies in Zionism,* no. 8 (August 1983): 217.

much less specifically Zionist, journals that could be found in Tunisia. Furthermore, none of the Algerian and Moroccan Jewish periodicals of the first two and a half decades of this century enjoyed the distribution or longevity of many of the Tunisian papers. It was not until 1926 that Morocco had a major Zionist publication, the monthly—and later biweekly—magazine *L'Avenir Illustré*, which was widely read in Morocco and throughout North Africa and continued to appear until 1940.[34]

Libya had the smallest and least westernized Jewish community in the Maghreb. It would seem that there was some awareness of the Zionist movement within the small circle of individuals in the main towns who had some modern education and contacts with Europe. A few Jews from Tripoli and Benghazi corresponded with the World Zionist Organization in the beginning of the century and apparently distributed some literature. In 1908, leaders of the Jewish community in Benghazi wrote to Zangwill's Jewish Territorial Organization pleading for help and protection after an incident in which Arabs had damaged Jewish shops. However, there do not appear to have been any groups—even small, informal cells—that might be described as Zionist at this early period when such groups were forming in the rest of North Africa.[35]

A short-lived Zionist association called Ōra ve-Simḥa was established in Tripoli in 1912 by a group of young people at the initiative of Elia Nhaisi, a photographer by profession who was also the local correspondent for *La Settimana Israelitica*, Italy's leading Jewish weekly. Although Nhaisi and his friends had been able to enlist some communal leaders into executive positions in the new association, they soon found that they had no support—and even outright opposition—from the pro-Italian mercantile oligarchy that dominated Jewish communal affairs in Tripoli, where the overwhelming majority of all Libyan Jews lived. Among this ruling group were men like Halfalla

[34] For the Algerian and Moroccan journals, see Attal, *Périodiques juifs d'Afrique du Nord,* pp. 45–67.

[35] For this early correspondence with the Zionist Executive in Vienna, see CZA (Jerusalem) Z 1/311, 316, 350, and 359; also Rachel Simon, "The Relations of the Jewish Community of Libya with Europe in the Late Ottoman Period," in *Les relations intercommunautaires juives en Méditerranée Occidentale, XIIIe-XXe siècles,* ed. J.-L. Miège (Paris, 1984), pp. 75–76; and Maurice M. Roumani, "Zionism and Social Change in Libya at the Turn of the Century," *Studies in Zionism* 8, no. 1 (1987): 6. On the correspondence with the Jewish Territorial Organization in London, see De Felice, *Jews in an Arab Land,* p. 25.

Nahum, who was a leading merchant, a counselor of the local committee of the Dante Alighieri Society, and an officer of the Bank of Naples' Tripoli branch.[36]

The young Tripolitanian Zionists channeled their energies into educational and cultural activities that included a night school for modern spoken Hebrew. Although almost all these young people were themselves Italian educated, they were opposed to the strong assimilationism of the wealthy pro-Italian clique. They viewed Jewish cultural revival and loyalty to the religious tradition as both being absolutely necessary for the achievement of national restoration. They propagated their ideas in the Italian Jewish press, which also circulated in Libya. The young idealists won considerable support from readers in Italy and from the editorial boards of such papers as *La Settimana Israelitica, Israel*, and *Il Vessillo Israelitico*.[37]

Nhaisi, together with about seventy of his fellow Zionists, succeeded in forming a new association, the Circolo Sion, in 1917. More than a Zionist group, the Circolo Sion became the opposition party to the Tripolitanian Jewish community's governing faction and put forward its own candidates for the Communal Council. The Zionists of Tripoli were youthful reformers who saw themselves as representing the masses of the *ḥāra* (the Jewish quarter) against the small, entrenched, Italianized elite. They depicted themselves as dedicated idealists versus selfish materialists and defenders of tradition versus assimilationists. The Libyan rabbis, who unlike their colleagues in Morocco and Tunisia had not been involved with the Zionist movement from the beginning, now threw in their support with the Circolo Sion because of the latter's strong stance against assimilation and secularization. In no other Jewish community of the Arab world was the struggle between Zionists and non-Zionists more strikingly delineated.[38]

The Balfour Declaration, the collapse of the Ottoman Empire, the San Remo Conference, and the stirrings of Arab nationalism in Libya itself all contributed to a rise in Zionist popularity in the aftermath of World War I. The Circolo Sion began to reach a growing audience with its programs and its Judeo-Arabic newspaper *Deghel Ṣion*, which appeared between 1920 and 1924. Zionist propaganda

[36] See Roumani, "Zionism and Social Change in Libya at the Turn of the Century," p. 6; De Felice, *Jews in an Arab Land*, pp. 26, 47, 317.

[37] Roumani, "Zionism and Social Change in Libya at the Turn of the Century," pp. 7–9; De Felice, *Jews in an Arab Land*, pp. 45–47.

[38] De Felice, *Jews in an Arab Land*, pp. 45–48, 86–96, 103–5; Roumani, "Zionism and Social Change in Libya at the Turn of the Century," pp. 10–15.

stirred interest in immigration to Palestine, not only among individuals, but among entire families as well.[39]

By 1921, the Zionists had captured a clear majority of seats on the Jewish Communal Council, which caused their opponents among the wealthy elite, who had never really been united themselves, to form an opposing organization, the Associazione Concordia e Progresso (Heb., Ḥevrat Aḥdūt ve-Hitqaddemūt), with its own rival organ *Hit'ōrerūt* (Awakening), published weekly between 1922 and 1924. A *modus vivendi* was eventually worked out, and even the Associazione Concordia e Progresso came to espouse a philanthropic form of Zionism. In 1923, the communal factions and Zionist associations united in a confederation, the Organizzazione Sionistica della Tripolitania, through the mediation of Abraham Elmaleh, the noted Sephardi intellectual and representative of the Jewish National Fund in Palestine.[40]

The Zionist activists would still have their ups and downs in the struggle for directing the course of Libyan Jewry, but they had made even their opponents into nominal Zionists by the mid-1920s. The Zionists themselves remained one of the two poles of communal leadership from the end of World War I until they finally won the loyalty of the Libyan Jewish masses in the period following World War II.

THE LEVANT

Jews in Syria and Lebanon do not seem to have entered into any sort of direct relations with the early Zionist congresses or the Zionist Executive in Europe. That is not to say that they were unaware or uninterested in the Zionist movement. The Jews of the Lebanese coastal towns, and of Beirut in particular, were perhaps the most aware of all the Arabic-speaking Jews of the pioneering activities of the New Yishuv because of their physical proximity to Palestine and the generally good communications. The more isolated and less

[39] On the "striking success" of the Zionists in Tripoli and their "feverish activity," see the report of the Alliance representative sent in 1923 in AIU Archives Lybie I.G.2 (Activités et agitation sionistes). On the interest in ᶜaliya, see CZA (Jerusalem) Z 4/1620, correspondence between Rafaelle Barda and the Zionist Office in London (1921–1922). For *Deghel Sion,* see Attal, *Périodiques juifs d'Afrique du Nord,* pp. 8–9.

[40] De Felice, *Jews in an Arab Land,* pp. 96–109, 123–35; Roumani, "Zionism and Social Change in Libya at the Turn of the Century," pp. 19–24.

sophisticated Jews of the interior centers of Damascus and Aleppo were somewhat slower in learning details about the Jewish national revival movement. Abraham Elmaleh, who visited Damascus in 1910, mentions that the Jews there had heard of Herzl and had a rather hazy idea about Zionism, some of which came from the none-too-sympathetic Arabic press.[41] But even these less well informed Jews of the interior had lines of communication with Palestine, and close ties bound Syrian Jewry with traditional segments of the Yishuv. For example, the Aleppan Jews had their own colony in Jerusalem, which was registered as a separate and distinct community (like the Maghrebis, the Bukharans, or the Ashkenazim) in 1880.[42] Some of the traditional Sephardi communal organizations in Jerusalem would eventually become important channels of contact between Syrian Jews and Zionism. Throughout the twentieth century, in fact, Syrian Jewry's links with Zionism were, in one way or another, established directly with institutions in Palestine itself.

Sympathy for Zionist aspirations was already widespread in Greater Syria early in the twentieth century. Yomtob Sémach, the director of the Alliance School for Boys in Beirut, writes in the beginning of 1907 that Zionism was already well established throughout Jewish communities and that nothing was to be gained by the Alliance's coming into conflict with it: "Since Zionism exists in all our communities . . . it would be better to look for the points we have in common. It is above all necessary to make concessions at times rather than start internal struggles which will ruin our work without any benefit to the communities."[43]

On the whole, the representatives of the Alliance in Syria and Lebanon do not seem to have heeded Sémach's advice during the decades that followed.

There were no Syrian Zionist associations prior to World War I, but Zionist cultural activity was considerable during the period. A Hebrew national school and kindergarten was opened in Damascus in 1910 by Elmaleh with a staff of several Palestinian teachers. Despite the vigorous opposition of the local Alliance director, the new school flourished and had nearly 500 pupils within its first year. The children received an education modeled closely after the curriculum taught in

[41] Abraham Elmaleh, *ha-Yehūdīm be-Dammeseq ū-Maṣṣāvām ha-Kalkalī veha-Tarbūtī* (Jerusalem, 1911/12), pp. 24–25.

[42] Walter P. Zenner, *Syrian Jewish Identification in Israel* (unpublished doctoral dissertation, Columbia University, 1965), p. 106.

[43] AIU (Paris) Liban I.G.2, letter from Y. D. Sémach to the president of the Alliance in Paris (January 14, 1907). A year earlier, Sémach had to defend himself

the schools of the New Yishuv. Modern Hebrew was popularized as a national, cultural medium and could be heard spoken by Jewish youth in the streets of Damascus.[44]

Zionist propagandizing increased in Syria during the war years when many members of the Yishuv were exiled to Damascus by the Ottoman authorities. Among the exiles were educators and intellectuals such as Elmaleh, Yehuda Burla, Joseph Joel Rivlin, and David Yellin, all of whom devoted their efforts to educational and cultural programs with a strong Jewish national orientation. Although Damascus was the center of their activity, Zionism spread to other communities as well, including the highly conservative enclave of Aleppo.

At war's end, Zionist proselytizing was stepped up throughout Syria, in both the French- and the Arab-administered zones. Burla and Rivlin remained in Damascus to direct the Hebrew National Schools for Boys and Girls, respectively, as well as to oversee new Zionist cultural and welfare institutions such as the kindergartens, adult education programs, youth clubs and organizations, an orphanage, and a clinic. All of these were staffed with personnel from the Yishuv and subvented by the Council of Delegates (Heb., *Vaᶜad ha-Ṣīrīm*) and the Council of Education (Heb., *Vaᶜad ha-Ḥinnūkh*) in Palestine. Burla and Rivlin also became active in communal affairs and were both elected to the reorganized Communal Council, some of whose leading members had been won over to Zionism.[45]

Zionism made deep inroads among Damascene Jewry in the immediate postwar years. Over two thirds of the children in Jewish schools attended Zionist institutions. More than 500 young adults attended classes sponsored by the Maccabee League, and the Kadimah Club became the focal point for the social life of Jewish youth. Hebrew newspapers from Palestine gained an audience,[46] as did the secular literature of modern Hebrew culture. Even a rabbi of the old school in Aleppo, while decrying the abandonment of religious tradition and the blandishments of Western culture, quotes both

---

against the criticism of the Alliance president that he was "un peu trop facilement entraîner sur le pont sioniste." See ibid., letter dated January 14, 1906.

[44] Elmaleh, *ha-Yehūdīm be-Dammeseq,* pp. 35–36.

[45] See Rivlin's report translated in Part Two, pp. 263–273; also CZA (Jerusalem) S 2/493, 578, 579, 628, and 691 and Z 4/2332.

[46] See Part Two, pp. 264–271. The section of this report dealing with the Maccabee and Kadimah organizations, however, is not included in the translation. On the initial success of Kadimah, see also the grudging testimony of an Alliance school director in Part Two, pp. 275–276.

Tchernichowsky and Bialik, referring to the latter as "the national poet"![47]

Lebanon, too, was the scene of intensive Zionist activity at the end of World War I. Beirut had a small Ashkenazi community that was already well disposed to the Zionist ideal. The Ashkenazim had been the mainstay of a Hebrew-language kindergarten that had operated in the city before the war. The Sephardi majority, on the other hand, had been rather "distant from the national movement."[48] The Balfour Declaration and the Allied victory, however, generated local enthusiasm for the Zionist cause, as it had done in other Arabic-speaking Jewish communities. Various emissaries such as Elmaleh, the chief rabbi of Jaffa, and Jack Mosseri from Egypt went to Beirut to meet with Jewish communal leaders during 1918 and 1919, and (much to the chagrin of the local Alliance representative) they "gained considerable sympathy."[49]

As in Damascus, much of the Zionist activity in Lebanon was primarily cultural rather than philanthropic in the early postwar years. There seems to have been little in the way of fund-raising until the mid-1920s and 1930s. The Jewish communities of Greater Syria had an even thinner upper stratum of wealth and, with the exception of Beirut, less of a middle class than most of the other Arabic-speaking Jewries already discussed in this chapter. Hebrew schools and kindergartens staffed by Palestinian teachers were opened in Beirut and Sidon in 1919 and 1920. The Jewish Youth Movement in Beirut had a Zionist orientation and by 1925 had become affiliated with the UUJJ (Union Universelle de la Jeunesse Juive). A pro-Zionist newspaper published in Arabic, entitled *al-ᶜĀlam al-Isrāʾīlī*, began to appear

---

[47] Isaac Dayyan, "Tōrat Yisrāʾēl ve-ᶜAm Yisrāʾēl," *Minḥat Yehūda,* ed. Nissim ᶜAṭiyya (Aleppo, 1924), pp. 21, 23, 30, 31. An excerpt is translated in Part Two, pp. 278–279.

[48] CZA (Jerusalem) S 2/657, letter from M. R. Cohen in Beirut to Dr. I. Luria in Jaffa, for the Council of Education (November 4, 1918).

[49] AIU Archives (Paris) Liban I.G.3, letter from E. Penso in Beirut to Alliance headquarters (February 23, 1919). According to Penso, these men have carried out "une propagande active." Six years later, his successor, Maurice Sidi, also reports on the "great sympathy" for Zionism in Beirut. See ibid., letter dated May 3, 1925. The director of the AIU school in Aleppo quotes his colleague in Beirut, M. Danon, as saying that Zionists "dominate the Beiruti Jewish Community Council and try to give all activities and organizations a nationalist character." See AIU Archives (Paris) Syrie I.G.1, letter from Dr. Joseph Rosenfeld (July 10, 1921). Concerning Elmaleh's activities in promoting Zionism and Hebrew culture, see CZA (Jerusalem) S 2/657, letter from the Conseil Communal Israélite de Beyrouth to the Council of Education in Jerusalem (July 15, 1919).

fortnightly in Beirut in 1921. The paper was read by Jews in the interior towns as well and remained until after World War II the only Jewish paper—Zionist or otherwise—in all of Greater Syria.[50]

Aside from the cultural and youth organizations, there was none of the proliferation of Zionist associations in the cities of Greater Syria as in Egypt, Morocco, and Tunisia. It was only in 1924 that a Syrian Zionist association was organized by Toufic (Tawfīq) Mizrahi, a journalist and owner of an advertising agency, together with Chief Rabbi Tagger of Beirut and seven provisionary committee members in Damascus. The association took on the name of the Club National Israélite in obvious imitation of the famous Arab Club, which was the focal point of Syrian and Pan-Arab nationalism. The Club National Israélite set out a nine-point program that in addition to moderate Zionist goals included working for friendly ties with the other native communities in Syria.[51] As the climate in Damascus became increasingly, even violently, hostile to Zionism in the late 1920s, the center of the club's activity shifted to the more cosmopolitan and laissez-faire atmosphere of Beirut.

The Zionist idea penetrated Iraq even more slowly and less directly than it did in Syria. Limited circles of Iraqi Jews first became aware of modern Zionism through the Hebrew press in the late nineteenth century.[52] A few individuals in Baghdad and Basra entered into correspondence with the World Zionist Organization in Berlin in the years just preceding the First World War. These individuals disseminated Zionist literature that had been sent to them from Europe and engaged in some extremely modest fund-raising activities. However, until 1913, there was nothing that might be called a Zionist society in Iraq. The first such society was organized in Basra in 1913 at the initiative of E. Issayick, a lawyer, and J. J. Aaron, a photographer. The group was informal and had only some ten members,

[50] Concerning fund-raising activities, see CZA (Jerusalem) Z 4/2332 and S 5/2204. Concerning the schools, see CZA (Jerusalem) S 2/493, 579, 657, and 777. On the youth movement, see AIU Archives (Paris) Liban I.G.3, letter from Sidi to Alliance headquarters (June 12, 1925).

[51] See CZA (Jerusalem) Z 4/2332, correspondence between Mizrahi and the Zionist Executive in London between June 1924 and January 1925.

[52] See Hayyim J. Cohen, *ha-Peᶜīlūt ha-Ṣiyyōnīt be-ᶜIrāq* (Jerusalem, 1969), pp. 27–28. Aaron Sasson b. Elijah Nahum, who became the first chairman of the Iraqi Zionist Organization in 1920 and was known as "the Teacher" (Heb., *ha-Mōreh*) in the movement, recalled that his introduction to Zionism was through the Hebrew newspapers.

although according to one of its founders, "many are anxious to enter into it but are afraid of the Turkish authorities."[53]

The Basra Zionists opened a modern Hebrew school at the end of 1913 or the beginning of 1914. At least one instructor was from the Yishuv. The school enjoyed immediate success and attracted approximately 200 pupils. However, it soon ran into opposition from the local Alliance school director, many of whose students had transferred to the new competing institution, and from the town's chief rabbi, who probably feared the reaction of the Ottoman authorities. The local Zionists felt compelled to close the school for a short time and to discontinue their public activities. They then reopened the school, which remained in operation until the British occupation of Basra in November 1914, after which it seems to have closed for good.[54]

The earliest Zionist activities in Baghdad were even more modest than in Basra. In May 1914, a certain Menaschi Hekim sent 18.75 francs to the Zionist secretariat on behalf of himself and two friends expressing their interest in the movement and requesting pamphlets. The literature was duly sent a month later with instructions that since the Ottoman Zionist Society was still not fully organized in Constantinople, the Baghdadi Jews should wait until told by Berlin when to establish their own branch (although in Basra the local Zionist group was already selling shekels).[55] This response from the movement's world headquarters does not seem to have offered the Baghdadis much encouragement. In any case, with the outbreak of the war several months later, all fledgling Zionist activity in Iraq appears to have ceased.

[53] CZA (Jerusalem) Z 3/981, letter from J. J. (Isaac b. Isaac) Aaron to the Zionist secretariat in Berlin (September 13, 1913). The writer goes on to request the Zionist Organization's help in obtaining the protection of either the German or English consuls for the new society. Only three months earlier, before the society had been actually formed, Issayick had written Berlin (ibid., letter of June 13, 1913) that:

> the information you have given has not quite enlisted our people's interests. The community naturally are not of very advanced ideas and nothing interests them but what would be of immediate benefit to the community and the pamphlets you have sent do not shew that joining the movement would raise the status of the community or in any way secure it some sort of influence or prestige.

[54] See Cohen, *ha-Peʿīlūt ha-Ṣiyyōnīt be-ʿIrāq,* pp. 31–32.

[55] CZA (Jerusalem) Z 3/982, letters of May 4 and June 9, 1914. Both of these letters are published in Cohen, *ha-Peʿīlūt ha-Ṣiyyōnīt be-ʿIrāq,* App. 3–4, pp. 219–21. Concerning the sale of shekels in Basra, see CZA (Jerusalem) Z 3/982, letter from Zionist headquarters in Berlin to J. J. Aaron in Basra (May 1, 1914), acknowledging

Zionist activities resumed in Iraq about a year after the war ended. Though still unorganized, serious fund-raising was undertaken at the initiative of a few individuals like Aaron Sasson, a Baghdadi schoolteacher, who had been active in the earliest Iraqi pro-Zionist circles before the war. Throughout the 1920s, very sizable sums of money were raised for the various Zionist funds, such as the Keren Hayesod and the Jewish National Fund. The total contributions to the Jewish National Fund alone for 1920 and 1921 amounted to 16,343 pounds sterling, the lion's share of which was given by one individual, Ezra Sasson Suheik.[56] (Together with Egypt, Iraq was the home of some of the wealthiest Jews in the Arab world.)

Despite the substantial sums given by a few wealthy philanthropists for development projects in Palestine, most of the Jewish mercantile elite of Iraq remained unattracted by Zionism. The movement seems to have appealed to a few intellectuals and middle-level members of the modern bourgeoisie. Leading members of the first organized Zionist group in the postwar period included a schoolteacher, a law student, and a police official. In 1920, they formed an association in Baghdad with the innocuous name of Jamᶜiyya Adabiyya Isrāʾīliyya (Jewish Literary Society). The society obtained legal recognition from the British Mandatory authorities and published a short-lived journal in Hebrew and Judeo-Arabic, *Yeshurun*.[57] In early 1921, a group within the Jewish Literary Society formed a separate Zionist association, The Mesopotamian Zionist Committee (al-Jamᶜiyya al-Ṣahyūniyya li-Bilād al-Rāfidayn), which also received a permit from the government. At first, the Zionists enjoyed considerable sympathy from the poorer Jewish masses, who demonstrated their support in vocal public gatherings that offended Arab public opinion and frightened members of the Jewish upper class. Such unrestrained behavior was, in the view of Menahem Ṣāliḥ Daniel, a leading Baghdadi Jewish notable and later a senator in the Iraqi Parliament, "altogether unenlightened

---

the receipt of five pounds sterling and the dispatch of twenty shekel blocks (200 shekels).

[56] See Cohen, *ha-Peᶜīlūt ha-Ṣiyyōnīt be-ᶜIrāq,* pp. 36–37, 99–101. Concerning Aaron Sasson, see also n. 52 above.

[57] It was not unusual for a cultural or a literary club to serve as a cover for a nationalist group. Several such associations had arisen in the Middle East since late Ottoman times. See Serif A. Mardin, "Libertarian Movements in the Ottoman Empire, 1878–1895," *MEJ* 16 (1962): 169–82; Irene L. Gendzier, *The Practical Visons of Yaᶜqub Sanuᶜ,* Harvard Middle Eastern Monograph Series, vol. 15 (Cambridge, Mass., 1966), pp. 41–42. See also the example of the Club National Israélite in Syria, p. 84 above.

. . . and more Messianic than Zionistic . . . merely a reaction of a subdued race, which for a moment thought that by magic the tables were turned and that it were to become an overlord."[58] British officials and the native Arab authorities also warned both local Zionists and visiting representatives of the movement against public activities and indiscreet statements. The nationalist press was more emphatic in this regard. Therefore, even though no actual ban was imposed upon their activities in Iraq until 1929, the Zionists found it necessary almost from the first to restrict their visibility. The weekly newspaper *al-Miṣbāḥ* founded in 1923 by Salmān Shina, secretary of the Jewish Literary Society and treasurer of the Mesopotamian Zionist Committee, appears to have studiously avoided Zionist propagandizing and to have limited itself to a few news items on Palestine buried amid the mainly cultural and literary articles that filled its pages. The need to maintain a low profile was increased when the Zionist Committee found that it could not renew its permit in 1922, although it was allowed to continue operating unofficially until 1929.[59]

After slow, fitful beginnings within the various Jewries of the Arab world from the late nineteenth century until World War I, Zionism penetrated the major urban Jewish centers and succeeded in arousing considerable popular enthusiasm in the wake of the Balfour Declaration, the Allied victory, and the ratification of Britain's promise of a Jewish national home in Palestine by the delegates at the San Remo Conference. In 1917, for example, thousands of Jews had gathered in Cairo and Alexandria in support of the Balfour Declaration, and similar scenes greeted Chaim Weizmann and the Zionist Commission when they passed through Egypt the following year.[60] The Jews of Tunis celebrated the Allies' triumph by marching through the streets in noisy demonstrations waving the Zionist banner.[61] In a burst of semimessianic enthusiasm, several hundred Jewish families emigrated from Morocco to Palestine between 1919 and 1923, much to the chagrin of the French authorities. There was a similar wavelet of *ᶜōlīm* from Iraq at this same time, comprising a little over a thousand

[58] CZA (Jerusalem) Z 4/2101, letter from Daniel to the secretary of the Zionist Organization in London (September 8, 1922). The full text is given in Part Two, pp. 331–333.

[59] See Cohen, *ha-Peᶜīlūt ha-Ṣiyyōnīt be-ᶜIrāq,* pp. 41–43; also Ṣādiq Ḥasan al-Sūdānī, *al-Nashāṭ al-Ṣahyūnī fī 'l-ᶜIrāq, 1914–1952* (Baghdad, 1980), p. 42; and the texts in Part Two, pp. 334–339, 342–344.

[60] Krämer, *Minderheit, Millet, Nation?,* p. 356; and also Part Two, pp. 307–308.

[61] al-Taymūmī, *al-Nashāṭ al-Ṣahyūnī bi-Tūnis,* pp. 77–78.

individuals, with smaller numbers coming from Syria and Libya.[62] A steady stream of several thousand *ʿōlīm* came from Yemen until the flow was staunched by an edict of the Imam in 1929 forbidding emigration.[63] Modern Hebrew schools, cultural associations, student and youth groups, and Maccabee sports clubs—all with a strong Jewish national orientation—sprang up all over the Arab world. Zionist lecturers from Europe and Palestine, especially Sephardi speakers like Elmaleh, drew large audiences in Beirut, Cairo, Tunis, and Casablanca throughout the 1920s.[64] In a few countries, such as Lebanon, Libya, and Tunisia, Zionists or Zionist sympathizers were in fact predominant in the communal leadership.

But the initial ardor soon died down considerably for several reasons. First in Syria and soon after in Iraq, the Jews found themselves facing a highly developed, impassioned, and militant Arab nationalism that by the end of the 1920s had come to identify itself wholeheartedly with the Arab cause in Palestine. In Damascus, where Zionist educational and cultural organizations had flourished in the years immediately following the First World War, where Hebrew had been spoken openly in the streets by young people, and where Zionists had held leading positions on the communal council, the Jewish community made a complete volte-face. In response to the virulent wave of anti-Zionist and, even more ominously, anti-Jewish agitation in the Christian and Arab nationalist press in the late 1920s, the Jewish organizations in Damascus tried to assert their total loyalty to the Arab cause with anti-Zionist demonstrations and public statements. In a public declaration disassociating itself from Zionism, the Jewish Youth Association in Damascus pointed out on August 27, 1929, that "certain newspapers do not distinguish between Arab Jews and Zionists." The statement went on to request that such a differentiation be made and concluded with the plea, "We, therefore, beg the population and the press to consider the Jews of Damascus to be Arabs who share entirely all the feelings of their fellow citizens

[62] See Part Two, pp. 314–317; and also Bensimon-Donath, *Immigrants d'Afrique du Nord en Israël,* p. 64, and the sources cited there in n. 81. For Iraq, see Zvi Yehuda, "Aliya from Iraq in the Early 1920s: Survey and Problematics," in *From Babylon to Jerusalem,* ed. Zvi Yehuda (Tel Aviv, 1980), pp. 3–16 [Heb.]. For Syria and Libya, see Part Two, pp. 329–330; and CZA (Jerusalem) Z 4/1620.

[63] Abraham Yaʿari, "ʿAliyyat Yehūdē Tēmān le-Ereṣ Yisrā'ēl," in *Shevūt Tēmān,* ed. Y. Yeshayahu and A. Ṣadoq (Tel Aviv, 1945), pp. 35–36.

[64] See, for example, Part Two, pp. 325–327.

both in good times and in adversity."[65] As shall be seen in the following chapters, even such extreme protestations of fidelity to Arab nationalism were to be of no avail.

Pan-Arab consciousness had not yet evolved outside of Syria and Iraq (and, of course, Palestine) into a powerful force in the other Arab countries. It was to spread and become predominant in these other lands as well over the next two decades. In the meantime, other by no means negligible factors were at work that put a damper on many Jews' initial enthusiasm for Zionism.

In the Maghreb, particularly in Morocco, which had the largest Jewish population by far of anywhere in the Arab world, the French authorities, who feared political activity of any sort among the natives, were totally opposed to Zionist activity. Beginning in 1919, they blocked any attempt to create a Moroccan Zionist organization and, for a while during the mid-1920s, banned the Zionist newspaper *Hā-ᶜŌlām* from the country.[66] Although the French authorities were not so restrictive in Algeria and Tunisia, or in the mandates of Syria and Lebanon, they nevertheless tried to discourage Zionism, which they viewed as a tool of their rival colonial power, Great Britain, as well as a potentially disruptive force.[67]

There was also considerable opposition to Zionism within certain segments among the Jews themselves. The Alliance Israélite Universelle, which had been overtly tepid and covertly hostile to Zionism from the inception of the movement, did everything that it could to dampen the early general enthusiasm, to check or undermine Zionist activities (especially in those countries under French control), and to woo the local Jews to what it considered to be a more positive course. The whole philosophy of the Alliance was one of regeneration by

[65] Quote by A. Silberstein, director of the Alliance school in Damascus in a letter to Paris headquarters, August 31, 1929, AIU Archives (Paris) Syrie I.G.2. The complete text of the manifesto is translated in Part Two, p. 328.

[66] CZA (Jerusalem) Z 4/2011A, 2149, and 2669 are filled with documentation and correspondence on this subject. See also Yehuda, *Organized Zionism in Morocco,* pp. 84–112 [Heb.]; David Cohen, "Lyautey et le Sionisme, 1915–1925," *RFHOM* 67, nos. 248–49 (1980): 269–300; and Part Two, pp. 314–315, 319.

[67] Both the Alliance and the Central Zionist Archives frequently mention official French disapproval of Zionist activities in the various Arab countries under their control. French colonial policy was "to prevent Jewish nationalism as well as Panislamism or Panarabism." See Henri Gaillard, "Le Sionisme et la question juive dans l'Afrique du Nord," *Renseignements Coloniaux et Documents,* nos. 1–3 (January–February 1918): 7. The French were also suspicious of Anglican missionaries and had their doubts about American Methodists. See, for example, Raoul Darmon, *La situation des cultes en Tunisie,* 2nd rev. ed. (Paris, 1930), p. 151.

assimilation to French culture and upward mobility within the Diaspora society, which was the antithesis of the Zionist ideals of Hebrew cultural revival and ᶜaliya.[68]

The small, wealthy Jewish upper class in the Arab world was generally unenthusiastic about Zionism. In North Africa and Egypt, the rich Jews were for the most part disinterested. According to Ralph Harari, a scion of an elite Alexandrian family who was pro-Zionist, the movement was simply "not very chic" as far as most members of his class were concerned.[69] In Syria, certain Jewish bankers were already opposing Zionist activities in the early 1920s.[70] Members of the Iraqi Jewish upper crust were also expressing their grave reservations about Zionism at this time, although they would not begin to vigorously campaign against it until the following decade.

Other factors inhibited the growth and vitality of the Zionist movement among Arabic-speaking Jewry. Prior to the Second World War, the World Zionist Organization had never placed a high priority upon activities in the Arab countries. From the earliest days of the movement, complaints about a lack of communication from the Zionist Executive were legion. In a confidential report filed from Tunis in the late 1920s, a visiting observer notes that even the dues-paying Zionists there "feel themselves in the position of lost sheep, about

[68] The Alliance journals such as *Bulletin de l'Alliance Israélite Universelle* (1862–1913) and *Paix et Droit* (1921–1940) maintained on the whole a studied, but frosty neutrality when mentioning Zionism. The private correspondence between Paris headquarters and the Alliance school directors and other representatives in the field were, on the other hand, filled with such derogatory references as "that pernicious movement," "this gangrene," or "this organization whose leaders exercise a harmful influence on the minds of these young people." Certain Alliance officials, such as Jacques Bigart, who was secretary of the Alliance Central Committee for most of the first three decades of the twentieth century, were virulently opposed to Zionism. A history of the Alliance's relation to Zionism has yet to be written and remains a major desideratum. In the meantime, see Aron Rodrigue, *French Jews, Turkish Jews: The Alliance Israélite Universelle in Turkey, 1860–1914* (Ph.D. diss., Harvard University, 1985), pp. 311–48; Laskier, *The Alliance Israélite Universelle and the Jewish Communities of Morocco,* pp. 124–225; Eliahou Cohen, *L'influence intellectuelle et sociale des écoles de l'Alliance Israélite Universelle sur les Israélites du Proche-Orient* (unpublished doctoral dissertation, Université de Paris, 1962), pp. 76–78.

[69] Krämer, *Minderheit, Millet, Nation?,* p. 380, citing CZA (Jerusalem) KKL 5/1143.

[70] CZA (Jerusalem) Z 4/2332. Letter from Toufic Mizrahi (Beirut) to director of Keren Hayesod (London), November 15, 1921. He mentions that these bankers were working together with the Alliance and French officials to create problems for Zionist activities.

whom the shepherd does not care a jot."[71] More discouraging still was the perception that the World Zionist Organization and the Jewish Agency favored European Ashkenazim in the allocation of immigration certificates and that Sephardim were not properly represented in the World Zionist Organization and its institutions.[72]

Although the vitality of Zionism among Arabic-speaking Jews waned in the late 1920s, events in the following two decades that were totally beyond their control would conspire to link irrevocably the destiny of the movement and the Jews of Arab lands.

[71] CZA (Jerusalem) Z 4/3262. The full text is given in Part Two, pp. 322–323.
[72] See, for example, the letters in Part Two, pp. 329–330, 340–341.

5

DARKENING SHADOWS: 1929 to 1939

The decade between 1929 and 1939 began with an international economic crisis and ended with a world war. During this period, relations between Jews and Arabs in Palestine deteriorated into violent, irreconcilable civil strife, and the Palestine conflict gradually began to command the attention and sympathies of Arabs everywhere, whose own political self-awareness was increasing from day to day. Also at this time, relations between the colonial powers and their Arab subjects were being progressively strained with the steady growth of Arab nationalism. The Jewish and Christian minorities in the Arab countries that had benefited more on the whole than the vast Muslim majority under imperial domination and that were closely identified with intrusive foreign cultures and foreign interests could not help but be affected negatively by the mounting tensions. Middle Eastern and North African Jewry's situation was made all the more precarious as the struggle in Palestine came gradually to be perceived in terms of a contest between the Muslim Arabs, on the one hand, and the Zionist Jews with British backing, on the other.

In addition to these immediate factors of conflict already at work in the Arab world, there appeared during this decade a new and totally foreign catalytic element that had an important role to play in precipitating the ultimate dissolution of Arabic-speaking Jewry. The rise in Europe of militaristic National Socialism and Fascism offered the Arab nationalists chafing under the colonial yoke not only new, seductive models to emulate, but also ones that were made all the more attractive because they were perceived as powerful opponents of the British and French imperialists, and hence, on the principle that "enemies of my enemies are my friends," powerful allies of the Arab cause. Even more ominously for the Jews of Arab lands, Hitler's

Third Reich (followed somewhat later and with less conviction by its ally, Italy) propagated the most virulent anti-Semitism as one of the cornerstones of its ideology. And although the Nazis' pathological hatred of the Jews—so palpably foreign as it was—made relatively little headway at first among Muslim Arabs (by contrast, the Arabic-speaking Christians had for some time been receptive to both the traditional and modern varieties of European anti-Semitism), it began to gain credence first with Palestinians and their closest supporters in neighboring countries, then with some Arab nationalist admirers of Germany, and finally with widening circles among the population at large.

THE PALESTINE ISSUE

Zionism, the Palestinian national movement, and events in the Holy Land made little appreciable impact upon the relations between Jews and Arabs in most of the Arab world until 1929. In August of that year, widespread rioting broke out among the Arabs of Palestine in the wake of a perennial dispute over Jewish prayer at the Western (Wailing) Wall. The rioters massacred 129 Jews and injured over 300 more, most of them defenseless members of the old religious communities in Hebron and Safed. The local police and British troops in turn killed more than 100 Arabs in suppressing the uprising. Even before the riots, Palestinian leaders such as the Mufti Ḥājj Amīn al-Ḥusaynī had depicted the Jews as attempting to usurp and dominate the Muslim sacred precincts in Jerusalem. The violence of August 1929 only inflamed Muslim feelings in this regard. Furthermore, the unequivocal response of the British high commissioner, Sir John Chancellor, in condemning the "ruthless and blood-thirsty evildoers" and his pledge "to inflict stern punishment upon those found guilty" was viewed by the Arabs as thoroughly biased in favor of the Jews, whom Palestinian leaders accused of having committed aggression against the Arabs. The Arabs killed, and their survivors were portrayed as victims, as were those arrested and facing trial.[1]

Prior to 1929, events in Palestine evoked little popular interest in much of the Arab world. That apathy was shattered by the Wailing

[1]Concerning the riots, the events leading up to them, and their aftermath, see Lt.-Col. F. H. Kisch, *Palestine Diary* (London, 1938; reprint ed., New York, 1974), pp. 248–94 (the text of Chancellor's statement is on p. 252); Y. Porath, *The Emergence of the Palestinian-National Movement, 1918–1929* (London, 1974), pp. 254–73; idem,

Wall riots. The strongest reaction was in neighboring Syria and Lebanon, which together with Palestine formed a single cultural entity and which were seething centers of frustrated Arab nationalism. The Syro-Lebanese press carried fantastic and lurid accounts accusing the Zionist Jews of desecrating the Muslim holy places and savagely massacring innocent men, women, and children. In Beirut, the protests were generally orderly, but in Damascus, they were noisy and threatening and had an overtly anti-Jewish tone.[2]

In Iraq, too, the Palestinian disturbances aroused a widespread and highly vocal reaction. The press carried exaggerated reports placing the Arab casualties in the thousands. A leading nationalist paper, *al-Waṭan* (August 29, 1929), claimed that the Jews had thrown a bomb into a mosque, killing seventy worshipers at Friday prayers. Several papers reported that the disturbances were spilling over from Palestine into neighboring countries. On August 30, some 10,000 Arabs gathered in Baghdad's Ḥaydar Khāna Mosque, where prayers were recited for the victims of British and Zionist aggression. A committee headed by Yāsīn al-Hāshimī was elected to work in Iraq for the Palestine cause. After speeches, the crowd poured out into the streets for a demonstration march, which turned into a violent clash with the police. Several protest leaders, such as Jaᶜfar Abu 'l-Timman, and most of the press, except for such extreme nationalist papers as *al-Nahḍa* and *al-Waṭan*, tried to differentiate publicly between Zionists and their own Iraqi Jews.[3]

Egypt at this time was not a center of Pan-Arab national sentiment as were Syria and Iraq. All of the mainstream political parties emphasized an Egyptian rather than an Arab identity, and some Egyptian leaders, such as Zīwar Pasha, had even shown a certain friendliness to Zionism. In fact, prior to 1929, "Zionist activity in Palestine aroused neither Egyptian resentment nor Egyptian sympathy for the

---

The Palestinian Arab National Movement: From Riots to Rebellion. Vol. 2: 1929–1939 (London, 1977), pp. 1–19.

[2] AIU Archives (Paris) Syrie I.G.2 is filled with detailed reports on reactions in Syria and Lebanon at this time. One of these is translated in Part Two, pp. 357–359. See also AIU Archives (Paris) Liban I.G.5 for reports from Beirut.

[3] ᶜAbd al-Razzāq al-Ḥasanī, *Ta'rīkh al-Wizārāt al-ᶜIrāqiyya,* vol. 2, 2nd ed. (Sidon, 1953), pp. 228–29; Ṣādiq Ḥasan al-Sūdānī, *al-Nashāṭ al-Ṣahyūnī fi 'l-ᶜIrāq, 1914–1952* (Baghdad, 1980), pp. 77–81; Khalid Abid Muhsin, *The Political Career of Muhammad Jaᶜfar Abu al-Timman (1908–1937): A Study in Modern Iraqi History* (unpublished doctoral dissertation, University of London, 1983), pp. 270–75. According to the director of the Alliance Boys School in Baghdad at the time, the crowds in the streets were chanting "Down with the Jews!" See AIU Archives (Paris) Irak I.C.3, Robert Mefano to the AIU president (December 14, 1934).

Palestinian Arabs."[4] In Syria and Iraq, by contrast, there already had been some public displays of anti-Zionism before the Wailing Wall riots, when Lord Balfour visited Damascus in 1925 and when Sir Alfred Mond, a well-known Zionist, visited Baghdad in 1928.[5] In Egypt, there simply were no such angry mass demonstrations at all on the Palestine issue during the 1920s.

Secularist, official circles in Egypt still maintained a rather detached view of events in Palestine immediately after the Wailing Wall riots, and the general Egyptian press gave a far more sober and sophisticated account of the news than either the Syrian or the Iraqi papers. But, the more traditional religious groups within Egyptian society, such as the Young Men's Muslim Association (*Jamᶜiyyat al-Shubbān al-Muslimīn*), the Society of Islamic Guidance (*Jamᶜiyyat al-Hidāya al-Islāmiyya*), the students at the Azhar, merchants in the bazaar, and some members of the professional class, were deeply affected by what was happening in Palestine. Although they did not take to the streets with protest marches, they responded with impassioned manifestos, newspaper articles, and fund-raising campaigns on behalf of the Palestinian Arabs. Their appeals were filled with accounts of Zionist aggression and wild accusations concerning Jewish attempts to destroy the Aqṣā Mosque in order to replace it with a new Temple. Their propaganda was heavily colored with traditional Islamic imagery of the Jews as deceitful and as the eternal enemies of the Believers. This sort of message appealed primarily to a broad popular audience. In a few short years, it would shake the attitudes of Egypt's aloof politicians as well.[6]

[4] Thomas Mayer, *Egypt and the Palestine Question, 1936–1945.* Islamkündliche Untersuchungen, Band 77 (Berlin, 1983), p. 11.

[5] On the violent demonstrations in Damascus, see AIU Archives (Paris) Liban I.G.3, letter from M. Sidi (Beirut) to Alliance headquarters (May 3, 1925), which includes a clipping from the Beirut daily *Le Reveil* (April 11, 1925); and also Stephen Hemsley Longrigg, *Syria and Lebanon under French Mandate* (London, New York, and Toronto, 1958), pp. 151–52. On the demonstrations in Baghdad, see al-Ḥasanī, *Ta'rīkh al-Wizārāt al-ᶜIrāqiyya,* vol. 2, pp. 140–41; al-Sūdānī, *al-Nashāṭ al-Ṣahyūnī fi 'l-ᶜIrāq,* pp. 65–73; Hayyim J. Cohen, *ha-Peᶜīlūt ha-Ṣiyyōnīt be-ᶜIrāq* (Jerusalem, 1969), pp. 44–45. Peter Sluglett, *Britain in Iraq, 1914–1932* (Oxford, 1976), pp. 159–60, seems to suggest that demonstrations against Sir Alfred Mond were more the result of internal Iraqi political intrigues than of spontaneous anti-Zionist sentiments.

[6] Mayer, *Egypt and the Palestine Question,* pp. 15–40; James Jankowski, "Egyptian Responses to the Palestine Problem in the Interwar Period," *IJMES* 12, no. 1 (August 1980): 3–9; also idem, "Zionism and the Jews in Egyptian Nationalist Opinion," in *Egypt and Palestine: A Millennium of Association (868–1948),* ed. Amnon Cohen and Gabriel Baer (Jerusalem and New York, 1984), pp. 314–20; and Israel Gershoni and James P. Jankowski, *Egypt, Islam, and the Arabs: The Search for Egyptian Nationhood, 1900–1930* (New York and Oxford, 1986), pp. 247–54.

In Tunisia, the events of August 1929 found a sympathetic audience in both traditionalist and nationalist circles. The French authorities tried to limit direct contacts between the local Arab population and the Middle East, but they could not cut off news from the region or keep out its ideological and political currents. The Tunisian nationalists were in communication with the Arab Executive Committee and the Mufti in Jerusalem. Palestinian emissaries who entered Tunisia as tourists were active in the year following the Wailing Wall riots, speaking in mosques at Friday prayers and meeting with individuals and small groups. The Tunisian nationalist papers, such as *La Voix du Tunisien*, were filled with attacks against Zionist pretensions and threats against Zionist activities in Tunisia itself. The Young Tunisians spread a rumor that the French had made sure that large numbers of Tunisian draftees in the French army were killed during World War I in order to hand Jerusalem over to the Jews. All of this agitation succeeded in exacerbating both anti-European and anti-Jewish sentiments in Tunisia.[7]

At the farthest end of the Arab world in Morocco, events in Palestine aroused anti-Zionist feelings among certain Moroccan intellectuals who did some fund-raising on behalf of the Palestinian cause. However, there does not seem to be much, if any, immediate anti-Jewish reaction at the time. This was probably because Morocco was much farther removed from direct contact with the Arab heartlands than Tunisia, its own nationalist movement was still only in its earliest embryonic state, and the Zionist movement was far less visible or active among Moroccan Jews than among their Tunisian counterparts.[8]

Pan-Islamic, Pan-Arab, and pro-Palestinian feelings increased throughout the Arab world in the early 1930s. Anti-Zionism was, of course, an important corollary. The Mufti Ḥājj Amīn al-Ḥusaynī endeavored to foster these sentiments by calling for universal Muslim

[7] On the futility of French attempts to keep out Middle Eastern influences, see Roger Le Tourneau, *Evolution politique de l'Afrique du Nord musulmane, 1920–1961* (Paris, 1962), p. 71. On reactions to the Wailing Wall riots and contacts with the Palestinian national movement, see the informative report of C. Ouziel, director of the Alliance school for boys in Tunis to the president of the Alliance in AIU Archives (Paris) Tunisie II.C.6 (October 17, 1932); also al-Hādī al-Taymūmī (Hedi Timoumi), *al-Nashāṭ al-Ṣahyūnī bi-Tūnis bayn 1897 & 1948* (Tunis, 1982), pp. 142–44; and Daniel Goldstein, *Libération ou annexion: aux chemins croisés de l'histoire tunisienne (1914–1922)* (Tunis, 1978), pp. 362–63.

[8] See John P. Halstead, *Rebirth of a Nation: The Origins and Rise of Moroccan Nationalism, 1912–1944,* Harvard Middle Eastern Monographs, vol. XVIII (Cambridge, Mass., 1967), pp. 155–56; also Charles-André Julien, *Le Maroc face aux impérialismes, 1415–1956* (Paris, 1978), p. 161.

solidarity in the defense of Arab Palestine and its Islamic holy places. To this end, he convened a World Islamic Conference in Jerusalem in December 1931. Delegates attended from every Muslim country except secularist Turkey, which declared its opposition to the "use of religion as a political instrument."[9] Among the various resolutions adopted by the conference were a number of anti-Zionist resolutions that called for defending the Holy Land against the *Jews*. After the delegates went home, the Mufti continued his ties with Islamic organizations, such as the Young Men's Muslim Association, and with nationalists in the various Arab countries. These groups actively disseminated Palestinian anti-imperialist and anti-Zionist (and not infrequently, anti-Jewish) propaganda materials in their own countries.[10]

The first responses among the Jews of Arab lands to the rising tide of Pan-Arabism, Pan-Islamism, and anti-Zionism in the wake of the 1929 Palestinian disturbances differed from country to country depending upon the intensity of the local Arab response and how threatened the Jews themselves felt. In Syria, for example, the small and rather poor Jewish communities were simply cowed into asserting their total loyalty to the Arab cause with anti-Zionist demonstrations, public declarations, and deputations of Jewish leaders before the Muslim notables. In Iraq, where the Jews were numerically and financially far stronger, the official communal leadership and most of the elite, who had never been very enthusiastic about Zionism, totally—albeit less abjectly—distanced themselves from the movement, which was officially banned by the end of the year.[11]

The leaders of Egyptian Jewry reacted with cautious concern, urging all members of the community, and especially the Zionists, to

[9] *Oriente Moderno* (November 1931): 579–80, cited in H.A.R. Gibb, "The Islamic Congress at Jerusalem in December 1931," in *Survey of International Affairs 1934,* ed. Arnold J. Toynbee (London, 1935), p. 102.

[10] On the Mufti's Pan-Islamic activities and the 1931 conference, see Porath, *The Palestinian Arab National Movement,* vol. 2, pp. 8–13. For an example of the kinds of propaganda material distributed in various Arab countries, see the pamphlet *Bayān lil-Umma al-Tūnisiyya ᶜan Ḥālat Filasṭīn al-ᶜArabiyya al-Muslima al-Mujāhida,* translated in Part Two, pp. 381–382.

[11] Detailed reports on reactions in the Syrian Jewish community at this period may be found in AIU Archives (Paris) Syrie I.G.2. For examples, see Part Two, pp. 357–359. See also p. 88. These reports indicate the need for revision of Hayyim J. Cohen's view that it was only in 1935 that the Jews of Syria began to experience problems of this sort. See Hayyim J. Cohen, *The Jews of the Middle East 1860–1972* (New York and Jerusalem, 1973), p. 45. Concerning Iraq, see idem, *ha-Peᶜīlūt ha-Ṣiyyōnīt be-ᶜIrāq,* pp. 23–34; Muhsin, *The Political Career of Muhammad Jaᶜfar Abu al-Timman,* pp. 270–71, 278; also Part Two, pp. 342–344.

maintain a discreet silence in public, while behind the scenes, they lobbied government officials to protect them if need be from the "fanatics" and to suppress anti-Zionist and anti-Jewish agitation, which the government in fact did.[12]

The Jews in the French-ruled Maghreb felt for the most part far safer than those in the Arab East and did not seem to have been particularly alarmed by Arab nationalist attitudes at this time. In Tunisia, for example, the Zionists waged their own propaganda campaign. The Revisionist *Reveil Juif* traded strongly partisan polemics with the Neo-Destour's *La Voix du Tunisien* until asked by the resident general to cease in 1932, after disorderly encounters broke out between Arabs and Jews in several Tunisian towns, the most violent of all taking place in Sfax.[13] Moroccan Jewry also did not seem to have been terribly alarmed by warnings in the local nationalist press "to preserve an absolute neutrality vis-à-vis the Palestinian conflict."[14] On the contrary, Morocco's leading Jewish periodical, *L'Avenir Illustré*, called upon the nationalists to close ranks with the Zionists in their country to work for the betterment of Morocco following the example set by the Jewish pioneers in Palestine, an idea that was, of course, angrily rejected.[15]

There were only isolated instances of physical hostility toward the Jews of Arab lands during the first half of the 1930s despite the dire warnings made by Saʿīd Thābit, the Iraqi delegate at the 1931 Islamic Congress, that "if the Jews continue their activities in Palestine, we shall be obliged to treat them in the way they know."[16] The implication was clearly that the Jews throughout the Arab world were included. Indeed, just five months later on May 23 and 24, 1932, anti-Jewish rioting that resulted in numerous injuries and extensive property damage erupted in Aden after Jews had been accused of having desecrated the courtyard of a mosque. Throughout Jewish history under Islam, accusations of this sort had been enough to set off such violent reactions, especially during the later Middle Ages

[12] Gudrun Krämer, *Minderheit, Millet, Nation? Die Juden in Ägypten 1914–1952.* Studien zum Minderheitenproblem im Islam (Wiesbaden, 1982), p. 298; Mayer, *Egypt and the Palestine Question,* pp. 19–20.

[13] See AIU Archives (Paris) Tunisie II.C.6, Ouziel to Alliance president (October 17, 1932); *Paix et Droit* 12, no. 9 (November 1932): 8.

[14] Othman El Fayache, "L'origine de la question de Palestine," *L'Action du Peuple* (November 17, 1933): 2.

[15] See Part Two, pp. 348–349.

[16] Joseph M. Levy, "Moslem Threatens Jews in Palestine," *New York Times* (December 14, 1931): 4.

and early modern times. However, in this instance, intercommunal tensions had probably already been exacerbated by the Palestine issue.[17]

An even worse incident took place in Constantine, Algeria, from August 3 to 5, 1934, after a drunken Jewish army tailor insulted some Muslims in the courtyard of a mosque and urinated on them. During the rioting that ensued, twenty-three Jews, including men, women, and children, were killed and thirty-eight injured according to the official statistics. Widespread damage estimated at approximately 150 million francs was done to Jewish homes, businesses, and synagogues. Throughout much of the pogrom, the French police and security forces stood by and did little or nothing to stop the rioters. Jewish opinion at the time blamed the incident on a plot by European anti-Semites in the Algerian bureaucracy and on Pan-Arab propaganda. Neither of these seems to have been the case. As Charles-Robert Ageron has shown, the violence was a spontaneous event resulting from the grave social and economic conditions obtaining in Constantine at the time.[18] Events in Palestine do not seem to have been much of a factor in this instance, although they threatened to be so shortly thereafter.

Pro-Palestinian, anti-British, and—more ominously for Middle Eastern and North African Jewry—anti-Zionist sentiments were raised to new heights in the Arab world in 1936. The Arab General Strike and Revolt that erupted in Palestine in April of that year gave the conflict there a new centrality in Arab politics. Not only did events in the Holy Land elicit widespread popular concern, but for the first time, they brought about the direct intervention of four Arab states—Iraq, Saudi Arabia, Yemen, and Transjordan—as interested parties in the conflict. What is more, this right to intervene was tacitly recognized as legitimate by Great Britain, which was responsible for the mandate.[19]

[17] For details concerning the Aden riots, see Part Two, pp. 360–362.

[18] Charles-Robert Ageron, "Une émeute anti-juive à Constantine (août 1934)," *ROMM,* nos. 13–14 (ler Semestre 1973): 23–40; Mahfoud Kaddache, *Histoire du nationalisme algérien: question nationale et politique algérienne, 1919–1951,* vol. 1, 2nd ed. (Algiers, 1981), pp. 303–20. For Jewish views on the incident, see Michel Ansky, *Les Juifs d'Algérie du Décret Crémieux à la libération* (Paris, 1950), pp. 67–70; Richard Ayoun and Bernard Cohen, *Les Juifs d'Algérie: deux mille ans d'histoire* (Paris, 1982), pp. 162–64; André N. Chouraqui, *Between East and West: A History of the Jews of North Africa* (New York, 1973), p. 153; and Part Two, pp. 365–366. For the views of a gallicized Algerian Muslim, see Part Two, pp. 363–364.

[19] Barry Rubin, *The Arab States and the Palestine Conflict* (Syracuse, N.Y., 1981), pp. 66–80; Porath, *The Palestinian Arab National Movement,* vol. 2, pp. 201–14.

The most violent reactions came, not surprisingly, in Syria and Iraq, where anti-Zionism and solidarity with the Palestinian Arab cause were linchpins of their own national politics. As in 1929, the press in both countries constantly issued hyperbolic reports filled with lurid details of the happenings in Palestine. Throughout the latter part of April and into May, Jews were accosted and beaten in the streets of Damascus. Gangs of young toughs from the neighboring Shāghūr Quarter would come into the Jewish Quarter "to reason with" passersby. Jewish businessmen were accused of sending supplies to Palestine, and trucks with Jewish-owned merchandise were attacked and destroyed by mobs. Rumors were spread by posters and in the press that Jews were giving poisoned candy to Muslim children, some of whom had died as a result. For a while calm was restored in mid-May, when the French authorities increased police protection in the Jewish Quarter and Syrian nationalist leaders, like Fakhrī al-Barūdī, who were eager not to jeopardize the negotiations for independence from France that were then going on in Paris, refuted the poison libel and urged restraint toward their Jewish neighbors.[20]

Although the press reports were equally vociferous, the initial reaction in Iraq to the Palestinian uprising was more controlled than in Syria,[21] since the Hashemite kingdom was then in the midst of finalizing delicate negotiations for a treaty with England that was only ratified at the end of June of that year. Furthermore, during the summer of 1936, the Iraqi foreign minister Nūrī al-Saʿīd was involved in mediating among the British, the Palestinians, and the Zionists in

[20] AIU Archives (Paris) Liban I.C.1, "Extraits de Presse": *al-Ayyām* (May 22–June 16, 1936), *Les Echos de Syrie* (May 27, June 2 and 8, 1936), *Ṣawt al-Aḥrār* (May 30, 1936); *al-Nahār* (May 30, June 2 and 3, 1936) *al-Bayraq* (May 24, June 2, 10, 16, and 17, 1936). See also the report of the Alliance school director in Damascus translated in Part Two, pp. 383–384.

[21] The Iraqi Jewish community petitioned the government to place controls on the press reports to avoid stirring up anti-Jewish animus. See AIU Archives (Paris) Irak I.C.3, unsigned, typed report from the College A. D. Sassoon, Baghdad (April 25, 1936). The British ambassador in Baghdad also requested that the government "restrain the press from publishing further tendencious matter," although for its own reasons. See Reeva S. Simon, *Iraq between the Two World Wars: The Creation and Implementation of a Nationalist Ideology* (New York, 1986), pp. 68–69, citing PRO (London) FO 406/74, E2653/94/31 (May 4, 1936). There were reports in the Palestinian Arab newspaper *al-Difāʿ* (May 28, 1936) of several anti-Jewish incidents, including student marches into one of Baghdad's Jewish neighborhoods, that ended in violence. These were taken up in the Hebrew press. However, the incidents are not substantiated elsewhere and appear to have been merely an attempt by Palestinian nationalists to stir up the situation even further. See al-Sūdānī, *al-Nashāṭ al-Ṣahyūnī fi 'l-ʿIrāq*, pp. 91–93.

an attempt to resolve the crisis and end the strike.[22] After the failure of Nūrī al-Saʿīd's diplomatic efforts and Great Britain's imposition of severe measures to end the disorders in Palestine, there was a rash of violent incidents against Jews in Iraq. During September 1936, the atmosphere in Baghdad became very highly charged. Anti-Jewish pamphlets were circulated by Saʿīd Thābit's Committee for the Defense of Palestine. (Thābit, it will be recalled, had threatened the Jews in general with retribution in his fiery speech at Jerusalem's Islamic Congress in 1931.) Over a four-week period extending from mid-September to mid-October, three Jews (one, a friend of the prime minister) were murdered in Baghdad and one in Basra, a bomb—which, however, failed to go off—was thrown into a Baghdadi synagogue on Yom Kippur (September 27), several other bombs were thrown at Jewish clubs, and a number of Jews were roughed up by street gangs. The president of the Baghdadi Jewish community, Rabbi Sassoon Khadduri, who was himself a staunch anti-Zionist, issued a public statement in response to demands from the nationalist press affirming loyalty to the Arab cause in Palestine and disassociating Iraqi Jewry from Zionism.[23] This did not bring about any improvement in the situation.

Amid the growing insecurity, the Jews of Baghdad went on a three-day protest strike from October 7 to 9. Owing to their disproportionate role in the nation's commerce, the strike immediately had a major economic impact. The government convened a meeting with the Jewish leadership at which it expressed its "benevolence" toward Iraqi Jewry and promised to "take all necessary measures to maintain the security of the Jews whom it rightfully considered to be outstanding Iraqi citizens." It also issued an official communiqué from the

[22] Norman Anthony Rose, "The Arab Rulers and Palestine, 1936: The British Reaction," *JMH* 44, no. 2 (June 1972): 220–26; Porath, *The Palestinian Arab National Movement,* vol. 2, pp. 207–11.

[23] National Archives (Washington) U.S. Department of State RG 890G.4016 Jews/12, James S. Moose (Baghdad) to secretary of state (October 14, 1936) in Part Two, pp. 386–388; AIU Archives (Paris) Irak I.C.3, letter from M. Laredo in Baghdad to Alliance president in Paris (October 18, 1936), the major part of which was published in *Paix et Droit* 16, no. 8 (October 1936): 12. See also Cohen, *The Jews of the Middle East,* pp. 27–28; idem, *ha-Peʿīlūt ha-Ṣiyyōnīt be-ʿIrāq,* pp. 156–57; and Rubin, *The Arab States and the Palestine Conflict,* pp. 75–76. Al-Sūdānī, *al-Nashāṭ al-Ṣahyūnī fi 'l-ʿIrāq,* p. 95, claims that the anti-Jewish leaflets were in fact the work of Zionist provocateurs. Elie Kedourie, *The Chatham House Version and Other Middle-Eastern Studies* (New York and Washington, D. C., 1970), p. 306, contends that the anti-Jewish violence in 1936 was only "on the pretext of making gestures against Zionism—with which the Iraqi Jews had no connection." This, of course, is

Ministry of the Interior stating that "events in Palestine . . . should not affect the Jews of Iraq and that any attempt at disorder would be severely repressed."[24]

In marked contrast to those in Syria and Iraq, the reactions in Egypt to the Palestinian Arab General Strike were remarkably subdued at first, although ever-growing numbers of Egyptians in all walks of life were beginning to take an active and concerned interest in the Palestine conflict. Still, with the exception of Islamic extremist groups, such as the Muslim Brotherhood, which called for a boycott (a call that seems to have been ineffectual) against local Jewish merchants in May 1936, some anti-Jewish remarks in religious radio broadcasts and publications, and the appearance of some Jew-baiting graffiti on the walls of the Jewish Quarter of Port Said in September after the president of the Palestinian Islamic Youth Organization visited that city, there was no harassment of Egyptian Jews. However, both Jewish and government leaders were worried about the possibility of violence erupting.[25]

In the French-controlled Maghreb, the reactions to the strike in Palestine were even more sporadic. There were some sympathy strikes and demonstrations in several of the main cities of Tunisia, Algeria, and Morocco. There were a few small-scale riots, but these were the result of local political and economic conditions no less than of events in Palestine. Only in a few instances were Muslim hostilities aimed at the local Jewish population.[26]

The recommendation of the Peel Commission Report in 1937 for partitioning Palestine into separate Arab and Jewish states, the renewed violence of the Arab Revolt, and the flight of the Mufti to Syria to avoid arrest by the British mandatory authorities all combined to arouse sympathies for the Palestine cause more than ever before

---

only partially true and reflects the author's own social milieu at that time. For the text of Rabbi Khadduri's public statement, see Part Two, p. 389.

[24] AIU Archives (Paris) Irak I.C.3 (October 18, 1936) and *Paix et Droit* 16, no. 8 (October 1931): 12. Al-Sūdānī, *al-Nashāṭ al-Ṣahyūnī fi 'l-ᶜIrāq,* p. 96, states that the government threatened the instigators of the strike with punishment, thus getting the Jews to return to work! He offers no documentation, and the statement is not corroborated in any of the sources.

[25] Mayer, *Egypt and the Palestine Question,* pp. 44–47; Krämer, *Minderheit, Millet, Nation?,* pp. 290–91; Jankowski, "Egyptian Responses to the Palestine Problem," pp. 15–16.

[26] "Unrest in the North-West African Territories under French Rule (1927–37)," in *Survey of International Affairs 1937,* vol. 1, ed. Arnold J. Toynbee (London, 1938), pp. 533–35.

throughout the Arab world. By this time, the fine line between anti-Zionist and anti-Jewish sentiments was being almost totally eroded in many quarters by the ever-increasing anti-Semitic overtones of Arab nationalist rhetoric.

THE PENETRATION OF ANTI-SEMITISM

European anti-Semitism of both the traditional ecclesiastical and the more recent pseudoscientific varieties had made some inroads among small circles of westernized Christian intellectuals in Syria and Egypt during the nineteenth and early twentieth centuries.[27] For most Muslims such notions were still too new and too palpably foreign to be lent much, if any, credence. By 1920, however, Palestinian nationalists began citing that classic of modern European anti-Semitic literature, *The Protocols of the Elders of Zion*, in their propaganda.[28] Anti-Jewish and anti-Zionist agitators in other Arab countries, like Ṣādiq Pasha al-Qādirī, who appeared in Iraq in 1924, also took up the libels of the *Protocols*, particularly the idea of a worldwide Jewish conspiracy. These ideas were played up in the Arab nationalist press. Jewish requests for government intervention to muffle such propaganda went unheeded. When some Baghdadi Jews wrote counter articles in their own newspaper *al-Miṣbāḥ*, officials warned the editor that if he continued to print such articles, the paper would be shut down. Communal leaders were sufficiently alarmed to request secretly the Zionist Executive in London (this was, after all, several years before the Wailing Wall riots) to intervene with the British Colonial Office.[29]

The *Protocols* spread even more rapidly in the Middle East with the appearance in late 1925 of an Arabic translation entitled *The Conspiracy of Jewry against the Nations* (*Mu'āmarat al-Yahūdiyya ʿala*

[27] For background on the early propagation of both traditional and modern anti-Semitism in the Middle East by the French, see Norman A. Stillman, in "Antisemitism in the Contemporary Arab World," in *Antisemitism in the Contemporary World,* ed. Michael Curtis (Boulder, Colo., and London, 1986), pp. 70–85; also idem, *The Jews of Arab Lands: A History and Source Book* (Philadelphia, 1979), pp. 104–7; and Sylvia G. Haim, "Arabic Antisemitic Literature," *JSS* 17, no. 4 (1955): 307–12.

[28] See Elyakim Rubinstein, "The 'Protocols of the Elders of Zion' in the Arab-Jewish Conflict in Palestine in the Twenties," *Hamizrah Hehadash* 26, nos. 1–2 (1976): 38 [Heb.].

[29] *Al-Miṣbāḥ* (September 25 and October 16, 1924); also CZA (Jerusalem) Z 4/2470, confidential letter from the secretary of the Zionist Organization in Baghdad to the Zionist Executive, London (October 30, 1924). The writer mentions that the community believed al-Qādirī to be a British agent!

'l-Shuʿūb) by a Lebanese Maronite priest Anṭūn Yamīn. This was the first in a long line of editions and translations. It caused considerable alarm among Syro-Lebanese Jewry. The president of the Jewish Community Council of Beirut petitioned the French mandatory authorities to ban the book throughout Syria. The French High Commissioner de Jouvenel, however, did not consider the publication to be worthy of so much fuss.[30]

The *Protocols* circulated in Egypt, where Yamīn's Arabic edition had been originally published, throughout the 1930s, but it was only in the latter part of the decade that it seems to have gained prominence, as its libels were increasingly echoed in the nationalist and militant Islamic press. Copies of it, along with other anti-Semitic works, were distributed at the World Parliamentary Congress for the Defense of Palestine, which was held in Cairo in 1938. This marked a new stage in the appropriation and assimilation of European anti-Semitic propaganda by the Pan-Arab and Pan-Islamic movements, which at earlier gatherings had generally disseminated more traditional Muslim anti-Jewish polemical material of the sort that had become popular in the darker days of the later Middle Ages.[31]

THE GERMAN AND ITALIAN IMPACT

This period of rising tensions between Arabs and Jews over the Palestine issue, on the one hand, and between the Arabs and the colonial powers of England and France over national aspirations, on the other, coincided with the rise of Fascism on the European continent. Italy and especially Germany had long been admired by Arab nationalists for their success in forging strong, independent, unified nation-states in the late nineteenth century. The Arab officer corps of the Ottoman army, from whose ranks emerged much of the later Iraqi political and military elite and at least one of the leading figures

[30] See Part Two, pp. 351–352. On the history of the *Protocols* in Arabic, see Stillman, "Antisemitism in the Contemporary Arab World," pp. 75–76; Haim, "Arabic Antisemitic Literature," pp. 308–9.

[31] Krämer, *Minderheit, Millet, Nation?,* pp. 277, 295. At the Bludan Congress a year earlier, delegates received a tract of the traditional variety entitled *The Jews and Islam,* which described the Jews as being perfidious and rancorous foes of Islam since the time of the Prophet. See Public Records Office (London) FO 371/20814, file E5515/22/31, published in Elie Kedourie, "The Bludan Congress on Palestine, September 1937," *MES* 17, no. 1 (January 1981): 123–24. On the images of Jews in late medieval Muslim polemics and the social background to this literature, see Stillman, *The Jews of Arab Lands,* pp. 64–87, especially p. 72.

in the Egyptian army, had been deeply imbued with the militaristic ideals of their Prussian teachers. These men and others, like Baᶜth ideologist Michel ᶜAflaq and the Pan-Syrian nationalist Anṭūn Saᶜāda, continued to exhibit an intense "germanophilia" (to use Bassam Tibi's apt expression) for decades to come.[32]

The Arab nationalists of the Maghreb were not as thoroughly germanophile as their Middle Eastern counterparts, but they also admired Germany for similar reasons. Furthermore, in North African eyes, Germany was free from the taint of colonialism and was the historic enemy of the French oppressors. The Moroccans in particular were grateful for Germany's efforts to block French and Spanish imperialist designs upon their country and had fond memories of Kaiser Wilhelm's visit to Tangier in 1905. The rapid reconstitution of German power in the 1930s only served to enhance its prestige among the North Africans.[33]

The conflict between Jews and Arabs in Palestine was, in the words of Polish historian Lukasz Hirszowicz, "as if made to order for the needs and aims of Nazi propaganda."[34] However, it was not until the late 1930s that the Third Reich began to exploit it or even to engage officially in actively propagandizing in the Arab countries. (Fascist propaganda broadcasts in Arabic were the monopoly of the Italian radio station at Bari until 1939.[35]) The influence of Nazi Germany upon many Arab nationalists was strong nevertheless. Sāmī al-Jundī, who was a young Syrian nationalist in the 1930s and later a Baᶜthist leader, observed in his memoirs: "We were racialists. We were fascinated by Nazism, reading its books and the sources of its thought, especially Nietzsche's *Thus Spake Zarathustra*, Fichte's *Addresses to the German Nation*, and H. S. Chamberlain's *Foundations*

[32] Bassam Tibi, *Arab Nationalism: A Critical Enquiry,* ed. and trans. Marion Farouk-Sluglett and Peter Sluglett (London and Basingstoke, 1981), pp. 91–96, 100–1, 126, 156–57, 165–67. See also Simon, *Iraq between the Two World Wars,* pp. 7–33; and the important article of Stefan Wild, "National Socialism in the Arab Near East between 1933 and 1939," *WI* 25, n.s. (1985): 126–47.

[33] Halstead, *Rebirth of a Nation,* pp. 152–53; Charles-Robert Ageron, "Les populations du Maghreb face à la propagande allemande," *RHDGM* 29, no. 114 (April 1979): 2–3; Mahfoud Kaddache, "L'opinion politique musulmane en Algérie et l'administration française (1939–1942)," *RHDGM* 29, no. 114 (April 1979): 98.

[34] Lukasz Hirszowicz, *The Third Reich and the Arab East* (London and Toronto, 1966), p. 27.

[35] Ibid., p. 41. Pro-Nazi, anti-Semitic broadcasts in Spanish were beamed nightly from Seville to northern Morocco as well. See AIU Archives (Paris) Maroc IV.C.11, report from A. Sagues (Tangier) to Alliance president (Paris), dated October 27, 1937.

of the Nineteenth Century."[36] Al-Jundī goes on to say that he and his friends considered translating *Mein Kampf* into Arabic.

Arabic translations of *Mein Kampf*, usually with the anti-Arab passages carefully expurgated, were available in both the Middle East and North Africa during these years. German tourists, businessmen, and individual members of the foreign service disseminated anti-Semitic (that is, anti-Jewish) propaganda.[37]

Paramilitary youth groups, such as the Green Shirts (al-Qumṣān al-Khaḍrā') of Miṣr al-Fatāt, the Phalanxes (al-Katā'ib) of the Muslim Brotherhood, the Iron Shirts (al-Qumṣān al-Ḥadīdiyya) of the Syrian National Bloc, the Phalanges Libanaises of the Maronites, and the Muthannā Club and the Futuwwa in Iraq, consciously emulated German and Italian models. In addition to their uniforms, martial displays, the cult of the leader, and a propensity for violence, many of these groups openly espoused, especially after the Palestinian Arab Revolt, the Judeophobic rhetoric of their European heroes. Thus Aḥmad Ḥusayn, the founder and leader of Miṣr al-Fatāt (Young Egypt), could write in the movement's journal:

> They [the Jews] are the secret of this moral desolation which has become general throughout the Arab and Islamic worlds. They are the secret of this cultural squalor and these filthy arts. They are the secret of this religious and moral decay, to the point that it has become correct to say "search for the Jew behind every depravity."[38]

36 Sāmī al-Jundī, *al-Baʿth* (Beirut, 1969), p. 27. See also Elie Kedourie, *Arabic Political Memoirs and Other Studies* (London, 1974), pp. 200–1, where a lengthy excerpt, including this passage, is translated.

37 On Arabic editions of *Mein Kampf*, see Wild, "National Socialism in the Arab Near East between 1933 and 1939," pp. 147–70; Ageron, "Les populations du Maghreb face à la propagande allemande," p. 2; idem, "Contribution à l'étude de la propagande allemande au Maghreb pendant la deuxième guerre mondiale," *RHM* (January 1977): 16–17; Stillman, "Antisemitism in the Contemporary Arab World," p. 76; Nissim Kazzaz, "The Influence of Nazism in Iraq and Anti-Jewish Activity," *Peʿamim* 29 (1986): 53 [Heb.]. On the propaganda activities of such individuals, see Michel Abitbol, *Les Juifs d'Afrique du Nord sous Vichy* (Paris, 1983), pp. 36–37; Ageron, "Les populations du Maghreb face à la propagande allemande," pp. 3–4; Krämer, *Minderheit, Millet, Nation?,* pp. 259–79; Kazzaz, "The Influence of Nazism in Iraq and Anti-Jewish Activity," pp. 52–55 [Heb.]; Maurice Le Glay, "Musulmans et Juifs marocains: Etude de moeurs et de l'état des esprits à l'occasion du mouvement antisémite d'Allemagne," *Afrique Française* 43, no. 11 (November 1933): 621–25; Ansky, *Les Juifs d'Algérie,* p. 76.

38 Aḥmad Ḥusayn, "Risāla min Yahūdī, *Jarīdat Miṣr al-Fatāt* (July 27, 1939): 1, 4. Cited by Jankowski, "Egyptian Responses to the Palestine Problem in the Interwar Period," p. 33, n. 118. See also Shimon Shamir, "The Influence of German National-Socialism on Radical Movements in Egypt," *Germany and the Middle East,*

The initial response of the Jews in the Arab world to the rise of Nazism differed markedly from country to country in proportion to the relative strength and security of each national community. The Jews of Syria, for example, who as noted were in a state of semipanic since 1929 on account of the threats of their nationalist Arab neighbors, were too cowed to show much in the way of an outward response beyond some modest collections taken up primarily by Alliance teachers, their students, and alumni on behalf of their brethren in Germany and Eastern Europe. Helping the handful of European Jewish refugees who arrived in Syria immediately after Hitler's accession to power was even more difficult because of the hostility of the local Arabs, who saw them as an unwanted vanguard of many more.[39] In neighboring Lebanon, where the overall situation of the Jewish community was considerably better than in Syria and where the Maronite Patriarch Monsignor Arida had issued a pastoral letter in 1933 strongly condemning Nazi persecution of Jews, the consensus among the Jewish leadership in Beirut was that given the mounting tensions in Palestine any sort of overt communal demonstrations would be disastrous.[40]

The large Egyptian Jewish community, which was prosperous, sophisticated, well organized, and far more self-confident than either

1835–1939, ed. Jehuda L. Wallach. Jahrbuch des Instituts für Deutsche Geschichte, Beiheft 1 (Tel Aviv, 1975), pp. 200–8.

[39] For the modest nature of collections on behalf of European Jews, see, for example, AIU Archives (Paris) Syrie I.B.2, where the Union de la Jeunesse Juive in Aleppo is recorded as raising 1,020 francs on May 22, 1933. Compare this with 12,245 and 16,551 francs collected by the much more comfortable (politically and economically) Beirut Jewish community on May 11 and June 11 of that same year. AIU Archives (Paris) Liban I.C.1. For a case of German Jewish refugee physicians in Damascus in 1933, see Part Two, p. 367.

[40] For the text of Msgr. Arida's pastoral letter, see Part Two, p. 370. For a personal expression of sympathy written by the patriarch to Maurice Sidi, director of the Alliance school in Beirut, see AIU Archives (Paris) Liban I.C.1, letter dated May 20, 1933. On the fears about taking too conspicuous a stance against Nazism, see the letter (in Hebrew) by Joseph Farhi, president of the Beirut Jewish community, to the Zionist Executive, Histadrut Department, January 22, 1937, in CZA (Jerusalem) S 5/2204. Both the Lebanese and Syrian Jews were apparently willing at first to send telegrams of protest to the German consul in Beirut. See Dan Eldar, "The Response of Oriental Jewry to German Antisemitism, 1933–1934," *Pe^camim* 5 (1980): 63 [Heb.].

Syrian or Lebanese Jewry, reacted swiftly and vigorously to Nazi anti-Semitism in Europe and to the activities of Nazi supporters in Egypt. A number of mass protests were organized at the initiative of the influential B'nai B'rith lodges in March and April 1933 in Cairo, Alexandria, Port Said, Mansura, and Tanta. Thousands of Jews, including the chief rabbis and representatives of the communal councils, took part. A defense organization called La Ligue contre l'Antisémitisme Allemand, Association formée par toutes les oeuvres juives en Egypte, was formed to counter Nazi activities and propaganda in Egypt. The league was headed by a committee of leading Jewish public figures from Alexandria and Cairo and soon merged with the Ligue Internationale contre Antisémitisme (LICA, the International League against Racism and Antisemitism), becoming its Egyptian branch. By 1935, it counted 1,500 members. In addition to LICA, Jewish students formed a youth association called La Ligue Internationale Scolaire contre l'Antisémitisme (LISCA), which in theory included all of the students in Egypt's Jewish schools. One of LICA's principal activities was countering German propaganda, whose principal local agents were the Nazi party members among Egypt's German colony. (The Cairene branch of the NSDAP [National Socialist German Workers' Party] had been founded by Alfred Hess, brother of later Deputy Fuehrer Rudolf Hess, in 1926.[41]) The league's other main activity was organizing a boycott of German goods. LICA's publicity efforts were facilitated by the significant number of Jewish journalists in Egypt who wrote not only for the Jewish newspapers, such as *L'Aurore*, *Israël*, *La Tribune Juive*, and *al-Shams*, but also for the major English- and French-language papers of the country, such as the *Egyptian Gazette*, *Egyptian Mail*, *La Bourse Egyptienne*, and *Le Journal du Caire*.[42]

The boycott of German imports, films, and local businesses was ushered in by a public appeal issued by Léon Castro, one of the leaders of LICA and for many years one of the leading Jewish figures in Egyptian nationalist politics. His appeal was published in the Jewish press and called upon the Jews of Egypt to "break every material, intellectual, social and worldly relation with them [the Germans]."[43]

[41] Krämer, *Minderheit, Millet, Nation?,* p. 260.

[42] Ibid., pp. 261–64; Maurice Mizrahi, *L'Egypte et ses Juifs: Les temps révolu (XIXe et XXe siècle)* (Geneva, 1977), pp. 103–7. The journal *L'Aurore,* in particular, became the mouthpiece for LICA. See Maurice Fargeon, *Les Juifs en Egypte depuis les origines jusqu'à ce jour* (Cairo, 1938), p. 227.

[43] Quoted in Krämer, *Minderheit, Millet, Nation?,* p. 267.

Castro's fellow Jews met the call, and the boycott was successful enough to hurt a number of German business interests, to drive German films completely out of the Egyptian movie houses, and to alarm some German officials, who launched a countercampaign of their own. Fearing a serious breakdown of public order and possible financial dislocations, Egyptian and British authorities finally stepped in during the summer of 1933 to halt the most vocal aspects of the campaigns of both sides. The boycott thereafter was carried out unofficially on the individual level.[44]

Although other actions taken by members of the Egyptian Jewish community, such as a highly publicized libel trial in 1933–34 against the head of Cairo's German Club, failed, the communal leadership continued to protest anti-Semitism and the persecution of Jews in Europe and in the neighboring Italian colony of Libya throughout the decade.[45]

The leaders of Egyptian Jewry were far more circumspect in responding to the anti-Jewish propaganda emanating from the militant Arab and Islamic groups, which augmented considerably as of 1936. Instead of embarking upon a highly visible offensive as they had against the Nazis, they made discreet, behind-the-scenes use of their still "excellent personal and business contacts" with the ruling elite and with influential members of the foreign diplomatic corps to keep anti-Semitic and anti-Zionist agitation in check as they had done earlier at the time of the Wailing Wall riots.[46]

In French North Africa, as in Egypt, the large urban Jewish communities also responded with a strong activist stance against German and Italian anti-Semitism. In Morocco, for example, Jews in the main cities held meetings in 1933 and declared a boycott of German goods that was highly effective since many Jewish merchants were the principal importers for these products. Protests were addressed to the German consular representatives. Similar meetings and boycotts

[44] Ibid., pp. 268–74; Eldar, "The Response of Oriental Jewry to German Antisemitism, 1933–1934," pp. 66–71 [Heb.]; Mizrahi, *L'Egypte et ses Juifs,* pp. 105–6. See also Part Two, p. 378.

[45] For details of the Jabes v. van Meeteren trial and appeal, see the Egyptian Jewish press between January 1934 and May 1935; and Krämer, *Minderheit, Millet, Nation?,* pp. 265–67. For examples of protests against Jewish persecution, see the lead articles "Les Juifs et la provocation allemande" and "Protestations des organisations juives d'Egypte contre les excitations nazis au meutre des Juifs," *Israël* (May 18, 1934): 1; and "Antisémitisme en Lybie," *Israël* (January 4, 1937): 3.

[46] Krämer, *Minderheit, Millet, Nation?,* p. 295.

were conducted in Tunisia. Italian banks were also targeted by Jews throughout North Africa for the mass withdrawal of assets.[47]

The reaction of Algerian Jewry differed somewhat from this pattern of response. During the 1930s, there was a virulent revival of *pied-noir* anti-Semitism. For the right-wing French colonists, the Nazis were natural allies against the Jews and the Bolsheviks. The official Jewish leadership in Algeria, embodied in the consistories, was, as has been noted in Chapter 3, prohibited from engaging in all but activities related to communal religious and charitable matters. Furthermore, some of the consistorial leaders believed that the best response to the rising anti-Semitic tide around them was "silence and contempt." Activist leaders, including Elie Gozlan and André Lévi-Valensi, therefore decided in 1937 to revive the Algerian Jewish Committee for Social Studies (CESA) and, at its first meeting in February of that year, issued a declaration that "in the face of the odious campaign of calumnies and hate . . . silence and contempt are neither wise nor courageous."[48] Jewish trade unions and professional organizations also took up their own defensive campaigns. Unlike the other North African Jews, the Algerians saw themselves first and foremost as Frenchmen, and even the activists of the CESA found it difficult to respond as Jews. As Michel Abitbol has observed, the leaders of Algerian Jewry "were more at ease denouncing the 'anti-republican' and 'anti-French' message of the antisemitic line than in condemning its particularist character, openly directed against a definite group in society."[49]

ON THE EVE OF THE SECOND WORLD WAR

By the late 1930s, tensions between Jews and the surrounding population were mounting everywhere in the Arab world. During the last two years leading up to the Second World War, there was a rash of sabotage incidents aimed at Jewish private and communal property in Iraq, Syria, Lebanon, and, for the first time, Egypt.[50] The primary

[47] "Maroc: Les troubles antisemites," *Afrique Française* 43, no. 11 (November 1933): 665; Abitbol, *Les Juifs d'Afrique du Nord sous Vichy,* p. 38; Elie Cohen-Hadria, "Les Juifs francophones dans la vie intellectuelle et politique en Tunisie entre les deux guerres," *Judaïsme d'Afrique du Nord aux XIXe-XXe siècles: Histoire, société et culture,* ed. Michel Abitbol (Jerusalem, 1980), pp. 62–63.

[48] Ansky, *Les Juifs d'Algérie,* p. 78.

[49] Abitbol, *Les Juifs d'Afrique du Nord sous Vichy,* p. 31.

[50] See, for example, Part Two, pp. 390–396.

factor was the conflict in Palestine, which between 1936 and 1939 had degenerated into an open rebellion against the British mandate and the Zionist enterprise. The appeals of the Mufti and his envoys for Arab and Islamic solidarity in the struggle against imperialism and Zionism struck a note of resonance in much of the Arab world, which was still under outright colonial rule or some form of European tutelage. In the highly charged atmosphere of Syria and Iraq, not only did all open Zionist activity within the Jewish community cease, but the communal leadership again and again disavowed any connection with Zionism in the futile hope of gaining some respite. By contrast, the leaders of Egyptian Jewry tried to emphasize their own patriotism, on the one hand, and to promote Egypt as the example of peaceful Arab-Jewish coexistence for all the parties in Palestine to follow, on the other.[51] These attempts proved to be no less futile.

Arab-Jewish relations were further strained by the rise of Nazi Germany and Fascist Italy, which offered Arab militant nationalists powerful alternative models to British and French liberalism. No less threatening was the increasing penetration of European anti-Semitism into the Arab world and the growing receptivity among Arabs to both its ideas and its vocabulary. In the French Maghreb, there was the added factor of a homegrown anti-Semitism among the colonial population, especially in Algeria.

In the ten years between 1929 and 1939, the Jews of Arab lands had witnessed the steady undermining of their position almost everywhere. During the decade that followed, the process of erosion would increase in rapidity and intensity, leading finally to a total collapse.

[51] See, for example, the letter written by the presidents of the Cairene and Alexandrian Jewish communities to the Egyptian prime minister on May 17, 1938, translated in Part Two, pp. 402–403.

6

WORLD WAR II AND ITS IMPACT

The Second World War was traumatic for the Jews of Arab lands—as for all world Jewry. The war would have a major transformational effect upon them and would contribute greatly to their sense of solidarity and common destiny with the rest of the Jewish people. As noted in the preceding chapter, many Arab nationalists admired German and Italian militarism, and there was widespread sympathy among Arabs for the Axis, which was the enemy of colonialist Britain and France. The Middle East and North Africa became actual theaters of war, and Jews in almost every Arab country were caught up in the maelstrom of events, not merely as inhabitants of their region, but as Jews. Indeed, in many Arab countries, the Jews would experience a brief but bitter foretaste of what awaited their brethren in Europe. Only in Egypt, in the Levant States, and in the isolated mountain fastness of Yemen did the Jewish communities go through the war years relatively unscathed.

EGYPT AND THE LEVANT STATES

The outward manifestations of anti-Jewish hostility that had begun to surface in Egypt during the late 1930s were suppressed when the government declared a state of emergency and introduced martial law and strict censorship at the onset of the war. However, Egypt's careful neutrality until almost the very end of the conflict, the nearness of Rommel's Afrika-Korps during 1941 and 1942, and the continued sympathy of the nationalists for the Germans (King Fārūq, for example, conveyed his "high respect and support" and that of "a 90 percent majority of his people" to the Fuehrer) gave Egyptian Jewry cause for anxiety.[1] The massive presence of British troops was the only real guarantee of the Jewish community's continued safety, and this guarantee was by no means assured until the rout of Rommel's forces at El Alamein in late 1942. Prior to the British victory, thousands of Jews, along with many other members of the large foreign community, fled from Alexandria. Many transferred to Cairo, although many fled from there as well. Others, including those who were known to have been active in either Zionist or anti-Fascist activities, were temporarily evacuated to Palestine. The assurances of Prime Minister Muṣṭafā al-Naḥḥās Pasha (who had been installed several months earlier with the backing of British tanks) to Chief Rabbi Ḥayyim Nahum in July 1942, when an invasion seemed imminent, that even if the Germans invaded the country, Egypt would not institute anti-Jewish measures, did little to assuage communal fears.[2] Egyptian Jews also had considerable cause for concern on account of the widespread popular belief that Jewish businessmen were profiteering from the war. It was commonly believed among the hard-pressed Egyptian masses, who had to face a 300 percent rise in the cost of living during the war years, that the Jews were in the words of a British Embassy report "mainly responsible for shortages and high prices of essentials of life."[3] German and Italian propaganda capitalized upon these sentiments and portrayed the Jews in Egypt "as acting as British agents to deprive the people of food supplies in favour of themselves and of British troops."[4]

The Jews in Syria and Lebanon were briefly touched even more directly by the war, although they too came through relatively unharmed. For almost a year, between July 1940 and 1941, Syro-

[1] Gudrun Krämer, *Minderheit, Millet, Nation? Die Juden in Ägypten 1914–1952.* Studien zum Minderheitenproblem im Islam, 7 (Wiesbaden, 1982), pp. 306–7. On German contacts with Fārūq at this time, see Lukasz Hirszowicz, *The Third Reich and the Arab East* (London and Toronto, 1966), pp. 239–43.

[2] Krämer, *Minderheit, Millet, Nation?,* pp. 308–9; Elie Politi, *L'Egypte de 1914 à "Suez"* (Paris, 1965), pp. 210–17. Jacques Berque, *Egypt Imperialism and Revolution,* trans. Jean Stewart (London, 1972), p. 571, notes that the dominant class was seized with panic as Rommel drew near, but "an even intenser panic swept over that small but economically important section of the population, the Jewish minority of Cairo and Alexandria." Rahel Yanait-Ben-Zvi, *Be-Shelīḥūt li-Lvanōn ūle-Sūrya (1943)* (Tel Aviv, 1979), p. 9, records the amazement of the Yishuv as Jews and Europeans began arriving in Palestine from Egypt at this time.

[3] PRO (London) FO 371/31576, Ambassador Lampson to Foreign Office (January 22, 1942), cited in Lois Gottesman, "Israel in Egypt: The Jewish Community of Egypt, 1922–1957" (unpublished master's thesis, Princeton University, 1982), p. 61.

[4] Ibid.

Lebanese Jewry found itself under Vichy authority. Shortly after the establishment of the Pétain regime, a delegation of Jewish communal leaders in Beirut headed by Joseph Farhi petitioned the French High Commissioner Gabriel Puaux, who had been in office since before the war, not to apply Vichy legislation concerning Jews in Greater Syria. Puaux could not accede to their request.[5] However, he was not an enthusiastic supporter of Vichy and did not do his utmost to implement its directives. His replacement, General Dentz, although a loyal servant of the regime, was too occupied with the deteriorating internal economic and political situation and, as of June 1941, with the Allied invasion, to single out the small, unobtrusive Jewish minority for attention. The Jews merely suffered from the severe shortages of food and fuel along with the rest of the urban population through the winter and spring of 1940–1941.

The Syrian Jews had additional cause for concern on account of the active presence of German agents who were in open contact with the Arab nationalists and were finding ready listeners to their propaganda among the masses who believed that an Axis victory would bring them independence at last. A popular children's ditty celebrated the coming time when there would be "No more 'Monsieur,' nor more 'Mister' / God in Heaven, and on earth Hitler."[6]

The Jews' sense of relief was greatly tempered when the Allies handed Lebanon and Syria over to the Free French in the summer of 1941, because of General Catroux's proclamation on the morning of the invasion promising that the two mandatory territories would finally be granted independence. Although it would be more than two years before the Free French began to make good on that promise, many young people, especially in Syria, concluded that there was no future for them there and, as will be shown later in this chapter, began turning toward neighboring Palestine.[7]

[5] The meeting with Puaux is mentioned by Yanait-Ben-Zvi, *Be-Shelīḥūt li-Lvanōn ūle-Sūrya (1943),* p. 13, where Farhi is the source of the information.

[6] *Balā misyū, balā mister/fī 'l-samā' Allāh, wa 'l-arḍ Hitler.* Cited by Stefan Wild, "National Socialism in the Arab Near East between 1933 and 1939," WI 25, n.s. (1985): 128. For a slight variant, see Michel-Christian Davet, *La double affaire de Syrie* (Paris, 1967), pp. 63–64; also Isaac Lipschits, *La politique de la France au Levant 1939–1941* (Paris and Amsterdam, 1962), p. 188, n. 7.

[7] Very little published material deals with Syrian Jewry during the year of Vichy rule other than the valuable preliminary survey by Irit Abramski-Bligh, "The Jews of Syria and Lebanon under Vichy Rule," *Peʿamim* 28 (1986): 131–57 [Heb.]. For general background, see Davet, *La double affaire de Syrie,* passim; Stephen Hemsley Longrigg, *Syria and Lebanon under French Mandate* (London, New York, and To-

The Jewish community of Iraq was not nearly so fortunate as those of Egypt and the Levant States in escaping physical harm. Even before the war, Iraqi Jewry, which was conspicuous because of its overall numbers, its prosperity, and its disproportionate prominence in the commercial and professional life of the capital, had been subject to threats and invectives emanating not only from extreme nationalist elements in the press and political opposition groups, but from within official state institutions as well. Under Dr. Sāmī Shawkat, who was a high official in the Iraqi Ministry of Education in the prewar years and for a while its director general, fanatic statism on the Nazi model, heavily imbued with anti-Semitism, was inculcated in the school system, often by Syrian and Palestinian teachers. In fact, in one of his addresses to educators, he branded the Jews as the enemy from within, who should be treated accordingly, and in another he praised Hitler and Mussolini for making the eradication of their internal enemies, the Jews, a cornerstone of their own national revivals.[8] The tone of anti-Jewish agitation in Iraq was raised even further after the arrival of the Mufti Ḥājj Amīn al-Ḥusaynī in Baghdad in 1940.

The position of the Iraqi Jewish community became exceedingly precarious when a military coup toppled the pro-British government of Prime Minister Ṭāha al-Hāshimī and forced the Hashemite Regent ᶜAbd al-Ilāh to flee the country. The new government of Rashīd ᶜĀlī al-Gaylānī was backed by the army, the Mufti (in whose home the conspirators had planned the coup and sworn allegiance to one another), the Pan-Arabists, and indeed most of the Iraqi people. Some of the leading members of the new regime, such as Yūnis al-Sabᶜāwī, were rabid Jew-baiters, and during the two months that the Rashīd ᶜĀlī government remained in power, Nazi propaganda in Iraq reached its zenith. One of the cardinal points of this propaganda was that the British and the Jews were allies. Thus, when Iraq entered into open hostilities with Great Britain in May 1941, the Jews were regarded by

ronto, 1958), pp. 296–328; Hirszowicz, *The Third Reich and the Arab East,* pp. 102–3, 112–14, 129–33, 173–92; and Bernd Philipp Schröder, *Deutschland und der Mittlere Osten im Zweiten Weltkrieg,* Studien und Dokumente zur Geschichte des Zweiten Weltkrieges. Band 16 (Frankfurt and Zurich, 1975), pp. 150–78.

8 See his collected addresses—Sāmī Shawkat, *Hādhihi Ahdāfunā, Man Āmana bihā fa-Huwa Minnā* (Baghdad, 1939), pp. 37, 63. See also Reeva S. Simon, *Iraq between the Two World Wars: The Creation and Implementation of a Nationalist Ideology* (New York, 1986), pp. 95—114, where the curriculum and textbooks used in the Iraqi schools at this time are discussed.

much of the population as a fifth column. Throughout this "Thirty Days' War," the Jews of Baghdad were subject to all sorts of harassment and intimidation. Paramilitary youth groups, such as the Futuwwa and the Youth Phalanxes (Katā'ib al-Shabāb), roamed the streets of the capital, arresting individual Jews whom they accused of signaling the enemy, sometimes executing the suspects on the spot. Members of the military or the civilian authorities made various attempts to extort contributions for the war effort from the Jewish bourgeoisie. In one or two incidents threats of anti-Jewish mob violence occurred, as on May 7, when an angry crowd broke into the Meir Elias Hospital (a Jewish institution), accusing the patients "of giving signals to airplanes."[9] However, the prompt intervention of the police averted any serious harm. Despite the tensions and the periodic harassment during the final month of the Rashīd ᶜĀlī regime, the Jewish community of Baghdad experienced no real misfortune.[10]

Ironically, disaster struck at the very moment when Baghdadi Jewry thought deliverance was at hand. On Thursday, May 29, 1941, as British troops from the south approached the outskirts of Baghdad,

[9] Abraham Twena, "The Diary of Abraham Twena," *The Scribe* 2, no. 11 (May–June 1973): 4.

[10] For general historical surveys of the Rashīd ᶜĀlī government of April–May 1941, see Majid Khadduri, *Independent Iraq, 1932–1958: A Study in Iraqi Politics*, 2nd ed. (London, New York, and Karachi, 1960), pp. 212–43; ᶜUthmān Kamāl Ḥaddād, *Ḥarakat Rashīd ᶜĀlī al-Kaylānī 1941* (Sidon, 1950), passim (Ḥaddād was the Mufti's personal secretary); ᶜĀbd al-Razzāq al-Ḥasanī, *al-Asrār al-Khafiyya fī Ḥarakat al-Sana 1941 al-Taḥarruriyya*, 2nd rev. ed. (Sidon, 1964), passim; Simon, *Iraq between the Two World Wars*, pp. 145-65. On the connections between Iraq and the Axis during this period, see Hirszowicz, *The Third Reich and the Arab East*, pp. 134–72; Heinz Tillmann, *Deutschlands Araberpolitik im Zweiten Weltkrieg* (Berlin, 1965), pp. 227–661 (a Marxist perspective); Fritz Grobba, *Männer und Mächte im Orient: 25 Jahre diplomatischer Tätigkeit im Orient* (Zurich, Berlin, and Frankfurt, 1967), pp. 216–48 (Grobba had been Germany's minister in Iraq before the war and was the chief liaison with the Mufti and Rashīd ᶜĀlī during the final month of the regime and thereafter in Berlin); Schröder, *Deutschland und der Mittlere Osten im Zweiten Weltkrieg*, pp. 63–149. Concerning the situation of the Jews in Iraq at this time, see Twena, "The Diary of Abraham Twena," pp. 3–7; Sylvia G. Haim, "Aspects of Jewish Life in Baghdad under the Monarchy," *MES* 12, no. 2 (May 1976): 192–94; Ezra Laniado, *The Jews of Mosul: From Samarian Exile (Galuth) to "Operation Ezra and Nehemia"* (Tirat Carmel, 1981), pp. 118–21 [Heb.]; Heskel M. Haddad, M.D., *Flight from Babylon: Iraq, Iran, Israel, America,* as told to Phyllis I. Rosenteur (New York, 1986), pp. 45–48 (a somewhat sensationalized personal memoir); Naim Kattan, *Farewell, Babylon,* trans. Sheila Fischman (Toronto, 1976), pp. 11–28 (an excellent fictionalized autobiographical account); and Anwār Shā'ul, *Qiṣṣat Ḥayātī fī Wādi 'l-Rāfidayn* (Jerusalem, 1980), pp. 244–48 (personal memoir of Iraq's leading Jewish writer of Arabic poetry and prose).

the four colonels who had staged the military coup, Rashīd ᶜĀlī and his close associates and the Mufti and his followers all fled the country. (Rashīd ᶜĀlī and the Mufti eventually reached Berlin, where they worked on behalf of the German war effort.) A three-man Council for Internal Security headed by the mayor of Baghdad was left behind as a transitional government. Yūnis al-Sabᶜāwī, the judeophobic minister of economics, had also remained behind and declared himself military governor of the capital.

On the morning of May 30, al-Sabᶜāwī summoned Rabbi Sassoon Khadduri, the president of the Jewish Communal Council, and ordered him to inform his people that they were to remain in their homes for the next three days and to refrain from using the telephone or communicating with one another. At the same time, al-Sabᶜāwī prepared an incendiary speech for broadcast on the radio later that day, calling for an uprising that would, among other things, purge the city of the enemy from within. It would appear that he was planning a massacre of the Jewish population. Before this could be done, however, al-Sabᶜāwī was arrested by the Council for Internal Security and expelled from the country. The council also dissolved the paramilitary groups, such as the Youth Phalanxes and al-Sabᶜāwī National Force (al-Quwwa al-Sabᶜāwiyya al-Waṭaniyya), and ordered them to turn in their weapons to the authorities.

The Jewish community was now convinced that the danger had passed. On Sunday, June 1, the first day of the Jewish holiday of Shavuᶜot, which in Iraq was traditionally marked by joyous pilgrimages to the tombs of holy men and visits to friends and relatives, the Hashemite regent, ᶜAbd al-Ilāh, returned to the capital from his exile in Transjordan. A festive crowd of Jews crossed over to the west bank of the Tigris to welcome the returning prince. On the way back, a group of soldiers, who were soon joined by civilians, turned on the Jews and attacked them, killing one and injuring others while both the civil and the military police looked on. Anti-Jewish rioting soon spread throughout the city, especially on the east bank of the Tigris, where most of the Jews of Baghdad lived. By nightfall, a major pogrom was under way, led by soldiers and paramilitary youth gangs, followed by crowds of men, women, and children from the urban masses. The rampage of murder and rapine in the Jewish neighborhoods and business districts continued until the afternoon of the following day, when finally the regent gave orders for the police to fire upon the rioters and Kurdish troops were brought in from the north to maintain order. The British army, which had been encamped on the outskirts of Baghdad the entire time, could easily have suppressed the Farhūd (the name given the pogrom by the Jews)[11] but refrained from entering the city, not wishing to give the appearance that the regent, who was friendly to England, was returning to power with the help of British arms. As Somerset de Chair, an intelligence officer with the British forces, ruefully observed: "Ah yes, but the prestige of our Regent would have suffered."[12]

In the Farhūd, 179 Jews of both sexes and all ages were killed, 242 children were left orphans, 586 businesses were looted, and 911 buildings housing more than 12,000 people were pillaged. The total property loss was estimated by the Jewish community's own investigating committee to be approximately 680,000 pounds (with some estimates ranging as high as four times that amount). An Iraqi governmental commission of inquiry appointed immediately after the incident advanced considerably lower casualty statistics, although one of its members later acknowledged that the government desired that the figures be minimized.[13]

None of the other, smaller Jewish communities of Iraq experienced such a disaster. Nonetheless, the Farhūd dramatically undermined the confidence of all Iraqi Jewry and, like the Assyrian massacres of 1933, had a highly unsettling effect upon all the minorities.[14] In the immediate aftermath of the pogrom, the British consular authorities received over 1,000 visa applications from Iraqi Jewish merchants for India, ostensibly for commercial reasons, but clearly in order to seek refuge, since they applied to take their families with them. Most of the applications were denied on the grounds that many more would apply if the visas were granted freely.[15] Nearly a year

[11] The word indicates a murderous breakdown of law and order.

[12] Somerset de Chair, *The Golden Carpet* (London, 1944), p. 118. For a devastating critique of British policy in this affair, see Elie Kedourie, "The Sack of Basra and the Baghdad *Farhud,*" in idem, *Arabic Political Memoirs and Other Studies* (London, 1974), pp. 283–314.

[13] See al-Ḥasanī, *Ta'rīkh al-Wizārāt al-ᶜIrāqiyya,* vol. 5 (Sidon, 1953), p. 234, n. 1; and also Kedourie, *Arabic Political Memoirs and Other Studies,* p. 298. Many Iraqi writers, including statesmen in their memoirs, have played down or ignored the Farhūd entirely. See Yehuda Taggar, "The Farhud in the Arabic Writings of Iraqi Statesmen and Writers," *Peᶜamim* 8 (1981): 38–45 [Heb.].

[14] See, for example, PRO (London) FO 624/34, Report No. 3097 (November 1, 1943), "IRAQ: Political. Restlessness among Minorities."

[15] PRO (London) FO 371/27116, India Office to Foreign Office (August 27, 1941). In a secret note, London responds that "H.M.G. feel that Bagdad Jews have good reason for alarm. . . . and they would be grateful if applications for visas could

after the Farhūd, a British military intelligence report noted that there was a feeling in the Jewish community "that whatever the outcome of the war that the Iraqis will punish the Jews eventually."[16] The same report also mentioned an increase in illegal emigration from Iraq to Palestine. Although no accurate statistics are available for this movement on account of its very nature, American intelligence (Office of Strategic Services) estimates placed the number of Iraqi Jews who entered Palestine in this way during the war years at over 1,000.[17]

Most Iraqi Jews could not go to Palestine or anywhere else for that matter, nor probably did the majority of them have any serious intentions of emigrating from the country as yet. Many tried to convince themselves that the worst had passed. But the undiminished predominance in Iraqi political and social life of a militant and uncompromising Arab nationalism in which minorities had no real place, the continued widespread sympathy for the Axis among the masses, and their own disillusionment with the British as protectors led many other Iraqi Jews to contemplate what social scientists refer to as "alternative strategies." Some young Jewish intellectuals flirted with communism,[18] and many more began to reconsider the Zionist option. As will be seen later in this chapter, Zionism started to make new inroads into the Iraqi Jewish community as it was to do in other major Jewish communities of the Arab world in the wake of the wartime experience.

---

be favourably entertained by you [i.e., the Government of India and the consular authorities], subject always to reasonable conditions."

[16] PRO (London) FO 624/29/374, Lieut.-Col. T. W. Boyd, Tenth Army, to Maj. D. E. Driver, British Embassy, Baghdad (April 29, 1942), in Part Two, p. 418.

[17] National Archives (Washington) RG 226 0SS Report L45124 Iraq. "The Zionist Organization in Baghdad" (August 31, 1944).

[18] On the beginnings of Jewish attraction to the Iraqi Communist party, see Hanna Batatu, *The Old Social Classes and the Revolutionary Movements of Iraq: A Study of Iraq's Old Landed and Commercial Classes and of Its Communists, Baᶜthists, and Free Officers* (Princeton, N. J., 1978), pp. 448, 461, 650–51. The party had voiced its disapproval of the harassment of Jews and of the government's pro-Axis policies in a letter sent to Prime Minister Rashīd ᶜĀlī on May 7, 1941, nearly one month before the Farhūd. The letter's criticism was tempered, however, with the statement:

> While thus expressing our disapproval, we do not in the least deny the existence of traitors who belong to the Jewish sect and who have made common cause with the wicked band of ᶜAbd ul-Ilāh and Nūrī as-Saᶜīd and their henchmen but we feel that punishment should be meted out to them according to the provisions of the law [p. 454].

Two thirds of all the Jews in the Arab world were living in North Africa when World War II broke out. Because of the region's geographical proximity to Europe, its outright colonial status (Algeria was in fact a part of France) with large European populations, and the fact that it became a major theater of military operations, the Jews in the Italian colony of Libya and in the French Maghreb came to experience a more direct and prolonged encounter with the war and with the anti-Semitic policies of the Axis and Vichy than did their coreligionists in the Middle East. Moreover, it was only in North Africa that large numbers of Arabic-speaking Jews came under outright Nazi control.

Even before the war, Libyan Jewry had become subject to the anti-Semitic racial laws that began emanating from Rome in September 1938. However, it was not until Italy entered the war in June 1940 that the overall situation of the community took a definite turn for the worse. Until that time, several factors mitigated the effects of Italy's new anti-Semitic policy. One of these factors was the indispensable role played by Jews in the Libyan economy. The other was the fact that the governor of Libya, Marshal Italo Balbo, although an ardent Fascist, was no anti-Semite, abhorred Nazism, and felt that the new policies were mistaken as far as colonial aims in Libya were concerned. He therefore attempted to delay the full implementation of the new policies, especially in the economic realm. (See, for example, his letter to Mussolini in Part Two.) Furthermore, some of the discriminatory legislation, such as the laws forcing Jews out of state schools and requiring them to attend newly established Jewish institutions, really had a negative impact only upon foreign Jews. The great majority of Libya's religiously observant Jewish community had, as Renzo de Felice has pointed out, "always wanted special classes or their own community schools, so that paradoxically, they were almost happy with the Fascist measures."[19]

Shortly after Italy's entry into the war Balbo's plane was mistakenly shot down by Italian gunners. His death marked the beginning of a period of increasing hardship for Libyan Jewry.[20] Discriminatory

[19] Renzo De Felice, *Jews in an Arab Land: Libya, 1835–1970,* trans. Judith Roumani (Austin, 1985), p. 169.

[20] On Balbo and the Jews, see ibid., pp. 143–67, 169–73, passim.

laws were now more strictly enforced. Certain Jewish organizations, such as the Maccabee Sports Association, which was considered subversive, were suppressed. Jews were blamed for the spiraling prices that resulted from wartime shortages, and more determined administrative attempts were made to break the Jewish dominance in the wholesale sector of the economy. In addition to the increased hostility on the part of the Italian authorities, the Jews of Tripoli suffered numerous casualties from French and British bombings, which also left many homeless.

The situation deteriorated further after the first British occupation of Cyrenaica, Libya's eastern province, between February and April 1941. The Benghazi Jewish community made the mistake of showing its enthusiasm at what it considered liberation and of fraternizing with the Jewish soldiers in the Palestine units. Reprisals were taken against collaborators when the Italians, who were now reinforced by their German allies, recaptured the province, and Jews throughout Libya were subjected to physical harassment and abuse by irate colonists and soldiers and by Arab youths. The situation worsened after the second British occupation of Cyrenaica which lasted from December 24, 1941, to January 27, 1942. In addition to executions and stiff prison sentences for collaborators, the Italians decided to "clear out" (*Sfollamento*) all Jews from Cyrenaica. Over 2,500 people were transferred to internment and labor camps in Tripolitania. Most were sent to Giado in the desert about 150 miles south of Tripoli, where 562 died, mostly from typhus.[21]

The Jews of the much larger Tripolitanian community were also victims of heightened repression in this period. Severe restrictions were placed upon Jewish commercial and professional activities in May and June 1942. On June 28, a law was issued requiring all Jewish males between the ages of 18 and 45 to register for labor assignments. About 3,000 individuals were sent to the Sidi Azaz camp near Homs. However, because of insufficient planning by the Italians, about two thirds of them had to be sent back to Tripoli. The rest were assigned to labor details along the Egyptian front and the lines of communication in Cyrenaica. The skilled personnel were employed in office work, and the others were put on road gangs. Most of them were

[21] Rachel Simon, "The Jews of Libya on the Verge of Holocaust," *Peʿamim* 28 (1986): 51–70 [Heb.]; and de Felice, *Jews in an Arab Land,* pp. 178–80. For a description of conditions in Giado, see B. Y., "Be-Gālūt Giado," in *Yahadūt Lūv,* ed. F. Zuaretz et al. (Tel Aviv, 1960), pp. 197–99.

simply abandoned when the Germans and the Italians retreated before the British offensive from October to November 1942 and had to make the long, difficult trek home on foot through the desert. Back in the towns of Tripolitania, the final month of Italian rule was marked by great hardship caused by continual aerial bombings and severe food shortages. Jews received smaller individual rations than either Europeans or Arabs and were the last to be provided for. Just before the very end, Jewish shops were plundered in Tripoli, Homs, and Misurata by soldiers from the Afrika-Korps.[22]

The Jews of Libya had undergone greater and more prolonged hardship than the Jews of either Iraq or the Levant States. Yet, they came through their ordeal with less dejection and an enhanced sense of communal solidarity and purpose than their Middle Eastern brethren thanks to their strong rabbinical and lay leadership, which had remained effective both during the period of Fascist rule and after liberation. The Libyan Jews' esprit de corps—and, as we shall see, their Jewish nationalism—was also strengthened by the large numbers of their coreligionists in the Palestine units of the British army with whom they came into close, intimate contact. Although they had been humiliated and mistreated by their former colonial masters whom they had once admired, they had never been cowed with violent threats by a powerful, militant Arab nationalist majority as had their fellow Jews in the East. Buoyed by a great wave of optimism, Libyan Jewry underwent a major rehabilitation during the remaining war years under British occupation with help from Jewish organizations in the Allied countries and especially with assistance from the Yishuv.

The Jews of the French Maghreb were also touched very directly and very profoundly by the Second World War. Despite the anti-Semitism of the colonial population, which in Algeria had been both endemic and virulent, the overwhelming majority of Jews identified strongly—even passionately—with France. This was the case not only in Algeria, where they had enjoyed French citizenship for three generations and were for the most part highly gallicized, but in Morocco and Tunisia as well, where there were only thin strata of Europeanized elites. Maghrebi Jews had watched with horror the rise of Hitler and the beginnings of the persecution of European Jewry, which were given extensive coverage in both the Jewish and the general press. Six months before the actual outbreak of hostilities, an Alliance school

[22] Simon, "The Jews of Libya on the Verge of Holocaust," pp. 70–75 [Heb.]; de Felice, *Jews in an Arab Land,* pp. 180–84; ᶜA. Guetta, "Be-Gālūt Sīdī ᶜAzāz ū-Buqbuq," in *Yahadūt Lūv,* ed. Zuaretz et al., pp. 200–1.

director in Tunis reported that the Jewish youth was committed "to defending dearly the threatened liberty by placing itself at France's service, and it was resolutely waiting the coming events."[23]

When war was declared in September 1939, Maghrebi Jews rallied to *la Patrie adoptée* in what Michel Abitbol has referred to as a "paroxysm of patriotism."[24] However, many young Jews who tried to register in Morocco and Tunisia were turned away or deferred by the authorities from military service for political reasons, which were understood to mean not offending the native Muslim population. Some young Moroccan Jews who had given up any hope of being accepted into the French army joined the Foreign Legion. As Frenchmen, Algerian Jews could not be so easily rebuffed, but in some instances Algerian Jewish recruits found themselves transferred out of their original units when they arrived in France.[25]

The fall of France was a tremendous psychological blow to Maghrebi Jewry, for whom it had been the embodiment of all that was good and enlightened. For most Jews, as for Marcel Aboulker, a young, demobilized army officer, "June 1940 was a moral as well as a military disaster."[26] Many of the right-wing colonists, on the other hand, saw the defeat as metropolitan France's, not their own, and enthusiastically supported Marshal Pétain's National Revolution. From Morocco to Tunisia, even before the promulgation of Vichy's anti-Jewish legislation, Jews found themselves facing a resurgence of colonialist anti-Semitism, which had many sympathizers among the Muslim masses as well. The anti-Semites soon regained their freedom of expression with the repeal on August 27, 1940, of the so-called Marchandeau Law, which had been issued only a few months before the war and had banned incitement in the press against any group on racial or religious grounds.

The Vichy regime issued a series of far-reaching anti-Jewish laws beginning with the Statute on the Jews (Statut des Juifs) of October

[23] AIU (Paris) Tunisie II.C.6, Elie Donio to Alliance president (March 27, 1939). Compare the very different attitude that prevailed during World War I. See Chapter 3, pp. 49–50.

[24] Michel Abitbol, *Les Juifs d'Afrique du Nord sous Vichy* (Paris, 1983), p. 41.

[25] Ibid., p. 42; Michael M. Laskier, *The Alliance Israélite Universelle and the Jewish Communities of Morocco, 1862–1962* (Albany, N. Y., 1983), p. 179; Doris Bensimon-Donath, *Evolution du Judaïsme marocain sous le protectorat français, 1912–1956* (Paris and the Hague, 1968), p. 108; AIU (Paris) Maroc XLVIII.E.743, letter of A. Cohen (Safi) to Alliance headquarters (Paris), December 18, 1939; and Maurice Eisenbeth, *Pages vécues, 1940–43* (Algiers, 1945), p. 11.

[26] Marcel Aboulker, *Alger et ses complots* (Paris, 1945), p. 16.

3, 1940, which defined Jews according to purely racial criteria that were in fact even more stringent than those used by the Nazis in occupied France. The new law was of a constitutional character and included in its scope all Jews under Vichy's jurisdiction, be they citizens, subjects, protégés, or resident aliens. It relegated all of them to a markedly inferior legal position and put various restrictions upon them in the public domain. In contrast to the case of Syria and Lebanon, the Statute on the Jews was not only rigorously applied in North Africa, but also "meticulously adapted to the juridical situation in each of the three Maghrebi territories" by the zealous authorities.[27] The culmination of this first series of anti-Jewish legislation was the law of October 7, promulgated at the urging of the new interior minister, Marcel Peyrouton, who was a former governor general of Algeria, abrogating the Crémieux Decree. More than 100,000 Algerian Jews were thereby stripped of their citizenship. (Exceptions were made for those who had received the Legion of Honor, the Croix de Guerre, or some other major distinction.) The parallel between their plight and that of their German coreligionists in the wake of the Nuremberg laws has been aptly noted by Marrus and Paxton: "having previously been citizens, they were reduced to subjects."[28]

Vichy's anti-Jewish laws were refined and expanded in 1941. On June 2 of that year, the government ordered a census of all Jews, including those in North Africa. The census demanded, among other data, a detailed inventory of personal wealth to facilitate the aryanization of Jewish property that was then being planned. With their usual alacrity in these matters, the Algerian authorities established their own bureau of aryanization (Service de l'Aryanisation Economique) not long afterward. They also set up a special Bureau for the Regulating of Jewish Affairs (Service de Réglementation des Questions Juives) parallel to France's own infamous General Commissariat for Jewish Affairs (CGQJ). Jewish commercial and economic activities were more severely curtailed at this time. In Morocco, for example, a Sharifan *dahir* on August 5 made any form of credit unavailable to Jewish subjects of the sultan, and another *dahir* on August 22 expelled Jews who had homes or businesses in the European neighborhoods of the principal towns. The professions were very hard hit everywhere. In each of the three Maghrebi territories, quotas were established limiting the number of Jews permitted to practice law to 2

[27] Abitbol, *Les Juifs d'Afrique du Nord sous Vichy*, p. 66.

[28] Michael R. Marrus and Robert O. Paxton, *Vichy France and the Jews* (New York, 1981), p. 193. For the text of the law of October 7, 1941, see Part Two, p. 426.

percent of the total number of Gentile members of the profession. As in France, a numerus clausus of 2 percent was set for doctors in Algeria, whereas in Tunisia the number was raised to 5 percent. (Morocco lagged several months behind before following the lead of Algeria and the Metropole.) In some instances Algeria was actually ahead of metropolitan France in instituting quotas. Thus, for example, the quota for Jewish midwives was set at 2 percent in Algeria on November 19, 1941, whereas a similar decree in France was not issued until December 26.[29]

In education the Algerian authorities showed their greatest zeal and innovativeness in instituting discriminatory measures that even exceeded those in force in France. Already by mid-December 1940, all of Algeria's 465 Jewish teachers—from humble schoolmasters to university professors—were dismissed (two were reinstated the following year). It was General Maxime Weygand, Vichy's proconsul in the Maghreb, who was among the first to suggest to Pétain that Jewish students be excluded from studying at the universities, a theme that was taken up by the Algerian Student Union (Association Générale des Etudiants d'Algérie). A numerus clausus of 3 percent was duly announced in June 1941. This measure was considerably more devastating for Algerian Jews than for French Jews, since the former constituted a much higher percentage of the university student body (14 percent in prewar Algeria versus only 0.6 to 0.7 percent in France). The Algerians went beyond Vichy's own restrictions by establishing quotas for primary and secondary schools as well. The quota was first set at 14 percent, effective January 1, 1942, and later cut in half. During the 1941–1942 school year, 11,962 Jewish pupils were eliminated from the public schools, and 13,168 remained. The following year only 6,582 Jewish children were left under the 7 percent quota.[30]

Unlike in Morocco or Tunisia, where most of the Jewish children in school went to Alliance institutions, which continued to operate during the war years despite the dissolution of the AIU Central

[29] For the general background to the legislation of 1941, see ibid., pp. 83–128; for its application in North Africa, see Abitbol, *Les Juifs d'Afrique du Nord sous Vichy,* pp. 66–79; for Algeria, in particular, see Eisenbeth, *Pages vécues,* pp. 17–56; and Michel Ansky, *Les Juifs d'Algérie du Décret Crémieux à la libération* (Paris, 1950), pp. 107–74.

[30] The most complete survey of Algeria's discrimination in education is Robert Brunschvig, "Les mesures antijuives dans l'enseignement, en Algérie, sous le régime de Vichy," *Revue d'Alger* 1, no. 2 (1944): 57–79. See also, Eisenbeth, *Pages vécues,* pp. 29–42; and Marrus and Paxton, *Vichy France and the Jews,* pp. 124–25, 195.

Committee, the overwhelming majority of Algerian Jews had attended state schools. In the face of this educational crisis, the Algerian Jewish community under the leadership of men like Chief Rabbi Maurice Eisenbeth and Robert Brunschvig, who had been a professor of Islamic history at the University of Algiers prior to the mass dismissals of 1940, created virtually ex nihilo an entire Jewish school system. Nearly 20,000 pupils throughout the country were taught in these private schools notwithstanding the numerous obstacles placed in their way by the hostile government.[31]

The great majority of Muslims remained relatively impassive vis-à-vis Vichy's anti-Jewish policies in spite of the tensions that had existed between themselves and the Jews up to the fall of France. As noted, the North Africans had been receptive to German propaganda, and many nationalists continued to have pro-German leanings. There were a few scattered anti-Jewish incidents involving Arabs. The worst of these was a mob attack against Jews coming out of a synagogue in Gabes, Tunisia, on May 23, 1941, in which six people were killed and sixteen others injured. The incident seems to have been touched off by news of the defeat suffered by Rashīd ᶜĀlī's troops at the hands of the British, who were invariably painted as the allies of international Jewry.[32]

Most thoughtful Maghrebi Muslims, however, saw that under Vichy's authoritarian and racist regime they were no closer to either independence or even a greater measure of equality under the French imperium. There was, therefore, little comfort that could be drawn from the official treatment of the Jews. On the contrary, this persecution evoked a certain degree of sympathy for the unfortunate Jews and at the same time reminded the more sophisticated Muslims of their own powerlessness under colonial domination. Aḥmad Bū Minjal (Boumendjel), an Algerian lawyer and close associate of Farḥat ᶜAbbās, summed up the general feeling among many Muslim intellectuals in his letter of November 29, 1942, that was widely circulated within the Algerian Jewish community:

Our adversaries were sure that by making the Jews inferior they could not help but bring the Muslims closer for their benefit. The majority believed that the Muslims would rejoice at the abrogation of the Crémieux Decree.

[31] Brunschvig, "Les mesures antijuives dans l'enseignement," pp. 61–73; also Ansky, *Les Juifs d'Algérie,* pp. 127–31.

[32] Concerning this incident, see National Archives (Washington) U.S. Department of State RG 59, 740.0011/European War 1939/11281, Telegram No. 58 from Consul Doolittle (Tunis), May 23, 1941.

The latter, however, could only draw the simple conclusion that a right of citizenship that could be withdrawn after 70 years of exercise was "questionable."[33]

Three months later, Farḥat ᶜAbbās would take this line of reasoning to its logical conclusion in his nationalist "Manifesto" and write:

> The time is passed when an Algerian Muslim will demand anything other than to be a Muslim Algerian. Especially since the abrogation of the Crémieux Decree, Algerian nationality and citizenship offer him more security and present a clearer and more logical solution to the problem of his evolution and emancipation.[34]

The plight of their Jewish subjects also elicited some sympathy from the Muslim rulers of Tunisia and Morocco, who had no choice but to countersign many of the discriminatory decrees issued in their names by the French Residency. Upon his accession to the Tunisian throne in June 1942, Munṣif Bey publicly expressed his solicitude for "all the population of the Regency," and in the following months, when French policy was of course to heap humiliations upon the Jewish population, he went out of his way to bestow the royal order of merit, the Nishān Iftikhār, upon a score of leading Tunisian Jewish personalities. The Bey could, so to speak, get away with these admittedly token gestures in part because of the French Resident General Admiral Esteva's own personal lack of enthusiasm for Vichy's racial policies and because of the opposition of the Italian Armistice Commission in Tunisia, which, despite its own official anti-Semitism, did not want to jeopardize the economic interests of the Livornese Jews through whom Italy had historically maintained a presence in Tunisia.[35]

The sultan of Morocco, Muḥammad V, also demonstrated his personal distaste for Vichy's anti-Semitic laws. In audiences granted during the spring and summer of 1942 to Moroccan Jewish leaders,

[33] This passage together with other excerpts from the letter is frequently cited in the literature, including Ansky, *Les Juifs d'Algérie,* pp. 296–97; Yves Maxime Danan, *La vie politique à Alger de 1940 à 1944* (Paris, 1963), pp. 46–47; Mahfoud Kaddache, *Histoire du nationalisme algérien: question nationale et politique algérienne, 1919–1951,* vol. 2 (Algiers, 1981), p. 617, n. 51; Abitbol, *Les Juifs d'Afrique du Nord sous Vichy,* pp. 171–72. The letter, which was countersigned by the Islamic reformist Shaykh Ṭayyib al-ᶜUqbī, was addressed to Dr. Loufrani, a leading activist for Muslim-Jewish entente.

[34] Cited in Kaddache, *Histoire du nationalisme algérien,* vol. 2, p. 643.

[35] Abitbol, *Les Juifs d'Afrique du Nord sous Vichy,* p. 82. See also the comments of Paul Raccah in *Proceedings of the Seminar on Muslim-Jewish Relations in North Africa* (New York, 1975), p. 28.

the sultan expressed his view that the French-imposed statutes were illegal and that in his eyes all of his subjects, Jews and Muslims alike, were equal. He assured them that he himself would never lay a hand "upon either their persons or their property." It later came to be widely believed that the popular sultan had played the role of protector of the Jews before the French authorities and had even refused to apply the discriminatory laws. However, as H. Z. Hirschberg and later, and more emphatically, Michel Abitbol have pointed out, there is no evidence that he ever did any more than personally reassure the various Jewish delegations that met with him. Most recently, David Cohen has argued that there is some evidence, albeit tenuous, that the Sharifan monarch did act behind the scenes on behalf of Moroccan Jewry.[36]

There were, of course, other cases of individual Muslims offering assistance, comfort, or protection to Jewish acquaintances. In the Algerian town of Batna south of Constantine, for example, local Muslims offered to hide their Jewish neighbors in the event that Rommel's troops invaded from Tunisia or the Vichy authorities decided to round up Jews for internment in concentration camps. (There were prison and labor camps throughout southern Algeria and Morocco that were primarily for political prisoners and foreign internees, with many Jews among them.) Nevertheless, these were exceptions, not the rule, and for the most part, the Jews of the French Maghreb found most of the native population, though not openly hostile, indifferent to their plight.[37]

[36] H. Z. [J. W.] Hirschberg, *A History of the Jews in North Africa,* vol. 2 (Leiden, 1981), p. 325; Abitbol, *Les Juifs d'Afrique du Nord sous Vichy,* pp. 84–85. For the sultan as defender of the Jews, see I. D. Abbou, *Musulmans andalous et judéo-espagnols* (Casablanca, 1953), p. 346; and Rom Landau, *Moroccan Drama, 1900–1955* (London, 1956), p. 209. For new evidence to support this view, see David Cohen, "Le roi Mohamed V et les Juifs du Maroc," *Information Juive* 38 (October 1986): 12.

[37] Elizabeth D. Friedman, "The Jews of Batna, Algeria: A Study of Identity and Colonialism" (Ph.D. diss., City University of New York, 1977), p. 174. David Ovadia, *The Community of Sefrou* (Jerusalem, 1975), vol. 3, p. 183 [Heb.], reports that some Arabs in Morocco took advantage of Jews at this time and became menacing, but this also seems to have been exceptional. Bensimon-Donath, *Evolution du Judaïsme marocain,* p. 110, argues that most Moroccan Muslims were too concerned that they might be the next victims of Vichy racism to be won over to the anti-Jewish campaign. Concerning the prison camps in the south, see André Moine, *La déportation et la résistance en Afrique du Nord (1939–1944)* (Paris, 1972); also Ansky, *Les Juifs d'Algérie,* pp. 260–81; Abitbol, *Les Juifs d'Afrique du Nord sous Vichy,* pp. 102–7; and Zosa Szajkowski, *Analytical Franco-Jewish Gazetteer, 1939–1945* (New York, 1966), p. 95.

For two years, the Jews of the French Maghreb endured severe economic and social discrimination and a continuous barrage of vilification under the Vichy regime. The Algerian Jews suffered the additional blow of political disenfranchisement and the humiliation of being reduced from Frenchmen to "natives" in a colonial society. All this was, admittedly, highly traumatic. Still, until late 1942, none of the three Maghrebi Jewish communities had come face to face with the imminent threat of general physical violence. The only Jewry to actually brush against the Holocaust in a brief encounter was that of Tunisia.

The Germans began their invasion of Tunisia on November 9, 1942, one week after the British breakthrough at El Alamein and one day after the Allied landings in Morocco and Algeria. By December 12, the Axis forces had established their bridgehead, securing the eastern third of the country, where most of the major towns and cities were located. Unsure of the reliability of the French colonial authorities, the Germans set up alongside the Residency parallel organizations manned with members of the extreme French right. They also tried to woo the Arab population into active collaboration and succeeded in winning a good measure of popularity.

Most of Tunisia's 80,000 to 90,000 Jews came under direct Nazi control. As Jacques Sabille has observed, the German's policy toward the Tunisian Jews was from the first more like their policy toward Eastern European Jewry than toward the Jews in occupied France and Belgium. It was only the logistical problems imposed by geography, their own military weakness, and the brevity of their occupation that prevented them from inflicting the Final Solution upon the Tunisian Jews.[38] Rudolf Rahn, the Nazi Foreign Ministry's chief representative in North Africa, explained that owing to the chaotic situation that prevailed during the first month of the occupation, "incitement to looting of Jewish shops, turning demonstrations into pogroms etc. [are] not practicable while our troops are not at least at the frontier of Algeria."[39]

The persecution of the Jews began on November 23, with a roundup in the middle of the night by the Gestapo of some of the

[38] Jacques Sabille, *Les Juifs de Tunisie sous Vichy et l'occupation* (Paris, 1954), p. 31. The Germans also encountered difficulties with their Italian allies who tried to protect Tunisia's Italian Jewish community. See Abitbol, *Les Juifs d'Afrique du Nord sous Vichy,* p. 128; also Marrus and Paxton, *Vichy France and the Jews,* p. 364.

[39] See Rahn's report to Berlin (December 24, 1942), published by Abitbol, *Les Juifs d'Afrique du Nord sous Vichy,* p. 192, Annexe VII.

leading members of the Jewish community of Tunis, among them the president, Moïse Borgel; a former president, Felix Samama; and the consul of Finland, Jacques Cittanova, who was also a well-known Free Mason. It was believed that the Nazis intended to execute the prisoners and in one fell swoop terrorize the community into abject submission. Officials of the Residency intervened, however, since the arrests violated the agreement between the occupying Germans and the Vichy authorities, according to which all police powers were left under the latter's jurisdiction. The prisoners were freed, although not all at once, and were soon to be replaced by other hostages.[40]

The Germans turned next to mobilizing Jewish labor to work on military fortifications along the front lines and at military bases. They established in each major city a Committee for the Recruitment of Jewish Manpower (Comité de Recrutement de la Main-d'Oeuvre Juive), somewhat reminiscent of the *Judenrat* of Eastern Europe. The committee was in charge not only of recruiting workers for the labor details, but also of providing them with food and equipment. In addition, it was charged with raising through internal taxation the enormous sums levied upon the community by the Germans as an indemnity for the damage caused by Allied bombings. The rationale was that the British and the Americans were the allies of "International Jewry." The community was also compelled to pay the salaries of non-Jewish laborers when it failed to fill its own quotas and to supply matériel requisitioned by the German army. From Tunis alone, approximately 5,000 Jews were mobilized between December 1942 and April 1943. In Sousse, the entire Jewish male population between the ages of 18 and 50 was pressed into reconstruction of the port facilities. In the southern town of Sfax, only about 100 men were taken.

To carry out its functions, the committee in Tunis created an entire bureaucracy—and a very effective one at that—manned by many leading members of the Jewish community's elite, men like Moïse and Robert Borgel; Paul and Henry Ghez; Elie, André, and Albert Nataf; Victor Cohen-Hadria; Guy Bocarra; Victor Bismut;

[40] For two firsthand accounts, see Robert Borgel, *Etoile jaune et croix gammée: récit d'une servitude* (Tunis, 1944), pp. 21–24 (the author is the son of Community President Moïse Borgel); and Paul Ghez, *Six mois sous la botte* (Tunis, 1943), pp. 13–15. See also Sabille, *Les Juifs de Tunisie sous Vichy et l'occupation,* pp. 35–37; and Abitbol, *Les Juifs d'Afrique du Nord sous Vichy,* p. 127. For the texts of protest notes sent by Admiral Esteva to Rahn, see Abitbol, *Les Juifs d'Afrique du Nord sous Vichy,* pp. 194–95, Annexe VIII.

Isaac and Edmond Smadja; and Georges Krief. Since the majority of the mobilized laborers were from the poorer classes, considerable animosity was stirred up among the Jewish masses against the communal leadership. Many felt as the hero did in Albert Memmi's autobiographical novel *The Pillar of Salt*:

> that the middle class had assumed these responsibilities to save themselves and their children. Rich men's sons were everywhere in the auxiliary offices: food supplies, ambulances, transport and medical services. But they had decided that certain categories of men were to be spared, for instance the intellectuals. . . . By some stroke of luck, as it turned out, most of the intellectuals were of the middle class. So the intellectual and the economic elites were confused. It seemed to the middle class only fair, since they had to pay the heavy cost of the camps, that their own sons should be exempted.[41]

This charge is also taken up by the historian Abitbol, who admits, however, that the communal elite was also motivated "by a profound sense of Jewish solidarity erasing all distinctions of class or origin."[42] This was certainly true as far as some of the leading communal figures such as Paul Ghez, who directed the Recruitment Service in Tunis, were concerned.[43]

There were numerous instances of Nazi brutality in the towns and in the camps—beatings and the shooting of individuals. However, during the six months of occupation, Jewish casualties remained relatively low. Only thirty-nine men from Tunis died in the labor camps, although scores were injured, mostly in the Allied bombing raids, which also caused considerable misery among the urban population. Hygiene in the camps was bad, of course, and many of the

[41] Albert Memmi, *The Pillar of Salt,* trans. Edouard Roditi (New York, 1955), pp. 281–82. See also the instances of verbal and physical attacks against communal officials and denunciations to the Gestapo reported by Ghez, *Six mois sous la botte,* pp. 55–56, 58–59, 64–65, 72–73, 79–80, 88–89, 117–18. Memmi's remark that the bourgeoisie was paying the heavy cost of the camps (and the indemnities) was in fact the case in Tunis, where all of the funds were collected from only 1,397 individuals out of a total Jewish population exceeding 40,000. See Itzhak Abrahami, "The Jewish Communities of Tunisia during the Nazi Conquest," *Peʿamim* 28 (1986): 114 [Heb.].

[42] Abitbol, *Les Juifs d'Afrique du Nord sous Vichy,* p. 136.

[43] In his diary, Ghez relates with the ring of conviction how he and his colleagues "decided to be untouchable" in the face of numerous solicitations for them to show favoritism. See Ghez, *Six mois sous la botte,* pp. 41–42. More apologetically, Robert Borgel, son and aide of the community's president, argued that it was necessary for the community's "elites, its people of experience, its technicians" to assume responsibility for the common defense. See Borgel, *Etoile jaune et croix gammée,* p. 72.

conscripts suffered from skin diseases and other maladies. Conditions were generally less harsh in the camps run by the Italians.[44]

The Tunisian Jews were the victims of terror, physical abuse, and extortion, but they experienced nothing comparable to the mass roundups and murders perpetrated by the Nazis in Eastern Europe, although it is clear from the reports of Rudolf Rahn and other evidence that the Germans had such ideas in mind. Fortunately for the Tunisian Jews, no rail lines connected their country with Europe. Toward the end of the brief occupation, a number of Jewish communal leaders, including Victor Cohen-Hadria, Benjamin Levy, Serge Moatti, and Victor Silvera were arrested on political charges and flown to Auschwitz and other concentration camps, from which a number of them never returned. Others were supposed to follow but were saved when the Allies entered Tunis on May 7, 1943.[45] Also toward the end of the occupation, the Germans intended to require the entire adult Jewish population of Tunis to wear the yellow star. (This badge had already been imposed upon Jews in other parts of the country.) But because of delays caused by the German's Italian partners and by the Vichy authorities, Tunisia's largest Jewish community was spared this too with the arrival of the victorious Allies.[46]

Liberation was, to say the least, a bitter disappointment for the Jews in French North Africa. In Morocco and Algeria, which were liberated six months before Tunisia, all of the Vichy officials were left in place by the Americans. These included everyone from the petty bureaucrats to the Governors General Nogues in Morocco and Châtel in Algeria, and even the high commissioner for all of North Africa, Admiral Jean François Darlan, who had been Pétain's vice premier and foreign minister between February 1941 and April 1942 and now continued to exercise his office in the name of the Marshal.[47] Not

[44] For descriptions of conditions in the camps, instances of brutality, and the names of those killed and injured, see Sabille, *Les Juifs de Tunisie sous Vichy et l'occupation,* pp. 81–115, 125–30; Borgel, *Etoile jaune et croix gammée,* pp. 104–27; Abitbol, *Les Juifs d'Afrique du Nord sous Vichy,* pp. 137–43; Memmi, *The Pillar of Salt,* pp. 283–95.

[45] See Sabille, *Les Juifs de Tunisie sous Vichy et l'occupation,* pp. 126–27; and Abitbol, *Les Juifs d'Afrique du Nord sous Vichy,* p. 146.

[46] Sabille, *Les Juifs de Tunisie sous Vichy et l'occupation,* pp. 127–30, 179–81, Annexe I, G. In Sousse, everyone above the age of six was supposed to wear the yellow star, but the order was not enforced (ibid., p. 149). See also Hirschberg, *A History of the Jews in North Africa,* vol. 2, p. 141; and Part Two, pp. 440–442.

[47] For the politics behind the American decision, see the highly critical exposé by Renée Pierre Gosset, *Algiers, 1941–1943: A Temporary Expedient,* trans. Nancy Hecksher (London, 1945). For an apologetic account by the chief agent of the

only did the Vichy officials remain in authority, but for the next four and a half months so did the notorious Bureaux for Jewish Affairs. All of the hated anti-Jewish racial laws continued in effect until March 1943, and it would not be for an additional seven months until abolition of the Crémieux Decree was finally revoked in Algeria.

In Morocco, Jews were subject to mob attacks as soon as General Patton's troops landed. Over the months that followed, in addition to all of the vexing restrictions of Vichy's racial laws, they were victims of unabated anti-Semitic propaganda, summary arrests, confiscations, and other punishments, including corvée labor. In tribal regions of the country, some of the old dhimmī restrictions were reintroduced. In the Warzazat region south of the High Atlas, for example, the local Jews were required to dress exclusively in black. These and other forms of harassment continued even after the Vichy anti-Jewish laws were abolished in March 1943.[48]

It was in Algeria, however, that the sting of betrayal and dashed hopes was felt most strongly. The bold Resistance putsch, which paralyzed communications and captured strategic points in Algiers on the night of November 7–8, 1942, to facilitate the Allied landing, was the work of 200 young men, mostly Jews (about 85 percent) under the operational leadership of José Aboulker, a twenty-one-year-old medical student and son of the lay leader of the Algerian Jewish community, Professor Henri Aboulker, from whose home the entire operation was directed.[49] The conspirators, who had had General Juin, the commander of the French army in Algeria, and Admiral Darlan himself in their hands, soon found themselves betrayed by their American contact, Robert Murphy, who cut a deal with Darlan, leaving them in a more precarious position than ever. Their predicament in the weeks just after the landing was described by members of the Aboulker group to an American correspondent as follows:

American policy in North Africa, see Robert Murphy, *Diplomat among Warriors* (Garden City, N. Y., 1964), pp. 66–185. For a dispassionate account, see Arthur Layton Funk, *The Politics of TORCH: The Allied Landings and the Algiers Putsch, 1942* (Lawrence, Manhattan, and Wichita, Kans., 1974).

[48] Abitbol, *Les Juifs d'Afrique du Nord sous Vichy,* pp. 153–55; Hirschberg, *A History of the Jews in North Africa,* vol. 2, pp. 325–26.

[49] Much has been written both about the Anglo-American landing in North Africa, known as Operation Torch, and about the role played by the Jewish urban guerrillas in Algiers. See, for example, José Aboulker, "La part de la Résistance française dans les événements de l'Afrique du Nord," *Les Cahiers Français,* no. 47 (August 1943): 3–45; Marcel Aboulker, *Alger et ses complots* (Paris, 1945); Ansky, *Les Juifs d'Algérie,* pp. 175–221; Danan, *La vie politique à Alger de 1940 à 1944,* pp.

> He [Murphy] shuns us like a case of an extremely contagious disease. The army brass hats and the people of the Prefecture whom we arrested hate us. . . . They hate us because we know what cowards they are. You should have seen how miserably they acted when they saw the tommy guns, the brave Jew-baiters. The chief of the secret police, who has been of course restored to his position, kneeled on the floor and wept, begging one of my friends to spare his life. Imagine his feeling toward the man who spared him! Another friend, a doctor, is to be mobilized—in a labor camp, of course—under the military jurisdiction of a general whom *he* arrested.[50]

After the assassination of Darlan by a young French royalist on December 24, 1942, a number of the principal Jewish Resistance figures, including José Aboulker and his father, were rounded up with other "suspects" and sent to the Laghouat prison camp in central Algeria, where they remained under harsh, primitive conditions for two months until finally released through American efforts.[51]

The anti-Semitic Vichy officials in North Africa, ensconced under American protection, explained their continued enforcement of the discriminatory regulations pertaining to Jews as necessary so as not to arouse the Arab population. This line of reasoning was accepted by Murphy, Eisenhower, and the American government, which now took the position that the status of the Jews in these territories was an internal French matter in which the United States had no right to intervene. A few journalists also seem to have gone along with these explanations.[52] Soon, however, American and British public opinion was stirred against these cynical policies by the press corps and by Jewish groups such as B'nai B'rith, the World Jewish Congress, and especially the American Jewish Committee.[53]

48–117; and most recently, the important work of Gitta Amipaz-Silber, *La Résistance juive en Algérie, 1940–1942* (Jerusalem, 1986). See also the works cited in n. 47 here.

[50] A. J. Liebling, *The Road back to Paris* (New York, 1944), p. 228, cited in Funk, *The Politics of TORCH,* p. 258. Aboulker and his comrades were in close contact with war correspondents to whom they imparted their own indignation. See Danan, *La vie politique à Alger de 1940 à 1944,* pp. 148–49.

[51] Gosset, *Algiers, 1941–1943,* pp. 189–99, 249–51.

[52] Thus, for example, Drew Middleton, "Giraud's Reforms Getting Under Way," *New York Times* (January 16, 1943): 3: "The Jewish problem is complicated by the large Arab population which contains many elements who nurse an old hatred for Jews founded on religion. The Arabs resent the relaxation of the Jewish laws." See also Murphy, *Diplomat among Warriors,* pp. 145–48. Needless to say, the Algerian Jews did not accept these explanations.

[53] On the American press reaction, see Abitbol, *Les Juifs d'Afrique du Nord sous Vichy,* pp. 162–63; in addition to the articles cited there, see, for example, "Sabotage, Pogroms Reported in Algiers," *New York Times* (January 20, 1943): 6, which mentions the arrests of the Aboulkers, Dr. Morali, André Temime, and others who are

On March 14, 1943, seventeen weeks after the Allies had landed in North Africa, General Henri Giraud, Darlan's successor as French high commissioner, declared that the anti-Jewish legislation, which he blamed on the German occupation of France, was null and void. At the same time, however, he issued his own ordinance abrogating the Crémieux Decree with the astoundingly disingenuous explanation that he was doing so out of "the same desire to eliminate all racial discrimination," since the 1870 decree had created "distinctions between Mohammedan and Jewish inhabitants." It was not until October 20, 1943, after much more lobbying in Washington, London, and Algiers, as well as public declarations of support by distinguished French intellectuals like philosopher Jacques Maritain, that General de Gaulle's French Committee of National Liberation, whose authority was now recognized in North Africa, restored the Crémieux Decree and gave Algerian Jewry back its citizenship.[54]

TRANSFORMATIONS

Like their coreligionists everywhere, the Jews of Arab lands were transformed in various ways by the Second World War. First and foremost among these transformations wrought by the war was a heightened Jewish consciousness and sense of common destiny. It was not only the universal threat posed by Hitler to world Jewry, but their own particular experiences that gave rise to this esprit de corps. From Iraq to Morocco, Arab sympathies had lain with the Axis, a fact not lost on the Jews of these countries. They also could hear the Mufti's broadcasts from Berlin calling upon the Arabs to "Kill the Jews wherever you find them, for the love of God, history and religion."[55]

In Iraq, the Jews had seen what could happen to them under a native regime. In Italian Libya and the French Maghreb, they saw what European colonial rule could do to them while much of the native population looked on with indifference. Even liberation proved

---

referred to as "our own friends and men who assisted the Allied landing." On the efforts of the American Jewish Committee, see Naomi W. Cohen, *Not Free to Desist: The American Jewish Committee, 1906–1966* (Philadelphia, 1972), pp. 267–68.

[54] See Ansky, *Les Juifs d'Algérie,* pp. 288-321, on the international lobbying effort. See also Hannah Arendt, "Why the Crémieux Decree Was Abrogated," *Contemporary Jewish Record* 6, no. 2 (April 1943): 115–23.

[55] Broadcast of March 1, 1944, quoted in Hirszowicz, *The Third Reich and the Arab East,* p. 311.

disappointing at first. In Iraq, the British troops held back while the Arabs went on a rampage, killing and looting the helpless Baghdadi Jews. (The British would show similar "restraint" during the anti-Jewish riots that took place in Libya right at the end of the war.[56]) In Morocco and Algeria, the Americans had, as a temporary expedient, not only confirmed the anti-Semitic Vichy oppressors in office, but also allowed them to keep on enforcing their discriminatory laws for months.

The war also transformed the attitudes and feelings of many Jews in the Arab world toward Europe. For more than a century, Middle Eastern and North African Jews had looked to the Western powers as protectors. Europe had represented to them what was modern and what was good. They had eagerly sought European educations and the benefits they bestowed. Many of them strongly identified with the colonial powers, especially in North Africa. Memmi's autobiographical hero eloquently sums up the profound disillusionment of many Jews at the time:

> It was the painful and astounding treason . . . of a civilization in which I had placed all my hopes and which I ardently admired. . . . I was all the more hurt in my pride because I had been so uncautious in my complete surrender to my faith in Europe.[57]

Memmi, like so many others throughout the Arab world, underwent a powerful reaffirmation of his Jewish identity, a "return to self" (*retour sur soi*), as the North African Jews called it. Even the most assimilated elements of the Jewish elite were affected by this return to selfhood, especially in Libya and the French Maghreb.

In the decade preceding the war there had been a marked decline in the vitality of the Zionist movement among Arabic-speaking Jewry. The wartime experience reversed this trend and engendered a new, intensified receptivity to Zionism among the Jewish population in every Arab country and among the younger generation in particular. These revived Zionist sentiments were fostered and strengthened by encounters with Jewish soldiers serving in the Allied armies. Enthusiastic young men and women from the Yishuv acted as emissaries for the Zionist movement in Iraq, the Levant States, Egypt, Libya, and Tunisia. There was also renewed contact with official Jewish bodies such as the Jewish Agency.

[56] Concerning these riots, see de Felice, *Jews in an Arab Land,* pp. 192–210; and Part Two, pp. 461–465.

[57] Memmi, *The Pillar of Salt,* p. 272.

Palestinian soldiers working on their own initiative or in cooperation with agents of the Mōsād le-ᶜAliya Bēt (the organization for illegal immigration) smuggled several thousand Jews from Iraq, Syria, and Lebanon (along with many European refugees) into Palestine, often using British military transports. An equal if not greater number of Syrian and Lebanese Jews took advantage of the relaxed security that followed the British and Free French takeover of the Levant States and simply crossed the porous southern frontier into the Galilee by themselves or with help from their own local Zionist organization. Menahem Louzia, a leader of the Damascus branch of He-Ḥalutz, helped 1,350 young people to make the border crossing.[58]

Palestinian soldiers and civilian emissaries also actively promoted youth clubs and sporting and cultural organizations, all with a strongly Jewish national emphasis. In Libya, Jewish soldiers in the British Eighth Army set up an entire network of Hebrew schools and ad hoc classes, at first with the permission of the British military authorities and later without it. In Iraq, they aided the fledgling underground movement that had developed spontaneously in the wake of the Farhūd among young Iraqi Jews who were mostly still in their teens. The small, locally formed groups like the Rescue Youth (*Shabāb al-Inqādh*) were soon replaced by the He-Ḥalutz movement, which counted over 1,000 members by the war's end, and by a much smaller arm of the Hagana.[59]

Not all Jews living in the Arab world—not even the majority, except perhaps in Libya—had become ardent Zionists by the end of World War II. Most Algerian Jews, for example, felt themselves vindicated as Frenchmen with the restoration of the Crémieux Decree. The Jewish haute bourgeoisie in Iraq and Egypt maintained for the most part their long-standing coolness toward Jewish nationalism.

[58] On the role played by Palestinian Jewish soldiers in the British army as Zionist emissaries in these countries, see the detailed study of Yoav Gelber, *Tōldōt ha-Hitnaddevūt, vol. 3: Nōs'ē ha-Degel* (Jerusalem, 1983), pp. 20–74. Yanait-Ben-Zvi, *Be-Shelīḥūt li-Lvanōn ūle-Sūrya (1943),* p. 64.

[59] On the activities of the Palestinian soldiers in Libya, see Gelber, *Tōldōt ha-Hitnaddevūt,* vol. 3, pp. 95–131; de Felice, *Jews in an Arab Land,* pp. 186–89; CZA (Jerusalem) S 25/5219, S 6/1984, and S 6/4582 contain numerous letters from soldiers and military chaplains, as well as longer reports on their work with the community. See also Part Two, pp. 452–456. For Iraq, see Gelber, *Tōldōt ha-Hitnaddevūt,* vol. 3, pp. 6–46; Hayyim J. Cohen, *ha-Peᶜīlūt ha-Ṣiyyōnīt be-ᶜIrāq* (Jerusalem, 1969), pp. 169–201; Yosef Meir [Yehoshafat], *Beyond the Desert: Underground Activities in Iraq, 1941–1951* (Tel Aviv, 1973) [Heb.]; Yehuda, *From Babylon to Jerusalem,* pp. 63–98, 153–73 [Heb.]; and Ruth Bondy, *The Emissary: A Life of Enzo Sereni,* trans. Shlomo Katz (Boston and Toronto, 1977), pp. 192–214.

But the movement had clearly penetrated more deeply and more widely among every stratum of the Jewish population, and especially among the youth, than at any time before the war. More important, there were no other ideologies, political or cultural, that could compete for Jewish loyalties. The assimilationist ideal of the Alliance Israélite Universelle had been badly discredited by the war, and even the Alliance itself, now reconstituted, had altered its position radically with regard to both the Jewish homeland and modern Hebrew culture. Arab nationalism had held little attraction for Jews before the war and certainly held none now, except for an infinitesimal handful of individuals.

As the war ended, most Jews of Arab lands probably believed that, as the world returned to some sort of normalcy, they could resume their lives for the foreseeable future without being forced to make great existential decisions. The rapid course of events over the next few years would prove otherwise.

7

THE LAST CHAPTER

RISING TENSIONS IN THE POSTWAR ERA

At the end of World War II, a concatenation of forces and events was set in motion that in relatively short order would totally undermine the position of the Jewish communities in the Arab world and result in their almost total dissolution. Within a decade, the overall Jewish population in the Arab countries was reduced by half through emigration. In several countries the decline was far greater. By the end of 1953, Iraq, Yemen, and Libya had lost over 90 percent of their Jews, and Syria approximately 75 percent. Most of the Jews who remained in the Arab world were in the French-ruled Maghreb. It was not long, however, before the three countries of that region achieved their independence. Within little more than two decades after the end of World War II, most of the North African Jews were gone as well.

The postwar years witnessed a renewed surge of Arab and Jewish nationalism. The Jews in the various Arab countries found themselves buffeted by centrifugal and centripetal forces. If, as has already been noted, the Jews on the whole emerged from the war years with a heightened sense of self-awareness, so too did the Arabs. Arab national aspirations had been frustrated during the war. Even independent states like Egypt and Iraq had found themselves unable to get free of British interference in their affairs. Overt political activities had been sharply curtailed everywhere in the Arab world during the war. By 1943, it was clear that the Allies would prevail and that any hopes placed on the Axis for deliverance from British and French colonialism or from Zionism were in vain. Those Arab leaders who had not made the mistake of hitching their fortunes to the losing side, as the Mufti and Rashīd ᶜĀlī had done, looked forward to a new geopolitical order that seemed sure to come. The tight political controls of the war years had led to a mounting of pent-up pressure among the Arab masses, whose rising expectations were coupled with deep dissatisfaction with the social and economic inequities that were heightened by the wartime experience. In Egypt, for example, the militant Muslim Brotherhood (al-Ikhwān al-Muslimūn) had become a great popular force by the end of the war, with a following of about 1 million members and sympathizers. Popular animus was directed against the wealthy ruling class, foreigners, and the non-Muslim minorities that were closely associated with the foreigners in the popular mind. Even more ominous for the Jews was the fact that the Palestine question, which had been temporarily dormant during most of the war years, returned to the forefront among the issues of primary Arab political concern.

Anti-Zionist agitation, with its corollary of anti-Jewish incitement, began to increase markedly after 1943, at the very time when Zionism was enjoying a resurgence among Jews throughout the Arab world and when Zionists in the West, especially in the United States, were pressing for unlimited immigration of Jewish refugees into Palestine when the war ended. The economic grievances of the masses, their xenophobia, and their anti-Zionism came to a head in November 1945 in a series of anti-Jewish riots that broke out in several Arab countries.

The first of these riots occurred in Egypt. Anti-Zionist demonstrations had been called for by such groups as Miṣr al-Fatāt, the Muslim Brotherhood, and the Young Men's Muslim Association. A few days before the demonstrations were to take place, the British assistant commandant of the Cairo city police noted an atmosphere of "considerable ill-feeling in Cairo against Jews." However, he believed that with proper security precautions, there was no need for undue concern.[1] Events proved otherwise, however. Mass demonstrations took place on November 2 (Balfour Declaration Day) in Cairo and Alexandria, with smaller ones in Port Said, Mansura, and Tanta. In Cairo, mobs pillaged Jewish businesses in the main part of town, in the Muski, and in the Jewish Quarter. The Ashkenazi synagogue was ransacked and burned. As often has been the case in the history of the Islamic world, violence initially directed against one non-Muslim minority easily spilled over into a generalized anti-dhimmī violence.

[1] PRO (London) FO 371/5333, Assistant Police Commissioner Speaight to Egyptian Department (October 30, 1945).

Coptic, Greek Orthodox, and Catholic institutions were also attacked, as well as shops owned by foreigners. Some 500 businesses were looted, 109 of these belonging to Jews. Damage was estimated to be in excess of 1 million Egyptian pounds. Injuries numbered in the hundreds, but amazingly only one person, a policeman, was killed. In Alexandria, the rioting claimed six lives, five of them Jewish, and another 150 persons were injured. Some disturbances continued on the following day. The king and some prominent public figures expressed their regrets at what had happened, and the government offered to bear the expenses for rebuilding the ruined synagogue. At the same time, however, there were calls from the Islamic religious establishment for Chief Rabbi Ḥayyim Nahum to issue a public statement repudiating Zionism. The chief rabbi responded with a letter to Prime Minister al-Nuqrashī Pasha, in which he included an earlier note that he had sent to the World Jewish Congress declaring the loyalty of the Jewish community to Egypt, observing the need for finding some less confined refuge than Palestine for the survivors of the Holocaust, and expressing the hope that Jews and Arabs would cooperate in solving the problem "in an atmosphere of complete accord."[2]

Neither the protestations of loyalty by the chief rabbi nor the expressions of regret and sympathy by government officials could restore Egyptian Jewry's sense of security, since the general atmosphere of hostility continued unchanged. As Thomas Mayer has rightly pointed out, "the critics of the riots did nothing to prevent the distribution of anti-Jewish propaganda in Egypt," and "the Egyptian Jews continued to be harassed by Pan-Arab and Islamic societies, as well as by Government officials, and pressed to make anti-Zionist declarations."[3]

Far more devastating anti-Jewish violence erupted in Libya only one day after the Egyptian rioting had quieted down. Early Sunday evening, November 4, attacks against Jews broke out in various parts of Tripoli after a minor altercation between a gang of Arab toughs and some Jews near the electric power station outside the Jewish

[2] "Les Juifs d'Egypte et la question palestinienne: une note de S. Em. le Grand Rabbin au Président du Conseil," *Le Progrès Egyptien* (November 10, 1945). For fuller discussions of the riots, see Gudrun Krämer, *Minderheit, Millet, Nation? Die Juden in Ägypten 1919–1952.* Studien zum Minderheitentproblem im Islam, 7 (Wiesbaden, 1982), pp. 318–22; and Thomas Mayer, *Egypt and the Palestine Question, 1936–1945.* Islamkundliche Untersuchungen, Band 77 (Berlin, 1983), pp. 297–300. See also PRO (London) FO 371/45395.

[3] Mayer, *Egypt and the Palestine Question,* p. 300.

Quarter. The riot took on major proportions on the following day when mobs numbering in the thousands poured into the Jewish Quarter and the Sūq al-Turk (the bazaar where many Jewish shops were located) and went on a rampage of looting, beating, and killing. According to one confidential report, weapons were distributed to the rioters at certain command centers, one of which was the shop of Aḥmad Krawī, a leading Arab merchant.[4]

Unlike the earlier disturbances in Egypt, the Tripolitanian incidents had no overt political coloring whatsoever, although some of the provocateurs may well have had political motives.[5] Again unlike in Egypt, in Libya only Jews and Jewish property were attacked. The rioters had no difficulty in distinguishing Jewish homes and businesses because prior to the attack, doors had been marked with chalk in Arabic indicating "Jew," "Italian," or "Arab." Mob passions reached a fever pitch when a rumor spread that the Chief Qāḍī of Tripoli had been murdered by Jews and the Sharīʿa Court burned. The terror then spread to the nearby towns of Amrus, Tagiura, Zawia, Zanzur, and Qusabat. Only in the Berber area of Yafran were there no attacks against Jews.

Throughout the first three days of the riots, the civil police stood by for the most part and did nothing, except in some cases relieving individual looters of their booty. Despite repeated pleas by leaders of the Jewish community, soldiers in the Palestine units of the British army, and American Jewish servicemen stationed on the outskirts of Tripoli, the British Military Authority waited inexplicably until Tuesday afternoon before sending in troops with orders to shoot rioters and impose a curfew in Tripoli. However, it was not until the following day that order was restored in the towns. One irate U.S. Air Force sergeant noted bitterly in a personal letter:

> The curfew stopped the violence. It could have been imposed last Sunday. In fact the fighting could have been stopped in five minutes flat. One mere gun shot—just to show the Arabs that the British were determined to protect

[4]CZA (Jerusalem) S 25/5219, anonymous typewritten report entitled "The Arab Anti-Jewish Riot in Tripolitania," p. 2.

[5]Suspicion pointed to members of the Nationalist party (al-Ḥizb al-Waṭanī), although this was never proved, and according to the British Military Administration's Annual Report for 1945, "the anti-Jewish riots could not be traced back to any concrete machinations of the Nationalist Party." Quoted by Renzo de Felice, *Jews in an Arab Land: Libya, 1835–1970,* trans. Judith Roumani (Austin, 1985), p. 201. The author of the report cited in n. 4 above, however, cites authorities within the British Military Administration who thought otherwise (pp. 2, 3).

the Jews—could have averted all the bloodshed. . . . I repeat: the British could easily have stopped the riots in five minutes flat.[6]

When the pogroms—for that is what the riots essentially were—were over, 130 Jews were dead, including thirty-six children. Some entire families were wiped out. Hundreds were injured, and approximately 4,000 people were left homeless. An additional 4,200 were reduced to poverty. There were many instances of rape, especially in the provincial town of Qusabat, where many individuals embraced Islam to save themselves. Nine synagogues—five in Tripoli, four in the provincial towns—had been desecrated and destroyed. More than 1,000 residential buildings and businesses had been plundered in Tripoli alone. Damage claims totaled more than one quarter of a billion lire (over half a million pounds sterling).[7]

The Tripolitanian pogroms dealt, in the words of one observer, "an unprecedented blow . . . to the Jews' sense of security."[8] Many leading Arab notables condemned the atrocities, but as the British Military Administration's *Annual Report* for 1945 noted, "no general, deep-felt sense of guilt seems to animate the Arab community at large: nor has it been too active in offering help to the victims."[9] Not that the British had inspired any confidence in the Jewish community. Quite to the contrary. The Military Administration, after demonstrating an appalling lack of initial concern, simply blamed the disorder on "the growth of Zionism," "Arab envy of the more prosperous Jews," and "fear, nourished from Arab sources in Egypt and Palestine, of Jewish supremacy."[10] What it failed to mention was its

[6] CZA (Jerusalem) S 25/5217, letter from S/Sgt Joseph Zweben 12037884, Sqdn A, 1262nd AAFBU to Ben and Tikvah (no last name). A handwritten note on the copy of the letter identifies Zweben as "editor of 'Prop Wash,' an American air force paper." Concerning the frustration and anger of soldiers in the Palestine units of the British army, see the extracts from the report by a company officer in CZA (Jerusalem) Z 4/10,221.

[7] A detailed statistical account of the casualties and material damage can be found in the official report of the Jewish community of Tripoli in CZA (Jerusalem) S 25/5219 (part of which is included in Part Two, pp. 461–465), in the British Military Administration of Tripolitania, *Annual Report, 1945,* and in de Felice, *Jews in an Arab Land,* pp. 194–95, 366–68, Tables N-5 to N-8 (which reproduce the appendices of the Jewish community's report).

[8] Haim Abravanel, director of Alliance schools in Tripoli, cited in de Felice, *Jews in an Arab Land,* p. 209.

[9] British Military Administration Tripolitania, *Annual Report 1945,* p. 13.

[10] Ibid., p. 9. See also British Foreign Office correspondence on the riots in which the tone is rather unsympathetic to the plight of the Jews and much of the blame is placed upon events in Palestine, where in the words of one internal

own anti-Zionist propaganda and the fact that not a few Egyptian and other agitators were actually employees of the Military Administration.

Many Libyan Jews, Jewish servicemen in the American and British armies, Italian colonists, and even some Arab notables believed that the British themselves were behind the pogroms. Renzo de Felice, after carefully weighing the known facts and allegations, comes to the highly persuasive conclusion that one cannot seriously believe the British organized the pogroms, but he also rejects the notion that the inaction of the British authorities during the early days of the rioting could be attributed merely to incompetence. Rather, he concludes:

> One can only think that the BMA's [British Military Administration's] conduct was strongly affected by a *political* concern not to adopt too harsh a position and not to annoy the Arab masses or alienate them, thereby playing into the hands of the nationalists. . . . This political concern is indirectly confirmed by the fact that, even though the British military authorities did not have large forces available and had to bring the whole region under control, they were careful not to deploy the soldiers of the Palestinian Brigade in restoring order, keeping them closely consigned to barracks.[11]

There was also some minor anti-Jewish violence in Syria a week and a half after the incidents in Tripolitania. On November 18, 1945, which was the Muslim holiday of al-ᶜĪd al-Kabīr, a mob broke into the Great Synagogue of Aleppo, smashed votive objects, burned prayer books, and beat up two elderly men who were studying there. The wave of anti-Jewish violence did not spread any farther at this time. In Iraq, for example, the government took precautions to maintain control immediately following the initial Egyptian rioting by banning public demonstrations that had been called for by students. The potential for violence, however, increased almost everywhere in the Arab world during the next three years as Arab and Jewish nationalism headed down a collision course.[12]

---

memorandum, "Palestine Jewry was at the moment indulging in not dissimilar violence, which could not help reacting on the Arabs." See PRO (London) FO 371/45395, Scrivener to Beeley (November 18, 1945).

[11] De Felice, *Jews in an Arab Land,* pp. 208–9.

[12] For the Aleppo disturbances, see S. Landshut, *Jewish Communities in the Muslim Countries of the Middle East: A Survey* (London, 1950), p. 58; and Joseph B. Schechtman, *On Wings of Eagles: The Plight, Exodus, and Homecoming of Oriental Jewry* (New York and London, 1961), p. 155. There had already been anti-Jewish rioting in Damascus earlier that same year. Concerning Iraq, see Hayyim J. Cohen, *The Jews of the Middle East, 1860–1972* (New York and Jerusalem, 1973), p. 32.

Arab-Jewish tensions reached new heights in the fall of 1947 as the United Nations debated the future of Palestine. Dr. Muḥammad Ḥusayn Haykal, the chairman of the Egyptian delegation, warned the Palestine Committee of the General Assembly that "the lives of 1,000,000 Jews in Moslem countries would be jeopardized by partition." Jamāl al-Ḥusaynī, representing the Palestinian Arab Higher Committee, was even blunter:

> It must be remembered, by the way, that there are as many Jews in the Arab world as there are in Palestine whose positions, under such conditions, will become very precarious, even though the Arab states may do their best to save their skins. Governments, in general, have always been unable to prevent mob excitement and violence.[13]

Such threats were not idle. In the wake of the General Assembly vote in favor of the partition of Palestine on November 29, 1949, a new wave of anti-Jewish violence spread through the Middle Eastern Arab countries, where demonstrations against the United Nations vote were called for December 2–5. As in the 1945 disturbances, mobs in Cairo turned upon Jewish, minority, and foreign businesses and other institutions. This time, however, the police prevented the attackers from storming the Jewish Quarter, and on December 5, the government clamped down by declaring a state of emergency and banning all demonstrations.[14]

In Bahrain, the first two days of demonstrations were marked only by some minor stone throwing at individual members of the small Jewish community. Beginning on December 5, however, crowds in al-Manama, the capital, began looting Jewish homes and shops, destroyed the synagogue, and beat up any Jews they could lay their hands upon. Miraculously, only one elderly woman was killed.[15]

The rioting in Aleppo, Syria, took a far greater toll. The venerable Jewish community was physically devastated. At least 150 homes, 50 shops, all of the community's 18 synagogues, 5 schools, its orphanage, and a youth club were destroyed. Property damage was estimated at $2.5 million. Many people were reported killed, but no figures have

[13] Frank S. Adams, "Arabs and Zionists Warn of Fighting: In Final Appeals to U.N., Each Pleges War to the Finish if Turned Down on Palestine," *New York Times* (November 25, 1947): 7.

[14] Krämer, *Minderheit, Millet, Nation?*, p. 410.

[15] Natan Alluf, *Bahrain—A Community That Was* (Tel Aviv, 1979), pp. 111–22 [Heb.]; and Part Two, pp. 469–470.

ever been advanced. More than half of the city's 10,000 Jews fled across the borders into Turkey, Lebanon, and Palestine.[16]

Similar devastation engulfed the Jewish community in the British-controlled protectorate of Aden. As in the Tripolitanian pogroms of 1945, the police, composed mainly of natives, proved unable to contain the rioting and in some cases took part in it themselves. Troops had to be called in to quell the violence. By the time order was finally restored on December 4, 82 Jews had been killed and a similar number injured. Of the 170 Jewish-owned shops in the Crater (the main town of Aden), 106 were totally destroyed and 8 more partially sacked. Hundreds of houses and all of the Jewish communal institutions, including the synagogue and the two schools, were burned to the ground. Many people had lost everything. Four thousand Jews had to be fed by the authorities. Rioters also wrought havoc upon the small Jewish communities in the surrounding towns and in the Hashed camp housing Yemenite Jewish refugees. The Adeni Jewish community claimed that the damage it had suffered exceeded over 1 million pounds.[17]

The wave of violence that followed the United Nations vote for the partition of Palestine had a demoralizing effect upon the Jews living in the eastern Arab countries. Expressions of sympathy from political leaders and reassurances that they had nothing to fear as long as they were not associated with Zionism offered little solace. The press, students, members of the political opposition, and religious leaders rarely maintained the fine distinction between Jews and Zionists. Calls for *jihād*, or holy war, heightened interreligious tensions. Prominent Jews were increasingly called upon to make declarations of solidarity with the Palestinian Arab cause, not to mention generous contributions.[18]

The Jews of the French-ruled Maghreb had been spared the fury of the latest storm. There certainly was tension between Arabs and

[16] Landshut, *Jewish Communities in the Muslim Countries of the Middle East,* pp. 59–60; Nehemiah Robinson, *The Arab Countries of the Near East and Their Jewish Communities,* unpublished report of the Institute of Jewish Affairs, World Jewish Congress (New York, 1951), p. 77.

[17] The complete Colonial Office *Report on the Commission of Enquiry into Disturbances in Aden in December, 1947* is given in Part Two, pp. 471–499. See also the detailed reports and related correspondence in AJDC (Jerusalem) 322A.7.

[18] Barry Rubin, *The Arab States and the Palestine Conflict* (Syracuse, N.Y., 1981), p. 192–93; Krämer, *Minderheit, Millet, Nation?,* pp. 408–11; Cohen, *The Jews of the Middle East,* pp. 32–33; Stephen Hemsley Longrigg, *ʿIraq, 1900 to 1950: A Political, Social, and Economic History* (London, New York, and Toronto, 1953), pp. 349–50. See also the report in Part Two, pp. 500–503.

Jews over the Palestine issue, but for the most part it remained beneath the surface at this time. This was due to a number of factors. The French still exercised tight, even repressive, control over the population. Palestine was geographically far removed and, no less important, was not the central issue of North African nationalist concern. Maghrebi Arab leaders consistently eschewed the kind of anti-Jewish rhetoric that had become commonplace in Middle Eastern political discourse. As André Chouraqui has noted, there was "a tacit understanding" between the Muslim and Jewish communities in North Africa "that the conflicts which plagued their coreligionists in the Holy Land were to be avoided."[19] Thus Maghrebi Jewry, although anxious about the future, maintained a much higher morale than its brethren in the East during this period.

THE IRREVOCABLE SPLIT

By the time Israel was established on May 15, 1948, and war was declared by the members of the Arab League against the newborn state, the very foundations of the Jewish communities in the Arab world had already been severely weakened. The waves of anti-Jewish violence that had struck almost every major Jewish community from Libya to Iraq, beginning with the Baghdadi Farhūd of 1941 and culminating in the widespread rioting of 1945 and 1947, had eroded the Jews' confidence in these countries. The Palestine issue was, of course, a major contributing factor in all of this, but it was by no means the only one. Indeed, it was more of a catalyst precipitating and sharpening other problematic issues.

More and more, Jews were finding themselves in the position of "odd man out" as the societies around them cultivated nationalisms with a strong ethnic and religious component (namely, Arab and Islamic), as well as what Bernard Lewis has characterized as "a new militancy that [left] no place for those who deviate from the rule."[20] This was as true in Iraq, where most of the Jews had roots going back two and a half millennia, as it was in Egypt, where most of them were of relatively recent foreign origin. Already in the late 1930s, Jewish civil servants were being weeded out of the Iraqi bureaucracy, utilities,

[19] André N. Chouraqui, *Between East and West: A History of the Jews of North Africa* (New York, 1973), p. 191. For the mood in North Africa in 1947, see the report in Part Two, pp. 467–468.

[20] Bernard Lewis, *The Jews of Islam* (Princeton, N.J., 1984), p. 190.

and public corporations to make room for "real Iraqis." Throughout the late 1930s and 1940s, Egypt enacted a series of legislative measures aimed at Egyptianizing the economy. The Company Law of 1947, for example, specified that at least 75 percent of the employees, 90 percent of the laborers, and 51 percent of the capital in companies incorporated in the country had to be Egyptian. Since the majority of Jews in Egypt either held foreign nationalities or were technically stateless persons, they could not help but be adversely affected by the Company Law. The president of Cairo's Jewish community estimated privately that the Company Law jeopardized the jobs of perhaps as many as 50,000 Jews. Already in 1945, Minister of Commerce and Industry Ḥafnī Maḥmūd was differentiating between "nominal Egyptians" and "real Egyptians" with regard to employment.[21]

The first Arab-Israeli war greatly accelerated the process whereby the Jewish minorities in the Arab countries were being alienated and isolated from the larger societies in which they lived. Compared with the violent mob reactions against them following the United Nations partition vote in 1947, the overall response at the outbreak of the war in May 1948 was relatively subdued. This was due perhaps to the universal popular expectation of a speedy and decisive Arab victory that was fostered by the unrealistic rhetoric of their leaders and the grossly exaggerated reports of early successes in their media. "The Zionist fortress will fall after the first attack," predicted King ᶜAbd Allāh of Transjordan, and ᶜAzzām Pasha, the secretary of the Arab League, declared, "[T]his will be a war of extermination and a momentous massacre which will be spoken of like the Mongolian massacres and the crusades." Egypt's leading newspaper *al-Ahrām* observed, "The history of the Egyptian army is one long list of victories."[22] Much of the attention and the passion of the Arab masses was directed almost exclusively toward Palestine and temporarily, at least, away from the local Jewish communities and, it might be added, from the serious internal problems plaguing their individual countries. The

[21] See Cohen, *The Jews of the Middle East,* p. 27; Krämer, *Minderheit, Millet, Nation?,* pp. 402–6; Krämer, " 'Radical' Nationalists, Fundamentalists, and the Jews in Egypt or, Who Is a Real Egyptian?" *Islam, Nationalism and Radicalism in Egypt and the Sudan,* ed. Gabriel R. Warburg and Uri M. Kupferschmidt (New York, 1983), pp. 354–71; and Don Peretz, *Egyptian Jews Today,* unpublished report for the American Jewish Committee (New York, January 1956), p. 16. In Syria, too, Jews were purged from employment in the public sector at this time, although the rationale was blatantly anti-Zionist. See Schechtman, *On Wings of Eagles,* pp. 161–62.

[22] The quotations are all taken from Rubin, *The Arab States and the Palestine Conflict,* pp. 200–2.

governments of Egypt, Iraq, Lebanon, and Syria also took concerted steps to prevent mob violence from erupting during the early days of the war by imposing a state of emergency and martial law. In Morocco, the popular Sultan Muḥammad V, addressing his Muslim and Jewish subjects as "all of you, Moroccans, without exception," publicly appealed for calm and the preservation of order.[23] Egypt's King Fārūq, meeting with a delegation of Jewish leaders on the eve of the war, assured them of his protection.[24]

While protected from the danger of mob actions, the Jewish communities in the Arab League states found themselves subject to a variety of harsh and intimidating administrative impositions. Known or suspected Zionist activists were arrested everywhere. In Egypt and Iraq, the governments took advantage of the state of emergency to round up communists, which in both countries included a considerable number of Jews. In fact, as far as Egyptian Premier al-Nuqrashī Pasha was concerned, "all Jews were potential Zionists," "all Zionists were Communists," and all communist activities "were directed exclusively by Jews." Some of Iraq's veteran politicians, like Nūrī al-Saʿīd, were of a similar mind.[25] In all, between 600 and 1,000 Jews in Egypt and around 310 Jews (nowhere near the figure of 2,000 charged by Israel at the time) in Iraq were taken into custody during the early days of the war. Most were held in prisons and internment camps for weeks. The treatment meted out to the internees was generally far better in Egypt than in Iraq. Many more non-Jews were also arrested at this time since the two governments took advantage of the imposition of martial law to suppress internal opposition. In addition to the communists, for example, many Muslim Brethren were rounded up in Egypt. The property of those arrested, both Jewish and non-Jewish, was placed under special stewardship during their incarceration. Most of the Egyptian Jews who were interned were eventually released and their property restored. In Iraq, most of the Jews arrested were brought before courts-martial and received fines, prison sentences of varying lengths, or both. The only individual to receive the death penalty was Shafīq ʿAdas, Iraq's richest Jew, who was condemned on the unlikely charge of having supplied scrap metal to the Zionist state. (Even more farfetched, he was accused of having communist ties.)

[23] The complete text of the speech is given in Part Two, pp. 513–514.

[24] Rubin, *The Arab States and the Palestine Conflict,* p. 202.

[25] Krämer, *Minderheit, Millet, Nation?,* p. 414; and Lois Gottesman, "Israel in Egypt: The Jewish Community of Egypt, 1922–1957" (unpublished master's thesis, Princeton University, 1982), p. 71 (both citing FO 371/69159/2410 and 371/69211). For Iraq, see Shiblak, *The Lure of Zion: The Case of the Iraqi Jews* (London, 1986),

ᶜAdas was fined 5 million pounds and publicly hanged in front of his palatial home in Basra on September 23, 1948.[26]

It was not until several weeks after the war began, when it was becoming clear that the Arab offensive in Palestine was encountering serious difficulties, that incidents of anti-Jewish violence began to break out in the Arab countries. The first such incidents took place on June 7 and 8 in the northeastern Moroccan towns of Oujda and Jerada. Forty-two Jews were killed and approximately 150 injured, many of them seriously. Scores of homes and shops were sacked.[27]

On June 12, the day after the first truce was declared between the Israeli and Arab forces in Palestine, mobs attacked the Jewish Quarter in Tripoli, Libya. (Thousands of Moroccan and Tunisian volunteers had been streaming through the city on their way east to join the Arab armies fighting in Palestine.) However, Jewish self-defense units, which had been organized here as in other cities that had suffered pogroms in recent years, repelled the attackers with stones, handguns, grenades, and Molotov cocktails, inflicting heavy casualties. The rioters then turned upon undefended neighborhoods outside the Ḥāra. Only thirteen or fourteen Jews were killed and twenty-two seriously injured, but property damage was very high. Approximately 300 families were left destitute. There were also attacks against Jews in the surrounding countryside and in Benghazi.[28]

A week after the Libyan riots, a bomb went off in the Karaite quarter of Cairo, killing more than twenty people. An anonymous

p. 65; and ᶜAbd al-Razzāq al-Ḥasanī, *Ta'rīkh al-Wizārāt al-ᶜIrāqiyya,* vol. 7 (Sidon, 1953), pp. 93–95.

[26] Krämer, *Minderheit, Millet, Nation?,* pp. 415–16; Gottesman, "Israel in Egypt," p. 71; Landshut, *Jewish Communities in the Muslim Countries of the Middle East,* pp. 34, 48–50; Cohen, *The Jews of the Middle East,* pp. 33–34; Schechtman, *On Wings of Eagles,* pp. 99–102, 189–90; Abraham Ben-Jacob, *A History of the Jews in Iraq: From the End of the Gaonic Period to the Present Time,* 2nd rev. ed. (Jerusalem, 1979), pp. 258–61 [Heb.]; Shiblak, *The Lure of Zion,* pp. 68–70; PRO (London) FO 371/82478; also "Iraqi Persecution Not Substantiated: U.S. Envoy Discounts Charge of Israel That 2,000 Jews Had Been Imprisoned," *New York Times* (November 2, 1949): 16.

[27] Chouraqui, *Between East and West,* pp. 181–82. Michael Laskier, basing himself on a report by a Zionist emissary operating in North Africa at the time, suggests that French officials may have been the agents provocateurs behind the pogroms. This, however, requires considerably more documentation. See Michael M. Laskier, "Hebbēṭīm Pōlītiyyīm ve-Irgūniyyīm shel hā-ᶜAliyya mi-Marōqō ba-Shānīm 1949–1956," *ha-Ṣiyyōnūt* 12 (1987): 336.

[28] De Felice, *Jews in an Arab Land,* pp. 223–25; Yosef Maymon, "Irgūn ha-Hagana be-Trīpōlī," in *Yahadūt Lūv,* ed. F. Zuaretz et al.(Tel Aviv, 1960), pp. 231–32; Ṣ. Shaked, "Nesheq la-Hagana," and "Pirqē ha-Hagana," in ibid., pp. 233–35. For a

note laid blame for the explosion on the Rabbanites, but this was rejected by all Jews as totally preposterous. A tense calm was restored for almost a month, during which time, according to one British diplomatic report, "Jews, both rich and poor, carry on their normal activities in satisfactory conditions," although they were "apt to be nervous of their position, as are the Copts and other minorities."[29]

Following the Israeli air force bombing raids over Cairo and Alexandria, which had resulted in heavy civilian casualties on July 15, and the declaration of a second truce in Palestine on July 18, anti-Jewish and anti-foreign agitation in the mosques and in the press reached a fever pitch. The atmosphere was even more highly charged by the coincidence of Ramadan, the holy month of fasting. There were sporadic assaults against Jews and foreigners in the streets in the days immediately following the air raids.[30]

A large explosion severely damaged the Circurel and Oreco department stores in the heart of Cairo's modern business district on July 19. Twenty minutes after the blast, an air raid alert was sounded. The explosion was officially blamed on "an aerial torpedo from a Jewish aircraft," although a truce was in effect, no plane had been sighted, and a former under secretary of the interior, Ḥasan Rifaᶜat Pasha, who was one of Circurel's Muslim board members, affirmed that the explosion "could not possibly have been caused by a bomb from the air." The attack on Circurel's was the signal for what British Ambassador Campbell described as "an orgy of looting" and stepped-up assaults upon Jews and foreigners.[31]

Over the next three months, bombs destroyed Jewish-owned movie theaters and large retail businesses, including the Adès, Gattegno, and Benzion establishments. In all, attacks on Jews claimed approximately fifty lives during the summer of 1948, with tremendous property losses. The injured, homeless, and unemployed numbered

---

detailed memorandum on the situation in Libya following the riots, see CZA (Jerusalem) S 32/1069, report from Samuel Auerbach.

[29] PRO (London) FO 371/69259, G. L. McDermott to C. P. Mayhew (June 2, 1948), "The Position of Jews in Egypt." For the incident in the Karaite Quarter, see Krämer, *Minderheit, Millet, Nation?*, p. 419; Landshut, *Jewish Communities in the Muslim Countries of the Middle East*, p. 36.

[30] For reports on such incidents, including casualty figures, see PRO (London) FO 371/69259, Sir Ronald Campbell to Foreign Office, telegram no. 1075 (July 19, 1948).

[31] The quotations are all from PRO (London) FO 371/69182, Ambassador Campbell's telegrams nos. 121 and 127 (July 23 and 31, 1948). See also Landshut, *Jewish Communities in the Muslim Countries of the Middle East*, p. 37.

in the hundreds. Public protestations of loyalty and condemnations of Zionism by Jewish notables and large contributions totaling nearly a quarter of a million dollars to the Welfare Fund for Egyptian troops fighting in Palestine did not bring security. A series of bombs in the Jewish Quarter killed 29 people on September 22, and fifty Jews were arrested on trumped-up charges. Morale in the community reached a particularly low ebb during this period, and according to a confidential American Jewish Committee report, there was a marked increase in conversions to Islam and Christianity.[32]

The Israeli victory and the Arab defeat in Palestine had enormous political consequences throughout the Middle East in both the short and the long run. No less important were the psychological consequences for the minority Jewish communities and for the Muslim majorities in the various Arab countries. But just what were these consequences was by no means immediately clear as the cease-fire agreements were being signed by the belligerents in the spring and summer of 1949.

Despite their feelings of insecurity, which had existed long before the first Arab-Israeli war, many Jews of the upper classes and some of the middle classes in several Arab countries still hoped that they could make the best of the new situation and return to some semblance of life as usual. In Egypt, Iraq, and even Syria for a brief time during the short-lived regime of Ḥusnī al-Zaʿīm, these hopes were fostered by the easing of some restrictions imposed during the war and the release of many individuals who had been imprisoned on flimsy charges. In Egypt, hope was reinforced by the restoration of much of the property that had been placed under government stewardship. Furthermore, it was clear that much of the violence against Jews had not been government sponsored, although the authorities were certainly responsible for allowing the development of (and in part fostering) an atmosphere conducive to such violence and for taking inadequate steps to protect their Jewish minorities. For

[32] AJC FAD-1: Egypt (1948–1949), Confidential Report on Egypt (October 1949), by Z. Shuster, cited in Gottesman, "Israel in Egypt," p. 104, n. 144. See also ibid., pp. 72–73; and Krämer, *Minderheit, Millet, Nation?,* p. 420. A British consular official reports that Baroness de Menasce had placed her house in Alexandria in the care of a recent Jewish convert to Catholicism; however, he doubted that the latter would be "a very effective protector of the property." See FO 371/69259, H. G. Jakins (Alexandria) to Cairo Embassy (June 30, 1948). As already noted, conversions to Christianity were not unknown among members of the Egyptian Jewish elite (see Chapter 1 above, p. 21, and Part Two, pp. 245–249). Conversions to Islam were rare and took place mainly among the lower class.

their part, government officials saw that, once unleashed, popular violence could get dangerously out of hand for all concerned, as the assassination of Egypt's Prime Minister al-Nuqrashī Pasha by the Muslim Brotherhood proved in December 1948. (This was only the first in a long series of political assassinations in the Arab world that may be viewed at least in part as a consequence of the Arab-Israeli war.)

THE MASS EXODUS BEGINS

The momentary optimism quickly evaporated in Syria and Iraq. In Libya, there had been none at all. Libyan Jewry had been thoroughy demoralized by the pogroms and saw no hope for the future in the country. Some members of the community, in an impassioned letter to the United Nations Security Council, described their collective plight as "unbearable materially, economically, as well as morally" and asked to "be free of this hell." According to the same letter, 60 percent of the community was living on welfare provided by Jewish philanthropy from abroad.[33] The Libyan Jews detested both the British and the Arabs and were totally unwilling to remain in an independent Libya under Arab rule. By 1949, many Libyan Jews were becoming desperate, feeling trapped by the British Military Administration, which would not allow them to emigrate either to Israel, where the vast majority desired to go, or to Italy, the refuge of choice for some of the more assimilated members of the elite. As in other Arab countries during this period, a considerable number of individuals resorted to clandestine emigration, much of it organized by emissaries from Israel. During the second half of 1948, 1,041 young people departed in this way.[34]

When the British Military Administration lifted travel restrictions on February 2, 1949, thousands of Jews lined up for exit permits. In Tripoli alone, over 8,000 were issued within a few days. Within a few

[33] Lengthy passages from the letter are cited in de Felice, *Jews in an Arab Land,* pp. 226–27. The full text is in "Gli ebrei di Libia e il loro triste destino," *Israel* (November 18, 1948). Most of the Jews who crowded into Tripoli from the provincial towns were living off subsidies, as were about a third of the city's 20,000 regular Jewish inhabitants. For extensive reports on the prevailing conditions and relief activities at this time, see AJDC (Jerusalem) Libya 265B.12–19; 306C/307A.4; 405A.34; and 438B.17; also CZA (Jerusalem) S 32/121–123.

[34] Barukh Duvdevani, "Perāqīm be-ᶜAliyyat Gōlat Lūv," in *Yahadūt Lūv,* ed. Zuaretz et al., p. 301. For descriptions of this illegal ᶜaliya, see K. Adadi and Ṣ. Fadlun, "ᶜAliya B.," in ibid., pp. 269–73.

months, approximately 2,000 individuals had left the country on their own—most of them for Italy, and from there, Israel. The rest of the community waited impatiently to be evacuated in a mass ᶜaliya. Between April 1949 and December 1951, over 31,000 of a total of 35,000 to 36,000 Jews left the country on Israeli ships, the last two of which sailed out of Tripoli harbor shortly after Libya gained its independence at the end of 1951.[35]

Practically the entire Jewish population of Yemen had also been gripped with a messianic enthusiasm after the establishment of the State of Israel. Already during the preceding five years, several thousand Yemenite Jews had made their way to Palestine individually and in small groups. The great majority came through the British protectorate of Aden, where most ended up for shorter or longer periods in refugee camps. The largest camp at Hashid, known in Hebrew as Maḥane Ge'ūla (Camp Redemption), was maintained by the American Joint Distribution Committee and the Jewish Agency. By the early autumn of 1948, the camp's population had swollen to nearly 7,000, far beyond its intended capacity.[36]

The British authorities in Aden, as elsewhere in the Middle East, were generally unsympathetic to Zionism and to ᶜaliya. They also feared a repetition of the disorders that had rocked the protectorate a year earlier and tried to stanch the flow emanating from Yemen and to repatriate the refugees. However, the lobbying efforts of Jewish organizations in London and the sudden, unprecedented, and completely inexplicable decision of the new Zaydī Imam Aḥmad to allow his Jewish subjects to leave Yemen unimpeded set in motion a mass migration from every corner of the country into Aden via the neighboring sultanates.[37]

[35] The most detailed account of this massive operation is Duvdevani, "Perāqīm be-ᶜAliyyat Gōlat Lūv," pp. 297–316. (Duvdevani was the Jewish Agency official who was in charge of the ᶜaliya in Libya.) See also Schechtman, *On Wings of Eagles,* pp. 140–47; and de Felice, *Jews in an Arab Land,* pp. 229–33.

[36] For a historical account of the Hashid camp that includes some documentary material, see Nissim Benjamin Gamlieli (Shukr), *Tēmān ū-Maḥane "Ge'ūla" (Qōrōt ha-Yehūdīm be-Tēmān, ba-Derākhīm, be-ᶜAden, ūve-Maḥane ha-Pelīṭīm)* (Tel Aviv, 1962), pp. 139–330. See also the important eyewitness account of Joseph Ṣadoq, *Be-Saᶜarōt Tēmān: Megillat "Marvad ha-Qesāmīm"* (Tel Aviv, 1956), pp. 9–55, 85–90, 164–68, passim; and the somewhat journalistic account of Shlomo Barer, *The Magic Carpet* (New York, 1952), pp. 39–106, passim. Extensive documentation on the camp can be found in AJDC (Jerusalem) Aden—Yemenites 322A.1, 7, 8, 12 and 322B.1–3 and 6–11.

[37] Jewish sources involved in the Yemenite exodus insist that no negotiations took place with the Imam. See Barer, *The Magic Carpet,* pp. 177–79. However, one

The Yemenite refugees poured into Aden at a rate and in numbers that were beyond anything that had been expected and overwhelmed the camp facilities and relief efforts. Many refugees arrived undernourished and in frightful physical condition after having trekked hundreds of miles over rough terrain, in many cases entirely on foot. Several thousand individuals were stricken with malaria, and 70 to 80 percent of all refugees were suffering from eye diseases. Approximately 600 people died in the camps, nearly half of these during September and October 1949, when the influx of refugees was at its height. Fearing the outbreak of an epidemic, the British authorities in Aden closed the border for five weeks during this peak period, causing near starvation among the hapless refugees stranded on the other side. The situation demanded that the facilities be expanded and the refugees transferred as quickly as possible. Between June 1949 and September 1950, approximately 44,000 Yemenite Jews were brought from Aden to Israel in a dramatic airlift, dubbed Operation On Wings of Eagles (see Exod. 19:4), later renamed Operation Magic Carpet. The airlift was carried out by a specially formed American charter airline, the Near East Air Transport Company, in 430 flights, with at times as many as eleven planes flying around the clock during the height of the exodus in the fall of 1949.[38]

Jews continued to trickle out of Yemen during the early 1950s. Many of these last emigrants were craftsmen who had been required by the Imam or by local tribal shaykhs to remain behind until they had taught their skills to Arabs who could replace them. (The Jews had traditionally been the principal artisans in the country.) By 1955, the exodus had ended. Less than 1,000 Jews were estimated to have remained behind, mainly in the remoter mountain regions of northern Yemen.[39]

---

meeting did take place between the Imam and the Israeli emissary Joseph Ṣadoq in November 1949 in Taᶜizz. See Ṣadoq, *Be-Saᶜarōt Tēmān,* pp. 101–9. Concerning lobbying efforts in London, see Part Two, pp. 517–518.

[38] Barer, *The Magic Carpet,* pp. 12–13; Schechtman, *On Wings of Eagles,* pp. 52–57, 70–72. For the personal account by one of the Near East Transport pilots who took part in the operation, see Edward Trueblood Martin, *I Flew Them Home* (New York, 1958); also Lawrence Resner, *Eternal Stranger: The Plight of the Modern Jew from Baghdad to Casablanca* (Garden City, N.Y., 1951), pp. 187–97.

[39] Estimates of the Jewish population that remained in Yemen have varied considerably, from approximately 600 in 1959 to only 200 in 1968. See Simon Federbush, ed., *World Jewry Today* (New York, 1959), p. 374; and Hayyim J. Cohen, "Yemen," *EJ* 16: 751. Recent, more informed estimates place the figure at around 2,000. See George Lichtbau, "Jews Who Still Live in Yemen," *Jewish Monthly* 98, no. 8 (April 1984): 10.

The Jews of Iraq were considerably more divided as to where their future lay after the birth of Israel than either their Libyan or Yemenite coreligionists. Many members, though by no means all, of the wealthy mercantile elite and most of the official communal leadership in Baghdad headed by Rabbi Sassoon Khadduri, a long-time and outspoken opponent of Zionism, still hoped that despite the intensely hostile atmosphere that prevailed in the country they could ride out the storm and eventually, with the easing of restrictions, continue their comfortable lives as before. Most other segments of Jewish society, however, were far less optimistic about their future in Iraq. In addition to the committed Zionists, who numbered only a few thousand, were many Zionist sympathizers, especially among young people. A secret British diplomatic report sent to the American secretary of state in March 1949 estimated that "many younger men, of the 'white collar' class, roughly those aged 30 and younger, would be interested in emigrating to Israel, in the belief that they would have better opportunities there than in Iraq."[40] Growing numbers of primarily young Jews began crossing the frontier illegally into Iran either individually or in small groups. Despite martial law, which was in force until December 1949, at least 1,500 of them succeeded in making the crossing. About two thirds of these went on to Israel.[41]

Throughout 1949, the general disaffection of Iraqi Jewry was exacerbated by frequent calls of the extreme nationalists for the wholesale expulsion of the Jews as a disloyal element from the country. This idea was even picked up briefly by veteran politician Nūrī al-Saʿīd as a possible retaliation for the expulsion of Palestinian Arabs from Israel. Such threats were complemented by broadcasts on the Voice of Israel promising the Iraqi Jews salvation and by the distribution of underground publications urging resistance.[42] Just how alienated the rank and file of the Jewish community was from its official leadership became apparent on October 23, 1949, when a large demonstration of Jews protesting arrests and other harassments took place in Baghdad, and the president of the communal council, Rabbi

[40] PRO (London) FO 371/75128 (March 8, 1949).

[41] Cohen, *ha-Peʿīlūt ha-Ṣiyyōnīt be-ʿIrāq,* p. 210.

[42] PRO (London) FO 371/75128 (February 14 and 18, 1949); FO 624/165 (October 24, 1949); FO 371/75197 (October 27, 1949). See also Elie Kedourie, *The Chatham House Version and Other Middle-Eastern Studies* (New York and Washington, 1970), p. 311; and Shiblak, *The Lure of Zion,* p. 75; Ṣādiq Ḥasan al-Sūdānī, *al-Nashāṭ al-Ṣahyūnī fi'l-ʿIrāq 1914–1952* (Baghdad, 1980), pp. 183–84. The idea of exchanges of Jewish and Arab minorities following the Greek-Turkish and other precedents was being discussed in diplomatic circles at the time and was favored by

Khadduri, was dragged from his home and manhandled by the crowd before being extricated by the police. He resigned a few days later (although his resignation was not officially announced by the government until mid-December). On October 25, most of the Jews of Baghdad stayed home from work to observe a day of special fasting and prayer and to express their general sense of grievance.[43]

Promises by Acting Premier ᶜUmar Naẓmī to a group of Jewish notables a few days after these incidents that some of the restrictions would soon be lifted had little effect on the Jewish masses. When martial law was finally lifted in December 1949 and the punishment for attempting to emigrate illegally was accordingly lightened, clandestine crossings of the Iranian border began to assume major proportions. Within the first few months of 1950, at least 10,000 Jews fled Iraq in this way. Only a small portion of these émigrés were spirited out of the country by the Zionist organization. The majority simply went on their own, often with the aid of Arab smugglers, bribed policemen, and other officials. Once in Iran, most Iraqi Jews were directed to the large refugee camp administered by the Joint Distribution Committee near Teheran, and from there they were airlifted to Israel. All of this was done in cooperation with the Iranian authorities.[44]

---

the Israelis, the Great Powers, and even some Arab politicans. See Joseph B. Schechtman, *Population Transfers in Asia* (New York, 1949), pp. 84–141. When the Iraqi government itself proposed such a scheme, the Israelis countered that they would only be prepared to agree if the Iraqi Jews were allowed to leave with their possessions, but "could not in any circumstances agree to receiving them as penniless, displaced persons." See FO 371/75128, Sir K. Helm (Tel Aviv) to Foreign Office (October 18, 1949); also FO 371/75152 in Shiblak, *The Lure of Zion,* pp. 138–39.

[43] PRO (London) FO 371/75128, Sir H. Mack (Baghdad) to Foreign Office (October 24, 1949); FO 624/165 (same date); FO 371/82477, clipping from *The Jewish Chronicle* (December 30, 1949, anonymous article by a supporter of Rabbi Khadduri, entitled "Baghdad Jewry's Leader Resigns"). See also Shlomo Hillel, *Operation Babylon,* trans. Ina Friedman (New York, 1987), pp. 222–23; and Heskel M. Haddad, M.D., *Flight from Babylon: Iraq, Iran, Israel, America* as told to Phyllis I. Rosenteur (New York, 1986), pp. 188–90.

[44] Cohen, *ha-Peᶜīlūt ha-Ṣiyyōnīt be-ᶜIrāq,* p. 210; Albion Ross, "Jews Leaving Iraq in a Steady Flow: Heavier Traffic across Border into Iran Is Attributed to Lifting of Martial Law," *New York Times* (February 7, 1950): 11. See also PRO (London) FO 371/91693, H. Beeley (Baghdad) to G. W. Furlonge (London), January 27, 1951: "total of illegal emigrants is slightly greater than the 10,000 which we had estimated it to be hitherto." On dealings with Iranian officials regarding the refugees, see Hillel, *Operation Babylon,* pp. 197–205; for a personal account of the Teheran refugee camp, see Haddad, *Flight from Babylon,* pp. 218–44.

The government of Iraq was being caused considerable embarrassment both domestically and internationally by the flood of illegal emigration. It also considered the continued presence of large numbers of disaffected people who remained in the country against their will to be a risk to security and economic stability. Because of the uncertain climate, many Jewish businessmen had stopped reinvesting their capital in local enterprises. Many more Jews were trying to dispose of their assets and to transfer funds out of the country. The national economy had also been seriously affected by a decline in oil revenues caused by the closing of the pipeline terminating at Haifa.

In an attempt to stabilize the situation and to solve its Jewish problem once and for all, the government of Prime Minister Tawfīq al-Suwaydī introduced a bill in the Iraqi Parliament at the beginning of March 1950 that would in effect permit Jews who desired to leave the country for good to do so after renouncing their Iraqi citizenship. The bill also provided for the denaturalization of those Jews who had already left the country. During the parliamentary debate, the elderly Jewish Senator Ezra Menahem Daniel urged the government to reassure the Jews who wished to remain in Iraq by removing the severe official restrictions and the no less debilitating unofficial discrimination to which they had been subject. Interior Minister Ṣāliḥ Jabr, who had introduced the bill, replied that Jews who remained in the country would be considered "as Iraqis equal with Muslim and Christian Iraqis so long as they obeyed the law and acted in accordance with the national interest," adding perhaps somewhat disingenuously, "the constitution was a guarantee of this." The measure was duly passed in the Chamber of Deputies on March 2 and in the Senate on March 4 as Law No. 1 of 1950 (Annexure to the Ordinance for the Cancellation of Iraqi Nationality, Law No. 62 of 1933). It was to remain in force for one year.[45]

Iraqi government officials thought that only about 6,000 or 7,000—and at most 10,000—Jews would take advantage of the new law and that most of these would come from the poorer classes. This view was shared at the time by the British diplomats in Baghdad and by a few Israelis as well. During the first few weeks following the enactment of the law, only a few dozen individuals presented themselves for denaturalization. Representatives of the Zionist organization in Iraq spread the word for Jews to hold back, while many unclarified

[45] For the text of the law and a summary of the debate in the Iraqi Senate, see Part Two, pp. 522–526. A lengthier summary may be found in al-Sūdānī , *al-Nashāṭ al-Ṣahyūnī fi'l-ʿIrāq,* pp. 192–211.

details as to just how they would be gotten out of the country were being clarified. (There was in fact a debate in Israel whether the financially beleaguered state, which was already overwhelmed with immigrants, would even be able to accommodate large numbers of Iraqi refugees.)[46]

When arrangements for an airlift of those Jews wishing to leave the country were finalized between Near East Transport, the same American company (now secretly a partner with El Al) that had carried out Operation Magic Carpet, and the Iraqi government, the Zionist organization in Iraq issued the call at the end of Passover (April 8, 1950) for Jews to come forward and register for emigration. By the end of the month, 47,000 people had appeared at registration centers set up at the major synagogues and had signed the following declaration:

> I declare willingly and voluntarily that I have decided to leave Iraq permanently and that I am aware this statement of mine will have the effect of depriving me of Iraqi nationality and of causing my deportation from Iraq and of preventing me forever afterward from returning.[47]

By January 13, 1951, a total of 85,893 people, or about two thirds of all Iraqi Jews, had registered for emigration to Israel. Because of the slowness of the airlift, dubbed Operation Ezra and Nehemiah (popularly called Operation Ali Baba), only a little over 23,000 of the would-be emigrants had been flown out of the country. The plight—not to mention the morale—of those who were still waiting to leave was becoming increasingly precarious. The number of stateless individuals without employment, and in many instances without homes, was growing daily. (It could take up to two months for a person to be officially denaturalized after having signed the preceding declaration.) The newly installed government of Nūrī al-Saʿīd increased the pressure to speed up the emigration process by threaten-

[46] PRO (London) FO 371/82478, H. Trevelyan (Baghdad) to Bevin, March 7, 1950; Hillel, *Operation Babylon,* pp. 227–32. Even a "maximalist" estimate like Hillel's envisaged only about 70,000 Jews choosing to leave. See also Yosef Meir [Yehoshafat], *Beyond the Desert: Underground Activities in Iraq, 1941–1951* (Tel Aviv, 1973), pp. 191–95 [Heb.].

[47] Text of declaration cited in Schechtman, *On Wings of Eagles,* p. 112. For the negotiations with Iraqi officials, which were actually carried out by Shlomo (Selim) Hillel incognito, see his own account, Hillel, *Operation Babylon,* pp. 233–60. For an Arab historian's view, see Shiblak, *The Lure of Zion,* pp. 115–19. The Zionist underground's call for Jews to register for emigration is translated in Part Two, p. 527.

ing to drive the stateless Jews across the border into neighboring Kuwait, if they were not out of the country by the March deadline.[48]

Tensions in Iraq mounted further after a hand grenade was thrown on January 14, 1951, into a group of Jews in the courtyard of the Masᶜūda Shemtov Synagogue, one of the main registration centers in Baghdad. Five people were killed and at least fourteen injured as they were about to leave for the airport. The incident remains unsolved to this day. Jewish sources tend to blame Arab extremists, whereas Arab sources and pro-Arab sympathizers blame the Zionist underground, whose caches of arms were discovered later that same year. The Iraqi government accused the Zionists variously of wishing to discredit Iraq, to pressure Israel into speeding up the protracted airlift, and to sow panic among the Jewish population in order to stampede those who had not registered for emigration into doing so. Much of the evidence for these accusations by Iraq came from the show trials of Zionists held in December 1951. Both sides in this historical dispute, over which a considerable amount of ink has been spilled, are certainly plausible. Neither side, however, has provided truly convincing evidence, and for any detached observer the point must remain moot.[49]

[48] PRO (London) 371/91689, several documents from which are included in Part Two, pp. 528–529.

[49] Meir, *Beyond the Desert,* p. 205 [Heb.], implies that circles within the police or the military may have been responsible. Shlomo Shina, Jacob Elazar, and Emmanuel Naḥtomi, *Perāqīm be-Tōldōt ha-Maḥteret* (Tel Aviv, 1970), p. 31, point either to the government wishing to frighten off the rich Jews in order to take their assets or, alternatively, to the opposition Istiqlāl party that wished to embarrass the government. Cohen, *ha-Peᶜīlūt ha-Ṣiyyōnīt be-ᶜIrāq,* pp. 211–212, summarizes Jewish and Arab views and judiciously concludes "the material available to the researcher at present is insufficient for judging." For the Arab view, see Shiblak, *The Lure of Zion,* pp. 119–27. Shiblak, however, in addition to a number of factual errors of his own, is overly dependent upon Marion Woolfson, *Prophets in Babylon: Jews in the Arab World* (London and Boston, 1980), pp. 182–99. Woolfson's work is a thoroughly unreliable polemic. Kedourie, *The Chatham House Version and Other Middle-Eastern Studies,* p. 312, finds the Iraqi government's allegations plausible, but merely notes dryly that "the Zionists were capable of using such tactics." Hillel, *Operation Babylon,* pp. 273–84, vigorously denies the charges made against the Zionist underground and dismisses any analogies made to the so-called Unfortunate Business (also known as the Lavon Affair) of the mid-1950s in Egypt. British diplomatic records from the period merely report the incident and some prevailing theories without drawing any conclusions. One report mentions "a rumour circulating in the bazaars" that an Iraqi army officer had been arrested for complicity in the crime. See PRO (London) FO 371/91689, T. E. Bromley (Baghdad) to Eastern Department, February 3, 1951. A later report filed at the time that arms caches were uncovered and Zionists arrested found the theory that Jews might have been responsible for the bombings "more

Whoever was behind the bomb attack, and whatever the motive may have been, it is an undisputed fact that over the following seven weeks leading up to the March 9 deadline, after which registration for emigration would no longer be accepted, nearly 30,000 additional Jews signed up for departure, and the pace of the airlift was accelerated dramatically. The Iraqi authorities even dropped their earlier insistence that the departing Jews fly first to Cyprus and, as of March 12, permitted the planes to carry them directly from Baghdad to Lod Airport in Israel.[50]

Only one day after the registration deadline passed, the Iraqi Parliament, convened in secret session by Prime Minister Nūrī al-Saᶜīd, passed Law No. 5 of 1951, which froze the assets of all departing Jews and placed them under the control of a government bureau, in effect stripping the émigrés of all they possessed. The Parliament also passed a second law (Law No. 12 of 1951), which declared that all Iraqi Jews who were abroad and did not return home within a specific period would forfeit both their nationality and their property. It is clear that Nūrī had waited until after the expiration of the registration deadline in order not to frighten off any prospective emigrants and thereby maximize the government's windfall. Estimates of the total value of the frozen Jewish assets at the time ranged from as low as the Iraqi government's figure of $50 million to as high as $436 million put forward by the Israelis. Less politically inspired estimates of $150 million to $200 million do not seem unreasonable. Although some individuals succeeded in smuggling out considerable sums after March 10, 1951 (often via the Beirut black market), many more were reduced to paupers, being allowed to take out only 50 dinars ($140) per adult and 20 to 30 dinars ($56 to $84) per minor depending upon age. Most émigrés were thoroughly searched—and frequently subjected to all sorts of abuse—upon departure.[51]

---

plausible than most." See FO 371/91693, H. Beeley (Baghdad) to G. W. Furlonge (Foreign Office), June 27, 1951.

[50] Schechtman, *On Wings of Eagles,* pp. 117–18.

[51] Al-Ḥasanī, *Ta'rīkh al-Wizārāt al-ᶜIrāqiyya,* vol. 8, pp. 189–92; al-Sūdānī, *al-Nashāṭ al-Ṣahyūnī fi'l-ᶜIrāq,* pp. 239–41; Shiblak, *The Lure of Zion,* pp. 89–90; Kedourie, *The Chatham House Version and Other Middle-Eastern Studies,* pp. 312–13; Schechtman, *On Wings of Eagles,* pp. 119–23; Robinson, *The Arab Countries of the Near East and Their Jewish Communities,* pp. 59–65; AJDC (Jerusalem) 321B.23 and 241A.9; PRO (London) FO 371/91690 contains the texts of the property laws and is published in Shiblak, *The Lure of Zion,* App. 5, pp. 144–52. Concerning funds smuggled out of the country, see FO 371/91691, A. B. Horn (Tel Aviv) to Eastern Department, April 17, 1951. On the treatment of departing Jews, see Resner, *Eternal Stranger,* pp. 150–51; and Hillel, *Operation Babylon,* pp. 257–58.

By the end of 1951, only about 6,000 Jews remained in Iraq. Operation Ezra and Nehemiah had evacuated 113,545 people. Another 20,000 had left the country illegally. Most of those who chose to remain in Iraq were prosperous and despite some restrictions and inconveniences were able, after the fury of the late 1940s and early 1950s had died down, to return to relatively normal, comfortable lives for at least another decade.

The exodus from Syria was of mass proportions in relation to the smallness of the community, but it was in no way organized. Most Syrian Jews simply melted across the country's borders individually or in small groups despite the considerable personal risks. (In November 1950, for example, thirty Syrian Jews were murdered at sea by a band of smugglers who had agreed to ferry them to Israel.) The outward flow had been going on steadily since the last years of World War II and gathered momentum just before and after the creation of the State of Israel. Reports emanating from Beirut in May 1950 indicated that the Syrian authorities were considering following Iraq's example of permitting Jews to emigrate freely upon their renunciation of citizenship. However, nothing came of these reports, and the illegal emigration continued. From 1948 to 1953, approximately 4,000 Syrian Jews succeeded in making their way to Israel. Many Syrian Jews settled in neighboring Lebanon, where they became the majority of the Jewish community of 11,000. Lebanon, with its generally tolerant, laissez-faire atmosphere and multiethnic composition, was in fact the only Arab country whose Jewish population increased after the first Arab-Israeli war.

By the mid-1950s, only about 5,300 Jews remained in Syria. Don Peretz, who visited there in 1957, describes the remnant of Syrian Jewry as living, "if not in terror, certainly in constant fear, bedeviled by the Syrian security forces." He also depicted the Jews in the three remaining communities of Damascus, Aleppo, and Qamishli as generally poor and dependent upon charity from abroad.[52]

There was a significant wave of Jewish departures from Egypt in the immediate aftermath of the first Arab-Israeli war, but it did not assume proportions comparable to the mass emigrations discussed so far. Between 1949 and 1952, 25,000 to 30,000 Jews left Egypt. About

[52] Don Peretz, *Jews in Egypt, Syria, Lebanon and Iraq, July 1957,* unpublished confidential report submitted to the American Jewish Committee (New York, 1957), pp. 23–24; AJDC (Jerusalem) 378A.5 Syria, C File (March 1951); Schechtman, *On Wings of Eagles,* pp. 164–66; Robinson, *The Arab Countries of the Near East and Their Jewish Communities,* p. 79.

15,000 to 20,000 of these went to Israel, usually via Marseille or Genoa, where they underwent preparation in Zionist training (*hakhshāra*) camps. Many Jews who left at this time belonged to the lower and lower middle classes, were technically stateless individuals, and had been hurt by the Egyptianization laws. In many cases their passage and other related expenses were paid by international Jewish organizations such as the Joint Distribution Committee and the Jewish Agency, as well as by wealthier members of the Egyptian Jewish community, who, as Gudrun Krämer has remarked, saw this as a "discreet way of promoting the departure of their poorest stratum."[53] The Egyptian government facilitated this exodus by lifting the travel restrictions that had been instituted during the war with Israel and by looking aside as travel agencies operated by agents of the Mōsād (the Israeli Organization for Clandestine ᶜAliya) made arrangements more or less openly for Jews who wished to leave for Israel.[54]

Although some members of the Jewish upper class emigrated at this time, mainly to Europe and the Americas, most of the middle and upper classes opted to remain in Egypt. The anti-Jewish violence of the late 1940s had been instigated by extremist groups like the Muslim Brotherhood and was not perceived to be government sanctioned. Indeed, the government viewed the Brotherhood as a threat to its own existence, had declared it illegal, and was probably behind the assassination of its leader, Ḥasan al-Bannā', in February 1949. With the exception of communists, most Jews were released from detention, and property sequestered during the Arab-Israeli war was returned to its Jewish owners. Furthermore, unlike Iraq and Syria, the Egyptian government did not pass specifically discriminatory Jewish legislation, nor did it even make "Zionism" a specific offense in the criminal code (although it did make "activities" for the benefit of a state with which Egypt had broken relations or was at war grounds for forfeiting citizenship). Finally, nationalist agitation and popular attention were turned primarily toward the British presence in the Canal Zone and only secondarily toward Israel and the Jews.

Despite some lingering anxieties, Jewish life in Egypt regained a certain degree of normalcy. Jews generally maintained their social and economic prominence. The leadership of the Jewish community was aging and noticeably weaker, but communal institutions such as schools and hospitals continued to function, albeit on a reduced scale.

[53] Krämer, *Minderheit, Millet, Nation?*, p. 425.

[54] Ibid., pp. 424–26; Gottesman, "Israel in Egypt," pp. 73–74; Robinson, *The Arab Countries of the Near East and Their Jewish Communities*, pp. 72–73.

Several Jewish journals still appeared, including the Karaite bimonthly magazine *al-Kalīm,* Albert Mizraḥi's political and business weekly *al-Tasᶜīra,* and Sol Mizraḥi's pro-Wafdist daily *al-Ṣirāḥa* (founded in 1950). Some Zionist cultural organizations continued as private discussion groups, and a Maccabee club openly played football matches again. The overall good relations between the Jewish community and the Egyptian authorities continued—and for a while even improved—after the Free Officers' Revolution overthrew the monarchy in July 1952.[55]

As in the case of Egypt, there was a significant though not overwhelming Jewish exodus from the Maghreb in the years immediately following the establishment of the State of Israel. Between 1948 and 1953, approximately 46,000 North African Jews went to Israel. More than half of them came from Morocco—28,781, or slightly more than 10 percent of Moroccan Jewry. The smallest group came from Algeria. Only about 1,000 Algerian Jews, or less than 1 percent of that country's Jewish population, immigrated to Israel during this period.[56]

This initial North African ᶜaliya was not the result of any urgent sense of fear for physical security or of outright political oppression, but rather it was the genuine expression of a quasi-messianic enthusiasm that swept over Maghrebi Jewry in the wake of Israel's victory in the Arab-Israeli war. Although Zionist emissaries had been active in the region since 1943 and conducted extensive propagandizing after 1948, most of the émigrés were not attracted by the ideologies of modern political Zionism (in fact, most Moroccan and Algerian Jews—though not the Tunisians—were shocked by the factional rivalries among the emissaries from the various movements). A considerable proportion of those who were members of the pioneering movements, about 1,500 young people, had already left clandestinely for Palestine from 1947 to 1948 to take part in Israel's struggle for independence. (Nearly half of them were caught by British coastal

[55] Krämer, *Minderheit, Millet, Nation?,* pp. 423, 428–29; Sihām Naṣṣār, *al-Yahūd al-Miṣriyyūn bayn al-Miṣriyya wa 'l-Ṣahyūniyya* (Beirut, 1980), pp. 70–76, 81–83; Gottesman, "Israel in Egypt," pp. 74–75; Cohen, *The Jews of the Middle East,* p. 51; Peretz, *Egyptian Jews Today,* pp. 43–46.

[56] For ᶜaliya statistics, see Schechtman, *On Wings of Eagles,* pp. 289–321, 334; also Doris Bensimon-Donath, *Immigrants d'Afrique du Nord en Israël: évolution et adaption* (Paris, 1970), p. 559, Annex 4 (where, however, the figures given for Algeria are much too high); and Michael M. Laskier, "The Jewish Agency and the Jews of Morocco and Tunisia," *Proceedings of the Ninth World Congress of Jewish Studies, Division B,* vol. 3 (Jerusalem, 1986): 95, Table.

patrols and interned in Cyprus until the end of the Mandate in May 1948.[57])

Many thousands more, particularly from among the poorer sectors of Moroccan Jewry, wished to immigrate to Israel in these early years but were prevented from doing so by a policy of Selective Immigration (Heb. *seleqṣeya*) which was adopted in mid-1951, placing severe restrictions upon Maghrebi Jews who could not pay their own way. Only families acompanied by a breadwinner aged eighteen to forty-five and in good health were accepted by the Jewish Agency. Even if the family had a breadwinner who had already gone to Israel, it could be turned away. If one member of the family was crippled or suffered from a serious illness, the entire family was rejected. Witnesses describe pathetic scenes in ᶜaliya offices. Even those who were selected often had to wait months, first in the camp near Casablanca, and later in the Arenas camp outside Marseille.

The rationale for this often-cruel policy was twofold. First, the State of Israel was undergoing an economic crisis and was already inundated with immigrants and thus, according to the prevailing opinion, had to exert some control where possible. Second, the North African Jews were not in any imminent danger and therefore did not have the same priority as the Libyans, Yemenites, and Iraqis, or the survivors of the European Holocaust. The *seleqṣeya* policy, which was applied exclusively to North Africans, may also have been influenced in part by a growing prejudice among veteran Ashkenazim in Israel against Oriental Jews in general and North Africans in particular—and most especially against Moroccans—as primitive and violent individuals. They were considered to be—to use a popular expression from the period—"poor human material." These unjust stereotypes may have been reinforced by the rather contemptuous attitude of the North African Jewish elite toward their own poor. For example, Isaac Abbou, the president of the Jewish community of Rabat, referred to "the great majority" of Moroccan emigrants as "the dregs of the mellahs."[58]

[57] Ephraim Ben Ḥayyim, "ha-Haᶜpāla mi-Ṣefōn Afrīqa: Shalōsh hā-Oniyyōt, 1947," *Shorāshīm ba-Mizraḥ: Qevāṣīm le-Ḥeqer ha-Tenūᶜa ha-Ṣiyyōnīt veha-Ḥalūṣīt ba-Arṣōt hā-Islām,* vol. 1, ed. Itshak Avrahami (Tel Aviv, 1986), pp. 241–320; Bensimon-Donath, *Immigrants d'Afrique du Nord en Israël,* pp. 85–91; Michael M. Laskier, "Hebbēṭīm Pōlīṭiyyīm ve-Irgūniyyīm shel hā-ᶜaliyya mi-Marōqō ba-Shānīm 1949–1956," *ha-Ṣiyyōnūt* 12 (1987): 334–35.

[58] Quoted in Bensimon-Donath, *Immigrants d'Afrique du Nord en Israël,* p. 95. The most virulent expression of anti–North African prejudice that describes Maghrebi immigrants in Israel as totally devoid of any redeeming characteristics and

The selective immigration policy engendered considerable bitterness among North African Jews, as did reports of anti-Oriental and anti-Maghrebi prejudice on the one hand and the difficult conditions of life in Israel on the other. Some *ᶜōlīm* in fact returned to North Africa during the early 1950s.[59]

THE SECOND STAGE OF THE EXODUS

The initial waves of Jewish emigration from the Arab world were followed by a period—longer in some places, shorter in others—of relative tranquillity and security.

The new revolutionary regime in Egypt, which came to power in July 1952, went out of its way to reassure Jews and other minorities that had been badly shaken by the events of the late 1940s and early 1950s. General Muḥammad Najīb, the popular figurehead of the ruling Revolutionary Command Council, made public visits to Jewish communal institutions in Cairo and Alexandria, including an unprecedented appearance for an Egyptian head of state at Cairo's Great Synagogue on Yom Kippur, just two months after coming to power. The new government pointedly refused to identify the local Jewish community with the Zionist enemy and vigorously rejected calls within the Arab League for freezing Jewish property in all the member states. As Jewish confidence began to be restored, some Jews began to hearken to Najīb's call and began bringing back capital they had abroad for reinvestment in Egypt.[60]

This brief halcyon period began to end in 1954, when Jamāl ᶜAbd al-Nāṣir, the real force behind the revolution, desposed General Najīb. During that same year, an espionage and sabotage ring composed of young Egyptian Jews working for Israel was uncovered. Two of the defendants, Dr. Moses Leito Marzouk and Samuel Azar, were hanged in January 1955 and six others sentenced to prison. This

---

compares them unfavorably to the Yemenites is the article by Aryeh Gelblum, "ᶜAliyyat Tēmān u-Vᶜāyat Afrīqa," *Haaretz* (April 22, 1949): 2.

59 Concerning *seleqṣeya,* see B. Gil, "The Selectivity of the North African Aliyah," *AR* 10, no. 29 (February 1955): 25–28; Laskier, "Hebbēṭīm Pōlīṭiyyīm ve-Irgūniyyīm shel hā-ᶜaliyya mi-Marōqō ba-Shānīm 1949–1956," pp. 341–43; Schechtman, *On Wings of Eagles,* pp. 289–91.

60 Maurice Mizrahi, *L'Egypte et ses Juifs: Les temps révolu (XIXᵉ et XXᵉ siècle)* (Geneva, 1977), pp. 56–57; Peretz, *Egyptian Jews Today,* pp. 23–24, 27.

fiasco could not help but undermine efforts to stabilize the position of the Jewish community in Egypt.[61]

The October 1956 war, in which Great Britain, France, and Israel attacked Egypt following the nationalization of the Suez Canal, provided the coup de grace to Egyptian Jewry. In marked contrast to 1948, there was no mob violence against Jews or their property. The government, however, responded swiftly with harsh measures aimed at Jews and foreigners. Most of the Jewish leaders of Cairo and Alexandria were rounded up in a wave of mass arrests. At least 900 Jews were detained or imprisoned. More than half of them were interned in the Jewish Sybil School in Cairo's Abbasiyya suburb. An additional 500 heads of households were summoned to police stations and summarily ordered to leave the country, either alone or together with their families within two to seven days. Proclamation No. 4 of November 1, 1956, provided for the freezing of bank accounts and the sequestration of property of both internees and suspects. Among those whose property was seized was Salvatore Circurel, president of the Cairene Jewish community and owner of one of Egypt's leading department stores. There were mass dismissals of Jewish employees everywhere. The undefined crime of "Zionism" was now specifically mentioned in the penal code and was grounds for loss of citizenship.

Panic spread rapidly through Egyptian Jewry. During the twelve months that followed the war, approximately 30,000 Jews, about 60 percent of the entire community, left Egypt. Most of the émigrés were required to leave behind almost everything they possessed except for a few items of clothing. The International Red Cross played a major role in facilitating this exodus with behind-the-scenes funding by the American Joint Distribution Committee. Most of the stateless individuals and Egyptian citizens who had been stripped of their nationality went to Israel. Although the pace of emigration eased considerably by mid-1957, the departure of Jews continued unabated. Three years later, only about 10,000 Jews remained in the country, and by the time the third Arab-Israeli war broke out in 1967, their number had shrunk to a mere 2,500 to 3,000 souls.[62]

[61] This security mishap precipitated Israel's notorious "Lavon Affair." For the very different perspectives of participants in the events, see Aviezer Golan, *Operation Susannah. As Told to Aviezer Golan by Marcelle Ninio, Victor Levy, Robert Dassa and Philip Natanson,* trans. Peretz Kidron (New York and London, 1978); and Avri El-Ad with James Creech, *Decline of Honor* (Chicago, 1976). See also Eliyahu Hasin and Dan Horowitz, *The Affair* (Tel Aviv, 1961) [Heb.].

[62] There is extensive documentation on the situation of Egyptian Jewry in the wake of the Suez War in AJDC (Jerusalem) 245A.7 and 16; 250B.51; 306A.3;

It was not the repercussions of the Suez conflict but the disengagement of France from its colonial empire in North Africa and the reintegration of the region into the the Arab world that set in motion the second great wave of Jewish emigration from that region. Already in 1954, there was mounting anxiety both within Maghrebi Jewry and within world Jewish organizations after French Premier Mendès-France proposed granting greater autonomy for Tunisia and gradual internal reforms for Morocco. Mendès-France's controversial initiative, which led to the fall of his government, was taken in response to a rising tide of nationalist agitation in the two protectorates. Most of the violence in North Africa during the early to mid-1950s was aimed at the French, not at the Jews. (It has even been claimed that the Moroccan resistance deliberately chose to throw a bomb into Fez's popular Café de la Renaissance on the eve of Yom Kippur because it knew that no Jews would be there at that time.[63])

Most Jews stood on the sidelines during the years of nationalist agitation, observing a studied neutrality, torn by conflicting feelings for their native land, for their French mentors, and for their reestablished Jewish homeland in the Middle East. Only a small handful of individuals, like André Barouche in Tunisia, Joseph Ohana in Morocco, and some leftist students at French universities, were actually attracted to the active ranks of the nationalists.[64]

In Algeria, where the long, bloody national revolution was only just beginning in 1954, "a significant proportion" of Jewish intellectuals was at first sympathetic to the FLN (Front de Libération Nationale), while the communal leadership maintained its traditional stance that the Jewish community was not a political entity and that individual members could only speak for themselves. At the same time,

---

306B.3 and 8; 307A.10–16; 307B.1–28; 307C.2–4; 308A.1–6; 308B.1; and 321A.67. Especially informative is the unpublished monograph of Edmond Muller, *Entre Juifs et Arabes: le conflit de Suez et ses consequences* in 306A.3. (Muller was head of the International Red Cross Delegation in Egypt between 1956 and 1962.) See also Peretz, *Jews in Egypt, Syria, Lebanon and Iraq, July 1957,* pp. 1–19; Mizrahi, *L'Egypte et ses Juifs,* pp. 128–32; Krämer, *Minderheit, Millet, Nation?,* pp. 429–30; Gottesman, "Israel in Egypt," pp. 82–85; and Michael M. Laskier, "From War to War: The Jews of Egypt from 1948 to 1970," *Studies in Zionism* 7, no. 1 (Spring 1986): 131–37.

[63] Joseph Levy, "Témoignage d'un militant juif marocain," in *Juifs du Maroc: Identité et dialogue,* Actes du Colloque International sur la Communauté Juive Marocaine (Paris, 1980), pp. 281–82. The same author also claims that the resistance attacked collaborators, but never attacked Jews, no matter what their position was vis-à-vis the national movement.

[64] Ibid., pp. 279–82; Michel Meyer Albo, "Militants juifs pour l'indépendance du Maroc," *Nouveaux Cahiers* no. 70 (Autumn 1982): 64–70; Doris Bensimon-

though, the leadership pointed out that the members of the Jewish community were French citizens. Jews on the whole kept their distance from both the Muslims and the European colonists. However, as Jews began to become the victims of FLN terrorist attacks from 1956 on, a small number were attracted to the counterrevolutionary OAS (Organisation Armée Secrète).[65]

Jewish emigration rose dramatically as Morocco and Tunisia neared independence despite frequent public and private assurance by the nationalists that Jews would be equal citizens in the new independent, democratic states. Most Jews were not convinced by these statements. The tense atmosphere, the sagging economy, increased competition between Muslims and Jews for jobs, and opposing sympathies with regard to the Middle East conflict made for considerable intercommunal friction. The smaller Jewish communities outside the main population centers felt especially isolated and vulnerable. So too did the Jewish urban poor who overwhelmingly wished to go to Israel. With an easing of the policy of *seleqṣeya,* nearly 25,000 Jews left Morocco for Israel in 1955, and over 36,000 in the first half of 1956. More than 12,000 Tunisian Jews also went on ᶜaliya during the same two-year period.[66]

Much larger numbers would have left Morocco had not the new Moroccan government placed a ban on organized emigration and ordered the local Zionist organization Cadima to dissolve itself in June 1956. This move by the authorities left stranded some 50,000 Jews who had already registered for ᶜaliya, as well as an equal number

---

Donath, *Evolution du Judaïsme marocain sous le protectorat français, 1912–1956* (Paris and the Hague, 1968), pp. 115–16; and Chouraqui, *Between East and West,* p. 267.

[65] Alistair Horne, *A Savage War of Peace: Algeria 1954–1962* (New York, 1978), pp. 59, 140, 410–11, 432; Richard Ayoun and Bernard Cohen, *Les Juifs d'Algérie: deux mille ans d'histoire* (Paris, 1982), pp. 167–78; and Régine Goutalier, in "Les Juifs et l'O.A.S. en Oranie," in *Les relations entre Juifs et Musulmans en Afrique du Nord, XIXᵉ-XXᵉ siècles* (Paris, 1980), pp. 188–96. See also Elizabeth D. Friedman, "The Jews of Batna, Algeria: A Study of Identity and Colonialism" (Ph.D. diss., City University of New York, 1977), pp. 177–90. For the thoughts of an Algerian Jewish intellectual on Muslim-Jewish relations during this period, see Part Two, pp. 542–547.

[66] On nationalist assurances, see Bensimon-Donath, *Evolution du Judaïsme marocain sous le protectorat français,* pp. 114–15; Schechtman, *On Wings of Eagles,* pp. 282–85, 314–15; Naomi W. Cohen, *Not Free to Desist: The American Jewish Committee, 1906–1966* (Philadelphia, 1972), pp. 515–17; and PRO (London) FO 371/108605, A. M. Williams (Tunis) to T. E. Bromley (African Department), August 12, 1954. On the economy, job competition, and intercommunal tensions, see Michael M. Laskier, "The Instability of Moroccan Jewry and the Moroccan Press in the First Decade after Independence," *Jewish History* 1, no. 1 (Spring 1986): 39–41; Robert Attal and Claude Sitbon, *Regards sur les Juifs de Tunisie* (Paris, 1979), p. 23. For

who had expressed interest in registering. Although Jews were still legally allowed to leave the country individually, the government ban on organized departures effectively put an end to the mass flight since, as one British diplomat in Rabat observed, "in practice . . . the type of Moroccan Jew who wishes to emigrate cannot do so without the aid of some organisation such as Cadima."[67] As of 1957, it became difficult for individuals—Jewish or Muslim—to obtain passports.

In contrast to the Moroccan government's restrictive policy, Tunisia continued to allow free emigration under the aegis of the Jewish Agency, although Tunisian officials openly deplored the steady outflow of the Jewish population to France (approximately one third of the country's Jews had French citizenship) and Israel. During the year following independence alone, more than 10,000 Jews left Tunisia. About two thirds of these went to Israel.[68]

When Morocco and Tunisia achieved independence in March 1956, genuine efforts were made by the respective leaders of the two countries, Muḥammad V and Ḥabīb Bourguiba, to show goodwill and win over their anxious Jewish communities. In each country a Jew was appointed to the cabinet. Dr. Léon Benzaquen was named minister of posts, telephone, and telegraph in Morocco, and André Barouche was appointed minister of planning and construction in Tunisia. Jews were also given positions in the government bureaucracy in both countries. In Morocco, an elite group for promoting mutual understanding between Muslims and Jews, called al-Wifāq (Entente), was formed within the Istiqlāl party under the leadership of Jewish political activists like Marc Sabbah, a follower of Mahdī Ben Barka.[69]

These initial gestures of goodwill, sincere though they may have been, were ultimately unsuccessful. They were quickly overshadowed

---

emigration statistics, see Laskier, "The Jewish Agency and the Jews of Morocco and Tunisia," p. 95, Table.

[67] PRO (London) FO 371/119528, Ambassador H.W.A. Freese-Pennefather (Rabat) to Foreign Secretary Selwyn Lloyd, June 21, 1956. See also the enclosures to ibid.; and Schechtman, *On Wings of Eagles,* pp. 298–30.

[68] Schechtman, *On Wings of Eagles,* pp. 322–24.

[69] Concerning Jews in government, see Muḥammad al-Ḥabīb b. al-Khōja, *Yahūd al-Maghrib al-ᶜArabī* (Cairo, 1973), pp. 175, 182–83; Ṣalāḥ al-ᶜAqqād, "al-Yahūd fi 'l-Maghrib al-ᶜArabī," *Majallat Maᶜhad al-Buḥūth wa 'l-Dirāsāt al-ᶜArabiyya* 3 (March 1972): 54; Michael M. Laskier, *The Alliance Israélite Universelle and the Jewish Communities of Morocco, 1862–1962* (Albany, N.Y., 1983), p. 57. Concerning al-Wifāq, see Michael M. Laskier, "Etre Juif modéré ou radical au Maroc indépendant," *Le Monde Sepharade* 5 (June–July 1983): 13–15; idem, "Zionism and the Jewish Communities of Morocco: 1956–1962," *Studies in Zionism* 6, no. 1 (1985): 121–24; Hal Lehrmann, "L'El-Wifaq chez les Juifs marocains: 'entente cordiale' ou collabora-

by events and trends that further undermined the confidence of most Jews regarding their future in postcolonial North Africa. Neither Jewish minister survived the first reshuffling of their respective cabinets. More significantly, no Jew was appointed again to a ministerial post in either Morocco or Tunisia. The proponents of intercommunal entente made little impression on the Jewish and Muslim masses from whom they were totally removed. The cordiality shown to Jews in some of the highest echelons of government did not percolate down to the lower ranks of officialdom, which exhibited attitudes that ranged from traditional contempt to outright hostility. The natural progression in both countries toward increased identification with the rest of the Arab world (first Morocco, then Tunisia, entered the Arab League in 1958) only widened the gulf between Muslims and Jews. Furthermore, government steps to reduce Jewish communal autonomy, such as Tunisian Law No. 58-78 of July 11, 1958, which dissolved the Jewish Communal Council of Tunis and replaced it with the Provisional Commission for the Oversight of Jewish Religious Matters, having far more circumscribed authority, had negative psychological consequences for Jews, who saw their traditional structures under siege. The official pressure on Jewish educational institutions for arabization and cultural conformity only succeeded in feeding the Jews' worst fears, rather than fostering their integration.[70]

Jewish emigration from Tunisia continued steadily and gained momentum after the crisis of 1961, when France and Tunisia became embroiled in violent confrontations over the continued presence of the French naval base at Bizerte. At the height of the crisis, Jews were accused in the nationalist press of being sympathetic to France and a potentially disloyal element. By the time the Six-Day War broke out between Israel and the Middle Eastern Arab states in June 1967, Tunisian Jewry had dwindled to about 23,000 persons.

The third Arab-Israeli war proved to be the final blow to the still not insubstantial remnant of Tunisian Jewry. On June 5, 1967,

---

tion," *L'Arche* (August–September and October): 32–36, 27–47, respectively; and idem, "Report from Morocco," *Midstream* 4, no. 3 (Summer 1958): 10–12.

[70] Laskier, "The Instability of Moroccan Jewry and the Moroccan Press in the First Decade after Independence," pp. 41–49; idem, *The Alliance Israélite Universelle and the Jewish Communities of Morocco,* pp. 321–23, 330–34, 339–42; Charles Haddad de la Paz, *Juifs et Arabes au pays de Bourguiba* (Aix-en-Provence, 1977), pp. 105–232; Schechtman, *On Wings of Eagles,* pp. 319–21; H. Z. [J. W.] Hirschberg, *A History of the Jews in North Africa,* vol. 2 (Leiden, 1981), pp. 144–45; AJDC (Jerusalem) 250A.49, A. J. Easterman, "Report on Visit to Tunisia. 28th September–3rd October, 1958." (This report contains a detailed and enlightening account

widespread anti-Jewish rioting in Tunis, the capital, where the vast majority of Jews lived, resulted in the looting of most Jewish shops and businesses and the desecration and burning of the Great Synagogue. A sense of almost total despair took hold of the community despite President Bourguiba's strong condemnation of the riots and government promises to punish the perpetrators and make restitution. In the words of one eyewitness, "It is the unanimous opinion of Jews one talks to that if there was any doubt about the question previously, it is quite clear now that there is no future for them in Tunisia." Most fled to France. Within a year, only about 7,000 to 8,000 Jews remained in the country.[71]

Although legal mass emigration from Morocco had been halted by the authorities in 1956, clandestine departures organized by agents of the Israeli Mōsād continued throughout the remainder of the decade and into the early 1960s. In the four years following the dissolution of Cadima and the imposition of the ban on ᶜaliya activities, nearly 18,000 Moroccan Jews were spirited out of the country. Moroccan officials frequently looked aside as this underground exodus was taking place. Only during the premiership of ᶜAbd Allāh Ibrāhīm (December 1958 to May 1960), who represented the radical wing of the Istiqlāl party, was there a serious attempt to clamp down on illegal movement, and a special emigration section was established in the police department that carried out numerous arrests of Jews attempting or even suspected of planning to emigrate illegally.

Shortly before his sudden death in February 1961, King Muḥammad V decided to reverse the policy banning Jewish emigration. This decision was prompted by a genuine desire—both pragmatic and benevolent—to settle the Jewish problem once and for all, to reverse the growing influence of Nasserism in the country, which had become painfully evident during the Casablanca Conference of African States in January of that year, and to counter the negative international publicity that had been generated by the drowning of forty-four Jews, whose small boat, the Pisces, foundered off the northern Moroccan coast on the night of January 10, 1961, as they were attempting to flee the country. With the door to emigration now opened, 70,000 more Jews left Morocco over the next three years

---

of the author's conversations with Bourguiba and portraits of the Jewish communal leaders.) For the text of Law No. 58–78, see Part Two, pp. 548–549.

[71] See Part Two, pp. 550–551. On the Bizerte crisis, see AJDC (Jerusalem) 242A.16.

under the aegis of American United HIAS Service, which was permitted by King Ḥasan II, who had ascended the throne upon his father's death, to operate discreetly in the country.[72]

Throughout the 1960s and 1970s, the Jewish community in Morocco steadily ebbed away, with the rate of departures increasing after the Arab-Israeli wars of 1967 and 1973 and the attempts against King Ḥasan's life in 1971 and 1972. Unlike those who had gone in the earlier waves, many of those who left after 1967 belonged to the well-to-do and professional classes. Most of them immigrated to France, Belgium, Spain, and Canada rather than to Israel. By 1967, Moroccan Jewry, which had numbered close to a quarter million souls after World War II, had declined to approximately 50,000. By the early 1970s, that number had been reduced by half to only about 25,000 as emigration continued inexorably.[73]

The decline of Algerian Jewry was far more precipitous and more complete than that of either its Moroccan or Tunisian counterparts. As the revolution began, approximately 140,000 Jews were living in Algeria. All of them were French citizens except for those few thousand living in the Saharan Mzab province. For the most part, Algerian Jews could identify with neither the Islamic nationalism of the revolutionaries nor the extreme right-wing, racist politics of the anti-Semitic *colons*. Caught in the cross fire, Jews began leaving the country for France as the savagery mounted on all sides during the late 1950s. Perhaps most symbolic of their predicament was the tragedy of the William Lévy family of Algiers. The father, a socialist leader, was murdered by the OAS in 1961, and his son was murdered by the FLN.[74]

On the eve of Algerian independence in July 1962, virtually the entire Jewish community joined the flood of European refugees going to France. (Only about 5,000 chose to go to Israel.) By the time of

[72] Laskier, "The Instability of Moroccan Jewry and the Moroccan Press in the First Decade after Independence," pp. 41–43, 46–49; idem, "Zionism and the Jewish Communities of Morocco: 1956–1962," pp. 130–38; Lehrman, "Report from Morocco," pp. 16–19; Samuel Segev, *Operation "Yakhin"* (Tel Aviv, 1984) [Heb.].

[73] For personal observations on one small Moroccan Jewish community during the 1967 and 1973 Arab-Israeli wars, respectively, see Lawrence Rosen, "A Moroccan Jewish Community during the Middle East Crisis," *The American Scholar* 37 (Summer 1968): 435–51; and Norman A. Stillman, "The Sefrou Remnant," *JSS* 35, nos. 3–4 (July–October 1973): 257. See also Victor Malka, "Morocco," *AJYB* (1968, 1970, and 1972): 524–26, 514–18, 590–92, respectively.

[74] Horne, *A Savage War of Peace,* pp. 410–11; Ayoun and Cohen, *Les Juifs d'Algérie,* pp. 168–78. For the effects of the revolution on one small Jewish community, see Friedman, "The Jews of Batna," pp. 177–91.

the Six-Day War, there were only 3,000 Jews in all of Algeria, most of whom were involved with the French Technical Cooperation Project. Two thirds of these had left by 1970, and most of those who remained behind were elderly. Organized Jewish life in the country had almost entirely ceased to exist.[75]

[75] Horne, *A Savage War of Peace,* pp. 532–33; Victor Malka, "Algeria," *AJYB* (1968, 1970, and 1972): 523–24, 514, 593–94, respectively. On relief and resettlement of the refugees, see AJDC (Jerusalem) 382A.19–20; and concerning those who remained behind 339B.17; 405B.43 and 48–51; 422B.2–4; and 489A.47.

EPILOGUE

The long history of the Jews of Arab lands, a history that is only a few centuries shorter than the entire post–Second Temple Diaspora, is now virtually ended. The collapse and dissolution of the Jewish communities in these lands had been rapid. Within two decades, beginning at mid-century, the overwhelming majority of Jews from Iraq in the east to Morocco in the west abandoned their countries of origin, primarily for Israel and France. Only a small, vestigial, and moribund remnant is left behind. No more Jews are left in Aden (now the People's Democratic Republic of Yemen). Perhaps half a dozen individuals remain in Libya, some sixty in Lebanon, about 300 each in Iraq and Algeria, and less than 200 in Egypt. Only four Arab countries can boast of a Jewish population of more than a thousand people—Morocco (less than 10,000), Tunisia (a little over 2,000), Yemen (perhaps over 2,000), and Syria (with 4,000). In the first two, life is rather tolerable, if somewhat tenuous, for the Jews who have chosen to remain. However, many Moroccan and Tunisian Jewish parents send their children to study abroad for their secondary or advanced education, and few return. These communities are declining slowly but steadily. In Syria and Yemen (now the Yemen Arab Republic), the Jews are virtual prisoners, living in a state of constant terror under strict surveillance in Syria, and under considerably less oppressive, if no less isolated, conditions in Yemen.[1]

The Arab-Israeli conflict may have been the catalyst for the mass exodus of Jews from most of the Arab countries (in the Maghreb,

[1] For the most recent statistics on the Jews remaining in the Arab countries, see Norman A. Stillman, "Fading Shadows of the Past: Jews in the Islamic World," in *Survey of Jewish Affairs 1989,* ed. William Frankel (Oxford, 1989), pp. 157–70.

the end of French colonial rule was also a major contributing factor), but it was by no means the sole cause. The underlying forces that paved the way and contributed to this seemingly sudden rupture had been at work since the dawn of the modern era and were part and parcel of the impact of the West and the process of modernization that affected both Jews and Arabs, albeit in different ways.

The growing economic, political, and cultural intrusion of the West into the Islamic world during the course of the nineteenth century and well into the twentieth was perceived as a serious threat by the dominant Muslim community, whereas by the Jews and most native Christians, it was viewed as a liberation from their traditional humble and subordinate *dhimmī* status, which since the later Middle Ages had been rigorously imposed upon them. The Jews and Christians of the Muslim world were quick to see that increased European interference and penetration into the affairs of their region meant a weakening of the traditional Islamic norms of society and could only better their own position, which was one of religiously and legally defined inferiority.

Non-Muslims in the Islamic world had for centuries served as the intermediaries between European commercial interests in the Middle East and North Africa and the surrounding Muslim society. In the nineteenth century, they began to take advantage of the protection these ties might afford them under the capitulations. They were encouraged in this by the European powers that had begun to take an interest in their welfare at this time for both humanitarian and imperialistic reasons. For their part, the European powers lobbied with the Islamic states—and particularly with the Ottoman Empire—to extend greater civil rights to their non-Muslim subjects.

Non-Muslims also began during the last century eagerly to avail themselves of the benefits of a modern European education provided by the various cultural and religious missionaries who flocked into the Middle East and North Africa. For the Jews, the Alliance Israélite Universelle became the chief provider of modern education in the major towns and cities of most Arab countries from the 1860s onward. French, rather than Arabic or Turkish, became the primary language of high culture for thousands upon thousands of Jews. The Alliance gave its pupils far more than an education. It gave them a new self-image, created new expectations within them, and helped to arouse a sense of international Jewish solidarity. It also produced cadres of westernized native Jews who now had a distinct advantage of opportunity over the largely uneducated Muslim masses as the Islamic world was drawn ineluctably into the modern world economic system.

Together with the rapidly evolving native Christians who benefited from missionary schools, Jews came to have a place in the economic life of the Middle East and North Africa that was far out of proportion to their numbers or their social status in the general population. Their foreign ties, Western acculturation, and economic success were deeply resented by the Muslim Arab majority. This conspicuous overachievement by some Jews and Christians would contribute to their undoing as a group in the twentieth century with the rise of nationalism in the Arab world.

Rapid acculturation, overachievement in certain economic spheres, and a weakening of tradition may seem to parallel the emergence of European Jewry from the ghetto. However, in Europe, the emancipation and modernization of the Jews resulted in greater assimilation into the surrounding culture. In the Islamic world, the result was quite the opposite. Jews there became further alienated from the society around them. Although Arabic-speaking Jewry had never been totally a part of Arab culture, it nevertheless shared many more cultural elements with its Muslim neighbors prior to the modern era than did its European brethren with their Christian compatriots.

The Jews of Arab lands had no vested interest in the old social and political order of their traditional Muslim overlords. Therefore, they welcomed European political domination that began with the French conquest of Algeria in the 1830s and culminated in the carving up of the Ottoman Empire at the end of World War I. It was their misfortune to discover that the hopes they placed in their British, French, and Italian masters would be disappointed again and again. In the nineteenth century, the European powers had sought to extend their protection to the non-Muslim minorities, in part, to gain greater influence in the region. Once much of the Middle East and North Africa were under European control in the twentieth century, the colonial and mandatory authorities were frequently more concerned with appeasing, or at least not offending, the Muslim majority than in protecting the Jewish and Christian minorities, especially as the tide of Arab nationalism began to rise and swell. It was this powerful tide that would eventually engulf and destroy the Jewish and some of the Christian communities in the Arab world.

It is at times suggested that the Jews failed to hear the call of Arab nationalism when they had the chance. On the contrary, they heard it only too well. There never really was a place for them in the militant national movements with their strong Pan-Arab and Islamic overtones. Furthermore, from 1929 onward, Arab nationalism became increasingly anti-Zionist. Despite frequent disclaimers, it became increasingly difficult for either nationalist leaders or the population at large to differentiate between Jews and Zionists. Growing Arab admiration of German National Socialism and Italian Fascism in the 1930s and 1940s and a concomitant receptivity to their anti-Semitic rhetoric also ensured that Jews would find no place for themselves in the Arab nationalist camp and the society it would create.

World War II demonstrated to the Jews of Arab lands with painful clarity just how vulnerable they were. In Iraq during the Farhūd, Jews had seen the kind of violence that could be visited upon them under a native regime. In Italian Libya and the French Maghreb, they saw what anti-Semitic European colonial rule could do to them while much of the native Arab population looked on with indifference. In Egypt, they could only imagine what might have befallen them if King Fārūq had been able to welcome Rommel into the country as he had hoped to do. The lesson of the European Holocaust was not lost upon most of the Jews of the Arab world either. They emerged from their wartime experience with a heightened sense of Jewish consciousness and esprit de corps. Among young people in particular, there was an increased receptiveness to Zionism as the ultimate answer to the anti-Semitism of both the European colonialists and the Arab nationalists.

Events moved rapidly in the years immediately after World War II, and in short order totally undermined the already weakened underpinnings of the Jewish communities in the Arab world. It made little difference whether Jews abjectly mouthed the Arab anti-Zionist line as in Syria, donated generous sums of money to the Palestinian cause as in Iraq, publicly proclaimed their loyalty as in Egypt, openly declared their allegiance to Zionism as in Tunisia and Libya, or completely identified themselves with a colonial power as in Algeria. In the end, they all shared a similar fate and chose to emigrate or flee from the lands of their birth.

PART TWO

SOURCES

1

THE NINETEENTH CENTURY AND THE IMPACT OF THE WEST

THE ʿAHD AL-AMĀN
(September 10, 1857)

Praise be to Allah Who has shown a path to what is right, has made justice as a guarantee for the preservation of universal order, has revealed laws commensurate with human welfare, has promised reward to the just and punishment to the unjust. Nothing is better than the word of Allah. Peace be upon our Master Muḥammad whom He has commended in His Scripture as gracious and merciful, singled him out and sent him with the true and tolerant religion,[1] making it clear and manifest for all.

We ask that You grant, O Lord, success that will lead to furthering that which pleases You and will be of help in the affairs of rulership, which is a heavy burden for him who bears it. We have placed our trust in You and have taken refuge with You. It is sufficient to have Allah as one's Trustee.

Allah has entrusted us with authority and with the affairs of His creatures in this region. He has imposed upon us binding laws and obligatory duties which cannot be fulfilled except with His help upon which we rely. . . . Allah sees that I accept this weighty authority for the welfare of the nation rather than for myself. . . . I have already begun with a reduction of taxation as is well known. The result of this has become manifest with Allah's help. Hopes are high, and people are looking forward to the fruits of their labors.

. . . .

We have seen the Sultanate of Islam,[2] and the Great Powers have wisely acted in annulling some laws while strengthening the personal security of

[1] Islam.
[2] The Ottoman Empire.

their subjects, seeing to it that their rights are observed. Both reason and nature dictate this. Just as good government is highly esteemed, so it is held in high regard by the Sacred Law, which was revealed to remove people from the call of their passions. Whoever adheres to what is just and swears by it, he is the closest to piety. Human hearts rest tranquilly in security and godliness.

We have been in correspondence with the *ᶜulemā'* of the Religion of the Five Pillars[3] and with some notables concerning our determination to set up administrative courts to look into criminal acts by various sorts of individuals and into commercial dealings from whence the prosperity of nations comes. We have drawn up their administrative organization so that they are not in conflict—God willing—with the principles of the Religious Law.

. . . .

The following are the fundamental principles (of this code):

1. Security is guaranteed for all our subjects and for those residing in our Regency irrespective of religion, language, or color, with regard to their respected persons, their inviolate possessions, and their sacred honor, except as required by law under the purview of the court with consultation. Such exceptions will be brought to our attention, and we shall have authority to execute or commute the sentence or to permit a reexamination of the case.

2. People are constitutionally equal in the payment of levies which have been imposed or will be imposed, even though the actual sums may be different, so that the great will not be exempt from the code because of their greatness, nor will the lowly be exempted because of their lowliness. This article will be clearly defined.

3. The Muslim and non-Muslim inhabitants of the Regency are equal in their claims for justice, because the right to justice is a human characteristic unlike any others. Justice on earth is a balanced scale in which the truthful is protected from the liar and the weak from the strong.

4. The dhimmī among our subjects may not be compelled to change his religion, neither is he to be prevented from performing what his religion requires. Their gathering places are not to be shown disrespect and are to be secure from harm or insult. For their protected status requires that they have what we have and that they be subject to what we are.

5. (Deals with the rights of soldiers)

6. When the criminal court recommends punishment for a dhimmī, there must be present an associate judge from among their notables so as to prevent any injustice being done to the individual. The Religious Law enjoins us to treat them well.

7. We shall establish a commercial court with a president and a secretary. Its members shall be composed of Muslim and non-Muslim subjects of the friendly nations. It shall have competence in commercial disputes. It

[3] Islam.

will be established after an agreement is reached with our friends, the Great Powers, as to how their subjects are to come under the jurisdiction of the court, in accordance with clearly defined regulations that preclude factious controversy.

8. All of our subjects, both Muslim and non-Muslim, are equal under the customary regulations and legal codifications. No preference is to be shown to one over the other.

9. There will be freedom of commercial endeavor without privilege for any individual, but rather it shall be licit for everyone. The state shall not engage in commerce, neither shall it bar anyone from engaging in it. The state shall, however, have general oversight of commercial activity in order to promote it and prevent anything which might obstruct it.

10. (Concerning the establishment of foreign industries and services in Tunisia)

11. (Concerning foreigners who wish to purchase homes and property in Tunisia)

We swear by Allah's pact and covenant that we shall carry out these principles which we have promulgated in the manner we have stipulated and they shall be followed up with clear elucidation of their meaning. I call upon Allah and this distinguished assembly[4] as witnesses that this is binding upon me and my successors. No one may accede to rulership without swearing by this Pact of Security upon which I have expended great effort.

. . . .

We, Allah's humble servant, have promulgated this introductory code after consultation as to its beneficiality to the general welfare. May Allah aid us with the blessing of the Koran and the mysteries of the Fātiḥa.[5]

Salutations from him who is in need of his Exalted Lord, His servant, the Mushīr[6] Muḥammad Pasha Beg, ruler of Tunisia. 20 Muḥarram, 1274.

Aḥmad b. Abi 'l-Ḍiyāf, *Itḥāf Ahl al-Zamān bi-Akhbār Mulūk Tūnis wa-ᶜAhd al-Amān*, vol. 4 (Tunis, 1963), pp. 240–44.

[4] The ᶜAhd al-Amān was publicly read out at the Bey's palace before a gathering of officials and foreign consuls and representatives of the non-Muslim communities on September 14, 1857. See Ibn Abi 'l-Ḍiyāf, *Itḥāf Ahl al-Zamān,* vol. 4, p. 240.

[5] The opening sura of the Koran and the principal Muslim prayer.

[6] The Bey's Ottoman title of "Marshal." See L. Carl Brown, *The Tunisia of Ahmad Bey, 1837–1855* (Princeton, N.J., 1974), p. 241, n. 3.

A RELIGIOUS GENERATION GAP IN ALGIERS
(1850)

Religious fervor has diminished considerably in Algiers, especially among the generation that has come along after the conquest. A good part of the youth are noted for a great relaxation in the observance of ceremonies and customs practiced by their fathers with so much rigidity. Many are even totally free of the yoke of religion, some following the natural inclination of their heart and their unregulated passions, others taking irreligion as the expression of civilization. We deplore these excesses, and we believe that it is not fitting to encourage them. We are not speaking in our capacity as minister to the Jewish religious community;[1] we make this observation merely as a moralist. We are speaking in your name, Gentlemen,[2] as the person in charge of the spiritual and temporal interests of a great community. There, where the moral sentiment is not very developed, only religion is the strict guardian of good morals. And it should be noted that those who have remained faithful to the ancient traditions distinguish themselves generally by purer morals and less reprehensible conduct. Furthermore, in showing contempt for that which their fathers and grandfathers respected and venerated, the young are creating a gulf between themselves and the older generation. A violent and continual struggle rages between father and son, between mother and daughter, between pious brother and irreligious brother. These things disturb family peace and replace love and respect, which are the guardian spirits of the home, with hateful feelings. Without demanding of the new generation the piety of their fathers or the devotion of their grandfathers, we desire that its aversion to the antiquated fanaticism does not push it toward contempt for all that is sacred. Between these two extremes there is a reasonable middle which the wise Ecclesiastes teaches us: "Be not overly righteous, nor overly impious."[3] It is around this middle ground that we wish to reunite reasonable minds and intelligently progressive individuals.

M. A. Weill, "Situation des Israélites en Algérie: Rapport général: Alger," in S. Schwarzfuchs, *Les Juifs d'Algérie et la France (1830–1855)* (Jerusalem, 1981), p. 348.

[1] The author of this report, Michel Weill, was chief rabbi of Algiers and, hence, of the Central Consistory of all Algeria from 1846 to 1889.

[2] This report was made by Rabbi Weill at the request of the Consistory (the gentleman here addressed). It was submitted to the French minister of religious affairs in Paris in January 1851. See S. Schwarzfuchs, *Les Juifs d'Algérie et la France (1830–1855)* (Jerusalem, 1981), pp. 54–55.

[3] Rabbi Weill is abridging Eccles. 7:16–17.

A PASTORAL LETTER FROM THE CHIEF RABBI OF FRANCE TO THE JEWS OF ALGERIA URGING REFORMS

(1873)

Cast ye up, cast ye up, clear the way, take up the stumblingblock out of the way of my people.[1]

Dear Coreligionists,

It would give me pleasure any time, and particularly on the eve of the august solemnities that we are about to celebrate,[2] not to have to address to you anything except words of praise and satisfaction. I would be happy to be able to state, to proclaim, that my exhortations have not been without success, that you understand the new responsibilities that have been imposed upon you, that you have listened to the counsel of a friendly voice that only wants what is good for you and has no more fervent desire than that the honor of the name of the Jew in Algeria should be as in France.

Unfortunately, it is not this at all, and to this day, my expectation, which is that of all good Jews, friends of their country and of their brethren, is still not realized.

Last year, in my pastoral letter addressed to all French Jews, I devoted a special mention to you. Among other things I said: "If in order to be French, you have to abandon practices that are dear to you, or customs that seem sacred, just look at our brethren in France and act like them. One glorifies his faith by showing it to be compatible with civilization. That is a veritable *kidousch-haschem*.[3] It is the first duty of an Israelite. It is the one that is most pleasing to God."

These words—I say with deep regret—have not had the success that I had reason to expect. I certainly would not wish either to give too severe an emphasis to the reproaches which my conscience obliges me to voice or to generalize in too absolute a fashion. Far from it. The majority of you, my Brethren, have it in your heart to obey the exhortations that I have just recalled and to prove to France that its sons in Algeria do not take second place in either devotion or morality to its other children. Your progress in European civilization is undeniable, and I less than anyone would want to deny it. However, this progress is still too slow, and there are still too many exceptions. the protests and complaints which are frequently addressed to us demonstrate to us that you are not doing everything to merit that beautiful title of Frenchmen, of which you are so jealous. You are not making all of the sacrifices that the circumstances require.

[1] Isa. 57:14.

[2] The reference is to Rosh ha-Shana, the Jewish New Year.

[3] Heb., *qiddūsh ha-shēm* (sanctification of the Divine Name). The term refers to any act that brings about a more profound recognition of God through either sacrifice or piety.

Let not this word about sacrifices alarm you. It has nothing to do—God forbid—with asking to abandon a single one of your beliefs, those sacred and cherished beliefs which you hold in trust, as do we. It is a trust that you ought to, and we wish to, transmit intact to your children, as you received it from your forefathers. . . .

No, I repeat, this has nothing to do with repudiating your beliefs or becoming unfaithful to the sacred traditions. What I am asking you is to renounce some of your prejudices, some false ideas, or rather, certain evil passions.

This has to do with practices in Judaism which do not have the absolute rigidity of a religious law and which are essentially subordinated to circumstances—practices which the greatest scholars of the Talmud and of modern temples have modified many a time and made to bend according to the demands of the situation; practices that were easy to carry out in other ages, but which have become incompatible with our new situation as French citizens and with the requirements that result from that for us. To this state of affairs, the wise maxim "dina de-malkhuta dina"[4] applies most aptly.

These reflections are applicable particularly to questions touching upon marriage, divorce, and the levirate. Moreover, I would say that this has to do with these questions which are so grave and so important for the family and for society that are producing the most frequent complaints, the most egregious abuses, upon which the most precious interests remain suffering and are shamefully sacrificed. Frivolous men, either malevolent or selfish, do not worry about covering their children with an indelible stain by evading civil marriage, or about condemning their brother's widow to perpetual isolation by refusing Halitsa.[5] This results not only in material prejudice for some unfortunate women, but also in moral prejudice, even shame, which reflects upon all of you. Yes, due to the ill will or the base egoism of some individuals, you all risk at passing for fanatic, intransigent people, unworthy of the noble title of citizen and of the benevolence of France. Many a time, we have had to respond to complaints coming from above and to accusations emanating from distinguished persons, not at all hostile, who reproach you with deeds that are painful for us and incomprehensible for non-Jews. Indeed, it is inexplicable in the society that surrounds us that some men under the cover of religion, would wish to circumvent so wise and so liberal an institution as civil marriage, or that others would be able to cast a relative into so painful a situation, and that the fate of the unfortunate widow could be at the mercy of a whim, at the mercy of her brother-in-law's veto!

[4] Aram., *dīnā de-malkhūtā dīnā* (the law of the state is law). This dictum of the Amora Samuel is cited four times in the Talmud and became an important principle in *halākha,* namely that Jews are subject to the laws of the country in which they reside. See Shmuel Shilo, "Dina de-Malkhuta Dina," *EJ* 6: 51–55.

[5] Heb., *ḥalīṣa* (removal). This is the name given to the ceremony that releases a widow from the obligation to marry her deceased husband's brother when there have been no offspring from the first marriage. Without performing *ḥalīṣa,* she is not free to marry anyone else other than the levir. See Louis Rabinowitz, "Levirate Marriage and Ḥaliẓah," *EJ* 11: 122–31.

. . . Look at your Brethren of Metropolitan France. Attached as much as you to the faith of their fathers, they nevertheless, with a meritorious willingness and unbounded sense of renunciation, knew how to submit to the exigencies of a new situation, because none of those exigencies were incompatible with the sound practice of Judaism. They renounced of their own free will outdated privileges, exceptional customs that isolated them from general society without any profit for true piety. They are rewarded for this today by the consideration that is shown them, by their complete fusion from the civil point of view with their compatriots of other confessions, and by the happiness of living under a flag of liberty and fraternity, under the aegis of laws which accord to all equal protection and equal benevolence.

You are today, dear Coreligionists, more or less at the same point at which your Brethren of France were a century ago. No longer oppressed, persecuted, or governed by special laws, you were attached and still remain attached to the most minute practices which have no longer any raison d'être and which have become nonsensical. Bear in mind that the times are no longer the same . . . you are no longer pariahs, but part of the French people. The sun of liberty has risen over you as well, and in its rays which make minds fertile, great and generous ideas ought to germinate in your souls as they did in ours.

Therefore, hasten, my dear Brethren, to make for the Motherland, for civilization, and for your own interests, of course, the sacrifice required. Show that you are neither backwards, nor fanatical, and that to the virtues of a believer, you know how to alloy that of a citizen—productivity, submission to law, and love of country. May France be proud to call you her children, even as you are proud to call her your mother!

These then, my friends, are the good things which I wish you—and I know of no more precious wish—as the New Year we are about to celebrate approaches.

. . . .[6]

Paris (September 1873) Tisri 5634

The Chief Rabbi of the Central Consistory
of the Jews of France,

L. Isidor[7]

Text published by Robert Attal, "Le Consistoire de France et les Juifs d'Algérie: Lettre Pastorale du Rabbin Isidor (1873)," *Michael* 5 (1978): 12–16.

[6]Here follow four paragraphs in Hebrew that reiterate in a more traditional rabbinic style the object of the letter with ample citations from halakhic sources. This Hebrew section is signed as follows: "From me, Eliezer Isidor, Teacher to the Nation of France and Algeria."

[7]Lazare Isidor was chief rabbi of France from 1867 until his death in 1888. See "Isidor, Lazare," *EJ* 9: 90.

STATUTES OF THE JEWISH COMMUNITY OF ALEXANDRIA, EGYPT
(1872)

Title I. On Jurisdiction

Article 1. The Jewish community of Alexandria comes under Austro-Hungarian jurisdiction.

Title II. On the Community

Article 2. All Jews resident and domiciled in Alexandria form a single Community with no distinction being made regarding origin, nationality, or *Minhag.*[1]

Title III. On Religious Direction

Article 3. Religious direction is entrusted to a Rabbi elected when there is a vacancy by a majority vote of the taxpayers, duly convened, and following a proposal from the representative Committee (cf. Art. 6)

Article 4. The rights and duties of the Rabbi are established by the convention as set by the taxpayers with the consent of the Committee representing the Community, and in accordance with the Regulation.

Article 5. Furthermore, within every three-year period it is incumbent upon the chief Rabbi to provide for the practical and theoretical instruction of two young men from the indigent classes in the professional practice of the *Scekita,*[2] and of another two in the professional practice of the duties of *Hazzanim.* The young men will be chosen by the Committee.

Title IV. On the Representative Committee

Article 6. The Community council is composed of Thirty-six individuals, elected by the general Assembly of taxpayers, by majority vote. Once elected, this Council will elect Twelve members from within its own ranks, by a majority vote, who will be in charge, under the title of representative Committee, of the direction and administration of community affairs. The other Twenty-four will assume the titles of Counsellors and will be consulted by the Committee regarding any important matter and any serious occurrence.

Article 7. The particular characteristics of the Committee and of the Counsellors will be established by internal Regulation as formulated by the entire body of the Thirty-six elect, and the Committee will elect from within its own ranks the President and two Vice-Presidents.

Article 8. In order that during the course of a three-year period, the entire Council may be renewed, four members of the Committee as well as eight Counsellors will be chosen annually to resign, by the drawing of lots,

[1] Heb., *minhag* (customary rite).

[2] Heb., *sheḥīṭa* (kosher slaughtering).

and the general Assembly of taxpayers will appoint twelve [new] members. The outgoing members can be re-elected.

Title V. On the Functions of the Representative Committee

Article 9. The Committee directs, administrates, and represents the Community.

— Formulates the annual preliminary and final budgets, the latter then being circulated to the taxpayers.
— Collects the *Arika*[3] from the taxpayers via the Commission; and compiles the list of electors and those eligible for election.
— Collects the burial taxes for the Cemetery.
— Oversees the smooth running of the Temples.
— Mediates with the local Government and with the Consulates of this City.
— Oversees, supervises, and represents the interests of the *Talmud Tora*, the girls' schools, and all the religious institutions and societies which it subsidizes.
— Distributes alms.
— Provides for the appointment of the medical surgeon to assist the poor and ill; provides for the free distribution of medications; promotes and patronizes charitable institutions.
— Convenes and presides over the Assemblies of the taxpayers.
— Establishes relations between the Rabbi and the Community.
— Elects a Treasurer from within its own ranks.

Title VI. On the Electorate and those Eligible for Election

Article 10. All Jews enjoying their civil rights who are over the age of eighteen and pay the *Arika* are electors.

Article 11. All electors who are over the age of twenty-one and can read and write are eligible for election to the Committee seats.

Article 12. The *Arika*, or annual contribution by subscription is individually determined by subscription for each case and obligatory for three years; whatever the sum paid, the taxpayers enjoy the same rights. It is the duty of the Municipal Administration to provide for a renewal of the subscription during the course of the third year.

Article 13. Individual contributions fall into three categories and are voluntary. 1st Category, not less than One Thousand Piastres. 2nd Category, not less than Five Hundred Piastres. 3rd Category, not less than One Hundred Piastres.

Article 14. The contributions are paid in advance by annual installments.

Article 15. Those contributors delinquent in their installments by six months are taken off the electoral register. They can be reregistered as soon as the arrears have been paid.

[3] Heb., *ʿarīkha*. This was the name given in Eqypt to the annual tax levied on individual members of the Jewish community according to estimated income. See

Article 16. In the event of it not being possible to obtain from a person in a financially viable position to subscribe or to pay having already subscribed, either the subscription to the contribution or the payment of the sum subscribed to, the consequences for the individual of his obvious refusal would be a voluntary withdrawal from the *Keila*.[4] This person and his family would also find themselves without assistance from the Community, whatever their circumstances. Permission would not be given either for them to exercise the religious functions they might require, at least, not unless the amount in arrears were paid prior to this. In addition, double the annual contribution from that category which the Committee judges to be applicable to the particular case will act as a fine, both in the case of having subscribed and not having paid as well as in the case of simply not having subscribed.

Title VII. On the Assemblies

Article 17. The Assembly is made up of the entire registered electorate in compliance with Article 10 of the Statutes.

Article 18. The Assemblies, which regularly convene, are quorate when those present constitute the absolute majority of the registered electorate.

Article 19. In the event of there not being an absolute majority at the first meeting, a second one is called which is then declared quorate, whatever the number of those present might be.

Article 20. The Assemblies discuss, approve or reject, by majority vote of those present, the proposals of the Committee, or those [proposals] which are initiated by the Assemblies, provided that they appear on the day's agenda.

Article 21. The Assemblies elect by a plurality, (a) the community Council, by secret ballot, as stated in Article 6, (b) the Rabbi, under the advice of the Committee, when there is a vacancy.

Article 22. The Assembly cannot convene for the purposes of reforming the Statues or for anything else unless the request is underwritten by a third of the registered electorate. Deliberations on the modification of the Statutes are valid when two-thirds of those who enjoy the right to vote are present, and when the proposal receives an absolute majority of the votes in the Assembly.

Article 23. The meetings of the Assembly are convened by the president of the representative Committee, by means of invitations sent to the homes of the taxpayers. The letter of invitation acts as an admission card to attend the Assemblies.

Title VIII. On Burials

Article 24. A Commission comprising five members must be appointed annually by the Committee for the purposes of directing and maintaining

---

Jacob M. Landau, *Jews in Nineteenth-Century Egypt* (New York and London), p. 58, passim.

[4] Heb., *kehilla* (congregation).

the cemetery and in order to promote the foundation of a *Gimilut Hassadim*[5] society, whose main aim will be to direct funerals and when necessary to provide the proper uniform dress for those participating in the funeral rites in accordance with their positions.

Article 25. The tariff on land destined as burial ground (*Deme Kebura*)[6] is set, for each member of the taxpayer's family and for the taxpayer himself, according to the annual contribution, *Arika*, paid by them. The tariff for those deceased between five and eighteen years of age constitutes a half of the annual contribution. Children under five years of age are exempt from the tariff.

Article 26. If the deceased were not a taxpayer, or did not belong to the family of a taxpayer, the Committee establishes the tariff payable, according to the different categories of age, taking into account the economic situation of the deceased's family and proceeding with the greatest of caution and fairness in setting the contribution.

Article 27. The indigent are exempt from tariffs.

Article 28. The Committee establishes to its personal satisfaction by negotiation, the tariff for those who want to have a larger plot of land than that usually deemed necessary.

Title IX. On the Temples and Their Administration

Article 29. The appointment and dismissal of the *Gabaim,*[7] the Administrative Directors of the Temples, and the Vice-*Gabaim* is the exclusive business of the Council in its entirety.

Article 30. The *Gabaim* must submit their annual budget proposals to the Committee, which either gives an approval in writing or imposes a veto.

Article 31. Once the total established in the preliminary budget has been subtracted from the excess income of the Temples, the remainder is transferred to the Community and is annually deposited in its coffers at the same time as submitting the Budget, which must not be presented later than *Tisri*[8] of every year.

Article 32. The sums to be distributed for restoration and embellishment of the temples are established from the preliminary Budget by agreement between the Committee and the *Gabaim*.

Article 33. The regulations for the internal organization of the respective Temples are formulated by the Council. The *Gabaim* and Vice-*Gabaim* must act in accordance with these regulations, but can submit to the Committee all those measures they deem necessary and expedient to the smooth running of said Temples.

[5] Heb., *gemīlūt ḥasādīm* (lit., doing acts of benevolence). In Egypt, this name was applied to the burial society.

[6] Heb., *demē qevūra* (burial fee).

[7] Heb., *gabbā'īm* (synagogue officials).

[8] That is, *Tishri,* the seventh month of the Jewish calendar (September to October), which also marks the beginning of the religious year.

Title X. On Charity

Article 34. Every year two collections (*Nedabot*)[9] are made for the Holyland, the first on the second day of the Feast of Weeks (*Scebot*)[10] and the other on the Sabbath of Hannuka. The purpose of the proceeds of these collections is to give aid to our coreligionists in Jerusalem, Safed, Tiberias, and Hebron, each in turn. The respective *Scialikim*,[11] who will be chosen at the established times, must provide for their own board and lodging.

Article 35. All supervision of the charitable institutions such as *Mohar Abetulot*[12] and others subsidized by the community itself is assigned to the representative Committee. The Council appoints representatives, following the norms established for the *Talmud Tora*, to participate on the Administrative Board of Advisors of each institution, and thereby having a detailed annual report on each of them.

Title XI. On the Taxation of Victuals

Article 36. No taxes on meat, wine, liquor, cheese, or other victuals can be established without the approval of the general Assembly of taxpayers.

Article 37. The Rabbinate has oversight in all matters pertaining to *Cacerut*.[13]

Article 38. The Committee pays the *Scioketin*[14] in accordance with the established norms, for both large and small livestock, as well as for poultry. Consequently the butchers cannot impose either any increase in price for meat or any tax. For poultry, the present tariff remains in force, payable by the customer to the individual *Scioket* involved.

Title XII. On Free and Obligatory Education

Article 39. Supervision of the free religious schools for boys and girls (*Talmud Tora* and *Sciadai Janzor*)[15] is assigned to the Committee which represents the Community, created with the assistance and by the authority of the Community itself.

Article 40. The Community contributes, to the extent to which its financial state allows, to the annual subsidy of the religious schools, with the intention of developing and propagating education for the young, in the best possible way.

Article 41. The directive and administrative Board of Advisors of the free religious schools is comprised of seven members, three of whom are delegates of the Council representing the community; four are elected by

[9] Heb., *nedāvōt* (charitable contributions).

[10] The holiday of Shavuᶜot, or Feast of Weeks.

[11] Heb., *shelīḥīm* (emissaries).

[12] Heb., *mohar ha-betūlōt* (the maidens' dowry). This is the name of a fund that assisted poor girls with a dowry so that they could be married.

[13] Heb., *kashrūt* (ritual fitness). The reference here is to the oversight of kosher food.

[14] Heb., *shōḥaṭīm* (ritual slaughterers).

[15] Heb., *Shadday yaᶜazor* (the Almighty assists).

the taxpayers to help maintain the Schools. The directive and administrative Board of Advisors elects the President from within its own ranks.

Article 42. The directive and administrative Board has its own autonomy with regard to the internal organization of the schools.

Article 43. The Committee representing the community does not give donations to the heads of families, or to the tutors unless they can prove that the children in their care, who are of the age established by the Regulations of the religious Schools, attend the *Talmud Tora* or other Schools, or that some other form of elementary education is given to them.

Article 44. A Report on the state of these Schools is presented annually by the Community representatives of the religious Schools (cf. Art. 41).

Title XIII. On Real Estate

Article 45. The Real Estate belonging to the Jewish Community of Alexandria, of whatever type, denomination, and title, cannot be transferred, given, sold, mortgaged, or leased for a period of longer than five years, except in the case of a deliberation by the general Assembly of taxpayers convened for that particular purpose. In order that it be legal and valid the following formalities must be observed:

A. Said gathering must be convened by the representative Committee by written invitation stating the purpose. The delivery of the invitations must be acknowledged by the addressee and the receipt collected for special circulation.
B. The invitations must precede the meeting by at least Fifteen days.
C. The number of those present at the meeting must represent two thirds of the taxpayers.
D. The deliberation must include a majority of two thirds of the total number present at that session.
E. The votes are verified by three examiners, if necessary elected from the same meeting.
F. The minutes of the previous meeting, upon being read, must then be signed by the three examiners, by the President, and by the Secretary of the Assembly.

Article 46. In the event that at a first meeting the number of taxpayers of which the preceding Article 45 speaks is not reached, the Committee will call a second meeting, by means of notices affixed in the *Kenessiod*,[16] in addition to a written invitation, setting the day of the gathering, where the presence of half the number of taxpayers is sufficient for a legal deliberation. The invitations are sent out at least ten days in advance of the session, and in case the attendance of the requisite number of taxpayers is not verified for the second meeting either, the gathering will be convened again, by invitation preceding it by eight days. In this event, if the number reached comprises a third of the taxpayers, the gathering is declared legal. The

[16] Heb., *kinēsiyyōt* (synagogues).

deliberations are only valid, however, when there is a majority vote of two-thirds of the number present at the gathering, and when all the formalities prescribed by Article 45 are observed.

Article 47. The agenda of things to be discussed, as compiled for the first meeting, cannot be altered and must be identical for the gatherings of the second and third convocations; nothing must be added or deleted, under pain of invalidation.

Article 48. At the second and third meetings, mention must be made of that which is stated in Article 45 and of the reasons for its application.

Article 49. The formalities as prescribed by the present law must be scrupulously observed, including the event that Real Estate is acquired by the Community itself.

Article 50. All previous statutory provisions valid to date are abrogated. The present Statutes are legally completed by Deliberation of the general Assembly of taxpayers, as witnessed on this day, September 11, 1871.

Approved as having been printed in conformity with the original
Alexandria, February 27, 1872
President of the representative Committee
G. Del Valle
Statutes of the Jewish Community of Alexandria, Egypt, 1872.

Stattuti della Communità Israelitica di Allessandria di'Eggito. Jacob M. Landau, *Jews in Nineteenth-Century Egypt*
(New York and London, 1969), pp. 183–91.

THE JEWISH COMMUNITY OF SIDON AT THE TURN OF THE CENTURY
(1902)

Formerly queen of the seas, Sidon, the flourishing city of the Phoenicians, is today nothing but a somber little town of 15,000 to 18,000 souls, a big village without commerce or industry. The great bulk of the population lives almost exclusively from the revenues of the numerous gardens that surround the town, from which the produce is exported to either Egypt or England, where the oranges of Saida[1] are, apparently, particularly in demand. The inhabitants are crammed pell-mell into tiny houses, which could not be more dilapidated, made of stones gathered from the fields that it was not even necessary to quarry.

I shall not even try to describe the maze of narrow streets, congested at practically every step by vaults supporting the houses, which are as if perched in the air, and where—without exaggeration—it is gloomy even at the height of noon. I have visited the oldest quarters of Jerusalem and Damascus, but I have never seen anything resembling the picture of desolate decay presented by Saida, a small town that knows no tourism and is still untouched by modern civilization.

It is one of the most somber of these alleys that leads into the Jewish quarter via a low, narrow, little gate. Passing through this portal, we are in the ghetto. Imagine a long courtyard, narrow and dark, a sort of corridor, as sinuous as can be, whose width is never more than two meters. On either side are two- and three-story houses—or rather cells cut into the walls, not receiving even a little of the dim light from the side of the narrow passage that forms the street. I asked myself more than once during my visits to the quarter whether people in Europe would be content to keep convicts in such a frightful prison where poverty is keeping a thousand of our coreligionists. . . . But continuing on our way, let us go further down this single street, which is not even paved. The unfortunate individuals who live there and to whom the street belongs (like the courtyard of a house) have asked in vain for the authorities to pave it at their own expense. The authorities are opposed to it! All the way at the end, we finally reach a small square of approximately 150 to 200 square meters, where the gay rays of sunlight are able to penetrate and where one can breathe a little more easily. It is on this square that the synagogue and Talmud Torah are to be found at the far end.

. . . .

I had just said that Saida is a town without commerce. The gardens which feed the great majority of the people belong almost exclusively to the Muslims who comprise about nine tenths of the population of Saida. The Christians, who are well protected by the consuls and by their priests who

[1] The Arabic name of Sidon.

have influence with the authorities, enjoy a certain degree of ease and consideration. Only the Jews, left to themselves, stagnate in dark poverty in which the others have little share, and they are the object of contempt and disdain in the eyes of their neighbors of other faiths. Peddling is practically the only way of making a living. Saturday night, they leave their ghetto and disperse left and right throughout the countryside painfully struggling to earn a few miserable piastres, which they leave at home when they return on Friday. This occupation is certainly arduous, at times humiliating, and always thankless. It does not feed its man—as they say. But can they do any better? They know nothing else. The few Jewish carders who work at Saida do not always even earn their daily keep, which is about two piastres, or 0.35 francs! What misery for a man who has a family to feed.

I stopped for a bit in each of the little shops maintained by those of our coreligionists who do business in town. I interrogated them one after the other. It was always the same sorry response: they are poor and they are unhappy. The richest among them considers himself fortunate when on the most fruitful day he realizes an earning of ten piastres, barely two francs!

Report by M. Angel, Beirut, May 1902.
AIU Archives (Paris)
Liban I.C.2.

2

SOCIAL TRANSFORMATIONS

A LETTER FROM THE ALLIANCE ISRAÉLITE UNIVERSELLE TO RABBI RAPHAEL ABENSUR OF FEZ REQUESTING HIS HELP IN COMBATING CHILD MARRIAGE (1903)

Alliance Israélite Universelle — Paris, 27 September 1903

Dear Rabbi,

We were visited a few days ago by several notables from Fez. We discussed with them the situation of the community, and we are happy to note the progress realized these last years in Fez. These improvements are due to a variety of causes, among which, we believe our schools are the principal factor. We would be completely delighted to congratulate the Fez community, if it would renounce the sorry custom of child marriages practiced by Jewish families.

Questioned by us on the means to putting an end to this deplorable practice, Messrs. Mimoun, David Cohen, and Raphael Azuelos were of the opinion that the cure for this evil depended upon you and your colleagues, Rabbis Vidal and Solomon Danan.[1] They urged us to beg you to act on

[1]Rabbi Vidal is probably Rabbi Vidal Sarfaty (1862–1921). Rabbi Solomon Danan is Solomon Aben Danan (1848–1929), who at this time was *Av Bēt Dīn,* or head of the rabbinical court of Fez. Aben Danan had been approached in 1897 by Joseph Bensimhon, the director of the Alliance School for Boys, with regard to this same matter. Aben Danan, however, had not been very helpful. See Michael M. Laskier, *The Alliance Israélite Universelle and the Jewish Communities of Morocco: 1862–1962* (Albany, N.Y., 1983), p. 119. This may explain why the Alliance was

behalf of this among your coreligionists in Fez. You know as well as we, Rabbi, that our foremost talmudic authorities are hostile to child marriage. Does not the *Pirka abot* V,24 fix the age of marriage at eighteen?[2]

There is no purpose for us to go on citing texts with which you are entirely familiar. Unfortunately, instead of following the advice of our sages, numerous communities have imitated the Arabs, who for a purpose that is hardly praiseworthy, marry off their children at an age when they should still be sitting on school benches. Morality and hygiene are no less opposed to this custom than is religion. Is it possible for two children who do not know all about life and its difficulties to set up a household already during their tender years, at age ten and even younger?

From the point of view of health, the dangers are of the greatest gravity: death during childbirth for many young wives, high infant mortality, and neglected hygienic care. What can one expect of a twelve-year-old mother and a fourteen-year-old father?

It is urgent that this custom disappear from our Moroccan coreligionists' way of life. In Tangier and Tetouan, marriages of girls under fifteen have become rare. The community of Fez under the enlightened prompting of its rabbis must follow suit. We beg you, Rabbi, to join our efforts to check this evil. Make the parents understand the dangers that they are courting for their children by not conforming to our counsels. We are convinced that thanks to your high religious authority, you are better placed than anyone in Fez to undertake such a task.

Bigart[3]

André Chouraqui, *Cent ans d'histoire* (Paris, 1965), Annexe 5, no. 1, p. 458.

---

turning in this letter to Rabbi Abensur, who was the scion of an equally distinguished dynasty of Fasi rabbis.

[2] Mishna Pirqe Avot 5:21.

[3] Jacques Bigart was the secretary of the Alliance at this time.

A EUROPEAN JEW TRIES TO RESCUE A GIRL FROM A CHILD MARRIAGE IN MOROCCO (1910)

A few weeks after we had moved in, we heard the cries and weeping of a child. These cries were coming from the undeveloped property facing our building, on which there were some shanties in which poor Moroccan Jewish families were living, six or eight to a room.

I went down in a bathrobe. A little girl of about eight years of age ran toward me in tears, begging me to protect her from a group of people who were gathered not far from there. I asked the others why the little waif was so frightened. They explained that the girl had been married the same day to a young man of twenty or thirty, whom they presented to me, and that the girl was afraid to go and pass the wedding night with her husband.

I was very upset. I called them savages and led the little girl away to pass the night in my house. The next day, I received a summons from the rabbinical court of Casablanca. I went there immediately.

At the court, I was told that I had been wrong to carry off this girl from her husband, who had married her in proper religious fashion. Moreover, this sort of marriage took place frequently in Morocco and was completely normal. I was then asked persistently to restore the little girl to her husband and his family, which I did with a heavy heart.

Afterward, the director of the Alliance Israélite confided in me that it often happened that parents remove their daughters from school at age eight in order to marry them off.

Ten or fifteen years after this incident with the little girl, a beautiful young woman came upon me in the old city of Casablanca, kissed my clothing, and told me that I had protected her from her husband and his family on her wedding night. She added that since then she was happy and had had two or three children.

Zede Schulman, *Autobiographie: l'histoire de ma collection* (Chatillon-sous-Bagneux, 1980), pp. 62–63.

THE JEWISH COMMUNITY OF SUEZ REQUESTS ASSISTANCE FOR YEMENITE REFUGEES

(1905)

Suez, 1 August 1905
Monsieur S. Somekh
Cairo

Sir,

The purpose of this letter is to let you know that in a short while some 2,000 Yemenite Jews should be arriving from Aden. They will certainly not be arriving all at once, but in groups. They have already been arriving—ten, twenty, thirty. We have spoken with them, and the others are awaited each week. We have to inform you, Sir, that the Jews of Suez are very few in number, not really to be counted.[1] Furthermore, what can five or six families who are barely able to take care of their own needs do for all of these poor unfortunates? The majority of these Yemenites arrive sick. They have to be restored to health, nourished, and then they must be sent on their way. We do not have the means to provide them with this. Consequently, I hope that you will take pity on these poor people and come to their aid. It would be preferable if you could arrange to leave a sum of money on deposit with one of your acquaintances here so that as soon as these people arrive, the money would be ready to pay for their feeding and their departure either to the interior or to Jaffa, according to their wishes. We are counting on you for the Love of God.

Thank you in advance. Please accept, Sir, my most respectful best wishes.

Moussa Tweg
President of the Jewish Community of Suez

AIU Archives (Paris)
Egypte, I.D.3

[1] The number of Jews in Suez was declining at this time. In 1897, 120 Jews were living there, and in 1907, two years after this letter was written, their number had fallen to just 74. See Jacob M. Landau, *Jews in Nineteenth-Century Egypt* (New York and London), p. 38.

A REPORT ON JEWISH EMIGRATION FROM TETOUAN (1891–1892)

In order to present an in-depth study on the emigration from Tetouan, tracing its ever-increasing dimensions up to the present, naming the principal points toward which it has flowed and continues to do so, I must go back to the first quarter of the century.

At no time, has Tetouan been able to feed the 6,000 Jewish souls that inhabit it. It is not a commercial town, nor an industrial one.

At first, they (the Jews) did not go far from their native town. They would venture into the Moroccan interior, or go to Alcazar, Larache, Casablanca, and Tangier. For people of sedentary habits like the Tetouanis, who had never traveled, it was a major thing to leave the paternal house and abandon the family. But that was only the beginning, and early manifestation of that spirit for distant enterprises which characterizes the young Tetouani generation of today. In these aforementioned Moroccan towns, having to deal with men who had similar customs and acted like them, there were only a few Tetouanis who could find a niche for themselves. Others, however, did not stop there. . . . Now the majority of the Jewish community of Gibraltar is composed of veteran émigrés or their descendants.[1] All of the commerce is in their hands, and Gibraltar has been for some years now the entrepôt of Moroccan commerce. Other Tetouanis went to Ceuta, where the Spanish have long been established, and they form an important colony there.[2]

But new centers have already been opening to Tetouani activity. When the French conquered Algeria, Oran, which is the nearest major city to Morocco, fell under their control. Encouraged by the successes of their compatriots in Gibraltar, the Tetouani Jews made their way to the Algerian port. The French, newly established in the country, received them well, finding in them clients, good resources for the prosperity of their conquest, and intermediaries who could open new markets for them in Morocco. The newcomers profited from this and quickly made a small fortune. Their successes encouraged others who followed them there. A small, though intermittent, stream was under way.

Later, when the Tetouanis became affluent in Oran, all of them engaging in commerce, it became necessary to expand their sphere of activity and

[1]The Moroccan Jewish emigration to Gibraltar goes back well into the eighteenth century. See A.B.M. Serfaty, *The Jews of Gibraltar under British Rule* (Gibraltar, 1953), pp. 5–14. For the close ties between Tetouani Jewry and Gibraltar, see Samuel Romanelli, *Travail in an Arab Land,* ed. and trans. Yedida K. Stillman and Norman A. Stillman (Tuscaloosa, Ala., and London, 1989), pp. 57, 59, 73, 146.

[2]The northern Moroccan coastal town of Ceuta (Ar., Sebta) has been in European hands since it was conquered by Portugal in 1415. It passed into Spanish control in 1580. Jews lived there intermittently from that time on, although the

extend into the interior. They headed particularly toward Sidi-Bel-Abbes, Mascara, Tlemcen, and Mostaganem, as well as other little villages. There too, as always, most prospered, occupying the primacy of place in commerce.

Having surveyed very briefly the beginnings of the emigration, we come to the year 1860, at the time when the Spanish-Moroccan War took place. It is well known that during this disastrous war the Tetouani Jews had to suffer terrible hardships at the hands of the Arabs, who abandoned the town of Tetouan in a cowardly manner to the invaders. Before running away, those fugitives sacked the Jewish Quarter. . . . The pillage lasted two days when the Jews saw the arrival of the Spanish as their liberators.

Already in 1862, when the Central Committee (of the Alliance Israélite Universelle) opened its first school in Tetouan, emigration was getting under way. In instructing the young Tetouanis, inculcating them with useful knowledge, and teaching them to read, write, and count, in teaching them another language, and—in a word—in shaping them, it was the Alliance in effect which gave them the courage to fight in life and the self-assurance and the means to earn their livelihood more easily.

But while waiting for this new generation to be formed in school, some hardy Tetouanis undertook to go to the New World. They went out on rickety sailboats—navigation has made great progress since then—to the Canary Islands. From there, they embarked on small vessels which took one and a half to two months to make the Atlantic crossing. The first city in the New World they visited was Rio de Janeiro, the capital of Brazil. The vast field of America was opened to their commercial enterprises, and 1865 marks the real stream of emigration which has continued till now and increases from day to day.

What then was the life of those first emigrants newly arrived in Rio de Janeiro? As one of them told me, and his route to making his fortune was not different from that of others: They arrived there stripped of any resources. In order not to die of starvation, they had to work hard and to create credit for themselves, because they could not find any coreligionists who could furnish them with it. Through honesty and hard work they were able to obtain it. They started out by *llevar el fardo,*[3] as they say it, selling pieces of cloth which they carried on their back. Then after a while, when they had realized some small savings, they hired some Negroes whom they charged with selling the merchandise. The savings grew thanks to a regimented life and all sorts of privations, so that they were able to buy carts which the Negroes pushed and on which were displayed all kinds of notions. Then in time the business grew. They had credit and were able to sell merchandise in bulk. Ease was not long in coming, and soon afterward, a modest fortune.

---

permanent modern community was only established in 1869. See David Corcos, "Ceuta," *EJ* 5: 316.

[3] Span. for "taking up the bundle."

We now come to the latest stage in the evolution of the Tetouani migration, that of today. Three places—Caracas, Buenos Aires, and Para—are simultaneously witnessing the arrival of Tetouani émigrés in large numbers. However, it is Caracas above all that is receiving the largest share.

It is to be noted that in recent years, emigration has taken on disturbing proportions. Each year it takes on a greater scale. Each year the flow increases. There is something dizzying about this fever to emigrate which pushes young people to regions across the Atlantic.

The child seated on his school bench studies only with a view to acquire knowledge that will be useful when he is abroad. He cannot hear resounding in his ears the geographical names of Caracas, Buenos Aires, Para, and Rio de Janeiro without his imagination transporting him to these points. The parents only send their sons to school with the goal of their knowing *una pluma,*[4] reading and writing a language. They point out to them the benefits of education, encouraging them to attend school regularly by citing the example of all the young people who have made a fortune abroad, where, in order to succeed, a certain sum of knowledge is indispensable. That is why the children leave the Alliance school quickly. At fourteen, they dream of making a fortune. At sixteen or seventeen they are already making the voyage.

. . . .

With the progress that has been made in navigation, the distances have become shorter. One sets sail for Caracas as easily as one went to Gibraltar or Oran twenty-five years ago. I know a number of these emigrants who have made the transatlantic crossing as many as six times and are prepared to do it again. In two or three days one is in Málaga, from where one takes the boat to America which deposits the emigrant at La Guaira, the port of Caracas, twenty days later. This is the route generally followed by the majority of those going to Caracas for the first time.

As to the sum needed for the expense of the voyage, it is often the father, brother, uncle, or cousin who supplies it when they engage the new emigrant to come and join them. . . . For this reason, one searches in vain in Tetouan for students who have reached the age of eighteen; they are all over there in America.

AIU Archives (Paris) Tétouan VI.B.25.
Maïr Lévy, "Rapport sur l'Emigration à Tétouan."
The complete French text is published in Sarah
Leibovici, *Chronique des Juifs de Tétouan*
(1860–1896)
(Paris, 1984), pp. 287–96.

[4] Span. for "a pen."

A JUDEO-ARABIC REPORT ON THE IRAQI JEWISH COLONY IN CHINA (1895)

The Jews whose original home was in Arab lands (Iraq) and whose present home is in China are few in number. More than forty years ago, Khawāja Elias David Sassoon[1] came to these parts and went into business. The reasons for this were as follows: The David Sassoon[2] clan was already known previously as people worthy of respect. They were merchants and communal leaders in the Arab lands (Iraq). They emigrated and went to India, where they were also merchants. One day, Khawāja Elias Sassoon went to pick up mail at the post office and saw that most of the packages and correspondence in all of the piles was between China and India. He recalled reports that he had heard and concluded that the business carried on must be very profitable, otherwise there would not be all of this mail between the two countries. Subsequently, he set sail from India on a ship, and six months later after many remarkable adventures, he reached the city of Canton.

At that time, the trade in opium was very lucrative, and Khawāja Elias saw that the time of opportunity had arrived and that he should give up any thought of leaving and should make a living like others there. One venture followed another, and he made a considerable amount of money. In the meantime, other people were attracted to come, and they made fortunes.

At the present, the number of Jews known to be in China is 175.[3] The most outstanding among them are the houses of David Sassoon and Elias Sassoon. Also of note are the House of Hezkel Joshua, the House of Ezra, and others. All of them deal in thread, cotton, and opium. Their synagogue is on Fuchow Road, which is most convenient for the majority of them.

Most Jews here are in the opium trade, spinning of thread, and brokerage. Their condition is a good one. The name of House of Sassoon in these parts is well known and highly regarded. They dress in the English fashion. They speak Arabic, Hindustani, and English.

Jacob b. Abraham b. Sudea, "Qiṣṣat Millat Yahūd Bilād ᶜArab fī Maṭāriḥ al-Chīn," edited by P. G. von Möllendorf, in *MGWJ* 39 (1895): 330.

[1] 1820–1880. *Khawāja* is a title of respect that is equivalent to "Sir."

[2] 1792–1864.

[3] This number is probably for heads of households and does not include women and children.

A VISIT TO THE JEWISH CAVE DWELLERS OF LIBYA
(1906)

In front of us loomed a rocky eminence, crowned by the ruins of a Berber stronghold. A little further on, to the rear of the ravine, we discerned the flourishing plateau of Beni-Abbes, the first village of the cave dwellers.

Very soon we were scaling the wild crags, reaching ever higher and higher. Finally a red plateau, dotted with fruit bushes, but utterly devoid of any trace of human habitation, unrolled before our eyes. A strange spectacle this—hills and fertile valleys, where, except for an occasional ruin or mosque, not a sign of a human habitation showed above ground, where the dead were entombed above the earth, and where the living dwelt in scarcely discernible subterranean caves. We wondered what sort of reception we would be accorded by the fanatical population.

Eager to look into the life of this curious corner of the earth, we passed by the Arab village of Beni-Abbes, and proceeded, still on foot, into Yehud Beni-Abbes, the village of the Jewish cave dwellers.[1] At a spot where the reddish ground sloped slightly upward, we came upon a group of young Jewish women, very white and slender, who seemed startled by our sudden appearance on the scene. We looked with admiration at these daughters of the cave-dwelling Jews—at the mobility of their features, their natural poise, the graceful folds of their bright-hued garments.

Then came along a number of men, bronzed and strongly built. They with surprise recognized the Rabbi of Tripoli, who, appearing suddenly in their midst on the Sabbath, must have seemed to them to have dropped out of the very skies.[2] Their astonishment seemed to be augmented by the fact that he was accompanied by an effendi,[3] who greeted them in Hebrew. In vain did we look amongst the palm trees, the olive trees, the fig trees—not a trace could be seen of any habitation, not a vestige of the caves we had heard so much about.

The appearance of the *Shohet,*[4] Saïd Shinani, who hailed Rabbi Mordecai as an old friend and extended a very cordial greeting to us, seemed to mark the end of our difficulties. We looked once more over the undulating plateau around us: at the olive trees, the fig trees, rare palms, the open fields; at the loungers, women clad in colored stuffs, men in bournous—in the

[1] Concerning these Jews and their transition to modern life in Israel, see Harvey Goldberg, *Cave Dwellers and Citrus Growers: A Jewish Community in Libya and Israel* (Cambridge, 1972).

[2] Slouschz traveled in the company of Rabbi Mordecai Cohen, who acted as his guide and interpreter. Because they were in dangerous country, the two had continued on, despite the advent of the Sabbath, in order to reach the Jewish community. See Nahum Slouschz, *Travels in North Africa* (Philadelphia, 1927), pp. 120–122.

[3] A Turkish title of respect for a person of rank.

[4] Heb., *shōḥēṭ* (a ritual slaughterer).

distance, a mosque half buried in the earth. Then we discerned a number of square holes, great pits almost concealed by the red hillocks around them; we could hear the wailing of infants, the lowing of cattle, the shrill cries of women, all issuing from the depths like the voice of the Sybil. Then we approached a hole, opening in the side of a hill like the entrance to a cave. But, as a matter of fact, a wooden door was opened for us by a wooden key, with which Saïd fumbled in the lock, reminding me of the biblical *manᶜul* in the Song of Songs.[5] We found ourselves in a sort of dark, uneven gallery, burrowed in the red soil, which led ever downward, and which long habit alone could teach one to pass through without mishap. At the end of about fifteen or twenty yards we found ourselves in a court, illumined faintly by rays of light slanting in from above. This was the stable, into which our animals were taken, and which preceded the central court of the human habitations.

Obviously everything is calculated among these cave dwellers, as Herodotus already noted,[6] with an eye to baffling the marauding bands who infest the surrounding desert; if these should invade the village, they would have the greatest difficulty in penetrating into a cave irregularly cut out and hidden from view. If, despite all precautions, a number of them should succeed in surprising the cave inhabitants, it would be better that they should first come upon and seize the cattle, although this comprises the sole wealth of these primitive people, and that the lives of the human beings should be spared. The same consideration accounts for the fact that the Jewish smiths and jewelers have their places close to the stables and in front of the walls. In this country of lawlessness and rapine, the individual always keeps in mind the biblical axiom: "Take all my possessions, but leave me my life."

We continue the descent by a straight passage, keeping to the side whence the light came, and we reached a square subterranean courtyard, fairly well lighted by a patch of sky visible at a depth of about ten or twelve meters from the surface of the earth; this provided all the light and air for the inhabitants. This court, which resembled a well in its rectangular depth, fulfilled the purposes of a central dwelling place, a kitchen and a factory; the living rooms, which were in caves either cut out from the walls themselves or dug out from the level of the subsoil, received a little of the light and air of the court. We were not exactly suffocated, but we must admit that we were not altogether comfortable, whereas the natives consider this underground life perfectly natural and even commodious.

Our host received us with the utmost cordiality. He was a handsome fellow, of a pure, brown Southern type; he was a *Shohet,* although almost entirely ignorant of Hebrew, having learned his profession from manuscript

[5] See *Song of Songs* 5:5.

[6] Herodotus, *The Histories,* trans. Aubrey de Sélincourt (Baltimore, 1963), Book IV, 183, p. 304.

treatises in Judeo-Arabic. Like all the Jews of the Jebel, he was a peddler[7] during the slack season, a field laborer and gardener in the busy season, and a blacksmith in between. His wife wove *ganduras,* or girdles, like the women of the Bible.

The news of our arrival spread through the village: men and women, all of a perfect type, which the underground air had failed to mar, came hurrying into the cave. The men gave us greeting, "salam," and the women kissed our hands and called us "Rebbi." We observed that here the Jewish women enjoyed much more liberty than in the oases near the coast. Even the young girls, who in Tripoli must cover their faces, here go unveiled, without any constraint; the women sit side by side with their husbands on the ground, for chairs and tables are entirely unknown. We took a sip of *oraki*, or date-brandy, of local manufacture. We were informed that the Jews are the only makers of these beverages, but that they themselves are also the largest consumers. This is characteristic of Jews of African origin; in a country of sand and sun they are very prone to indulge excessively in liquor and in the red pepper plant, which, with its sharp taste, they like almost as well as alcohol.

After a refreshing glass of *lagbi* (date-tree juice) we climbed back to the surface in order to inspect the village and its surroundings.

Yehud Beni-Abbes is on the very margin of the desert which lies between the oasis and Tripoli; the village comprises two hundred and forty inhabitants, who take up six underground courts. At one time the Jews were very numerous in this country, holding most of the land and defending it successfully against all invaders. We were shown the fertile ravine, which ends in a well-watered valley and which commands the approach of the region toward Tripoli. Here, on the slopes, we found grottoes and traces of mines of an ancient civilization. We were led across spaced-out fields and were told that all of this splendid country belonged at one time to the Jews. But toward 1840 the plague ravaged the Jewish population; the only survivors were four families of Beni-Abbes, while many of the neighboring villages were completely wiped out.

The Ulad Beni-Abbes Arabs took advantage of the unhappy plight of the Jews to deprive them of their lands; the rightful owners kept on struggling against the invaders, but to no purpose; besides this, the Arabs, with that meanness characteristic of the servile *fellah,* took possession of the cemetery, the resting place of a whole line of ancestors, and plowed it up. They could not have conceived a more malignant act, nor one which would have wounded so deeply the "infidels," who now, with tears in their eyes, led us across this field which contained the desecrated remains of their ancestors and their rabbis.

[7]Concerning the importance of Jewish peddling in the socioeconomic life of this region, see Harvey Goldberg and Rachel Rosen, "The Itinerant Jewish Peddlers in Tripolitania at the End of the Ottoman Period and under Italian Rule," in *Commu-*

The Arabs, however, had not dared to dispossess the last native Jews entirely; they managed, instead, to force them into collective ownership of the whole village, so that the Jews, having no distinctive property of their own, are yet forced to till fields and cultivate fruit trees belonging exclusively to the Mussulmans, and at a distance from their homes. The outcome is that the Jewish farmer must look on, without daring to protest, while his Arab neighbor appropriates the first-fruits of his olive-groves and the best produce of his own plot of land, which is swallowed up in the vast Arab fields.

Even this did not satisfy the oppressors. There is in the village an ancient synagogue, a sanctuary held in deep veneration. It is situated in a hollow surrounded by an open court, and its roof is colored like the soil in order to conceal it from view. This spot affords them the only moral gratification they have; it is the one meeting place where they can offer up their prayers or pour out the plaints of the *Piyyutim*, which mourn the sorrows and proclaim the hopes of Israel.

The fanatic Mussulmans, jealous of this sanctuary, planned, after the desecration of the cemetery, the ruin of the synagogue, on the pretext that the neighboring mosque would, according to Mohammedan law, be profaned by its proximity.

Fortunately, there were judges in Tripoli and money in the hands of the Jews. By a happy chance the Jews have in their possession a document which proves that the synagogue was in existence on its present site five hundred years before the foundations of the mosque were laid, that is to say, seven or eight centuries ago. The administration, basing its decision on the right of priority, was able to rescue the synagogue, to the unbounded joy of the Jews. Looking through the Geniza of this sanctuary we found, among other things, a tablet dating from 5359—that, is 348 years old. Surely these Jews, swallowed up in the Sahara, have deserved a better fate. Nowhere would there be found better proof of the moral superiority of our race, which holds firm even in the most primitive conditions.

In the caves of the Jews everyone must work; the men are blacksmiths before the time comes for work in the fields, farmers in due season, and itinerant merchants during the period of unemployment. The women weave *ganduras* for the natives and work in the fields and orchards. The children help their mothers and then the animals.

Among the Arabs the filth and stench are simply indescribable; they are so lazy that, were it not for the Jews, who lend them seed, provide them with implements, and urge them to their work, they would never get anything done. It is true that the entire existence of the Jew is dependent on the goodwill of his Arab customer, for the Jews are the only artisans in a country where money is hardly known. Generally payment is made in kind, so many bushels of barley, of figs, or of olives, and that not according to work done,

---

nautés juives des marges sahariennes du Maghreb, ed. M. Abitbol (Jerusalem, 1982), pp. 303–20.

but according to the success or failure of the crops. But it is just as true that the Arab must tolerate the Jews because he cannot do without him; without his labor, his energy, and his initiative life would be impossible in a country where laziness is a tradition.

The life of the Jews of the cave country is primitive in the extreme. They are generally content with barley bread, with dates and figs, with *cus-cus* and with *bazin.*[8] White bread, which comes from Tripoli, is an unheard-of luxury, even during festivals, which are rigorously observed. To make up for it they overindulge in date-whiskey and in red pepper.

Almost every Jew possesses an ass; and again the Arab shows his unspeakable malice. On Saturday the Arabs, insisting that there is no reason why the beasts should lose a day simply because the Jews do so, appropriate the animals and set them to work.

Through everything the Jews cling faithfully to their traditions; they still believe in the coming deliverance of Israel, and look forward to better days.

This is all the more surprising in view of the prevailing ignorance. The Talmud Torah, where a single instructor teaches reading, has sixteen children, but the Rabbi and the Shohet are as unlettered as the pupils.

We return to the cave of Saïd, our host, for the night. Here among the mysterious mountains of Libya, in a cavern fifteen meters below the surface of the earth, suffocating for lack of air, a prey to vermin—here, fifty centuries away from civilization and modern man, I passed a sleepless night. I meditated on the evolution of human civilization and on the strange lot of Israel among the nations. Now more than ever did I feel my close relationship, my brotherhood, with these cave dwellers, with these prehistoric people snoring around me.

Nahum Slouschz, *Travels in North Africa*
(Philadelphia, 1927), pp. 122–31.

[8] *Cus-cus* (more usually couscous) is a staple of the North African diet and consists of very fine grains of semolina pasta served as a starch with meat and vegetables or as a porridge with milk. *Bazin* is a popular Libyan dish consisting of maize or barley meal mixed with oil, red pepper, and spices into a heavy porridge.

MORE AMONG THE CAVE DWELLERS
(1906)

Tigrena: The Rabbi of the Caves

The next morning, after attending morning prayers and partaking of a light breakfast, we mounted our camels to continue our journey. We had hardly left the village, when a young Jewess, who was busied in picking the figs from an enormous fig tree, motioned me, drew near, and offered me a handful of fresh figs, saying courteously: "Hod,[1] Rabbi, hod!" ("Take, Rabbi, take!").

I thanked her and, true to my role of Rabbi, blessed her as best I could. The young woman, deeply moved, kissed my hand, as was fitting to my rabbinic dignity, and disappeared among the trees.

We continued our rhythmic march across the picturesque hills and valleys of the Jebel Gharian. The soil of this region is red and exceedingly fertile, and there is an abundance of water. As we went along, the invigorating wind tempered the heat of the African summer, which had caused me so much discomfort in the lowlands. The further south we advanced from the Turkish administrative center, the more frequently were the signs of cultivation: the vine flourishing in abundance on this vast mountain oasis in the heart of the desert. The remains of ancient ruins looked down from hilly eminences, while the young fruit trees scattered here and there bore witness to human habitations.

After a march of three and a half hours, we came upon a square building, dominated by a rather squat cupola and—which is strange enough in these parts—rising clear above the soil.

This was the new synagogue of Tigrena, which the population was anxious to have built above the ground. Apparently civilization is advancing, even in the country of the cave dwellers. However, I was shown an ancient synagogue, highly venerated, which was situated underground, and which reminded me of the one at Beni-Abbes. I made a tour of the village, with its twenty subterranean courts and its 650 or 700 inhabitants; in the synagogue I found a young man by the name of Ebani Hajaj, who was teaching some forty urchins to read Hebrew.

But I looked forward with impatience to the arrival of the most important person in the district, Rabbi Halifa Hajaj, the Haham Bashi (Chief Rabbi) and physician of the Gharian, the only one in the village who can speak Hebrew fluently. He was away at the market, which is held every Sunday at Ksar Gharian, and someone had gone to look for him.

[1] Ar., *khudh* (take!).

Meanwhile we proceeded to the underground home of the rabbi of the caves. His wife welcomed us respectfully and brought us the inevitable draught of *lagbi* (date juice), which refreshed us.

Men were scarce. Nearly all of them were at the market, but the news of our arrival having spread even as far as the marketplace, the foremost citizens hurried back to bring us a brotherly "salam." Less than an hour after my arrival there were already more than a dozen of my coreligionists returned from the market, all of a fine, dark type; they surrounded us, and poured forth all their troubles and all the details of their life.

I was informed that our host, Rabbi Halifa, who was still absent, was descended from a family of physicians and rabbis which immigrated from Morocco more than seven centuries ago; that one of his ancestors had even succeeded, in the days when the Jews were still numerous in these parts, in rising to the headship of the Jebel Gharian. They showed me in the distance the *Kasr* (fort) of Tigrena, dominating the village and bearing inscriptions in Hebrew and in Arabic which testify to the curious fact of the Jewish supremacy in the Gharian.

They told me further that Halifa had never taken any course in medicine, owing all his knowledge to his ancestors and to manuscript treatises in Hebrew-Arabic. He is a physician of great ability—the only one among the Mussulmans of the district. His fame has traveled as far as Tripoli, whither he has been called on two occasions, to perform surgical operations which were crowned with success. Like the Rabbis of the Middle Ages, he draws his whole income from his practice, and discharges his rabbinic functions without any compensation whatsoever. His success has only succeeded in making him an object of jealousy to the fanatic Mussulmans and rapacious officials.

In this country, cut off as it is from all effective supervision, and separated even from Tripoli by the desert, the religious head of the Jews has on two occasions been the victim of false accusations on the part of certain of his coreligionists who also practiced medicine, and has suffered the most savage persecution—which completes his resemblance to the Jewish savants of the Mussulman medieval age.[2]

But his ability, his probity, and his large humanity, which are the admiration of friends and enemies, finally overcame these jealousies. A commission of physicians from Constantinople finally put a stop to all these annoyances. This self-taught man obtained from the medical commission the official permit to practice medicine.

As I was learning all this, Rabbi Halifa himself appeared in the courtyard; he greeted Rabbi Mordecai warmly, and kissed my hands.

[2] It is not clear to which medieval savant Slouschz is referring here. Perhaps he had in mind Samuel ha-Nagid, who was once falsely denounced by Jewish rivals in Granada. See Eliyahu Ashtor, *The Jews of Moslem Spain,* vol. 2 (Philadelphia, 1979), p. 59.

I looked at this Rabbi, this survivor from the Middle Ages, recalling so vividly the doctors of the Arabian period: of small stature, but of venerable appearance, with large brown, lively eyes, a long beard, and a lofty forehead, which gave him an imposing air. He was some fifty years of age, but hardships and an eventful life had left their mark on his face.

Just now he was happy; it was the happiest day for him, he told us, as host, since the untimely death of his only son, who left a little boy, now the one consolation of his life.

Our appearance seemed to throw him into confusion; he was unable to show me sufficient respect and friendliness, and he ended by showering on me a whole flood of benedictions and cabalistic conjurations with which he adorns his medical knowledge.

We conversed in Hebrew, which this rabbi of the caves spoke fairly well, while poultry strutted on every side of us, a young he-goat skipped about, asses brayed, and several black sheep rubbed against us—all this swarming at the bottom of the underground pit where the rabbi's wife was busy preparing a meal over a fire lit in a heap of stones in the form of a primitive oven.

Men, women, and children, beasts and fowls, garbage and smoke—all moved and mingled restlessly in this pit, into which a glowing strip of the sky threw a deep blue light which seemed to envelop the entrance to the dwelling.

After I had satisfied his curiosity as to the condition of the Jews in the far north countries, Rabbi Halifa invited me to dinner in his "drawing room," a cave cleaner than the others, where a curious spectacle unceasingly unfolded itself before my eyes.

At the entrance there was a *mezuzah*; near that hung a piece of ground glass; through this the doctor examines certain cases of illness. Inside, on a plank suspended by the wall, I discovered a number of manuscripts in Hebrew and Arabic and even some printed books. On the floor was laid a straw mat, and a beam, which served as a table when any patient had to lie down.

But still stranger was the opposite wall. There, in place of an ornament or painting, stood a straw chair battered and worn out. This chair, Halifa told me, he brought from Tripoli in order to astonish everyone with a luxury unknown in this country; my umbrella, moreover, broken as it was, did not fail to evoke amazement by its complicated mechanism.

We seated ourselves on the mat. On my special behalf Halifa laid down a little cushion; he placed the beam at my side to serve me as a table. We spoke of underground life, and my host stated his conviction as a doctor that caves make much better habitations than do the houses in Tripoli: in winter they are not as damp, in summer they are not as hot. As for light and air, living in the heart of the Sahara where there is a little too much of these, one does not object to the reduction.

Seated on the ground, we prepared to dine. I was given a portion of warm barley bread, roast chicken seasoned with red pepper, and some red wine; the others sipped eagerly at their *araki*, or date whiskey. The rabbi's wife brought in a large clay dish full of a thick broth, glimmering with oil and abundantly overflowing the rim.

This is the *bazin*, the national dish of the Sahara. It is made of barley meal mixed with oil, strong pepper, and goodness knows what else, which gives it a yellowish, unappetizing color. I overcame my distaste and, a wooden spoon having been found by good luck, I took a taste, and found the dish too sharp, too fat, and too heavy for my European digestion. I decided firmly against going on with it. And my decision was an excellent one. I had hardly drawn out my spoon when twenty hands—one hundred fingers—of very questionable cleanness, were thrust into the dish. Each one took a handful of broth and squeezed it through his fingers, until the oil oozed out, mingling with the perspiration and forming a highly original mixture. They told me amiably that the *bazin* is only good after it has been mauled about between their fingers for several minutes, and that it is only after this delicate treatment that it acquires a really delicious taste.

As I declined firmly to follow their example, these people regarded me with feelings of alternate pity and vexation. "This *bazin* is *mazon* (nourishment) itself," someone told me dogmatically. But I did not give way to their importunities, happy to find a moment in which to examine at leisure the manuscripts on the plank, among which a collection of local Piyyutim particularly attracted my attention.

An Evening among the Cave Dwellers

The sun began to set. The burning African heat gave way to the refreshing shadows of the evening. The guests departed, this one for his anvil, that one for his loom, and ascended as it were into space, followed by the boys. The women came in from the fields with baskets of fresh figs. We proceeded to the synagogue for the *Minhah*[3] service. Tigrena boasts two *zla,*[4] or houses of worship: one entirely subterranean, the other lifting its roof of *pisé* (rammed clay) above the level of the soil. Prayers were said in the deep yard surrounding the building. Then we ascended a knoll overlooking the neighborhood. We sat down for a chat till the hour of *ᶜarbit.*[5] How many of us were there? About a score of men, including two or three Mussulman neighbors, who, in Africa, mingle everywhere in Jewish life with that indelicacy which is characteristic of the natives. A number of women—who are

[3] The afternoon prayer service.

[4] Jud.-Ar., *ṣlā.* This ancient word of Aramaic origin is used for "synagogue" in the Maghreb and at the opposite end of the Arabic-speaking world in Iraq. See Paul Wexler, "Terms for 'Synagogue' in Hebrew and Jewish Languages. Explorations in Historical Jewish Interlinguistics," *REJ* 140, nos. 1–2 (1981), pp. 101–38, especially pp. 118–19.

[5] The evening prayer service.

excluded from divine service—remained somewhat apart, seated on the brink of a dwelling pit.

I observed this world around me, and conversed with Rabbi Halifa, while my interpreter, Mordecai, expatiated with enthusiasm to several prominent members of the community on the object of my travels. I interrogated the Rabbi in regard to the beginnings of the Jewish settlements in this cave country. Savage invasions and devastating wars, replied the Rabbi, had robbed them of their ancient documents. There are in the district numerous villages where one may find traces of deserted Haras[6] and of Jewish cemeteries now abandoned. The ancestors of the Jews of the cave country have transmitted the tradition that in very ancient times the Jews formed the majority of the population, but that wars and epidemics decimated their numbers. There were, moreover, frequent conversions to Islamism for many generations. And, in addition, as a result of the frightful epidemics, a large part of the Jewish population of the recent generations had preferred to leave the Gharian in order to settle in the oasis on the coast of Tripoli.

"As for my family," continued the Rabbi, "we know with certainty that the first ancestor of the Hajaj family came, some seven centuries ago, from Maghreb-el-Aksa[7] (Morocco). Like myself he was a physician and a rabbi, but he was no less a warrior. He took part in the struggles which were then laying waste the country, and, having taken possession of the Tigrena fort, which dominates the countryside, he succeeded in having himself proclaimed the chief of the Gharian.

"For several centuries our ancestors governed the country; then came the Ishmaelites (the orthodox Arabs, as opposed to the heretical Berbers); with them came bloodshed and pillage, which were destined never to leave our unhappy country. Our family was gradually impoverished, declining in numbers and in importance. Today all that is left to me is my medical practice, and the honorary title of Haham Bashi, or Grand Rabbi, which was already borne by my grandfather.

"But God is just; misfortunes of every kind have beset me. I have been denounced to the authorities for the illegal practice of medicine; I have even tasted the sweets of a Turkish prison, the *zekut* (merit) of my fathers (peace be with them) delivered me. I lost my only son; but God was merciful. He has been pleased to leave me his child, who is my only heir, and my one consolation.

"May it be His will to deliver us from the hand of the Barbarians, to take us out of the *Galut*. Amen!"

Thus spoke Rabbi Halifa.

I followed up my inquiry concerning the local traditions of the Jews and the abandoned Haras. I found that there are numerous Jewish families

[6] Ar., *ḥāra* (a quarter). The reference here is to a *ḥārat al-Yahūd,* or "Jewish Quarter."

[7] Ar., *al-Maghrib al-Aqṣā* (lit., the furthest West).

of Tripoli who came originally from the Gharian, among them the Attras, the Hassans, the Hajajs, the Seroz, the Abbani, the Bahdish, the Saduebs.

Among other things Halifa told me that of the heroes of the Jewish wars, local tradition has preserved the name of one Arun ben Arun. It appears that the father of the Rabbi read in one of the caves in the Jebel Nefussa an inscription in Hebrew characters which bore the following legend:

> Ana Arun ben Arun, ya Rejaba, etc. (I, Arun son of Arun, who delivered his people in battle . . .)

A number of the men present spoke with me on the precarious position of the Jews of the Sahara. They complained of the arbitrary treatment which the minor Turkish officials mete out to them on every occasion, of the humiliating attitude of the neighboring Mussulmans, who are one of the most degenerate races it has ever been my lot to meet.

Their complaints were bitterest against the *askeria* duty, a tax for exemption from military service, which the Jews are forced to pay in kind, in a country where the natives are excused from army service.[8]

While they were pouring out their complaints to me, an Arab, who had just come from the Kasr Gharian (Turkish fort and administrative center), thrust himself into our conversation and announced solemnly that at that very moment an order had arrived from Constantinople, exempting the Jews from the *askeria* in all countries where the Mussulmans are not subject to military service.

Poor people! This announcement, fabrication though it was from beginning to end, was enough to rouse everybody to enthusiasm. Even the women came running up to share in the general rejoicing.

Date whiskey and red pepper, hotter even than alcohol, were brought to celebrate the great deliverance. The Mussulmans, total abstainers when at home, have no scruples about drinking among Jews. As for the bringer of the good tidings, he helped himself to drinks with the greatest freedom, which confirmed, in my eyes, the improbability of his story. It was just an Arab ruse to have a little feast at the expense of the credulity of the Jews.

However, business is business, even among the cave dwellers. The most prominent men of the village took advantage of our presence to bring up for trial a dispute, or *mahaloket*, which was dividing the community over the question of a *shohet*—for all the world like an orthodox Polish community. It need only be said that this profession, which everywhere else among orthodox Jews calls for talmudic scholarship of more or less profundity, can be assumed in most small Arabian communities at the cost of very little effort. It is sufficient for the candidate to have learned by heart a few pages from

[8]Concerning this levy, known in Turkish as the *bedel-i askeri,* see Part One, p. 9.

a manual in Judeo-Arabic, and to have taken a few practical lessons from an established *shohet.* This post, while carrying no remuneration, is very much sought after as an honorary title. The result is constant squabbling and rivalries in the midst of the communities.

A dark young fellow was brought before us as the defendant. A cave citizen of advanced years upbraided him for not having examined his knife before slaughtering a kid. He demanded, therefore, in the name of the law, that the practice of the *shehitah* be absolutely forbidden to this young man.

The onlookers were divided into two camps. They vociferated, shouted, swore, insulted one another. The uproar was terrific, such as only Orientals could make without coming to blows. Finally our authority prevailed, and we had the young man reinstated in his post.

The arrival of a new personage put an end to this scene. A Jewish itinerant merchant from Nefussa, returning from Fezzan, gave me some very lively details of the mode of living and of trading of the Jewish itinerant merchants, who follow all the routes of the Sahara and face all the dangers which infest them. As for the Jews of the southern Sahara and of the Sudan, he did not remember ever having met them, but he assured me that there exists, at least in the east Sudan, a black-skinned population which some call the Felici and which are generally known among the Tuaregs as the Krit. They observe the Sabbath and are known to be of Jewish origin.

This picturesque evening, from which I had gathered such a rich harvest of facts and observations, taught me one thing more.

In these, inaccessible regions of the Sahara the "vendetta," or *lex talionis*, still reigns supreme. Already at Msellata I had been able to observe a case of vendetta between a tribe of ordinary Arabs and a tribe of Shurefa, noble descendants of Mohammed.

Because they had seen one of their number slain by the Arabs, the Shurefas, the holy descendants of Mohammed, massacred forty of their neighbors, and would have exterminated them to the last man had it not been for the energetic intervention of the Turkish government, which does not permit too much of this sort of thing in its territories.

The further south one goes, the ruder become the customs and the bloodier the vendetta. Local tradition attributes the disappearance of villages to acts of the vendetta.

Indeed, it only suffices for a Mussulman to have been killed by a Jew, even by accident, for the whole village to find itself faced by the terrible alternatives of expatriation or extermination. Fortunately, the Arabs of the desert, who are the laziest people in the world, are, in their love of money, not behind their coreligionists of the towns, and nothing is more natural, in a case of this kind, than the blood redemption of the murdered man, which his family permits for a consideration and which finally puts an end to hostilities.

The most curious thing is that the vendetta is not unknown among the Jews. However, it must be said in justice to them that, as among themselves, one never hears of assassinations. But between Jews and Mussulmans it is different.

Formerly, when the Jews were more numerous, they did not let a single case pass without avenging the blood of one of their number, and whenever it came to a question of punishing an Arab tribe, the Berbers were ready with effective cooperation. Today the Jews and Berbers of the Gharian are powerless to exact reprisals from their Arab neighbors, who outnumber them overwhelmingly.

But what the Jews of the Gharian have retained is a certain courage, which is characteristic of a large number of them. I was introduced to a Jew by the name of Hai who scours the desert and whose heroic exploits are the terror of the degenerate natives and the Turkish authorities.

Several years ago some Arabs surprised, in the open desert, a brother of Hai, a young Jew, whom they murdered on the spot. His elder brother, who, by right of vendetta, was bound to avenge him, and who is known for his courage, swore solemnly to take vengeance on the entire family of the assassins. For many years this avenging brother has scoured the desert routes, and has lain in wait for his prey. Every time he succeeds in surprising a member of the family which he holds responsible for his brother's death, the avenger murders the man on the spot. Three of the aggressors are already dead, but the savage avenger is not appeased. It would have been vain for me to have sought to dissuade this primitive man from a purpose which he had made the aim of his life.

Nahum Slouschz, *Travels in North Africa*
(Philadelphia, 1927), pp. 132–47.

THE CHIEF RABBI OF CAIRO'S RESPONSUM ON PROSTITUTES' GIFTS TO THE SYNAGOGUE
(LATE NINETEENTH TO EARLY TWENTIETH CENTURIES)

Concerning the matter of prostitutes from the daughters of Israel—far be it from our straight paths—who dedicate a new ark curtain or Torah scroll cover, it is permissible from a legal point of view to accept these from them because the fabric is not the actual "harlot's pay," as Rabbi Moses Isserles has written in his gloss to the *Shulḥan ᶜArūkh, Oraḥ Ḥayyim*, Section 153, paragraph 21, citing Rabbi Jeroham.[1] However, the gift should not be accepted from them if their contemptible name is inscribed on it, for that would be a memorial to them in the house of our Exalted God, Who detests prostitution and considers all evil strange.

An actual case occurred here in Cairo of a prostitute who dedicated a curtain of new fabric for the Holy Ark. However, that wicked woman had her name conspicuously embroidered upon it in gilded letters that could be distinguished and read from a distance. I spoke with the leaders and officers of the congregation—may God grant them long life and protect them—telling them that this was a very reprehensible and disgraceful thing. That harlot was continuing to sit in her brothel and, alas because of our many sins, numerous young Jewish men continue to be ensnared in her net, while at the same time her despicable name is emblazoned across the Holy Ark. When those young men were in synagogue and looked up at the ark curtain and saw her name there, they would without a doubt be brought to thoughts of sinning even while at prayer. Thus, we would be causing the many to go astray—God forbid—in addition to the fact that a memorial to sin, prostitution, and abomination in God's house is in and of itself loathsome. We, therefore, ordered them to bury that ark curtain immediately—may God reward their good deed.

It is fitting for the officers of congregations to be protective of their Master's honor, and if those evildoers should dedicate an ark curtain, a Torah scroll, Torah crowns, or the like, they should accept it on condition that their name is not indicated on the ritual object. For their name is to be obliterated.

There was another case of a prostitute who dedicated a Torah scroll to the synagogue. It was accepted on condition that her name not be inscribed upon it or memorialized. And so it was.

[1] "It is forbidden to use a 'harlot's pay' or the price of a dog for a sacred purpose such as the synagogue or a Torah scroll. However, this refers specifically to the item given as payment, but if money was given, it is permitted to buy with it a holy object. This does not refer to ordinary matters of prostitution, but to adulterous or incestuous relationships, but from ordinary unmarried prostitutes who make a dedicatory offering, it may be received. (Rabbi Jeroham, *Tōledōt Adām ve-Ḥavva,* 23:1.)"

The leaders of the holy people must keep on the alert in such instances. Honoring God requires that such things be anonymous. Let this remark suffice.

Raphael Aaron Ben Simeon, *Nehar Miṣrayim*
(Alexandria, 1907/8), p. 12a.

A SYRIAN RABBI PREACHES AGAINST THE NEW IMMORALITY

(PRE-WORLD WAR I)

There has increased in our times a new prohibited activity which never happened before. Many girls have desecrated God's Holy Name, singing and dancing in public. Men and women say to them, "Show me your face. Let me hear your voice, for your voice is pleasing."[1] There they sit—men, their wives, and their children.

Men—why do they go to graze in such places in the shade of the tree that Naaman has planted?[2] Women—why do they go to display their beauty before commonfolk and notables alike? Children—why do they go to get an education in sinning? Woe to the eyes that see such things and to the ears that hear them. The city that was praised as the perfection of beauty, how has the faithful city become a harlot![3]

I am not angry with the dancing girl, for she is from a lowly family. She dances out of greed for a silver coin. But I am angry with the decent people of respectable families. All of this leads to neglect of Torah study. There are some four hundred youths—God grant them life and prosperity—who have no learned master to teach them Torah and ethics. How can such a boy do anything without sinning?

Jacob Saul Dwek, *Derekh Emūna*
(Aleppo, 1913/14), p. 17b.

[1] Cant. 2:14.

[2] Naaman was the Aramaean commander who came to the Prophet Elisha to be cured of his leprosy (see II Kings 5). He is used here as an eponym for Gentile Syrians. Rabbi Dwek is saying that such places of public entertainment are not for Jews.

[3] Rabbi Dwek is combining phrases from Lam. 2:15 and Isa. 1:21.

THE RABBIS OF ALEPPO PRONOUNCE A BAN OF ANATHEMA UPON SABBATH DESECRATORS (1906)

Due the fact that certain scoundrels from within our midst have thrown off the yoke of the Sabbath and do their work on it just as on weekdays, I, together with the other rabbis and scholars, took it upon ourselves to try and repair this terrible breach as best we could for the sake of Heaven. We therefore wrote a proclamation and affixed our signatures to it. The rabbis and scholars of the four holy cities (may they be built up speedily) assisted us with their own stern proclamations in order to correct this serious matter.

The following is the proclamation agreed upon by the rabbis and scholars of Aleppo (may God protect it):

It is well known how serious is the prohibition against Sabbath desecration, and against eating nonkosher meat in a spirit of defiance, abandoning the permitted and eating what is forbidden, especially if done in public. It is clearly indicated in the Bible, the Talmud, and the homiletic and exegetic literature. Our Master[1] of blessed memory has ruled in the *Shulḥān ᶜĀrūkh* that the Sabbath desecrator is to be considered as a Gentile in all things. . . . He has cut himself off from the congregation of Israel. He has no religion at all. He is unfit to give witness, to take an oath, or to do anything. His meat is forbidden, as is all his food and drink, because he has lost his trustworthiness. There is no difference between opening his shop halfway or entirely. It is clearly specified, furthermore, that even if the desecration did not take place before ten witnesses, if he committed it in an open place and it became public knowledge, it is considered to have been committed publicly.[2]

Therefore, we have heard this day and are deeply distressed that there are unruly young men making trouble among the people, who defy the prohibition of the holy Sabbath by the merit of which we live. They also violate the prohibited forms of labor.[3] They seek to throw off the yoke of Heaven and to breach the fence around the Torah. It is our high duty, therefore, in judgment of sins and for the sake our holy Torah, to try with all forcefulness to break the jaws of wickedness and to give ourselves over body and soul to the santification of the Divine Name—may it be exalted. May God help us for the sake of His Name.

Therefore, we the undersigned rabbis and scholars of Aleppo have taken it upon ourselves to raise the banner of the sacred Torah for the unity

[1] Rabbi Joseph Karo, the author of the *Shulḥān ᶜĀrūkh,* the most authoritative code of Jewish law.

[2] The proclamation cites from a variety of places in the *Shulḥān ᶜĀrūkh*—Oraḥ Ḥayyīm 23 and 395; Yōreh Dēᶜa 2, 128, 158; Ḥoshen Mishpāṭ 36 and 125.

[3] Thirty-nine primary classes of work are forbidden on the Sabbath, according to Mishna Shabbat 7:2.

of the Holy Name. We have given our unanimous consent in council that anyone who violates the prohibitions of the Sabbath, even the nonbiblical ones instituted by the sages, and anyone who eats nonkosher meat out of willful defiance, we shall publicly declare him a heretic in accordance with the *Shulḥān ^{c}Ārūkh*. We shall not permit him to marry any of our daughters. Neither shall we accept his sons for our sons-in-law. We shall not perform any wedding for him. We shall not bury him among the graves of proper Israelites. He is unfit to give witness or to take oaths as previously stated.

We know with perfect faith that all the people of Israel are holy. The stock resembles its roots. They are careful to avoid even minor prohibitions. We have only to encourage and exhort those who will take caution. Whoever heeds us will be secure.

Enacted here in Aleppo, Tammuz 5666. "And the Children of Israel shall keep the Sabbath."[4]

Signed with abundant love and peace:

Jacob Saul Dwek
Jacob Diqnis
Isaiah Khaski
Michael Mish^{c}an
Saul Khaski
Abraham ^{c}Abbadi
Abraham ^{c}Antebi
Raḥamim Mizraḥi
Elijah Ḥamawi

Meir Sason
Ḥayyim Naḥmad
Solomon Laniado
Judah David Kohen
Isaac Sawid
Elijah ^{c}Abboud
Judah ^{c}Aṭiya
Abraham Eliezer

Moshe Harari
Ezra Ḥamawi
Ezra ^{c}Abbadi
Raḥamim Ben Dayyan
Isaac Avigdor
Jacob Shomer
Ezra Dwek
Ezra Levi

David Menashe
Reuben Ancona
Solomon Malchishoba
Ḥayyim Eli Kohen
Raphael Marcus
Jacob Lopes
Elijah Kohen
Issac Laniado

Jacob Saul Dwek, *Derekh Emūna*
(Aleppo, 1913/14), pp. 120a–121a.

[4] Exod. 31:16.

A TWENTIETH-CENTURY YEMENITE VERSION OF THE PACT OF ᶜUMAR[1]
(1905)

In the Name of Allah, the Merciful, the Beneficent

This is a decree which the Jews must obey as commanded. They are obliged to observe everything in it. They are forbidden to disobey it. It is intended to remind them of what the governors of the Ottoman Empire abolished . . . which are required by the principles of law.

That is that these Jews are guaranteed protection upon payment of the *jizya* by each adult male: from the rich, 48 silver qafla, which is equivalent to 3 3/4 riyal; from the middle class, 24 qafla, or 2 7/8 riyal; from the poor, 12 qafla, or 16/17 riyal. In this way, their blood is spared, and they are brought into the pact of protection. They may not avoid it. It is incumbent upon each individual to pay it prior to the year's end into the hand of the person whom we have commended to receive it from them. This is religious law revealed by Allah unambiguously in His Scripture.

Furthermore, they are required to pay on their commercial transactions whose value is equal to the legal taxable minimum, five percent per annum. However, they owe nothing on whatever falls below the taxable minimum of about 10 riyals. The aforementioned *jizya* and tariff are incumbent upon them.

They are not to assist each other against a Muslim. They may not build their houses higher than Muslim homes. They shall not crowd them in their streets. They may not turn them away from their watering places. They may not belittle the Islamic religion, nor curse any of the prophets. They shall not mislead a Muslim in matters pertaining to his religion. They may not ride on saddles, but only sit sidesaddle. They may not wink or point to the nakedness of a Muslim. They may not display their Torah except in their synagogues. Neither shall they raise their voices when reading, nor blow their shofars loudly. Rather, a muffled voice will suffice. They are forbidden from engaging in reprehensible relations[2] which bring down the wrath of Heaven. It is their duty to recognize the superiority of the Muslim and to accord him honor.

The Jews of Sanᶜa have chosen the dhimmīs Aaron Al-Kīhūn, Yiḥya Qāfiḥ, Yiḥya Isaac, and Yiḥya al-Abyaḍ to correct any of their misdeeds and to conduct their affairs according to rules of their religious law. The Jews are hereby ordered to obey them and to comply with their directives. It is incumbent upon those leaders not to let them deviate from the right path.

[1]Cf. the pact and various medieval decrees based on it in Norman A. Stillman, *The Jews of Arab Lands: A History and Source Book* (Philadelphia, 1979), pp. 157–58, 167–68, 273–74.

[2]The reference is to prostitution. See Part One, p. 37.

They are not to change anything from their religious law. They shall not make themselves aloof from them out of greed, so that the weak will not be destroyed by the strong. They may not prevent any of their people who wishes to seek justice according to Muḥammad's religious law.

We have appointed Yiḥya Danokh to be Shaykh[3] over them. He shall act in accordance with the commands that we issue for Sanᶜa. The Jews shall conduct themselves as is required. They shall live in their homes and shall refrain from whatever is to be avoided. He is to carry this out and to conduct wisely the affairs of all who are under the Prophet's pact of protection and under ours.

Sulaymān b. Yiḥya Ḥabshūsh, *Eshkōlōt Merōrōt*, in *The Yemenites*, ed. S. D. Goitein (Jerusalem, 1983), pp. 190–91 (Arabic).

[3] The Yemenite Arabic term used here is *ᶜāqil.* The person referred to is the secular head of the community who bears the parallel Hebrew title of *nāsī.* Concerning this office, see Erich Brauer, *Ethnologie der jemenitischen Juden* (Heidelberg, 1934), pp. 281–83; also Yehuda Nini, *Yemen and Zion: The Jews of Yemen, 1800–1914* (Jerusalem, 1982), pp. 103–9 [Heb.].

REACTIONS IN MOSUL TO THE CONSTITUTIONAL REFORM OF THE YOUNG TURKS (1908)

We have not had in Mosul—unlike our unfortunate coreligionists in Baghdad[1]—much to suffer from the fanatic and reactionary movement among the Muslims in recent days. The delegates of the Committee of Union and Progress of Salonika, whose arrival I have previously announced to you, have very simply been expelled from the city. They vainly tried to form a small Young Turk committee in secret. When the masonic methods employed by them to win adherents (obligation to put on a red shirt soaked in blood, oath of loyalty to the C.U.P., etc.) were uncovered, the fanatic Muslims meant to do harm to these two "cafers,"[2] who without the quick thinking of the governor who made them leave hastily in the night, might have been massacred.

The Christians of Mosul were less fortunate than we. The fanatic population killed five of them because they had declared publicly that they were partisans of the new constitution. Our brave Jews, on the other hand, strongly recommend to each other in our synagogues to never even pronounce the words "constitution" or "liberty," and as they have to howl with the wolves, they are always declaring when they are in the presence of Muslims that the constitution is disorder, anarchy, that the Young Turks are misguided individuals who must be set aright, and that after all, the old Hamidian regime was the best one can find in this world.

I do not consider it a good idea for me to mix into these dangerous political affairs, but I always counsel our coreligionists to stay completely aloof from both these parties and to keep their personal convictions to themselves so as not to upset either the Young Turks who are running things or the reactionaries who are predominant.

Letter from Maurice Sidi, director of Alliance School for Boys in Mosul, to the president of the AIU in Paris (November 13, 1908).

AIU Archives (Paris)
Irak I.C.8.

[1] A mob had attacked the Jews of Baghdad only a month earlier. See Part One, p. 48, and the sources cited there in n. 2.

[2] Ar., *kāfir* (infidel).

A JEWISH EGYPTIAN PATRIOT CALLS FOR DEEMPHASIZING RELIGION IN HIS COUNTRY'S PUBLIC LIFE FOR THE SAKE OF NATIONAL UNITY (1912)

I wish to discuss something that has a clear relationship to religion. I wish to speak about the national community, because being a healthy national society requires that there be in its extended national life a complete distancing from anything that might harm it from the realm of religion. Every single nation or kingdom always needs a community which calls to it the essence of nationhood, especially when it happens that the nation or kingdom belongs to people who are not of a single religion or rite as is the case in Egypt. When the adherents of various religions and rites arm themselves, some of them kill others. I do not mean real killing, but rather the killing of fraternal sentiments and the national feeling in people's hearts. There is no worse slaughter than this because it always bequeaths a legacy of burning fire which cannot be extinguished, or it is a war without end. If a nation has progressed in its conception, the smallest thing from the domain of religion which might be harmful to it should immediately be considered the greatest thing in proportion to this progress. No one will deny that interfaith relations in Egypt before now were heavier than the Juyushi Mountain or more terrifying than the savage in the wilderness who lies in ambush to assault the passerby on the way. However, the present advance in the concept of the nation, or in the concept of that which is meant to be denoted now by the term "the Egyptian nation," is far more advanced than the actual present state of things. We promote the state in its conception. We do not promote a religious association in accordance with this concept.

Forgive me, my brothers—and all under heaven are my brethren—if I speak, for there is nothing more beneficial than these words nowadays. They are the efficacious medicine for our societal sickness in this country of ours. If we want to improve our condition externally, we must first improve internally. Health begins properly with the internal remedy. We want to have a nation. We want a constitution or a general code. We want to be a sovereign state in our own sight and in the sight of others. It is a duty to work truly and effectively for this goal in a way that there is no doubt as to its efficacy, as it is said in His glorious Book: "Verily, God does not change a people's condition until they change what is in their souls."[1] It is a lofty maxim in language that can almost be grasped with the hand. The power of the work can only come from the will in the soul. When it lacks that will, it does not work, or it performs a false labor. If we want to have a nation, then we must have it in actuality. Moreover, we will have it by transforming ourselves

[1] Sura 13:11. It is interesting that the author, who is Jewish, refers to the Koran as "God's glorious Book."

altogether. We must change our souls and make them all into a single soul facing the nation. That is, in order for there to be a single soul, it is necessary for the individual souls to be dedicated to that which they share among one another. This dedication comes from abandoning everything religious which serves as an obstacle on the path to achieving it. I have before me now a palpable witness to this, a witness upon which there is the unspoken consensus of the Ottoman Empire in its entirety, just as there is consensus about it in every kingdom that has progressed before it. That witness is what we have seen and are seeing, namely the unity of the Muslims as an entity and marching together in step with their Ottoman brothers on a single path, proclaiming officially at the top of their lungs, "Our condition will only be improved by general, national unity and a lack of discrimination between one religion and another and between one rite and another through mutual association, moral conduct, and good social relations. It is henceforth no longer proper to be called 'Khawāja' or 'Effendi.'[2] Rather everyone, whether Muslim or non-Muslim, should be called 'Effendi,'" in order to unify all the sons of the one nation, to bring their hearts together, and to prevent that antipathy which afflicts human nature when someone addresses someone else as "Khawāja," meaning "O Christian" or "O Jew."

Would that I were better informed with a special knowledge of the condition of everyone in the Ottoman Empire and in Egypt with respect to the general morals, whether the Empire was more advanced or Egypt? The reader should pardon me that I am not better informed on this matter. However, he should also forgive me for saying that the Exalted Empire is working for the reform of general morals, while we are not.

. . . .

I do not belong to the party of the Prime Minister (the late Buṭrus Pasha). I support him or attack him not from a partisanship which tries to hinder leading dignitaries in the country, but rather as an Egyptian man, the son of an Egyptian, who defends the national union or attacks it in order to loosen its ties somewhat from the influences of religion.

The reason for this section of the essay in which I am now is that someone came into my presence and began to greet me with the words "Peace be upon you."[3] However, he did not finish it, but cut it in half to rectify the matter and changed the greeting to "May your day be auspicious."[4] But then he greeted someone else with the full "Peace be upon you" of course.

[2] The first title was reserved for non-Muslims, and the latter title was for Muslims.

[3] Ar., *al-salām ʿalayk.* This salutation is reserved for Muslims. See C. van Arendonk, "Salām," *Shorter EI,* p. 490; also Edward William Lane, *The Manners and Customs of the Modern Egyptians,* (reprint ed., London, 1908), pp. 203–4.

[4] Ar., *Nahāruka saʿīd.* This is a neutral greeting.

I will not hide from the reader that I was embarrassed and ashamed. I returned to my feelings thinking about the incident. It was not the first time, but rather one of a number of times that it had happened to me, while I kept silent and lowered my eyes. However, I did not find in my heart protection from the words, rather I found the words particularly necessary and required. My heart could not bear it any longer. I have regained my composure from it on the one hand, and I serve the national union on the other. I oppose anything of this sort that harms feelings of human brotherhood, let alone national feelings. When people distinguish between people with a greeting, there is in it an alerting of the mind that this is a Muslim or a non-Muslim. What is more than this warning, the person who is giving the greeting is charming every time the "Peace be upon you" is in order, while he almost pays no attention to the fact that non-Muslims are present with Muslims. But we are the people of a single nation who are working for one commonweal. Seldom is there a gathering of the three—Muslim, Christian, and Jew—without an insult being given as soon as the mental alert is sounded by a simple warning as to who is a Muslim and who is not. Furthermore, there is in this warning an indication to the soul that there is some sort of aversion or loathing, or at least a lack of equality in public morals and manners. Every etiquette, like the etiquette of social greeting, requires equalizing. When you are alone with a Muslim there is no harm in saying "Peace be upon you" a thousand times. Similarly, when there is a Christian or a Jew with him, there is no need for specifying and distinguishing. Then it will never be proper to cut a greeting short after beginning to utter it and to change it to another which distinguishes and specifies even more emphatically than at first. If the Exalted Empire has granted equality between Muslim and non-Muslim in its social policy by prohibiting the term "Khawāja" and by generalizing the use of the title "Effendi" for all, that is equality in its true sense. It is even stronger than according equality in the greeting "Peace be upon you." Is it not fitting, therefore, that we should at least follow the example of that great Islamic Empire which is the possessor of the Prophetic Caliphate with a similar acknowledgment of equality in the greeting "Peace be upon you"?

Murād Faraj, *Maqālāt Murād*
(Cairo, 1912), pp. 201–8.

THE JEWS OF BEIRUT COMPLAIN ABOUT THEIR NEW CHIEF RABBI TO THE HĀKHĀM BĀSHĪ *OF THE OTTOMAN EMPIRE*

(1909)

Beirut, 24 December 1909

To Imperial Chief Rabbi Nahoum,
Constantinople.

Dear Chief Rabbi,

Following the granting of the constitution in the Empire, there was an awakening throughout the Beirut Community, which, disorganized and lacking a chief rabbi at its head, wanted to regenerate itself too and have as a guide an enlightened man worthy to be its representative before the authorities.

Counting upon your enlightenment, the Community did not hesitate to bring to your attention the ill that it was suffering so that you might indicate the remedy, declaring itself ready to make any sort of sacrifice in order to merit it.

Alas! Vain sacrifices, vain hope! The man who should have sought to unite the hearts of all has done everything to divide them. He whose moral dignity is equivalent to that of the magistrate has succeeded only in sowing discord by his arbitrary and senseless acts. By his inconsistent character and lack of dignity, he has done everything to discredit himself in the eyes of the people and, what is worse, to discredit his office.

Some men of goodwill with the interests of Jewry at heart worked hard to support him at first, and as much by persuasion as by the influence they enjoy, succeeded in creating a climate of respectful sympathy for the new head of the Community.

He, unfortunately, did not know how to profit at all from this purely selfless cooperation. Blinded by a power which he exaggeratedly thought he wielded, he threatened at every turn the newcomer and the notable alike, and this, in the name of the firman[1] in his possession. The firman is for him a sword that he brandishes at the least trifle when it must strike. It was like this only recently when he threatened one of the members of the Communal Committee that he would have him brought before him by force if he did not answer his summons, and when he wanted to force the Treasurer to deliver over to him the Communal funds and valuables in his possession, threatening that if the Treasurer did not comply, he would have recourse to the local authorities. To these authoritarian acts which should demonstrate a total lack of experience and tact, you should add the childish tantrums

[1] Turk. for "an imperial edict."

that compel him to use the most violent language toward the elected leaders of the community.

Instead of setting the example for a certain elevation of heart and spirit by not mixing into the handling of communal receipts (since his honoraria have been fixed), he has been spending a great deal of his time in forcing a detailed accounting of the *gabella*.[2]

This tax which the Community has imposed upon itself voluntarily to aid in the better functioning of its institutions, he has had pretentions of monopolizing for the sole profit of the Hahamhane,[3] only consenting after long struggles and the sight of 300 poor children left out in the street by order of the Alliance, to divert a part of the revenues of the *gabella* to educational uses.

This man, who should have been the model of unselfishness, has shown an intemperate zeal in preoccupying himself with his own interests, which have not been threatened at all, at the expense of the interests of the poor.

We believe that the office of the Chief Rabbi ought to be of a higher order, which is the sole condition for it being respected by its flock and having a benevolent influence upon them. Unfortunately—and we say it to our great regret—the person charged with representing you is far from being of the high caliber required for such a role.

Instead of listening to the advice which the city notables have not failed to give unstintingly to him, he has chosen an entourage of self-interested individuals to sow discord in order to play a role in the Community. People of ill repute have free access to him, and he shows more regard for their opinion than for that of the elected officers of the Community.

To top off the inconsiderate measures taken by him which have no other result than to ruin the Community and turn the entire population against him, he has just taken forcible control of the locks of the Jewish cemetery for which he has the new keys in order to personally collect the tax on burials.

The tax was collected until now by the Committee, and the revenues were deposited in accordance with the statutes of the Community in the Anglo-Palestine Bank to be reserved for the free burial of the poor. Chief Rabbi Danon appointed as banker for these revenues in place of the aforementioned Jewish bank an individual to whom he personally owed money, and he intended to settle his debts at the expense of the burial fund.

A month ago, there was a death in one of the most honorable families of our Community (the Greenbergs). The family would have immediately after the eight days of religious mourning hastened to pay the prescribed tax to the Anglo-Palestine Bank. This displeased the Chief Rabbi. While the family was still grieving during that week for the loss of its head, the Chief Rabbi had the unheard-of, inconceivable idea of forbidding anyone from

[2] A sales tax, usually levied upon meat.

[3] Turk. for "the chief rabbi's office."

proceeding with the burial, or even with the preliminary funeral ceremonies. He demanded that he himself should be paid on the spot (the affair took place between midnight and two in the morning) a tax fixed abusively high by him at 1,000 francs. It was necessary to negotiate with the Rabbi until dawn while the corpse lay on the floor and the family, in tears at the latest misfortune to have struck it and torn between grief and indignation, did not know what to do. In place of the most elementary human sentiments and respect for the dead which the circumstances required, the Chief Rabbi committed a revolting abuse of power and displayed an unqualified cupidity in aggravating circumstances. Moreover, considering the fact that this concerned one of the most charitable and justly respected families in the city, the entire populace was outraged at these unheard-of goings-on which even a person totally devoid of tact or manners would not have done.

We beg you, Chief Rabbi, to please put an end to this state of affairs by withdrawing from Rabbi Danon the dignity with which he has been invested. His remaining in office would spell the ruin of the Community, which instead of gaining prestige, would only come to dishonor. The Jewish Community of Beirut will be eternally grateful to such an extent that it would unite the diverse factions now existing, but which are unanimous in asking you to recall their present Chief Rabbi.

Please note in examining the attached petition signed by the great majority of Jews in Beirut that the signatories are none other than the notables who asked you to help them to reorganize the Community. They are those who had hoped for the coming of the present Chief Rabbi, whom they had freely given their cooperation and counsel. You can judge Chief Rabbi Danon's conduct by noting that even his most ardent partisans from the beginning, his friends who were sympathetic to him in advance because they saw in him the Regenerator of the Community, are obliged today, in order to save the Communal Institutions that he has endangered, to ask you for his recall.

. . . We have sought to calm the people while waiting for a telegraphic response to our request from you. . . . We have been careful to abstain from presenting our request to you through the channel of the local authorities and thus making them aware of communal affairs.

We hope that, given the importance of the case submitted to you and the urgency of the measures to be taken, that you will not delay in issuing the orders that the circumstances require.

Please accept, dear Chief Rabbi, this expression of our respect and devotion.

P.S. Please address your telegram as well as your letter to Mr. Anzarut, the President of our Community.

signed:

Abouhab A.
Alkalay Y.
Anzarut L.
Anzarut M.
Attié M.D.
Attié M.H.
Barzel
Benjamin E.
Calef L.
Dana H.
Dischi H.
Dweik S.
Enriquez V.
Epstein
Farhi H.
Farhi Sasson
Farhi Y.
Farhi J.D.
Grasowsky
Greenberg M.
Greenberg J.
Grumberg W.
Haiat D.
Haiat R.
Hadda
Hakim Isaac
Halfon S.
Hallak I.
Lévy J.
Lévy S.
Lipawsky
Mizrahi A.
Mograbi M.
Moyal B.
Mubazbaze I.
Metalon R.
Nahon Y.
Rosensweig F.
Rabbinowitz
Safadi Y.
Sasson B.
Sasson D.
Sasson Ibrahim
Sroure S.
Sroure Saad
Totah A.
Yédid M.
Yédid H.
Yédid D.

AIU Archives (Paris)
Liban I.G.4.

THE CHIEF RABBI OF BEIRUT DEFENDS HIMSELF
(1910)

The Chief Rabbi of Beirut
Beirut, 25 August 1910

The President of the Alliance Israélite Universelle
Paris

Dear Sir,

I have the honor to bring to your attention by the present letter that as of a year and a half ago, I was named Chief Rabbi of this city.

Seeing the abnormal state and negligence of the directors of the Community which had remained for a long time without a chief, I was resolved to work for its resurrection. My first thought was to introduce the gabella, an indispensable measure which would provide for the expenses of all the Community.

I encountered many obstacles against this innovation which I overcame one by one. However, the opposition of Mr. Y. Semah,[1] the former director of your schools in our city, paralyzed all of my undertakings. Taking advantage of his influence among the notables, he knew how to imbue them with his opinions, and in concert with them, he opened a fierce polemic against this tax. It is almost a year now that the gabella has been abolished. You can imagine how much all of the communal institutions in general and the rabbinical corps in particular suffered by this lack. Due to the lack of any resource, disorder and discord began to be stirred up in the Community. And in order to remedy this, I wanted to try a second time to reestablish the gabella. I am requesting of you, therefore, dear Sir, to please write to Mr. Y. Semah and recommend that he not mix in any more in the affairs of our community.

If he had followed the good example of Mr. Carmona, the community would have been better organized.

With this hope, please accept, Mr. President, this expression of my highest regard.

N. Danon

AIU Archives (Paris)
Liban I.B.3.

[1] Yomtob David Sémach (1869–1924) was a veteran Alliance teacher, principal, and troubleshooter. In 1910, he undertook his famous mission to Yemen. From 1924 until his death in 1940, he was the Alliance delegate to Morocco.

THE TRADITIONAL JEWISH SCHOOLS OF SAN^cA
(1910)

Synagogue and school are called here by the same name, *knīs* (assembly). Both establishments are places of worship, but one studies in them more than one prays. I went first to the teachers' *knīs*. I returned disenchanted and disheartened. The educational system is stupefying, the hygienic conditions deplorable. Coupled with a regimen of overworking, they are made to completely annihilate the student population more than to develop their minds. It is a veritable source of joy to the community that we are going to establish an educational institution to guide the children on the path of health and reason at the very moment that the community is being numerically reconstituted.[1]

Let us go to visit the *melamed tinokot* (elementary school teacher): A courtyard of a few square meters, a little door on the right. I push it. What a horror! In a small room lower down, there was a crowd of shadows from which emanated a penetrating odor of foul air and of perspiration. It was suffocating, and I was obliged to take a step back. As I was coming from the bright sunlight, the darkness seemed total; however, I became used to it. I perceived three large holes in the wall the size of a hand. They were plugged with pieces of frosted glass that admitted a little light. This sort of cave was three meters long, two and a half wide, and two meters high. Forty-eight children ranging from three to eleven years of age were crammed in there, one against the other, sitting on the floor on tattered mats. Poor little things! I went to sit on a stone in the courtyard and called the schoolmaster.

"He's an excellent teacher," the Chief Rabbi, who was accompanying me said. "He is sought out by families."

And indeed, I could make out at the far end of the court the children of some notables. The youngsters arrive at dawn for prayer. Then they go to have breakfast, after which they return to work until noon, when there is a new recess for lunch. Then they go back to studying until sundown without any moving around at all. The youngest ones, overwhelmed in this closed-in atmosphere, fall asleep right there, stretched out on the mats on the ground, in the dust and the intertwining of legs. These forty-eight pupils were divided into ten classes, all working simultaneously in this single room. Some were reading the first part of the alphabet, others the last part. Some were doing syllables, others words, and still others the Parasha,[2] the Targum,[3] or the Tafsir.[4] There was an indescribable clamor, a deafening cacophony.

[1] Many people had been killed or fled the city during the siege of San^ca in 1905 by the rebellious Imam Yaḥya and his tribal supporters. The school Sémach is referring to was never established.

[2] The weekly portion of the Torah.

[3] The Aramaic translation of the Torah attributed to Onkelos, which in ancient times was read aloud in the synagogues along with the weekly Torah portion for those who could not understand Hebrew. Although the practice disappeared elsewhere, it continued in Yemen until modern times.

[4] This is the Arabic translation of the Scripture by Sa^cadya Gaon (882–942), which was also read in the synagogues of Yemen.

The little ones excited one another. Each child tried to outvoice his neighbor. What power of attention it took them to read their part while their comrades recited theirs. The teacher went from group to group, trying to set those who stumbled on the right path. By evening, both teachers and students must go out exhausted from this hell.

I asked if I might examine some of the children. They tried to bring me a tiny tot of three. He still wore his hair long under a girlish bonnet. They had just awakened him. He was completely covered with wisps of straw, and he howled with terror. I had him taken back. I asked if at that age he could understand anything. I was then apprised of the most odd, amusing, and absurd pedagogy. At this tender age of three, the children are taught the alphabet by heart to a simple, monotonous melody which is engraved in their mind. After this, they put the written alphabet in their hands and have them recite their melody while placing their finger in succession on the symbols written on the paper. Next, new oral instructions—the letters in combination with the vowel points, *alef-pataḥ* (*a*), *bet-pataḥ* (*ba*), etc. At the same time that he is learning this, the little tyke learns by heart every day a verse from the Parasha, and after four years, when a Bible is placed in his hand, given that he knows more or less the forms of the letters and vowels, given that he knows entire chapters by heart, he is able to read without too much difficulty the Parasha of the week. As soon as a child deciphers the first syllable of a word, he immediately guesses the word in its entirety. As soon as the youngster recognizes the first word of a verse, he easily recites the entire verse. The Yemenite, moreover, has an extraordinary memory for sounds, and forms, and an acuity of vision that is equally remarkable. There are few books in the schools or synagogues. One volume can serve ten people—opened wide on a low stool, they sit around it. Each one follows attentively whether he is looking at it from the front, the side, a seventy-five-degree angle, or upside down.

I interviewed, therefore, a biggish boy of seven. He read the Parasha glibly, but only the parts he knew by heart. In other places, he was not even able to spell out the letters. It was the same with the Targum and the Tafsir. A child learns, in effect, three languages at once: Biblical Hebrew, Aramaic written in Judeo-Arabic script, and the Tafsir of Saadya in literary Arabic, but also written in Hebrew characters. These three languages, he does not understand at all. But since, grownups can all speak Hebrew—not fluently, but correctly—When do they learn it? Without a doubt, during the readings in the synagogue.

I stayed for more than an hour in Joseph Dahabani's *knis*. I now knew all about the local pedagogy. I could run more quickly through the other institutions. They had the same methods of instruction and the same deplorable conditions.

Yomtob Sémach, *Une mission de l'Alliance au Yémen* (Paris, n.d.), pp. 51–53.

THE MODERN JEWISH SCHOOL IN SANᶜA
(1910)

I reserved the visit to the mehtep[1] for the end. It was exactly two months ago at the time I was disembarking at Hodeidah that the Turkish authorities organized a school for Jewish children. They hired a rabbi[2] to teach Arabic and Hebrew and a drill instructor and teacher for Turkish who was supposed to come three times a week. The Turkish administration rented two rooms in the quarter, and the school was opened. In order to avoid any conflict, the administration of the school was given over to the rabbi, with the Turkish authorities contenting themselves with paying the 100 francs a month it cost to maintain the institution. Despite this restraint, our Jews did not respond with enthusiasm to the call. In every family people were saying, "They are attracting our children to the school in order to hand them over to the army." It required unheard-of efforts in order to gather together the fifty pupils there—all admitted gratis.

Let us go up the little stairway to the mehtep. There was a tempest roaring, cries that would shake the eardrums of the deaf. It was the same pedagogy as in the *knis*, the same practices. However, the little courtyard we entered was clean. Three steps away on the right was one classroom, five steps to the left was another. At the moment, all of the pupils were assembled in the first room for a Hebrew class. As soon as the youngsters became aware of my presence, they stopped right in the middle of the verse. I entered. The fifty children were seated on the floor on worn mats, on strips of black carpet, and on little cushions. They were formed into groups around low stools made of old petrol cans. The schoolmaster was seated propped against a cushion. His assistant was standing, cracking a little whip. They all got up with a jump and greeted me. How happy and proud these little ones were! How their eyes sparkled! They were aware that they were beginning a new era. For are they not the first Jewish mehteplis (pupils in a modern school)? I had them seated. They were well behaved and very clean. Their wavy *simanim*[3] gave their young faces an original frame. They wore a short tunic of Indian material with small checks, and in pulling their thin legs under them, they revealed little pantaloons or foutas[4] covering their nudity.

[1] Turk. for "school," but here used for a modern, state-run institution.

[2] The rabbi referred to is Yiḥye Qāfiḥ (1850–1932), who is discussed on p. 22 and the sources cited there in n. 59.

[3] Heb. for "distinguishing signs." In Yemen, this was the term used by Jews for their sidecurls (Heb., *pē'ōt*). See Ahroni, *Yemenite Jewry: Origins, Culture, and Literature* (Bloomington, Ind., 1986), pp. 112–14; and Erich Brauer, *Ethnologie der jemenitischen Juden* (Heidelberg, 1934), p. 54.

[4] Ar., *fūṭa* (loincloth). See Brauer, *Ethnologie der jemenitischen Juden,* pp. 80, 82–83.

I asked the director if he was satisfied with them. "Not overly," he replied. "Oh, they work hard, but can you believe that they neglect the study of our holy law to think only about their Arabic and Turkish lessons?"

This brought me back thirty years to the time when my old rabbi also felt that I was neglecting Hebrew for the study of other things. In the future when we organize the schools, these complaints will increase. But they will not be the complaints of the students. The pupils today prefer reading in Arabic and Turkish to this disagreeable singsong recitation of the parasha. They can write in Arabic and are beginning to say a few words in Turkish, the language of the masters of the country. However, this instruction is done in only a slightly more sensible manner than the Hebrew teaching. The Turkish teacher has the pupils read and gives them formidable lists of words to memorize. What becomes of the children's intelligence in all of this? I can see in the future these youngsters put in contact with our modern teaching methods, becoming enthusiastic about mathematics, geography, and the various sciences.[5]

The mehtep, nevertheless, constitutes an enormous step forward over the knis.

Yomtob Sémach, *Une mission de l'Alliance au Yémen* (Paris, n.d.), pp. 54–55.

[5] The Alliance project to open a school in Yemen never came to be realized.

AN ENGLISH TRAVELER AND MIDDLE EAST EXPERT VISITS THE ALLIANCE ISRAÉLITE SCHOOL IN MOSUL (1910)

One other memory of the days at Mosul stands very freshly in my mind. There exists in the town a small and indigent Jewish community—neither too small nor too proverty-stricken to have attracted the watchful care of the Alliance Juive. Under their auspices, M. Maurice Sidi, a courageous and highly cultivated Tunisian, has opened a school for the children, and by precept and example he imparts the elements of civilization, letters, and cleanliness to young and old. The English vice-consul, who had witnessed his efforts with great sympathy and admiration, invited him to bring a deputation of his coreligionists to the consulate while I was there, and a dignified body of bearded and white-robed elders filed one morning into the courtyard. We returned their visit at the school, where we were received by a smiling crowd, dressed in their best, who pressed bunches of flowers upon us. The classrooms were filled with children proudly conscious that their achievements in the French, Arabic, and Hebrew tongues had called down honor upon their race. The scholars in the Hebrew class, who were of very tender years, were engaged in learning lists of Hebrew words with their Arabic equivalents, Hebrew being an almost forgotten language among the Jews of Mosul. M. Sidi drew forward a tiny urchin who stood unembarrassed before us, and gazed at him expectantly with solemn black eyes.

"What do you know?" said the master.

The black-eyed morsel answered without a shadow of hesitation: "I know Elohim." And while I was wondering how much of the eternal secret had been revealed to that small brain, he began to recite the first list in the lesson book, which opened with the name of God: "Elohim, Allah"—I do not remember how it went on, neither did he remember, without M. Sidi's prompting. Elohim was what he knew.

Gertrude Lowthian Bell, *Amurath to Amurath* (London, 1911), pp. 260–61.

THE CHIEF RABBI OF ALEXANDRIA COMPLAINS ABOUT THE TREATMENT OF HIS SON IN AN ALLIANCE SCHOOL
(1904)

February 12, 1904

The President of the Alliance Israélite Universelle
Paris.

Mr. President,

It is my duty to inform you that, despite all my good feelings toward the Alliance schools, which you have known about for a very long time, I was obliged, with deepest regrets, to place my son in a non-Jewish school.

I believe it is only fair to make you aware so that you yourself might judge my situation, and furthermore *ve-hayyittem neqiyyīm.*[1]

Here are the facts: My son who had attended your school in Alexandria for over four years was corporally beaten on January 8 by a teacher. Marks on his arm and back which remained for a long time denoted strong blows from a switch. Since then, the boy no longer went to the school.

I had hoped that M. Danon,[2] as a friend and neighbor, would come to me to ask after the reasons for this absence and then I would have shown him the marks from the beating, which is something I cannot believe would be permitted by the Central Committee.[3] Indeed, corporal punishment with a rod has been prohibited even in our popular Talmud Torah schools.

I waited for M. Danon until the 29th. Seeing that he was indifferent and that it was no longer possible to keep the child at home, I telephoned M. Danon, asking him to come by the Rabbinate. I wanted to share with him all the unhappiness I was feeling in sending my son to another school, I who had always preached on behalf of the Alliance's activities and who had chided in writing and in speech all the Jews who did not send their children to Alliance schools. I also wanted to know why he did not care whether my son remained in the school.

M. Danon, to my great astonishment, refused to come and see me. I would like to send my son to the Alliance school in Cairo, but seeing that he is sickly and weak (and besides that his mother refuses to send him out of town), I am therefore obliged to place him in another school until the day when I can put him in an Alliance school.

I am sending this very same day a copy of this letter to M. Danon so that if he has serious claims against me that would justify breaking the friendly relations of a neighbor, even to the point of refusing my request to

[1] "And you shall be clear" (Num. 32:22).

[2] The director of the school.

[3] The governing body of the Alliance in Paris.

come to the Rabbinate, he will tell them to you so that I shall at least know them through you.

Please be assured, Mr. President, of my deepest respect.

Elijah Bekhor Hazzan

P.S. The copy of the letter was sent to M. Danon on Friday, the 12th of this month, in the morning, with the hope that he would send me a copy of his reply so that I might verify the arguments that he would give you; however, he has sent me nothing until now.

You be the judge, Mr. President, of M. Danon's conduct in this circumstance as well.

AIU Archives (Paris)
Egypte I.B.7.
The French text is published in Jacob M. Landau,
Jews in Nineteenth-Century Egypt
(New York and London, 1969), pp. 309–10.

A BAGHDADI RABBI DECRIES THE DECLINE OF TRADITIONAL MORALS (1913)

As for examining our acts, there is no need for an exhaustive search, because they are clearly manifest and well known. They are heaped up like so many bundles, and the earth reeks from their stench. For in addition to the old misdeeds which we used to commit, new and very serious transgressions have sprung up among us which our forefathers never even considered, such as the public desecration of the Sabbath. You can find it among those of our people who are clerks in the banking houses and other high places. They go there even on the Sabbath and come home to do work, each according to his own occupation. Whatever he does on a weekday, he does on the Sabbath. Not only that, but the riffraff in our midst has developed a craving for forbidden food, seeking to fill their bellies with unkosher carrion and all the rest of the prohibited viands in Gentile restaurants, where they eat the impure and the pure together. May their tables be a snare for them, their food be bitter vipers' venom in their inwards, and may the accursed waters come into their intestines to swell their bellies and cause their thighs to sag.[1]

And what can we say about the sin of adultery—God preserve us!—which has spread among us? And what about the brothels that have multiplied among us? "Each man is neighing at his neighbor's wife, and they line up in troops at the harlot's door."[2] They are like dogs that surround a trampled corpse or a stinking carcass without any shame. And what about the sin of homosexuality, which is found among the other peoples in whose midst we live? Has even this come into the House of Israel?

Our heart is also greatly pained by people going to theaters to see women dancing on the stage and to hear erotic songs sung by vile, sensuous women who are like a fire in the chaff—God protect us! It is not only by the youth who have cast aside morals, have transgressed the covenant, and have broken the law, that we are shocked, but by the important people of good repute in the world of commerce, whose position among the leading citizens of the city has been shaken. It is by them that we are taken aback. Even if we were to suppose that they are not concerned by this terrible sin, whom then do they have to care about their honor, because according to general etiquette, going to this sort of despicable show is considered a dishonor, a disgrace, and a shame for a man of stature and nobility. They had to learn from well-mannered people among the Gentiles that they had

[1] The imagery is from Num. 5:22.

[2] Jer. 5:7–8. However, the verses are cited here in reverse order.

complained bitterly against the frequenting of these vile houses of entertainment in the city. Satan had so blinded them that they exchanged their honor for hopeless disgrace. Heaven forbid!

And how much more are we heartsick at the immodesty that has arisen of late among women and at their high audacity in modifying their clothing to be like the clothes of wanton Christian women. They have done this despite the fact that we are warned against resembling the Gentiles in dress or in actions, as is clearly stated in the *Shulḥān ʿĀrūkh, Yōreh Dēʿa,* Section 178.[3] These women use up their husbands' money to embellish the dresses with decorations and buttons that cost more than the original garment itself. They cause their husbands to go broke and to swallow up the wealth of others. The honor of Israel is lowered in the eyes of non-Jews since most of the bankrupts are Jews.

Worse than this are those women who have cast off the yoke of modesty and go about bareheaded for all to see and are not ashamed. Woe to the eyes that see such things! . . . Woe to the generation in which such things have arisen!

This sort of evil which has infected us is the fault of the Alliance schools, those bitter grapes,[4] that have been established in our city. All of the teachers in those schools are deceitful individuals who have shaken off the yoke and do all sorts of evil and abomination. How can students not sin when they see their teacher doing that, and thus they fall upon wicked ways? And thence it extended and spread to the rest of the masses. (The Chief Rabbi and the rabbis and scholars see all this, but they place their hand over their mouth out of weakness. No one demands anything, no one asks anything, even though according to the rules of the Alliance and the rules of etiquette, they have the power to exert oversight upon all of this.)

It was not enough for them until they established schools like these for Jewish girls as well in order to capture precious, pure, and innocent souls. The schoolmistresses in those institutions are the lascivious wives of the male teachers, and whatever their husbands do, they do as well to separate these daughters of Israel from their God and from the customary religious laws of their pure and modest mothers. Thus, they destroy the world from both ends.

Simeon Agasi, *Imrē Shimʿōn*
(Jerusalem, 1967/68), pp. 124–44.

[3] The section is entitled "One is not to wear the clothes of idolaters."

[4] A play on the Hebrew words *askōlōt* (schools) and *eshkolōt* (cluster of grapes). Cf. Deut. 42:42.

A WAVE OF CONVERSIONS AMONG JEWISH YOUTH AT CHRISTIAN SCHOOLS IN EGYPT SHOCKS THE COMMUNITY
(1914)

Last February and March, a rumor was running around Cairo that some young Jews, students or former students of the Brothers,[1] had converted to Christianity. Their names were cited and their parents apprised. When interrogated, the young people affirmed that they were good Jews, that they had never been converted, and that they had exhibited some Christian sentiments occasionally only to make fun of their teachers or to win their favor in order to obtain good marks and prizes or to be more certain of passing the course. It was noted that nearly all of them gave the same response in the same words, which gave us to assume that this answer had been dictated to them in order to lull their parents' vigilance (see Item Nos. 2, 5, 15).[2] But upon being pressed with further questions, nearly all ended up by admitting that they had been baptized or were on the point of being baptized (case of Félix Lévy, etc.).

The parents, whose attention had been aroused, followed the actions and gestures of their children and came upon them carrying out the practices of the Christian religion. They found in their possession sacred images, crosses, and significant letters (see the Dayan letters, Item Nos. 6–11 and the Halfallah Guetta letters, Item No. 2),[3] letters which left no doubt as to the state of these young peoples' souls and beliefs.

The names of those who had converted in Cairo are:

Joseph Azulai	18 years of age	French	Government employee
Raphael Dayan	18 years of age	French	Public Works employee in Alexandria
Salomon Lagnado	18 years of age	Local	Government employee
Léon Dayan	20 years of age	Local	Government employee
César Lévy	20 years of age	French	Anglo Egyptian Bank employee
Mansour			Employed in commerce
David Dayan			

The following are the names of the youngsters from 12 to 15 years of age who had converted, but who refuse to admit it:

[1] That is, the Brothers of the Congréganiste Order.

[2] The reference here is to the other documents gathered in the course of the community's investigation into the affair.

[3] Guetta was a businessman in Cairo who was asked by the French Jewish Consistory to conduct an inquiry into the affair. The item referred to here is his letter to Maurice de Cattaoui Pasha, president of the Cairene Jewish Community (March 19, 1914).

Edouard Forti, Elie Lichàa, Goldstein, Rosensweig, Hamawi, Karmann, Joseph Pinto, Bialobos, Eugène Lévy, Depaz, Victor Is. Léon (see H. Guetta's letter of May 10, 1914—Item No. 2).

The names of the young people who converted in Alexandria are:

Jacques Adès	19 years of age	Employee of the Deutsche Orientbank
Jacques Abram	18 years of age	
Félix Lévy	19 years of age	
Albert Chalem	10 years of age	Pupil at the Ecole de la Sainte Famille

How had these young people been brought to apostasy? We interrogated some of them on this, and here is what they replied.

At the college, we are all—Jews, Muslims, and Christians—without exception, required to take the catechism courses, and since the grade coefficient for catechism has a double value, we pay particular attention to this course of study. The teacher was able to discern quickly those boys who have a vivid imagination, a tender heart, and a soul inclined toward mysteries. They hovered around them, attached themselves to them, inspired them with contempt and hatred for Jews and Judaism, exalting Christianity, flattering, promising, threatening (H. Guetta's letter, Item Nos. 5, 14, 16, 18).

The teachers are not satisfied with giving tendentious oral instruction. They put into the hands of their pupils works in which historical events are denatured, where Protestants, Greek Orthodox, and Jews are presented in an unfavorable light. The Jews in particular are treated with a complete lack of charity. These books were brought to the attention of the Consul of France in Alexandria.[4] . . . .[5] All of these works and others which we could also cite, far from being appropriate for educational establishments to which children from different confessions and nationalities come for instruction, tend to create misunderstandings and to form a society where men rather than respecting and loving each other, hate and fight each other, which is the very opposite of all religion and moral teaching.

It is the Brothers Reposit, Félix, Edouard, and Absalom in Alexandria and Brother Louis in Cairo who are above all animated with missionary zeal. When the youngster seems ripe for apostasy, he is catechized, introduced into one of those organizations that flatters his amour propre such as the academy, club, or patronage (Dayan's letter of January 8, 1914, Item No. 6.71). Father Veillat is the missionary to whom the baptism is entrusted when the boy is not sent to take this decisive act in Cairo (declaration of Jacques Abram). The Brothers take every precaution so as not to incur legal responsibility. They catechize the boys, convert them, even baptize them, but they advise them not to declare their Christianity until they reach their majority. Since it concerns God's glory and their well-being, they can lie to

[4] France subsidized the Congréganiste schools in part. See the minutes of a meeting between Jewish leaders from Cairo and Alexandria and the French Consul on May 8, 1914, in Alexandria (Item No. 1 in the documents).

[5] A list of titles, authors, and publication data follows in the original report.

their comrades and to their parents; they can swear that they are good Jews since only those who believe in Jesus as the Messiah and son of God are really reputable (case of Jacques Abram and Félix Lévy).

You can imagine the state of mind of the Jews who have their children in the Congréganiste schools, their emotion, their anxiety. Are their children Jews or Christians? Do they have their esteem, their affection, or are they the object of their hatred and contempt? Who knows whether or not there are tens of young people who are in the same situation as Félix Lévy, who affirmed that he was a good Jew, who demanded that it be proclaimed in the synagogues, and who was ready to swear on the Bible by God that he was a good Jew and who, when called upon to declare under oath that he had never been baptized, asked to reflect and then ended by admitting he had received baptism at the same time as Jacques Abram!

Some individuals have gotten together and taken upon themselves the task of calming the emotion produced by all these conversions and to prevent the legitimate indignation provoked by these machinations of the Congréganistes from extending to those French institutions which must be protected and encouraged on account of the love that we must profess for France.

"Notes relatives aux conversions qui se sont
produites au Caire et à Alexandrie de quelques
jeunes Israélites appartenant ou ayant appartenu aux
Ecoles Congréganistes,"
AIU Archives (Paris)
Egypte I.C.15.

A CONVERTED YOUTH RETURNS TO JUDAISM
(1914)

Chief Rabbinate of Alexandria — Item No. 4
Egypt

Copy
Register of the Bet-Din IV.—Page 118

I the undersigned, Jacques D. Abram, declare that it was in a moment of mental aberration that I embraced the Catholic religion, while being a Jew. Having repented of having done that and regretting having abandoned the religion of my fathers in which I deeply believe and to which I absolutely want to remain attached until the end of my life, I of my own free will ask His Eminence the Chief Rabbi of Alexandria to please accept me back among his coreligionists and today have accomplished the necessary ceremony for my admission into the religion of Israel, and I declare that I am a Jew and agree to follow all the prescriptions of the Hebrew religion to which I belong.

Alexandria, May 6, 1914
(Signed) J. Abram[1]

For a conforming copy delivered to Mr. Jacques Abram for legal validation.

Alexandria, May 29, 1914
The Chief Rabbi
(Signed) Prof. Raffaello Della Pergola

AIU Archives (Paris)
Egypte I.C.15.

[1] An identical statement was signed by Félix Lévy on May 15 (Item No. 3).

A LETTER FROM ONE EGYPTIAN "JEW FOR JESUS" TO ANOTHER
(1914)

Item No. 6 January 8, 1914

My Dear Friend Salomon (Lagnado),

You were greatly shocked that I am taking accounting and asked me whether I wouldn't prefer doing "latinam linguam."

I am not doing the latter language all the time because it is difficult for me—impossible at home, at a friend's house it would arouse suspicions, at the office in the afternoon it is forbidden. You see, therefore, the obstacles.

While you take three courses a week, each an hour and a half at a time, I only take two lessons of a half hour each. You see, how can I advance quickly, and I do a lot of exercises. But what I know, I know well.

Apropos of that unfortuante sentence which slipped from your pen and which made me worry, I pray you to be certain of such a piece of news next time before informing me. And then, haven't I been right to keep myself ready for everything?

You say "the newspapers are talking about it." I asked you for clarifications and you fall silent. More risks. One does not write such things on an open postcard which can fall into everyone's hands.

I attended midnight mass at Christmas, like yourself.

I hope you haven't forgotten to wish a happy New Year to all of the members of the Patronage without exceptions as I told you before.

Yours in Our Lord,
(no signature)

AIU Archives (Paris)
Egypte I.C.15.

THE GALLICIZATION OF A TUNISIAN JEWISH BOY IN THE YEARS JUST PRIOR TO WORLD WAR I

In 1906 we left these old quarters for an apartment in the European part of town. We were not the only ones who wanted to get out of the Hara[1] in this way. That pile of dilapidated and frequently squalid buildings constituted without a doubt the most unhealthy and the most overpopulated quarter of Tunis. Whoever had the means sought to escape it by taking up residence in the new town. But there were two ways of leaving the ghetto, or more precisely, two steps to be accomplished in order to get out completely, just as there were two stages to be traversed in acquiring a modern education: the schools of the Alliance Israélite first, then the French schools proper.

Set within the Medina,[2] and bordered by the Arab town and the souks,[3] the ghetto could not scarcely burst open except at the point where it touched the suburbs: the Place Bab Carthagene. From there, two compact overflows of population extended, either by the Avenue de Londres in the direction of the Jewish cemetery . . . or toward the Alliance Israélite School, which was also built in a quarter which at that time was relatively on the outskirts. In these two massive overflowings, a person still remained among his own. The buildings were occupied exclusively by Jews. One did not feel strangeness, and one could conform without difficulty or bother to all the traditional rites and practices. But certain more adventurous, more audacious, more determined individuals went even further than there into the still newer zones of the new city, into buildings where not all the neighbors were Jews, or even where the Jews were not in the majority. It was generally in this latter category of buildings that the families whose children attended the real French schools, rather than the Alliance Israélite, lived.

For in the Alliance school, too, a person remained among his own. He had only neighbors from the block or the building as schoolmates. And above all, he maintained contact with the Jewish tradition. One did not go to class on Saturday or on the Jewish religious holidays. While becoming initiated into modern culture, one had the feeling of being closely tied to the entire Jewish past, to the entire Jewish milieu. One resisted an uprooting that was too brutal. In the French schools, quite to the contrary, one set sail on the open sea with all the advantages and, too, all the risks which that entailed.

One would be committing an error in thinking that it was the richest who followed this new path. On the contrary, quite frequently the children of well-to-do families were readily satisfied with the modest baggage of the Alliance Israélite which allowed them to return quickly to take part in the

[1] Ar., *ḥāra.* The Jewish Quarter of Tunis.

[2] The native quarter, as opposed to "the new city" where the Europeans lived.

[3] Ar., *sūq* (the bazaar).

paternal business in the souks while trying vaguely to modernize its methods. Those who went to real French schools, and in particular to the lycée, were more often the children of those whom I would permit myself to call—while keeping a due sense of proportion—the small new intellectual Jewish elite: former good students of the Alliance who, since the beginning of the Protectorate, had found employment in banks, insurance companies, and capitalist ventures of all sorts, and who wanted the best for them. . . . The latter found in their daily professional contacts, which were more directly with the modern world and European circles, better reasons than did the traditional type of businessman to give their children a more thorough education.

Like my brothers, I went, therefore, from the elementary class to the Lycée Carnot, where I continued until I obtained my baccalaureate. Family legend has it that I knew only Judeo-Arabic when I entered the lycée and that within a few months I had totally forgotten it in order to speak only French. That is doubtlessly an oversimplified and embellished view of things. While it is true that while alone at home with my mother and especially my grandmother, I spoke only Judeo-Arabic with them, I nevertheless heard my older siblings and my uncles speaking French, both among themselves and with my mother. I certainly could not have been completely ignorant of the language. However, it is quite true that it was not my mother tongue and that I am indebted to my first teachers and even more, without a doubt, to my first French schoolmates for familiarizing me with it so quickly, to the point that it is today the only language that I speak and write fluently.

I have no qualms in saying that I did outstanding work at the lycée. In the upper level, I chose Classical Studies, as had my older brother, who had also been an outstanding student. This again separated me from the mass of my fellow Jews and appears to have caused me to mingle even more with Frenchmen of good stock. Out of some thirty students in our class, there were only two Tunisian Jews and three Muslims. The Tunisians—Jewish and Muslim—were much more numerous in the modern classes, without however succeeding in making up a majority.

As a matter of fact, I had only rather superficial relations with my French schoolmates. I did indeed go to the homes of one or another of them to work or, more rarely, to play, but I had no friends among them. Relations with my Muslim classmates were even rarer. The latter were generally the sons of Caids[4] from the interior and for the most part lived in the dormitories. As for the Jews, the "moderns" formed a rather tight-knit group with whom I had no contacts on the whole. Most of them lived in the new Jewish quarters along the Avenue de Londres. Many of them had taken their primary classes at the Alliance. Especially numerous were those whose primary language at home remained Judeo-Arabic and who likewise used that language for intercourse among themselves. I found myself, therefore, having real affinities only with the young Jews who like myself spoke French

[4] Ar., *qā'id.* The title of certain native officials.

more or less exclusively both at home and among themselves. There were but a few of these each school year.

As for my fellow students who came out of the primary grades at the Alliance, whose homes I visited and with whom I kept close company, some of their traditional preoccupations were foreign to me and their habits were palpably different from mine. I felt myself vaguely somewhat different.

Not that my family had renounced religious practices. On the contrary, as long as my maternal grandmother was alive at least, one conformed to them very precisely. Mezuzahs on the doorposts, Friday evening prayers, no cooking or touching fire on Saturday; regular observance of the dietary prohibitions, strict enough at ordinary times and complicated still further during Passover; family celebrations of religious occasions—nothing was missed. Nothing except (for me at least) the heart.

They had tried to give me some religious instruction. A rabbi, not too famished-looking and not too threadbare, would come to teach me to read the sacred books three times a week. How difficult was that alphabet! And that language so obscure! Above all, how rudimentary was the good man's pedagogy, how mediocre his culture! Comparing him to my French teachers made him look ridiculous. Thus it was that I was always completely atheist. It was an atheism, however, that was perfectly tolerant and accommodating, except when one wanted to coerce me into practices which I judged to be outmoded.

I had a happy life at the lycée. Aside from a few minor incidents, I practically never perceived the least bit of anti-Semitism among my teachers. When one of my fellow students, more sensitive perhaps than I to certain acts or certain remarks, said that about one of them: "He is an anti-Semite!"—I vigorously defended him against that accusation. My academic successes after all bore witness to the teachers' impartiality. On this point, someone answered me with a certain spitefulness not devoid of insight, however, that my scholastic achievements were protecting me no doubt, but they would not protect me forever.

Indeed, immediately after receiving my baccalaureate, I went to learn to my cost that a Tunisian Jew, even if he was a brilliant student, did not have the same rights as others.

Elie Cohen-Hadria, *Du Protectorat français à l'indépendance: Souvenirs d'un témoin socialiste* (Nice, 1976), pp. 9–13.

3

BETWEEN NATIONALISM AND COLONIALISM IN THE AFTERMATH OF THE FIRST WORLD WAR

A TUNISIAN JEW'S STRUGGLE TO SERVE HIS ADOPTED COUNTRY IN WORLD WAR I

When the war broke out, Henry Bonan[1] of an honorable Jewish family originating in Algeria, but long established in Tunis, could have pleaded in good faith his status as a Tunisian subject to remain in his villa by the seashore and not serve. He did not wait for his class to be called up and wanted to enlist as a volunteer. However, the Office of the Resident General, contesting the French citizenship of his father Isaac Bonan, opposed in the name of the State and with a view toward the public interest Henry Bonan's inscription in the recruitment lists. Anyone else rebuffed like this would have put aside his patriotic sentiments, his ardor, and his aspirations and blame the administration for the fact of not having been able to serve as he had so ardently desired. But Henry Bonan fought in court to obtain the right to serve. At his insistence, M. Isaac Bonan subpoenaed the Resident General before the Court of First Instance in Tunis, and the latter, in its session of December 7, 1914, rendered a decision declaring the plaintiff a French citizen.

Henry Bonan then enlisted. He went through the training school at Fountainebleau and was named an officer cadet at the same time that he was accepted into the Central School. He was just recently killed at the age of twenty, standing by his gun facing the enemy for the Motherland which he had recently entered by the force of law. He was decorated with the Croix de Guerre.

C. Ouziel, "Les Juifs tunisiens et la guerre,"
typed report (Tunis, 1917), p. 17.
AIU Archives (Paris) Tunisie II.C.5.

[1]The name Bonan and its variations are common among Algerian and Tunisian Jewry. See Maurice Eisenbeth, *Les Juifs de l'Afrique du Nord: démographie et onomastique* (Algiers, 1936), pp. 103–4.

TURKISH EXACTIONS WEIGH HEAVILY UPON BAGHDADI JEWS DURING WORLD WAR I

(1917)

A much simpler method of extortion was the compulsory exchange of gold for notes. By this system nearly all the available cash of the Arabs, Jews, and Christians in the city passed into the hands of the Turks. When debts were paid in paper currency a profit of from 60 to 75 percent accrued. And when there was no opportunity for a transaction, the officials summoned the Jews to their houses at night; they came with gold and went away with paper. The most dreadful penalties were held out against those who would not accept Government paper on its face value. In the meanwhile, notes fell to a third, and even a quarter, of their accredited value; and orders kept coming through from Constantinople that, as the depreciation of Government paper in Baghdad was greater than elsewhere in the Empire, immediate steps must be taken to revive credit. The officials were frightened and vexed, and the weight of their displeasure fell chiefly on the Jews. There had been actual trafficking in notes. Merchants had been selling them at a discount for a third of their value. This was viewed officially in the light of a studied conspiracy to depreciate Turkish credit. The higher officials, of course, understood; but the slow-witted Turk genuinely believed that the motives of the Jews were political and mischievous. When Government ordains that paper is the same value as gold, he argued, then paper becomes gold by law; or "if not gold for you or me, gold for Mirza, Abdul, Ezra, and Johannes."[1] A proclamation was issued that all trade transactions and purchases must be made in paper money. The result was a financial panic. Shops were shut; there was no market; you could not buy meat or bread in the bazaar. To keep his household alive, the Baghdadi had to slink about and make surreptitious purchases in cash after dark. Another proclamation was issued. Merchants were to open their shops. Those who did business secretly, or hid, or refused to sell their goods would be deported and their property confiscated.

The Jews who had been guilty of trafficking with notes were summoned secretly to the Court of the Prefect of Police at night. They were confined by day and taken out after dark and tortured. Finally, they were murdered and thrown into the Tigris. When their families brought round breakfast, they were told that they had gone down river to see Khalil Pasha in Kut. Or that is the story in Baghdad, and everybody believes it. The nineteen Jews have never been seen alive since, though the bodies of five of them were restored by the Tigris. Haron Mealem, Abdullah Isaac Mesafy, and Ibrahim Dabool were identified on March 7th, Shelomo Siom and Isaac Messim

[1] That is, for Shiᶜite, Sunni Arab, Jew, and Christian.

Mina a few weeks afterways. The two legs of Haron Mealem had been cauterized, apparently by a hot iron, just above the ankle.

When the police came round, a cousin of one of the men who was wanted and who had fled was sleeping in the house of his relative, the accused, and he was taken as a hostage, in the hope that he might betray the fugitive's whereabouts. As he was not actually implicated, his case was left to the last, and he managed to slip away in the confusion caused by our approach to the city.[2] He and other prisoners in the house at the time bear witness to the groans and cries for mercy uttered by the Jews at night. These torturings and assassinations were by way of a deterrent. The Turks argued that by no milder methods could they give discredited paper the value of gold. The idea was that if they killed one or two, the others would soon come to their senses and the mischievous trafficking would cease.

Edmund Candler, *The Long Road to Baghdad*
(London, 1919), pp. 120–21.

[2] The writer was with General Maude's forces, which were then advancing upon Baghdad.

THE JEWS OF BAGHDAD PETITION FOR BRITISH CITIZENSHIP AT THE END OF WORLD WAR I

Baghdad, 18th, November 1918

To

The Civil Commissioner.
Baghdad.

Sir,

We have the honor on behalf of the Jewish Community of Baghdad to bring the following to your kind consideration:

The Allied Great Powers have triumphantly brought to an end the greatest war that ever scourged mankind to find themselves confronted with a work of pacification and reconstruction of unprecedented magnitude. One of the most important problems which face the Allies is the satisfactory solution of the complicated questions of nationalities.

The Allied Powers have repeatedly proclaimed that they are determined, as regards the small nations to take into account and respect any just aspirations or legitimate claims with the view to precluding any popular friction and eliminating all causes for future wars.

As far as Mesopotamia is concerned, the Allied policy, it is understood, will be to promote indigenous government and encourage the establishment of an autonomous administration. This scheme is excellent in principle and reflects the greatest credit on the Governments of Great Britain and her Allies as a fresh manifestation of the elevation of principles with which this war has been waged. But its immediate execution is coupled with such difficulties as render it hardly recommendable.

It is too early now to have an accurate idea of the exact form of this future government, but the semi-official assurances given suggest the assumption that the local administrative body may be vested with wider powers than perhaps advisable in consideration of the following reasons:

The state of utter unpreparedness of the inhabitants for serious political or administrative responsibilities hardly qualified them to undertake with success the management of their own affairs.

A local government in accord with the desire of the local majority cannot but bear a very strong theocratical character due to the dominance of religious feelings which are unconciliable with the idea of giving to alien confessions any sort of privilege or rights. This cannot be consistent with the democratical views of the Allies.

Owing to the absence of scientific institutions, this country cannot furnish men capable to take up any branch of administration. Even the subordinate staff, fresh from the Turkish bureaucratic practices, may be a calamity for the country if freed from control. The higher functionaries under Turkish rule were mostly Turks especially prepared in the Constantinople universities.

A small nation abandoned to itself with no adequate preparation for efficient self-government cannot even maintain its rank of small nation but is inevitably destined to be crushed in the great economical strife. It is feared therefore that the results which are to be apprehended might not only be disadvantageous to the progress of the country, but also contrary to the views of the Allied Great Powers and the principles proclaimed by the regretted liberator of Baghdad the late Lieutenant-General Sir Stanley Maude.[1]

The Jews of Baghdad feel it their duty to declare that their aims in the present juncture would be to have a free opportunity for economic and educational development, these having proved through the ages the two main elements which guaranteed the existence of their race in adversity. Two centuries of active commercial relations with Great Britain have slowly cemented a community of interests which in these days are greatly inspiring their determination: they wish to submit through the undersigned a request that they may be graciously taken under the shield of the British Government and considered true subjects of His Majesty, holding themselves prepared to accept all obligations and rights of true citizens. They are confident that their brethren in all Iraq will formulate the same desire. We may recall on this occasion that since 50 years Baghdad has furnished to the British Empire important colonies of Jewish Traders, established mostly in India and England,[2] who enjoy without exception the rights of British citizens. Our Community trust that an agglomeration of 80,000 Jews in a country like Mesopotamia may prove as good subjects to His Majesty as their brethren in England.

This request, however, we fully realize, may raise complicated questions of political and legal character, which we do not propose to examine, this application purporting only to record the desire of the Community and referring to the competent authority the right issues to frame.

We beg to request you, Sir, to kindly communicate with the Government at Home on this subject, and solicit your personal assistance in this connection.

We have the honor to be,

Sir,
Your Obedient Servants.

President of the Jewish Lay Council

Acting Chief Rabbi & President of Religious Council

[1] Maude took ill and died of cholera on November 18, 1917, after attending a theatrical performance in his honor at the Alliance school in Baghdad. See Richard Coke, *Baghdad, The City of Peace* (London, 1927), pp. 299–300.

[2] See Part One, pp. 38–39.

A. M. Somekh
A. Haim
Shoua Bekhor
Simon Hay Isac
S. Hougi
Ezra S. Shasoue
Sasson Murad
Yamen Cohen
Frayem Djedda
Abr. E. Djouri
S. Bekhor
Isac Ruben
Yamen
E. D. Bassous
Yona M. Yona
Ezra A. Salem
Abdulla S. Ini
Saleh Y. Naftali
S. Birshan
Sion E. Gourgi
Heskel Hindee
Ezra M. Bekhor
Shelomo Shooker
Manashi Djedda
M. S. Shashoue
Menashi Sehayek
Fraim Toeg
Meir H. Gareh
Sion E. Dengoor
Sion Is. Mikhael
S. Sabha
Sasson H. Toeg
A. H. Elikibir
Isac Tweina
Gourji Mokamal
Menahem Gahtan
Ezra S. Sehayek
Ezra Abd. Menashi
Y. Y. Zelouf
Menahem Daniel[3]
Sasson Khezam
Saleh M. Cohen
Moshi Shashoue
Isac M. Iny
Saleh E. Sasson
Murad Djouri
M Jos. Shemtob
Abr. A. Bashi
E. Khezam
Daoud Somekh
Saleh F. Haim
Abr. E. Yehouda
Yehouda Y. Noonoo
Ruben Gahtan
Heskel Ezra Naftali
Abraham Denoos

AIU Archives (Paris)
Irak I.C.4.

[3] See the letter written by him four years later to the secretary of the World Zionist Organization in London, pp. 331–333.

AN IRAQI NATIONALIST APPEAL TO NON-MUSLIMS
(1920)

To all our Brothers, Christian and Jewish fellow citizens:

It is to be made clear to you, our brothers, that we in this country are partners in happiness and misery. We are brothers, and our ancestors lived in friendship and mutual help. Do not consider in any way that the demonstrations carried out by the citizens affect any of your rights. We continue to value and respect our friendship. All demonstrations being made do not indicate a lack of respect for you or any citizen. We have no other object than to claim from the present government[1] the fulfillment of its pledges to the Iraqi nation which it has published many times in the newspapers. We therefore invite you to take part with us in everything that is good for the nation. Be assured that our union and mutual support will be illustrious in the future of our fatherland on which our common happiness depends. We again invite you in the name of the fatherland and patriotism to unite, in order to form a single land to work for the realization of our principles and our future happiness whereby you will render us thankful to you.

Leaflet distributed in coffeehouses frequented by non-Muslims. Text in Khalid Abid Muhsin, *The Political Career of Muhammad Jaᶜfar Abu al-Timman (1908–1937): A Study in Modern Iraqi History* (doctoral dissertation, University of London, 1983), pp. 129–30, n. 83.

[1] That is, the British governing authorities.

AN EXCERPT FROM A SPEECH GIVEN BY KING FAYṢAL TO THE JEWISH COMMUNAL LEADERS OF BAGHDAD

(JULY 18, 1921)

There is no meaning in the words Jews, Muslims, and Christians in the terminology of patriotism, there is simply a country called ᶜIraq, and all are ᶜIraqīs.

I ask my countrymen, the ᶜIraqīs, to be only ᶜIraqīs because we all belong to one stock, the stock of our ancestor Shem; we all belong to that noble race, and there is no distinction between Muslim, Christian, and Jew. Today we have but one means to our end: the race.

al-ᶜIrāq (July 19, 1921), translated in Philip Willard Ireland, *ᶜIraq: A Study in Political Development* (London, 1937), p. 466, App. VII (iii).

OBSERVATIONS ON THE COMMERCIAL LIFE OF BAGHDAD
(1920s)

In the wholesale circles of the city's business life, the foreign element is dominated by the British, with the Italian a very active second, and the local by the Jew. Banking is also monopolized by these three races. Much of wholesale business at its selling end is done in the bazaars by strolling brokers or "*dalals*,"[1] who make a specialty of being *au fait* with changes in the market, and to some extent perform the functions allotted in Western countries to business newspapers and trade reports. Here, as might be expected, the local Jewish community finds a profitable and congenial opportunity for a "*carriere ouverte aux talents.*" In retail circles in the Great Bazaars the Jews are again strongly represented; in the smaller bazaars Muslims predominate. Christians, strangely enough, play an almost negligible part in commercial life, confining their attention mainly to enterprises such as hotels, cinemas, and shops catering to Europeans. Bargaining is in universal use; by general consent the commercial morality of the Muslims is a good deal higher than that of the Jews or Christians, and even black sheep among the Muslims tend to be more open and sporting in their methods; like the gentleman who attempted to steal an entire bungalow from a British camp, and seemed only mildly surprised when his coolies were caught in the act of taking the building to pieces and walking off with it. The hold of the Jews on the commercial life of the city is greatly helped by the local habit of living on credit by means of *compialas*, or notes of hand, redeemable at so many days' notice; the Jew gains also by the tendency of the property owner to run into mortgage on the slightest provocation, and by the custom of the British Army and Air Force of selling surplus stores by private tender instead of by public auction. One peculiar but highly creditable feature of local business procedure is that a man's word, once he is known, will be accepted as his bond, and even the local Jewish banks will issue money to their customers if necessary without a cheque or written order of any kind; sometimes large sums are dispatched in this way to distant khans, through the medium of a servant or underling, and this trust is but rarely abused. As elsewhere, the Jews display the business talent at an early age; the city coffee shops of an evening are full of small boys running round with trays of miscellaneous articles, from socks to handkerchiefs to watches and safety razors, swearing to the quality of their goods "bi nebi Musa"—by the prophet Moses.

As a trader the Arab is outclassed only by the Jew, but he is less influenced by modern ideas, and his business is in many respects entirely his own. He is not afraid of enterprise and will cheerfully risk large sums on speculations which would give an Englishman many sleepless nights. To his

[1] Ar., *dallāl.*

friends and old customers he is generous to a fault, and will not infrequently grant far more credit than his business warrants. His love of good living, of entertainment and pleasure, and of generally "going the pace" when he has had a good turn of fortune tend to place him at a disadvantage with the ever-watchful Jew or Armenian, on the look-out for every move in the game. For them, business is a lifelong occupation, combining profit with sport; for the Arab it represents merely a means of getting money for living in the expansive, extravagant way that his soul loves. By nature, in fact, the Arab strongly resembles the old aristocratic, country-family class of prewar England, and in this prosaic modern world in which the virtues of the heart count for so much less than the virtues of the head, he tends to suffer the same handicap. He falls a victim to the climbing Jew or Armenian—the local equivalent of the British *nouveau riche*—and then is apt to turn with a sudden fury, unjust, but natural, upon his wily conquerors.[2]

Richard Coke, *Baghdad: The City of Peace*
(London, 1927), pp. 313–15.

[2]This passage reveals as much about the prejudices of many of the British Arabists of the period as it does about Baghdadi life.

My trip to Damascus had two main objectives: (A) To observe the overall condition of the community at the present time and all that has been done there over the three quarters of a year period from the time of the conquest until now, and (B) To visit the educational and welfare institutions which the Council of Delegates and the Council of Education[1] support. I have devoted almost all of my time in Damascus to these two objectives. I shall discuss these two matters, especially the second, in detail:

A. The Community

1. COMMUNAL ADMINISTRATION

Only someone like myself who has been acquainted with the Jewish Community of Damascus and its administration (or, more accurately, its lack of any administration during the war years)[2] can fully appreciate the significance of the progress that has taken place within the community lately. When I and other Palestinians aroused the community last October to the necessity of electing a municipal council on the basis of legal elections, we doubted very much whether such a council would be established and whether it would continue to operate if established. Indeed, in view of the state of affairs then, there was no reason to think otherwise. There was once a community council that either by itself or with the assistance of the *Ḥākhām Bāshī* extended its authority over the people without having been elected by them and without taking them into consideration at all. However, this council did not meet to discuss reforms that had to be made in communal affairs to improve the community and to raise its status. It did not worry about fulfilling its needs, nor did it look for ways to make the wealthy members of the community conscious of their duty toward their poor brethren. Every single member of this council had his own special fund from the municipal income, and he controlled it in most instances without even asking the opinion of his fellow councillors. Furthermore, funds that came from abroad to aid the poor, as for example the support from B'nai B'rith out of Constantinople which was a conduit for American monies during the war, were drawn in the name of one of the members of the council. In this too, he alone had control, and complaints by members of the community increased considerably. But they could not find the internal fortitude to change the

[1]That is, the Vaᶜad ha-Ṣīrīm and the Vaᶜad ha-Ḥinnūkh of the Yishuv in Palestine.

[2]The author, Joseph Joel Rivlin (1889–1971), had been exiled to Damascus in 1917. After the war, he headed the Hebrew language school for girls until 1922. He later became a noted Arabist. See Benjamin Rivlin, "Rivlin, Joseph Joel," *EJ* 14: 201–2.

situation. The community members, and even the best among them, did not believe that there was any possibility of steady, organized work on the part of the council. They themselves recognized the element that is habitually missing in work done in the Levant, namely, the element of following through. The community generally looked upon this matter of elections of a council by the entire group as something strange and shocking. How could a council be appointed by the majority opinion of the community that did not arrogate for itself the reigns of power?

Nevertheless, what actually took place demolished all our doubts and skepticism: a plenary committee of fifty men was elected by all the members of the community. These fifty in turn chose an executive committee of nine men, and this executive committee meets every week, performs the work of the community, organizes new institutions in a community that did not have until now any public institution, collects funds from the members of the polity themselves, and tries to find financial means from outside the community as well. It collects all the sums that were in the hands of individual members of the previous council. It keeps exact accounts of all income and expenditures and precise minutes of all meetings. In other words, it does all of those things and others of the like that are so elementary and self-evident in every general public institution in the enlightened countries, but are not usual and not known in the ancient communities of the East.

The vibrant spirit in the workings of the council is Mr. Joseph ᶜAbadi, a respected, educated, and very talented businessman. He has energy and initiative and wields great influence within the community, before the government, and with the Arab notables, all of whom he knows. (This year he was nominated as justice of the peace, but he resigned after a time.)

2. COMMUNAL INSTITUTIONS AND WELFARE SOCIETIES

In addition to the educational institutions founded in this city by the Palestinian Council of Education, the community this year established the following institutions:

a. *A second kindergarten*, about which I shall speak in the section below on educational institutions in general.

b. *A Talmud Torah*, also discussed below in the same section.

c. *An orphanage for children.* I still remember the dreadful sights while passing through the main street of the Jewish Quarter at night and seeing orphaned children in ragged clothes lying on the garbage heaps in abandoned shops. These were heart-rending sights. Aid is now coming to these miserable, abandoned children with the establishment of this institution.

There are forty-one orphans in the institution. Thirty-three of these have lost both father and mother. Many of them are afflicted with skin diseases which they contracted from the filth in which they were to be found until now. However, they are slowly recovering under the care of the doctor and the nurses.

The children are fed according to a detailed list made up by the orphanage physician, Dr. Efron.

Their clothing is clean. Each one has several outfits which were sewn for them from cloth which the community received as a gift.

They receive their education in our educational institutions, and during the vacation period, one of the Talmud Torah teachers took it upon himself to come and look after them and even teach them a little. My wish was to send them all during the vacation period to Mezeh, which is a summer retreat of the Damascenes. But the plan never came to fruition.

There is, of course, a need to get more household utensils—a wash cup for each of them (there are now only six for all of them). There is also a need for a place for them to wash (for now they wash in the kitchen). However, the greatest single thing lacking is proper housing. The quarters they are now in consist of four not very spacious rooms plus one small room which is only the height of a man. According to the doctor's calculation, in all of the rooms together, there is only enough space for twenty, not forty-one children. . . . There is no dining room, and the children eat in the courtyard, which they will not be able to do in winter. There is only one toilet for the entire institution, and it is in the kitchen.

I brought this to the attention of the Community Council and advised them to immediately rent another house instead. There is in fact a large house that can be rented for 100 Egyptian pounds a year. In my opinion, the institution cannot be expanded until they rent an appropriate facility, and it is incumbent upon the Council of Delegates to inform them of this in no uncertain terms.

In looking at the male and female orphans with neither father nor mother who are still to be found without any shelter, the community is demanding that a similar institution be opened for orphan girls. In our opinion, the fate of Damascene Jewish maidens who have no source of livelihood is to go astray and bring shame upon the community. I believe, therefore, that it is imperative that this demand be considered.

d. *Travelers' Aid.* A few months ago, some young people in the community, seeing the distress of Jews passing through Damascus on their way to Palestine, founded a society called Hakhnāsat Ōreḥīm.[3] This society now has eighty members, each of whom pays from one half to one shilling a month. In addition, there are some 400 families who pay half a piastre each a week. With the money that has been collected, they have rented for the time being a single room with eight beds which they received as a donation. This became a place where people passing through may stay for free. When a traveler leaves, they assist him by paying the train fare, giving some food for the way, and a little pocket money. To date, 132 people have passed

[3] Heb. for "hospitality" (lit., taking in guests). Since this is considered a very important commandment in Judaism, societies of this name were to be found in traditional Jewish communities throughout history.

through this institution. While I was there, some twenty people came from Kurdistan on their way to Palestine. Their next stop was Samaḥ and thence to Tiberias to work in the agricultural settlements.

The municipal council lends support to this society from time to time when it is necessary. The society now wants to rent another room, also with eight beds, that would be exclusively for women.

e. *ᶜŌzēr Dallīm*[4] *Society.* If one no longer sees all over the main street of the Jewish Quarter poor people going from door to door of every house, it is thanks to this society which distributes various sums of money every week to 160 of these people so that they will not have to make the rounds begging. It also supports about seventy women so that they will not have to serve in brothels. The society has approximately 300 members who pay between a shilling and a half to six shillings a month. The society takes in about thirty Egyptian pounds each month.

f. *Shevet Aḥīm*[5] *Society.* This society organizes and manages the operations of the abovementioned ᶜŌzēr Dallīm Society. One of its goals is to collect funds from its members for the purchase of land in Palestine for settlement. It takes upon itself part of the work of the municipal council by distributing money and provisions to the poor. It is their members who made allocations from the Egyptian Aid money to 4,200 souls. During a three-month period they distributed half a *raṭl*[6] of flour or bread twice a week and also approximately one *raṭl* per person of rice from 100 (98 to be exact) sacks which the Communal Council received from the Council of Delegates. Before and during the intermediate days of Passover, they distributed to every individual close to two shillings from the Egyptian Aid funds. Likewise, they distributed over a three-week period during the month of Iyyar[7] one *raṭl* of flour per person, per week, to the very neediest, from 80 sacks received by the community from the government. Of these, 48 sacks were given to the orphanage for the maintenance of the orphans until next Tishre.[8]

g. *Rōdefē Ṣedeq Society.* This society has made it its objective to combat prostitution in the Jewish Quarter. When it was first founded, it had collected funds and supported poor young women who, it was feared, would fall into bad ways, and got them married to husbands. Lately, however, they have begun to employ means that have brought dishonor to the community. They turned to the government and obtained an order for the police to send gendarmes every night to patrol the main street of the Jewish Quarter, and

[4] Heb. for "helper of the poor" (it is one of the Divine epithets mentioned in the daily liturgy).

[5] Heb. for "brothers dwelling" (together in unity). See Ps. 133:1.

[6] A *raṭl* is a measure of weight, which in Damascus during this period was equivalent to 3.202 kilograms. See A. Barthélemy, *Dictionnaire arabe-français, dialectes de Syrie: Alep, Damas, Liban, Jerusalem,* fasc. 2 (Paris, 1936), p. 284.

[7] In 1919, the Hebrew month of Iyyar coincided with May 1–29.

[8] That is, until September 1920.

any woman or girl found in the street after eight in the evening is to be arrested and taken to the police. At first, members of the society went with the gendarmes so that they could differentiate between respectable and disreputable women. But when many people began to complain, they stopped going, and only the gendarmes kept patrolling, and they made no distinction between one woman and another. One ugly incident already took place in which twenty women, most of whom are of respectable families, were tied together with a rope and brought to the police. This incident caused a controversy in the community and a split between the council and the society. Furthermore, it was brought before the government authorities and caused the community's honor and that of its leaders to be stained.

When I saw this tremendous disturbance and its consequences, I called a meeting of the leaders of the society and the members of the municipal council and other societies. At the meeting, matters were clarified, and the leaders of the society saw that they had made a mistake. It was decided by the consent of all assembled that, henceforth, no one (not even the *Ḥākhām Bāshī*) was to turn to the government authorities with regard to communal matters except the Communal Council. It was also decided that the society had to cancel night patrols of the gendarmes in the street of the Jews. Furthermore, it was incumbent upon the society and together with the Council to seek other means to fight prostitution, which, to our regret, brings down the honor of the Jews throughout the city. It was agreed that the fight would be more successful if they could create work and sources of income for the needy.

3. COMMUNAL INCOME AND EXPENDITURES

I was interested in knowing exactly what were the income and expenditures of the Communal Council. For an entire day, I spent time with the accountant in order to get out the account of every single matter individually (because until now all the accounts are mixed together, and they have only one ledger with all of the income and the outlays together). After the inspection, I found that this year was a felicitous one for the community generally because it received large sums from members of the community who are in America, as well as from the Committee for Syria which operates in Egypt, and from private philanthropists in both Egypt and Syria. In addition to this, there is the sum which Mr. Mosseri[9] and I transferred to them on behalf of the Council of Delegates. It was only due to these sums together with the income from within the community itself that they were able to meet all the demands of the various institutions that were established in the community this year.

The following are the amounts of income and expenditure that passed through the Council:

[9] The name is not entirely clear in the manuscript.

Income:	*Eg. £*
From members of the Damascene community itself (in addition to the income of aforementioned societies)	1,054
From America	1,497
From the Committee for Syria in Egypt	1,000
From Egyptian Philanthropists (Smooha and Gatenio)	300
From Syrian Philanthropists	195
From the Council of Delegates in Palestine	350
	4,396.00

Expenditures:	*Eg. £*
For Educational Institutions	962.40
For the Orphanage	617.40
For the Distribution of Flour, Bread, and Money to the Poor	800
Communal Expenses, Support for the Poor, and Salaries for the Rabbis	550
	2,929.80
Remaining in the Communal Treasury	1,466.20

5.[10] MEDICAL ASSISTANCE

Dr. L. Efron is kept very busy giving medical assistance. He was assisted up until July by Mrs. Efron, who completed her studies as a medic in Beirut. In the beginning of July, Mrs. Bogen came as a medic, but while I was in Damascus, she received a message from the director of medical affairs in Jerusalem to return there.

Dr. Efron does his job with dedication, and despite the fact that he devotes more time to his work than was stipulated in his contract, he still does not have enough time for all the work that is requested of him. The sick that come to ask his advice are continually growing in number—about a thousand per month on average. The schools have expanded to three times what they were. The number of children is now more than 1,000. And if the doctor wishes to carry out his duties faithfully (and Dr. Efron is such a man), it would require two hours a day just for this part of his work.

There is another difficulty with regard to providing medical assistance, and that is the matter of medicines. There is no Jewish pharmacist in Damascus. The medicines are made up by an Arab pharmacist who always demands high prices for them, and it is not always certain that he is giving the correct prescriptions. It would be good if there was a possibility of finding a Jewish pharmacist who would open a general pharmacy there. All of the medicines would be prepared at his place in accordance with the doctor's prescriptions at reasonable, fixed prices, and the doctor would be on the medical assistance

[10] There is no paragraph 4.

account. It would even be better still if a small pharmacy could be opened in the clinic with a pharmacist coming one or two hours a day.

Medical instruments are also needed for the clinic. Those that are there are few, and not all of them are of the most necessary.

The Regular Monthly Expenditure for This Institution	*Eg. Piastres*
For the Doctor	1,500
For House Calls to the Homes of the Sick	715
For Medicines	2,225
For the Maid's Salary	240
Miscellaneous Expenses	140
	4,820

Not included in this account is the rent for the facility, which has already been paid up till May 1920, and also the medic's salary, which she received from a different fund.

. . . .

There is in Damascus another clinic (Dispensaire) named after Baron Eduard Stern that perhaps can be joined with this institution. There would then pass over to here all of the pharmacy that is within it and the £ 10 a month that it receives. The question, however, is whether it is worthwhile to do that since the person who has power of attorney for it here in Damascus is the director of the Alliance School for Boys, who insists that the entire institution bear Baron Stern's name and that they should accept the Egyptian doctor who receives 100 francs a month and the Egyptian pharmacist who receives 40 francs a month.

Besides this institution, there is in Damascus the Biqqūr Ḥōlīm[11] Society, which pays five Egyptian pounds for milk for the sick who need it according to the doctor's orders.

6. EDUCATIONAL INSTITUTIONS

In place of the School for Boys that had about 100 pupils, the kindergarten that had about 160, and the beginning of a girls school that had some 50, which were operating in Damascus last year, there are the following institutions of Hebrew education:

The School for Boys	480 pupils
The School for Girls	210 "
Talmud Torah	120 "
Kindergarten A	245 "
Kindergarten B	220 "
	1,275 pupils

[11] Heb. for "visiting the sick." This is another important commandment in Judaism, and many societies bore this name in traditional Jewish communities.

Before I go on to talk about each of these institutions, I must make the following comments:

A. As the Hebrew schools grew larger, the Alliance schools grew smaller. At present, there are in the Alliance School for Boys 160 pupils, and 250 in its School for Girls. (The principal of the latter complained to me that *100* of her pupils transferred to the Hebrew school.) Everyone who knows how highly French studies have been regarded till now by the Damascene Jews and how they could not comprehend that it was possible to study the sciences in Hebrew will see just how powerful is an idea that will clear a path at any cost.

B. There is no longer in Damascus any other Talmud Torah or *ḥeders* and malameds.[12] All of the education now is secular.

C. The number of approximately 1,800 children in Jewish educational institutions out of an overall population of 15,000 Jews indicates that there are many more children, boys and girls, who are not receiving any education, or who are leaving school while still very young.

D. The school facilities are good by the standards of Damascene buildings. In one of them (the Boys' School), the bathrooms still need to be repaired in a hygienic manner, and it would be best to do it now during the vacation.

E. The growth and expansion of the schools did not develop in a natural, gradual way. Rather, it came about, on the one hand, by the consolidation of various institutions (the Talmud Torahs with the Boys' School), and on the other, by students leaving those schools in which they received a completely different kind of education in another language (as in the case of the Hebrew School for girls which received students from Alliance and the Christian schools), and finally, by gathering children from the marketplace and placing them in an educational institution (as in the case of Kindergarten B). This fact has its effect upon the schools and makes the implementation of proper arrangements difficult. Doubtless, it will be several years before everything in these schools will be fully in order.

F. All of these institutions, together with the evening courses for girls, the Maccabee Leagues for teenage boys, for teenage girls, and for small children, have brought about a complete revolution in the Jewish community. Hebrew has become the "fashionable" language. One can hear Hebrew songs in homes and in the streets even from those who are not studying in school. Sometimes, national interests also spread outside of the Jewish Quarter. (For a celebration in the Hebrew School for Girls, the rich and well-to-do girls had sewn for themselves dresses decorated with blue ribbons and buttons. A week later, Christian and Muslim girls did likewise, thinking that it was the latest fashion.) It is especially gratifying to note the fact that the well-to-do have begun sending their sons and daughters to the Hebrew schools. The teachers, both men and women, are the vital spirit in all public

[12] Teachers in the traditional schools of the *ḥeder* type.

work. The school directors are all members of the Communal Council, and not just the males, but also the *female*—the first example of a woman on the municipal council. One can already see readers of Hebrew newspapers in the streets. Two of the Jerusalem papers already have subscribers (and what is more important, readers) in Damascus.

. . . .[13]

Joseph Joel Rivlin, *Dīn ve-Ḥeshbōn ᶜal Devar Nesīᶜātī le-Dammeseq* (August–September 1919), handwritten report, pp. 1–22. CZA (Jerusalem) S 2/657.

[13] The report goes on to describe in lengthy detail each of the individual schools and their programs, the night courses, youth organizations, and clubs. The report concludes with a brief description of contacts between Zionists and Arab nationalists, which is given in translation in the following reading.

CONTACTS BETWEEN ZIONISTS AND ARAB NATIONALISTS IN DAMASCUS (1919)

In addition to observing the state of the Jewish Community and of the educational enterprise, I also dealt a little with the general state of affairs while I was in Damascus. I visited the Amir Fayṣal[1] together with the *Ḥākhām Bāshī*. He received us in his private house most cordially. I thanked him for what he had said to the Ḥākhām Bāshī and the notables of the Jewish Community regarding the working and mutual assistance between Arabs and Jews. I also thanked him for the good things he said about Zionism and its leaders. And he said that these had always been his views, and he asked after Dr. Weizmann and Frankfurter[2] and inquired where they were at present.

Together with Mr. Klavariski, I saw again two members of the Arab Congress—Riyāḍ Bey al-Ṣulḥ,[3] the son of Riḍā Bey al-Ṣulḥ, who is shortly to be the Governor of Aleppo or the Minister of the Interior in the Arab government, and also with Hāshim Bey, who is now chairman of the Drafting Committee for the Arab Constitution. These two are favorably inclined toward us, and we had a long conversation about our aspirations and rights and what would be our relations with the Arabs. Both of them promised to disseminate these views among their ardent nationalist friends "who do not differentiate between what is possible and what is impossible." We also spoke with the former on the matter of the telegram that has to be sent to the Peace Commission in Paris concerning the annexation of Sidon to Palestine and not to Syria.

We were informed that the Arab Congress is about to send a delegation of seventeen men to Paris and America. Among them, there are those whom the two of us have known for a long time. According to Mr. Klavariski, in his last letter to me, it would be a good idea if both of us were in Paris at the time that the delegation is there, because we could do a lot for a

[1] At this time, Fayṣal was commander in chief of the forces occupying the O.E.T.A. (Occupied Enemy Territory Administration) East, which included most of Syria east of the Lebanese coast, held by France, and the Palestinian south, held by Great Britain. Already, however, he was preparing for the establishment of his short-lived Syrian kingdom. See Stephen Hemsley Longrigg, *Syria and Lebanon under French Mandate* (London, New York, and Toronto, 1958), pp. 66–93.

[2] Fayṣal had met with both Weizmann and Frankfurter in 1919, with the former in January in London, and with the latter in February at the Paris Peace Conference. See Walter Laquer, *A History of Zionism* (New York, 1972), pp. 236–38; also Elie Kedourie, *England and the Middle East: The Destruction of the Ottoman Empire, 1914–1921* (London, 1956), pp. 152–156.

[3] He later became the first prime minister of independent Lebanon.

compromise between us and the Arabs. If the Council of Delegates[4] considers this to be a good idea, it will be necessary to obtain Baron Rothschild's permission for Mr. Klavariski to leave Palestine for a while.

I spoke with Mr. Tawfiq Mizrahi[5] on the subject of contemporary Arabic journalism, and it was explained to me that recently the newspapers have stopped speaking about Zionism by order of the Amir Fayṣal.

There are now eleven newspapers in Damascus, seven of which are dailies. The biggest paper does not have more than a thousand subscribers. But all of them are receiving support from the authorities.

There was a paper *al-Ḥayāt* that had begun to speak favorably about the Jews, and they closed it down with the argument that the editor was a former Turkish spy. He is presently a partner in the newspaper *Lisān al-ᶜArab,* in which there appear reports about Jews from time to time. It is interesting to note that after an article was printed in this paper about his visit to the *Ḥākhām Bāshī* and about what he said, the Amir sent for the editor and ordered him not to report anything more about him without his signed consent.

I also spoke with young Mr. David Zaja, who completed his studies in pharmacology in Beirut. He is a young, enthusiastic Zionist, and he wants very much to work for Zionism in Damascus or in Palestine. He gave me an account of a conversation that he had had with Dr. Aḥmad Shahbandar,[6] the secretary of the Society for Syrian Unity in Egypt, and I am conveying it along with this for the Council. I think that it will be possible to make a good deal of use of him for the sake of our political work in Syria.

Joseph Joel Rivlin, *Dīn ve-Ḥeshbōn ᶜal Devar Nesīᶜātī le-Dammeseq* (August–September 1919),
handwritten report, pp. 35–38.
CZA (Jerusalem) S 2/657.

[4] That is, the Vaᶜad ha-Ṣīrīm of the Yishuv.

[5] He apparently was an active Zionist, and correspondence from him to various Zionist bureaus may be found in the Central Zionist Archives (Jerusalem) Z 4/2332.

[6] He is apparently referring to Dr. ᶜAbd al-Raḥmān Shāhbandar, a leading Syrian Arab nationalist who had fled to Egypt in 1916 and later returned to become minister for foreign affairs in Fayṣal's short-lived government in 1920. See C. Ernest Dawn, *From Ottomanism to Arabism: Essays on the Origins of Arab Nationalism* (Urbana, Chicago, London, 1973), p. 156; and Longrigg, *Syria and Lebanon under French Mandate,* p. 100, n. 3.

A DIRECTIVE BANNING HEBREW AS THE LANGUAGE OF INSTRUCTION IN SYRIAN JEWISH SCHOOLS

(1922)

Damascus Government
Office of the Inspector General
of Education
No. 185

To the Honorable Director of the Israelite Kindergarten:

It is necessary that instruction in your school be in the Arabic language as opposed to any other, because it is the official language. You can teach Hebrew as a foreign language only. The school which teaches its curriculum in the Hebrew language after this date will be closed by the Bureau of General Education. Peace./ 3 Tammuz 922[1]

Director General of Education
(illegible signature)

CZA (Jerusalem) S 2/628.

[1]July 3, 1922.

THE VICISSITUDES OF JEWISH YOUTH CLUBS IN DAMASCUS (1923)

Damascus, February 2, 1923

Mr. President,

I have the honor to apprise you of a newly founded institution in Damascus; it is the circle of Jewish youth. An analogous organization already existed in our quarter several years ago, but in another form and with other goals. Immediately after the armistice, when many Jews exiled to Damascus as foreigners during the hostilities had to return to Palestine, they did not want to depart without leaving behind them a club where one could propagate the Zionist spirit. They rightly thought that all of the ideas which they had disseminated with such care would disappear upon the departure of those who had preached them. They thought, therefore, to found a club where the Jewish youth of Damascus, guided by the teachers of the Hebrew language school, could continue to work for the propagation of the Zionist ideal. The club took the name of National Kadima Club.

During the first months following its foundation, the club fully answered the hopes of its founders. In fact, all of Damascene youth was engaged in learning Hebrew, and something really amazing here, they were even speaking Hebrew in the streets. However, this ardor did not last long. The passion for Hebrew and Zionism was only a flash in the pan. Here, as throughout the East, people are quickly enthused, and they are just as quickly cooled again. Furthermore, Messrs. D. Yellin, Eitan, and other intelligent and active Zionists left, and the only people remaining to forward the expansion of the club are barely competent and overly fanatic individuals like Mr. Bourla,[1] the director of the Hebrew language school, and Mr. Albert Totah, your former teacher.[2]

These individuals exaggerate their own importance and exceed the task assigned them. Regarding the Damascenes from the height of their own grandeur, they consider them uncivilized and poorly informed. What is more, following their usual method, they think they can reraise Zionism's

[1] Yehuda Burla (1886–1969), who headed the Hebrew language schools in Damascus for five years following the conclusion of World War I, later became prominent as the first major Sephardi writer of modern Hebrew literature. Concerning him, see Curt Leviant, "Burla (Bourla), Yehuda," *EJ* 4: 1524–26. Much important documentation on Burla's activities in Damascus at this time and on the rivalries between the Zionists and the Alliancists may be found in the Education Department (*ha-Maḥlāqa le-Ḥinnūkh*) files for Syria of the Central Zionist Archives (Jerusalem), as for example, S 2/492, 493, 578, 579, 628, 657, and 691.

[2] That is, a former Alliance teacher. He seems to have had pro-Zionist inclinations at least as far back as 1918, at which time he made a number of pro-Zionist speeches to the Club Mixte in Damascus. See CZA (Jerusalem) S 2/578. His name indicates that he was a Syrian Jew.

prestige by denigrating the work of the Alliance, that society, which they say, has only given its graduates a veneer, an artificial sheen of modern civilization, without molding their hearts and minds. The young people were indignant at being considered so lightly and at seeing newcomers attacking an institution that for more than fifty years has molded the more enlightened spirits of the Damascene community, and they wanted to reject the tutelage of these strangers. They turned out Mr. Bourla, who was president of the club and named a local person in his place. However, the club did not last much longer. The Arab government closed it,[3] contending that it was a political center where people worked against Arab interests.

It was never known who had denounced the club to the government. In any case, people did not fail to attribute this denunciation, as always, to the Alliance. The Damascenes were made to believe that the poor Zionists were being oppressed by the representatives of the Alliance, which had used its influence with the Frence authorities to denigrate Zionism. Furthermore, this is now the only weapon of the Zionists, who, having failed all of their undertakings here, now throw upon others the responsibility for their own misfortunes.

The Jewish youth here remained for the past three years without having any place to meet. The young people have been going to the cafe or getting together in the homes of certain families to play cards. Girls have been promenading in the main street of the quarter until midnight, causing strangers to gossip about their conduct. We, therefore, thought to put an end to this state of affairs by establishing a club. We tried the experience two years ago and last year, but we were always encountering the indifference of various individuals. Finally, this winter, having brought together some young people of goodwill, we succeeded in founding a club.

We wanted to give this organization the name of the Association of Alliance Alumni. However, a few pretentious young people found this name too modest. They wanted a "Circle" just like the Maronites, the Greek Orthodox, etc. We accepted their proposal since the name was of little importance.

Just to be in order and not have problems from anyone, we asked the High Commissioner's Office for authorization to open the club. M. Catroux gave it to us immediately. He was even kind enough to send us the permit on a Sunday and promised us the cooperation of the High Commissioner's Office. The latter, in fact, has supplied our club with reviews, pictorial magazines, and all sorts of daily newspapers for the club reading room. His office also sends us the military cinema once a month. We are, ourselves, now in the process of drafting the statutes of the society. Among other

[3] At the war's end, Greater Syria was divided into three occupied zones, with the Amir Fayṣal's forces controlling Damascus and eastern Syria. This lasted until Fayṣal was run out of Syria by the French in July 1920. See Stephen Hemsley Longrigg, *Syria and Lebanon under French Mandate* (London, New York, and Toronto, 1958), pp. 61–108.

things, we are inserting two articles: one prohibiting gambling, the other forbidding members of the club from engaging in political activities.

The goal of the society is to instruct the youth with lectures and interesting public readings, to give them a taste for reading by furnishing them with good books and journals. In short, to keep the members from going elsewhere by procuring for them such distractions as parlor games, dominoes, checkers, chess, etc., and by organizing dances.

Establishing the club was not achieved without difficulties. We encountered many fierce opponents. Some, like the Chief Rabbi, contended that it was not permissible for young men and women to come together to read, to chat, or to dance. Others, like the Zionists, who watched unhappily as they lost all influence upon the youth, have tried to stir up problems for us on the Communal Council of Notables. Someone even went to the Chief of Police to say we had established a cabaret. Fortunately, we knew how to overcome all of these calumnies. The Chief Rabbi of Beirut, M. Tagger, helped us in this.

During his stay in Damascus, we invited him to a soiree organized at the club in his honor. At the party, to which all of the notables were invited, he delivered a speech in which he praised our initiative. He took advantage of the occasion also to recall the good that the Alliance had done in all of the towns of the East. He concluded by exhorting all of those who were present to take part in our club or at least to lend it their assistance.

The club now enjoys a good reputation. Everyone frequents it except the teachers at the Hebrew language schools because Mr. Bourla has expressly forbidden them to do so.

The club is open four times a week. On Saturday nights, one of us gives a lecture or a reading. M. Kahanoff[4] has already given two talks this winter: one on aviation, the other on wireless telegraph and telephone. For my part, I gave one lecture on the Alliance and its work and another on Pasteur. One of our former teachers, M. Kandalaft, gave an informal talk on the responsibilities of young people. We hope to be able to continue in this vein. On the other days, some read, some take a dance course, while others play while chatting.

We think we have done a useful piece of work in bringing together the young people under our roof and in trying to give them some instruction. This is without even taking into account that the club contributes to making them like the Alliance.

We assume that this will entail an increase in our work, but we are rewarded when we consider the usefulness of our action.

Please accept, Mr. President, our devoted sentiments.

Anna Kahanoff

AIU Archives (Paris)
Syrie I.G.2.

[4] The writer's husband and head of the Alliance School for Boys in Damascus.

A SYRIAN RABBI CRITICIZES "THE NEW INTELLECTUALS"
(1924)

The first intellectuals during the period of the scholars of Spain were enlightened and knew well the profundity of the spirit of Judaism and its glorious power. Torah and enlightenment were like twin sisters that went together. There was true harmony between their two spiritual trends.

But the new intellectuals of the past generation did not comprehend this. They did not penetrate deeply into the great ideas of Judaism. They did not understand that the spirit of the Bible and the homiletic literature and the lofty ideas that are within them, these are the spiritual homeland of the people, developed and perfected over thousands of years. They were unable to grasp, moreover, that whoever seeks wisdom and is well versed in wordly fields of knowledge must fulfill his natural duty to honor the sacred tradition just as a man must honor his father and his mother. And so, they went far afield to other pastures. They gave first priority to secular studies and made sacred studies secondary. They were unable to recognize or find the illumination that is in the Torah and tradition. Rather, they went in search of sparks that shed no light even on the surface of things. They imbibed mockery like water.

They gave the outward appearance of being friends and allies, but this was only to hide the hatred buried in their hearts. With smooth tongues and flowery words, they thought to destroy our spiritual possessions which we had acquired through personal sacrifice. . . . They even dared to speak insolently about divine matters and about the rabbis of old and of recent times who are the heroes of the spirit, the elect of the people, who did not assume their authority by force, but rather were raised to distinction by their extensive knowledge, acquired throughout a long life of hardship, and by virtue of their personal qualities, their expertise, their warmth, their humility, their self-sufficiency, and their piety.

The new intellectuals were not able at all to penetrate the hidden inner depths of either the general or the particular spirit of the people of Israel. . . . Thus, with all their enlightenment they have not been able to enrich their people spiritually. They have not produced any vital, lasting spiritual contribution for the nation. They have stirred up people's hearts and confused their minds and have led them astray with tremendous doubts and delusions.

Our national poet[1] has expressed this bitterly in his verses:

And when an eagle grows up from among your sons and takes to wing—
From his nest you will send him forth forever;

[1] Ḥayyim Naḥman Bialik.

Even when he soars through the sky, strong and thirsting for sunlight—
It will not be to you he brings down the lights;
Far from you atop rocks he will shriek
But the echo of his voice will not reach you.[2]

They thought to improve and reform education, but they only turned the pot on its head. They purport that their desire is to benefit us, but either intentionally or unwittingly they are taking our souls.

It is incumbent upon us, therefore, to put all of our work and effort into educating our children in our own spirit. We must implant in their hearts our ethics, our language, our history, our studies, the contents of the Bible and the talmudic and midrashic narratives. We must teach them that the pure spirit and high ethics in these works, these are the test of the spirit and soul, while other studies and foreign languages are the test of the body; they are an outer garment. We must take care of our children's spiritual needs before taking care of their bodily needs. Then these two kinds of knowledge can exist within them. They will become educated, successful, and good people, who give benefit to God and His Torah, to their people, to themselves, to others, and to all the world.

Isaac Dayyan, "Tōrat Yisrā'ēl ve-ᶜAm Yisrā'ēl," *Minḥat Yehūda,* ed. Nissim ᶜAṭiyya (Aleppo, 1924), pp. 40–43.

[2] These verses are from the poem "Ākhēn Gam Ze Mūsar Elōhīm." See *Kol Kitvē Ḥ. N. Bialik* [The Complete Works of H. N. Bialik] (Tel Aviv, 1959), p. 49.

A SYRIAN JOURNALIST IS STUNNED THAT JEWISH STUDENTS EXCEL IN ARABIC EXAMS (1939)

The degree of success this year was to a very great extent related to the proportion of time wasted during the course of the academic year because of serious political strikes and violent upheaval, about which I shall say nothing. But an astonishing occurrence revealed something that amazed me; namely, the proportion of successful students from the Alliance Jewish School, not only in quantity, but in quality as well. These students attained the highest marks on the written exams in both the Arabic and French languages, while the average of grades in Arabic among the students from the Arab schools were very much inferior. Is this not astounding—the Jewish students excelling in the Arabic language more than the Arab students?!! O how strange! The Jews' children excel in Arabic above its own sons. What a humiliation it must be for these Arab students. What a source of heartache it must be for you, dear readers.

I do not know who is their (the Jewish students') teacher, but I do not doubt for an instant that he is a giant of giants, and if I ever saw him, I would extend my hand to shake his, embrace him warmly, and congratulate him sincerely. For what he has done deserves praise, acknowledgment, and respect.

O Arab students! Take a lesson from the Jewish students. You are more entitled to your language if you learn it. We understand your hatred of French. Therefore, you have not been successful in it. But what do you think about your not succeeding in Arabic!! Is there not in your fall something to make one weep and cut one's soul to the point of killing it with grief and anxiety?!

I do not know what I want to say. Pain has risen up in my heart and alighted within my breast. Have I shown you, O Arab students, that from now on you must be concerned and apply yourselves with your utmost efforts, sincerity, and love!?

Mamdūḥ Ḥaqqī

Clipping from the Syrian newspaper *al-Inshā'* (June 25, 1939) in AIU Archives (Paris) Syrie XI.E.94.

SPEAKING JUDEO-ARABIC IN MIXED COMPANY
(BAGHDAD, 1940)

The coffee pot had just gone around again and we were all holding cups of bitter coffee when Nessim made his entrance. . . .

We got together at the Yassine Cafe every evening, making plans for the future based on our day's reading. It was an endless debate that we resumed night after night. We were painfully tracing our path, each of us seeking in the others' approval a confirmation of the dictates of his temperament; and under cover of discussing the future of our culture, we were defending our own first writing.

That evening was marked by an unusual note. Nessim spoke in the Jewish dialect. We were the only Jews in the group. All the others, except for a Chaldean and an Armenian, were Muslim and their dialect served as our common language. In Iraq the presence of a single Muslim in a group was enough for his dialect to be imposed. But was it a true dialect? All of us—Jews, Christians, or Muslims—spoke Arabic. We had been neighbors for centuries. Our accents, certain words, were our distinguishing marks. Why did the Christians draw out certain words? We were told that in this way they were perpetuating the traces of their Nordic origin. But then the Nordic Muslims, those from Mosul, should have spoken like Christians. The Jewish manner of speaking was sprinkled with Hebrew words, explained by long familiarity with the Bible and prayers. But how to explain the presence of Turkish and Persian words in our dialect? We would have had greater contact with invaders and pilgrims than the Bedouins. Then what about the Muslims who during the Ottoman era were forced to learn, not Arabic, but Turkish in school?

We had only to open our mouths to reveal our identity. The emblem of our origins was inscribed in our speech. We were Jew, Christian, and Muslim, from Baghdad, Basra, or Mosul. We had a common language, that of the Muslims of the region. An inexhaustible source of confusion and cruel ridicule. What better entertainment for a young Muslim than listening to an old Jewish woman from the poor section of Abou Sifain speaking to some Muslim official? She mispronounces several Jewish words, following them with a couple of common Muslim expressions. With many contortions of the mouth, she finally succeeds only in mispronouncing her own dialect. The effect is inevitably comic.

Semiliterate Jews always studded their phrases with one or two Muslim terms when they spoke to other Jews. Borrowing a few words from the Muslims proved that one had dealings with them, that one associated with them, and that one was not content with the poor company of other Jews. The rich Jews were no less ashamed of their accent, and they never missed the chance to slip a few words of English or French into their conversation. A child who called his father "papa" or "daddy" was already guaranteed a future aristocracy.

The Muslims borrowed only from literary language. They felt no need to cast an unfavorable judgment on their dialect. And they turned to the dialects of Jews and Christians only to amuse visitors. A typically Jewish word in the mouth of a Muslim was synonymous with ridicule. In emancipated intellectual circles there was no thought of borrowing the Jewish accent and even less of making fun of it.

It was unusual, then, for Nessim to speak in his own accent among so many Muslims. Was it another joke? No, he was not speaking exclusively to me. He was not even looking at me. He was speaking to Nazar, Said, and the others.

It was very important not to attach too much importance to this new whim. Everyone tacitly wanted to attribute this outburst of comic dialect to Nessim's bantering nature. It was of no consequence. Most of all, we must guard against giving any special import to this jesting.

Nessim persisted, straight-faced. It was as though he were taking special care to choose all the Jewish words that usually got a laugh from Muslims. Imperturbably, he pleaded Balzac's case and talked of his enthusiasm for Stendhal, whom he had just discovered. Like a coward, I chose silence. Still displaying all his enthusiasm for the French novel, he called on me to participate. Finally he asked me a question directly. It was useless for me to escape. He would persist.

I chose a middle course. My words were neither those of the Jews nor the Muslims. I spoke in literary Arabic, the Arabic of the Koran. Then, in a supercilious tone and with contained anger, Nessim corrected me: "You mean. . . ." And he translated into perfect Jewish dialect. He compressed his lips in a gesture of hatred. He exaggerated our accent. I could see in his look a mixture of sorrow and commiseration. I was betraying him. I was ashamed to utter in the presence of others the words of intimacy, of home, of friendship. Nessim was forcing me to take a stand against the solidarity of the group. I could not reject our common language without humiliating myself. It was no longer the language of friendship, but of the clan. I listened to myself, and the Jewish words stood out in all their strangeness, coldly naked. My sentences were frozen. But I uttered them, I heard them echo in my ears. I was reciting a lesson I had learned. I slipped in a French word. Nessim, pitiless censor, immediately translated into the Jewish dialect.

No one smiled. The new rules of the game had been accepted by common accord. The Muslims with good grace paid no special attention to the new language that was stating its unaccustomed presence. Generally they looked at us without seeing us. Now, mysteriously, they recognized our features. They were noting a new color in the panoply. Later, everything would be restored to order, as no one would want to admit the existence of particular cases.

In our group we were neither Jew nor Muslim. We were Iraqis, concerned about the future of our country and consequently the future of each one of us. Except that the Muslims felt more Iraqi than the others. It was no use for us to say to them, "this is our land and we have been here for twenty-five centuries." We had been there first, but they were not convinced. We were different. Was our coloring not lighter than the Bedouins'? Did we not know foreign languages? The fact that the best students in Arabic in the final examinations were Jews, that the Alliance Israélite school produced the best Arabic grammarians, changed nothing. Our identity was tainted. So be it. Nessim was assuming this difference. He wanted it admitted. He did not intend to convince and he had no evidence to produce. He was presenting a fact. We were Jews and we weren't ashamed of it.

By the end of the evening, we had won the game. For the first time the Muslims were listening to us with respect. We were worthy of our dialect. We were clothed in our own garments. Our mouths were restored to their true form, the one they had worn for generations in the secrecy of the home. . . . The masks had fallen. We stood there in our luminous and fragile difference. And it was neither a sign of humiliation nor a symbol of ridicule. In a pure Jewish dialect we made our plans for the future of Iraqi culture. We did not take shelter behind the veil of an artificial equality. Our features were emerging from the shadow; they were being drawn. They were unique. Our faces were uncovered, recognized at last.

Naim Kattan, *Farewell, Babylon,*
translated from the French by Sheila Fischman
(Toronto, 1975), pp. 5–9.

Sunday 8 December. At daybreak we are in Baghdad. A car takes me to the hotel via a broad avenue. I do not recognize a single building in this city where, thirty years ago, I spent five years of my life. Only the site of the palms is familiar to me.

I settle in and prepare to leave the hotel to go to the school. A young man comes up to me and greets me effusively. He was waiting for a traveler and was surprised to see me there. It was one of my former pupils. Wherever I would go, I would similarly be stopped. The old school master who raised so many generations is remembered!

We penetrate the maze of ancient lanes, somber and cheerless—veritable mires. We cross them hopping on the bricks which are set at intervals. The high gray walls with only a few windows fitted with iron bars and the massive doors with their large, round-headed studs give the impression of prisons. I am recovering my way: it was indeed through here that I used to pass four times a day to go to and return from my work. . . . I hasten my steps, my heart beating. I am in front of my school. I want to restrain the flood of my memories. I force myself to hold back the past from surging out of the forgotten, but it is stronger than I am.

I see myself in November 1899, coming into this school yard like today. They were at recreation. The little and the big ones were wearing the robe whose skirt lifted when walking to expose the large white pantaloons. They were chatting or shouting. Their guttural speech was incomprehensible to me. I experienced a strange impression, I felt sad. When I knew them, when I saw them at work, it was a revelation. Their intelligence delighted me. I admired in them that desire to know everything, to understand everything. Impossible to do an approximation; one had to be clear and precise. Often it was wiser to admit ignorance at their questions or objections. I set myself to work; I had to relearn what I had forgotten, acquire new knowledge. It was in this school that I understood the talmudic dictum: "I have learned much from my teachers, still more from my friends, but it is to my students that I owe the most."[1] Through their willingness, through their increasing effort, the level of studies gradually rose, and this primary school became an institution of secondary instruction. Afterward, the Turkish authorities put the Albert Sassoon College[2] on the same level as the lycées. The diploma it granted was made comparable to the baccalaureate, allowing the young people entrance into the university departments.

[1] Taᶜanit 7a and Makkot 10a.

[2] Alliance school named after Sir Albert (Abdulla) Sassoon (1818–1896), who donated 50,000 francs for the building in 1873. See Abraham Ben-Jacob, *A History of the Jews in Iraq: From the End of the Gaonic Period to the Present Time,* 2nd revised ed. (Jerusalem, 1979), pp. 290, 294 [Heb.]; and David Solomon Sassoon, *A History of the Jews in Baghdad* (Letchworth, 1949), p. 171.

This buzzing hive contains at this moment 500 pupils, 500 "Europeans," well dressed, eager to learn about modern science, about progress. The task is being accomplished under difficult conditions. We were more favored. Our programs included the study of Turkish, Arabic, English, and Hebrew; however, the language of instruction was French. When a student reached the end of his studies, he thought in French, he wrote in French, but he was able to express in one of the other languages studied the idea he had conceived in French. Our scholastic population at that time was a select one. We had succeeded in bringing together in the four schools 1,500 pupils, boys and girls. One could demand of this elite a considerable effort. There are today in the various Jewish schools of the city close to 7,000 pupils. The mass has happily been called to the benefit of instruction, although the intellectual level overall is not as high. Incidentally, the Arabic language is reclaiming supremacy; English, the language of the protecting nation, is seeking to occupy second place; Hebrew, in this era of Jewish awakening, is gaining ground, while French does its best to maintain its position. . . .

I pass rather rapidly through the elementary classes and want to give the better part of my time to the upper-level courses, the culmination of scholastic work. This class attains on the whole the knowledge of a Third at a lycée. These young people are seventeen years old. They answer with ease the questions I pose on all subjects: history or geography, science or mathematics. They read with understanding a passage from the great French authors and can explain its ideas. Hebraic studies have pushed forward a long way. Instructors who have come from Palestine teach Hebrew and Jewish history.

The personnel is excellent: young people coming out of this Ecole Normale Israélite Orientale who have acquired so much learning, teachers trained in Palestine or in Baghdad, Muslim Iraqis, Syrian Christians, all of them animated by the desire to fulfill their task well, to maintain the good name of the institution, working side by side for the same ideal. I admire here, as I did in Persia, this new sentiment which brings closer Jewish youth with those of other faiths. This is the new fact in the Middle East, a beautiful conquest, a consequence of the Great War. This spirit of broad tolerance permits everyone to have hopes—would that the governments would jealously watch out to maintain it. It is the gauge of humanity's march toward a better future. Some uneasy spirits perceive precursory signs of struggles that will provoke economic rivalries. It is possible that the difficulties of life create antagonisms, but let us hope that these will not take the confessional forms. Here union exists between all elements of the population: the school is the crucible in which the living forces of the nation are amalgamated in the sentiment of justice and equality. That is comforting.

I cross the alleys of the old Jewish Quarter in order to go to the Laura Kadoorie School for Girls.[3] It is the first, the largest, and most beautiful of

[3] This Alliance school originally founded in 1893 was rebuilt in 1911 by Sir Elly Silas Kadoorie (1867–1944) in memory of his wife. See Ben-Jacob, *A History of the Jews in Iraq,* p. 295 [Heb.]; and Rudolf Loewenthal, "Kadoorie," *EJ* 10: 667.

Mr. Kadoorie's foundations. It was a gamble twenty-five years ago to build such enormous buildings in an overpopulated quarter, where the little houses squeezed one against the other sheltered numerous families—several people in the same room, the bed superposed against the walls like bunks of a ship.

The facade of the building is simple: two vast interior courtyards forming patios; all around wide galleries onto which the classrooms open. Those are supported by massive marble columns on the ground floor and on the second floor by tall, thin wooden columns. This school was the "wonder" of Baghdad when it was built. Over the years, the masses would come to gaze at it. Now that vast educational institutions are rising up on the outskirts of the city, the 1,400 pupils populating this school are feeling cramped and the generous philanthropist is buying up by payment in gold the surrounding homes. He is having them demolished in order to give more air and light on all sides.

The majority of the children belong to the well-to-do class. One would not at all say looking at them, Baghdadis. Their simple bearing is very gracious. They are given the education of young girls of "family." Their open spirit has the gleams of all. I have heard them read and explain with full understanding a page of good literature. They draw nicely. They know sewing, hygiene, and housekeeping. I see in the library some alumnae perusing the latest issue of *l'Illustration*. Others are cutting aprons and dresses for the poor pupils—they purchased the fabrics from their savings. A workshop for dressmaking adjoins the school. As soon as the poorer students have learned to read and write, they are sent there to be taught a trade—sewing, cutting, embroidery—that will allow them to earn their living. The works produced by these skillful hands have a supervising finish, the colors are put together with taste; some of them deserve to be represented in the collections of the department stores of Europe.

Monday 9 December. I visit this morning the Revka Nouriel School.[4] I had founded it with the cooperation of so many friends who are gone today! We gave it the name of the virtuous woman who had bequeathed her fortune for the education of children and care for the sick. Two hundred and fifty boys follow the elementary curriculum there of Albert Sassoon College.

The Noam School bears the name of Revka's sister, another benefactrice of children.[5] Five hundred little girls learn French, Arabic, and Hebrew there; a major place is reserved for needlework.

Thus, there are in the Alliance schools 2,700 children; 4,300 others attend the schools maintained exclusively by the community and received Arabic and Hebraic instruction, or English, Arabic, and Hebrew. I shall visit

[4] Alliance school for boys funded by a wealthy Iraqi Jewish woman, Rivka Nuriel, in 1902. See Ben-Jacob, *A History of the Jews in Iraq*, pp. 296–7 [Heb.].

[5] This school was founded in 1923/24 with a bequest from Rivka Nuriel's sister. See Ben-Jacob, *A History of the Jews in Iraq*, p. 297 [Heb.].

them all in turn, but I must make note now of this great effort by the community.[6]

The Iraqi government is opening the public schools to the Jews; however, they are still too few in number for the needs of the population. It has created a special school reserved for the Jews which has been able to gather 175 children out of 12,000 of school age according to the community's reckoning. It is said: "The Jews, from the point of view of education, have such a head start!" Precisely because they have sought after modern education since 1864, because they inhabit the cities and engage in commerce, they, more than others, need to be educated. Five thousand children still grow up in ignorance.

Y.-D. Sémach, *A travers les communautés israélites d'Orient*
(Paris, 1931), pp. 39–45.

[6] The author was on an inspection tour of Alliance schools in the Middle East.

THE THEOSOPHIST CONTROVERSY AMONG THE JEWS OF BASRA
(1931)

A.

An excited crowd numbering about 300 and including women and children appeared before Basrah City Police Station on Saturday night, and later in the evening H. E. the Mutasarrif[1] ordered the arrest of the Jewish Mukhtar.[2]

Earlier in the evening a party of about twenty boys tore down the signboard of the hall of the Theosophical Society, near the Jewish synagogue, thus taking the first overt step in the quarrel that has arisen following the establishment a year ago of the Society. In all, seven people are now under detention.

The Theosophical Society was formed in Basrah by Mr. Khedoouri E. Ani last year. The present issue was raised when the Basrah Chief Rabbi Hakham Sasson delivered a sermon in which he asked the Jews not to join this new society, being, he said, a kind of new faith, and so forbidden by the Jewish religion. This sermon was received from the Council of Rabbis at Baghdad.

The Chief Rabbi also requested the Mutasarrif to eject the society from its present premises, on the grounds that by ancient law, no church, Muhammadan mosque, and synagogue may be situated together in the same street, on account of the possibility of quarreling and bloodshed among followers of the different faiths.

"Jewish Demonstrations in Basrah City—Anti-Theosophy Protests," *The Times of Mesopotamia* (April 13, 1931).

B.

The seven persons arrested in the Jewish demonstrations in Basrah City on Saturday night were released yesterday morning.

H. E. the Mutasarrif is understood to have communicated to Baghdad the Chief Rabbi's request to eject the Theosophical Society from its present premises, as it is surrounded by Jewish synagogues and schools and so may be thought liable to be a source of trouble.

[1] Provincial governor.

[2] Secular chief of the Jewish community.

The President of the Rabbinical Court of New York, Dr. Leo Gung,[3] wrote as follows, in reply to an enquiry addressed to him by a Basrawi:

> Jews do not need Theosophy. In the Torah they are taught a philosophical life, not a mystic nothingness.
>
> Theosophy leads Jews away from their solid duties with which our Lord has crowned us.
>
> I would certainly warn my brothers against the surrender of their religious identity, which is inevitable as they lose themselves in the unprofitable mazes of theosophical thought. . . . It is not a religion for men. It robs women of their grace and strength. It deprives youth of its moral stamina.[4]

"Basrah Jews and Theosophy—Arrested Persons Liberated—Appeals to Be Orthodox," *The Times of Mesopotamia* (April 14, 1931).

C.
A JEWISH THEOSOPHIST REPLIES

Sir,—As you have seen from our open letter which was published in your Arabic section of 28th March 1931, the Acting Hacham Heskell Sasson has distorted the truth by alleging that the Theosophical Society, founded here in 1927, is a new religion which is contrary to the Jewish faith and has enjoined all not to elect those affiliated to it either to the Jewish Lay Council or to any committee which has any sort of control over the Community's funds.

Reference to Pears' Cyclopaedia, Theosophical Literature, History of Modern Philosophy, and other historical literature will show that Theosophy is not a religion but is a Philosophical Science which has been taught for thousands of years by the ancient Egyptians, Romans, Israelites, Christians and Arabs and that the Theosophical Society is a scientific, literary, ethical and philosophical society. Its aims are three, as follows:

1. To form a nucleus of the universal brotherhood of humanity, without distinction of race, creed, sex, caste, or color
2. To encourage the study of comparative religion, philosophy, and science
3. To investigate the unexplained laws of nature and the powers latent in man

Is it possible for anyone with the least common sense to imagine that this Society conflicts with other religions or that it offends against other beliefs? It is with this illusion that the Acting Hacham and his satellites have

[3] Misprint for Rabbi Leo Jung, a leading figure in American and world Orthodoxy.

[4] Other foreign rabbinic authorities were also contacted. See the excerpts from the letter of Great Britain's Chief Rabbi, Dr. J. H. Hertz, quoted in *The Times of Mesopotamia* (April 13, 1931).

wanted to mislead public opinion and to detract from the good reputation of the Society. They have circulated provocative reports in the Synagogues in a manner calculated to excite the public against it, rendering those affiliated to it subject to the risk of persecution, humiliation, and even evil intent.

The result of this was made evident on Saturday, when weak and narrow-minded members of the Jewish Community rushed the premises of the Theosophical Society, howling and shouting, each armed with whatever might enable him to attack the members of the Society.

Fortunately, no one happened to be present and the onslaught was made on the locked door. When they found they could not break it, they pulled down the signboard which was shattered to pieces in front of the house of the President, which was also pelted with stones.

The strongest proof of the intentions toward those connected with the Theosophical Society in Basrah is their circular, which was prepared at will and in conformity with no legal code, without any observations having been indicated to any member of the Society, and without addressing any question to or obtaining a reply from any of them.

Would it ever have occurred to you, Mr. Editor, that in this Century of Light the Acting Hacham would play the role of Jeroboam, son of Nebat (Kings I, Chap. XIV), by sowing discord among the individuals of the Jewish Community in Basrah who are day and night toiling to earn their living in peace and harmony, in full obedience to the Law.

I am, etc.
K. E. Ani,
President.

"The Case for the Theosophists—(To the Editor)," *The Times of Mesopotamia* (April 14, 1931).

AN ALLIANCE OFFICIAL'S VISIT TO THE JEWISH COMMUNITY OF DAMASCUS IN 1929

Since Antiquity, Damascus has possessed a very important Jewish community, noted for its opulence and learning. . . . These people of Damascus knew how to make for themselves amicable relations with highly cultivated, highly refined, old Arab aristocracy. They rose by this contact with them to a great distinction—the fine manners which still to this day are held in esteem among them. Material prosperity kept pace with intellectual progress. Damascus, the commercial capital of Syria, sent out its caravans south to Arabia, east to Baghdad, as far as the Indies and China. There were many Jews who acquired fabulous riches. The Jewish Quarter was newly rebuilt, ostentatious homes went up there, real palaces of stone and marble.[1] . . . Some of these houses have preserved some vestiges still of those splendors which the tourists come to admire. Then, there was decadence. A stupid accusation of ritual murder in 1840 put a barrier between the various confessions.[2]

The events in Lebanon in 1860 had their backlash in Damascus.[3] The opening of the Suez Canal in 1869 reduced the caravan traffic. Turkish bankruptcy in 1876 gave the coup de grace to this prosperity. Damascus lost its wealth, although it preserved a taste for luxury and the love of pleasures.

During the last revolt,[4] it was via the Jewish Quarter that the rebels believed they could enter the city. Our coreligionists found themselves in the crossfire, and their losses were heavy. Many families left the city with no intention of returning. Those who remained are the poorest—the artisans and those without work.

We spoke of the catastrophe of the last century. This community, which did not wish to die, turned instinctively toward the manual occupations and specialized in copper work in particular. The Jews are almost the only ones producing these curious objects of infinite variety which the Oriental bazaars retail throughout the four corners of the world: trays, flowerpots, ashtrays, lamps, boxes, knickknacks of all sorts. These artisans can be counted in the thousands. In former times,[5] I saw workshops in which dozens of young

[1] For a nineteenth-century traveler's description of such a home, see Norman A. Stillman, *Jews of Arab Lands: A History and Source Book* (Philadelphia, 1979), p. 353.

[2] See ibid., pp. 105–6, 393–402.

[3] Ibid., pp. 403–5.

[4] Sémach is probably referring to the uprising of 1925–1926, led by the Amir Sulṭān al-Aṭrāsh. During the revolt, Damascus was attacked on several occasions, with extensive damage and loss of life resulting. See Arnold J. Toynbee, *Survey of International Affairs, 1925, vol. I: The Islamic World since the Peace Settlement* (London, 1927), pp. 425–32.

[5] Sémach first came to Damascus in 1898.

children of five and six years of age were hammering large trays from morning till evening. The blows that they struck on certain parts painted black rough-hewed the work that an experienced worker would quickly finish.

Cabinetmaking in engraved walnut and inlay of bone and mother-of-pearl is also an industry in which the Jews excel. They are also in the weaving of fabrics: cushions, drapes, tapestries of cotton and silk with threads of gold and silver. Some workmen produce "Persian carpets." There exist blacksmiths, carpenters, and many who practice the callings that have always been Jewish specialties: tinkers, tailors, jewelers, hairdressers, etc.

These artisans were recruited from among the youth who could not find a place in school. Today, all the children are in class thanks to a happy entente between the Alliance and the community, which requires heavy sacrifices for the sake of education. Nine hundred pupils attend our schools. Four hundred others go to different institutions. Of these, 300 are at the school of the Protestant Mission.[6] These children do not receive an education in the Jewish spirit and do not learn French.

I visited the classrooms of the four (Alliance) schools. The male and female teachers use all of their ingenuity to train the minds of the children and to give them the knowledge appropriate to their age. In the kindergarten, the little ones learn to speak French and Hebrew, to sing, to play, to execute little works which employ the fingers and exercise the spirit of observation. In the elementary classes numerous hours are devoted to the French language, the tool that will make the studies possible. In the advanced classes, I found select subjects appropriate for ensuring success on examinations and in competitions. The teaching of Hebrew and Arabic is done efficiently, and the students know the main events of Jewish history.

Here, as elsewhere, the premises have something to be desired. It is an old princely home that is completely dilapidated. The small rooms are insufficiently lighted for classrooms. The worm-eaten woodwork is falling to dust. The marble slabs have come off in places, while those that remain are broken.

"Help us to construct quarters better suited to the needs of school!" the members of the local Committee said to me. The generous philanthropist Kadoorie, who, from Persia and Iraq,[7] has extended his benefactions to Syria and Palestine, put at the disposal of the Alliance a considerable sum of money for building purposes. The community promised its cooperation, but the hour was allowed to pass, and the credits available were not sufficient.

The case is not peculiar to Damascus. There is need to envisage an overall policy regarding such quarters. There is everywhere a pressing need

[6] Concerning the educational activities of the Protestant missionaries among Middle Eastern Jewry, see Stillman, *Jews of Arab Lands,* pp. 101, 104–5, 377–83, 422.

[7] Concerning the Kadoorie schools in Iraq, see pp. 285–286.

to accommodate the children in large, airy classrooms. It is necessary to prepare a general plan to be realized by steps over a certain number of years.

I visited the Stern Dispensary in Damascus, with which I had occupied myself in former times. A young, active doctor and a zealous staff take care of a large, indigent population. The installation is unfortunately very poor.

Our former students, animated by excellent sentiments, are exerting themselves more than ever before to direct the community in a good course. They dedicate their spare time to Jewish activities, to the young, and to the indigent. They deserve to be encouraged.

Y.-D. Sémach, *A travers les communautés israélites d'Orient* (Paris, 1931), pp. 62–66.

A PLEA FOR HELP FROM THE JEWS OF HODEIDA TO THEIR CORELIGIONISTS IN LONDON (1923)

To you honored gentlemen, sons of holy men, lovers of benevolence, who repair every breach, who have fulfilled the Scriptural Word "Each man helps his neighbor, and they say to one another: Be strong!"[1] to you our brethren, the members of holy congregation of the capital city London (may the Lord on High make its foundations firm). May the Lord be with you.

After asking after your honors' health and well-being, we now bring to your attention a most urgent message. Whoever hears it—his heart will melt and his ears will ring. Know that even as we are astonished by the great suffering, the long exile, and the Yemenite government's oppression of our fellow Jews who live under its dark shadow, beneath its leaning wall, there reached the city of Hodeida[2] sixty men, women, old people, and infants. We received them, and they told us all of the hardship that had befallen them on the way and from which the Lord had delivered them.

After they had recovered their composure somewhat, we asked them what was the reason for their journey, and why were their faces so disturbed? Woe unto the ears that hear such things, and woe unto us who have seen our brethren in such a state! They answered us: "Did you not know that the turmoil has grown in all of the cities and a great cry has gone out because the enemies are rising up with a strong hand and an outstretched arm to destroy us[3] or to force us to renounce our faith for the corrupt, abominable[4] faith of the Arabs. Furthermore, when they hear about the condition of our brethren the children of Israel in the Holy City, their hate and envy have greatly inflamed. We fled to save ourselves, abandoning our homes and everything we possessed in order to escape death or the profanation of the Divine Name."

And now, Gentlemen, for the sake of your people, try with all your might to save your brethren, to aid them, and to provide some refuge for these wretched souls. Let each one try to persuade his fellow, and the latter

[1] Isa. 41:6.

[2] The principal port of Yemen on the Red Sea coast. At the time this letter was written, Hodeida was not under the control of the Imam of Yemen, having been handed over by the British to the Sharīf of ᶜAsīr in 1918. This is the reason that the city served as a refuge for those fleeing the persecutions of the interior. See L. O. Schuman, "al-Ḥudayda," *EI*[2] 3: 539–40.

[3] A paraphrase from the Passover liturgy. This letter is replete in almost every line with allusions to scripture, liturgy, and the traditional sources.

[4] These words have been dropped in the published Hebrew text of this letter. See Yosef Tobi, "An Epistle from Yemenite Jews to the London Jewish Community," in *The Jews of Yemen: Studies and Researches,* ed. Y. Yeshaᶜyahu and Y. Tobi (Jerusalem, 1975), pp. 412–14 [Heb.].

his fellow, so that funds might be collected for them, together with necessary provisions, and passage by boat to Aden, where they can keep themselves alive and find permanent shelter.

Please save a few souls from the House of Israel, make an effort on their behalf, and do not ignore them. Save them from the hand of those Arabs[5] and from their land, a country in which no Jew ever settled.[6]

Now it is not fitting to turn aside or to tarry, for this is a serious matter. There is nothing more fitting for us than to sanctify God and to deliver the oppressed from the hand of the oppressor. Everyone is obliged to sanctify God with all his heart, with all his soul, and with all his might, as it is written: "And thou shalt love the Lord thy God, etc."[7] Whom can we rely upon, if not upon our Heavenly Father and your compassion for your aforementioned brethren. We have offered them words of comfort, but because of their great anguish they have not been comforted, preferring death over life. We are continually lamenting, but we know that you are all of the true seed, that we all have one forefather, and that the seed of Abraham our father—peace be upon him—are compassionate people who perform deeds of kindness. Therefore, you will not reject their plea. To You O' Lord Who dwells on high, I lift up mine eyes, that they may be rewarded many times over as it is written: "May the Lord bless you from Zion, and may you see the goodness of Jerusalem all the days of your life."[8] May it be His will. Amen.

Furthermore, there is another matter which concerns forty-two people who were seized by the enemy who claimed that they are orphans. They seized them, beat them, and gave them bitters to drink. It was decreed that they must convert.[9] A few of them managed to escape into the wilderness. And now, they scream and weep on account of their terrible suffering which is even worse than the cruelty that had overwhelmed them and worked its

[5] The Hebrew text has Kedarites (cf. Ps. 120:5), which since the Middle Ages was commonly equated with the Arabs and particularly Muḥammad's own tribe of Quraysh. See Norman A. Stillman, *Jews of Arab Lands: A History and Source Book* (Philadelphia, 1979), p. 41, n. 21.

[6] Jews, of course, were settled in considerable numbers in the interior of Yemen. Perhaps the writers wish to say that no Jew ever felt really at home there.

[7] Deut. 6:5.

[8] Ps. 128:5.

[9] One of the worst of the many sufferings endured by Yemenite Jewry was the forced conversion of children whose father had died. This practice, which seems to date back as far as the eighteenth century, was, of course, totally at odds with mainstream Islamic law. However, the Zaydī Shiʿite authorities in Yemen apparently interpreted the well-known tradition attributed to Muḥammad that "every child is born in the natural state [i.e., Islam] and it is only his parents who make him a Jew, a Christian, or a Zoroastrian" as justifying this practice. See Yehuda Nini, *Yemen and Zion: The Jews of Yemen, 1800–1914* (Jerusalem, 1982), pp. 33–34 [Heb.]; also S. D. Goitein, *Jews and Arabs: Their Contacts through the Ages,* 3rd revised ed. (New York, 1974), pp. 77–79.

will with them. They (i.e., those who did not escape) renounced their faith, the faith of the living God and ruler of the world, for the ugly, abominable, and corrupt[10] religion, the religion of the Arabs. For this reason, every heart trembles and every ear tingles about these men and women, young and old alike.

Furthermore, there was the case of a very old man, some seventy years of age, who was seized by the enemy who claimed he was an orphan. It is their custom to call anyone whose father has died and who has not reached majority, an orphan. They ordered him to renounce his faith, which he refused. How many beatings and tortures were inflicted upon him! Afterward, they chained him, threw him on the ground, and brought him cooked carrion, insisting that he eat it. He still refused. They then brought an iron pincer and forced his mouth open, breaking his jaws and knocking out his teeth. They took him in chains and put him in the marketplace for every passerby who saw him to spit in his face and stone him. He was naked, barefoot, and completely played out from hunger and thirst.

Our eyes are therefore turned to the Lord our God in the hope that He will say "Enough!" to our sufferings and our exile.[11] We also ask God that He grant redemption to you and to us in our lifetimes. May Judah and Israel be granted salvation and dwell in security. Amen.

These are words of the petitioners from the holy congregation of Yemen.
(Week of the Pericope "And the Lord delivered Israel")[12]

Ms Sassoon 215 (photograph in Ben-Zvi Institute File 145).[13]

[10] See n. 4 above.

[11] On the intensity of messianic expectations in Yemen, see Nini, *Yemen and Zion,* pp. 142–59, 179–82 [Heb.], and the sources cited there. Messianic movements and false redeemers have appeared in Yemen from time to time as far back as the twelfth century. See, for example, Maimonides' Epistle to the Jews of Yemen, in Stillman, *Jews of Arab Lands,* pp. 233–46, especially pp. 240–41.

[12] Portion of *Be-Shallaḥ* (Exod. 13:17–17:16).

[13] In the text published by Tobi (see n. 4 above), the Ben-Zvi file number is incorrectly printed 3145.

The Bazaar of the Livornese Jews (Sūq al-Grāna) in the Ḥāra of Tunis, early twentieth century. (*From Carthage to Jerusalem: The Jewish Community in Tunis* [No. 85]. ©Beth Hatefusoth–Photo Archive, The Nahum Goldmann Museum of the Diaspora: Tel Aviv, 1986; with permission.)

A busy thoroughfare in the Jewish Quarter of Oran, Algeria, in 1907. (Gérard Silvain, *Images et Traditions Juives.* Editions Astrid: Milan, 1980.)

Iraqi Jewish merchants in their distinctive attire, late nineteenth or early twentieth century. (Yūsuf Rizq Allāh Ghanīma, *Nuzhat al-Mushtāq fī Ta'rīkh Yahūd al-ᶜIrāq*. Baghdad, 1924.)

A Jewish family in Mosul, Iraq, early twentieth century. (Ezra Laniado, *The Jews of Mosul: From Samarian Exile [Galuth] to "Operation Ezra and Nehemia."* Tirat Carmel, 1981.)

A commercial street with Jewish shops in Cairo's Muski District, alongside the Ḥārat al-Yahūd (Jewish Quarter), early twentieth century. (*Juifs d'Egypte: Images et Textes.* Editions du Scribe: Paris, 1984, p. 47.)

Jewish dancing girls in Beirut, early twentieth century. (Gérard Silvain, *Images et Traditions Juives.* Editions Astrid: Milan, 1980.)

LEFT: Anti-Semitic cartoon on the front page of the Algerian journal *Le Charivari Oranais & Algérien* (May 31, 1896), showing an Algerian in traditional dress and a European member of the Oran City Council. Each holds one end of the Crémieux Decree, and the Jew is saying (in broken French), "Vatch out, mine friend, eets going to brek." (Geneviève Dermenjian, *Juifs et Européens d'Algérie: l'Antisémitisme Oranais, 1892–1905.* (Ben-Zvi Institute: Jerusalem, 1983, Pl. VII.)

RIGHT: Anti-Semitic cartoon on the front page of *Le Charivari Oranais & Algérien* (July 12, 1896), showing the leader of the Anti-Jewish League of Oran firing a cannon salvo at M. Kanoui, the president of the Jewish Consistory, who has taken refuge at the synagogue and who is saying (in broken French), "Isn't you ashaymt, mine friend, to brek an monument that cost so much!" (Geneviève Dermenjian, *Juifs et Européens d'Algérie: l'Antisémitisme Oranais, 1892–1905.* Ben-Zvi Institute: Jerusalem, 1983, Pl. VIII.)

Mori Yiḥye Qafiḥ, head of the Dar Da[c] (Heb., Dōr Dēʿa, "Generation of Knowledge") movement in Yemen and founder of the first modern Jewish school in Sanaʿ, portrayed here with scientific instruments, early twentieth century. (Schwadron Collection, Jewish National University Library, Jerusalem.)

Rabbi Raphael Aaron Ben Simeon, the modernist *Ḥākhām Bāshī* of Cairo (1891–1920) and a leading Sephardi legal authority. (Jacob M. Landau, *Jews in Nineteenth-Century Egypt.* New York University Press: New York and London, 1969, Fig. 17.)

Interior of the Eliyahu Hannabi Synagogue, looking toward the ark. The building was inaugurated in 1850 and enlarged considerably in 1865. (*Juifs d'Egypte: Images et Textes.* Editions du Scribe: Paris, 1984.)

Gallicized Jewish children in front of the synagogue in Orléansville, Algeria, late nineteenth or early twentieth century. (Gérard Silvain, *Images et Traditions Juives.* Editions Astrid: Milan, 1980.)

Alumnae of the Alliance Girls' School in Tetouan, Morocco, ca. 1925. (*Jewish Communities in Spanish Morocco.* ©Beth Hatefusoth–Photo Archive, The Nahum Goldmann Museum of the Diaspora, Tel Aviv, 1986; with permission.)

Jewish junk dealers, Morocco, early Protectorate period. (Gérard Silvain, *Images et Traditions Juives.* Editions Astrid: Milan, 1980.)

Jewish seller of rolls, Morocco, early Protectorate period. (Gérard Silvain, *Images et Traditions Juives.* Editions Astrid: Milan, 1980.)

AN ARAB JOURNALIST'S IMPRESSIONS OF THE JEWISH QUARTER OF SANᶜA (1930)

What struck me when we first sighted the ghetto was the dead level of the low houses. So different from Sanᶜa and Bir'ul-ᶜAzab;[1] not a house more than two stories, and nothing projecting above the roofs, not even the pinnacle or the dome of a synagogue. When I expressed my surprise, Hezam[2] said: "And should the houses of the Yahoud be like those of the Muslemin!?"

Abjectly indeed the little village crouches in the shadow of Mt. ᶜUsor. But instinct with the feeling of preservation and self-protection, it is compact and consolidated, its roofs leading to each other. Nor does it look slummy. The little terraces are whitewashed and hedged with flower pots; in the principal street, a broad thoroughfare leading to the outer gate, the children play; and neither the dense crowd nor the unctuous raggedness of the slums is evident except in its business section. There the streets are narrow and the shops—stalls—as small, but not as interesting, as those of Sanᶜa. There is nothing, in fact, in the ghetto, except perhaps some ancient Hebrew Mss., which one cannot get in the city. The best jewelers, the big merchants, and those who have ambition that rises above the two-story equality have their business in Sanᶜa, but their homes are here among their fellow Jews.

Through a narrow path we made our way to a row of stalls raised about four feet from the ground, where men with long frowsy sidelocks and beards are seated in a kneeling posture, like their Muslim lords, and waiting, patient and composed, for the bounty of the day, which is in the hand of Allah beyond the square and in the hand of Jehova here. But Hezam, with the butt of his rifle, was the busiest man, and when our way was blocked by a few donkeys he lost the patience which hitherto had kept his tongue in check. "Thou art the father of this nuisance, O Yahouda, Allah strike thee, O Yahouda, in thy soul." Whereupon he lifted his hand vicariously and struck him in the face. It was outrageous, it was sickening. I protested to Saiyed Muhammad[3] and refused to go any further. Then Saiyed took the soldier by the sleeve, not too violently, I observed, and chided him in half-uttered words. But we did return to the square, and thence, across the principal street and through a narrow lane to the heart of the ghetto.

Here I experienced a very pleasant sensation. My idea of the ghetto, as it exists on the East Side of Manhattan, or even in the Bronx, was totally but happily upset. I looked for clotheslines, for rags, for overflowing garbage cans, for accumulated filth, for babble and confusion, for ragamuffin chil-

[1] Bi'r al-ᶜAzab is the suburb that lies between the main town and the Qāᶜ al-Yahūd, or Jewish Quarter.

[2] A soldier in the service of the Imam, assigned to guard the writer.

[3] A government official accompanying the writer.

dren, for slatterns with infants at their breasts, for dingy and smelling doorways; but I found instead a labyrinth of incredibly clean lanes, narrowing in places into footpaths, with little doors on either side, far apart, a few people shuffling sluggishly and quietly hither and thither, a woman's face in a window, a flower pot, a sweet-basil plant. No cries, no noise, no confusion, no smells. When we heard a voice—a woman calling her child or speaking with her neighbor—it was subdued and mellow. A cozy little village indeed, whose people, lived so snugly and peacefully, thought I, must be highly civilized.

The men shave their heads, cultivate sidebraids, wear black skull caps, a blue tunic down to the knee, and sometimes a robe over it and a sash. The women are not veiled, but they throw a big kerchief of print or of silk over their heads, and they sometimes hold it, in a coquettish manner, across the face. Their pajamas, tight around the ankle, are like those of a Muslim woman, but the robe above them does not trail, only reaches to a little below the knee in fact, and is invariably blue.

Physically and physiognomically, however, there is little or no difference between the Jew and the Muslim. They are both natives of Al-Yaman, both Arabs, Semites. The Jew has even been in Arabia as long perhaps as the Arab, and longer certainly than the Muslim. But he has been conquered by his brother Semite, made a tributary, and held in subjection. His status in Al-Yaman today is similar in every respect to that of his ancestors of Khaibar in the days of the Prophet. There are things which he does not do by choice, and things which he must not do. His blue smock, for instance, is obligatory, and the two-story limitation of his house is a condition of tenure. He is permitted to distill wine and trade in it, but not to sell it to the Muslim; he is permitted to do business in San^{c}a, but not to live in it; he is exempt from service in the army, but he must pay tribute.[4]

The Jews of Al-Yaman call themselves Timonim,[5] which is a branch, I was told, of the Sephardim;[6] and there are not more than 20,000 in the Imamdom,[7] most of whom are in San^{c}a, Yarim, Ibb, and Zamar. The ghetto of San^{c}a is the largest, having 6,000 souls, 2,000 of which pay the tribute.[8] But the 6,000 souls have sixteen synagogues, to keep them in the ancient faith, which is the cause of both their subjugation and independence, and a few schools, where the children are taught to speak Hebrew and continue to live in the shadow of the synagogue. There are no big fortunes among them—the richest merchant is not worth more than $100,000; they have heard of the Zionist Movement and the National Home; they receive newspapers from Palestine and they believe that the King of the Jews now sits on

[4] See pp. 225–226.

[5] Heb. for "Yemenites" (in the Yemenite pronunciation).

[6] Actually, the Yemenites constitute a rite unto themselves, which is distinct from that of the Sephardim or the Ashkenazim.

[7] This figure is much too low. The actual number was certainly double.

[8] That is, only the adult males.

his throne in Jerusalem; but they have no desire to leave Al-Yaman. "Are you contented here?" I asked one of the Rabbis. "We live in security," he replied.

In security! One of the latter Himyar kings, Zu'n-Nawwas, in whose days the Muslim Arabs of Al-Hijaz invaded Al-Yaman, first embraced Al-Islam and soon changed his mind and embraced Judaism. . . . The Muslims he had infuriated by first embracing and then renouncing their faith. The Jews may proudly say that a Jewish king once ruled Al-Yaman, but they are still paying for it.[9]

The common people, like the *dowshan*[10] and Hezam, may be rabid in their hatred, but the cultured are subtle and more malevolent. Saiyed Muhammad is even ironic. "The Jews must wear sidelocks, ya Ameen,[11] that we may not kill them by mistake in times of war. They must ride donkeys only, because they cannot ride horses; safety, ya Ameen, before gentility. They must not build their houses more than two stories high—if one of them fell from his roof, he will not break his head. They must pay tribute so as not to forget their origin, and to appreciate always the tolerance and benevolence of the Prophet, the peace of Allah upon him. . . . We give them a lease on the land for ninety-nine years, but do not encumber them with absolute ownership. We permit them to make wine, but not to sell it to us. We deprive ourselves that they may have more to drink. But we permit them to offer their daughters to us as servants, whom we take into the harim and treat like our own slaves. We also bestow upon those of them who deserve it the boon of Al-Islam."

Their daughters! The Arabs who, like the *dowshan* and Hezam, would not soil their feet in Qa'ul-Yahud, are not honest about it. For those who cannot order pleasure to their homes must walk barefoot to it; and in the ghetto are the three joys of which the poet sings—wine, a fair face, and flowers. There was also *hasheesh* in the days of the Turks, and there is still a lute and a voice to charm. The Zaidi[12] may hate and fulminate, but he cannot resist.[13]

Ameen Rihani, Arabian Peak and Desert:
Travels in Al-Yaman
(Boston and New York, 1930), pp. 183–87.

[9] Actually Dhu 'l-Nuwās ruled the Yemenite kingdom of Ḥimyar a century before the rise of Islam. See Norman A. Stillman, *The Jews of Arab Lands: A History and Source Book* (Philadelphia, 1979), p. 4, and the sources cited there.

[10] Ar. for "troubadour." Here, it refers to another native accompanying the writer.

[11] Ar. for "O, Ameen" (addressing the writer).

[12] That is, a member of the ruling Zaydī Shiᶜite sect.

[13] The reference here is to Jewish prostitution, which had existed in Sanᶜa since the Turkish occupation. See pp. 37, 225.

ARTICLES DEALING WITH MOROCCAN JEWS IN THE STATUTE OF THE INTERNATIONAL ZONE OF TANGIER (1923)

Article 26

Subject to the maintenance of public order, the free practice of the religion of the natives and of its traditional customs, and the observance of the traditional Mussulman and Jewish festivals and their ceremonial, shall be respected and guaranteed in the Zone.

Article 27

The three contracting Powers[1] undertake to draw up with as little delay as possible rules regulating the administrative and juridical status of the Moroccan Jewish community of Tangier.

Article 28

Moroccan subjects, whether Mussulman or Jews, shall enjoy complete equality with the nationals of the Powers in the matter of duties and taxes of all kinds.

They shall pay exactly the same duties and taxes.

They shall have the benefit, under the same conditions as foreign nationals, of any relief, hospital, or educational institutions which may be created or subsidized by the Zone.

Article 29

His Shereefian Majesty will nominate a Mendoub[2] to represent him at Tangier. The Mendoub will promulgate the legislation passed by the international Assembly and countersigned by the President of the Committee of Control. He will directly administer the native population.[3] He will fulfill the functions of Pasha and exercise those administrative and judicial powers which fall normally under this head within the Empire. He will have the right of expulsion as regards Moroccan subjects, and will exercise the same right in the case of persons justifiable by the Mixed Court on a decision to that effect by a full meeting of the titulary members of the Court.

. . . .

It will be his duty to ensure the observance and execution by the persons whom he administers of the general clauses of the statute of the Zone, and especially to ensure by the administrative and judicial means at his disposal the exact payment of the duties and taxes due from the native population.

[1] Great Britain, Spain, and France. This was revised by the Protocol of July 17, 1928, to include Italy. See Stuart, *The International City of Tangier,* 2nd ed. (Stanford, 1955), pp. 100–2, 235–41 (text of the Protocol).

[2] Ar., *mandūb* (representative).

[3] That is, Moroccan subjects, both Muslims and Jews.

The Mendoub shall preside over the international legislative Assembly and may take part in its deliverations but will not vote.

Article 34

In consideration of the number of nationals, the volume of commerce, the property interest, and the importance of local trade at Tangier of the several Powers signatories of the Act of Algeciras,[4] the international legislative Assembly shall be composed of:

4 French members
4 Spanish members
3 British members
2 Italian members
1 American member
1 Belgian member
1 Dutch member
1 Portuguese member

nominated by their respective consulates, and in addition:

6 Mussulman subjects of the Sultan nominated by the Mendoub, and,

3 Jewish subjects of the Sultan nominated by the Mendoub and chosen from a list of nine names submitted by the Jewish community.

The Assembly shall appoint from among its members three vice presidents, a French citizen, a British subject, and a Spanish subject,[5] responsible for assisting the Mendoub in presiding over the Assembly and of acting as deputy for him in his absence.

Convention Regarding the Organization of the Statute of Tangier Zone, signed at Paris, December 18, 1923, in Graham H. Stuart, *The International City of Tangier*, 2nd ed. (Stanford, 1955), pp. 208–10.

[4] Agreement adopted by the thirteen Western countries meeting in Algeciras, Spain, on April 7, 1906. The agreement aimed at preserving Moroccan territorial integrity and reforming its finances, while giving special recognition to French and Spanish interests in the country. It helped to prepare the way for the takeover of Morocco by these two powers in 1912.

[5] The vice presidency was expanded in 1928 to include an Italian as well. See n. 1 above.

A GALLICIZED MOROCCAN JEW CALLS UPON HIS CORELIGIONISTS TO IDENTIFY TOTALLY WITH FRANCE
(1926)

In the future evolution which North Africa must pursue under the aegis of the new Rome, France, the Jews have been called upon to play a very great role. To be sure, they are only a minority, but an intelligent and active minority, whose past services are guarantees of future ones. Was it not Judaism which spread among the Berber tribes, bringing them the first glimmers of civilization?[1] Was it not the Jews who, coming from Andalusia already from the seventh century, were the founders of that merchant aristocracy of Fez, which, converted to Islam, was during the period of the Almoravids as well as that of the Sa^{c}dians the essential element of Morocco's economic prosperity? And ever since the French conquest, was it not the Algerian, Tunisian, and Moroccan Jews who have primarily offered a prime living example for their Muslim fellow citizens of the diffusion of Western civilization?

The Algerian Jews are today Frenchmen. The Jews of Morocco and Tunisia must strive more and more each day to become so, following their example, not just in their hearts—for they are already French there—but in their spirits and culture. It is in the service of the French idea that they ought to put that energy, that suppleness, that faculty of adaptation which are the chief qualities of their race.

. . . .

There has been reason to worry at the sight of Russia, directed by Jews, putting itself at the head of a Pan-Asiatic crusade.[2] The North African Jews must testify by their intellectual and political action, by their words and their deeds, that in the course of the duel which one day must bring the culture of Europe and that of Asia to grips, that they will be resolutely on the side of Europe, whose greatest synthetic expression is the French genius.

Léon Abensour, "Messages," *L'Avenir Illustré,*
no. 2 (August 10, 1926), p. 20.

[1] This and the other historical observations that follow are highly fanciful.

[2] The writer has actually assimilated the anti-Semitic ideas of the French political right, which saw Jews as the major force behind Bolshevism.

A MOROCCAN JEWISH TEACHER ON THE NEED FOR ARABIC IN THE ALLIANCE SCHOOLS IN MOROCCO
(1939)

Marrakesh, 28 December 1939

Salomon Elbaz
Instructor at Marrakesh
To the President of the
Alliance Israélite Universelle, Paris

Secretary's Report

The instructors of the Marrakesh school recently had the pleasure of having Monsieur Tadjouri,[1] who was going to be—if the war had not broken out—the Alliance Delegate to Morocco. Among the numerous questions which he discussed informally with us, one has continued to hold my attention: namely, the absence of any Arabic instruction in the Alliance schools of Morocco.

One has to be a Moroccan in order to feel the seriousness of this lacuna. One has to have seen the relations existing between the two populations, Jewish and Muslim, in order to foresee the happy results of a rapprochement between them. And is not language one of the wonderful factors that creates a bond between men?

I was a little Moroccan Jew, and I can testify that there exists between Arabs and Jews a hostility nourished and developed from birth, a hostility that may be seen from all points of view, from that of domicile and from that of life-styles. This barrier which separates Jews and Muslims has not allowed the complete diffusion of the language of the country among the Jews. The latter have always spoken, and they continue for the most part to speak Arabic—if one is not mistaken.

It is enough to have lived in Morocco for some time in order to be able to distinguish quite easily Arabic speech and the speech known as "Judeo-Arabic." The latter borrows most of its words, expressions, and simple forms from Arabic. But what a difference in accent and construction! The Arabs know this Judeo-Arabic accent, which "smacks Jewish" only too well, and they often parody it. On the other hand, and above all, Judeo-Arabic is eminently *incorrect*. The grammar is literally murdered even in its most

[1] Reuben Tadjouri was, from 1940 until his death in 1960, the Alliance delegate (chief representative) in Morocco. For two decades before that, he was a teacher, a school director, and an Alliance activist in Morocco. Concerning him, see Michael M. Laskier, *The Alliance Israélite Universelle and the Jewish Communities of Morocco: 1862–1962* (Albany, N.Y., 1983), index, s.v.

elementary principles. What rules, what neglected, distorted forms! And what a vocabulary! It is made of a mélange of Arabic, Hebrew, Spanish, French, and even some English.

The only bond that exists between Jews and Arabs is in commerce, determined purely by self-interest.

The absence of any real bond between the two peoples (rendered still more sensitive by the "modernization" of the Jews) makes these inhabitants of the same country not know one another. Both groups are unaware of the kinship between their religions and do not see that, on the whole, their customs resemble each other and are disguised only to each other's eye.

The Alliance has done enormous good for the little Jews, but one cannot fail to notice that their schools, which are exclusively "Jewish," stand as the symbol of Judaism in the face of Islam, which widens the gap that already exists. Why not rather fill in the gap and establish a bridge between the two populations? Create a path between them, bring them together so that they will know one another, and for this, they will have to speak to one another. However, the Moroccan does not look with a kind eye upon the Jew who martyrs his language. He is annoyed by it, and he will not listen to the Jew.

Let us, therefore, teach the Jew to speak Arabic correctly. Because he receives his instruction in Alliance schools, let us organize systematic, progressive courses in Arabic, giving the same amount of time employed in teaching Hebrew, and parallel to the history and geography of France, let us teach the history and geography of Morocco.

Every day upon returning from school, I am grieved to see little Jews and Arabs looking for a fight with each other, waiting on street corners with rocks in their hands. Surely if the little Arab saw the little Jew studying his Arabic lesson seriously, he would feel sympathetic toward that child speaking the same language as he. And thus, language would bring about this miracle by replacing the notion of religion with that of citizen. . . .

The material and moral advantages that would result from this fusion between Arabs and Jews would be considerable. It would be, in any event, an act of integrity, of "decency" (to use the very word employed by Monsieur Tadjouri), toward our Muslim compatriots to speak the language of the country where we have been living for centuries.

I took it upon myself to draw your attention to this question in the hope that the Central Committee might wish to take it up one of these days after the war.

Please accept, Monsieur President, my respects.

Elbaz

AIU Archives (Paris)
Maroc XXV.E.396.

4

ZIONISM AND THE JEWS OF ARAB LANDS

A LETTER TO THEODOR HERZL FROM EGYPT'S FIRST ZIONIST SOCIETY
(1897)

"Bar Kokhba" Jewish Society
Cairo, Egypt
Founded the 1st of Adar I 5657
February 1897

Central Headquarters
Mr. Theodor Herzl
Editor of the "Neue Freie Presse"
Vienna

Sir, dear coreligionist in your Jewish State,

Over a year ago, the "Carmel"[1] was not only the first to salute your solemn entry into the Zionist ranks, but also to encourage your project which is as ingenius as it is patriotic. You know, Sir, that it was in Bulgaria[2] that you achieved your first success. Today, still, most of your partisans are the Zionists of Bulgaria.

Well, Sir, you will be happy to learn of the founding in Cairo through patience, perseverance, and action, of a patriotic Zionist society "Bar Kokhba," whose program is the same as that outlined by the "Carmel."

[1] Carmel was the name of both the Zionist society and the newspaper founded by Marco Barukh in Bulgaria. See Jacob Weinschal, *Markō Barūkh: Nevī Milḥemet ha-Shiḥrūr* (Jerusalem, 1980), p. 20. Barukh, as noted in Part One, p. 68, was the founder of the Bar Kokhba Society in Cairo.

[2] Herzl was hailed by Jewish crowds in Sofia in 1896, while on his way to Constantinople. See G. Hirschler, "Bulgaria, Zionism in," *EZI* 1: 169.

Would you please, Sir, we pray you, bring us up to date about everything that is taking place in the Zionist world at Vienna and at the same time send your pamphlet "The Jewish State" in French translation if it is possible.

Long live "The Jewish State!"

Please accept, Sir, the assurance of our most distinguished sentiments, together with our warm greetings of Zion.

Joseph Leibovitch — J. Harmalin
Secretary — President

Cairo (Egypt). April 8, '97

CZA (Jerusalem) Z/H.VIII.43.

MASS DEMONSTRATIONS BY EGYPTIAN JEWS IN CELEBRATION OF THE BALFOUR DECLARATION (1917)

Report No. 5.
November 26th, 1917

Recent Developments in the Palestine Situation

JEWISH ACTIVITIES

Following the publication of the Balfour Declaration a large mass meeting was held at Alexandria, where wild enthusiasm was shown among all classes and categories of Jews; orthodox and unorthodox Jews, non-Zionists as well as Zionists. Herewith, is given a copy of a report of the meeting written by Miss Landau, a prominent orthodox Jewess, but not a Zionist.

MISS LANDAU'S REPORT

Alexandria has witnessed two great demonstrations in the cause of Zionism within the last three months.

The first took place on Shekel Day[1] at the Alhambra Theatre, which was packed from floor to ceiling for the occasion. Ziwer Pasha, the Governor of Alexandria, and most of the leading members of the Jewish Community were present and a goodly sprinkling of British Jewish Tommies was amongst the audience. An outstanding feature of the afternoon was a one-act playlet in French (this being the language understood by most people in Jewish Egypt) which vividly showed the agony of the Jews' life in the Russia of the recent past and ending with the vista of a life true to Jewish ideals in Erez Israel. The proceedings terminated with an impassioned and eloquent oration by Mr. Jack Mosseri, the President of the Zionist Organization of Egypt; his theme being "Le Zionisme, une prétendue chimère devenue une réalité vivante."[2] Mr. Mosseri, at the close of his speech, referred to the meaning of "Jom Hashekel"[3] and called upon Egyptian Jewry to awaken from its lethargy in Jewish matters, and appealed to the Jews of Egypt, if they had nothing to offer in place of Zionism, to rally to that cause.

The Second Great demonstration took place on Sunday, November 11th, when a Mass Meeting, held at the Jardin Rosette was called under the auspices of the Central Committee of the Zionist Organization of Egypt, and organized by the Zeire Zion Society of Alexandria (president, Mr. Leon Nachmias).[4] The meeting was attended by between 7,000 and 8,000 people.

[1] The shekel was the fee and card of membership in the World Zionist Organization.

[2] "Zionism, an alleged chimera become a living reality."

[3] Heb., *Yōm ha-Shekel* (Shekel Day).

[4] Concerning this organization, see p. 310, n. 3. Leon Nachmias (Nacmias) was an Alexandrian Sephardi notable, who, in August 1918, together with Felix de Menasce, Joseph Elie de Picciotto, Victor Naggiar, and Alfred Cohen, founded a

The governor of Alexandria was again present. Twenty different organizations and institutions were represented by delegates. The Chief Rabbi of Alexandria, Professor Della Pergola,[5] with Miss Landau on his right and Mr. Wolf Gluskin on his left, was present. Among the chief organizations represented were the Alliance Israélite (M. Danon), the Menasce High School (M. Antabi), the Bene Berith (M. J. de Picciotto), the Ecoles Hebraïques, Jaffa-Alexandria (Dr. Perlman), and the organizers of the Maccabean and Asmonean Boys, Scouts, and Girls Guides.

Extraordinary enthusiasm permeated the atmosphere of this meeting, caused by the publication, on the preceding day, of what is called here the "Balfour Declaration." When M. Felix Tuby,[6] the Chairman of the Comité d'Assistance for Palestine Refugees (elected chairman of the meeting upon the suggestion of M. J. Mosseri, President of the Zionist Organization of Egypt) who opened the meeting and welcomed those present, stood up with an outspread copy of the day's "Reforms," containing the Declaration, in his hand, thunderous applause greeted him. A resolution was immediately passed to send the following telegrams:[7]

The High Honorable Lloyd George,
Prime Minister,
Downing Street, London.

Mass meeting of 8,000 Jews held today in Alexandria, manifested indescribable enthusiasm during reading Mr. Balfour's Declaration and expressed its deepest gratitude to His Majesty's Government.

Jack Mosseri
President of the
Zionist Organization of Egypt

Report from William Yale, American Diplomatic Agency, Cairo, in National Archives (Washington), Department of State Records 59, 763.72119/———.
Published in Muḥammad ᶜAbd al-Ra'ūf Salīm, *Ta'rīkh al-Ḥaraka al-Ṣahyūniyya al-Ḥadītha, 1898–1918* II, Documentary Referencies [*sic*], pp. 207–9.

Pro-Palestina Committee for humanitarian assistance to the Zionist enterprise. See Gudrun Krämer, *Minderheit, Millet, Nation? Die Juden in Ägypten 1914–1952.* Studien zum Minderheitenproblem im Islam, 7 (Wiesbaden, 1982), p. 359.

[5] Chief rabbi of Alexandria from 1910 until his death in 1923. See Maurice Fargeon, *Les Juifs en Egypte depuis les origines jusqu'à ce jour* (Cairo, 1938), p. 248.

[6] Felix Bey Tuby was a Sephardi banker and president of the Alexandrian Jewish Community Council from 1917 to 1935. See Krämer, *Minderheit, Millet, Nation?,* p. 161.

[7] The text of the second and much longer telegram to Chaim Weizmann has not been included here.

A CALL TO ALEXANDRIAN JEWRY TO CELEBRATE THE SAN REMO RECOGNITION OF THE BALFOUR DECLARATION AND TO CONTRIBUTE TO THE ZIONIST ENTERPRISE

(1920)

The hour of deliverance has sounded!

Like the sentiment which our forefathers felt when they saw the walls of Jericho crumbling before them, all of us felt once again a relief, an infinite joy, when the brazen cable transmitted to us, like a song of victory, the San Remo declaration, which consecrated the legitimacy of our rights and aspirations—Palestine as the National Jewish Home. . . . It is indeed the deliverance, the end of our miseries, of bondage, and of exile!

. . . .

To commemorate this declaration and in order that the Jewish people dispersed over the face of the earth might rejoice together at the same time, the Executive Committee of the World Zionist Organization has decided that the week commencing with the Feast of Shavuᶜot will be the "Week of Ge'ula,"[1] in the hope that all Jewish communities, great and small, will find it in their hearts to celebrate it with the greatest possible display.

We Jews of Alexandria join all our brothers in Egypt and abroad in celebrating our deliverance! We who have unfailingly preserved in our hearts a vivifying faith in the justice of our cause, all of us who have directed ourselves toward the same goal, toward Zion, which shines from afar guiding us as the lighthouse shines over the crests of the waves for the lost navigator, we seize this formal occasion to reunite all of us without distinction and to take part in our celebrations in order to give free rein to our overflowing joy.

. . . But we must remember the actual situation in our recovered homeland. We left it beautiful and prosperous, the star of the East, shining with the most lively brilliance, and we find it bruised, arid, almost bitter!

Brothers! There is but one solution, and it imposes itself upon us in a most pressing fashion. We must rebuild it and restore its former fertility, splendor, and beauty. This task is not beyond our powers. On the contrary, it is within our means.

Rebuilding Eretz Israel is a sacred duty which no one can evade or shirk.

Jews of Alexandria! We will give all—our money, our work, our health. Our people are sounding the supreme call, and we shall respond to it. We who are on the breach at the frontier of Zion, we perhaps feel more keenly than anywhere else the enormity of the task to be undertaken, but the more formidable the task, the greater will be our sacrifice!

[1] Heb., for "deliverance."

A committee made up of representatives of the Community, of the Pro-Palestina Committee,[2] and of the Zéiré Zion Society[3] is in the process of forming in order to collect the funds needed for the restoration of Palestine. It will be appealing to you—men, women, and children—to do your duty. Rich or poor, each of you will give all that you can.

Brothers! The hour of serious resolve has sounded! It means showing the world which watches our actions and letting it know that if we have preserved our national identity in the dispersion despite all the persecutions, we shall know how to restore our homeland in order to live in it!

. . . Above all, let us not forget that everything depends on what we actually do. You must all contribute to the restoration of our Homeland, and the result will be worthy of us and of our people.

Alexandria, May 22, 1920 — Zéiré Zion Society

PROGRAM OF THE CELEBRATIONS

Thursday, May 27 at 3:30 PM:	Children's Celebration in the Courtyard of the Eliahou Hannabi Temple
Saturday, May 29 at 8:30 PM:	Grand Soiree to celebrate the "Yom Ha-Ge'ula" (see posters)
Sunday, May 30 at 3:00 PM:	Sports Day on the field of the Maccabee Organization
at 6:30 PM:	Solemn Service at the Eliahou Hannabi Temple
Saturday, June 5 at 8:30 PM:	Soiree organized by Hadassah (by invitation)

Handbill entitled "La Semaine de la Guéoula:
Appel aux Juifs d'Alexandrie!"
AIU Archives (Paris)
Egypte I.G.5.

[2] Founded in 1918 by Alexandria's leading Sephardic families, this organization was headed by Felix de Menasce, scion of one of the richest Jewish families in all of Egypt. See Gudrun Krämer, *Minderheit, Millet, Nation? Die Juden in Ägypten 1914–1952.* Studien zum Minderheitenproblem im Islam, 7 (Wiesbaden, 1982), pp. 159, 359.

[3] This organization was founded in 1907 by Ashkenazi immigrants. See Zvi Yehuda, "hā-Irgūnīm ha-Ṣiyyōniyyīm be-Miṣrayim (1904–1917)," *Shevet ve-ᶜAm,* 2nd ser., 3 (April 1978): 164; also Krämer, *Minderheit, Millet, Nation?,* p. 361.

THE FIRST FUND-RAISING EFFORTS BY MOROCCAN ZIONISTS
(1901)

Mogador (Morocco) May 1, 1901

Monsieur le Docteur O. Kokesch[1]
9 Turkenstrasse
Vienna IX

Sir,

I have the honor to inform you that for this year this organization[2] has collected approximately 300 pesetas to aid the campaign undertaken by the Zionists. Would you please let me know to whom I should direct this sum which I would like to change first into English or French notes.

Please accept, Sir, the assurance of my highest regard.

On behalf of the Committee,
Samuel S. Bendahan
Secretary

CZA (Jerusalem) Z 1/321.

[1] Ozer Kokesch (1860–1905) was a member of the Zionist Executive. See Getzel Kressel, "Kokesch, Ozer," *EJ* 10: 1156–57.

[2] The Sha^carē Ṣiyyōn Society, concerning which see Part One, pp. 72–73.

A LETTER TO THEODOR HERZL FROM THE ZIONISTS OF SAFI, MOROCCO
(1903)

Ahavat Zion Society
Safi—May He Who is on high make its foundations firm
(Morocco)

March 17, 1903
18 Adar 5663

To His Honor, the Exalted President, Lover of His People, Glory of His Nation, Our Distinguished Lord, Dr. THEODOR HERZL (may God preserve him and grant him life).
Vienna.

Abundant Greetings!

President of God! Although this city is still far from every glorious thing and lofty idea connected with society, and although every good and useful institution that raises the soul and spirit from their torpor is still unknown to it, and although the spiritual state of its inhabitants is extremely poor—nevertheless, thanks to those precious newspapers *ha-Melīṣ* and *ha-Yehūdī,* the Zionist idea throbs intensely within the hearts of some of us, and it has given us no rest until we founded an association which we have named "Ahavat Zion."[1]

Moreover, our hearts exult in the fact that through our effort, the cornerstone of this exalted institution has successfully been laid. We stand ready with warm hearts and soaring spirits to work for it and establish it to the best of our ability. This, then, is our goal from this time forth, as we grope like blind men along a wall, for we still have no correct idea or clear knowledge with regard to everything that pertains to Zionism. We have no book that can shed light upon our ignorance and clarify for us what is Zionism and what is its nature. No one among us knows what is the character of its leaders. We have only heard its name. We know about the holy shekel which one has to pay. But, believe us, that all we can make known is that Zionism is founded upon the shekel and that only by virtue of the shekel which he pays once a year is a person raised up and exalted to be called by the name of "Zionist" and to be numbered in the congregation of the Zionists who are the standard bearers of the nation, exalted in rank, doing great deeds. However, without a doubt, it is a most lofty goal of great value for the life of our nation that is in the care of Zionism. There has still not been specified for the individual who pays the shekel what are the many heroic and sublime deeds to be done, whose results will be of consequence for Zionism, and only upon the basis of which he will be worthy to profess the name of Zion.

[1]Heb. for "love of Zion."

Therefore, we are asking: What exactly is Zionism? What is the task that we must perform in order to achieve the desired end? What are the rules and regulations that we must follow? We wish confirmation of what we know. Since His Excellency is the author and creator of the present idea and is the father of Zionism overall, we are taking the liberty to present this letter of ours before his exalted and majestic glory, requesting that from his high seat, he instruct his distinguished secretary to clarify in writing for us everything we have to know about Zionism and to inform us how and in what way we too can assist in accordance with our abilities in the building of this great enterprise. He should also instruct him to send us the esteemed book *The Jewish State* in HEBREW TRANSLATION together with any other books WRITTEN IN HEBREW that shed light on Zionism. We are prepared to pay the price we are charged for them. Then, having correct, specific ideas that have been carefully explained and clarified, we can trust confidently that Zionism will develop and spread throughout our entire community here, and without much difficulty, it will strike roots in all the cities of Morocco—with God's help.

We are pleased to announce that at the time of the founding of the present society, we raised a glass to the health of His Excellency and blessed his good name from the bottom of our hearts with the wish that he who established this enterprise might bring it to fruition, and we have named him Honorary President[2] of our society. We, therefore, request that he be so kind as to honor us with his esteemed picture so that it can be placed in the council room of the society, to be a shining light in whose presence we can bring out feelings in all matters pertaining to Zionism with the help of God Exalted.

Respectfully yours, and with Zion's blessing

Me'ir Bar Sheshet, Chairman
(May his end be good)

Jacob Murciano, Secretary
(May his end be good)

Correspondence should be addressed to the Chairman.[3]

CZA (Jerusalem) Z 1/343.

[2] In the original, this title is written in French and Hebrew.

[3] This is followed in the original by an address in Latin script: Mayer Barché-chath, Saffi (Maroc).

A REPORT TO THE COLONIAL AUTHORITIES ON EMIGRATION TO PALESTINE AND ON ZIONISM IN MOROCCO BY A FRENCH-APPOINTED JEWISH OFFICIAL

Casablanca, September 6, 1919

Inspection of Jewish Institutions

The Inspector of Jewish Institutions
to the Commissioner Resident General of
the French Republic in Morocco,
DIPLOMATIC CABINET

Rabat.

Upon my return from Mazagan and Marrakesh where I spent several days organizing the Rabbinical Court and the Communal Committees,[1] I turned my attention to your letter No. 156 D of August 26, regarding Jewish emigration.

I have the honor of hereby responding with the information which you kindly requested of me:

1. The Jewish emigration toward Palestine began in April 1919. The tables which you will find included will indicate to you the monthly number of emigrants from April 1st to August 31, 1919.

2. The regions most particularly affected are Casablanca and Marrakesh.[2] The departures took place from Casablanca for Marseille.

3. The causes of this emigration: There exists among the Jews of North Africa, and especially among those of Morocco, a belief (more superstitious than religious, but which is anchored like an article of faith for certain fanatics) that in Jerusalem, in the sacred Jewish soil, bodies will not undergo putrefaction after death, but remain intact until the future life when the Messiah has arrived.

Furthermore, from time immemorial in this country, old men and pious people have had but one wish, which is to go and end their days in Jerusalem.

[1] The committees of the Jewish communities of Morocco were given official status by a *dahir* (decree) prepared for the sultan by the French authorities and signed on May 22, 1918. See André Chouraqui, *La Condition juridique de l'Israélite marocain* (Paris, 1950), pp. 180–89; Paul Marty, "Les institutions israélites au Maroc," *REI* 4 (1930): 301–3.

[2] Another such movement emanating from Fez occurred in 1923. See pp. 316–317.

It is in this belief that one must—in my opinion—seek out the primary cause of the emigration movement which I have noted.

The news of the Peace and of the occupation of Palestine by one of the European Great Powers, which assures the Jews of that country complete security and great religious freedom, has set this emigration in motion. One would not be able to find among these emigrants people having a modicum of modern culture. They are for the most part very pious, superstitious families possessing some resources who have marked this movement.

Others, without any assured means of existence, have followed this movement, counting on their arrival upon public charity and inexhaustible resources, the easy life, etc., which some propagators of the idea have dazzled before their eyes.

Zionism is not completely foreign to this movement. If it is not one of the determining causes, it has exercised, I think, a certain influence and has made up the minds of some of the hesitant to be the first to profit from the new Jewish state.

Zionism, which I consider to be a great danger for Moroccan Jews—and in this I am in agreement with the Alliance Israélite Universelle and some eminent members of French Jewry—has tried to influence some minds.

In Casablanca, apart from a few insignificant adherents who have tried to form a group and to engage in some propaganda, it was easy for me to block, very discreetly, all Zionist activity.[3]

In the event that the Resident General's Office shares my point of view, it would be in our highest interest to keep watch and to discreetly prevent any Zionist propagandizing in Morocco.

Y. Zagury

AIU Archives (Paris)
Maroc I.G.1.

[3] Zagury came to be viewed by the Moroccan Zionists as one of the primary obstacles to their work. See the document translated on pp. 318–319.

AN ALLIANCE REPORT ON A WAVE OF ᶜALIYA FROM FEZ TO PALESTINE WITH SUGGESTIONS ON HOW TO STEM THE TIDE
(1923)

The daily papers have related the departure for Palestine over these past weeks of numerous Jewish families from Fez. They add that the exodus has been continuing uninterrupted and that, according to reliable sources, the mellah (Jewish Quarter) of Fez will have lost half its inhabitants within a year's time.

The figures have been singularly exaggerated. The truth is that out of a population of approximately 9,000 Jews, 340, of whom 95 are men, 125 women, and 120 children, have left Fez with Jerusalem as their destination. It is likely, on the other hand, that the movement would have grown stronger without regulation as much for the departure from Morocco as for entry into Palestine. Before issuing a passport, the French authorities require a guarantee of 1,000 francs from each emigrant so that if after arriving at his destination he should wish to return to Morocco, he would be able to pay the costs of his repatriation.

Since those departing come mainly from among the petty artisans and shopkeepers, these prohibitive measures are an obstacle to mass emigration. Furthermore, the selection carried out among the immigrants by the British High Commissioner's Office in Palestine constitutes an impediment to emigration.

What motives can be attributed to this exodus which has taken place? Without a doubt, the propagation of Zionist ideas is not foreign to it, and the desire, notably among the old people of the mellah, to go end their days in the Holy Land has prompted a number of them to leave. As for the young people, they thought that the difficulties of living will be less in a country whose unlimited prospects for the future have been incessantly vaunted to them. The underlying reasons for these departures appear to be above all economic, however.

. . . .

Legal inferiority and disabilities in the economic domain, these already explain the discouragement of certain elements of the Jewish population of Fez. The present crisis, the scarcity of business in the city and the region, the taxes and duties which have been augmented in enormous proportions, these have made life difficult for many poor people. What is more, Palestine has been presented to them as an immense construction site bustling with activity, where life is sweet and pleasant and which is run by a government favorable to Jewish interests.

It did not require more of this to influence the simple minds to seek refuge there and an improvement over their present condition. But, barely settled, they could attest that they had been the victims of a deceptive mirage.

The prospects for living were not what they had been promised. The struggle had begun again for them, harsher than ever before, because they had arrived in a country in the midst of an economic crisis. They were in danger of adding to the number of those without work. Would the government under these conditions tolerate their prolonged stay and not oblige them in the near future to set out and return to their native soil?

The Central Committee of the Alliance Israélite has asked the government of the Republic to look favorably upon the request presented to President Millerand[1] and to raise as far as possible the disabilities which fall upon the Jewish population and which have contributed in large measure to the unfortunate departure for Palestine of Fasi Jews.

The Central Committee has also made known to the Alliance's representatives in Morocco, and in Fez in particular, the sorry lot which, given the present circumstances, is reserved for the immigrants who without proper consideration make their way to Palestine. It has instructed its representatives to stem the exodus movement which can only be disastrous for those unfortunate people who have yielded to incompetent or culpable suggestions.

"L'exode des juifs vers la Palestine," *Paix et Droit* 3, no. 1 (January 1923): 6–7.

[1] The petition was presented to the French president during his visit to Morocco during the summer of 1922 and included requests for: (1) permission for Jews to live and own property in the Muslim quarters of Fez, (2) permission for Jews to open businesses in the Muslim quarters, and (3) legal equality with Muslims in the native courts and before the Sharifan authorities. (Excerpts from this petition were included in the full text of this report but were not translated here.)

FRENCH AND JEWISH OFFICIALS OPPOSE THE FORMATION OF A ZIONIST SOCIETY IN MOROCCO
(1923)

Hadida Frères
Casablanca
Morocco

Casablanca, January 21, 1923

Please address correspondence
P.O. Box 170—Casablanca

World Zionist Organization
Central Office
77, Great Russell Street
London, W.C. 1

Mr. President,[1]

Immediately upon receiving your honored letter of September 21, 1922, we went to see Monsieur Zagury,[2] President of the Consistory[3] and Inspector of Jewish Institutions in Morocco, on the subject of founding a Zionist Society in Casablanca. He replied to us in an unpleasant manner as if angered and in a way one might say as if he himself were the Resident General and Zionism would be harmful to him if it were to exist—saying, "No!!! No!!! No!!! The Residency does not want any of this!!!" This accursed response discouraged us from writing to the Resident General's Office and from corresponding with you.

Since we are the publishers of *Or ha-Maᶜarab*, a newspaper in Judeo-Arabic, the language of the country, and since this journal already pursues a campaign against the Consistorial Committee, we do not want to get ourselves mixed up in Zionist activities, to which only the President of the Consistory is opposed. We would add on the basis of information that we have gathered that, in our opinion, the single, solitary person responsible for the nonexistence of Zionism in our midst is Zagury. For why is it that

[1] The president at the time was Weizmann.

[2] The Hadida brothers were not the only ones to see Yahya Zagury as a primary obstacle to Zionist activity in Morocco. See the letter from Joseph H. Levy (Fez) to Dr. S. Bernstein of the World Zionist Organization (London), March 4, 1921—CZA (Jerusalem) Z 4/2669. See also Michael M. Laskier, *The Alliance Israélite Universelle and the Jewish Communities of Morocco: 1862–1962* (Albany, N.Y., 1983), pp. 208–9. It is quite clear from Zagury's own letter to the resident general, in which he reveals his personal views on Zionism and how to deal with it, that these writers were not mistaken. See pp. 314–315.

[3] The writers are using the word loosely to refer to the organized Jewish community.

in France—in France itself—there is organized Zionism? Why in Tunisia, a country under the protection of France, is there also? Is not our country under a French protectorate? It is because—we would answer—that we have a leader whose ideas are "Alliancist."

We hasten to add that we remain forever faithful to Zionism, and we will work whenever we can with great pleasure and for the love of our cause.

Recently, we spoke with Monsieur Mardochée Dahan, a Jew with heart, asking if he would please take over Zionist affairs in Casablanca, and we promised him our assistance in work and in our newspaper. The gentleman replied that he would gladly accept and that he is only waiting for an authorization from you in order to be able to work.

Please write to this gentleman on our behalf, as we have promised him to tell you.

Looking forward to your reply. Please accept, Mr. President, our most enthusiastic Zionist greetings.

(signed) Hadida

CZA (Jerusalem) Z 4/2149.

A TUNISIAN UNITED JEWISH APPEAL
(1922)

To the Jews of Tunisia!

At San Remo, the great powers of the world have recognized our people's right to establish its national home in its historic fatherland, and England has accepted the mission of overseeing the development of the new state.

Thus, the civilized world has solemnly saluted the Jewish renascence in Palestine. It views favorably the return there of the exiles who, when living at last under normal conditions, will be able to give full scope to their national genius and, consequently, contribute more effectively to the progress of civilization.

Political guarantees have been given to us. It is for the Jews themselves to make the necessary efforts, which are enormous.

For this unique and formidable enterprise—namely, the restoration of Palestine—a fund has been created, the Keren Hayesod, which for five years has brought together the contributions of the Jews of the entire world and has undertaken the great works of a general order that are indispensable to the development of Jewish colonization.

The commanding and sacred responsibility for every Jew to make his contribution to Keren Hayesod is today particularly urgent. As a matter of fact, our brethren in Eastern Europe have been cruelly martyred. Hundreds of thousands would like to flee the lands of suffering, such as the Ukraine, where, for example, their situation has remained unspeakably lamentable for an even longer time.

Where can they go? No refuge is open to them: The United States has in effect since 1921 closed immigration to them by legislation. Canada and Australia barely let them in.

One sole country can offer them a material and a moral refuge. It is our ancient Palestine, toward which Israel has not ceased to aspire since its exile, and which, peopled with several hundred thousand souls, will be able to contain easily several millions.

Jews of Tunisia, whether native sons or citizens of other states, a great duty imposes itself upon you. You do not want to shirk it. Although struck by the general economic crisis, you want to collaborate with your more favored brothers in assuring a home for several million of your unfortunate brethren. You will respond with dignity to the Allies' offer. With Jewish pride you will help in the resurrection of Israel.

The hour is tragic, the hour is great.

Jews of Tunisia, you will understand without distinction of political opinions; you will respond to our appeal. You have in your hearts to contribute to the reconstruction of Eretz Israel, as much out of Jewish solidarity as out of humanitarianism.

Rabbi Moche Sitruk
Chief Rabbi of Tunisia

Eugene Bessis
President of the
Jewish Community
Council of Tunis
Knight of the Legion
of Honor

Alfred Valensi
President of the
Zionist Federation
of Tunisia

Albert Bessis
Chief of the Office of
Jewish Emigration to
Palestine

Dr. Joseph Boulakia
Delegate to the Advisory Conference

Joseph Cohen-Boulakia, Samuel Bellaiche, Victor Bessis
Delegates to the Native Consultative Chamber for Commercial
and Industrial Interests

Leon Ghez
Past President of the Jewish Benevolence Committee
Municipal Counsellor
Knight of the Legion of Honor

M. Salomon Tibi
President
of Keren Hayesod, Sousse

Victor Guez
Municipal Counsellor of Sfax
Government Delegate
to the Benevolence Committee
President of Keren Hayesod, Sfax

La Voix Juive (July 10, 1922), p. 1.

CONFIDENTIAL

TUNIS

Since the departure of Alfred Valensi[1] to Paris a few years ago following on his resignation of the post of Chairman of the Federation as a result of attacks against his paid K.H.[2] work, the Federation had practically ceased to exist. Though this country has a Jewish population of over 100,000, the majority of whom are Zionists and not as Frenchified as the Jews of Algeria, or even Morocco, the lack of initiative which is peculiar to Sephardim, and rivalry between Tunis and Sousse Zionists prevented united work until the arrival of Mr. N. Halpern, the Keren Hayesod delegate, in the summer of 1926, who was compelled to devote a lot of time to putting the Federation again on its feet. His first attempt was not successful, for the organization he set up crumbled away after his departure. Such is the common fate of all voluntary bodies set up by delegates in Sephardi countries. During his present visit, however, he has revived it again, and though retaining the same Chairman, Maître Cattan,[3] a local lawyer, he has installed as Secretary an Ashkenazi secondary school teacher of Alsatian origin, and who took his degree at the Sorbonne.[4] This Committee was to have been confirmed by regular elections during this month. It is too early to say how it will work, though here, just as in Egypt and other parts of North Africa, people do not yet understand how to carry on propaganda on a large scale, nor do they appreciate the need of basing the Federation on a membership basis. To bring these two essentials home to them, it is necessary to have a representative of the Executive to reside in North Africa (excepting Egypt) for at least one year. No other section of Zionists is so much impressed by a living personal contact with the Executive as the Sephardim. As it is, they feel themselves in the position of lost sheep, about whom the shepherd does not care a jot and who are subject to all sorts of crosscurrents. Thus Jabotinsky,

[1] Concerning Valensi, see Part One, p. 77.

[2] Keren Hayesod.

[3] Victor Cattan (1870–1944), a French-educated lawyer with large agricultural land holdings in Tunisia. He served as chairman of the Tunisian Zionist Federation from 1927 until his death in 1944. See Shlomo Barad, *Le Mouvement sioniste en Tunisie* (Tel Aviv, 1980), p. 141 [Heb.]; also al-Hādī al-Taymūmī (Hedi Timoumi), *al-Nashāṭ al-Ṣahyūnī bi-Tūnis bayn 1897 & 1948* (Tunis, 1982), p. 87.

[4] The writer is referring to Robert Brunschvig, who was then a classics professor at the lycée in Tunis and later became a noted Orientalist. Concerning him, see David Corcos, "Robert Brunschvig," *EJ* 4: 1420. Brunschvig was a member of the Executive Board, but not secretary of the Federation in 1927. See Barad, *Le Mouvement sioniste en Tunisie,* p. 25 [Heb.].

who fully knows his popularity among Sephardim, is now endeavoring to gain a foothold for Revisionism in North Africa.[5] A number of leading members of the Tunis Federation are Revisionists, and the result is already seen in the refusal on the part of the Federation to handle Romano's book, on the plea that it is partisan.[6]

Excellent work is being done by the *Reveil Juif* of Sfax, which is edited by a bright and devoted young Zionist, Felix Allouche, whom Halpern praised a great deal. Negotiations are now proceeding for transferring the paper to Tunis, where it would appear as the organ of the Federation. Meanwhile, it has published several Revisionist articles and is now featuring a series of articles by Jabotinsky on present Zionist problems. A few months ago a Hitachduth branch was opened in Tunis.[7] The Tunis UUJJ[8] is entirely Zionist and is doing practically all KKL[9] work.

CZA (Jerusalem) Z 4/3262.

Unsigned, undated (probably 1927) copy of a report.

[5] In the 1927 elections for representatives to the Fifteenth Zionist Congress, the Revisionists won an overwhelming majority in Tunisia. Revisionists represented Tunisia at every subsequent Zionist Congress until 1935, when the Revisionist Organization broke away from the World Zionist Organization. Brunschvig was himself a Revisionist. See Barad, *Le Mouvement sioniste en Tunisie,* p. 26 [Heb.].

[6] The reference apparently is to Marco Romano, *Problèmes politiques de l'organisation sioniste; nos rapports avecs les arabes et l'Angleterre* (Paris, 1927).

[7] That is, Hitaḥdūt ᶜOlāmīt shel ha-Pōᶜēl ha-Ṣāᶜīr ū-Ṣeᶜīrē Ṣiyyōn, a Labor Zionist party formed by the union of the Eastern European Ṣeᶜīrē Ṣiyyōn and the Palestinian ha-Pōᶜēl ha-Ṣāᶜīr, which lasted from 1920 to 1932. The person who read this report has underlined Hitachduth and has written a question mark in the margin. The author of the report may have been referring to the unofficial following of two Belgian trainees of ha-Shōmēr ha-Ṣāᶜīr, Itzhak Guintzic and Haim Nussbaum, who were in Tunis at this time on their way to Palestine. See Barad, *Le Mouvement sioniste en Tunisie,* pp. 28–29 [Heb.].

[8] Union Universelle de la Jeunesse Juive. The Tunisian branch was founded in December 1924. On its activities in Tunis, see Barad, *Le Mouvement sioniste en Tunisie,* pp. 27–33 [Heb.].

[9] Keren Kayemeth Le-Israel (the Jewish National Fund).

THE CIRCOLO SION APPEALS FOR PUBLIC SUPPORT DURING THE COMMUNAL ELECTIONS IN TRIPOLI (1918)

Brothers!

For the second time in a few months you are called to the important task of electing your representatives on the Council of the Community.[1]

The time for contests between personalities is past: today you must choose between two programs.

What are these two programs?

Ours is well known: we want to defend our tradition; spread education, especially Hebrew language and Jewish history; strengthen the Jewish national consciousness. We have faith in our people's glorious past and want to prepare it for its great future soon to come.

The largest Jewish organizations in America, Russia, Britain, and Italy are behind us.

What is the opposing program? It is not even a program: its greatest shortcoming is that it is not even a program. Just because they are rich and enjoy greater social influence, some men think that they have the right to be called to lead our Community. But what do they want to do with it?

What direction do they want to lead it in?

They do not know and do not care about knowing. They do not know, or pretend not to know, that without a strong culture, without respect for tradition, without national consciousness, Jewish life will collapse. This would not be the first case: other great centers of Jewish life, such as Tunisia, have been ruined within a few years by administrators who were incapable of Jewish idealism.

We must not allow that to happen to us.

We must want to increase and pass on to our children the glorious heritage received from our parents. If we do this we know that we are fulfilling our duty as Italian citizens,[2] citizens of that great country which together with its allies has declared itself in favor of the rebuilding of a Jewish national home in Palestine.

Anyone betraying Zion is, today, betraying Italy!

Voters!

Would you be traitors? Do not have regard for rich men or poor, but let yourselves be guided by the idea alone; then you will be able to say that you have done your duty toward your people.

"Agli elettori," *Israel* (December 23, 1918), in Renzo de Felice, *Jews in an Arab Land: Libya, 1835–1970,* trans. Judith Roumani (Austin, 1985), pp. 327–28, n. 51.

[1]Elections had to be held again after the Executive Board of the Community Council resigned after only a few months in office. See Renzo de Felice, *Jews in an Arab Land: Libya, 1835–1970,* trans. Judith Roumani (Austin, 1985), pp. 103–4.

[2]Most Libyan Jews were in fact not Italian citizens, but rather Italian subjects.

ABRAHAM ELMALEH PROPAGANDIZES FOR ZIONISM AND SEPHARDI REVIVAL AMONG THE JEWS OF BEIRUT
(1927)

Beirut, December 26, 1927

Sephardi Federation[1]
Jerusalem

Gentlemen:

I arrived safely in Beirut on Friday shortly before evening. . . . A beautiful welcome had been arranged for me. Representatives of all the institutions, organizations, and the community were waiting for me at the hotel.

. . . .

Several days prior to my arrival invitations were sent to leading figures of the community to come to the lectures which would take place in the synagogue and at the club of the Union Universelle de la Jeunesse Juive and afterward to a gala reception that would be held in my honor on Sunday in the late afternoon. The general Arab press announced my coming, and the paper *al-ᶜĀlam al-Isrāʾīlī*[2] gave more details so that the community was already prepared for the lectures.

On Shabbat morning, I was invited to the service in the Great Synagogue and was honored with opening the ark and being called up third, of course, to the reading of the Torah.[3] This splendid and beautiful synagogue which can hold approximately 1,000 men was filled to capacity with worshipers who had come to hear my lecture. After the prayers, which had lasted until ten o'clock, an enormous crowd began to stream in from the rest of the synagogues to hear the lecture. The women's gallery, which also holds more than a thousand places, was filled with women and young ladies. . . . I began my speech in Arabic after having expressed my great regret at being unable to speak in my people's language since most of the audience did not understand Hebrew.

[1] The Federation had arranged for a series of lecturers to come to Beirut, one each month, to speak on Zionist activities in Palestine and on the part played by Sephardi Jews there. See Abraham Haim, "Teᶜūdōt Lifᶜīlūt Ṣiyyōnīt ve-Ḥevrātīt be-Qehillōt Sūriya u-Lvanōn bēn shettē Milḥāmōt ᶜŌlām," *Hāgūt ᶜIvrīt be-Arṣōt hā-Islām,* ed. M. Zohori et al. (Jerusalem, 1981), p. 292.

[2] Concerning this biweekly Arabic-language Jewish newspaper, see Part One, pp. 83–84.

[3] The first two men called up are, according to custom, a Kohen followed by a Levite.

I took as my subject the verse from the weekly Torah portion—"And Joseph recognized his brothers, but they did not recognize him."[4] Around this verse, I spoke on the revival of the people of Israel and in particular about the revival of Sephardi Jewry. I talked at length about Sephardi Jewry in its days of greatness and glory. . . . I traced the terrible decline of Sephardi Jewry from the days of the Expulsion from Spain down to our own time. I went on to sketch briefly the history of Herzl's political Zionism and Ahad Ha-ᶜAm's spiritual Zionism. I spoke about the settlements and agriculture in Palestine, about the pioneers, etc., etc. I then got to the point of my speech: the revival of Sephardi Jewry and the work of our own Federation. . . . From the expressions on the faces of the people, I could see that my words had sparked great interest among them. They were all actually hanging upon my every word.

Just before evening, I was invited back to the Great Synagogue for evening prayers and the ceremony of lighting the Hanukka menorah.[5] . . . The number of men and women who came was some 2,000. Members of the Maccabee Organization and the orchestra came in their blue and white attire. . . . Greatly impressed to see strong and vigorous young people in blue and white, I spoke warmly and with feeling in Hebrew on the role of youth in the National Revival, on the Hebrew language, and especially on the Hanukka festival and the Maccabees of old. I concluded with a call for all the people to assist in building the Land and for the youth to carry with pride the national banner.

The highlight of my mission, however, was my major speech in French at the Club of the Union Universelle de la Jeunesse Juive. . . . I spoke for about an hour and a half—in French, naturally—on ten years of history in Palestine, beginning with the Balfour Declaration and ending with the current state of affairs.

In the course of my remarks, I talked about settlement activity, the pioneers, the Hebrew language, Hebrew education, the period of Sir Herbert Samuel,[6] and the tremendous work being done by the Keren Hayesod and the Jewish National Fund. And by the way, I asked them to come to the assistance of the Funds and to increase their contributions to them.

On Monday night, a gala affair was held in my honor. . . . At the party, Mr. Joseph Bey Dishi stood up and in a beautiful speech thanked me again on behalf of the community and on behalf of Bene Berith[7] for my lectures, which had helped to stir a tremendous movement among the inhabitants of Beirut. He thanked the Sephardi Federation, which kindly took it upon

[4] Gen. 42:8.

[5] It was the seventh night of Hanukka.

[6] He was the first high commissioner of the British Mandate of Palestine (1920–1925). Under his administration, the Yishuv doubled in size and there was extensive new settlement building. See Vivian David Lipman and Daniel Efron, "Samuel, Herbert Louis," *EJ* 14: 797–800.

[7] Dishi was the local president of the Bene Berith (B'nai B'rith) lodge.

itself to arrange these lectures, whose very positive result is raising the community's cultural level.

Respectfully yours,

A. Elmaleh

Archives of the Sephardi Communal Council (Jerusalem) ASh 7. Hebrew text published by Abraham Haim in *Hāgūt ᶜIvrīt be-Arṣōt ha-Islā*m, ed. M. Zohori et al. (Jerusalem, 1981), pp. 295–97, Doc. 3.

A PUBLIC DECLARATION BY THE DAMASCENE JEWISH YOUTH ASSOCIATION DISAVOWING ZIONISM AND PLEDGING LOYALTY TO THE ARAB CAUSE

(1929)

The Association of Jewish Youth has published on Tuesday in the city as well as in the newspapers the following manifesto:

Certain journals having not distinguished sufficiently between Arab Jews and Zionists, we take this opportunity as Arab citizens from time immemorial to bring the following to the attention of our fellow citizens and Syrians:

The Jews of Syria have no connection with the Zionist question. On the contrary, they share with their Arab fellow citizens all their feelings of joy and sadness. Not long ago *al-Sha^cab* published an article signed by a Jew from Damascus repudiating Zionism and explaining that it was founded by the Jews in Northern Europe and the Jews of Damascus are totally estranged from it.

It is for this reason that we have come to declare by the present note to our Arab fellow citizens and to the members of the press our attitude vis-à-vis the Zionist question, and we ask them to differentiate between the European Zionists and the Jews who have been living for centuries in these lands.

We ask that the population and the press consider the Jews of Damascus to be Arabs sharing completely all of their sentiments in good times and in adversity.

AIU Archives (Paris)
Syrie I.G.2.
Report from A. Silberstein (August 31, 1929).

A SEPHARDI LEADER IN ALEPPO COMPLAINS THAT THE JEWISH AGENCY IS IGNORING WOULD-BE ᶜOLĪM FROM HIS CITY

(1933)

Aleppo, 5 Tishre 5694[1]

The Central Council of the World
Federation of Sephardi Jews, Jerusalem

Gentlemen:

We hereby acknowledge receipt of your letter of the 22nd of last month and direct your attention again to what you have written us, because we hope that the Jewish Agency will allocate part of the immigration certificates to ᶜōlīm from Aleppo. It is astounding that the Jewish Agency has already received 1,000 certificates, and in *Do'ar Ha-Yom*[2] we read that this number was for ᶜōlīm from Eastern Europe, Yemen, and Salonika, but for ᶜōlīm from Aleppo nothing was given. Good Lord! Do those immigrants have a better pedigree than the Aleppan ᶜōlīm? Doesn't everyone know that in our city a great ᶜaliya movement can be felt among all classes? Nearly everyone has the desire to travel to Palestine. In addition to the number of requests that we sent you, there are hundreds requesting ᶜaliya permits. There are many people who are sacrificing themselves for the Land. We have heard of hundreds of people who have been caught at the frontier and were returned. We have heard of not a few people who were imprisoned in Acre. They went back again, made the journey, and were caught, suffered, and returned, weeping bitterly that they were unable to enter Palestine. Would it not be appropriate to give these people permits? Because these brethren of ours know the language of the country and understand the mentality of the Arabs and can live with them, is it not worthwhile to give them a portion in Palestine? Why should these Jews' share be any less than that of the rest? Indeed, those who submitted requests have been waiting for nearly four and five months for certificates.

For our part, we are advising all the perspective ᶜōlīm not to break the law and not to cross the border. This is for their own good. However, they have been waiting and waiting and are losing patience. We are amazed at Mr. Gaon,[3] who is one of the members of the Federation. He should have tried to petition and press for these would-be ᶜōlīm. The Central Council of

[1] September 25, 1933.

[2] Concerning this newspaper, which was published in Jerusalem from 1919 to 1936, see Getzel Kressel, "Do'ar Ha-Yom," *EJ* 6: 142.

[3] The reference is to Moses David Gaon, a leading Sephardi educator and Zionist figure. Concerning him, see Getzel Kressel, "Gaon, Moses David," *EJ* 7: 324–25.

the Federation should please lobby, protest, and urge the Zionist Executive to give us the number of 100 certificates as soon as possible, and also to explain to Mr. Gaon the vigor of Aleppan Jews' ᶜaliya and their desire to go to Palestine. Explain to him also that there are already young people there doing agricultural work and hard labor while at the same time their fathers are respected merchants there. They are sacrificing themselves for the Land. Please convey what we have to say to the ᶜAliya Bureau.

Respectfully yours,

In the name of the Committee of the World Federation of Sephardi Jews in Aleppo,

M. Nahmad[4]

Archives of the Sephardi Communal Council (Jerusalem) QH 10. Hebrew text published by Abraham Haim in *Hāgūt ᶜIvrīt be-Arṣōt hā-Islām*, ed. M. Zohori et al. (Jerusalem, 1981), pp. 300–1, Doc. 7.

[4] The author of this letter, Me'ir Nahmad, had for many years been one of the leaders of the Aleppan Jewish community and was active on behalf of Zionist causes. A little less than a year after writing this letter, he himself settled in Tel Aviv. See M. D. Gaon, *Yehūdē ha-Mizraḥ be-Ereṣ Yisrā'ēl* II (Jerusalem, 1937/38), pp. 462–63.

AN IRAQI JEWISH NOTABLE EXPRESSES HIS RESERVATIONS ON ZIONISM
(1922)

Baghdad, 8th September 1922
The Secretary
Zionist Organization
London

Dear Sir,

I have the pleasure to acknowledge receipt of your letter of the 20th July 1922.

It is needless to say that I greatly appreciate and admire your noble ideal, and would have been glad to be able to contribute toward its realization.

But in this country the Zionist Movement is not an entirely idealistic subject. To the Jews, perhaps to a greater extent than to other elements, it represents a problem the various aspects of which need to be very carefully considered. Very peculiar considerations, with which none of the European Jewish Communities are confronted, force themselves upon us in this connection.

You are doubtless aware that, in all Arab countries, the Zionist Movement is regarded as a serious threat to Arab national life. If no active resistance has hitherto been opposed to it, it is nonetheless the feeling of every Arab that it is a violation of his legitimate rights, which it is his duty to denounce and fight to the best of his ability. Mesopotamia has ever been, and is now still more, an active center of Arab culture and activity, and the public mind here is thoroughly stirred up as regards Palestine by an active propaganda. At present the feeling of hostility toward the Palestinian policy is more strong, as it is in some sort associated in the mind of the Arab with his internal difficulties in the political field, where his position is more or less critical. To him any sympathy with the Zionist Movement is nothing short of a betrayal of the Arab cause.

On the other hand the Jews in this country hold indeed a conspicuous position. They form one third of the population of the Capital, hold the larger part of the commerce of the country, and offer a higher standard of literacy than the Moslems. In Baghdad the situation of the Jew is nearly an outstanding feature of the town, and though he has not yet learned to take full advantage of his position, he is nevertheless being regarded by the waking up Moslem as a very lucky person, from whom the country should expect full return for its lavish favors. He is moreover beginning to give the Moslem an unpleasant experience of a successful competition in Government functions, which, having regard to the large number of unemployed former officials, may well risk to embitter feeling against him.

In this delicate situation the Jew cannot maintain himself unless he gives proof of an unimpeachable loyalty to his country, and avoid with care any action which may be misconstrued. This country is now trying to build up a future of its own, in which the Jew is expected to play a prominent part. The task will be of extreme difficulty and will need a strained effort on the part of every inhabitant. Any failing on the part of the Jew will be most detrimental to his future.

On the other hand, the large majority of the Jews are unable to understand that all they can reasonably do for Zionism is to offer it a discrete financial help. We have had, since Dr. Bension's arrival to this country,[1] a sad experience of the regrettable effects which an influx of Zionist ideas here may have. There was for some time a wild outburst of popular feelings toward Zionism, which expressed itself by noisy manifestations of sympathy, crowded gatherings, and a general and vague impression among the lower class that Zionism was going to end the worries of life and that no restraint was any longer necessary in the way of expressing opinions or showing scorn to the Arabs. This feeling, it is needless to say, was altogether unenlightened. It was more Messianic than Zionistic. To an observer it was merely a reaction of a subdued race, which for a moment thought that by magic the tables were turned and that it were to become an overlord. Very few stopped to think whether the Promised Land was already conquered, and if so how long it would take till all the Jews of Mesopotamia repaired to it, and whether any reasonable policy was in the meanwhile desirable. In this state of raving the Jews could not fail to occasion a friction with the Moslems, especially as the latter were then high up in nationalist effervescence, and a feeling of surprise and dissatisfaction ensued, which caused a prominent member of the Cabinet to remark to me reproachfully that after so many centuries of good understanding the Moslems were not at all suspecting that they had inspired the Jews with so little esteem for them.

During my first interview with Dr. Bension at a time when the internal political situation was particularly critical, I explained to him my anxiety as to the effect of the rather sonorous success of his mission on the political difficulty of the Jews at that juncture and requested him to postpone his mission, if possible, till the political outlook should be more reassuring. I am not aware that he actually took any steps in this direction, but the enthusiasm of the Jewish population has never abated since then.

In view of the above circumstances I cannot help considering the establishment of a recognized Zionist Bureau in Baghdad as deleteriously affecting the good relations of the Mesopotamian Jew with his fellow citizens.

[1] Dr. Ariel Bension was the representative of the Palestine Foundation Fund to the Middle Eastern countries. He came on a mission to Iraq in the spring of 1922. See Hayyim J. Cohen, *ha-Peʿīlūt ha-Ṣiyyōnīt be-ʿIrāq* (Jerusalem, 1969), p. 43; and Zvi Yehuda, ed., *From Babylon to Jerusalem: Studies and Sources on Zionism and Aliya from Iraq* (Tel Aviv, 1980), p. 12, n. 23 [Heb.].

As stated above, some misunderstanding has already occurred which, if allowed to take root, might well lead to a breach, which will have for the Jews grave consequences. The Jews are already acting with culpable indifference about public and political affairs, and if they espouse so publicly and tactlessly as they have done lately, a cause which is regarded by the Arabs not only as foreign but as actually hostile, I have no doubt that they will succeed in making themselves a totally alien element in this country and as such they will have great difficulty in defending a position, which, as explained above, is on other grounds already too enviable.

I hope you will fully understand the point of view which I have tried to set forth. I am the first to regret having to take it, because, I repeat, I have, on principle, great sympathy with your aims and warmly appreciate the devotion of your distinguished leaders of the Jewish cause. But you will realize that in practical policy the Jews of Mesopotamia are fatally bound to take for the time being a divergent course, if they are to have a sound understanding of their vital interests. I am not qualified to speak for them. The opinions expressed above are my own personal opinions. The community is unfortunately too helplessly disorganized to have any coordinate opinion, and that is indeed why it is the more exposed.

For Dr. Bension personally I have nothing but high esteem, but I regret that his mission, having had the practical consequences described above, I am forced to regard its development here with some misgiving. He is regarded both by Moslems and Jews as representing the Zionist Mission, as nobody here is realizing the distinction between that Mission and the Keren Yesod.[2]

I again express to you my deepest regrets at being unable to respond to your call, and at the unfortunate difficulty of our position vis à vis your movement.

I am, Dear Sir,
Yours faithfully,
Menahem S. Daniel

CZA (Jerusalem) Z 4/2101.

[2] Keren Hayesod is the Hebrew name of the Palestine Foundation Fund.

THE IRAQI ZIONIST FEDERATION REPORTS ON ITS ACTIVITIES FOR 1923 TO 1925

The Mesopotamian Zionist Federation

Baghdad, 12 Sivan 5685[1]

BRIEF SUMMARY OF OUR WORK DURING THE YEARS 1923–1925

A. The work of our federation during the years 1923–1925 was slow due to the political situation in our country, for we cannot carry out public propaganda activities, nor publish in any newspaper—even in the paper which we own—anything that has a Zionist appearance. Occasionally, even our friends who are devoted to the Zionist idea hide themselves and will not enter our office lest they be recognized as Zionists. In other words, all our propagandizing has been carried out secretly, and all our gatherings have been cloaked in a scientific guise, etc. Nevertheless, our movement has not ceased to spread, but rather has penetrated all ranks of our fellow Jews so that even many of those who opposed us have turned to be supporters. Of course, if the situation had been helpful to us, the number of our members would have risen to the tens of thousands.

B. For these reasons, our monthly number of members never reached more than 300.

C. In Iyyar 5684,[2] our federation established the Pardes Yeladim School.[3] It currently has 350 pupils. It is divided into two levels: a kindergarten with four classes and a preparatory school of three classes. In the preparatory, they study Hebrew, English, Arabic, Bible, Jewish History, Natural Sciences, etc. Hebrew is the language of instruction.

D. In Nisan 5684,[4] one of our members received a permit to publish a newspaper in Arabic, entitled "The Lamp."[5] It appears regularly despite frequent maligning by those who scent a whiff of Zionism in it.

E. On Friday evening of each week, academic lectures are held by the federation's literary circle, which is called Ṣeʿīrē Benē Yehūda.

[1] June 4, 1925.

[2] May 5–June 2, 1924.

[3] This school was established by Aaron Sasson after he was threatened with dismissal from his teaching position in one of the community's Jewish schools because of his Zionist activities. The school came under government scrutiny in 1929 (see p. 342) and was almost forced to close for lack of a proper permit, which, however, was eventually received. The school remained open until at least 1932, and perhaps as late as 1935, when Sasson was forced to leave the country. See Hayyim J. Cohen, *ha-Peʿīlūt ha-Ṣiyyōnīt be-ʿIrāq* (Jerusalem, 1969), pp. 85–87.

[4] April 5–May 4, 1924.

[5] The Arabic-language weekly *al-Miṣbāḥ* (Hamenorah) was published by Salman Shina from 1924 to 1929. See his letter to the Zionist Executive in London, pp. 337–339.

F. Pamphlets and announcements have been published by the Keren Hayesod Committee in Judeo-Arabic.

G. Through our efforts and directions, a few individual members have purchased hundreds of dunams in various places in Palestine.[6]

H. In 5684, the quarrels and conflicts between our membership and the leaders of our community increased. In the end, the scales tipped markedly in our favor. They were forced to replace the Chief Rabbi and to choose one who is not opposed to us.[7] Furthermore, three of our members were elected to the City Council, and in the Parliament of the local government, which has only two Jewish representatives, it so happens that one of them is a member of ours.

I. Our federation has collected close to 4,400 sterling for the two Funds[8] and for other Palestine projects.

For the Jewish National Fund:

Pounds Sterling	
110	Tishre through Tevet 5683[9]
230	Shevat 5683 through Shevat 5684[10]
80	Adar through Av 5684[11]
70	Elul 5684 through Shevat 5685[12]
85	Adar through Iyyar 5685[13]
575	
3,500	Collected for Keren Hayesod between 5683 and Nisan 5685
4,075	
325	For other projects and for shekels
4,400	

These are in addition to the large donations that were sent directly to the Jewish National Fund, such as the donations by the founder of Kefar Yehez-

[6] The sale of land in Palestine to Iraqi Jews through the Hakhsharat ha-Yishuv Company turned out to be a fiasco. The lands were tied up in legal complications. The titles were never delivered to the purchasers, and the Mesopotamian Zionist Federation suffered a serious loss of prestige. Concerning this episode, which dragged on for several years, see Cohen, *ha-Peʿīlūt ha-Ṣiyyōnīt be-ʿIrāq,* pp. 104–12.

[7] The report is referring to the appointment of R. Ezra Sasson Dangoor (1848–1930) to the office of *ḥākhām bāshī* in 1923 upon the death of R. Moses Ḥayyim Shammash. Dangoor resigned in 1928 as a result of communal strife. Concerning him, see Abraham Ben-Jacob, *A History of the Jews in Iraq: From the End of the Gaonic Period to the Present Time,* 2nd rev. ed. (Jerusalem, 1979), pp. 172–74 [Heb.]; and Abraham David, "Dangoor, Ezra Sasson Ben Reuben," *EJ* 5: 1274.

[8] The Jewish National Fund and the Keren Hayesod.

[9] September 23, 1922, to January 17, 1923.

[10] January 18, 1923, to February 6, 1924.

[11] February 6 to August 30, 1924.

[12] August 31, 1924, to February 24, 1925.

[13] February 15 to May 13, 1925.

kel, and the like, as well as the bequest on behalf of the Keren Hayesod, as for example the late Shemtob, and others.[14]

II.
Report of the Palestine Office[15]

(Tourists)

	Individuals
70	Tourists in 1923
400	Tourists in 1924
80	Tourists to end of April 1925
550	

Over 30 percent of these tourists were able to manage in Palestine.

Those Emigrating to Settle in Palestine with At Least 500 Sterling:

Individuals	Families	
25	8	1923
50	15	1924
75	18	1925 (to April)
150	41	

Travelers on Visas from the Zionist Executive in Palestine:

Individuals	Visas	
50	15	1923
163	35	1924
125	25	1925 (through end of March)
338	75	

Emigrants Who Intended to Settle or Those Traveling on Palestine Visas Who Returned to Mesopotamia:

Percentage	
30	1923
20	1924
25	1925

The above demonstrates that Iraqi Jews are going and adapting themselves to life in Palestine.

CZA (Jerusalem) Z 4/272.
Hebrew text published in Zvi Yehuda, *From Babylon to Jerusalem* (Tel Aviv, 1980), pp. 107–10.

[14] The founder of Kefar Yehezkel was Ezra Sasson Suheik, Iraq's single largest contributer to the Jewish National Fund (see p. 86). Between 1920 and 1923, he donated some 36,500 pounds sterling for the establishment of a moshav in the Harod Valley, which was named after his brother. See Cohen, *ha-Peʿīlūt ha-Ṣiyyōnīt be-ʿIrāq,* p. 101; and Efraim Orni, "Kefar Yehezkel," EJ 10: 896. Shemtov is Ezekiel Gurgi Shemtov, a wealthy merchant from Basra, who left his fortune to the Jewish National Fund. See Cohen, *ha-Peʿīlūt ha-Ṣiyyōnīt be-ʿIrāq,* pp. 99–100; see also p. 341, n. 8.

[15] This was the ʿaliya office adjoining the Zionist Federation in Baghdad.

THE FOUNDER OF AN IRAQI JEWISH NEWSPAPER REQUESTS THE WORLD ZIONIST ORGANIZATION TO INTERVENE WITH THE BRITISH GOVERNMENT ON BEHALF OF HIS PUBLICATION

(1924)

That Mesopotamian Jewry is still slumbering deep in front of all the efforts displayed by their coreligionists abroad is proved by the fact that their contribution to the various funds is rather insignificant.

Owing to the poor education acquired by our brothers, here, no act of national feelings is manifested by them, with the exception of a few young men who begin to peep forth and unite their strength, though with a small success.

Notwithstanding the prominent situation which they occupy among the Arab citizens, the Jews do not avail themselves of the opportunity and are indifferent to the national redemption. They do not possess the slightest idea of securing a brilliant future for the coming generation.

To the most of them, love of motherland is to be recited in prayers only and reconstruction of the temple is to be achieved by the Almighty.

Who is to remedy to this indifference? Who can convey to this recalcitrant community the spirit of virtual love of the Homeland?

We cannot deny the existence of sparse Zionists but this batch of uninfluential people does not carry weight, in view of the virulent antipathy of the high class.

We could not stand quiet in the presence of this dilemma, and in 1920 the Jewish Youth headed by the late Mr. Ahaya (the Assistant Commandant of Police who was assassinated in 1921) formed a Society with the purpose of uplifting the moral situation of our brethren.[1]

It was named the Jewish Literary Society, where I occupied the post of Honorary Secretary. But the treacherous hand which took away the president in the flower of his life did not permit of further progress in spite of our strenuous efforts.

By the time the Zionist Committee was formed and our people began to understand the necessity and the importance of our institutions, we had the chance to attract a few young men who, hitherto unimbued with Judaism even, backed up our cause.

Yet another strong want was felt in our midst. A Community of 80,000 souls cannot overcome the difficulties besieging its way without a paper defending its sacred rights.

[1]Concerning the Jewish Literary Society (Ar., al-Jamᶜiyya al-Adabiyya al-Isrāʾīliyya), see Part One, p. 86.

Local Arab papers were ransoming the Community whenever the opportunity presented itself to them. The gap ought to be filled, but who is going to start?

Surrounded by an army of enemies a paper though literary and communal, how can it survive?

I tried to gain the sympathy of some Arab influential personalities and my fellow law students, and after a half year of continuous efforts, I finally obtained the permit for the publication of an Arabic magazine "AL MISBAH." Suddenly awakened, the Jews did not hail the paper with the sympathy it deserves with the exception of the Youth.

Several suggestions were put forth by the prominent Jews here. Many showed indignance and preferred to live in peace, as they allege that a Jewish paper does not but reveal our true position to our fellow-citizens.

But the truth is they want to put out national feelings and prevent them from taking root in our midst.

Now that four months have elapsed, I came to observe during this period, the existence of two elements which should not remain unheeded, as they constitute a danger to our weekly "MENORAH"[2] i.e.:

1. The Local Press.
2. The Jewish Enemies.

In order to resist these foes, a strong hand is of great benefit to the promotion of our national ideal; otherwise no substantial success can be expected from this organ.

The anti-nationalist feeling prevailing throughout cannot be checked unless a free hand is lent to this weekly.

Our Youth is promising well, but how the war is to be waged without a strong weapon? A heavy task is incumbent upon us, that of clearing the road leading to our salvation, a thorny and dreary road as it is.

I am working incessantly, in spite of the scarcity of my time, for the welfare of the Community as far as my capacity permits, and I am devoting a good deal of it too, for other communal purposes; and beside a portion of money—though small—for the weekly is not paying its costs though published in a rich Community.

I am not asking any pecuniar [*sic*] subvention or anything of the kind; a moral support will do much to solidify the foundations of my Journal and will cause a great development of the national ideal.

As a matter of fact a good army of nationalists can be made within a very short time and Mesopotamian Jews will not stay behind forever deaf and dumb admirers in front of the activities displayed abroad.

It is essentially necessary and absolutely indispensable for us to maintain this paper, and nourish it in its actual state of infancy, so that no inimical trick be played to undermine the foundations erected.

[2] The Hebrew title of *al-Miṣbāḥ*.

A word from the British Government might considerably respond to the purpose, and for this reason I found no other clue to the problem, elsewhere than in your benevolent institution, and I kindly request you to use your auspices at the Colonial Office for a worthy recommendation to be made through the British Residency at the ᶜIraq Ministry of Interior.

Solomon S. Shina
30-7-24

CZA (Jerusalem) Z 4/2470.

IRAQI ZIONISTS COMPLAIN ABOUT THEIR LACK OF REPRESENTATION IN THE JEWISH AGENCY AND OF ASHKENAZI BIAS
(1925)

28th Nisan.[1]

From: The Mesopotamian Zionist Committee, Baghdad
To: The Zionist Executive, London

We desire to inform you herewith that we have waited until today for your invitation to the Iraqi Jews numbering about 150,000, to participate in the Jewish Agency, as you have invited other communities consisting of fewer Jews with whom the Zionist question is not of such political importance as it is with the Jews of Iraq, but we have waited in vain.[2]

We would therefore put the following questions to you:

a. Is it your intention not to invite the Jews of our country to participate in the Jewish Agency to be composed at the 14th Congress?[3]
b. Is your attitude towards the Sephardim different than towards the Ashkenazim?

Is the article in *Haaretz* true that the Executive intends deferring the question of electing Sephardi representatives to the Agency until the general Sephardi Congress will be convened, when two delegates will be elected on the Jewish Agency? If that is so, then it is unjust and offensive, for the question of delegation to the Agency is not connected with the Sephardic Congress, which will not be convened for some years, and the nature of which is unknown.

We cannot refrain from making the following comment: If the Sephardim require a Congress in order to appoint representatives on the Jewish Agency, why should not the Ashkenazim require such a congress too? We therefore wish to say that unless you give us an affirmative reply and an opportunity is given to all Zionist and non-Zionist[4] institutions in Iraq to elect representatives as behooves our standing and the sacrifices we have made for Palestine during the last few years (such as [a] Ezra Sassoon,[5] [b]

[1] April 22, 1925.

[2] A handwritten note at the top of this draft copy of the translation reads: "*Dr. Lauterbach.* Nobody has yet been invited to join." (Leo Lauterbach was director of the Organization Department of the World Zionist Organization at the time.)

[3] The Congress was scheduled to meet in August of that year in Vienna.

[4] The proposal to expand the Jewish Agency to include non-Zionists had been put forth at the Thirteenth Zionist Congress in Carlsbad in 1923. See Getzel Kressel, "Zionist Congresses: The Thirteenth Congress," *EJ* 16: 1172.

[5] The reference is probably to Ezra Sasson Suheik's gift to the Jewish National Fund in the early 1920s. See Part One, p. 86.

Elias Kadoorie, deceased,[6] [c] E. S. Kadoorie,[7] and last, [d] Ichezkal Gurgie Shem Tov.[8] It is offensive for us to hear from tourists returning from Palestine that Mr. Sacher[9] belittles the value of the bequest whereby the letter of the illustrious deceased will be refuted), we shall be compelled to sever our connections with the Zionist Organization and to work for Palestine independently.[10]

CZA (Jerusalem) Z 4/2470.

[6] Sir Ellis Kadoorie of Hong Kong (d. 1922). He left a bequest of 150,000 Palestinian pounds for the establishment of an educational institution in Palestine. The money was used to build two agricultural schools, one for Jews at Mount Tabor, the other for Arabs at Tul Karm. See Abraham Ben-Jacob, *Babylonian Jewry in Diaspora* (Jerusalem, 1985), pp. 382–83 [Heb.]; also Rudolph Loewenthal, "Kadoorie," *EJ* 10: 667–68.

[7] Sir Elly Silas Kadoorie (1867–1944), brother of Sir Ellis. He was an ardent Zionist, was president of the Palestine Foundation Fund in Shanghai, and had contributed a substantial sum of money for the building of the Hebrew University. See Ben Jacob, *Babylonian Jewry in Diaspora,* pp. 378–82 [Heb.]; also Loewenthal, "Kadoorie," *EJ* 10: 667–68.

[8] When this wealthy Zionist from Basra donated all of his property, estimated at 140,000 pounds sterling to the Jewish National Fund, the Zionist Organization in London did not even send him a letter of thanks until prodded by Dr. Ariel Bension. See Hayyim J. Cohen, *ha-Peᶜīlūt ha-Ṣiyyōnīt be-ᶜIrāq* (Jerusalem, 1969), p. 141.

[9] Harry Sacher (1881–1971), a British lawyer and Zionist activist, who at that time lived in Jerusalem. See Getzel Kressel, "Sacher, Harry," *EJ* 14: 591–92.

[10] This threat was never carried out.

A REPORT ON THE BAN UPON ZIONIST ACTIVITIES IN IRAQ
(1929)

Baghdad, 16 Kislev 5690
December 18, 1929

Main Office of the Jewish National Fund
Jerusalem

Honored Sirs,

We hereby give a general outline of the state of the Jewish National Fund in Baghdad.

1. The events of the month of Av[1] made a tremendous impression here on both Jews and Muslims alike, and as a result of the tense situation in which we find ourselves, we have refrained from any propagandizing or collecting funds.

2. In an interview which the chairman of our organization[2] had with the British adviser at the Ministry of the Interior, September 8, 1928, at the end of the conversation which lasted about half an hour, the aforementioned adviser requested that the chairman of the Zionist Organization sign a declaration in which he obligated himself "to put an end to all Zionist work in Baghdad," specifically:

a. Aliya matters
b. Fund-raising for the Jewish National Fund
c. Selling shekels

Furthermore, he had to obligate himself not to carry on any Zionist propaganda and not to disseminate Zionist ideas in the Pardes Yeladim School (the school directed by the chairman of the Zionist Organization).

3. Naturally, signing such a declaration was impossible. We, therefore, turned to the High Commissioner in a detailed letter in which we set out the entire matter and in particular emphasized the following points:

a. We have been carrying on our work unobtrusively for several years among the members of our community without anyone taking notice of us and without annoying anyone.
b. It is incumbent upon us to seek the advice of the World Zionist Organization in this matter.

[1] The reference is to the Wailing Wall riots that broke out on August 23, 1929. See Part One, pp. 94–97.

[2] That is, the writer of the report himself.

c. Since we have permission from the Minister for Colonial Affairs to engage in activities here, we consider it imperative to seek his advice in this matter. And if in any event a declaration is required from us that we will not engage at all in Zionist work (for the time being in effect we are refraining from any activity without a declaration on our part), we are prepared to sign a declaration of the following sort:

Not to engage in Zionist activity for the time being with respect to:
1. Emigration matters
2. Public fund-raising for the Jewish National Fund
3. Selling shekels

With regard to the Pardes Yeladim School, the children range in age from five to eleven, and the school's program is like the program in the government schools.

d. We sent the High Commissioner a copy of the document from the Adviser for Legal Affairs of the Palestinian Government, according to which the work of the Jewish National Fund is charitable in character and, therefore, it is legally impossible to forbid fund-raising for the Fund.

4. All these items, together with copies of the negotiations we had with the Government, we have sent to the Zionist Executive in London, requesting that it get involved in this matter. However, three months have passed since then, and the matter seemed to have resolved itself. We received no reply from the High Commissioner, neither did the Zionist Executive answer our letter.

5. Last Thursday (December 12, 1929), the chairman of the Zionist Organization was summoned to appear before the Central Police and there—upon orders from the Interior Minister—compelled to sign a declaration according to which he obligated himself to stop collecting funds for the Jewish National Fund and to refrain from organizing a Zionist Society here.

6. We turned again to the Zionist Executive in London regarding this matter, and we are asking you to also take an interest in this question. Until the matter is solved, we request that you send us only a single exemplar of propaganda materials to the following address:

A. S. M. ELIAHOU NAHOM[3]
15/140 Ubaid Street, Baghdad, Iraq

[3] The writer's full name was Aaron Sasson Mu^c^allim ("the Teacher") b. Elijah Nahum, but he was commonly known as Aaron Sasson. Apparently, he believed that using his other names on the address would be less easily spotted by the authorities.

Please confirm receipt of this letter and inform all departments of the main office of the change in our address due to the special situation in which we presently find ourselves.

With blessings for the redemption of the Land,
Aaron Sasson
Chairman of the Zionist Organization and JNF Committee, Baghdad

CZA (Jerusalem) KKL 5/481.
Hebrew text published in Zvi Yehuda, ed. *From Babylon to Jerusalem* (Tel Aviv, 1980), pp. 135–36.

AN ARAB JOURNALIST ACCUSES IRAQI JEWS OF ZIONIST INTRIGUES
(1933)

Is it not a joke of the times that parasitic elements are infringing upon the rights of a nation that has enveloped them with its benevolence, which has given them a part of its glory, and which has pulled them out of humility and poverty?

We are free from blame if we unmask the ruses and intrigues which are given free rein under our very eyes. The goal is on the verge of being attained, and what we today consider a dream is on the point of being realized. The unity which we are striving to maintain and to protect in silence has been struck to the heart by the destructive acts of agitation and is on the point of succumbing. Silence has become a crime and a shame. Unmasking the reality is a sacred duty that imposes itself upon every Arab concerned about safeguarding the interests of his people and upon every Muslim who feels Islamic blood coursing through his veins.

Ever since the beginning of the Zionist movement, we have observed among a large part of the Jews of Iraq abnormal signs and suspicious movements hinting at a desire to develop this movement and to encourage those who direct it by concealed means and under diverse guises. However, we abstained from making this state of affairs known publicly, anxious to safeguard unity and to avoid disquieting events. This attitude was interpreted by the Jews as weakness or as impotence on our part. They, therefore, invited Alfred Mond[1] to visit Iraq with a view to controlling the bases of Zionist propaganda and of taking up collections to this end. The people are taking account of this flagrant aggression against the Iraqi nation; namely the Jews wanting to make Iraq the source of death for Arabs and Muslims. An unprecedented turmoil was produced within the nation which decided either to die or to assassinate this visitor and, were it not for the wise intervention of the reformers, a terrible human slaughter would have taken place.[2]

We hoped that the Jews would remember this incident and take heed from it by abandoning this stupid fancy which will cause them to fall into the deepest abyss.

But what was the result? They believed above all that the Iraqis were inattentive to what they were doing in their synagogues, their establishments,

[1] 1868–1930. Concerning this well-known British Zionist, see Moshe Rosetti, "Mond (Melchett)," *EJ* 12: 241–42.

[2] Mond's visit to Baghdad on February 8, 1928, was marked by the first anti-Zionist demonstrations in that city. Because of the violence, the government was forced to cancel the official welcome that had been planned for him and to bring him into the capital by an alternate route. See Hayyim J. Cohen, *ha-Peʿīlūt ha-Ṣiyyōnīt be-ʿIrāq* (Jerusalem, 1969), pp. 44–45, and ʿAbd al-Razzāq al-Ḥasanī, *Ta'rīkh al-Wizārāt al-ʿIrāqiyya,* vol. 2, 2nd ed. (Sidon, 1953), pp. 140–41.

their clubs, and their schools. They reserved for the Iraqis a great hatred and set about to fight them in secret while appearing to make peace with them. They have insisted on following this policy and have begun to comment on events and politics according to their desires, imbued with fanciful dreams devoid of conscience and having no pity themselves. Several educated, well-informed individuals among them have advised them to abandon this state of mind and return to reason. But they have not listened to these counsels, and they themselves have begun to provoke a return of the horrors of history.

The fact that we have hesitated to deal with this subject for a long time justifies these declarations perhaps. We want to make them recognize the degree of our attention and our vigilance with regard to what they are doing openly, after having followed these movements closely and having gathered information from reliable sources. If they are contemptuous of Arab unity, we have before us Islamic unity, before which these contemptible elements will melt.

We do not know what these Jews have found among the Iraqis that they have attached themselves so to Zionism. Perhaps they do not know that it is pleasing to Iraq to die for the Palestine cause. If we abstain today from fighting against the intrigues of the Jews in Palestine, it is not because Iraq is hesitant to sacrifice itself for this cause. It is rather because Iraq considers all these dealings to be like a light cloud which will soon dissipate by itself.

As to the diffusion of Zionist books which the Jews have brought in clandestinely and which they continue to bring into Iraq, sometimes through the mails, sometimes by motor vehicles entering Iraq, and as to the distribution in public of Zionist journals—all of this will be of no avail to them in the face of Islamic power and the great concern of Muslims to protect their sacred religious traditions.

Another manifestation is to be noticed among these people. They have begun publishing long articles in foreign Zionist newspapers on the activity of the propagandists of this project and of the energetic efforts expended in this domain. In fact, these publications are of little concern to us. What does concern us is the unfortunate impression which this false propaganda creates in the minds of our brother Arabs and Muslims who regard us with admiration and respect and who place all their hopes in our country. But that is what these people want—that Iraq should be the center for the ruin and the misfortunes of the Arabs. The Government propagandizes for the benefit of Iraq, while this element destroys in its ignorance what the Government has built. The Government strives to strengthen relations with all foreign countries and this element provokes hostilities and tensions. The newspaper *Israël*[3] published in the twentieth issue of its fourth year the following:

[3] The writer is apparently referring to the Egyptian Jewish weekly, published in Cairo between 1920 and 1939, which was pro-Zionist. However, the passage cited must be from the fourteenth year of the publication and not the fourth.

The German Consul in Iraq has protested to local authorities against the aggressions of male and female students and accused the director of the Alliance, Mr. Sassoon, for this. He presented another protest to the French Consul with regard to what the Alliance Schools were doing against Germany.

Here is a Jewish witness testifying to the degree of Germany's impression of Iraq. It is Iraq's duty in the present circumstances to maintain good and amicable relations with Germany given the assistance that that country has lent us on several occasions and the sympathy it has demonstrated for our cause. The persecution of the Jews by Hitler should not prevent us from maintaining our friendship with his government. When we wanted to boycott Italian products during the persecutions of the Arabs in Tripoli, the Jewish merchants doubled their orders from Italian firms with an aim of hurting our feelings. They did the same thing with France at the time of the Berber Dahir question.[4] It is now time for Arab merchants to enter into relations with German firms. Within a few weeks, German products would flood the Iraqi market.

In spite of all that we have said above, it must be recognized that there exists certain Jews who feel genuine patriotic sentiments, who mock these foolish dreams, and who fight the Zionist tendencies with all their strength. Unfortunately, however, they constitute only a minority.

We shall content ourselves today with this general survey. We shall expose in detail everything that is going on here in a study entitled "The Zionist Movement in Iraq" which we will continue to publish in this review.

Amīn Aḥmad

Amīn Aḥmad, "Préludes du Sionisme en Irak," traduction d'un article paru dans le journal arabe *Al-Hedaye* (June 1933).
AIU Archives (Paris)
Irak I.C.3.

[4] On May 16, 1930, the French Residency drafted a decree for the sultan (the Dahir Berbère) that gave full authority to courts of Berber customary law as opposed to Islamic Sharīʿa courts in Berber regions of Morocco. This obvious attempt at driving a further wedge between the Arab and Berber populations had quite the opposite effect and became the catalyst that helped to unify various nascent nationalist forces within the country. See Jean Brignon et al., *Histoire du Maroc* (Casablanca, 1967), pp. 392–93; John P. Halstead, *Rebirth of a Nation: The Origins and Rise of Moroccan Nationalism, 1912–1944* (Cambridge, Mass., 1967), pp. 178–90. On the furious anti-Berber dahir campaign throughout the Muslim world, see ibid., pp. 184–86.

A MOROCCAN ARAB JOURNALIST ATTACKS ZIONIST ACTIVITIES IN HIS COUNTRY
(1934)

Our campaigns against Zionist intrigues in Morocco seem to have unnerved beyond all limits those gentlemen of *L'Avenir Illustré*.[1] One would have expected them to show more discretion in the way they exposed the Zionist theory and the attachment they demonstrate for it! Are they hoping to convince us and end up by our admitting this unwelcomed agitation in Morocco? I think that this is a wasted effort on their part, because whatever the reasons invoked by them to justify the existence of Zionism, we would not—in the interest of the Moroccan people as a whole—depart from our line of conduct and take a position of neutrality on a question so important for the future of Judeo-Muslim relations.

We have already denounced the machinations of the Zionists in Morocco, ever since several particular incidents have occurred which corroborate our apprehensions.

It is as if the Zionist Jews, in responding to our legitimate emotion, have wanted to hurl a challenge.

On the one hand, what has been shown by *L'Avenir Illustré,* where two high Sharifan functionaries were represented, has not failed to elicit righteous indignation in those circles which follow the development of this gangrene which is Zionism in Morocco.

The Jewish scouts of Tangier have just recently flown the Zionist flag, an act which has unleashed a widespread protest movement on the part of the Muslim element of the city.

The press, French as well as Arab, has not failed to brand this state of affairs as being very dangerous for Morocco. In reading these articles, one can only come to the conclusion that the Tangerine Jews actually marched with a banner that was not Morocco's—and in a country where they are considered to be subjects of H.M. the Sultan.

Fortunately, the local authorities, upon the intervention of more than 2,000 persons, saw fit to ban any further display of the Zionist banners, which we would describe as tactless and contrary to the patriotic sentiments of Moroccan Jews.[2]

On the other hand, the Zionist press has not failed to comment unfavorably upon our thoughts on this problem and to distort them for the needs of their cause.

[1] This biweekly illustrated magazine published by Jonathan Thursz appeared in Casablanca from 1926 until 1940.

[2] Two years later, the scouts in Tangier caused a similar stir by marching in public with Zionist banners. See p. 350.

We have said that we will not tolerate any Zionist demonstration in Morocco.

We repeat it today, more insistently, more vehemently than ever. If our anxiety displeases the staff of *L'Avenir Illustré,* we are sorry about it.

. . . .

Let us read the editorial from *L'Avenir Illustré* for March 31 and April 8, 1934. What do we see? A call to *L'Action*[3] to close ranks with the Zionists and to reinforce the struggle that they are waging for Moroccan nationality. After many insinuations which appear to be addressed to us, it says the following: "Finally, because we consider the creation being realized in Palestine to be a credit to all of Jewry . . . and because we see that the Jews there are providing a fine example of physical, intellectual, and moral health, we want to tear away our readers now and then from their material preoccupations to give these beautiful examples to contemplate so that they might practice here for Morocco's sake these fine virtues which are practiced there."

Thus, the facts come to light that not content to have already violated the rights of the Palestinian people, Arab and Jewish, the Zionists want *to practice these fine virtues* here.

. . . .

There is no need then to deceive oneself, nor to be taken in with regard to the character of this systematically anti-Moroccan movement which seeks to expand and which is encouraged by all sorts of silent accomplices. . . .

In the face of incontestable evidence, it is only proper for us to continue with all our strength to unmask the machinations of Zionism in Morocco. We shall do it implacably, knowing that we are serving thereby the future of the Jews and at the same time the entire Moroccan cause.

Mohammed El Kholti, "Les Sionistes au Maroc sur la défensive," *L'Action du Peuple* (April 27, 1934), p. 1.

[3] *L'Action du Peuple,* the writer's paper.

JEWISH BOY SCOUTS IN TANGIER CAUSE A STIR AMONG ARAB NATIONALISTS

(1936)

The Arabs' nationalist sentiments were further exasperated a number of days ago by the maladroitness of the Jewish Boy Scouts. Returning from Gibraltar where they had taken part in a scout jamboree, they proceeded through town bearing French and Zionist banners without a trace of the Sharifan flag, which is the only one they should have been flying.

Since then the atmosphere has been quite troubled. There have been numerous attempts at rapprochement. . . . These attempts have not yielded the results hoped for, and the Jews, in order to prevent the reoccurrence of similar incidents, must avoid doing anything which could hurt the sensitive self-esteem of their Muslim fellow citizens. Only on this condition will they always be able to declare that anti-Semitism does not reign in Tangier and will they be able to continue to enjoy a situation which our coreligionists in many other countries would envy.

Report on anti-Semitism by B. Yahni (Tangier), dated March 11, 1936.
AIU Archives (Paris)
Maroc IV.C.11.

AN ARABIC EDITION OF "THE PROTOCOLS" IN BEIRUT (1926)

The Jewish Community Council of Beirut was alarmed by the publication of an Arabic translation of *The Protocols of the Elders of Zion* by a Lebanese Maronite priest. This priest had previously tried to blackmail the well-to-do Jews of Beirut, seeking to get some money out of them. Failing in that, he carried out his threat to spread throughout the country that infamous book which only found buyers among a dozen of our coreligionists curious to become acquainted with the lucubrations of the author.

The President of the Community has addressed a letter to the High Commissioner, a copy of which I am forwarding for your information.[1] In it he requests that the sale of this work be banned in Syria. Although M. de Jouvenel[2] had promised to study the matter, he has declared that the affair appears ridiculous to him and that it cannot have any effect on the morale of the population.

Report of Maurice Sidi, director of the Alliance School for Boys, Beirut, to Alliance Headquarters in Paris (March 25, 1926).
AIU Archives (Paris)
Liban I.C.1.

[1] For the text of the letter, see the following document.
[2] The French high commissioner.

THE JEWS OF BEIRUT PETITION THE AUTHORITIES FOR A BAN ON THE SALE OF "THE PROTOCOLS"

(1926)

February 10, 1926

To His Excellency the High Commissioner
of the French Republic in Syria, Greater Lebanon

Beirut

Excellency,

We have the honor to bring to your high attention the book entitled *The Protocols of the Elders of Zion*, which, ever since its appearance some years ago, has been the object of polemics in Europe, and has just been translated into Arabic by a member of the clergy named Antun Yamin and published in Cairo.

It is not without regret, Excellency, that we who have always been peace-loving, and along with us, all who aspire to the pacification of hearts and minds, have seen it circulated in Beirut.

In fact, this book, which was translated with the very clear intention of defamation, can have no other result than to inflame minds that are not sufficiently freed of caste prejudice and to create among a certain class of the population, an atmosphere hardly sympathetic to the Jewish community living in Greater Lebanon and Syria.

Under these circumstances, it seems to us that the circulation of this book in Syria cannot but counteract the policy of social appeasement inaugurated by Your Excellency, the very happy results of which we see each day.

Furthermore, feeling ourselves warranted by the solicitude that Your Excellency has continually shown to all that touches the public interest, we have allowed ourselves to ask you very respectfully to please issue a decree throughout the length of the territories under the Mandate, forbidding the sale and confiscating the existing copies of this work, which we believe falls under the application of article No. 26 of the Ordinance No. 2464 of May 13, 1925.

Please be assured, Excellency, of our thanks in advance and of our very highest regard.

AIU Archives (Paris)
Liban I.C.1.

ADENI JEWS AND ZIONISM
(1920s)

All Jews who believe in the Bible must of necessity be Zionists unless another Bible is invented. The Jews of Aden belong to the Orthodox section of Jewry and they are therefore all Zionists. There is no such term as non-Zionist known in our ranks. To our community the rebuilding of Eres Yisrael is a religious as well as social motives. They believe in Rabbi Simeon's dictum that to live in Palestine outweighs the performance of all the commandments of the Torah.[1] They also lend support to the belief that he who makes his home in Palestine is certain of a share in the world to come.[2] Others go to Palestine in order to improve their conditions to live in a more healthy and congenial surroundings and to escape from the oppressive climate of Aden. To them the political situation is not of such concern as the economical position. Many of the Jews of Aden after selling their houses and all their belongings with a view to make their permanent home in the Holy Land, had to return destitute after trying to carry on the hardest and meanest work in order to eke out an existence. However, our Yemenite coreligionists fare better in Palestine by reason of their having been inured to a harder and humbler way of life in their former place of exile, and it is very rare to hear of a Yemenite family returning from Palestine by reason of unemployment. Our Yemenite brother is fit by nature to do work which is a hardship to his fellow-Jew who comes from the more liberal countries of the Diaspora. In fact the Yemenites in Palestine have got an organization of their own which deals with their needs in and outside of Eres Yisrael.

The Role of Aden Jewry

It was only in the early part of the year 1922 that our Community started to play its part by contributing its quota towards the up-building of our National Home, when Dr. Ariel Bension[3] visited Aden on behalf of the Keren Hayesod. As a result of his mission of sum of #800/-was collected at that time. A Keren Hayesod Committee was formed and glowing hopes were entertained for the future, but owing to the absence of a properly organized association to arouse the smouldering interests of the community, these hopes unfortunately failed to blossom. The Zionist Movement was

[1]This dictum is found in several places, as for example, Tosefta ᶜAvoda Zara 5:2.

[2]BT Ketubbot 111a.

[3]Bension was one of the most successful Zionist representatives to the Jews in various Arab countries. He was particularly dedicated to involving more Sephardim in the Zionist movement. See, for example, his article "Zionism and the Sephardim," *The New Judaea* (March 18, 1927): 223. See also above, p. 332.

most welcome by the masses here, not only out of religious sentiments, but they looked to it as a movement destined to infuse into the community a new spirit of independence and democratic organization. By the influence of Zionism, our community was to keep its head erect and cast off the spirit of sufferance. A Zionist Association is very essential to Aden which is far removed from the centers of Zionism. Moreover, Aden is a center of emigration for the Yemenite Jews who incessantly stream from Yemen on their way to Eres Yisrael and there is no institution which provides these transmigrants with the necessary permits, information and encouragement which they need. To fill such a gap, the Reverend Meshumor Shemuel Nissim, a saintly communal worker, is voluntarily carrying on the task of applying for permits for these transmigrants and supplying them with all the necessary encouragement and assistance. He does all his work single-handed and with zeal and devotion.

Aden's Love for Eres Yisrael

Once more our community was given the opportunity of manifesting its love for Eres Yisrael as the result of the visit of two Zionist envoys, Rabbi Menachem S. Levy and Mr. Michael Naamani, in March this year. In response to a general invitation many members of the community assembled at the hall of the Succath Shalom Synogogue to listen to the appeal on behalf of the Keren Hayesod. At the end of the address made by the Zionist delegates, some of the audience thought fit to place their so-called grievances before the said delegates. They pleaded that the Jews of Aden could not fare well in Palestine by reason of the fact that they did not receive the same aid and encouragement which their brethren from other parts of the Diaspora got at the hands of the Zionist Organization. To this the delegates retorted that the hands of the Zionist Organization was there to help all Jews without distinction and irrespective of the countries they hail from; and if the Jews of Aden did not get the same help, it was because they did not approach the Zionist Organization. Had the Jews of Aden organized themselves and placed their case before the Zionist Organization they would have received all help and encouragement. It was eventually resolved to appoint Reverend Menachem S. Levy as the Community's spokesman at Palestine which the Reverend Rabbi kindly accepted assuring the audience that he would do all he could on behalf of our community. On the following Sabbath the said Rabbi Levy delivered addresses in Hebrew in two Synagogues. His fiery addresses were full of pathos, and by his sweeping eloquence he infused into the people a new spirit and aroused the dormant interest of the community.

The material response was satisfactory for the amount donated reached the sum of 900 pounds and the pledges amounted to Rs. 6000/-. In many instances real sacrifice was made as the community consists mainly of artisans. Besides looking after its own poor, it has also to look after the poor Jews who flock from Yemen. Although charity begins at home as the slogan goes, our community placed the call of Eres Yisrael above their pressing needs and gave unstintingly of their substance towards the rebuilding of their National Home. On the eve of his departure, Rabbi Levy was accorded a hearty send-off and the Synagogue was crammed up with an unexpected multitude bubbling with anxiety to hear the last words from the lips of the learned Rabbi. At the conclusion of his speech, he announced the formation of the Keren Hayesod and Keren Kayemeth Committees. In reality, we cannot help mentioning that Rabbi Levy has proved himself to be the right envoy for Aden as by his natural tact and ingenuity he won the wholehearted cooperation from all and sundry. Amongst the list of those who gave the largest donations, stand the names of Messrs. Menahem Messa,[4] leaders of the Community and Mr. Jacob S. Mesha, a staunch Zionist. While Mr. Hahalla S. Jacob spent neither time nor energy to render the mission of the delegates a success. As in the previous occasion, the residents of Aden received the present delegates kindly and showed every interest and sympathy in their mission.

In conclusion, we can only hope that the impetus which the Jewish National Movement has already given to Jewish learning and unity of Israel will react on the community here and will be the means of establishing an organized and virile Jewish community free from the spiritual slavery of ignorance and indifference. We also look anxiously forward to the day when the economic position in Palestine will enable all our coreligionists to live an easy life in the land of their forefathers.

B. J. Yaish, "The Jewish National Movement in Aden," *Israel's Messenger* 24, No. 4 (July 8, 1927):22.

[4] Menahem Messa appears as a frequent correspondent of the Alliance Israélite Universelle in Aden during the late nineteenth and early twentieth century. A local merchant, he seems to have been active in relief work among the Jews in Yemen. See AIU Archives (Paris) Petits Pays Divers: Aden 1–4. The reference here is perhaps to his sons—hence, Messrs. Menahem Messa.

5

DARKENING SHADOWS: 1929 to 1939

THE STATE OF SYRIAN JEWRY IN THE IMMEDIATE AFTERMATH OF THE WESTERN WALL DISTURBANCES (1929)

No. 8 Damascus, September 9, 1929

A. Silberstein[1]

Mr. President,

Life in Damascus

The situation in our quarter has returned to normal after the noisy demonstrations of last week. People are back at work. Our coreligionists go about their business peacefully both in town and outside. The posts taken up by the French troops here have been evacuated, and the quarter has returned to its everyday life.

But there is a subject which is tormenting some of our coreligionists!

Didn't the Jews of Damascus go too far in their anti-Zionist demonstrations? Was the quarter really in such danger to issue manifestos disapproving of the Zionist enterprise?

Those who entertain friendly relations with our coreligionists to the south are really worried about the consequences of the demonstrations locally and worldwide! Whereas throughout the entire world, Jews have shown their attachment to the Zionists and their sympathy for the victims, those of Syria have made common cause with the Arabs![2]

[1] Director of the Alliance School for Boys in Damascus.

[2] Silberstein was certainly no Zionist, and hence his criticism of the community's behavior is all the more telling. Only a month earlier, Silberstein had accused the

"We deplore the Zionist acts of violence," the President of Beirut's Jewish community declared in the mosque. "We are Arabs from time immemorial, and we disapprove of the Zionist enterprise instituted by Jews from Eastern Europe," declared the Jewish Youth Organization of Damascus in all the newspapers.[3] In Beirut, many young Jews took part in the anti-Zionist demonstrations which rolled through the streets!

The Tel Aviv paper *Haaretz* rose up in indignation against the attitude adopted by Syrian Jewry during the bloody events in Palestine. It called them cowards and fulminated against the Damascene community in particular!

It was in fact the community in Damascus that was the first to demonstrate its sympathy for the Palestinian Arab victims. These demonstrations won over the other communities little by little. In Beirut, Sidon, and Aleppo, the Jewish communities demonstrated their solidarity with the Arabs. In Lattakia, capital of the Alawi State, the two sole Jews living in town, one a functionary and the other a laborer, addressed a letter to the Muslim Committee condemning the Zionist aggressions and expressing solidarity with the Arabs.

Some have found an excuse for the community's attitude.

The first news from Palestine published in the newspapers was the most tendentious! All of the papers in common accord reported that thousands of Arabs had been slaughtered in Jerusalem; that bombs had been thrown into the Mosque of ᶜUmar; that women and children had been butchered without pity!

As soon as the demonstrations began to circulate throughout the city, the Jews found themselves helpless, not knowing what to do. If they ought to be blamed, it is for adding credence to the new lies published by the newspapers and for acting precipitantly.

The Arabic and even the French newspapers of Syria and Lebanon continue to be very violent in their attacks against the Zionists. The term "anti-Semite" has disappeared from Syria; today there are no more anti-Semites among us, but rather anti-Zionists! In employing this term, the papers believe they are permitted to say anything against the Jews! Should our Syrian coreligionists rejoice by this change of vocable? I think not, since for the masses, Zionist and non-Zionist are Jews. It is true that for a few of our neighbors, the Zionists are something else entirely, and many have gone so far as to ask us whether the Zionists have the same religion as other Jews.

Despite the measures taken at the Syro-Palestinian frontier to keep Syrians from penetrating Palestine, the newspapers are announcing that several hundred patriots have already crossed the border to bring aid to the

---

Maccabee Sport Association before the authorities of being Zionist. See AIU Archives (Paris) Syrie XI.E.94, letter from Joseph Farhi, vice president of the Damascene Jewish Community Council, to Alliance headquarters in Paris (July 31, 1929).

[3] The text of their manifesto is translated on p. 328.

Palestinian Arabs. I think the lure of booty gave more of a push to these patriots to go and "fight in the Holy Land."

Our coreligionists are poltroons by nature. At the slightest alert, panic seizes the entire population! It is no doubt the troubled period of 1925–26 which is still in everyone's mind.[4]

Last week a bomb exploded not far from the quarter, killing two Christians and injuring four others. Immediately, the word spread among our people that this bomb had been intended for the quarter, but had gone off too soon. Throughout the day, all the streets were deserted because people feared an attack. Throughout the night, people kept watch at their windows. One girl thought she saw an Arab walking about in the streets armed with grenades! The French military post was alerted at midnight and a patrol of Senegalese soldiers made the rounds through the streets. People wanted representations to be made before the authorities to have a military post in every house. Fortunately, for the Jewish population, the bombing affair was cleared up.[5]

. . . .

If our coreligionists were moved by news of the events in Palestine, the emotion was even greater the day they learned of the misfortune which struck the Sephardi community of Safed. A commemorative service was held for the victims.[6]

Although life in Damascus is calmer, it still inspires some anxieties. People are terribly overwrought. This week two Jews were beaten right in the center of town not far from a police station. None of the attackers could be arrested!

Please accept, Mr. President, this expression of my devotion.

A. Silberstein

AIU Archives (Paris)
Syrie I.G.2.

[4] The writer is referring to the Druze uprising, which began in July 1925. During the rebellion, Damascus was severely bombarded by the French in October 1925 and May 1926. Calm was not restored until the autumn of 1926. See Stephen Hemsley Longrigg, *Syria and Lebanon under French Mandate* (London, New York, and Toronto, 1958), pp. 148–69. During October 1925, the Jewish Quarter of Damascus was first sacked by Druze and then shelled by the French. See "Les événements de Damas et la population juive," *Paix et Droit* 5, no. 9 (1925): 8–10.

[5] The bomb was from the time of the Druze uprising and had been used by an itinerant merchant as a scale weight.

[6] The attack on the Jewish Quarter of Safed began in the Street of the Sephardim, which was completely destroyed. See Lt. Colonel F. H. Kisch, *Palestine Diary* (London, 1938; reprint ed., New York, 1974), p. 255.

AN ACCUSATION OF MOSQUE DESECRATION RESULTS IN MOB VIOLENCE AGAINST THE JEWS OF ADEN

(1932)

On the pretext of throwing excreta in a Mosque, the Arabs began to assemble in large numbers in the streets incited by racial hatred and venomous propaganda against the Jews, as Jewish houses in the neighborhood were accused of the alleged misdeed. Restlessness and fanatical feelings ran high and just on the evening of the 23rd May a formidable Moslem mob stormed the Jewish Quarter and assaulted men and women. The defense action of few Jewish houses by throwing bottles served to keep the mob at bay; however, the assailants turned from the Jaffran entrance toward the isolated Jewish places where greater violence was inflicted. The Yemenite Shelter was forcibly entered and women and babies beaten mercilessly. Sporadic attacks were also made in all the Jewish streets and after the reinforcements of the armed Police the disturbances subsided at midnight. The 24th May passed off quietly till 4 P.M., when again a large Moslem mob was seen in the Jaffran Avenue planning a general attack on the Jews, and after a few hours' deliberations the hooligans broke into the Jewish streets and the outrages of the first night were repeated till midnight. The Jews were terror-stricken and could not venture out, but kept within their houses closed like chickens. The cry of the whistles for help were heart-rending, but when the Police arrived the assailants had already made good their escape; in fact the native Police could not cope with the situation.

The 25th of May was the last but the most fateful day of the riots. Moslem aggressors started on their lust for looting early in the morning. "El Damool," a house comprising many Jewish inhabitants, was entered and everything consisting of money and valuable articles was looted and carried away. Many residential shops in the same locality were entirely looted and the Yemenites were rendered utterly poor. El Farhi Synagogue was invaded and contents destroyed. The hooligans finally were chased by the Police and they left the ravaged area and turned to the Esplanade Road where the house of Jacob N. Moses, a tobacco merchant, suffered much damage. The said man suffered injuries on his head, while his wife hid herself in a room with her children whose mouths she kept closed, lest their cries might bring the assailants to their hiding place. The said house has since been immediately vacated. It is situated in an isolated locality and therefore exposed to danger. The loss of property sustained by Jews during the riots is estimated at 20,000 Rupees and application for payment for these damages has already poured on the Government. The fact should be mentioned that a number of phylacteries and Hebrew books disappeared in the course of the riots. The disturbances on that day did not abate till about 10:30 A.M., when few Officers arrived as well as armored cars which patrolled the city and sent the looters to their shells. In the height of the trouble, the Armed Police were stoned, and they had to open fire in the air.

The shops at Tawahi were also looted after the Jews evacuated that little spot of trade on the first night of the riots under police escort. A large number of the Jewish Goldsmiths had their share of looting as their workshops were cleared of all the tools as well as gold and silver and their condition is very pitiable.

The fact should be mentioned that the riots could have been checked if early vigorous action was taken, but the freedom allowed for large assemblies and deliberations mentioned earlier until the disturbances assumed alarming proportions is very regrettable. About fifty Jews were wounded, some very seriously; also, a small number of Moslems were injured.

Few Jewish enthusiasts did their very best to bring succor to their coreligionists by moving the Government and invoking help of their Jewish brethren in London, America, and Palestine. Cables were sent freely everywhere, giving details of the attacks on the Jews. Up till last Saturday there was anxiety, as further attacks were expected; the sense of insecurity was so strong that Jews dared not open their business shops until the 1st June. The fear exists that in view of the wanton looting, and violence which occurred, the assailants have now become encouraged and accustomed to looting, and it is therefore imperative that efficacious steps should be taken in order to prevent the recurrence of similar excesses in the future.

It may be stated that there was not the least offense on the part of the Jews, but the Moslems, whose true objective was to loot, tried to make the alleged defiling of their Mosque as the *casus-belli* for a general attack. The disturbances cannot be minimized, as in a small country like this, and directed against an innocent and helpless Community, they are comparatively too great. A suggestion has been made to pacify the Moslems by building walls round the Mosque which is tantamount to making concessions to violence.

In view of the critical time through which we have passed, the need for courageous and devoted leaders to look after the interests and welfare of the Jewish Community has become very insistent. It is very clear that the Jews lack spokesmen who would make strong representations to the Government with a view to the future protection of this helpless Jewish Community. Unless an organization of leadership takes place, the Jews are exposed to risks and danger for they are at present like "a cattle without a shepherd."

Joseph J. Yaish, "The Disturbances at Aden,"
The Jewish Advocate 3, no. 5 (July 1932): 439–40.

AN OFFICIAL BRITISH STATEMENT ON THE ANTI-JEWISH RIOTS IN ADEN
(1932)

On the 23rd of May 1932 a communal riot broke out at Aden between Arabs and Jews. The outbreak was caused by the defilement of a mosque by the alleged throwing of filth into the courtyard from an adjacent Jewish house. In the opinion of the local authorities the defilement was accidental and not of deliberate intention. The number of persons injured in the rioting was sixty-one, of whom only seven were detained in hospital for treatment. They included twenty-three Jews and thirty-eight Muslims, eleven of the latter being Police. There were no deaths. The disturbance was dealt with by the police, who were in the final stages reinforced by troops.

Response of Mr. H. A. Metcalfe to a question put by Mr. Gaya Prasad Singh in the Indian Legislative Assembly, quoted in the *The Jewish Advocate* 3, no. 9 (November 1932): 576.

A GALLICIZED ALGERIAN MUSLIM REFLECTS UPON THE CONSTANTINE POGROM OF 1934

Ever since the fifth of August (1934), there has been a lot of talk about the natives' resentment of the Jew. It has been stressed that the explosion was the result of a profound discontent provoked by the traditional arrogance of the nouveau-riche Jew, by the airs of superiority that he has been putting on ever since he became a French citizen and has been sticking his hands a little bit everywhere in local politics thanks to the ballot. This privileged position, which had been granted him by the Crémieux Decree of October 24, 1870, has created a feeling of jealousy among the Muslims and has caused an injury to their amour propre, which could only get worse since they were the former masters who had been used for centuries to having precedence over their submissive neighbors.

That a certain arrogance that really does exist among some Jewish elements—particularly the young—could have antagonized the urban native population, which is in continual contact with them, is possible. But that this sentiment had developed to the point of pushing the Muslims of Constantine to commit their horrors—we cannot subscribe to that. We have clearly stated that this resentment could only be found among the townspeople. However, the perpetrators of the lootings and murders of August 5 were all, or almost all, country folk, people who only see the Jew when they come to town to shop or to ask him for his financial services. For this reason, the man from the *bled*[1] has something of that kind of consideration for the Jew which a rich man inspires in one who might have need of him.

As for the rights of citizenship, only some intellectual natives, mainly those who know the value of the vote, have made reproaches—not against the Jews, who had known how to take advantage of a moment of disarray[2] to get a good deal—but against France, which had agreed to a veritable social upheaval in Algeria. The rest of the Arab population is incapable of understanding the significance of the Crémieux Decree and makes no mention of it in its complaints. Moreover, the natives, having no taste for citizenship, which had been made available to them since the Senatus-Consulte of 1865,[3] cannot be jealous of the Jews for an advantage that they still disdain after a century of contact.

[1] The Maghrebi Arabic term for "the countryside."

[2] The Crémieux Decree was issued by the provisional government of France following the country's defeat in the Franco-Prussian War and the fall of the Second Empire. See Part One, p. 17.

[3] On July 14, 1865, the Senatus-Consulte granted Jews and Muslims the status of French subjects, though not of French citizens. It also made provision for individuals to apply for French citizenship, which, however, involved renouncing their personal status under their traditional religious law and accepting the French civil code. Few Muslims were prepared to accept these conditions, which in any case did not

The natives, therefore, cannot harbor resentment toward the Jews either in the political sphere, because that still does not interest them, or in the economic sphere, since they are aware of their own inferiority and take account of the special attributes of their neighbors in business.

It is a completely different story with the Europeans of this country, almost all of whom have the spirit of domination by virtue of their being conquerors and who do not like being caused trouble of any sort in their business dealings. Now the Jew, who has evolved quickly, profitting from his particularly brilliant racial qualities, constitutes a tough adversary, or rather, a tough opponent, for the European who is in a hurry to get rich.

With whom can one work in Algeria? From whom can one extract serious profits? And who is the most numerous clientele which needs to consume, and who will allow for the increase of business? It is the native, always naive, always improvident, and always easy to fleece. It so happens that the Jew has more facilities for entering into relations with Muslims, whose language he knows and whose needs he understands. The European finds himself handicapped in the commercial realm and looks resentfully at the business dealings of even the most ordinary Jew prospering while he encounters all sorts of difficulties because he cannot succeed in reaching the native and in breaking the ice that stands between them. There, the resentments against the Jews are serious. The European, whose amour propre is offended and whose material interests are affected, manifests toward his competitor feelings which are not always very elevated and maneuvers to belittle him and to discredit him for his own profit. There is the source of Algerian anti-Semitism.[4]

R. Zenati, "La question juive: le problème algérien vu par un indigène," *Renseignements Coloniaux,* no. 6 (May–June 1938): 121–22.

---

guarantee that citizenship would be granted. See Vincent Confer, *France and Algeria: The Problem of Civil and Political Reform, 1870–1920* (Syracuse, N.Y., 1966), pp. 3–4, 27–28. Most Jews, on the other hand, viewed the decree in quite a different light. See Michel Ansky, *Les Juifs d'Algérie du Décret Crémieux à la libération* (Paris, 1950), pp. 34–35.

[4] The writer goes on to say that the Europeans also hate the Jews because they have invaded higher education and because they show such solidarity in politics. What is most startling is that he himself seems to accept all of the anti-Semitic stereotypes.

AN ASSESSMENT OF ARAB NATIONALIST FEELINGS TOWARD THE JEWS IN NORTH AFRICA (1934)

Paris (IIIe) August 28, 1934

1005
N.G.
CONFIDENTIAL

Mr. M Shertock, Member
Executive Member of the
Jewish Agency
Jerusalem—P.O.B. 92

Dear friend and comrade,

As agreed upon, I am sending you a report on the Constantine pogrom.[1] I have deleted from my survey the most pessimistic impressions, which I did not want to express in the report that you will read, because the latter is destined for too large a number of readers. However, I am sharing these impressions with you for your information and guidance.

In my opinion, all of North Africa presents at this moment the aspect of a volcanic territory, at the center of which an explosion can erupt from one instant to the next. The Constantine pogrom was only a small, insignificant manifestation which could, however, be repeated one day in the three North African countries.

I have not the slightest doubt that this pogrom had been organized and executed by the young Arab nationalist movement. According to the information that I was able to gather, this movement has expanded tremendously in the past three or four years.

In Tunisia, the Destour party,[2] which calls for Tunisian independence (officially only for autonomy) and which was made up a few years ago of some intellectuals living in the capital, today has followers in the smallest and most far-flung villages of the country. This was reported to me by a lawyer in Sfax who knows the situation extremely well.

In Algeria, the "Young Turk" movement—so called because it is centered around Clubs which, oddly enough, are named "Union and Progress"[3]—has spread a great deal, although perhaps not as widely as the Destour in Tunisia, but which is the harbinger of a more important development.

[1] The pogrom took place August 3–5, 1934, just three weeks before this letter was written. See Part One, p. 100.

[2] The Destour (Constitution) party was founded in Tunisia in 1920. Five months before this letter was written, the breakaway Neo-Destour party was formed by Habib Bourguiba and his followers. See Jamil M. Abun-Nasr, *A History of the Maghrib,* 2nd. ed. (Cambridge, 1975), pp. 342–48.

[3] The official name of the Young Turk organization in the Ottoman Empire had been the Committee of Union and Progress.

I have no more detailed information on Morocco, but only a few years separates us from the ᶜAbd al-Krīm uprising.[4]

In all of the countries the nationalist movement has taken on in the course of the last few years an anti-Semitic orientation. It stands up against the Jews, whom it considers the line of least resistance, against whom it is easy to stir up the native masses given the Jews' privileged social status compared to the latter's.

What is most worrisome is the fact that all these movements are in touch with the Arab movements in Palestine.

The anti-Semitic troubles in Tunis of two years ago, which were not serious in and of themselves (just some street demonstrations), were a disturbing proof of the angry state of mind. They took place a little while after the visit of Palestinian envoys to the Tunisian Arabs.

The Arab press of Cairo, Jerusalem, and Damascus is strongly represented everywhere, even in the towns of the Department of Constantine. This press shapes public opinion, orients it toward Pan-Islamic and Pan-Arabic ideas, and incites it against the Jews, whom it depicts as a docile instrument of English and French imperialism.

This state of affairs imposes upon us the most serious thinking.

We are today in conflict with practically the whole Islamic world. This conflict dates back to the events of 1929. Prior to that year, there were no anti-Semitic manifestations in the North African countries. An anti-Semitic movement existed, but it hailed from the European element and appeared as a foreign import. This time, we are facing a fierce anti-Semitic movement which emanates from the Arabs themselves.

It seems to me that our attempts to find a common language with the Arabs ought to take account of this state of affairs.

Please accept, dear comrade and friend, my cordial Shalom.

J. Fisher[5]

CZA (Jerusalem) S 25/5217.

[4] ᶜAbd al-Krīm (al-Karīm) was a Rifi Berber leader, who rebelled against the Spanish in northern Morocco in 1921 and in the following year set up an Islamic republic, which lasted until 1926, when he was defeated by the combined forces of Spain and France. See Abun-Nasr, *A History of the Maghrib,* pp. 364–66. ᶜAbd al-Krīm became a hero of the Moroccan nationalist movement.

[5] Joseph Fisher was the secretary general of the French branch (which included the Maghreb) of the Jewish National Fund. He was a frequent visiter to North Africa. Although he has perhaps overstressed the intensity of native anti-Jewish feelings at this time, he shows himself to be far more aware of the gathering strength of the Arab nationalist movements in French-ruled North Africa than most Frenchmen and, indeed, most Jews at this period.

THE ARRIVAL OF REFUGEE JEWISH DOCTORS IN SYRIA STIRS OPPOSITION (1933)

Two Jewish doctors fleeing the Hitlerian persecutions in Germany arrived in Damascus and have addressed a request to the Ministry of Hygiene for authorization to exercise their profession in Damascus.

This news has provoked great emotion in the city, above all within the association of doctors and pharmacists whose union will be meeting in the coming days to protest against "any hospitality to refugee Germans."

"Other physicians will arrive after the first two," they declared, "and the press has already anticipated following Baron Maurice de Rothschild's visit that it was a matter of 'placing' 200 doctors. There is no room for them in Syria."

"Nouvelle de Damas: Des médecins israélites allemands s'installent dans la capitale," *L'Orient* (June 13, 1933): 2.

THE ALLIANCE IN BAGHDAD AIDS THE FIRST JEWISH REFUGEES FROM GERMANY IN ITS MIDST AND TRIES TO RALLY COMMUNAL ACTION
(1934)

German Jewish Émigrés. We have a few of them in Baghdad. We have offered them help according to the limit of our means. Collections organized in our classes have provided some funds for them. A physician has been employed at the Wreis Elias Hospital at thirty a month plus room and board. A woman has been given employment as a nurse at the same hospital. A third individual, a chocolate manufacturer, I have put in touch with a member of our community in order to create a chocolate industry in Baghdad. This last individual, who is here with his wife, is already working and easily earning his livelihood. The authorities are according him all sorts of facilities because they are happy to see new industries being created in this country.[1] This gentleman, who has remained here at our advice, is actually happy and even considering bringing his parents to aid him in his work. He does not stop thanking the Alliance by name, which by its presence in Baghdad has facilitated his stay here and permitted him to remake his life. Others are continually coming, and their first footsteps are to the vicinity of our school.

I have just informed the President of our Community that it is incumbent upon us to create an assistance fund and to organize a special committee to deal with the question of these unfortunate émigrés. The President has just advised me that he has put the question on the agenda for the next meeting of the Communal Council.

I am chagrined to see that our large community, out of fear or indifference, has done nothing until now on this subject, while the small communities of Syria and Persia have done relatively more than it in these unhappy circumstances.

AIU Archives (Paris) Irak I.C.5, Extract from a report from the director of the Sassoon School, Baghdad, March 7, 1934, p. 2.

[1] Iraq had gained independence only two years before.

THE IRAQI GOVERNMENT INITIATES SEVERAL ANTI-JEWISH MEASURES (1934)

Anti-Jewish Movement. I am pained to inform you that for the last few months a movement of hostility against the Jews has been taking shape around us and is becoming more accentuated from day to day. It began with the more and more systematic dismissal of Jewish employees from government service. After tens of lower and middle senior employees, the secretary of the Ministry of Public Works and the Assistant Director of Posts and Telegraph, both Jews, were dismissed after so many others had been previously sacrificed. These continual dismissals have greatly alarmed our Community, which has met to study the situation and see in what measure it can react. Some have advised a mass protest; others have suggested the need to still remain silent. No solution was adopted and the situation remains unchanged.

2. Furthermore, in secondary and superior schools, a numerus clausus has been established for Jewish pupils, whose number may not exceed 10 percent of the non-Jewish students, even though the Jewish population of Baghdad (80,000) is one fourth of the total population.

3. Jewish businessmen would have sent funds to Palestine with the aim of undertaking certain commercial transactions. These transfers of money have encountered diverse opposition and multiple hindrances.

4. The Jewish newspapers from Palestine and Europe have been placed on the index and their entry into Iraq is forbidden. On the list is *The Jewish Chronicle, l'Univers Israélite,* and *Paix et Droit.* The result of this is that we are ignorant of everything going on in the Jewish world.

Sasson.

AIU Archives (Paris)
Irak I.C.3.
Report from the Baghdad School (October 3, 1934).

THE MARONITE PATRIARCH ISSUES A PASTORAL LETTER DEPLORING NAZI PERSECUTION OF THE JEWS
(1933)

His Beatitude the Maronite Patriarch has just published a pastoral letter, from which we cite the following passage, denouncing the Hitlerian persecutions:

> Hitler's Germany is hereby transgressing the teachings of the Christian faith. It is persecuting the unfortunate Jews whose sole crime is to be Jewish. Where then is the freedom of conscience that the Germans proclaim? It is rightful that we see our brother Catholics of all parties in the civilized world reproving Germany's attitude and testifying to their sympathy for the persecuted Jews. We associate ourselves with this good movement inspired by the Gospel. Let us not forget that the Jews are brethren in humanity, that God has chosen them to safeguard the faith in the unity of the Creator, that it was from the bosom of this people that there came forth Jesus Christ, the immaculate Mary, St. Joseph, St. John the Baptist, the apostles, the patriarchs, and the prophets. We pray God for the speedy deliverance of the Jews.

"Dans les communautés: Le Patriarche Maronite
et les persécutions hitlériennes,"
L'Orient (June 13, 1933): 2.

A POSITION PAPER BY LEBANESE AND SYRIAN JEWISH LEADERS AT THE TIME OF THE FRENCH-ARAB NEGOTIATIONS IN PARIS FOR TERMINATION OF THE MANDATES (1936)

Beirut, June 18, 1936

Negotiations are presently under way in Paris between the Syrian delegation and the French government for the purpose of concluding a Franco-Syrian treaty putting an end to the Mandate regime. What will the modalities of the future treaty be, and what will be the conditions for Syria's admission to the League of Nations, we still do not know. However, we learned from a generally well-informed source that the current negotiations are encountering a double difficulty: territorial delimitation of the State of Syria and protection of minority rights.

What interests us Jews in particular is that the future regime safeguard our rights and assure our security. Before examining in detail these two essential points—rights and security—let us look for a moment at how things presently appear.

The Syrian delegation demands from France a treaty that is identical to the one concluded between Great Britain and Iraq. Thus, it is on the basis of the Anglo-Iraqi treaty of June 30, 1930, that the negotiations in Paris are being conducted.

We objectively note that the latter does not include a single clause, or any allusion to the protection of minority rights. Later, at Great Britain's recommendation, Iraq was admitted to the League of Nations, in its capacity as a sovereign state. *We presume* that it was invited to make a simple unilateral declaration of terms according to which it would obligate itself to accord the national minorities exactly the same treatment and security which are accorded to the ethnic or national majority of the population as a whole.

It is probably a similar simple undertaking that some day or other Syria will take vis-à-vis the League of Nations, and the lot of the Jewish entities will thereby be regulated.

One cannot fault either Iraq or Syria if the minorities' protective net is not well constituted. It is the League of Nations itself that should be incriminated, because it is the League which has elaborated the special treaties providing for the protection of minorities in all the countries belonging to that body and who thereby come to be included in the Covenant.

You are certainly aware of the insufficient protection offered by the treaties presently in force and of the extremely long and complex procedure which the minorities have to adopt every time it is a question of obtaining their violated rights. It is unnecessary to cite examples because the Alliance

Israélite Universelle,[1] the traditional protector of the Jewish minorities, has had frequent occasion to intervene on their behalf and to appreciate the inefficacy of the system as it has been instituted by the League of Nations.

Our interest compels us, therefore, to go beyond this method and to ensure our defense by other more appropriate means. We do not believe that the League's Covenant opposes a direct and exclusive entente between two sovereign states, whereby one of them—in this instance, France—agrees to protect directly, effectively, and permanently, the Syro-Lebanese minorities by assuring to safeguard equally all of their rights. An explicit pact between two parties is worth more than a labyrinth of Genevan laws based upon collective security.

The day when we can count on immediate intervention by France, without any intermediary, is the day we will consider ourselves satisfied. In the event of the contrary, all our efforts should be exerted toward prolonging the period of liquidating the Mandate (that is, from the signing of the treaty until admission into the League of Nations).

This then is our immediate plan of action.

Let us return to the first part of our paper, because we must continue to take for granted that the negotiations are advancing very rapidly[2] and that soon Damascus will be cheering its delegates bearing the parchment of independence and liberty.

We do not believe that it is necessary to draw your attention to the situation of the Jews in the Muslim countries (North Africa, Yemen, Afghanistan, Iraq, etc.), to their (de facto) inferior position, which they occupy with regard to the other elements of the population, to the anti-Semitic persecutions to which they are subjected, or to the numerous attempts against their life, liberty, and goods.

You follow very closely these various vexations, and you are the better to judge them. However, as far as Syria and Lebanon in particular are concerned, the prejudices and animosities against the Jewish collectivities, far from ceasing, are growing from day to day.

Notwithstanding the French occupation, anti-Jewish demonstrations follow one another at an accelerated pace, assuming a dual aspect—nationalist and religious.

[1] The position paper was drafted by M. Penso, the director of Alliance schools in Beirut, together with leading Jewish communal leaders and is addressed to the president of the Alliance in Paris. See Penso's accompanying letter in AIU Archives (Paris) Liban I.C.1 (June 19, 1936). Penso makes clear that the document is to assist the Alliance in its lobbying efforts in Paris but asks that it not be "given the least publicity."

[2] The negotiations, which began in April, moved slowly until after May, when the new socialist government of Leon Blum came to power. See Stephen Hemsley Longrigg, *Syria and Lebanon under French Mandate* (London, New York, and Toronto, 1958), p. 222.

We know that the evolution of the Near Eastern peoples that has occurred since the armistice has provoked an awakening of Pan-Arabism and Pan-Islamism. These factors accentuate among the native elements the aggressive state against the minorities in general, and especially against the Jews, who are considered the weakest because they are without recognized protection.

In Damascus, where the Jewish community is plunged in complete misery and enjoys no influence with the local authorities, the Arabs do not hesitate to adopt a clearly aggressive attitude. No Jewish association can operate peacefully. The attacks of the Muslim population against the places where Jews gather can no longer be counted. Right in the heart of the Jewish Quarter, bloody incidents have frequently taken place.[3] On a vain pretext, the Arabs create agitation, sow terror to such a point that the police post installed in the heart of the Quarter to prevent disorders has not been able in many cases to control the situation.

In Aleppo, where the Jewish inhabitants occupy a situation which is relatively much better than that of Damascus, isolated troubles are recorded from time to time; isolated incidents, it is true, but all are also typical.

We shall say nothing of the towns of the Syrian interior, where Jews are rarely encountered. Our coreligionists who have to go to these villages for their business never stay for the night.

In Lebanon, one feels more sheltered perhaps, but the mood of overexcitement of people's feelings is almost continual.

Yet, France maintains in all of these territories forces which should impose security and assure the tranquillity of the minorities. We anxiously ask ourselves the question: What will be after the treaty is concluded and the transition period from the Mandate has expired?

All of these real threats which hover over the Jewish communities of Syria and Lebanon are increased by the danger of our close proximity to Palestine. The troubles which are erupting in that country have their direct repercussions here, and our situation is worsening to the point that we remain continually on the alert and in constant touch with the Mandatory authorities in order to prevent disorders.

We are annexing to the present report some extracts from the press, which amply prove the gravity of the situation and justify effective and permanent French protection, which is what we are requesting.[4]

It may be easily deduced, therefore, that urgent action before the competent authorities is required. It is a matter of our rights and our security.

Let us try to define them. The first article of the Mandatory Charter expressly stipulates that the organic statute will be prepared in agreement with the indigenous authorities, AND WILL TAKE INTO ACCOUNT the

[3] See Part One, p. 101.

[4] This annex has not been included here.

rights, interests, and WISHES of all the populations living in the said territories.[5]

If we make no claims, if we express no wishes, how can we force ourselves upon the attention of the French and Syrian negotiators? We are accorded an exceptional privilege, and out of modesty (or excess caution), we act as if we were ignoring it.

Here are the principal claims that we are making for the Jewish communities of Syria and Lebanon:

1. The same civil and political rights as those recognized for the other elements of the population without regard to birth, nationality, language, or race, whether they be Syrians or foreigners living in these territories.

2. The protection of their life, liberty, and also the free exercise of their religion both in public and private.[6]

3. The equal right to any of the other citizens to create, operate, and control charitable, religious, or social institutions, schools, or other educational establishments.

4. An equitable share in the distribution of subventions allocated by the State or the local administrations for educational, religious, or charitable purposes.

5. The free use of the Hebrew language whether in private life, religious matters, the press, or publications of any sort.[7]

6. The freedom from having to undertake any act incompatible with the sanctity of the Sabbath (testifying in court, etc.).

7. The maintenance of ritual slaughtering.[8]

8. Finally, no measure of discrimination may be taken with regard to us.[9]

It is impossible to foresee all the claims that we can rightfully formulate. We count on your competence and experience in the matter to complete finally these main wishes.

[5] This is an almost verbatim quote of Article One of the Mandatory Charter for Syria and Lebanon of July 24, 1922. For the full text of the document, see Longrigg, *Syria and Lebanon under French Mandate,* App. D, pp. 376–80.

[6] Under the stipulations of the document known as the Pact of ᶜUmar, Islamic society has traditionally tolerated the practice of Judaism, Christianity, and Zoroastrianism in private. Public manifestations, however, are not permitted. See Norman A. Stillman, *The Jews of Arab Lands: A History and Source Book* (Philadelphia, 1979), pp. 25–26, 158, passim.

[7] The use of Hebrew had been severely restricted in Syria for more than a decade by this time. Many Hebrew newspapers and other publications had been banned, and the use of Hebrew as the language of instruction in Jewish schools had been forbidden since 1923. See p. 274.

[8] The text of this clause has been amended in pen. It originally read: "Ritual slaughtering, known as Shehita, is under no circumstances to be prohibited or restrained."

[9] This clause has been entirely crossed out in pen in the original.

It is very good to safeguard our rights. It is better still to assure our protection. The constitutional guarantees are not worth as much as the guarantees resulting from a Franco-Syrian or Franco-Lebanese treaty which provides for the permanent presence of French troops and immediate intervention by occupying forces at the slightest infringement against the rights or life of the minorities.

It appears that the Syrian negotiators would be inclined to accept permanent control by France, even after the admission of Syria to the League of Nations, if, as they claim, this control would never have occasion to be made public.

This exposition has of necessity been summary, and we cannot by any means claim to have exhausted all the problems arising from the Problem of the Jewish minorities in Syria and Lebanon.

"Le problème des minorités juives en Syrie
et au Liban,"
typed report in the AIU Archives (Paris)
Liban I.C.1.

THE JEWISH COMMUNITY OF BEIRUT RECEIVES THE MARONITE PATRIARCH

(1937)

The Jewish community made a point of reserving a particularly grandiose reception for His Beatitude. Monsignor Arida was received by the Jews of Beirut with unequaled enthusiasm. Our demonstrations assumed a special character: we were, in effect, showing "the great friend of the Jews" our gratitude and our affection.

Thursday, April 22, will remain a historic day in the annals of the Beirut community.

The Jewish Quarter had been decorated with minute care. Flags with the Lebanese and French colors, palm branches, "parokhets,"[1] festoons, hangings, and carpets decorated the walls and main facades.

The entrance to the synagogue was decked with a magnificent triumphal arch. Our students, boys and girls, the scouts from the Alliance Israélite, and the Maccabee youth were lined up all along the street leading to the synagogue, forming a superb honor guard. Everyone admired their discipline and good conduct. On the rooftops of the neighboring buildings, clusters of people appeared as if suspended, while from the balconies, women threw flowers and trilled the traditional "you-you."[2]

Preceded by police motorcyclists, His Beatitude arrived at the synagogue at noon in the car of the President of the Lebanese Republic. Their Eminences the Maronite Bishops and Reverend Fathers accompanied the Patriarch. Our distinguished guests were received by our Chief Rabbi, the President and members of the Communal Council, and the Director of your (i.e., the Alliance) schools.

In the communal hall, Mr. Joseph D. Farhi delivered a beautiful speech in Arabic, the essentials of which were:

Beatitude,

The visit with which you are honoring the Jewish Community of Beirut today constitutes for us an historic event of the highest order. This is the first time that we are favored with the presence among us of the venerated head of the largest Christian community in the Near East, who is in our eyes the recognized and beloved head of all Lebanon, the spiritual father of all its inhabitants. You are, in effect, the very embodiment of the enlightened and fruitful patriotism which brings together all hearts and good wills for the greatest well-being of the country as a whole.

For us Jews, our attachment to this country is not of a recent date. It goes back thousands of years. . . . Time, far from weakening our attachment to the land we inhabit, has only strengthened our feelings of loyal devotion to Lebanon,

[1] Heb., *pārokhet,* the embroidered curtains hung before the ark in a synagogue.

[2] The reference is to the shrill ululating sounds made by women in the Middle East and North Africa to express joy. They are known in Arabic as *zaghāghīṭ*.

which in our own days, following the example of its glorious ally France, has known how to maintain in law and in fact a regime of liberty and equal justice for all citizens without distinction of race or confession.

This ideal of concord and brotherhood is especially characteristic of Your Beatitude, so much so that you have wished to see applied outside of Lebanon the principles of humanity and Christian charity which make you the defender of all who are oppressed and the supporter of the victims of hatred and intolerance. Our eyes well up and we remember ever gratefully Your Beatitude's famous pastoral letter addressing all the churches of the Orient, and eloquent protest against the persecutions of which our coreligionists are today the object in so-called civilized countries which want to bring the world back to paganism and barbarity.[3]

It is not only we, but world Jewry, indeed the civilized world that is infinitely grateful to you.

Monsignor Arida, visibly touched by the reception we had prepared for him, thanked the Chief Rabbi very warmly. . . . Then His Beatitude made declarations in favor of the Jews which were wildly applauded by the entire audience. . . . I reproduce those passages which I was able to retain:

The Jews are not only our ancestors, but our brothers. Our origin is the same, our language is almost common, our father is their father. We are proud to belong to the same race. We owe all to Judaism, our teachings are taken from their sacred law. Our faith is similar. We love the same God. We love Jerusalem as much as they do. We sincerely want that our relations with them will be constant and always fruitful. We assist each other and we hope with all our heart that God will deliver the oppressed Jews from those persecutions of which they are the object. We express our best wishes that all Jews will be assured of peace and tranquillity, because we feel how precious and sincere is their love for us.

His Eminence, Monsignor Ignace Mubarak, the Archbishop of Beirut, made a statement inspired by similar sentiments.

These declarations were greeted with thunderous applause and by cries of "Long live the Patriarch! Long live Lebanon!"

"Le voyage de Mgr Arida, patriarche maronite,"
Paix et Droit 17, no. 5 (1937): 8–9.

[3] For part of the text of the pastoral letter issued in 1933, see previous reading, p. 370.

THE TEN COMMANDMENTS OF THE EGYPTIAN JEWISH BOYCOTT OF AXIS GOODS
(1938)

1. Every time you are in a store, make it your duty to check the various items for an indication of the country of origin. The indication is ordinarily found marked on the object, the label, or the packaging.
2. Every article produced in Germany usually bears the mark: "Made in Germany: or "D.R.G." Every article produced in Italy regularly bears the mark "Made in Italy."
3. When you are certain of the German of Italian origin of an item, demand to see the owner, the director, or the department head. Let them witness your indignation; protest vigorously and insist upon these points:
   a. Why aren't these articles Egyptian-made, when it is the duty of all Egyptians and residents of the country to favor local industry?
   b. If the local industry does not produce similar items, why aren't they imported from friendly democratic countries?
   c. Point out how shameful it is in the present circumstances to favor trade with enemy countries.
4. Demand from your interlocutor the immediate suppression or replacement of the products from enemy nations.
5. Finally, leave without purchasing anything, declaring frankly that at no price would you buy what you need there, where the products of "aggressor" nations are sold.
6. Combat morally every wholesaler and every individual who does not comply with the boycott.
7. Advise members of LICA[1] when you know of flagrant cases that merit their intervention.
8. Always keep in mind that every piastre earned by the enemy increases the arms that they are forging for the war they wish to wage and augments the resources of their venomous propaganda of hate, falsehood, and diversion.
9. Remember that every piastre taken away from the aggressor countries is a blow that you are striking at those who are preparing a chain of slavery or death for you.
10. In the street, at home, during your leisure hours, everywhere and always, propagate the boycott and the Ten Commandments of the boycotter.

"Les Dix Commandements du Boycotteur," flier distributed in Cairo and Alexandria and published in the Egyptian Jewish press. Text in Maurice Mizrahi, *L'Egypte et ses Juifs: Le temps révolu (XIXe et XXe siècle)* (Geneva, 1977), Annexes, pp. 224–25.

[1] La Ligue Internationale Contre le Racisme et l'Antisémitisme. See Part One, p. 109.

ANTI-JEWISH DEMONSTRATIONS IN EGYPT ON THE PROPHET'S BIRTHDAY (1938)

Tanta, May 14, 1938

No. 110

Alliance Israélite Universelle

Paris

Subject: *Anti-Jewish Propaganda*

Mr. President,

I have the honor to bring the following to your attention:

You know from my previous letters that our Egyptian coreligionists have been the objects of anti-Jewish agitation during the demonstration by the theology students of the Azhar, who were protesting against the Partition of Palestine.[1] I added that strong measures were taken to stop this malevolent campaign, which is inexplicable, since the Egyptian Jews have always had the greatest attachment to this country and have not ceased to work for its prestige and development with all the means at their disposal.

On the occasion of the Prophet Muḥammad's birthday—the *mawlid al-Nabī*—processions were organized throughout all of Egypt. Taking advantage of these popular gatherings, an engineer from the Arsenal distributed anti-Jewish tracts. The Jews of Palestine, it was written there, are continually in conflict with the Arabs. They are assisted morally and financially by their coreligionists in this country. It is necessary for Muslims to boycott the Egyptian Jews who are in direct touch with their brothers in Palestine. This brochure was seized by the police, and the engineer who distributed it was taken into custody for questioning.

However, this arrest upset the Azharis, who, profitting from the Mawlid vacation, organized a demonstration yesterday morning after the religious ceremonies which took place at the Azhar University.

The demonstrators, who had at their head some Palestinian students, traversed the native quarters of Cairo with hostile cries against the Balfour Declaration and supporting Palestinian Arab claims. They moved in the direction of the Jewish Quarter in the Mousky[2] where a few minor scuffles took place. Since they refused to disperse despite the orders given by the authorities, the public force intervened and some of the demonstrators were arrested and held in police stations to be remanded to the Public Prosecutor.

Furthermore, in order to avoid an incident, significant police forces were posted in the Jewish Quarter of Cairo.

[1] The demonstrations had begun in April. See, for example, Nassi's detailed letter of April 29, 1938, in AIU Archives (Paris) Egypte I.C.27. The partition of Palestine had been suggested almost a year earlier by the Peel Commission.

[2] The Muskī is a quarter of Cairo containing Jewish and Christian neighborhoods. The Azhar lies right off its southeast boundary.

The most absolute calm reigns almost everywhere. However, anti-Jewish tracts were again distributed in Cairo, in the Ezbekiyya and Darb al-Aḥmar quarters.[3] The police were obliged to go ahead and make some arrests.

All of these facts constitute, one must admit, very serious symptoms. The Egyptian religious university youth is at this moment being worked upon without any doubt by foreign propaganda, which the Government's stringent investigation was quick to reveal. Let us point out that by a very significant coincidence, a similar demonstration was taking place in Beirut the same day.

Please accept, M. President, my expression of respect and devotion.

Nassi

AIU Archives (Paris)
Egypte I.C.27.

[3] Both quarters of Cairo. The Ezbekiyya lies just to the northwest of the Muskī and the Darb al-Aḥmar to the south of it.

AN ANTI-BRITISH AND ANTI-ZIONIST TRACT DISTRIBUTED IN TUNISIA (1934–1935)

A Manifesto to the Tunisian Nation on the State of Muslim Arab Palestine's Struggle for Freedom

In the Name of Allah, the Merciful, the Beneficent

O Muslim People!

Your society, the Muslim Young Men's Association, is grieved to inform you of the atrocities of the British government in Arab, Muslim Palestine, your sister-nation in Islam, in language, in feelings, in pain and hope; and thus she will always remain, if the Muslims will help her with financial and moral support.

This holy land has set the record for heroism, manliness, and courage in defending her rights, which have been violated, her legitimate goals, and her will to remain Arab and Islamic and not a haven for strangers, the refuse of the peoples.

. . . .

Here now, O people, is a report which was published by the Arab Women's Association in Jerusalem. It contains unimaginable atrocities. Let it touch your heart so that you will contribute funds.

1. The *zinzāna* is a narrow prison cell barely big enough for a man. The prisoner's food consists of a small crust of moldy bread and a little water.

2. Beating: They beat individuals with whips, hands and feet, until they faint, and their feet swell from the many blows. Then they place them under a cold shower to increase their agony.

3. Glass and nails: They force them to walk over pieces of glass and nails and make them jump on them. If they just stand, they beat them with whips. Then they cannot keep standing and fall, while blood flows from their feet, hands, and all the rest of their body until they collapse from exhaustion or lose consciousness. They then strip them of their clothes and beat them with wooden paddles studded with nails and the blood flows.

4. They tie their sexual organs with a cord that is attached to a pulley on the ceiling. Then they pull the cord little by little until the prisoners pass out. Often, they cut off the generative organs.

5. The fingernails and hair are pulled out with special pincers. They pull hair from mustaches and beards and pluck it from the head.

. . . (more of the same, including branding, electrical shocks, sexual assaults, etc.)

. . . .

O Zealous Muslim People!

These are only a fraction of the atrocities committed over the past thirteen centuries or more in a Muslim Arab land, namely Palestine, which must be redeemed.

We are addressing this manifesto to you, O people, hoping that you will aid Palestine with all of your strength and your tender feelings. You have already aided her in the past with more than 160,000 francs in addition to private contributions. This is a small amount compared to the donations sent by the Tunisian Zionists to the Zionists of Palestine for land purchases and to strengthen the Zionist movement. And what power is greater than that of money in this age?

Do you not know, O noble people, that in Palestine there are 18,000 orphans looking for assistance and crying out to the Islamic world? So help them, help them!

The Muslim Young Men

Jamᶜiyyat al-Shubbān al-Muslimīn, *Bayān lil-Umma al-Tūnisiyya ᶜan Ḥālat Filasṭīn al-ᶜArabiyya al-Mujāhida* (Tunis, 1353, A.H.).

REPERCUSSIONS FROM THE ARAB GENERAL STRIKE IN PALESTINE UPON DAMASCENE JEWRY

(1936)

Damascus, May 19, 1936

The events in Palestine have had their repercussion in Damascus. For several days, all the Jewish population lived in anguish.

The first incidents broke out in the Jewish Quarter immediately after the Passover holiday. Some young men of the plebeian class from the neighboring Arab Quarter would daily accost Jewish women and girls.

The ringleaders sought to work up all of public opinion against the Jews of Damascus. Calumnies were spread throughout town by the press and by means of posters. The worst one of which the Jews were accused just recently, and which could have had disastrous consequences, was the charge that they sold poisoned chocolate and bonbons to Muslims and caused the death of several Muslim children. The most serious newspapers spread this false report.

Incidents could not fail to break out. Jews were savagely beaten in the streets. A Jewish doctor whose clinic is situated in the Arab Quarter was assaulted by a Muslim woman who tried to kill him. When brought to the police station, she declared to the superintendent of police that she wanted to take revenge "because the Jews in Palestine are killing Muslims."

The leaders of the Community, alarmed by this grave situation, appealed to M. Fauquenot, Counsellor for the Interior, who intervened on behalf of the Jews and demanded that the local authorities install a police post in the Jewish Quarter.

The members of the Community, in order to calm public opinion which was overagitated by the events in Palestine as well as by the false accusations, appealed also to M. Fakhrī Bey al-Barūdī, assembly deputy and leader of the Nationalists. The latter issued the following statement to the population:

> There are people in this country who do not fear God, who have been corrupted and betray their homeland. They weave intrigues and spread mendacious rumors in order to sow discord among the citizens of a single nation. They accuse the Jews of having placed in the streets poisoned chocolates and bonbons. This rumor has no foundation. Whoever hears such noises has an obligation to silence the intriguers who are spreading them and to conduct them to the nearest police station so that they might receive the punishment they deserve.
>
> On this occasion, I ask all my fellow citizens to watch over their Jewish compatriots who have no relation with Zionism and reject it. The Jews of Damascus live with us, share our rights and our duties. Everyone should look after them just as one looks after oneself.

This statement, which was published by all the newspapers and posted in all the streets, has produced a profound impression. For a week now, calm has returned to people. Jews have gone back to work. They believe that they should not suffer from all these false accusations which have caused so much innocent blood to be spilled in the course of centuries past.

"La répercussion des événements de Palestine en Syrie," *Paix et Droit* 16, no. 5 (May 1936): 8.

AN ANTI-JEWISH PAMPHLET DISTRIBUTED BY ARAB MILITANTS IN CAIRO
(OCTOBER 1938)

O Young Men,
Towards the revolution . . .
In Palestine today monstrous slaughterings are being carried out by the English and the Jews, the enemies of Islam. . . . The English soldiers and the Jewish police are violating the Mosque of Omar . . . and they are destroying its dome and walls. The Arabs are threatened with extinction in the Holy Land as a result of this savage torture and mutilation for which humanity can show no precedent. . . .

O Moslem and Christian youths alike:
The jihad (holy war) on behalf of Palestine has become a sacred and holy obligation. . . . Your duty in this severe affliction is to make of the Palestine revolution a general revolution whose flames will spread to Egypt and burn up the English and the Jews, the opponents of the Arabs and Islam.

O Youth of the University:
Proclaim an implacable strike. . . .

O Merchants:
Boycott the English and the Jews. . . .

O Politicians:
. . . Tear up the unjust treaties. . . . Compare democratic England in Palestine with dictatorship Germany in the Sudetenland, and know that the foremost enemies of Islam are the English, the catspaws of the Jews, the lowest race on earth.

O Egyptians:
To the Palestinian arena, where your brethren, the fighters in the jihad, are raising the standards of God in striking and majestic manner.

O Youths:
TO THE REVOLUTION
Either a victory which raises up God's word, or a martyrdom for which there is an immortal reward. . . .

English translation of an Arabic pamphlet in *The Egyptian Gazette* (October 29, 1938), quoted in Gudrun Krämer, *Minderheit, Millet, Nation? Die Juden in Ägypten 1914–1952.* Studien zum Minderheitenproblem im Islam, 7 (Wiesbaden, 1982), p. 293.

THE AMERICAN CHARGÉ D'AFFAIRES IN BAGHDAD REPORTS ON THE REPERCUSSIONS OF THE PALESTINIAN ARAB GENERAL STRIKE FOR IRAQI JEWS
(1936)

LEGATION OF THE
UNITED STATES OF AMERICA
Baghdad, October 14, 1936

No. 708—Diplomatic
Subject: Anti-Jewish Agitation in Iraq
CONFIDENTIAL

The Honorable
The Secretary of State
Washington, D.C.

Sir:

I have the honor to refer to the Legation's telegram No. 23 of October 14, 1 P.M., and to report that on Thursday, October 8, 1936, another Jew was murdered in Baghdad, allegedly by a Moslem.

Baghdad papers were forbidden to report the incident, but it is generally believed that a Moslem who had been outbid in a government contract by a Jewish competitor took advantage of the tension between the Jewish and Moslem communities of Baghdad to settle a personal grudge, and at the same time to eliminate competition in future bids for contracts.

After the murder, several Jews called on the Prime Minister, Yasin Pasha al-Hashimi, and asked for police protection for Jewish families. Extra detachments of police were stationed in the Jewish quarter of Baghdad, and also in quarters inhabited by both Jews and Christians.

Simultaneously, Sassoon Khadduri, Grand Rabbi of Baghdad, issued a statement, a copy of which is annexed hereto as Enclosure No. 1, announcing that the Jewish community of Baghdad does not support the Zionist movement in Palestine.[1] Although this announcement was well received, by Moslem papers, its value is doubtful in allaying the antagonism already aroused.

The day following the publication of the Grand Rabbi's statement, a group of Jews called upon him and protested against something. Moslems interpreted the protest as being against the Grand Rabbi's statement, and even intimated that the group insisted that Baghdad Jews do, in fact, support the Zionist movement in Palestine. The Grand Rabbi's following, however,

[1] See the document that follows immediately below.

is quite positive that the group protested against the anti-Jewish agitation in Baghdad. Possibly both versions are correct.

On Monday, October 12, 1936, services were held in the mosques of Baghdad to commemorate the miraculous ascent of the Prophet, Mohammed, to heaven on the equally miraculous steed, al-Boraq.[2] For the first time, apparently, Christians were invited to attend such services, and it was announced that after suitable prayers, speakers would "explain" the Palestinian situation.

Between the time when the services were announced, however, and the time when the people assembled in the mosques, the announcement was made that the Palestinian strike had been settled. Consequently, the following morning "The Iraq Times" announced that the meetings had been held for the purpose of celebrating the end of the strike—a manifest absurdity since the meetings were called before the strike was settled.

A Christian eyewitness who attended two of the meetings reports that the services were inoffensive and devoid of political implications. The same eyewitness further reports that both meetings were well attended by police observers in plain clothes; and it is not improbable that an order from the Government was more effective in rendering the meetings innocuous than the settlement of the Palestinian strike.

On October 13, 1936, another Jew was murdered on the streets of Baghdad, and a Christian has been arrested and accused of his murder. Unconfirmed (and probably unreliable) rumors are afloat that three other Jews have been killed in Baghdad, one in Basrah, and one in Hillah.

Yesterday morning, October 14, 1936, a Jew mounted a chair in front of a coffeehouse in Exchange Square, the busiest corner in Baghdad, and, after recounting the discrimination from which Jews suffer, exhorted his listeners, who were in the majority Jewish, to do something about it. About this time a Moslem stepped up and slapped the speaker's face, and a street fight immediately ensued between Moslem and Jewish bystanders. No arms were used, and there were no casualties. Police were called and order was quickly restored.

All Jewish shops, both in the bazaar and elsewhere, were immediately closed as a protest, and are still closed.

If the Government permits certain anti-Jewish Moslem agitators, notably Saʿīd Thābit, to continue their work, and if the Jewish community maintains its present belligerent frame of mind, further trouble is an eventuality which cannot be entirely eliminated. There is no present indication, however, that the present situation will develop into any serious conflict between the two communities.

[2] Ar., *al-Burāq*. Concerning this mythical creature, see R. Paret, "al-Burāḳ," *EI*[2] 1: 1310–11.

As of possible interest to the Department, there are enclosed herewith suggested translations of a communication and its annexure which was addressed to the Legation on September 19, 1936, two days after the murder of the Jews reported in Despatch No. 707—Diplomatic.[3]

Respectfully yours,
James S. Moose, Jr.
Chargé d'affaires ad interim

National Archives (Washington) Department of State
RG 59 980G.4016
Jews/12.

[3] The two items, not included here, are letters by Saʿīd Thābit, president of the Palestine Defense Committee, to the American representative and the British ambassador in Iraq, protesting anti-Arab atrocities in Palestine.

A PUBLIC DECLARATION BY THE HEAD OF IRAQI JEWRY DISASSOCIATING HIMSELF AND HIS COMMUNITY FROM ZIONISM AT THE TIME OF THE ARAB GENERAL STRIKE IN PALESTINE

(1936)

In order to clear away any doubts and prejudices against the Jews of Iraq with regard to the Zionist movement, and in order to make known the bare truth in respect to this issue, I find it incumbent upon me to make the following announcement in the name of the Jewish community in Iraq:

The whole body of the Jewish community in Iraq has no connection with the Zionist movement and is in no way related to any of its Zionist institutions or activities. It never helps or sponsors this movement whether within or outside Palestine. The Jews of Iraq are Iraqis, bound to the people of Iraq, and they participate with their brethren, the Iraqis, in their times of prosperity and trial. They are animated by the same feelings, sympathize with the Iraqis in their difficulties, and share their affections.

I have issued this announcement to make known the truth.[1]

Sassoon Khadduri
Chief of the Jewish Community in Baghdad.

National Archives (Washington) Department of State
RG 59 890G.4016 Jews/12, Enclosure No. 1 to
Despatch No. 708—Diplomatic, October 13, 1936.

[1] This declaration was published in the newspaper *al-Istiqlāl* (October 8, 1936).

A BOMB IN THE JEWISH QUARTER OF SIDON AND A SABOTAGE ATTEMPT AGAINST JEWISH PROPERTY (1938)

Mr. Isaac Diwan, a Jew and longtime wholesaler in Beirut, has lived for several years in Saida,[1] where he opened a currency exchange. His prosperous business permitted him to amass gradually a large fortune.

A Failed Attempt

Walking the day before yesterday in a field recently acquired by him, Mr. Diwan wanted to visit the plot where an electric motor had been installed to operate a small nearby noria.[2]

During his inspection, his eyes fell upon a small cord, at the end of which were attached two sticks of dynamite. The fuse cord, which had been lit by a murderous hand, had gone out by itself on account of the dampness. Mr. Diwan ran immediately to notify the police at the nearby station.

The Police on the Scene

The police immediately encircled the area and opened an investigation. They took prints found on the spot and photographed the site.

Interrogated, Mr. Diwan declared that he suspected a certain Aḥmad al-Harārī, a gardener formerly in his employ, who could well have set the charge in order to get even with his ex-employer.

A Bomb in the Jewish Quarter

Around nine in the evening of the same day, an unusual noise put all of the city's Jewish Quarter into a panic.

An individual, who has still not been identified, taking advantage of the darkness and seeing no passersby in the area, threw a bomb into the entrance of the Jewish Quarter. All of the windows of the nearby buildings were shattered, and in an instant, all of the Quarter was topsy-turvy.

The police were on the scene at once and succeeded only with difficulty in restoring calm.

An investigation was opened to discover the perpetrator of the attack.

* * * * * *

[1] The Arabic name of Sidon.

[2] Ar., *nāʿūra,* "waterwheel."

In the wake of these two incidents, permanent patrols were set up in order to prevent any possible disorder.

People are busy conjecturing as to the reasons for these two attempts. The investigators are asking themselves among other things whether these attempts ought to be considered isolated or, on the contrary, whether a direct correlation ought to be established between them.

We have learned only a short while ago that the Public Prosecutor of the Republic of Southern Lebanon has just signed several arrest warrants for various individuals suspected of involvement in the affair.

"Une bombe éclate dans le quartier juif de Saida sans
causer de victimes," Le Jour (July 16, 1938).
Clipping in AIU Archives (Paris)
Liban I.C.4.

SOBER THOUGHTS ABOUT THE CAUSES OF THE ANTI-JEWISH INCIDENTS IN SIDON AND ABOUT THE UNCERTAINTY OF THE FUTURE

(1938)

TERRORIST CAPRICES IN LEBANON?

On July 14, at approximately 9 o'clock in the evening, a bomb was thrown in the Jewish Quarter. There were no victims. Elsewhere, an infernal machine was placed that day in a garden belonging to a well-known Jewish banker, Mr. Isaac Diwan.

The Jewish population of Sidon feels a legitimate nervousness, in spite of the standing police forces that have been set up since the attack in the Jewish Quarter for its protection against any eventuality.[1]

Should one see in these events a repercussion from the Palestinian terrorism in a town situated 40 km from the Palestinian frontier, an important center of contraband arms, which affords active assistance in men and material to the insurgents?

It seems legitimate to think so. Let us recall that in May 1936, when the Palestinian tragedy was only in its early stages with more violence than at present, demonstrations were taking place all through the streets of Sidon, roaring that imbecilic slogan "Palestine is our country, the Jews are our dogs." Attempts were made to put an end to the Jewish Quarter. Jews were attacked in the streets; stones were thrown at Jewish homes and shops and at the Alliance School, breaking windows and injuring youngsters in their classes. The merchants have been partially boycotted for two years now.

Lately, anonymous letters have been sent to Christian hotel owners in Djezzine, an important country resort near Sidon, threatening them with reprisals if they rent their facilities to Palestinian Jewish vacationers.

For the past ten consecutive days following the major attack in Haifa, attributed by the Arab and the English press to the Revisionist Jews, in which there were more than 120 dead and wounded, part of the Lebanese Arabic press—*al-Maqshūf* in particular, which has devoted a special issue of its weekly to the Jews that is entirely Hitlerian in inspiration—has been attacking the Lebanese Jews in the most vehement terms.

Merely terrorist caprices easily checked—or the beginning of a strong, organized Judeophobic movement, supported by foreign countries and calling for increasing expansion?

Tomorrow will tell.

A. Rahmany
Director of the Alliance Israélite School

AIU Archives (Paris)
Liban I.C.4.

[1] See the Lebanese newspaper report of these two incidents in the preceding text.

AN EGYPTIAN JEWISH NEWSPAPER COMMENTS ON A RISING WAVE OF ANTI-SEMITIC AGITATION IN EGYPT
(1939)

It is no longer possible to pass over in silence or to take lightly the anti-Jewish agitation which is taking place in Egypt. In the space of two weeks, four bombs have been left in front of synagogues and Jewish homes: one in Cairo another in Mansourah, the third in al-Mahalla, and the fourth in Asyut.

During this time, four newspapers (one in French and three in Arabic), as well as a party called "The Youth Party,"[1] are openly conducting a violent anti-Jewish propaganda campaign on Egyptian soil.

As a matter of fact, the results of this mischievous action are rather meager, at least up till now. The Egyptian, with his characteristic good sense, detects all that is false and artificial in this frenzied agitation carried on by a few unconscionable and unscrupulous individuals who are seeking the limelight or to make their living in this fashion for want of more honest means.

People should not, therefore, become unduly alarmed. They represent in all half a percent of the total population of the country (70,000 out of 14 million). Their role in the press is almost nil in contrast to the Syrians, who occupy the primary place.[2] In commerce, they do no not come near the position of the Greeks, the English, and the Italians. In banking, they are surpassed by the French. Even in industry, they come, if our information is correct, after the Egyptians.

None of the reasons that allowed the spread of anti-Semitism in other countries come together here. Another point that is important to raise: The Jews do not constitute here the only element which is differentiated from the majority of the inhabitants of the country. In Germany, Italy, Poland, and Hungary, there are more or less only Germans, Italians, Poles, Hungarians, and Jews. Such is not the case in Egypt, a cosmopolitan country par excellence, where the Copts, the Syrians, and even the Greeks and Italians are ever so much more numerous than the Jews.

Furthermore, it would be a great misunderstanding to think that those who are conducting this anti-Jewish agitation really have the Jews as the targets. The Jews, in the end, are only a pretext for reaching a much more important goal. This goal will be understood more easily when one sees who is hiding behind these agitators, who, in fact, are simply acting as puppets with others skillfully pulling the strings.

[1] There were several paramilitary youth parties. The reference here is probably to Miṣr al-Fatāt.

[2] From its very beginnings in the nineteenth century, the Egyptian press was dominated by Syrian Christians.

Nothing could be simpler than to know the true authors of this pernicious agitation. It suffices to look first of all at the method in order to recognize immediately the mark of origin. The method is the lie and the calumny.

A certain Shaykh has published a brochure on the Jews which was reproduced with the sort of haste one might imagine for all these anti-Jewish sheets. This brochure, naturally, accuses the Jews of all the misdeeds on earth, and among other things, of controlling all the cinemas and dancing establishments (what misdeeds!) of the country. One cabaret is even mentioned by name—the Kit Kat of Cairo. However, if the Jews run nightclubs, just as they run commercial establishments, it is thanks to their work, their spirit of initiative, and their money. As for the Kit Kat, there is no one who does not know that it belongs to a Greek.

. . . .

We have before us examples of certain anti-Jewish canards which have appeared for some time in Egypt. Strangely enough, the arguments . . . curiously resemble one another. Even stranger still, these arguments bear a curious resemblence to those developed in Germany in the Hitlerian *Stürmer* and *Weltdienst*, as well as those published in Italy in the Fascist *Tevere* and *Difensa della Razza*.

Draw your own conclusion. One can see where these individuals got their inspiration. One sees as well where they get their orders. Who profits by this maladroit agitation?

Certainly not Egypt. Egypt in the midst of the process of development needs the union and concord of all its inhabitants. And these sad specimens sow hatred and disunion.

Not the Arab and Islamic countries. They have no greater enemy than the Nazis and the Fascists who have destroyed Abyssinia, enslaved Libya, annexed Albania, and harbor the blackest designs for the countries of the Near East, notably against Egypt. These gentlemen do not make a peep about the aggression and ambitions of the Hitler-Fascists, but they make a great hue and cry when an unfortunate refugee tries to enter Palestine.

. . . .

We repeat: WE DO NOT FEAR ANTI-SEMITISM IN EGYPT. For the reasons we have outlined above, we believe moreover THAT IT IS IMPOSSIBLE TO CREATE A SPECIFICALLY ANTI-JEWISH MOVEMENT IN THIS COUNTRY.

But by sowing the wind, one ends up by reaping the whirlwind. This whirlwind would be a general xenophobia touching everyone, bringing discord, disunity, and hatred, of which Egypt would be the greatest victim. The tactic of sowing hatred and discord is indeed pursued by the Hitlerian-Fascists in all the democratic countries to better divide and weaken them.

We are convinced that every Egyptian, every sincere friend of Egypt, envisages such an eventuality with horror. Those who at this moment hold the governance of the country in their hands and whom we know to be conscientious and proven patriots certainly desire this less than anyone else.

Therefore, let them act, and let them act speedily.

L.T.J.I., "Agitation anti-juive: Quatre bombes en deux semaines," *La Tribune Juive* (July 26, 1939): 1–2.

A PLEA TO THE FRENCH AUTHORITIES FOR PROTECTION IN THE WAKE OF ANTI-JEWISH INCIDENTS IN BEIRUT
(1939)

Beirut, July 27, 1939

(Copy for the President of the Alliance Israélite)

TO HIS EXCELLENCY MONSIEUR PUAUX
AMBASSADOR OF FRANCE, HIGH COMMISSIONER OF THE FRENCH REPUBLIC
IN SYRIA AND LEBANON.

IN TOWN

Excellency,

I have the honor to draw your benevolent attention to the following:

You have learned that during the night yesterday, Wednesday, the 26th, at approximately 2:30, an unknown person threw a bomb at our school and disappeared without anyone being able to stop him. Very fortunately we have recorded only light physical damages. You also know that Mr. Jamāl al-Ḥusaynī, a member of the Arab Supreme Committee of Palestine and nephew of the Mufti of Jerusalem, Ḥājj Amīn al-Ḥusaynī, declared a few months ago at the Arab Congress in Cairo that if the Arabs of Palestine do not succeed in obtaining from the English authorities the realization of their national claims, they will attack the Jews residing in the Arab countries.

It appears that they are putting these threats into execution. Already bombs have been hurled on three occasions in the synagogues of Cairo and Mansourah,[1] and now they are attacking the Jews of Beirut.

The two bombs thrown in the space of two days, in the Jewish Quarter and at our school buildings, have sown panic among our coreligionists.

In their name and in the name of the Alliance Israélite, I am allowing myself to make an appeal to the leading representative of France, our secular Protectress, and beg Your Excellency to please take the necessary measures for protecting us against the machinations of these misguided men, unknown to us, who are so savagely making attempts upon our lives and property.

We here all know that as long as the French flag flies over our heads, we can count upon your help and your protection. We likewise know that the personal interest you take in the fortunes of all the minorities who live in the country will cause you to follow up this supplication favorably.

Please accept, Excellency, the expression of my highest regards together with my respectful homage.

E. Penso
Director of the Alliance Israélite
Schools in Beirut

AIU Archives (Paris)
Liban I.C.1.

[1] See p. 393.

AN ALGERIAN MUSLIM WARNS THAT EVENTS IN PALESTINE THREATEN MUSLIM-JEWISH RELATIONS IN ALGERIA
(1938)

But alas! We greatly fear that this lull is only on the surface.[1] The situation could change from one moment to the next, so difficult are the prejudices to destroy. We fear that affairs in Palestine contain the ferment of discord, a germ for war between the Muslims and the Jews of the world.

Arab agitation in Palestine is supported, as everyone knows, by the Supreme Arab Committee, creator and instrument of Pan-Arabism. Now, this essentially revolutionary Committee has branches in North Africa, branches which are, moreover, very active and enterprising. If the partition of Palestine is achieved, the Arab nationalists will not accept the fait accompli and will turn against the Jews of Palestine first and then against all those in the Islamic countries. The Pan-Arab organizations of North Africa would not be able to do otherwise than to conform, should the occasion arise, to the orders of the Supreme Arab Committee, formally the Syro-Palestinian Committee, and the difficulties would certainly begin again.[2]

R. Zenati, "La question juive: le problème algérien vu par un indigène," *Renseignements Coloniaux,* no. 6 (May–June 1938): 122.

[1] That is, the lull after the Constantine pogrom of 1934.

[2] The writer gives a somewhat misleading impression here that the Syro-Palestinian Committee merely evolved into the Supreme (or Higher) Arab Committee, whereas it was only a forerunner of the latter.

LIBYA'S ITALIAN FASCIST NEWSPAPER EXPLAINS A GOVERNMENT ORDINANCE BANNING SHOPKEEPERS FROM CLOSING ON THE SABBATH (1936)

The commission's ordinance is putting an end to an anachronism. Modern Tripoli, "European Tripoli," was entirely built by the Italians, for a pace of life no different from that of the most advanced cities in Italy. The Jewish shopkeepers came out from behind the ancient walls and took over the new high streets. They took over the best business locations in the area and set up new shops and outlets for businesses in the souk. This is all very well. Anything which stimulates local trade can only be welcome. But the anachronism was that the new modern Italian city on certain days of the week took on the appearance of a Jewish city, such as, let us say, Tel Aviv. That was what Corso Vittorio Emanuele—the former Via Azizia—looked like on Saturdays. Many of the shops were tightly bolted, ignoring the needs of the population. On November 27, 1935, the Governor-General had issued an ordinance to eliminate the absurd competition by which the shops would be open on Sundays. That is the day when shops run by Italians, in respect for the law regarding holidays, must be closed.[1]

The present ordinance is the logical consequence of the earlier one, and was taken as the final step to complete it. . . . Those Jews who are intelligent must have understood already that the first ordinance would lead to the second. . . . If this progress is not feasible in certain strata, never mind; there is a place for everyone. The refractory ones can stay inside the old walls, from which they have emerged before acquiring the flexibility necessary to follow the new rhythm. The old city and souks preserve the old, traditional local habits in trade. . . . Even the most inflexible old people have a right to exist. But the old city is there precisely for them. They can certainly not presume to make their mark on the Tripoli which the Italians have built from scratch. Through sacrifice and determination, and the completely new neighborhoods which they have brought into being, New Tripoli must live to the full. It must follow our own rhythm. The new Tripoli, a doubly Italian city, must remain purely Italian. Tripoli is not Tel Aviv.

L'avvenire di Tripoli (November 5, 1936),
quoted in Renzo de Felice, *Jews in an Arab Land: Libya, 1835–1970,*
trans. Judith Roumani (Austin, 1985), pp. 161–62.

[1]The original ordinance of 1935 only required that all shops in the new city close on Sundays. It did not, however, prohibit them from closing on other days as well. See Renzo de Felice, *Jews in an Arab Land: Libya, 1835–1970,* trans. Judith Roumani (Austin, 1985), p. 160.

TWO TRIPOLITANIAN JEWS ARE PUBLICLY WHIPPED FOR DEFYING THE GOVERNMENT'S BAN AGAINST SATURDAY SHOP CLOSING

(1939)

I
An Egyptian Jewish Press Account

We have largely reproduced in our last issues letters from our correspondents in Libya on the frightful events that have been unfolding recently in Tripoli. . . . The reports received and published have all been entirely confirmed and we were able yesterday to obtain from the highest authorized source the poignant details which deeply pain us as well as arouse our indignation, anti-Jewish acts which have taken place in a colony of Fascist Italy and which appear to be the first result of the Italo-German rapprochement.

It is known that the decree of the Governor General was promulgated during the first days of December. He formally forbade Muslim and Jewish merchants in the new city to close on any day other than Sunday, which clearly meant that the Muslims and Jews had to open on the day which is according to their religion and tradition holy for them.[1]

Serious corporal punishment would deter an infraction.

On Saturday, December 5, most of the Jewish shops remained closed despite the authorities' express orders. The Jewish merchants could still not believe that liberal Italy would allow itself to carry out such an inhuman procedure to force them to bend before its laws. Unfortunately, that was indeed the case. Two and three days later 92 Jewish merchants exactly were thrown into prison, and several of them had their license to conduct business taken away. . . . Three Italian Jews were condemned to be publicly whipped at once for having replied to the court that their religious convictions forbade them to work on a sacred day like the Sabbath.

L'Avvenire di Tripoli, which unceasingly wages a hate campaign against the Jews, did not conceal its enthusiasm for the decision.

We have reported that administration functionaries were charged with announcing the sentence in every corner of the city. It took place on Tuesday, December 8, at 2:30 P.M. in the public square near the Tobacco Company.

Thousands of people responded to the authorities' invitation. . . . A battalion of mounted carbinieri had great difficulty in containing the diverse movements of the crowd.

[1] The reference to the Muslim holy day here means Friday, which is a day of communal prayer that takes place at noon. It is not a day of rest in the same sense as the Sabbath, since the Koran specifically permits the believers to return to business

A few moments before being conducted to the place of punishment, one of the condemned, Benedetto Meghedesc, saw his sentence commuted to three months' imprisonment, after the government physician had noted the deplorable state of the poor man's health. The two others, Sion Barda, age 40, father of seven and considered one of the leading merchants of the country, and Saul Nhais, 26 and also married, were trembling so at the idea of such a degrading and cruel punishment that they were dragged more than led before the backwards mob which applauded nonstop.

The condemned were forcibly made to lie face down on the ground. Then a Muslim Arab, whose face was hooded and who held a long whip, beat them by turns while the crowd followed with shouts of encouragement.

This ordeal was terrible for the condemned. Sion Barda could not resist the blows he received and lost consciousness. His unfortunate comrade experienced a nervous shock so profound that he had to be transported immediately to a hospital. There is fear for his sanity. His wife, who was present at the punishment and was in a family way, had a miscarriage upon hearing the wrenching cries of her poor husband.

These truly barbaric actions have had their repercussions in all Jewish circles, particularly in North Africa and the Near East. The Muslims of Tunis were as revolted as the Jews and could not conceal their great indignation; Arab nationalist circles have addressed a moving complaint to the League of Nations.

In Palestine, the leaders of the Jewish National Council have energetically renewed their representations to the Italian Consul General, Count Mazzolini. . . .

In Egypt, the Jewish community has followed the events in Tripoli with sustained interest, and even among the local Italian Jews who wholeheartedly support Fascist policy, it is rare to find anyone who has not expressed his deep disgust at these actions.

Can one still hope that the Fascist government will see the useless injustice of which Tripolitanian Jewry, which has time and again given proofs of its loyalty, is the victim? And will it revoke in time these measures which it has put into law and which even Germany in all its barbarity has not enacted?

S.S.,[2] "A Tripoli, Colonie de l'Italie Fasciste et liberale! Les deux Juifs flagellés publiquement sont dans un état critique," Israël (January 26, 1937): 1, 4.

---

after worship (Sura 62:10). See S. D. Goitein, "The Origin and Nature of the Muslim Friday Worship," in *Studies in Islamic History and Institutions* (Leiden, 1966), pp. 111–25.

[2] Perhaps S. Shaool, who wrote for *Israël* during this period.

II
An Italian Fascist Press Account

Yesterday, in the early afternoon, following the fruitless attempt at rebellion against the hierarchy, of which we spoke in Monday's *Avvenire di Tripoli*, on the part of a minority of the local Jewish population, in the square in front of the Tobacco Factory, just and timely punishment was meted out to some of the most typical of the malefactors. In accordance with the law, the regulations, and local custom regarding the subject in relation to the Libyan indigenous population, ten strokes of the *kurbash*[3] were given to two disobedient Jews, Sion Barda fu Abramo and Nhaisi Sual di Nessin. A third, Benedetto Meghidesc fu Vittorio, who had been determined by medical examination to be unfit for the punishment due, was exempted: his punishment has been changed to three months' imprisonment.

With exceptional clemency, a punishment which was moral rather than material in nature was provided for: those punished, in fact, experienced hardly any physical harm from the flogging, which had an important meaning as an example. The public event naturally attracted to the square and its surroundings a large crowd composed of metropolitans,[4] Arabs, and even, for the record, some Jews.

It should also be said for the record that a German Jew living in Tripoli who had been expelled from Tunisia shouted "Cowards!" at the Arabs present.

This Jew, a certain Wolfgang Pinner, was immediately handcuffed and taken to the Prison together with the Jews who had been punished and with whom he had inappropriately expressed his rash solidarity.

There is no need to add that the entire population of Libya received the administration of justice yesterday with the most complete, absolute, and legitimate satisfaction.

Excerpt from *L'Avvenire di Tripoli*
(December 8, 1936) in Renzo de Felice
Jews in an Arab Land: Libya, 1835-1970,
trans. Judith Roumani (Austin, 1985), p. 353, n. 78.

[3] For Turk. *kirbac,* originally a leather whip, but here apparently a long rod.
[4] That is, the Italian colonists.

A LETTER FROM THE PRESIDENTS OF THE JEWISH COMMUNITIES OF CAIRO AND ALEXANDRIA TO THE EGYPTIAN PRIME MINISTER
(1938)

Cairo, May 17, 1938

His Excellency
The President of the Council of Ministers[1]
Cairo.

Excellency,

In the name of the Jews of Egypt, represented by the two communities of Cairo and Alexandria, we are addressing to you our heartfelt thanks for the benevolent interest which you have kindly taken in the Palestine Question which preoccupies the Muslim world to such a high degree, even as it does the Jewish world.

Like Your Excellency, we are convinced that, whatever will be the solution of this problem, it will not be complete and lasting unless it is solidly based upon a cordial and sincere understanding that precludes any cause for misunderstanding and gives above all full and complete satisfaction on the subject of the Holy Places, concerning which, moreover, there has never been a question at any time and in any place of violating in any way whatsoever, as has been declared many a time. Once again, we are authorized by all to proclaim this loudly and formally.

Living in a blessed land, which is essentially Muslim, we know how precious is the fraternal understanding that unites all its children without distinction, irregardless of the religion to which they belong. Would that the inhabitants of Palestine, whatever their faith, were able to understand, through the example of their Egyptian neighbors, that only a loyal cooperation can constitute the basis of a happy and prosperous life where all collaborate with a single heart for the progress and grandeur of a common homeland.

It is, therefore, with confidence in your wisdom that we hope that calm will soon return among people, and we are assured that, thanks to your wise intervention, it will not be long before an overall peace will reign everywhere.[2]

[1] Muḥammad Maḥmūd.

[2] The Egyptian government was at this time attempting to mediate between the British and the Palestinians. In fact, on the very day this letter was written, Prime Minister Maḥmūd and chief of the Royal Cabinet, ʿAl Māher, were meeting with representatives of the Mufti. See Barry Rubin, *The Arab States and the Palestine Conflict* (Syracuse, N.Y., 1981), pp. 111–12.

Please accept, Excellency, the assurance of our highest regard.

Robert J. Rolo President of the Jewish Community of Alexandria	Joseph Cattaoui President of the Jewish Community of Cairo

AIU Archives (Paris) Egypte I.G.5.
Newspaper clipping enclosed in a letter from
M. Nassi, director of Alliance Schools in Tanta to
Alliance president in Paris (May 20, 1938).

6

WORLD WAR II AND ITS IMPACT

THE REPORT OF THE IRAQI COMMISSION OF INQUIRY ON THE FARHŪD (1941)

The Iraqi Government
Committee for the Investigation of
the Events of June 1 and 2, 1941

In accordance with the resolution of the Council of Ministers issued on June 6, 1941, no. 3288, the committee presided over by Mr. Muḥammad Tawfīq al-Nā'ib and whose members were Mr. ᶜAbd Allāh al-Qaṣṣāb, representing the Interior Ministry, and Mr. Saᶜdī Ṣāliḥ, representing the Ministry of Finance, met in twelve sessions to investigate the events that took place on June 1 and 2, 1941. On the basis of the evidence brought before it, it concluded the following:

Summary of the Affair

On June 1, 1941, it was announced to the public that His Exalted Highness[1] was officially returning, and people rushed to greet him. Some Jewish individuals also went out happy and rejoicing on account of the advent of the Feast of Nabī Shūᶜa[2] and on account of the easing of the

[1] The regent ᶜAbd al-Ilāh, who had just returned from exile.

[2] The Arabs gave this name to Shavuᶜot, because many Jews were accustomed to making pilgrimages to the tomb of Joshua the High Priest (Ar., Nabī Shūᶜa) at this time. The tomb was located in the western part of the city, where this attack took place.

emergency that had resulted from the armed conflict.[3] When they reached the Khurr Bridge,[4] they encountered some soldiers. The latter, seeing them in this state, were not pleased, and their resentment was stirred up. They showered them with blows, punches, and stabbed them with knives. Whoever could fled. Those who could not were wounded. The soldiers were joined in this incident by some civilians. This assault took place while the civil and military police looked on. Afterward, the police took the wounded and transported them to the central police station in al-Karkh.[5] The number of wounded came to sixteen individuals, and one person was killed. They were sent to the hospital.

A great mob of people gathered in front of the hospital wanting to murder the Jewish medics and nurses. The hospital director, Mr. Jamīl Dallālī, went out to them and pleaded with them to disperse. But they demanded that he hand over to them the Jewish men and women. When he replied that the women were servants of humanity, they demanded the men, particularly the Jew Heskel, the medic. So the director promised them, but went to tell the police. Then a detachment of the mobile force appeared and broke up that crowd, arresting a number of individuals among them. No investigation was conducted at that time against the soldiers and civilians who had taken part in the assault. News of this spread—as was only natural—among the various social classes, and those with evil in their hearts. Another assault took place in the Ruṣāfa area,[6] where the body of a murder victim was sighted on the pavement of Ghāzī Street[7] near the cinema. The police were informed, and the precinct officer arrived on the scene and found that it was the body of a Jew and that the murderer was unknown. At this time, an injured Jew came, fell down, and died immediately before telling who had killed him. At the same time, word reached the police about a number of murder victims found in the Abū Sayfayn district.[8] So they went and collected the corpses, whose number was eight. It turned out that the perpetrators were individual soldiers who had been joined by civilians.

On the heels of this, a crowd gathered in Ghāzī Street. The police wanted to break up the mob, but were unable to do so. They therefore requested an armored car, which began to open fire into the air. At first the crowd, which was convinced that the fire was being directed against it, began

[3] That is, between the invading British troops and the Iraqi army.

[4] The bridge over the Khurr River, which runs through the western portion of the city.

[5] The name given to the western portion of the city on the right bank of the Euphrates.

[6] The eastern half of the city on the left bank of the Euphrates, where the principal Jewish neighborhoods were located.

[7] One of the main streets in Ruṣāfa. Part of Ghāzī Street cut through the Jewish Quarter. (The name of the street today is Kifah Street.)

[8] A Jewish neighborhood on the eastern edge of the Jewish Quarter that bordered upon Muslim sections of town.

to disperse. However, when people realized that the shooting was only in the air, they suddenly fell upon Jewish homes, broke into them, and began wounding, killing, and looting. When the police appeared upon the scenes of the events, the mobs greeted them with applause and cheers for long life, thinking that they were there to assist them in looting and pillaging. This was because there was no firing into the crowd, as has already been noted. Killing and looting went on that entire night right before the eyes of the police. In addition to which, some individuals from the police and the commissariat took part in the looting, pillaging, and killing.

The Mutaṣarrif[9] of Baghdad made the rounds through al-Amīn Street[10] accompanied by the Chief of the Baghdad Police. They came upon some soldiers with a machine gun who were shooting into Jewish homes. The Mutaṣarrif claimed that he ordered the police to open fire, but that they shot into the air. Furthermore, some of the soldiers began shooting at the Mutaṣarrif and the Police Chief, in the manner described, and the two of them had to take cover behind a wall there to avoid being hit by the hail of bullets.

On the second day, June 2, 1941, at 6:00 A.M., some soldiers began looting, pillaging, and breaking down doors. A military vehicle was seen in al-Amīn Street carrying household furniture from Jewish homes. When Mr. ᶜAlī Khālid al-Ḥijāzī[11] protested against this, he was told that there had been an air force office here that had been moved and that they were transferring its furniture—even though it was clearly household furnishings. He intervened again with a civilian car and a wagon that were carrying belongings from the same house. He was then surrounded by a crowd of people who demanded that he not interfere with them. He saw some policemen firing into the air, and whenever he asked one of them the reason for that, he was told that the Mutaṣarrif and the Police Chief had given orders not to fire upon civilians. He then left them and went to Police General Headquarters.

At that same time, an army lorry with no number came by through the al-Sunak[12] district. In it was an officer with the rank of first lieutenant and with him four armed soldiers carrying pickaxes (heavy metal tools for breaking and entering). The truck stopped at the Trade School and was joined by students of the school and members of the Youth Phalanxes.[13] They proceeded to attack houses belonging to Jews in the quarter. They broke down the doors of nine homes and plundered them of all their furniture and belongings. The owners fled, leaving them as spoil in order to save their lives. Even when the police searched in the main office of the

[9] The military governor of the city.

[10] Another main street running perpendicular, westward from Zubayda Square at the northern end of Ghāzī street to the Euphrates.

[11] He was appointed Chief of Police shortly after this.

[12] A predominantly Muslim and Christian neighborhood in Ruṣāfa, in which there were a few Jewish families.

[13] One of the nationalist paramilitary youth groups.

Trade School that same day, they found looted property belonging to the daughter of Abraham Ḥayyim, Parliamentary Representative for Baghdad, who resided in that neighborhood (al-Sunak). Some policemen went into Jewish homes demanding a fee for their protection. The Jews handed over to the police whatever they had with them toward the sums demanded, but the police were not satisfied with that. Indeed, some of them assisted the civilians in looting and pillaging and even took part in it with them. Some of the students from the Military High School also took part in this aggression.

As for Mr. ᶜAlī Khālid al-Ḥijāzī, after seeing soldiers filling cars with plunder—as we previously mentioned—and being unable to stop them, he went in great agitation to Police General Headquarters and reported to the Police Chief, the Mayor, and the Mutaṣarrif that some soldiers had begun looting, pillaging, killing, and injuring. Lieut. Col. Ḥamīd Ra'fat, the Deputy Commander of the First Division, was present when this took place and vigorously disputed what Mr. al-Ḥijāzī had to say, claiming that not a single soldier could be found in Baghdad. He said that it was members of the police force who perpetrated these outrages.

The aforementioned Mr. al-Ḥijāzī asked him to accompany him to the scene of the incident in al-Amīn Street, and he, together with the Mutaṣarrif, went with him. When they arrived at al-Amīn Street, they found that the vehicles had gone with the belongings. However, they did find some soldiers coming out of Jewish homes with looted valuables in their pockets and on their backs. Ḥamīd Ra'fat got out of his car and ordered the soldiers to drop whatever spoils they were carrying, and he struck one of them. When the Mutaṣarrif saw that the situation had reached alarming proportions, he asked Ḥamīd Ra'fat to assist him with reinforcements in order to calm the situation. Then the two of them went off to Division Headquarters leaving Mr. al-Ḥijāzī where he was.

The mobs finished looting the homes and came pouring out into the street. They then started to break into the shops and loot their contents. So Mr. al-Ḥijāzī returned to Police General Headquarters and asked the Chief of Police to give the order for his men to fire directly upon the mobs. If not, anarchy would prevail throughout the city. The Chief informed him that the police had exhausted their ammunition shooting into the air. The Assistant Director General of the Interior Office, Mr. Muṣṭafā al-Qarah Dāghī, was present at this moment, and he charged the Director General of Police to give the order to fire directly. However, the latter replied that he had not received any order concerning direct fire upon civilians. Mr. al-Qarah Dāghī retorted that the situation did not require that such an order be issued to him. The Director General of Police then said that Ḥamīd Ra'fat forbids any shooting. He then charged the Mutaṣarrif to give the order to fire upon the looters, but the Mutaṣarrif refused, answering that he would not give the order to kill anyone.

At this point, the Mayor telephoned His Exalted Highness the Regent and asked him to issue the order to fire upon the rioters. His Highness gave the order. The Mayor then issued a written directive following His Exalted Highness the Regent's command to fire upon the rioters and gave it to Mr. al-Ḥijāzī. Thereupon, Mr. al-Ḥijāzī took two armored cars with machine guns, went out, and fired upon the rioters. They took to flight, leaving behind them the looted possessions in the street. The Mutaṣarrif came to Police Headquarters when His Highness the Regent's written order arrived and was handed to him. Then he also took two armored vehicles and went out for the same purpose. Within an hour or so, the streets were completely cleared of people, and the Mounted brigade entered the city together with an infantry regiment to restore calm. They began collecting the booty. Some of them acted as if the loot was theirs. A number of individuals carrying stolen property were seized and were conducted to police stations together with what they had looted. Throughout the third and fourth days, the army remained in command of the situation, although there were still instances of looting by some individual soldiers and officers.

With regard to the incidents of looting and pillaging in al-Karkh on June 2—it was also at the very beginning some soldiers who were joined by riffraff from among the civilian population that was incited by them. They looted four homes and thirteen shops.

As for al-ᶜAẓamiyya[14]—some soldiers attacked a number of houses, breaking down the doors, and plundering their contents after the news of the looting in Baghdad proper reached them. They too were joined by civilian hooligans. The police rushed to the scene and dispersed them after they had looted ten or more homes. However, there was no killing or injuring there.

Nothing happened in al-Karāda al-Sharqiyya[15] on June 1. However, on June 2, at 9:30 A.M., some soldiers began killing, looting, and causing injuries. Six Jews were killed. One Muslim was also killed when he stood up to protect a Jewish home. Six Jews were wounded. Two rioters were killed. The identities of four of the murderers are known. They are Ḥassūn b. Majīd, serial no. 167, Third Regiment, Third Brigade, Support Squadron; Sergeant Major ᶜAbd Muḥammad al-Ẓāḥī from the same aforementioned military unit; a train guard called Muṣṭāf; and another soldier from the air force whose identity remains unknown. The sergeant major was taken into custody and sent to his unit. He is now in the army camp at Jalula'.[16]

The looting of homes was carried out by some officers and soldiers who prepared transport vehicles (lorries) in which they loaded the furniture and valuables. The civilians who joined them were incited and encouraged by them. Sixty-one homes and three shops were looted. The greater part of the

[14] A district in the northeastern part of the city in which is located the tomb of the Imām Abū Ḥanīfa. It was a predominantly Muslim quarter with a Jewish minority.

[15] A mixed neighborhood on the eastern bank of the Euphrates, south of Ruṣāfa.

[16] A town approximately 80 miles northeast of Baghdad not far from the Iranian border.

spoils are still in the hands of the populace. As for what was taken by the officers and soldiers—nothing has been returned, since they are still not identified. Many civilians who took part in the looting have been arrested and have been handed over to the Military Tribunal, where they have received various sentences.

Nothing took place in al-ᶜAlawiyya or in al-Batāwīn.[17]

The total number of killed, according to the view expressed in the report of the Investigating Judge,[18] was 110 Jews and Muslims, including 28 women. Many of the victims have not been identified. Two hundred four were injured, likewise both Jews and Muslims. The President of the Jewish Community claims that the number of killed and wounded is greater than that.[19]

As to the number of houses looted, no statistics have been made available by the police, even though this committee did request lists of the numbers of looted homes and businesses from the various police stations, but received no reply. The committee concluded that the police did not undertake any accounting. The President of the Jewish Community claims that 586 shops and warehouses were sacked completely and that the value of what was taken came to a total of 271,301 dinars.[20] He claims that 911 houses were looted in which were living 3,395 families, totaling 12,311 souls. This committee doubts the accuracy of these figures since they are not based upon fact. If the government wishes to know with accuracy the extent of the losses, it must form a special committee for that purpose. There were no complaints concerning outrages against the chastity of families. However, the President of the Jewish Community claims that there were three or four such incidents.

Those Responsible for the Disorders

It is evident from what has been stated above that the disorders started directly with some soldiers who were joined by civilians. This progression of events could have been stopped if the Department of Military Discipline had arrested them on the first day in al-Karkh and held them in check, and if they had deployed their men (the Military Police) to prevent the incidents

[17] These two adjacent quarters bordered upon the southern end of Ruṣāfa. Both were mixed neighborhoods. In al-ᶜAlawiyya, there was only a very small number of Jews.

[18] Chief Justice Maᶜrif Dayyāwuq, who headed a separate governmental commission appointed to recommend ways to rehabilitate those who had suffered losses in the disturbances.

[19] For its own reasons, the government wished the casualty figures to be kept down. See ᶜAbd al-Razzāq al-Ḥasanī, *Ta'rīkh al-Wizārāt al-ᶜIrāqiyya,* vol. 5 (Sidon, 1953), p. 234, n. 1; and also Elie Kedourie, *Arabic Political Memoirs and Other Studies* (London, 1974), p. 298.

[20] The Iraqi dinar was more or less equivalent to the pound sterling at the time.

from reoccurring. It certainly had the power to do that and thereby prevent what took place on the second day in al-Ruṣāfa. However, its negligence, dereliction of duty, and disregard, together with the participation of some military policemen in these activities, encouraged others to spread what was happening to al-Ruṣāfa.

Likewise, had the civil police acted with resolve and done its duty to preserve public safety and prevent danger by arresting those soldiers and civilians who were committing the very first acts of aggression in al-Karkh (since arresting soldiers openly observed in the act of committing crimes is the police's duty)—it would have quashed the movement on the spot and prevented it from spreading to al-Ruṣāfa. Regrettably, however, the police stood by in the role of onlookers. Furthermore, when a large crowd gathered at the entrance of the al-Karkh hospital to lynch the Jews, Precinct Commander Muḥammad ᶜAlī was called to disperse them. But when he asked those who were gathered to disperse, they ridiculed him and laughed at him. He then asked the policemen to strike them with batons, but they refused to do so. At this, he became enraged and started hitting members of the police force so that they would carry out the order. It was only after this farce that they began beating the crowd. After that, they evacuated the Jewish nurses and medics and escorted them to their homes, fearing the possibility of an assault against them at the hospital. It has been ascertained on the basis of the hospital director's testimony that the rabble rousers in this incident were Mufīd b. Yāsīn, Shākir the coffeehouse owner, and the soldier Ḥusayn. The committee has requested that legal proceedings be taken against them.

These travesties led to the spread of what had taken place across the river to al-Ruṣāfa in a more widespread and atrocious manner. Once again, if only the police in al-Ruṣāfa had taken proper precautions and instituted the necessary measures to insure the safety of the civilian population and their property after what had happened in al-Karkh, and if orders had been issued to fire directly upon the crowds (as legally required), the situation would have been calmed and the movement nipped in the bud. However, the police's refusal to fire upon the rioters contributed to what took place. This is proven by the fact that the disorder was not suppressed until after deadly force was employed. Indeed, many senior civil servants had indicated the urgent need to fire upon the perpetrators to the Director General of Police, Mr. Ḥusām al-Dīn Jumᶜa, and to his assistant Mr. ᶜAbd Allāh ᶜAwnī, as well as to the Mutaṣarrif of Baghdad, Mr. Khālid al-Zahāwī. However, their reply was that they had no orders to that effect. They forgot—or they pretended to forget—that in these kinds of circumstances, every policeman has the right to fire upon the perpetrators. Mr. Jumᶜa claimed that the army was forbidden to use deadly force, but this committee could not ascertain the degree of accuracy in this statement because the aforesaid individual went on leave to Istanbul. Therefore, the committee was unable to hear what he had to say about this matter and about the other events.

On the basis of the above, the committee finds that the primary degree of responsibility lies with the Director General of Police, Mr. Husām al-Dīn Jumᶜa; the Mutaṣarrif of Baghdad, Mr. Khālid al-Zahāwī; the district police chiefs, Mr. Ibrāhīm al-Shāwī in al-Karkh, Mr. ᶜAbd Allāh ᶜAwnī in al-Sarāy, Mr. Darwīsh Luṭfī in ᶜAbākhāna and Karāda; and with the Police Chief of Baghdad, Mr. ᶜAbd al-Razzāq Fattāḥ. The secondary degree of responsibility lies with the Commander of the Military Police, Major Muẓaffar Ibrāhīm and the officers and soldiers under his command. Similarly, with the commander of the first Division ᶜAbd al-Ḥamīd Ra'fat, who could have prevented his soldiers from leaving their barracks after what had happened in al-Karkh.

With regard to the Council for Internal Security which had been set up to maintain order[21]—it did indeed draw up a plan for the preservation of order which was approved by the High Command of the Army General Staff at the time and was conveyed to the Director General of Police, the Mutaṣarrif, Colonel Ḥamīd Naṣrat (the Commander of the Military Police), the Commander of the Border Police, the Director of the Police Academy, the Commandant of the Police Guards, the Director of the Customs Police, the Director of the Railway Police, and the Director of the Detective Force. Unfortunately, not a single clause of this plan was put into effect. If it had been applied in its entirety, this dangerous situation would not have resulted. Knowing this, our committee is not able to absolve the members of the Council for Internal Security from responsibility for calming the situation in view of the fact that it initially took this responsibility upon itself.

The Council committed an especially grievous error that may well have played a major part in these disturbances; namely, in allowing Yūnus al-Sabᶜāwī and Ṣiddīq Shanshal to leave Iraq, giving the former 100 dinars (for a monthly allowance).[22] By so doing, the Council encouraged the followers of al-Sabᶜāwī, the Youth Phalanxes, the Iron Guards, al-Sabᶜāwī's National Force, and other vicious criminal types who had gathered around him and who joined together in these tragic events. . . . The committee cannot understand what the Director General of Police and the Council for Internal

[21] This Council, headed by the mayor of Baghdad, was appointed by Rashīd ᶜĀlī as he fled the capital on May 28, 1941, with approach of the British troops. See ᶜAbd al-Razzāq al-Ḥasanī, *al-Asrār al-Khafiyya fī Ḥarakat al-Sana 1941 al-Taḥarruriyya* 2nd rev. ed. (Sidon, 1964), pp, 239–40; and idem, *Ta'rīkh al-Wizārāt al-ᶜIrāqiyya,* vol. 5, pp. 229–30 (where the material is verbatim).

[22] Yūnus al-Sabᶜāwī, one of Rashīd ᶜĀlī's most enthusiastic supporters, had been finance minister in the latter's pro-Axis government. When most of the members of the regime fled the city on May 28, at the approach of the British army, al-Sabᶜāwī declared himself military governor of the capital, a post he held for only a few hours before being arrested by the provisional Council for Internal Security. Although allowed to leave the country, he was later recaptured and hanged. See Majid Khadduri, *Independent Iraq: A Study in Iraqi Politics,* 2nd ed. (London, New York, and Karachi, 1960), pp. 227, 236–38; and Stephen Hemsley Longrigg, *ᶜIraq, 1900–1950:*

Security intended or what was its purpose in letting al-Sab^cāwī go. Neither can it comprehend the reason for giving him 100 dinars from public funds when the Council knew that he was not entitled to a penny, and had in fact taken 15,950 dinars from the State Treasury. Indeed, the cabinet in which he served was unconstitutional and illegal. He should have been considered an extortionist who deserved punishment rather than a reward. This committee will leave the assessment of the Council for Internal Security's responsibility in this specific instance to the distinguished members of the Cabinet.

This committee recommends that the following individuals be stripped of all authority and brought before the Military Tribunal: Police Director General Ḥusām al-Dīn Jum^ca, the Mutaṣarrif of Baghdad Khālid al-Zahāwī, District Police chiefs Ibrāhīm al-Shāwī, ^cAbd Allāh ^cAwnī, Darwīsh Luṭfī, and ^cAbd al-Razzāq Fattāḥ, Lieutenant Colonel Ḥamīd Ra'fat, Military Police Commander Muzaffar Ibrāhīm, his assistant, all his officers, and the military policemen who were on duty and under his command at the time of the incidents.

As for the police officers, station commanders, deputies, and individual policemen—those of them who took part in looting, pillaging, and killing have in part been arrested and have received the punishment they deserve. However, as for those whose part in this affair is not clearly evident—the committee did not find it possible to assign responsibility to any one of them since it is certain that it was their superiors who instructed them not to fire directly upon the crowd. . . .

Causes of the Riots

It is clear to this committee on the basis of the investigations that it conducted that the primary causes underlying these riots were Nazi propaganda as will be explained in detail below:

1. The German Legation: The German Legation had been spreading Nazi propaganda over a long period of time. It disseminated it among army officers by various ways and means. It employed beautiful and lissome German female agents to advocate this propaganda among the officers and young men, to win their hearts, and to channel their feelings in the direction they intended. Even the movement headed by Bakr Sidqī was a result of Nazi propagandizing and its many effects.[23] This became clear after Bakr Sidqī's coup succeeded, and he entered into contacts with the German

---

A Political, Social, and Economic History (London, New York, and Toronto), pp. 296, 304–5. Shanshal was propaganda minister under Rashīd ^cĀlī.

[23] He was military strongman in Iraq from October 1936 until his assassination in August 1937. See Khadduri, *Independent Iraq,* pp. 73–125.

authorities to obtain arms. The German envoy Herr Grobba[24] provided Bakr Sidqī with a German woman with the aim of spreading Nazi propaganda as widely as possible among the army and its officers. . . . Herr Grobba worked with complete freedom, spending money generously on his spies and propagandists until Nazism became rampant, penetrating all strata of society.

When Germany declared war on England, the Iraqi government broke off relations with it, but not with its ally Italy, which took over the operations of the German Legation. Banco de Roma took over the dispensing of necessary funds to those whom Germany designated. Thus German propaganda activities never ceased within Iraq's borders, but rather continued to inject its venom within all levels of the army and civilian society in the widest fashion. When the recent governments discovered this danger, they wanted to break off relations with Italy. However, great difficulties stood in the way, because one group of men within the government itself had embraced the Nazi ideology either out of conviction or for material reasons—especially the military leadership. These men opposed any steps taken by the government against Nazism.

2. The Mufti of Jerusalem Amīn al-Ḥusaynī and His Entourage Which Accompanied Him to Iraq:[25] This man was received by Iraq with tremendous enthusiasm, and he took full advantage of the situation. Once he was firmly established, he began disseminating Nazi propaganda with great cunning, while decrying the injustice done to Palestine and under the guise of Pan-Arabism and the Islamic religion. He exerted a considerable influence upon people in authority and positions of military leadership—to such a degree in fact, that orders were issued from his home. His entourage also engaged in wide-scale anti-Jewish and anti-British propaganda activities among all classes. The contributions that were collected on behalf of victims in Palestine were employed by him for his own propaganda purposes. It is even said that he had a code for communications between himself and Germany. Unfortunately, the successive governments paid no attention to him until the state of affairs which is all too well known. He has fled the country with those officials whom he had led astray.

3. The Palestinian and Syrian Schoolteachers: The influence of these men upon students in the schools was even more powerful than that of their leader, the Mufti, since they poisoned the pupil's minds and turned them into instruments of their propaganda. Whenever they perceived that the

[24] Dr. Fritz Grobba was a Middle East specialist of the German Foreign Office who represented Germany in Iraq from 1932 until the Second World War. Concerning his untiring efforts to woo the Arabs and extensive propaganda activities, see Reeva S. Simon, *Iraq between the Two World Wars: The Creation and Implementation of a Nationalist Ideology* (New York, 1986), pp. 37–43; Lukasz Hirszowicz, *The Third Reich and the Arab East* (London and Toronto, 1966), passim; and Grobba's memoir, *Männer und Mächte im Orient. 25 Jahre diplomatischer Tätigkeit im Orient* (Göttingen, 1967), passim.

[25] See Part One, p. 116.

government was taking any steps against Nazism, they went into action, arousing the students who would then go out in demonstrations and issue harmful manifestos. The present government[26] has done well by dismissing them and expelling them from the country.

4. The German Arabic-Language Radio Station: This station went a long way to aiding the German propaganda effort in Iraq, especially more recently after the Rashīd ᶜĀlī government made it legal to listen to it. This station disseminated false propaganda concerning Palestine and maligned Iraq's loyal leaders in the eyes and minds of the masses and made accusations against them. Thus, public opinion was poisoned. It created a favorable climate for Rashīd ᶜĀlī and his henchmen to carry out his infernal plans. There are some people whose minds have been poisoned that are still listening to these broadcasts in secret in spite of the government ban against doing that.

5. The Iraqi Broadcasting Station: Over the past two months of April and May 1941, during which the government of Rashīd ᶜĀlī was in power, this station broadcast false reports about misdeeds in Palestine. The broadcasts contained patently inflammatory agitation against the Jews and powerful appeals to Nazism. This had an electrifying effect upon the common folk and the weak-minded of Baghdad. It sowed hatred and anger among them toward the sincere leaders of Iraq.

6. The Futuwwa and the Youth Phalanxes: These groups imbibed Nazism from the Palestinians and the Syrians. When they took charge of guarding Baghdad, their first act was to show hostility toward the Jews. They would arrest Jews on all sorts of slanderous, trumped up charges and drag them off to police stations, sometimes murdering individuals before delivering them to the station. When no punitive actions were taken against their most unruly members, this led to even greater extremes of misconduct, especially among those associated with Yūnus al-Sabᶜāwī. He supplied them with money and fed their minds with malicious anti-Jewish notions. It was apparent to this committee that this man already had the intent to annihilate the Jewish community prior to the events, because he had summoned the President of the Jewish Community and instructed him to tell the members of the community that none of them was to leave his house on Friday, Saturday, or Sunday of May 30 through June 1, 1941. Neither was anyone to speak with anyone else by telephone. It appeared to us from the events that took place that his intention in this was to order his soldiers and guards to surprise the Jews in their homes and finish them off. The conclusion is strengthened by the fact that he had drafted a fiery speech calling for a revolution inside Baghdad that would leave nothing remaining. However, circumstances prevented him from carrying out what he had resolved, when the Council for Internal Security arrested him and did not allow him to

[26] Established on June 3, 1941, by Jamīl Midfaᶜī. See Khadduri, *Independent Iraq,* pp. 245–48; and al-Ḥasanī, *Ta'rīkh al-Wizārāt al-ᶜIrāqiyya,* vol. 6, pp. 5–10.

deliver his speech. The text of the speech is in the hands of the Mayor, Arshad al-ᶜUmarī. According to what he has told us, the text is written in al-Sabᶜāwī's own handwriting. Once again, the committee expresses its regret that this man was allowed to slip out of the hand of justice by men who are responsible for governing this country.

These then are the most important factors which brought about these riots. . . . It is certain that the goal was not loot and plunder alone. Rather, the motivation was a desire for vengeance. This was demonstrated during these events when looters who were unable to carry off some of the booty due to its bulk would simply smash it on the spot so that no one else might benefit from it. They smashed plate glass, doors, and windows. They took apart electrical equipment. They opened water taps and left them running to flood houses. These things indicate the spirit of vindictiveness. The clearest proof of these sentiments, however, is the carnage which included even women and children.

Because a considerable portion of the looted property has still not been recovered and because this committee finds that the loot entered many homes in Baghdad and its suburbs, it therefore considers it essential that comprehensive inquiries be made in all homes and that these inquiries be conducted under strict surveillance so that such property cannot be removed surreptitiously from a house that has not been searched to one that has been already, otherwise our efforts will be in vain.

There has been no cessation in acts of intimidation by some officers and soldiers even up till now. Many such instances have taken place recently, when officers and soldiers roaming the alleys of the Jewish Quarter threaten and intimidate anyone who might give damaging testimony against military men or civilians. A group of privates and corporals have begun frightening Jews with threats and are extorting money from them. For this reason, the Jews will continue to hold back from giving information concerning the killing and looting to any authority until the government takes the measures necessary to punish the perpetrators and to stop their torrent of threats. It is the opinion of this committee that the soldiers and officers—if at all possible—be sent to camps outside of town for the present in order to calm the Jews and make them safe from intimidation, so that they will come forward with information.

The committee finds that the baneful propaganda is continuing unabated—albeit in a lesser form. Firm and resolute measures should be taken to put an end to it. The committee also finds that is is imperative that all fire arms and dangerous weapons in Baghdad be collected, since they pose a dangerous overall influence upon security. If the government agrees to conduct house to house searches, it can within that scope easily confiscate weapons.

These, then, are the main findings of the committee's investigations, as well as the measures that it recommends being taken.

Submitted 14 Jumāda II, 1360, corresponding to July 8, 1941.

Member	Member	Member
Sa[c]dī Ṣāliḥ	[c]Abd Allāh al-Qaṣṣāb	Muḥammad Tawfīq al-Nā'ib

[c]Abd al-Razzāq al-Ḥasanī, *al-Asrār al-Khafiyya fī Ḥarakat al-Sana 1941 al-Taḥarruriyya*, 2nd rev. ed. (Sidon, 1964), pp. 246–56.

A BRITISH MILITARY INTELLIGENCE REPORT ON JEWISH ATTEMPTS TO LEAVE IRAQ FOR PALESTINE AND ELSEWHERE AFTER THE FARHŪD
(1942)

MOST SECRET.
No. 2399/1/ 18 /GSIx
HQ, Tenth Army,
29 Apr 42

To:-HBM Embassy, BD
CICI, BD
Maj D. E. Driver, HBM Embassy
Subject:— *POLITICAL—IRAQ.*
Ref. telegram (M) 903 27 Apr 42.

The following information has been obtained from a reliable Jewish source:—

The emigration from Iraq is taking place under two classes:—

(a) poor Jews who either have no money, or were looted last May–June, are paying money to friendly Jewish lorry drivers and in some cases soldiers of H. M. Forces, to take them over the frontier into Palestine. Most of these Jews are joining or intend to join Jewish forces in Palestine i.e., the Buffs.[1] The Jews usually contact drivers at Rutba;[2]

(b) rich Jews who have listened to bazaar rumors and are apprehensive about their future. They feel that whatever the outcome of the war that the Iraqis will punish the Jews eventually. Some rumors are to the effect that those Jews who escaped last June will not escape the anti-Jewish riots that will coincide with Hitler's Spring Offensive. It is stated that these Jews are willing to pay large sums for visas to the passport authorities, and actually do have to pay before they can obtain the necessary visa.

No organized movement is in force but the emigration is the result of fear inspired by Moslem threats.

(signed) T. W. Boyd
Lieut-Col
GSI.

WHM.29.4

PRO (London) FO 624/29/374, facsimile published in Yoav Gelber, *Tōldōt ha-Hitnaddevūt,* vol. 3: *Nōs'ē ha-Degel* (Jerusalem, 1983), p. 21.

[1] Apparently a sobriquet for the Palestinian Jewish units in the British army.

[2] A small town approximately 200 miles east of Baghdad, just before the cross-desert highway forks northwest to Syria and southwest to Transjordan and Palestine.

THE GOVERNOR OF LIBYA ADVISES MUSSOLINI TO MODIFY THE APPLICATION OF ITALY'S ANTI-JEWISH LAWS IN LIBYA
(1939)

My Leader,

The laws for the defense of the race are being applied in Libya. We have made arrangements to dismiss from government service officials who are of the Jewish race, and Jewish pupils have been expelled from secondary schools. Changes have been made in banks' discount committees and in the managing boards of official and semi-official bodies and municipal councils for the purpose of implementing the provisions of the law.

I have diligently examined the local Jewish problem as a whole. Certain situations and aspects have emerged which deserve much consideration and to which I feel it my duty to call your exalted attention.

In this region the Jewish population has special characteristics both in quality and numbers. It is an important ethnic element, since about one-fifth of the total population of Tripoli is Jewish. The presence in Libya of strong groups of Jews dates back to time immemorial. . . . Even before the Italian occupation the Jews received protection from Italy, set up schools, and spread the Italian language. Most of them live in very backward social conditions, and do not take the slightest part in political activities. They are mostly peaceful and timid, craftsmen and peddlers keeping to their modest little workshops and stalls, intent only on making a living from their occupation.

In contrast with this vast majority, a few dozen wealthy Jews run almost all local industry and trade, are the banks' main clients, and provide the funds for most of the Muslim business enterprises.

If the Jews stopped participating in the economy before they could be replaced by a group of Catholic merchants and industrialists, there would be economic imbalances in Libya. Looking at the local situation on a general level, I can point out several special cases that could not be readily solved:

(a) Hospitals in Libya treat numerous in-patients of the Jewish race, cared for by Jewish employees. This is essential because they obviously cannot be cared for by Muslims. Medical care for Muslim women giving birth is also provided by Jewish women, since Muslim nurses are lacking. Replacing this staff with metropolitans is both unacceptable and impossible. . . . Hence, strict application of the measures would mean that Jews would be deprived of hospital services.

(b) Monopoly industries whose main factories are in Tripoli largely use trained Jewish female workers, especially for the manufacture of cigars and cigarettes. These workers may no longer be employed by the governing authorities. It is not possible to find in Libya Italian nationals who are both skilled and willing to accept the same modest wages.

(c) The Government and municipalities employ Jewish clerks whose conduct is irreproachable. They have been working for a long time as Arabic and Hebrew interpreters; if they were dismissed, they would have to be replaced. Though in time this would be easy for Arabic, it would be impossible for Hebrew, since only those who profess the Jewish religion know it.

I have already described all these difficulties officially to the Ministry and asked for instructions, but I have not yet received any reply. Nor have I received a precise reply to this inquiry: whether the regulations applying to Jews having full Italian citizenship should definitely be applied to Jews with Libyan citizenship. In a country like this one, which has always had the virtue, compared with neighboring countries, of allowing Jews and Arabs to live together in full harmony, it would in my opinion be advisable to avoid making the struggle for the defense of the race a harsh one. The Jews are already a dead people; there is no need to oppress them cruelly, especially since the Arabs, the traditional enemies of the Jews, now show signs of feeling sorry for them.

No one can suspect me of weakness, since—as everyone remembers—two years ago I did not hesitate to order the public flogging of Jews, even those of high social standing, who were guilty of adopting an attitude of passive indifference to certain official measures.[1] But I have a duty to portray the situation frankly and as it really is.

Accordingly, may I venture to advise you to give the Government of Libya authorization to apply the racial laws "to the extent desirable in view of the very special local situation."

With my sincere respect,
Your faithful servant.

Mussolini Replies

Reply to your letter regarding Libyan Jews. No changes should be made regarding the situations listed under your headings (a), (b), and (c). Nonindigenous Jews, that is, those with metropolitan citizenship, should be given the treatment they receive in Italy under the recent laws. I therefore authorize you to apply the racial laws as above, remembering that though the Jews may seem to be dead, they never really are.

Texts published in Renzo de Felice,
Jews in an Arab Land: Libya, 1835–1970,
trans., Judith Roumani (Austin, 1985), pp. 171–73.

[1]Concerning this incident, see pp. 399–401.

ABOVE LEFT: Jacob Cattaoui Bey (1801–1883), patriarch of a dynasty of Egyptian Jewish bankers, courtiers, and communal leaders. (Jacob M. Landau, *Jews in Nineteenth-Century Egypt.* New York University Press: New York and London, 1969, Fig. 18.)

ABOVE RIGHT: Joseph Aslan Cattaoui Pasha (1861– 1942), member of the committee that drafted Egypt's first constitution, minister of finance in 1924, and minister of communications in 1925. (*Juifs d'Egypte: Images et Textes.* Editions du Scribe: Paris, 1984.)

RIGHT: Sir Sassoon Heskel (1860–1932), first finance minister of Iraq and the only Jew ever to serve in an Iraqi cabinet. (Yūsuf Rizq Allāh Ghanīma, *Nuzhat al-Mushtāq fī Ta'rīkh Yahūd al-ᶜIrāq.* Baghdad, 1923.)

Jewish banker and communal leader, Halfallah Nahum, conversing with Mussolini during the latter's visit to Tripoli in 1926. (Renzo de Felice, *Ebrei in un paese arabo: gli ebrei nell Libia contemporanea tra colonialismo, nazionalismo arabo e sionismo (1835–1970)*. Società editrice il Mulino: Bologna, 1978.)

Jews of the Ḥāra of Tripoli, lined up to give Mussolini a festive welcome (1937). (Renzo de Felice, *Ebrei in un paese arabo: gli ebrei nell Libia contemporanea tra colonialismo, nazionalismo arabo e sionismo (1835–1970)*. Società editrice il Mulino: Bologna, 1978.)

Portrait of an Egyptian Jewish girl, dressed for a modernist religious initiation ceremony (confirmation), Alexandria, 1927. (*Juifs d'Egypte: Images et Textes*. Editions du Scribe: Paris, 1984.)

Jewish girls' basketball team, Cairo, in the 1930s or 1940s. (*Juifs d'Egypte: Images et Textes*. Editions du Scribe: Paris, 1984.)

Partisans for Elie Samama, candidate for president of the Jewish Communal Council of Tunis, rally outside the polling station in the courtyard of the Alliance Israélite Universelle School, 1934. (*From Carthage to Jerusalem: The Jewish Community in Tunis* [No. 202]. ©Beth Hatefusoth–Photo Archive, The Nahum Goldmann Museum of the Diaspora, Tel Aviv, 1986; with permission.)

One of the buildings of the Jewish Community School of Alexandria, twentieth century. (Editions du Scribe: Paris, 1984.)

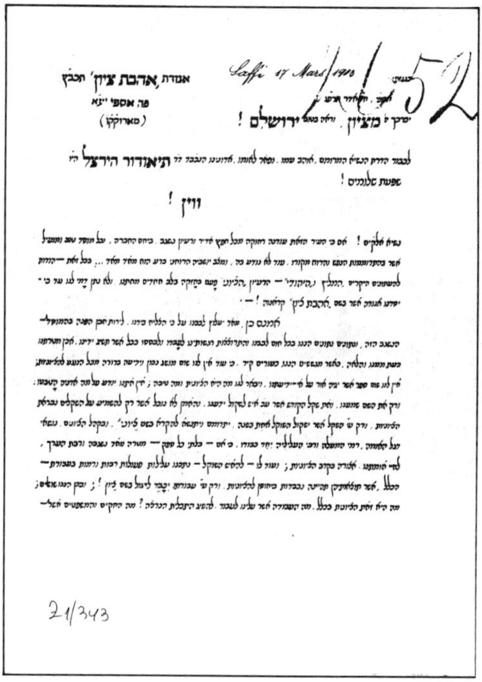

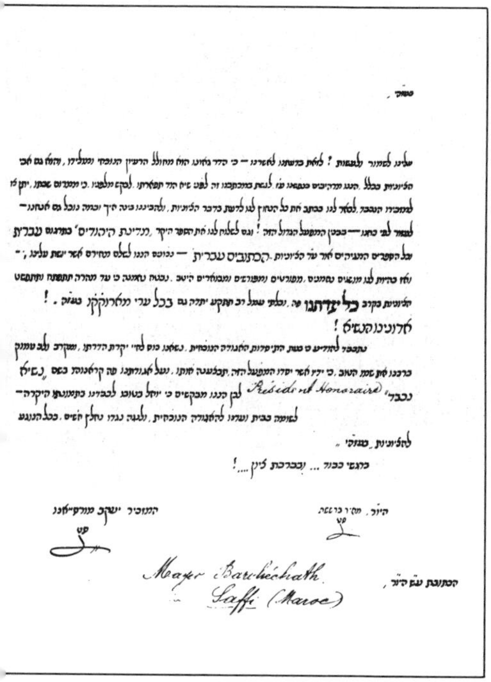

Letter to Theodor Herzl, from the Ahavat Ṣiyyon Society of Safi, Morocco, 1903. (Central Zionist Archives, [Jerusalem] Z 1/343.)

Rabbi Jacob Boccara of Tunis (standing center), with the North African delegates to the Tenth Zionist Congress, Basel, Switzerland, August 1911. (*From Carthage to Jerusalem: The Jewish Community of Tunis* [No. 285]. ©Beth Hatefusoth–Photo Archive, The Nahum Goldmann Museum of the Diaspora, Tel Aviv, 1986; with permission.)

Rabbi Joseph Brami, Zionist and modernist educator, with his Hebrew students, La Goulette, Tunisia, 1922. (Courtesy of Dr. Itzhak Avrahami, Kibbutz Regavim, Israel.)

Albert Mosseri (1867—1933), founder of the pro-Zionist Egyptian Jewish newspaper, *Israël.* (Jacob M. Landau, *Jews in Nineteenth-Century Egypt.* New York University Press: New York and London, 1969.)

العدد ١٠٦ ثمن النسخة آنات السنة الثالثة

המצביח

المصباح

المصباح
مجلة ادبية اجتماعية اسبوعية
صاحبها ومحررها
المحامي سلمان شينة

كلمات خالدة
قد لا يكون دائماً الاخ
صديقاً ، اما الصديق، فهو
اخ ابداً . فرنكلن

بغداد : الخميس في ١٥ تموز ١٩٢٦ ٤ آب ٥٦٨٦ عبراني ٤ محرم الحرام ١٣٤٤

مصرع الجنرال بتلورا

ما زالت الصحف الاسرائيلية تهتم في قضية شوارصبر اهتماما عظيما والراي السائد هو ان حالة القاتل تدعو الى الاشفاق اكثر منها الى اللوم بالرغم من استنكار معظم الصحف لهذا العمل لصراحة النهي الوارد في الكتاب المقدس (لا تسفك دما)

غير ان ثمة ظهور اناس امثال (شوارصبر) تقع على عاتق السفاكين امثال الجنرال بتلورا الذين اهرقوا دماء شعب مسالم لا هم له سوى ان يعيش بوفاق ووئام مع ابناء جنسه . هذا وان صحف فرنسا تنظر بعين ملؤها العطف على القاتل وانتصب كبار الرجال للدفاع عنه . وقد سعى البعض لافساح المجال الى المتهم للاثبات بانه مختل العقل غير ان شوارصبر افاد انه سليم العقل وان عمله كان انتقاما لدم مئة الف من ابناء جلدته المسفوك ظلما وعدوانا

تصريح (شوارصبر) الى مفوض الشرطة

حمل الينا البريد في هذا الاسبوع تفاصيل تسليم شوارصبر نفسه الى مفوض الشرطة بعد اطلاقه الرصاص على الجنرال . فقد فه المتهم لدى استجوابه بالعبارات التالية :

لقد انتقمت بعملي هذا لدم مئة الف من ابناء جلدتي الذين ذهبوا ضحية لمطامع هذا القاسي ولست نادما على ما فعلت وسأكرر ما قلته الان عند اللزوم

ثم اردف كلامه قائلا : لقد علمت بوجود بتلورا في باريس منذ مدة يسيرة وسمعت بانه يصدر جريدة باللغة الاوكرانية اسمها (لا تريدنت) وبما انني لا اعرفه شخصيا فقد قطعت رسمه من قاموس (لاروس) واخذت بتعقيب اثره في شارع اللاتين الى ان عثرت عليه للمرة الاولى بينما كان خارجا من المطعم وكان معه سيدة وابنة صغيرة ولذا لم تسنح لي الفرصة لتنفيذ مقصدي اما اليوم فقد نلت مرامي بعد التأكد من شخصيته وبعملي هذا قد انتقمت عن دم امي وابي الصالحين واني مستعد لاضحي حياتي من اجل ذلك

شهادة عقيلة شوارصبر

افادت السيدة شوارصبر عقيلة المتهم الى محرر جريدة الـ (بتي جورنال) بان زوجها كان قد ترك حانوته في الساعة الثانية عشرة والنصف وقال لها انه ذاهب لابتياع بعض اللوازم الى البيت . ولم يتناول طعام الفطور في ذلك اليوم وان زوجها مبتلى بداء الرئة منذ تركه خدمة الجيش الفرنسي وقد نال وسام (صليب الحرب) اكراما لشجاعته ويتناول الان راتب التقاعد من الحكومة الفرنسية . وعندما اخبرت السيدة عن قتل الجنرال من قبل بعلها اجابت انه لم يخبرها عن عزمه هذا غير انها لاحظته حينما كان يقرأ في جريدة (لا تريدنت) كان يقول : (مساكين اخواني اليهود) وختمت قائلة: (ان زوجي رجل ساكن لا يستعمل الخمر ولا يأكل اللحم)

راي محامي المتهم

صرح الاستاذ هنري تورس المحامي في قضية (شوارصبر) الى مندوب شركة التلغرافات الاسرائيلية ما يلي :

ان محاكمة شوارصبر لم تكن سوى محاكمة الاتسبيت العالمية . ان شوارصبر قام بعمله بجسارة فائقة منتقما لدم الابرياء وسيكون لمحاكمته صدى عظيم في جميع انحاء العالم حيث انها ستكون بمثابة احتجاج ضد الاعمال البربرية التي يدبرها الطغاة القساة

وزاد المحامي قائلا : لا اساس للاشاعة القائلة بان لشوارصبر اتصالا مع البلشفية وساداقع امام القضاء الفرنسي وامام ذلك الشعب الذي كان اول من اعترف بحقوق الشعب الاسرائيلي الدينية والوطنية وسأعمل جهد طاقتي لتخليص المتهم . فهو رفيقي في ساحة الوغى حيث حاربت معه جنبا لجنب واعتقد ان النصر سيكون حليفنا بالنتيجة .

Front page of the Iraqi Jewish newspaper, *al-Miṣbāḥ* (June 15, 1926).

Members of Snunit, the senior girl's group of Hashomer Hatzair, Tunis, 1931. (*From Carthage to Jerusalem: The Jewish Community in Tunis* [No. 309]. ©Beth Hatefusoth–Photo Archive, The Nahum Goldmann Museum of the Diaspora, Tel Aviv, 1986; with permission.)

The first senior group of the socialist Zionist Hashomer Hatzair, Tunis, 1930. (*From Carthage to Jerusalem: The Jewish Community in Tunis* [No. 306]. ©Beth Hatefusoth–Photo Archive, The Nahum Goldmann Museum of the Diaspora, Tel Aviv, 1986; with permission.)

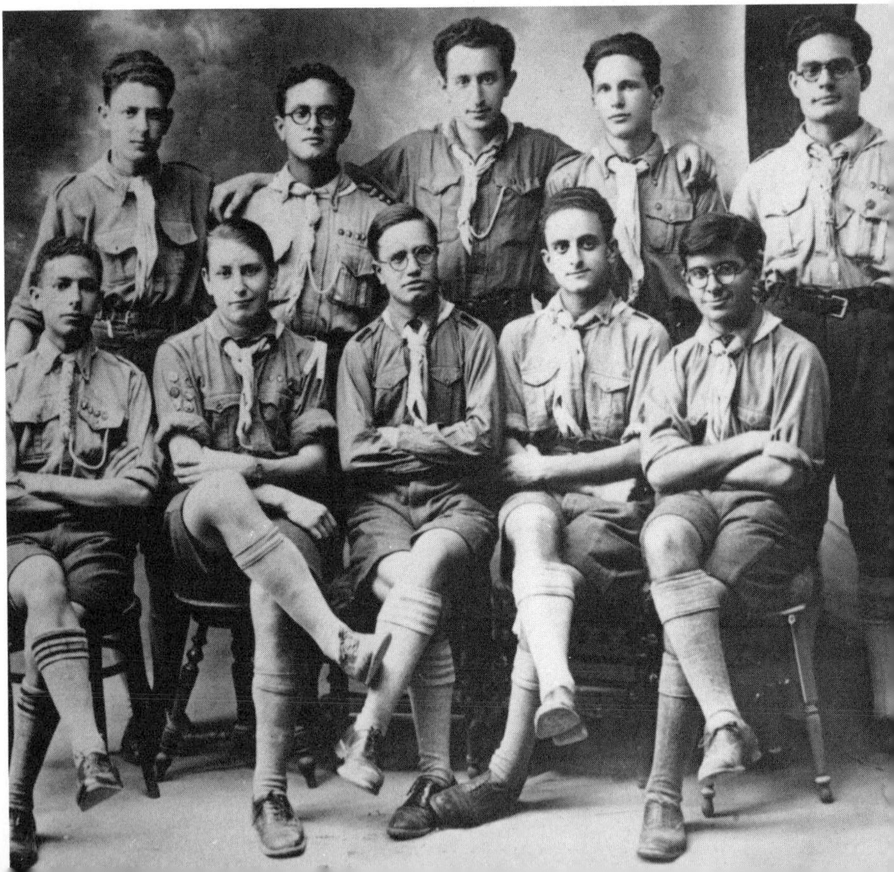

AN ITALIAN REPORT ON THE JEWISH INFLUENCE ON THE LIBYAN ECONOMY AND THE NEED TO TAKE ACTION AGAINST IT (1941)

The Jewish population of Libya amounts to roughly fifty or sixty thousand. It consists of a minority which, having considerable capital available, wields a major influence, and a mass of Jews with very limited means.

Jews form a good proportion of the total Libyan population. Their situation is quite different from that of Jewish communities in Italy and other European countries, since Jews can be viewed as one of the elements composing the population here, almost a local race.

Very little land is owned by Jews: They own more buildings, but most of their capital is invested in commercial and, to a lesser extent, industrial enterprises. Their business as franchise holders for Italian and foreign firms is especially important. Until a month or so ago most imports from Italy and abroad were ordered through Jews. This business has shrunk because of the smaller volume of imports due to the war. Still, almost all the requests for import licenses come from Jews.

The poor masses engage in petty trade and dominate the widespread distribution network, in which even Arabs take part, despite their traditional racial hatred.

Since the Jews control so much business activity, it is obvious that it is they who most frequently speculate and corner markets. Previously, until strict controls were introduced for military purchasing on the market, the strange phenomenon existed of the German Expeditionary Force largely using the Jewish network for major purchases of all sorts of provisions in Libya.

Moreover, some Libyan Jews have subsidiaries in Tunisia and even Egypt and thus tend to transfer their funds—which are generally liquid or easily encashable—from Libya to Tunisia or vice versa. This occurred particularly during the British offensives, when these Jews withdrew their deposits from banks and either hoarded cash or tried to smuggle their lire to Tunisia. This may be one of the main sources feeding the clandestine currency trade between Tunisia and Libya.

Apart from the general regulations to suppress speculation and monopolies, which all branches of the police are enforcing strictly, the government has adopted various sorts of measures to suppress the Jews' activities.

The General Commissioner for War Supplies and Economic Coordination, together with the Party,[1] has decided to exclude Jews from the wholesale trade in rationed goods; higher authorities wish to apply this criterion gradu-

[1] That is, the Fascist party.

ally rather than totally. Thus the Jews' participation in the wholesale business has been reduced considerably.

The Commissioner for Supplies has also promised two measures, which are presently under study by the appropriate agencies. One of them aims at regulating all business transfers, and the other will prohibit Jews from owning real property. Recently there has been a tendency among Jews to buy land.

All the measures adopted can only be partial solutions to the problem. Effective results can only be achieved by radical steps—such as putting the Jews in concentration camps—since excluding Jews from particular activities will only exacerbate the situation and make control more difficult. (Jews officially excluded from commerce might practice it under other names.) One should remember that the distribution network is composed almost entirely of Jews, and thus eliminating them would cause a disruption of the market.

It would be advisable, though, to exclude Jews from the activities of importing, franchise holding, and commercial representation, since these are easier to control.

It can be stated, in conclusion, that the Jewish problem in Libya is being viewed and dealt with as a political issue. The economic aspect is merely a consequence and can only be resolved within the framework of a decisive racial policy.

Archivio Storico del Ministero dell Africa Italiana (Rome), Archivio de Gabinetto, file 99/IX, fasc. "Varie—1941," published in Renzo de Felice, *Jews in an Arab Land: Libya, 1835–1970*, trans., Judith Roumani (Austin, 1985), pp. 175–77.

A GERMAN CONSULAR OFFICIAL'S OBSERVATIONS ON FASCIST ANTI-JEWISH LEGISLATION IN LIBYA
(1942)

German Consulate
Tripoli, October 21, 1942

No. 279g *Confidential!*
7 copies
In reference to the Reports
No. 208g of 5.19.42 and
No. 285 of 6.9.42
Subject: Legislation concerning the Jews in Libya

Following the law of May 2, 1942, which recently made Jewish commercial activity in Libya subject to a special regulation,[1] the ordering of the "Civilian mobilization of Italian and Libyan nationals of Jewish race" has come under the law of June 28, 1942.[2] The law covers Jews aged 18 to 45 residing in Libya. Since prior to the Italian occupation of Libya there was no statistical record of Jews, and thus for the present only those Jews up to the age of 31 can be registered, compulsory registration was introduced concurrently. The work force of mobilized Jews is to be assigned to areas correlating to the military and commercial exploitation of the colony of Libya. Each Jew will be employed according to his physical and professional capabilities. The Acorguerra[3] is charged with the implementation of this regulation.

On the basis of this new law, some 3,000 Jews who had been assembled in Homs were recently mobilized. However, since no preparation had been made for the allocation of labor, it was found necessary to send the majority back home. There remained some 600 skilled workers who were sent to work in Cyrenaica and were divided there among the various military work sites; moreover, some of the Jews were placed in military administrative offices. Due to organizational difficulties, their collective assignment to specific workplaces was not possible. Due to this fiasco, a commission was formed in which the Acorguerra, the Vice Governor, the Police, the Military Authorities, and other interested parties were represented. This commission

[1] The reference here is to the provincial governor's decree no. 105 of May 30, 1942, which went into effect on June 2 (not May 2 as in this document). The decree aimed at regulating Jewish economic and professional activities. Among other things, "it forbade Jews to sell, purchase, or lease property or farms to or from Aryans, Italians, or Muslims." See Renzo de Felice, *Jews in an Arab Land: Libya, 1835–1970,* trans. Judith Roumani (Austin, 1985), pp. 180–81.

[2] This mobilization law followed similar legislation that had been passed in metropolitan Italy. See ibid., p. 181.

[3] The general commissariat for war supplies and economic coordination.

was to determine the details of the future allocation of Jewish labor. It was agreed to conscript for the present only those Jews between the ages of 28 and 38. Unless they possess specialized professional training, these Jews are to be organized into labor battalions and, as far as possible, employed collectively in railway construction. Prior to conscription, registrants are to be examined by a medical commission for their fitness for service. Since two doctors have already had to be suspended from duty because of their amenability to bribery, the commissions are now drawn by lot; in addition, police officers attend the examination. An economic commission is determining whether remaining family members should receive support, based on their financial condition. The conscripts themselves will receive payment as high as that of the corresponding Arab work force. A progressive rate of pay is projected based on performance, whereby the top group gets 80 percent above the minimum. Some 4,000 to 5,000 of the 16,000 Tripolitanian Jews are affected by this "Mobilization."

The fundamental factor distinguishing this from German legislation concerning Jews is that the basis of the law is not the suppression of the Jews, nor even their seclusion from the rest of the populace, rather it is based on the necessity of turning the Jewish work force to account given the great labor shortage in Libya. To a certain degree, this has probably been accomplished; however, the law's political success is negligible.

The law's principal weakness lies in the fact that it does not cover the Jews in their entirety. Moreover, those with the real upper hand retain the potential to continue their activity, no doubt of a damaging nature to the Libyan economy and administration. Furthermore, the mobilized Jews are not being rigorously concentrated in labor camps, but are distributed among different fields of work. They are thereby given the potential to infiltrate operations of military importance, which is not completely without risk. It seems particularly disquieting to me that the work rendered by the Jews is not limited merely to manual tasks, but that they are also being employed in offices. A Jew who works for payment in a Tripoli government office is not necessarily any worse off, and possibly has greater opportunities than before to carry on illegal activities. (The original fear that the Secret Service was availing itself of the Libyan Jews has turned out to be more baseless than was first assumed. To date, it has not been possible to prove a single case, and even the agents provocateurs occasionally brought in by the Italian police have without exception had their offers rejected.)[4]

The main difficulty in the implementation of the law may well be the fact that hardly any of the important local officials are tackling the abovementioned implementation with conviction. The majority will readily admit the destructive activity of the local Jews, but fear a collapse of the Libyan economy from measures that are too drastic. A small number of the

[4]The concern expressed here stems from the fact that at this time the Italians and Germans were facing the British at El Alamein.

officials also have personal or material ties to Jews. Those arguing for drastic measures are in the minority. The handling of the whole question has caused acute tensions within the civil service. Oddly enough, the Party[5] is keeping a low profile.

One major reason for the labor law and further anticipated is that the very anti-Semitic Arab population keeps pointing to the fact that they themselves have lost their best men at the first retreat, where three Arab divisions were completely wiped out or taken prisoner, while the Jewish population has so far come through the war unscathed and has simply pocketed large business profits.[6]

Furthermore, the leading officials in Libya probably have the feeling that they must do something so that they do not someday lose the initiative to Rome. All leading positions here are occupied by "veteran colonials," who—to be sure—feud amongst themselves occasionally, but are united in their opposition to a homo novus. On top of that are their fears vis-à-vis the German authorities here, from whom one assumes a special interest in the Jewish question. Each of the important officials is taking pains to show me a quite marked fervor about the Jewish question and to prove that he is the very man to do anything that is at all possible. The same observation has been made by SS-Hauptsturmführer Saevecke, liaison officer for the Security Police and the Italian Africa Police.

(signed) Walther

Text published in United Restitution Organization, Ltd., *Judenverfolgung in Italien, den italienisch besetzen Gebieten und in Nordafrika* (Frankfurt a. M., 1962), pp. 108–10.

[5] That is, the Fascist party.

[6] Concerning Arab attitudes at this time, see de Felice, *Jews in an Arab Land,* p. 183.

ABROGATION OF THE CRÉMIEUX DECREE BY THE VICHY REGIME
(1940)

We, Marshal of France, Chief of the French State, with the understanding of the Council of Ministers, decree:

Article 1.—The decree of the Government of National Defense of 24 October 1870[1] regulating the political rights of the Jewish natives of the departments of Algeria and declaring them French citizens is abrogated.

Article 2.—The political rights of the Jewish natives of the departments of Algeria are regulated by the texts defining the political rights of the native Algerian Muslims.

Article 3.—Regarding their civil rights, the civil and personal status of the native Jews of the departments of Algeria continues to be governed by French law.

Article 4.—Those Jewish natives of the departments of Algeria, who, having belonged to a combat unit during the war of 1914–1918 or of 1939–1940, and who attained a military Legion of Honor, the Military Medal, or the Croix de Guerre, retain the political status of French citizens.

Article 5.—This status[2] may be retained, by a decree countersigned by the Keeper of Seals, the Ministerial Secretary of State for Justice, and the Ministerial Secretary of State for the Interior, by native Jews of the departments of Algeria who have distinguished themselves through services rendered to the country.

Article 6.—The present law is applicable to all the beneficiaries of the decree of 24 October 1870 and to their descendants.

Artice 7.—The present decree will be published in the *Journal Officiel* and executed as the law of the State.

Done at Vichy, 7 October 1940.[3]

Ph. PÉTAIN

By the Marshal of France, Chief of the French State:
The Keeper of Seals,
Ministerial Secretary of State for Justice
Raphaël ALIBERT

The Ministerial Secretary of State for the Interior
Marcel PEYROUTON

Text from the *Journal Officiel de l'Algérie* (October 8,1940), in Michel Ansky, *Les Juifs d'Algérie du Décret Crémieux à la Libération* (Paris, 1950), p. 88.

[1] That is, the Crémieux Decree.

[2] Of French citizenship.

[3] The final regulation with certain adjustments of this decree was made by Law no. 252 of February 18, 1942, the text of which is published in Michel Abitbol, *Les Juifs d'Afrique du Nord sous Vichy* (Paris, 1983), p. 183, Annexe 1.

THE LEADERS OF ALGERIAN JEWRY PROTEST THE ABROGATION OF THE CRÉMIEUX DECREE AND DECLARE THEIR CONTINUED LOYALTY TO FRANCE

(1940)

MEMORANDUM[1]
To Monsieur le Marechal PÉTAIN
Chief of the French State
VICHY (France)

The abrogation of the Crémieux Decree, regulating the political rights of the native Jews of the departments of Algeria and declaring them French citizens, reverberates painfully in the hearts of all Algerian Jews.

The Crémieux Decree of 24 October 1870 bore the signatures of the members of the delegation of Tours: Gambetta, Glais-Bizoin, Crémieux, Fourichon.[2]

This decree was not made on the spur of the moment. As a matter of fact, as far back as 1847, Monsieur De Baudicour, in his book *The Colonization of Algeria,*[3] wrote that "the French government had a major interest in attaching to itself the Algerian Jews."

. . . . [4]

Glais-Bizoin,[5] one of the signatories of this decree, would later write: "Among the thousands of decrees issued by the Government of National Defense, this was surely one of the most just."

The Algerian Jews themselves had asked to become French citizens; notably, in 1864, they addressed a moving petition to the Senate requesting this citizenship. Again, in 1869, the Consistories demanded by petition to the Emperor complete and obligatory emancipation for native Jews.

To this end, the Algerian Jews were willing to be deprived of their personal status which was an integral part of their religious obligations. This important sacrifice, which at the time profoundly changed their social structure and their family relations, proved the sincerity with which they would integrate themselves into the French nation.

The promoters and authors of the Crémieux Decree were not mistaken in according the statutes of citizenship to the Algerian Jews.

[1] The memorandum was included with a letter of protest to Marshal Pétain, dated October 10, 1940. The text of the letter is included in Maurice Eisenbeth, *Pages Vécues: 1940–43* (Algiers, 1945), p. 15.

[2] Concerning the circumstances, see, p. 17.

[3] The reference is to Louis de Baudicour, *La colonisation de l'Algérie* (Paris, 1856). The author was one of the great proponents of French colonialism.

[4] A detailed history of the process leading up to the Crémieux Decree is given.

[5] Alexandre Glais-Bizoin (1800–1877) was a member of the Government of National Defense and a delegate at Tours in 1870. The reference here is to his book *Dictature de cinq mois: mémoires pour servir à l'histoire du gouvernement de la défense national et de la délégation de Tours et de Bordeaux* (Paris, 1873).

Overall, the new citizens contributed to the strengthening of French authority in Algeria, which was one of the principal aims of this decree.

They had a great part in the economic and intellectual development of this country, which is today, rightly, one of the glories of the French Empire.

Not shirking any of their duties, they responded loyally in 1914–1918 and 1939–1940 to the call of the Fatherland. They fought valiantly in the defense of the country as is proved by the number of their dead, wounded, those cited and decorated, and the significant number of bereaved parents, war widows, and orphans. There is not a single family that the two wars have not touched.

The decree of abrogation provides, however, in Articles 4 and 5 two categories of exception:

1. In favor of native Algerian Jews who belonged to a combat unit during the wars of 1914–1918 and 1939–1940 and had been awarded the military Legion of Honor, the Military Medal, or the Croix de Guerre, thereby retaining their political status as French citizens (Art. 4).

2. In favor of those who distinguished themselves by rendering services to the country, for whom the same political status of French citizenship would be preserved (Art. 5).

While gratefully acknowledging the sentiments that dictated these two categories of exceptions, we do not know how to express our sorrow in seeing such distinctions established between citizens of the same origin who are animated by the same French sentiments and who on the strength of these sentiments consented together to the same sacrifices for the Fatherland, some of them brilliantly and others unseen.

Without wishing to give the impression in what follows of seeking new categories of exceptions, it is our duty, nevertheless, to observe that the decree of abrogation leaves out widows and bereaved parents of those who died on the field of honor and war orphans who have, notwithstanding, a right to the Fatherland's recognition.[6]

The exceptions stipulated also result in dividing families, distinguishing one brother from another, a son from a father, even though they received the same moral education and the valor of one was a product of this same common education. Does not this division of a single family run counter to the policy which tends to strengthen the family and develop familial feelings?

The forfeiture of the political rights which had been enacted by the decree of abrogation of 7 October 1940 is all the more painful since the withdrawal of such rights after exercising them for seventy years evokes the harsh punishments of the French Penal Code regarding those condemned by common law to loss of their civil rights which entails precisely the deprivation of political rights. The situation would have been entirely different had the Algerian Jews never exercised these rights.

[6] The final law (Loi no. 254 of February 18, 1942) fixing the status of Algerian Jews did in fact take into consideration widows, orphans, and bereaved parents of

This decree of abrogation intervened only a few days ago, recognizing the special situation of Algeria which is, to take up the expression consecrated by historians and general opinion, a great crossroads of races, the government finds it necessary not to apply to it the metropolitan legislation concerning the sons of foreigners. So it is that in Algeria, a French citizen, a citizen of seventy years, who had lived the same joys and the same sorrows as his fellow citizens, who has taken part in two wars, finds himself rejected from French citizenship, while the son of a foreigner is maintained in his rights; and beyond that, the naturalized person who did not even take part in the two wars remains a French citizen. This simple observation does not entail—it goes without saying—any feeling of acrimony vis-à-vis the categories indicated.

We could have produced other arguments and refutations to contradict the press commentaries concerning notably the supposed influence of the Crémieux Decree on the Muslim problems. However, the object of our Memorandum is entirely other. It in no way intends to respond to the very delicate questions which have been raised publicly. As Frenchmen and Patriots our hearts command us to be silent.

However, we would have been unworthy of the name of French citizens, which has been taken away from us while still in a state of armistice and without having heard the parties involved of whom a great number remain prisoners or listed as missing, if we were not to raise a legitimate protest.

We do not intend by this protest to create any difficulty of order for the French Government. A large part of France is occupied. Our duty is to say nothing and to do nothing that would add to the present difficulties.

The excercise of the rights of citizens entails not only rights, but also duties. If the decree of abrogation of 7 October 1940 withdraws our rights, we keep our duties. We will carry them all out, as in the past, entirely selflessly, animated only by concern for the Greatness of France.

Long live France.

Long live French Algeria.

The Chief Rabbi of Algiers
The President of the Consistory of Algiers
The Chief Rabbi of Oran
The President of the Consistory of Oran
The Chief Rabbi of Constantine
The President of the Consistory of Constantine[7]

Text of the memorandum in Maurice Eisenbeth,
Pages Vécues: 1940–43 (Algiers, 1945),
pp. 93–96, Document No. 2.

---

war heroes. For the text, see Michel Abitbol, *Les Juifs d'Afrique du Nord sous Vichy* (Paris, 1983), p. 183, Annexe 1.

[7]They are R. Maurice Eisenbeth, Joseph Kanoui, R. David Askenazi, Albert Smadja, R. F. Halimi, and André Bakouche, respectively.

THE GOVERNOR GENERAL INFORMS THE CHIEF RABBI OF ALGIERS OF A NUMERUS CLAUSUS FOR JEWISH CHILDREN IN PUBLIC PRIMARY SCHOOLS

(1941)

Government General of Algeria
Office for Jewish Questions and Secret Societies
No. 343 QJ

Algiers, 30 September 1941

Monsieur Eisenbeth, Chief Rabbi of Algiers
62, rue Constantine

Algiers

Monsieur Chief Rabbi,

You kindly asked me in your letter of September 21 what decision had been taken concerning the admission of Jewish children to the primary schools.

I have the honor to inform you that, as I had informed you during a previous audience,[1] a numerus clausus has been established for primary education, fixing the number in each school at 14 percent of the total student body. This numerus clausus will be applied to all new pupils from the next term.

However, in order to facilitate your organizing elementary Jewish instruction, I have decided not to apply temporarily this numerus clausus for pupils already in school. This postponement, in any case, will be in effect only until this coming December 31.

As of January 1, 1942, the figure of 14 percent will be valid for all Jewish pupils, and the elimination of all children over that figure will be immediately announced.

I can only urge you, therefore, to make the most of this delay for creating the schools that will be needed to receive the children who will find themselves in excess of the abovementioned numerus clausus.

Please accept, M. Chief Rabbi, the assurance of my highest consideration.

The Governor General
(signed:) WEYGAND

Text of the letter in Maurice Eisenbeth, *Pages vécues: 1940–43* (Algiers, 1945), pp. 33–34.

[1] According to Eisenbeth's note here, there was no such audience. See Maurice Eisenbeth, *Pages vécues: 1940–43* (Algiers, 1945), p. 34, n. 1.

THE AMERICAN CONSUL IN ALGIERS ADVISES AGAINST U.S. INTERVENTION ON BEHALF OF ALGERIAN JEWRY UNDER THE VICHY REGIME
(1941)

985 Algiers, Algeria, November 11, 1941.

CONFIDENTIAL.

SUBJECT: Factors in Algerian Pro-British Sentiment.

THE HONORABLE
THE SECRETARY OF STATE,
WASHINGTON.

SIR:

. . . .

The Jews in Algeria, hitherto classed with the European population, number about 150,000 or about 15 percent of the total. They are considered a class apart from the rest of the population on which they can exercise little influence. Their position is as much the result of their own attitude as that of the rest of the population towards them. There is no doubt that the recent legislation of the French Government[1] is arousing them to protest through various channels to more liberal governments, such as those of the United States and Great Britain. It would be fatal, I submit, to accept the role of champion of the Jewish population in either France or Algeria and thereby give an implicit pledge that, in the defeat of Hitlerism, France should be forced to restore fully the former position of its Jewish inhabitants. Such a policy would almost entirely alienate the active and passive sympathy now felt by Algerians of French nationality for the great democratic powers and thus provide an additional obstacle to the anti-German cause.

. . . .

Respectfully yours,

Felix Cole
American Consul General

National Archives (Washington, D.C.) RG 226.
Records of the Office of Strategic Service, 21554.

[1] For examples of Vichy anti-Jewish legislation, see pp. 124–126.

A DAHIR *EXPELLING MOROCCAN JEWS FROM EUROPEAN NEIGHBORHOODS*
(1941)

Article 1.—Moroccan Jewish subjects occupying residential locations, in whatever capacity, in the European sectors of the municipalities, must evacuate the said locations within a month of the date of the publication of the present dahir in the *Bulletin Officel,* unless they can prove their having taken up residence prior to September 1, 1939.

Article 2.—Property owners, principal renters, and every person having entered upon a written or verbal lease corresponding to the conditions provided in Article 1, must make a declaration of the fact to the Bureau of Housing instituted by our dahir of April 23, 1941 (25 Rabīᶜ I 1360) within eight days of the publication of this dahir.

Article 3.—Notwithstanding any contrary stipulation, these leases will be legally canceled at the end of the period of one month stipulated in article 1.

Article 4.—Moroccan Jews residing in the European sectors of the municipalities prior to September 1, 1939, will evacuate their dwellings within a time period that will be set by an executive order of Our Grand Vizier.

Article 5.—Jews who fulfill one of the following conditions will not be subject to the dispositions of Article 1:

a. Are holders of a combat veteran's card instituted by article 101 of the law of December 19, 1926;
b. Were awarded a citation during the 1939–40 campaign giving the right to wear the Croix de Guerre instituted by the decree of March 28, 1941;
c. Were decorated with the Legion of Honor or the Military Medal for deeds in war;
d. Are the parents, widows, or orphans of a soldier who died for France;
e. Are the holders of Sharifan civilian or military Order of Merit.

Article 6.—Infractions of the dispositions of the present dahir and any attempted maneuver to obstruct them will be punished with a fine of 500 to 10,000 francs, in addition to the total amount of the rents. Furthermore, the recalcitrant tenant can be expelled by administrative decision.

Bulletin Officiel du Maroc (August 22, 1941),
text in Michel Abitbol, *Les Juifs d'Afrique du Nord sous Vichy*
(Paris, 1983), p. 189, Annexe V.

MEMBERS OF THE GEO GRAS GROUP THAT TOOK PART IN THE ALGIERS INSURRECTION

(NOVEMBER 7–8, 1942)

The Prefecture

Zermati, Jacques
Levy, André
Atlan, Emile
Bouchara, Charles
Atlani, Henri
Benaiche, Paul
Aich, Fernand
Guez, Fernand
Guez, Eugène
Mesguich, William
Smadja, Arsène
Biribi, Fernand
Benhayo, Jacques
Bedjai, Gilbert
Oualid, Sadia
Fitoussi, Alfred
Papero, Henri
Ayoun, Félix
Azoulay, Albert
Tabet, Michel
Sultan, Claude
Albou, Marcel
Jais, Fernand
Ayache, Albert
Nenhomo, Benjamin
Sessas, Georges
Sebaoun, Paul

Main Post Office

Dreyfus, Jean
Gozlan, Jean
Boumendil, Charles
Timsit, Martial
Gozlan, Julien
Elbaz, Raphaël
Chemla, Prosper
Kamoun, Lucien
Kamoun, André
Tibika, Victor
Smedja, Albert
Chemoulli, Charles

XIX Corps

Pillafort, Cap. Alfred
Daridan, Lieut.
Jais, Roger
Fredj, Fernand
Temime, André
Faivre, Mario
Morali, Roger
Loufrani, Georges
Siksik, Léon
Bitoun, Georges
Darmon, Adolphe
Albou, Roger
Libine, Germain
Bouana, Elie
Cohen, Eliezer
Gamzon, Robert
Taouss, Jacques
Taouss, Maurice
Abrami, Henri
Bouchara, Joseph
Boshen, Jean
Cohen, Adad Raoul
Adda, Charles
Benaim, René
Zeraffa, Jean-Claude
Sonegon, Marcel
Tordjman, Armand
Temime, Elie
Temime, Roland
Ayache, Alfred
Asfes, Lazare
Quibech, Joseph
Mesguich, Jacques
Mesguich, Henri
Mesguich, J. C.
Belaloum, Gilbert
Cohen, Sauveur
Benarous, René
Ayoun, Jacques
Zitoun, Jacques
Tedri, Maurice
Achouche, Simon
Oualid, Paul
Amran, Vitalis
Bendavid, Sam
Beladina, Paul
Dahan, Philippe
Driguez, René
Ankaoua, Robert
Nebot, René
Smedja, Robert
Ayache, Sylvain
Benhamou, Edmond
Cassis, Marcel
Bakry, André
Bouchara, André
Tedri, Léon
Belhacem, Maurice
Hini, ?

Commissariat of the Tenth Arrondissement

Aboulker, Raphaël	De Saint-Blancat, P.	Roberty, Jean-Louis
Aboulker, Stéphane	De Roquefort, ?	X. Chauffeur
Bokaborski, Olivier		

Michel Ansky, *Les Juifs d'Algérie du Décret Crémieux à la libération* (Paris, 1950), pp. 361–62, Annexe 10.

THE NAZIS' REQUISITION OF JEWISH LABORERS IN TUNIS

(DECEMBER 1942)

The President[1] left his office around 11 o'clock and, accompanied by the Chief Rabbi whom he had picked up at his home, went to the Kommandantur,[2] arriving there a quarter of an hour later.

Noon. One o'clock. Two o'clock. Three o'clock. They still had not returned. An intense anxiety took hold of the Jewish population, among whom any item of news spread rapidly, often inflated and distorted.

Three thirty. Finally, they returned with the look of defeat. They asked that the Communal Council and all the notables be convened immediately at the Chief Rabbi's residence. It was not possible to get them all together. Only a few arrived, along with the many curious onlookers.

The President gave an account of what had taken place.

They had been received by Colonel Rauff, Chief of the Gestapo.

. . . .

Colonel Rauff indicated to them that by way of reprisals "on account of the presence of Jewish political agents in the Anglo-American army," General Nehring had decided to compel the Jews between the ages of 17 and 50 to forced labor. They would be employed in making earthworks, trenches, etc., but they would not be sent into theaters of operations. The Colonel indicated that General Nehring had made these arrangements with the consent of Admiral Esteva, the Resident General.

Finally, with the inevitable zest in the style of Hitler's and his henchmen's speeches, Rauff added that it was the Jews who had launched this war and that they ought, therefore, to bear the burden of this generic responsibility. Here in Tunisia, their share of the suffering would be this labor which had been imposed upon them and which they should not try to shirk. If they did not do it in good faith, they would then be constrained under a much more brutal form, with heavy sanctions upon the population.

Our venerable Chief Rabbi, a simple and pure old man, exclusively preoccupied with talmudic studies, having always lived in the exercise of an active charity which was his supreme goal, tried to get the German to be flexible and did his best with his naive honesty to find a path to his heart. The President, with fewer illusions it is true, persisted in protesting, or to be more precise, arguing that these measures would turn the country's economy upside down, that they would cause hardship and desolation for a multitude of poor people, who make up the great majority of the colony, and that they would be in the end too brutal.

Nothing helped.

[1] Of the Jewish Communal Council of Tunis.

[2] German Command Headquarters.

Colonel Rauff specified that he thought a figure of 3,000 to 4,000 workers would be sufficient, that he was charging the Jews themselves with the task of organizing their maintenance in the camps, their outfitting even down to the digging tools, and the distribution of aid to their families. The workers would have to wear a large, visible yellow star sewn on their clothing front and back. "In order to allow them to be recognized even from afar and shot down in case of escape," added Rauff.

He intended that all this would be organized most efficiently, that the Chief Rabbi would put together a team of people, other than the Community Council members who were destined for Heaven knows what sacrifice, to organize each service. The aforesaid organization would be responsible to the Germans for the proper execution of their instructions. Their names would have to be submitted to him that very same day at 5:00 P.M. While on the following morning at 8 o'clock, he had to have a list of 2,000 names from which would be selected the required workers as needed.

On behalf of the Chief Rabbi and the Community, M. Borgel[3] reiterated that the task was unrealizable. For one thing, it was impossible to find such a large number of laborers within a population that counted a large proportion of handicapped and ill persons. Furthermore, they could never satisfy such an exorbitant and unexpected demand in so short a time. Lastly, the Community lacked the means for any team whatsoever to take a census and then to organize and carry out such a project on the run.

The Chief Rabbi pleaded again with his tears, unable to make himself understood any other way.

The tears of a Jew could not move a man like Colonel Rauff, even if it was an elderly clergyman.

He broke off the interview with these words: "If you do not know how to find 2,000 Jews by yourselves, I will be forced to round up 10,000 with my own men. That is what will happen to you if I do not get all that I have just required carried out in the allotted time." Then he turned on his heels and added: "The visit is terminated as far as I am concerned."

Robert Borgel, *Etoile jaune et croix gammée: récit d'une servitude* (Tunis, 1944), pp. 32–36.

[3] Moïse Borgel was president of the Communal Council.

A NAZI PROCLAMATION OF AN INDEMNITY LEVIED AGAINST THE JEWS OF TUNISIA (1942)

It is International Jewry that wanted the war and prepared for it.

The inhabitants of the land of Tunisia—French, Italian, and Muslim—have suffered cruelly from the war on account of the aerial bombardment which struck the country in recent days.

Therefore, I have decided to impose an indemnity upon the wealth of Tunisian Jews in the sum of 20 million francs for aid to the civilian victims of the bombardment. The distribution of the aid will be in the hands of a committee organized under the name of "Committee for Immediate Relief," which will come directly to the assistance of everyone who has personally suffered harm either to his person or his property due to the criminal Anglo-American aerial bombardment of unarmed civilians.

Consequently, all civilian inhabitants of Tunis, whether French, Italian, or Muslim, who have suffered damage because of the Anglo-American aggression, should come forward with a detailed request setting forth the damage incurred to the office of the aforementioned committee in the Center for National Relief in the Palais des Sociétés Françaises, Avenue de Paris. As for the inhabitants of other cities, they should present their requests to their municipality which will promptly forward it to the central office of the aforementioned committee.

The grants of assistance will be given as soon as possible to the victims of the aerial bombings themselves. Whoever presents himself to receive the aforesaid aid unrightfully will incur severe punishment.[1]

Tunis, 23 December 1942.

The Commander-in-Chief of the Axis Forces,
General von Arnim

"Iʿlām li-Ḍaḥāya 'l-Rami 'l-Jawwī Anglo-Amīrikānī,"
Ar. text in Robert Attal and Claude Sitbon, eds.,
Regards sur les Juifs de Tunisie
(Paris, 1979), p. 187.

[1] The proclamation was issued in three languages: Arabic, French, and Italian.

THE JEWS OF TUNIS RAISE THE FUNDS TO PAY THE INDEMNITY

(1942)

Anxiety reigned at the Community Office. M. Borgel had been summoned by Colonel Rauff for a special and important communication. What was going to happen now? We trembled for our hostages.[1]

After an hour's wait, the President came back looking very downcast.

"We must have 20 million francs before tomorrow evening."

He related the Nazis' latest demand.

The Anglo-Saxons had bombed the city, creating many victims and causing considerable damage. The Jews, being their allies, had to bear the consequences of these crimes. A beginning contribution of 20 million would have to be immediately turned over to be divided among the victims and their families. If these orders were not carried out, the hostages would be shot.

. . . .

There was no delaying. It had to be carried out. But how to find such a sum in so short a time? Our well-to-do coreligionists had already paid over significant contributions approaching on average half a million a day for the needs of the recruitment.[2] It was impossible to put together that kind of sum in ready cash in such a short time.

On the other hand, it would be criminal to allow even one man to be shot for a matter of money.

M. Borgel, accompanied by Lawyer Nataf, the Honorary President, immediately went to the Resident General's Office and demanded an audience.

Admiral Esteva[3] would not permit any financial participation by the government. The Germans were demanding moreover that it be the Jews alone who paid. However, he agreed to give instructions to the Land Fund, an institution for real estate loans, to get in touch with us. The first conversation with the director of the institution took place that very evening.

22 December

The negotiations with the Land Fund were conducted at full speed thanks to the understanding and the practical sense which the director showed his board. This high official exerted himself to extricate us from this predicament, but he was bound by the obligations of his office, and we had to furnish substantial guarantees.

Within a few hours we were in the process of bringing as collateral some of the finest agricultural estates and the choicest pieces of urban real

[1] That is, the large number of Jewish laborers in the work camps.

[2] For the labor details.

[3] The French Resident General.

estate. The guarantees thus put together exceeded 100 million. The margin of security was by any standards more than enough.

The contracts were drawn up and signed on the spot.

Later in the evening, M. Borgel went back to the Kommandantur and handed over the required ransom to the Nazi gangster chief.

The bourgeois Jews have been frequently denigrated and caricatured. However, they knew how to prove in tragic circumstances that they are capable of selflessness and sacrifice.[4]

Paul Ghez, *Six mois sous la botte*
(Tunis, 1943), pp. 43–44.

[4] After liberation, the Jewish community was threatened with foreclosure by the Land Fund. Receiving no sympathy from French officials, the communal leadership turned to the United States. President Roosevelt himself instructed the secretary of state to intervene on the Tunisian Jews' behalf. See *FRUS 1943* 2: 280–301.

A VICHY OFFICIAL DISCUSSES A GERMAN PROPOSAL TO REQUIRE JEWS TO WEAR THE YELLOW STAR IN TUNIS

(1943)

Residency-General of France
at Tunis
and
Secretariat-General of the
Tunisian Government
Office of Judicial and Legislative Affairs

Tunis, March 20, 1943
From the Chief Appeals Attorney
of the Council of State,
Judicial and Legislative Counselor
to the Tunisian Government
to
Admiral Esteva
Resident General of France at Tunis

SUBJECT: Wearing of the yellow star by Jews

As per his letter of March 17, 1943, the Prefect for General Security has informed you that Colonel Rauff, Chief of the German Police, has advised him that it would be appropriate for the Jews of Tunisia to be required to wear the yellow star, and he has charged him to ask you to make a decision in this regard which would be submitted beforehand for General Von Arnim's approval. He added that the Italian Jews would be subject to a special measure on the part of the German High Command.[1]

You kindly communicated this letter to me, asking me to prepare a text right away with M. Lamotte.[2]

M. Lamotte, with whom I got in touch immediately, forwarded the following note to me concerning the advisability of this measure:

. . . .

If wearing of a distinctive badge would be imposed upon French and Tunisian Jews, but not upon Italian Jews, His Highness[3] would not fail to see it, insofar as his subjects are concerned, as a measure taken against their nationality rather than against their race.

Furthermore, obligating Jews to wear a distinguishing badge would be interpreted by the unsophisticated Muslim opinion as an indication that the Jewish race has been denounced to public humiliation, and the masses would not miss the opportunity to inflict harm upon Jewish persons and property.

[1] The Germans were constrained to do this by their Italian allies.

[2] The French delegate to the Tunisian Department of Justice.

[3] The bey.

Finally, numerous Muslim youth groups: the Red Crescent, the Destour Youth, the Lion Cubs of the Flag, the Muslim Scouts, etc., who already have a tendency to sow disorder in the country, would find in the proposed measure a pretext to further aggravate the confusion.

Perhaps you would consider it useful to call the German authorities' attention to the difficulties indicated in this note which a measure imposing the yellow star on the Jews would arouse.

Whether or not this measure will be decided upon, we have gone over, according to your instructions, the details of form and content according to which it could be put into effect.

. . . .

We have therefore proposed the following preliminary draft of a police ordinance:

The Prefect for General Security of Tunisia

In accordance with the Beylical Decree of October 30, 1941 determining the powers of the Prefect for the General Security of Tunisia, and

In accordance with the Beylical Decree of March 12, 1942 concerning the status of the Jews,

Issues the following ordinance:

Article 1.—In all of the territory of the Regency, all persons of either sex considered Jews under Article 2 of the decree of March 12, 1942, will be obliged as of the age of eighteen to wear a yellow badge representing a six-pointed star.

This badge will be made of lemon yellow fabric and should be 5 cm in diameter. It must be firmly sewn along all its points in the manner that escutcheons are attached to garments on the left side of the chest, and it is to be clearly visible.

Article 2.—Contraventions of the present ordinance will be pursued in conformity with the laws in force. Furthermore, contraventions will be subject to administrative internment.

Article 3.—The police force and the gendarmerie will be charged with the application of the present ordinance, which will go into effect on April 1, 1943.[4]

. . . .

With regard to the age from which the wearing of the yellow star will be mandatory, it seems to us at the minimum, the age of eighteen should be chosen, after which Jewish workers are required. This will avoid the badge being worn in schools, even secondary schools, where it would present certain inconveniences.

As to the persons who are to be subject to this badge, it seems to us impossible for us to refer to any definition other than the legal definition in Article 2 of the decree of March 12, 1942, on Jewish status.

. . . .

It is up to the German military police to take any special measures that it judges necessary with regard to the Italian Jews. However, in our own

[4] The ordinance, however, did not go into effect in Tunis.

opinion, the Protectorate authorities would not be able to make any distinctions according to nationality without violating the decree of March 12, 1942, on Jewish status.

. . . .

Finally, a certain delay, at least until the end of the month, will be necessary so that those concerned would be able to produce the badges.

(signed) De Font Reaux[5]

CDJC Archives FA 50, Published in Jacques Sabille, *Les Juifs de Tunisie sous Vichy et l'occupation* (Paris, 1954), pp. 179–81, Annexe I, G.

[5] According to Jacques Sabille, *Les Juifs de Tunisie sous Vichy et l'occupation* (Paris, 1954), p. 128, he was "a convinced antisemite, who collaborated with the representatives of the CGQJ [Bureau for Jewish Affairs] at Tunis." Despite their own anti-Semitism, Vichy officials were becoming more resistant at this time to going along with the Germans on further anti-Jewish measures for reasons discussed by Michael R. Marrus and Robert O. Paxton, *Vichy France and the Jews* (New York, 1981), pp. 326–27.

TRIPOLITANIAN JEWRY WELCOMES THE SOLDIERS OF THE EIGHTH ARMY AS LIBERATORS (1943)

"You have saved us all."

"This is the happiest Sabbath of our lives," said the Jews of Tripoli as they watched, yesterday morning, a parade of Jewish soldiers of the Eighth Army enter a Tripoli synagogue for a solemn service of thanksgiving.

On the saluting base, as the troops marched past, was Brigadier F. H. Kisch, C. B., C. B. E., D. S. O., Chief Engineer of the Eighth Army and himself a Jew. At his side stood Major L. Rabinowitz, Senior Jewish Chaplain to the M. E. F.[1]

Hundreds of members of the Jewish faith, who have been so cruelly oppressed under the Nazi-Fascist regime, lined the square and cheered when the parade was welcomed at the synagogue by the Chief Rabbi of Tripolitania, Dr. Aldo Lattes.[2]

The parade was headed by Major C. J. O'Shaughnessy, G. C., D. S. O., O. C., of an R. E. Coy.,[3] and Capt. C. W. Wellington.

Jewish soldiers drawn from many units of the Eighth Army, and wearing a bewildering variety of headdresses, marched smartly through the main street of Tripoli, headed by the pipes of a famous Highland Regiment.

After the service, the parade marched to the H. Q. of an R. E. unit, where members of the Jewish Community of Tripoli had prepared cakes and wine for the soldiers.

The ceremony of sanctifying the Sabbath was performed by Major Rabinowitz, who said prayers over the first goblet of wine.

Major O'Shaughnessy, on behalf of the Jewish soldiers of the Eighth Army, thanked the Jewish Community of Tripoli for entertainment afforded.

Replying, the Chief Rabbi of Tripolitania, Dr. Lattes, said that this was a great day in the history of Jewry and marked their first liberation from Axis domination.

He quoted a Hebrew poem, "Come in peace, ye messengers of peace of the Most High."[4]

Leading representatives of Tripoli's 20,000 Jewish population cheered the parade. Many of the women were in tears.

[1] Concerning each of these men, see the entries on each in *EJ* 10: 1061–62, and *EJ* 13: 1477, respectively.

[2] He was an Italian, appointed by the Union of Italian Jewish Communities to be chief rabbi of Libya in 1937. See Renzo de Felice, *Jews in an Arab Land: Libya, 1835–1970,* trans. Judith Roumani (Austin, 1985), p. 91, passim.

[3] Royal Engineers Company.

[4] From the hymn *"Shālōm ʿAlēkhem,"* which is sung upon returning home from synagogue on Friday evening.

Speaking to Cyril James, *Tripoli Times* representative, a Jewish leader said:

"Soldiers of Eighth Army can never know what they have done for the Jews of Tripoli. The Nazis had issued orders that all able-bodied Jews were to be sent to Tunisia on forced labor, with no exceptions. The order was to have come into force in fifteen days' times. You have saved us all. But thousands of our community have already been deported by the Axis powers, and there have been many cases of death through starvation.

"We can never forget this glorious day."

CZA (Jerusalem) S 25/5217, "Tripoli's Chief Rabbi Thanks the Eighth Army," copied from *Tripoli Times* (January 31, 1943).

PALESTINIAN JEWISH UNITS IN THE BRITISH ARMY AID THEIR BRETHREN IN LIBYA AND TUNISIA

(1941–1942)

What a difference when the advance of the Eighth Army brought the Jewish units into contact with their suffering brethren of Cyrenaica, Tripolitania, and Tunisia! No words of praise could be too high for their admirable conduct, in which sympathy, understanding, and practical assistance were the most prominent features. They regarded themselves as ambassadors of the Jewish people, with a positive duty to raise them from their lowly state, restore to them their self-respect and pride, intercede on their behalf, and act as their mentors. In every town and village they entered, from Derna to Tunis, they made a beeline for the Jewish community, heard their woes, gave them encouragement, and, from the wells of their pity, sent accounts—as often as not exaggerated—to Palestine of these lost tribes of Israel. Woe betide the reputation of the chaplain were he backward in acting upon their information![1] In Tobruk, in 1941, 5 M. T.[2] restored the damaged synagogue. It was but an omen for the future. During the 1942 campaign, 1039[3] restored the desecrated Jewish cemetery in Tobruk, 738[4] did the same in Derna. In Misurata and in Sirte, in Takrouna and in Ben-Gardane, in Mokhnine and in Tunis, they brought their message of good cheer to these downcast communities.

But it was in Benghazi and Tripoli that they were able to do their most lasting work: first, because of the size of the communities and, secondly, because they were stationed there for some time. Benghazi was entirely disorganized; chaos ruled supreme in the community. All but 200 of its 3,500 Jews had been deported to a concentration camp. At last, after many delays, they were sent back. The Palestinian Jewish units received and assisted them, and *established a Hebrew school for the children.*[5] That school was the showpiece of Benghazi. Its moving spirit and "acting principal" was Lieutenant Reifenberg,[6] R. A. S. C., a lecturer in peacetime in the Hebrew University, its teachers all humble Palestinian Jewish soldiers. The progress made was remarkable, the effect on the spirit of Benghazi Jews indescribable; and when the unit which took the initiative was ordered to Malta, their joy was tempered, not by the danger of the journey (to which they fell victims), but by the mournful thought, "What will happen to the school?"

[1] The writer was senior Jewish chaplain in the British army.

[2] The number of a specific unit.

[3] See note 2.

[4] See note 2.

[5] The writer's italics.

[6] The reference is to Adolf Reifenberg, the distinguished chemist, concerning whom see *EJ* 14: 52–53.

So in Tripoli they were instrumental in obtaining the reopening of the Maccabi Club, to which they sent P. T. instructors, and the Ben Yahuda organization, for which they provided teachers. Palestinian Jewish doctors with the hearty approval of the D. D. M. S., volunteered to attend at the Jewish eye-clinic, and the soldiers awaited only the reopening of the schools to provide teachers. One day, shortly after the capture of the town, the *Tripoli Times* bore an announcement of a football match between Tel-Aviv and Maccabi. "Tel Aviv" was the pseudonym for a Palestinian Jewish unit, since, for security reasons, they could not give their designation.

The effect of all this on the morale of these downtrodden Jews cannot be exaggerated, and Jewry as a whole has cause to bless the public spirit of its Palestinian sons.

Louis Rabinowitz, *Soldiers from Judaea: Palestinian Jewish Units in the Middle East, 1941–43* (New York, 1945), pp. 67–69.

A REPORT ON THE STATE OF TRIPOLITANIAN JEWRY IN 1943

Comunita Israelitica della Tripolitania
TRIPOLI

Tripoli, August 13, 1943
12 Menahem,[1] 5703
No. 7256

Subject: *Situation of the Jewish Community in Tripoli*
To the JEWISH AGENCY
JERUSALEM

Now, after few months, having resumed our work with quietness and serenity, after the most difficult period, we would like, first of all, to send you our brotherly salute.

Consequently allow us to submit you an exact sketch of the situation of the Jews in Tripoli, during the last years, showing you the wide and serious problems which must be urgently solved.

The Jewish Community at Tripoli, which counts today more than 20,000 souls (not included the 8,000 Jews living in small centers of Tripolitania), has suffered a great deal these last years, either due to anti-racial laws or due to war.

But even before racial laws, this Community was very badly hurt in his deepest Jewish feelings by government proclamations compelling the Jewish youth to frequent Medium[2] Schools also on Sabbath, which law practically deprived the youth of any education, beside much of elementary schools, as the scrupulous observation of the Sabbath, as well as the laws for food (cacher) is absolutely totalitarian in our City and further laws against us hurt the Jewish soul, when the government compelled Jewish shopkeepers and merchants to keep their shops open on Saturdays in the new quarters of the town.[3] Afterward came the official anti-racial laws and the war, which put this Community in a moral and material condition, so serious and grave, as never before in our life.

Wishing to limit report only to the material damages, as the moral sufferings could never be expressed adequately, we beg to inform you that:

1. four Synagogues were completely destroyed and several seriously damaged;

2. the Cemetery, which due to its position and site was used for numerous anti-aircraft batteries, has been bombed repeatedly and had the external wall almost destroyed and hundreds of tombs were devastated and ravaged;

[1] That is, the Hebrew month of Av.
[2] Secondary or high school.
[3] See pp. 398–401.

3. the Jewish quarters were, more than any other part of the town, bombed for several times and dwelling houses were completely destroyed and others seriously damaged and became uninhabitable;

4. the proclamation against the Jews in Tripoli and the fact that they were forced to do hard labor in far-reaching military areas has compelled the Community to serious sacrifices, as the Italian Government refused to give any allotment or aid to their families and paid the Jewish laborers less then six pence a day;

5. the sending of all Jews of Cyrenaica to concentration camps had as immediate consequence for our Community the moral obligation to provide at least to their elementary exigencies of life, because the Italian Government did not give them even the minimum food required for not starving. Notwithstanding our great sacrifices, the diseases and death rate were very high, during 10 months out of 3,000 interned Jews, we have had about 500 deceased;

6. the application of anti-racial laws, which produced serious restrictions on the wholesale and retail trade, the dismissal of all Jewish employees from the Government and public administrations, the prohibition for the Jews to sell real estate property, etc., had reduced seriously the capacity of earning a living of the Jewish merchants and traders;

7. the limited possibility of labor and work raised the number of paupers needing subsidy to several thousands.

When our general conditions reached a point which left us almost desperate and hopeless for the future, the victorious forward march of the Allied troops whom we greeted as real messengers of God gave us back our dignity as human beings and allowed us the possibility of hoping again for a future under a better omen. Since these few months of the reconquest of our liberty, we are happy to affirm that the wounds made to our souls and bodies from Fascist oppression are slowly recovering.

The possibility of labor after British Military occupation has reduced the number of our paupers. The invalids for any work due to old age or other physical conditions, the orphans and widows to be assisted completely by this community are today 848. But the assistance of those poors requires enormous expenses, because of the high cost of living due to the devaluation of the Italian lire and lack of sufficient essential foodstuffs and other necessary articles on the markets. To this category of very indigent people, there is to be added to our budget the sick and those poors who require aid from the Community because their wages or salary are not sufficient to live with their families, under actual conditions.

For our assistance work, we need also specially blankets, clothing of any nature, and milk for sick and children.

We have many other difficulties actually concerning education. Since three years, about 3,000 children between 6 and 13 years of age are deprived of any education, whereas other 1,000 of 13 to 16 years old must through a professional school be prepared to be citizens and Hebrews, useful for themselves and for others. The expenses for building Schools and their functioning are very high. Even to reduce them to the strict necessity, the estimates of such a project are about 15,000 for installations expenses (to adapt and repair the premises, purchase of school and education material, which has been mostly destroyed or dispersed) and for the functioning of these school, based on a minimum program, there will be about £ 28,000 expenses a year.

It is just and fair that the community is entitled to a grant in aid or subvention from the British Government, specially for the elementary Schools, and besides, in a relative modest amount, we rely upon school taxes and the contribution of Tripoli Jews, who of course will help as much as they can. But the figures of needed funds are reaching such importance that we are compelled to call for aid and assistance on our Jewish brothers. If we would like to try to resolve the problem with a complete program, in all points concerning Jewish education and formation, supplying the schools with all modern pedagogic material, opening a free refectory for paupers, medical assistance for sick (specially trachoma cases very high among school children), foundation of a medium school, an asylum for children of 3 to 6 years of age, taking them away from the streets and preparing them to discipline and school life, etc., in this case the estimates would have to be raised accordingly.

We must not forget that for the life and regular development of the communal activities, we need very important funds every year, for which we think that we could provide ourselves: functioning of 22 synagogues, beneficence, economical improvement of personnel for the creed and for administration, pension and allowances, Jeshivoth and Hebroth, etc.[4]

We feel that we would fail to our principal duty in front of God and our consciousness, if soon after our autumnal holidays, which this year will be in thanksgiving God, full of joy and happiness for the new definite victory, we do not open the schools for all our youth and children, which are very thirsty of education and knowledge.

Shalom.

JEWISH COMMUNITY OF TRIPOLITANIA
THE PRESIDENT
(Halfalla Nahum)
signature

CZA (Jerusalem) S 6/4582.

[4] Yeshīvōt and Ḥevrōt (Ḥavarōt). A Ḥevra is a society dedicated to pious works.

A BRITISH OFFICER SURVEYS THE STATE OF CYRENAICAN JEWRY AT THE TIME OF LIBERATION (1943)

Lt.-Col. H. M. Foot
HQ.
British Military Administration
Cyrenaica, M. E. F.[1]

My dear Goor,

You will remember that when you were in Cyrenaica you asked me the position about the Cyrenaican Jews who were exiled by the Italians in Tripolitania and said that there were various individuals and organizations in Palestine anxious about their condition and ready to help if necessary.

Since then I have had the opportunity of visiting the camps at Giado and Gharian, where the 2,300 exiles have been living, and hearing something of their experiences. It is an astonishing story—not the least remarkable factor being the apparent lack of all reason for such a senseless action on the part of the Italians. The move must have required a great deal of transport at a time when the Italians were short and subsequently entailed an additional drain on the depleted food supplies of Tripolitania.

The camp at Giado was kept very short of food throughout the autumn of 1942, and typhus caused over 300 deaths. Since we took over, things have of course greatly improved. The cleanliness of the camp is now all that could be desired, and the food is good and quite sufficient. I found the exiles in excellent spirits, very excited at the prospect of returning to Cyrenaica after a year or so away from their homes. Disease is now practically absent, and everyone looks well fed (especially the children). The few young officers who were running the camp have done magnificent work and taken a very great interest in the welfare of their charges.

The first 500 of the returning exiles arrived back a week or so ago. I have not seen them yet, but I inspected the arrangements made by Capt. Evans-Jones (whom you may have met in Benghazi), and I am sure that everything was done to receive them properly. Kitchens were equipped, blankets provided, rations issued, water distributed to the houses, latrines built, and, in cooperation with the Jewish community reception committee, everything possible done to make the houses inhabitable. They have now scattered to their own homes, and small parties have been sent to Barce and Derna.

The slow work of rehabilitation now has to go forward, and it will be many months before anything like normal conditions return. Many of the houses in Benghazi particularly have been damaged by bombs, and everywhere they are bare of furniture except for rush mats. The poorer sections

[1] Middle East Forces.

of the community are in undoubted need of assistance, and any amounts that Palestine Jews feel they can contribute will, I am sure, be put to a very good purpose. Distribution of the money contributed would be made entirely by the Jewish relief committee.

I think the best course would be for any organization which proposes to collect funds for this purpose to write first of all to Civil Affairs Branch, G. H. Q. Cairo, and ask whether facilities may be given for forwarding money to the Jewish relief committee. Once that approval is obtained, no further obstacle appears to exist.

I am sending this letter to you through Civil Affairs Branch so that they can see what line I have suggested.

Yours sincerely,
H. M. Foot

A. Goor, Esq., M. B. E
Jerusalem

CZA (Jerusalem) S 6/4582
(undated, unsigned copy).

THE BRITISH MILITARY COMMANDER OF BARCA COMPLAINS ABOUT PALESTINIAN JEWISH SOLDIERS TEACHING IN A LOCAL SYNAGOGUE AGAINST ORDERS

(1944)

228 Town Major
Middle East Forces
Ref: 228/22
Dated 18 Jan. 44

Subject: Discipline
To: O. C. 544 and M Coy RE.,
Cyrenaica.

1. The attached AFsB of two men of your unit have been seen by A. Q. M. G., HQ Cyrenaica Area, and approved. Copies of action taken by you are to be forwarded to Town Major, Barce, and HQ Cyrenaica Area.

2. *Statement by Town Major Barce.*

On or about the 10th January 1944 I was informed by Major Douglas, C. A. O., that two members of H. M. Forces, namely Pal/46178 Sapper SHLOMO VITKI and Pal/45139 Sapper WEINSHALL THEODOR, both of No 544 E and M Coy RE, after having been told by C. A. O. that it was an offense for serving members of H. M. Forces to teach in schools, were found by him giving instruction in Barce Synagogue.

I informed the N. C. O. i/c Detachment 544 E and M Coy RE that this breach of discipline had taken place, and he would order his detachment to cease this illegal practice. He consented.

On the 18th January 1944, Major Douglas informed that the same two men had committed this crime again on the 17th January 1944. I placed both men under arrest and, on going with the C. M. P. to take them into custody, found that they were both teaching in the synagogue again.

Obviously they were completely indifferent to Military Law and have to be kept under close arrest until such time as their O. C. can take them over.

3. Major Douglas C. A. O. and the District Security Officer will make their statement in due course.

Copies to: (signature)

A. Q. M. G. HQ Cyrenaica Area
C. A. O. Barce
A. P. M. Cyrenaica Area

228 Town Major
A. G. Cruickshank RAC

CZA (Jerusalem) S 25/4971, facsimile published in Yoav Gelber, *Tōldōt ha-Hitnaddevūt, vol. 3: Nōs'ē ha-Degel* (Jerusalem, 1983), p. 121.

A PALESTINIAN JEWISH SOLDIER IN THE BRITISH ARMY WRITES HOME ABOUT MEETING HIS LIBYAN BRETHREN (1943)

February 19, 1943

Finally let me tell you about my most precious experiences on this trip—my encounter with the Jews here. As we passed through a little town in our cars marked with the Star of David both in front and in back, we suddenly saw people dressed in European clothes shouting to us in excitement, "*Shalom*!" I stopped and two boys jumped on my running board. "Shalom, Yehudim!"[1] they said and we shook hands. Their first question was, "Do you have any newspapers from Palestine?" I searched around in confusion and finally found a copy of *Hegeh*[2] (I used it to teach one of the refugees Hebrew) under the car seat, and gave it to them. One of them took it with his eyes shining, looked at the Hebrew letters, kissed the paper, and said with moving sincerity, "We shall read this aloud in the synagogue." . . . Behind me the trucks were blowing their horns and I was unable to hold up the convoy any longer. All along the street of this little town stood Jews cheering us with, "*Shalom Yehudim*!" and waving their hands in excitement. . . . Our hearts were warmed by all this. But all this was only an introduction to what was to happen to us in the big city, from which I am writing you.

There are twenty thousand Jews in this city.[3] The streets that we drove through were loud with cries of joy, cries of "Shalom." Ecstatic greetings were pouring upon us from all sides. We felt as if we were dreaming all this excitement. We drove straight through the city to the outskirts, let the Negroes get out, and camped there. I went back immediately to the city, in search of Jews. At the gate to the city I met a man wearing spectacles and I approached him in Arabic, "Where do the Jews live here?" He answered in Arabic that most of them live in the Jewish Quarter, and he looked rather startled. I suspected that he was a Jew. However, I hesitated to ask him about this and went on in Arabic, "Where is the nearest synagogue? Could I go to worship there?" At this he smiled and asked, "Are you a Jew?" Then he looked at my epaulettes and saw "Palestine" there and shook my hands with a warm "*Shalom Aleichem*."[4] From then on he did not leave me alone. Simon L. is his name. I went along with him, and he told me in fluent Arabic about the Jews in the city. He explained that wealthy Jews had built the suburb we were in and that poor Jews used to rent rooms there to escape the bombings. In the days of the German occupation there was a joke

[1] "Greetings, fellow-Jews!"

[2] A Palestinian daily newspaper in vocalized Hebrew and on a somewhat easier level than the regular papers.

[3] Tripoli.

[4] The traditional Hebrew greeting, "Peace be upon you."

circulating to the effect that the Allies would have to save them from the Germans, the Italians, and the British Air Force. . . . I went with him to his house. There we found his wife, his sister, two younger brothers, and a little daughter of five called Eliza. All of them, except for the mother, speak Hebrew fluently. Little Eliza didn't leave me alone for a moment, singing me Hebrew songs and laughing with joy. In the meantime two neighbors came in. I was amazed at their fluent Hebrew. It seems that most of the Jews of Tripoli know the language.

It was hard for me to get up to leave them. They simply did not let me. I promised that I would return shortly. I would only go to tell my sergeant that I was going to spend some time with the Jews in the city. But Simon refused to let me go alone. He accompanied me to the camp, and I spoke to the sergeant there and came back. When we entered the house the table was set and the family was sitting and waiting for me. I saw some of the neighbors coming in with pots and realized that they were helping the mother to prepare a fitting meal for the occasion. I knew that this was not to be one of their ordinary meals and that they were not in the habit of eating their fill. But there were all kinds of delicacies at this meal. After the dinner many of the neighbors came in. I talked to them about Palestine, and I gathered that they had heard nothing about the fate of our people in Europe. I told them about the atrocities the Nazis committed upon the Jews in occupied countries. How intently they listened! After that they opened their hearts and told of what they had been through. Simon L. asked that all of the Jewish soldiers come to the Jewish Quarter on the next day to have their Sabbath meal there. I told him that there were sixty of us. He replied, "We'll divide you among us. Every family will take a soldier." Thus I sat there until it grew late.

From their tales I gathered that the Jews of Tripoli were also due to be carried off to the concentration camps in Tunis. And probably these 20,000 Jews would be dead today if Montgomery had not attacked before the Germans were able to complete their plans for the liquidation of the Jews. It was from them that I heard of the concentration camps for the Jews of Cyrenaica in Jiddo.[5] This camp was erected 200 miles deep in the desert. There the last remainder of the lovable Jews whom we met a year and a half ago in Bardia, Tobruk, Derna, Berci, Benghazi, and other places were gathered.[6] They also told me that there were present about 200 refugees from the concentration camp in the city. During the retreat some of them tried to escape into the desert. The Italian guards shot them while they were escaping, but 200 of them succeeded in reaching Tripoli. As for the rest—no

[5] The writer is referring to the Giado camp, concerning which see, pp. 122, 450.

[6] The Cyrenaican Jews were exiled because of their collaboration with the British during the first two times the area came under the latter's control. See, p. 122.

one can tell what happened to them. The Allied authorities announced that typhus fever was rampant in the camp at Jiddo and that it was quarantined—that nurses, doctors, food, and supplies were sent there and that the internees were found to be without any food and water and in a dreadful condition. The authorities also announced that all the exiles would be returned to their homes. But the Jews of Tripoli, at least those with whom I spoke, had heard nothing of the fate of their brethren. . . . In the evening, as I was still visiting with the L. family, a neighbor came in with a copy of *Davar*[7] that he had received from one of the Jewish longshoremen who are stationed in the city. The letter that I had written about the Jews of Libya had been published in that issue. It was read aloud in public in the synagogues and proved something of a balm in their affliction.

I heard many wonderful things that evening. I heard legendary stories of our exploits—the exploits of a Jewish Motor Unit that managed to save the lives of hundreds of Jews, bringing them in military autos to Tobruk or to the Egyptian frontier. Legends. . . . The stories were embroidered with imaginary details, as is the way with unhappy people who transform the most simple acts into epic deeds. I realized then that every one of our good deeds, every act of brotherly solidarity was engraved in the memory of these people. Their children will be brought up on these stories of brotherly love.

This morning a group of us went out to the Jewish Quarter. At the entrance we saw a sign saying, "Out of Bounds." I went up to one of the military police with a red cap and told him that we were Jews from Palestine and that we wanted to visit the Jews in the town. He consented to this immediately but cautioned us to "behave properly." Only after this did I hear that some colored soldiers had burst into some Jewish houses and had violated a number of Jewish women; that was why the sign had been put up. I heard further that the unit of Jewish longshoremen from Palestine here had organized a guard for the Jewish Quarter at night, although they were not granted the permission of their British officers.

In the Jewish Quarter we were simply carried through the streets. Such joy! On every side we heard greetings of welcome. I felt the way I had on the day that I returned from Tobruk to Naan,[8] a year and a half ago. We went to Simon's shop and found it almost completely bare of merchandise. Simon knocked a few of the tiles out of the floor and pulled out a tin can in which was hidden a "blue box" of the Jewish National Fund.[9] He put it down on the table, his eyes shining with excitement. We opened our purses and filled the precious box that had to be kept secretly under the Fascist regime. We wanted to buy some things from him, but he refused to take money from us. We had to insist strongly before he would agree to accept

[7] The Palestine Hebrew daily newspaper published by the labor movement.

[8] The writer's home kibbutz, near Rehovot.

[9] These little boxes for contributions could be found in every Zionist home throughout the Jewish world.

it. And so it was wherever we came. We entered a restaurant and ordered food. The room was crowded with people. On the table were cups with Hebrew letters on them saying, "Jews! Speak Hebrew." The Jews of Tripoli had ordered these cups from Italy before the war. What a wonderful type of Jew! After our meeting with the cold, assimilated Jews of Egypt, our hearts were full of gratitude to these Jews. We got up feeling somewhat intoxicated, and when we tried to pay we were refused again.

. . . .

These were very precious hours. We wandered about the streets, our faces shining with excitement. One of the soldiers, A. M., came up to me and said, "Listen, I simply want to cry now, my heart is so full." I understood him very well!

. . . Finally we came to the synagogue. We stood on the veranda outside and took part in the prayers. The children—how beautiful they are here!—clung to us, and many of us stood there during prayers with our hands on a child's head.

After prayers we were divided among the different families. They actually fought over us. At the end some families were left without a soldier to take home: "Why should some have two and I none?" When they received one they asked again, "Why should they have two and I only one?"

Finally after some coaxing and good-natured laughter everything was straightened out and we scattered to our different families. B. and I were Simon's guests. Before five minutes had passed a family that had been left without a soldier came and joined us. They simply added some more bowls and another table and we ate together. . . . They didn't want to eat alone.

The meal was fit for a king. Sometimes my mouthful would stick in my throat when I remembered that this was the ration of weeks. Sabbath hymns were sung. B., who was with me, sang in his melodious voice and entertained the family. Little Eliza sang us the "Song of the Port" and "Hatikvah."[10] The mother's face was radiant with happiness and she murmured in Arabic, "I have had many joys in my life, but never one like this evening."

My letter has grown lengthy, but I have not finished telling you all about it. It's three in the morning now. I am sitting in the car and writing this letter. The other boys are sitting outside singing, or lying in their beds. The boys who are singing say that they can't fall asleep. We have had so many rich experiences in these last few days.

Moshe Mosenson, *Letters from the Desert*,
trans., Hilda Auerbach (New York, 1945), pp. 171–78.

[10] The Zionist anthem, now the anthem of the State of Israel.

EXCERPTS FROM A ZIONIST PAMPHLET EXHORTING IRAQI JEWS TO LEARN FROM THE LESSON OF THE FARHŪD

(1944)

Memories

Every Jew of our community well remembers these two sorrowful days during which cruel killings took place instead of seeing our way to enjoy them as they were the days of 'visits festivals' . . . which turned to be days of sadness and terror.

Every child remembers these two frightful days which turned to be days of weeping and appeals for help. . . . We should hear the appeal for help of those girls and women who were touched by the dirty hands. We should share with those children their feelings of terror when they saw with their own eyes their fathers and mothers being killed and dishonored.

We should look upon the memory of those days as a guiding light that will show us our way in the dark of the future.

. . . .

We tell every man, woman, young man, and girl, and children too, in this day: "Slavery will not save us from being looted, disdain will not prevent us being annihilated, and caring not for ourselves will not guarantee our lives, so you should beware companions, because the day is today."

We have decided not to keep quiet and not to forget our sorrows until the day will come when Israel and its lost people get back to rescue the land of their forefathers.

We shall remember. . . .

What Happened in Baghdad

The disturbances of Rashīd ᶜĀlī were over within a month of commencement, after which the Jews felt free again, and they began to show themselves out in the city with gay appearances. This might have increased the hatred of their enemies to them. So it might have been better for the Jews to have been wiser in the manner of showing themselves out again after the disturbances.

It was on the first day of the 'Jewish Festival of Visits' when a Jew was wounded in Ghazi Street. The effect of this event was dreadful among the Jews in general, and they began to run to their homes. They all disappeared after a few minutes of the event, and their enemies, seeing this, were encouraged to treat them with killings, especially when no sign of defense was seen from them. The mob attacked the houses of the Jews and looted them, treating their inhabitants in the way they desired. Jewish men were afraid and were looking for escape from death. Their cries and appeals filled the air, and many of them did actually run away, leaving their women and children struggling in the hands of the enemies.

Bands of enemies were wandering inside the Jewish quarters and were killing and looting. Such events lasted until midnight, and many were killed. Heads of children were cut off like sheep, old men were killed, while women were disgraced. . . . This was how the night passed. In the morning the Jews did not know what had happened to their brothers during the night, and they went out for work as usual, but it was only a short interval given by the killers, after which they resumed their terrorism under the management of policemen and ex-soldiers. They began at 9:30 A.M., completing their program of the night before. Their action was begun in Rashid Street and Shorja, where they broke into the shops and commercial stores belonging to the Jews and looted all they could find in them. They moved thereafter to the neighboring Jewish houses and did similarly in them. Ghazi Street found trouble again that day, later on Amīn Street, as well as the Jewish quarters of Abū Seifayn, ᶜAbbās Effendī, Aqūliyya, and other far and nearby quarters.

Killing and looting lasted until 11 A.M. that day. . . . Bodies of the dead were thrown on pavements on both sides of the street, and this drama did not stop until its conductors wished it off, i.e., some units of the Kurdish Iraqi soldiers gave a hand and all trouble was over within a few minutes.

Every Jewish house sustained the loss of one of its members, or it had at least had one of them wounded. The remaining people lived in terror.

What Do We Learn from the Massacre of Baghdad?

What was it that the Baghdad Jews did not do to be trusted by the Arabs? They gave up their Hebrew language. Did they not stop giving money for the sake of the Land of Israel?[1] They accepted participating with the Arabs in every activity that was in the interests of the country. They were always the first in giving money to help achieving any national scheme in Iraq and especially in Baghdad. Some of the rich Jews have generously contributed to the funds gathered for the followers of the Mufti, who were called the Palestinian Patriot Fighters.

The Jews in Baghdad, for the sake of buying safety for themselves and a comfortable life for their families, abandoned their human dignity and their liberty. Their rich families in Baghdad lived comfortably, but with fear and disdain, while they forgot their brothers who were astray in Europe and who are working hard in the land of Israel. But did they gain any benefit

[1] The translator's typescript reads: "They did not stop giving money for the sake of the future of the Israel Land." This, however, seems to be at variance with the gist of the paragraph.

from all this during the days of slaughter? Could they buy their lives with their dignity, or have they found safety for themselves after having so heavily sacrificed? Never. They never did gain any benefit from all this, as slavery will never make them free from being looted and disdained, or from being annihilated.

Death is the result of giving up our rights and all efforts to show the others that we do not cling to Judaism and awakens hatred in the hearts of our enemies. Every endeavor on the part of the Jews to mix with others and do as the others do leads to butchery. Iraq is just like Yemen. Our luck is the same in all the Eastern countries. It is not enough for the Jews to experience such difficulties. Does our history, which is full of news of killings, teach us nothing of the past? Are our memories so feeble that we forget all that has been done against us so long as we gain profits?[2]

Our aim is a Hebrew National State with Hebrew Power, and our hope lies in defending ourselves and our dignities in life.

PRO (London) FO 624/38/502
Translated Extracts from "The Tragedy of 1st and 2nd June, 1941 in the Capital of Iraq" (Arabic or Hebrew original not in file).

[2] Obviously, this tract was prepared by members of a Zionist Socialist movement. Another pamphlet in the same file, entitled "Hebrew Commandoes," denounces the Irgun and Stern Gang as "terrorists" and "enemy of our people with their foolish actions."

7

THE LAST CHAPTER

THE JEWISH COMMUNITY'S OFFICIAL REPORT ON THE ANTI-JEWISH RIOTING IN TRIPOLITANIA (1945)

1. *General Survey*

From the 4th to the 7th of November, 1945, mobs of Arabs, old and young, made a vicious and sudden attack on the Jews in different parts of Tripolitania. Never in the history of Tripolitanian Jewry, not even in the darkest periods of their existence, has such a pogrom been launched against them.

In Tripoli and the smaller provincial centers of Suk el Jouma, Tagiura, Kussabat, Zanzur, and Zavia, more than 100 Jews, law-abiding and unarmed (including a large percentage of women, old people, and children), were savagely massacred, some after cruel torture, others by being burned alive. A great number of houses, shops, and stores were plundered and set alight, five synagogues in Tripoli, two in Amrus (Suk el Jouma), one in Tagiura, one in Zanzur were profaned, plundered, and fired, together with the Scrolls of the Law, all equipment and the sacred books. Well-to-do families were reduced to abject poverty overnight. Scores of widows, orphans, and others who lost relatives who had supported them now swelled the ranks of the already numerous poor Jews.

2. *Outbreak and Development of Riots*

In the later afternoon of Sunday, 4th November, the President of the Jewish community received news of the first serious attacks, which occurred simultaneously, as if by a prearranged signal, in different parts of Tripoli. He rushed to police headquarters to report the attacks and urged that immediate measures be taken to prevent further trouble.

No police officer, however, was to be found at headquarters, and it was also impossible to trace them elsewhere. Noncommissioned police officers who were at the station confined themselves to assuring the President that all the police were on duty. It seemed that order would be promptly reestablished. Though the reports on 4th November had been numerous and simultaneous, they did not last so long, nor were they so extensive as to give reason for the belief that they would increase with greater severity on the two successive days.

On Monday morning the riots broke out afresh. (The rioters in the town were joined meanwhile by several thousand Arab villagers.) The heads of the Jewish community proceeded early in the morning to report to Headquarters of the Senior Civil Affairs Officer of the Province, Lieutenant-Colonel Oulten. This officer, who had been out of Tripoli, returned to Headquarters at about 9 that morning. He was immediately informed of the gravity of the situation and urged to take steps at once to quell the disorders with the aid of British troops, since the civil police had revealed their inability to keep the situation under control. Lieutenant-Colonel Oulten promised that he would give his immediate attention to the matter. Unfortunately, however, the British Forces were not actually called upon to intervene until more than forty-eight hours after the outbreak of the riots, despite the fact that on the same day, Monday, both the Chief of the Tripolitania Police and Colonel Mercer, Chief Secretary to the British Military Administration (since the Chief Administrator, Brigadier Blackely, had been out of town for some days), were also informed by Jews and Arabs of the increasing severity of the riots and exhorted to take energetic and proper measures against them. Indeed, notwithstanding the curfew imposed of the Monday, that same evening, and on the following Tuesday, 6th November, large-scale, renewed attacks, plundering, and firing of Jewish homes occurred. On Monday evening the few troops that began to appear on the streets took no action against the mob or used their arms to repress the rioting.

Only on Tuesday evening (6th November) and on Wednesday (7th November), did the Military Commander finally take action. At first he prohibited the assembly of crowds and the carrying of sticks and other offensive articles, and later he proclaimed a State of Emergency. British patrols began to patrol the streets and to search passersby and Arab houses.

In Tripoli this firm stand on the part of the authorities was sufficient to diminish the disorders considerably, without resort to arms, as from Tuesday night. The arrest of Arabs guilty of acts of plundering and aggression did not, however, take place until Wednesday. The Jewish quarter of Hara had been previously attacked by bands of Arabs at different external points, but they did not succeed in penetrating the quarter, owing to active defense measures taken by the Jewish inhabitants. Meanwhile thousands of Jews swarmed from the more exposed places to take refuge there.

In other places, at Zanzur and Zavia, for instance, the mass slaughter of Jews occurred on Tuesday night.

In Tripoli, the most serious attacks occurred in the streets of the old city, where there was a mixed population, and the busy parts of the new town, where the Jews lived in isolated houses and were therefore unable to resist the attackers to any appreciable extent. And indeed the rioters could make no mistake, since some mysterious band had previously marked the doors of houses and shops of non-Jews with suitable signs. During the riots only one Arab was killed, presumably by one of those attacked in self-defense.

On Wednesday, 7th November, and Thursday, 8th November, it was possible to provide for the burial of the victims of Tripoli and Zanzur. The funeral, directed by the President of the community, aided by the personnel of the Burial Society, took place at the beginning of the curfew, following a route largely patrolled by armed troops but, as a sign of protest, unaccompanied by relatives or coreligionists. Administrative and military authorities, however, were represented at the funeral. The other communities arranged the burial of their dead on the spot. British officials inspected and photographed some bodies, especially those on which signs of the attackers' cruelty were more evident. With the exception of two (Rabbi Saul Dabuse and Rabbi Abraham Tesciuba), the victims were buried in only one section of the Jewish Cemetery of Tripoli (Kever Ahim).

3. Arms and Methods

In order to carry out the slaughter, the attackers used various weapons: knives, daggers, sticks, clubs, iron bars, revolvers, and even hand grenades. Generally, the victim was first struck on the head with a solid, blunt instrument and, after being knocked down, was finished off with a knife, dagger, or, in some cases, by having his throat cut.

In Zanzur and Amrus (Suk el Jouma) in particular, after having killed or injured their victims, the attackers poured benzine or petroleum over them and set them on fire, and ultimately those killed were so charred as to be unrecognizable. Grenades were used especially at Amrus (Suk el Jouma) against the synagogue as well as the houses. On some of the bodies signs of unimaginable cruelty could be discerned.

4. Direct and Indirect Victims

Up to December 31, 1945, the number of killed (increased by the number who had succumbed to their injuries) amounted to 130, divided as follows (see Appendix A):[1]

[1]Pages 8–12 of the report, giving the names and statistical data of Jews killed in the riots. Not included here.

Tripoli:	35, of whom 31 were killed in the riots, 3 succumbed to their injuries, and 1 was unaccounted for.
Amrus (Suk el Jouma):	38, all killed in the riots (buried on the spot).
Tagiura:	7, of whom 6 were killed in the riots (buried on the spot) and 1 succumbed to injuries (buried in Tripoli).
Kussabat:	3, all killed in the riots (buried on the spot).
Zanzur:	34, of whom 33 were killed in the riots and 1 succumbed to injuries (all buried in Tripoli).
Zavia:	13, of whom 8 were killed in the riots (buried on the spot) and 5 succumbed to injuries (buried in Tripoli).

In consequence of the slaughter, 30 widows and 93 orphans have been registered. (See Appendix B.)[2]

In certain cases whole families were exterminated; others have lost a great part of their members.

There were other crimes, not less painful to record, even though the facts cannot be ascertained fully. In Kussabat, many of our women and girls were violated under the eyes of their own relatives; and many men and women, in order to save their lives, were compelled to abjure their faith and to embrace Islam.

5. *Material Damage*

The damage caused in the riots was various: plunder, rape, fire, etc.

The most affected areas in Tripoli were Suk el Turk (variety shops, modes, mercery shops, ironmongeries, tailor shops, shoe shops, goldsmith shops, household articles, etc.), Suk el Siaga (silverware market), Suk el Attara (grocery market), Suk el Harrara (imported textile and locally made silk shops), Suk el Muscir (mercers and ironmongeries), Suk el Naggiara (where the shops are wholly of Jewish ownership or in overwhelming majority).

Nothing was spared by the attackers; whatever they did not want or could not carry away owing to bulk or weight was damaged, destroyed, or set on fire. Massive safes were demolished; pieces of furniture destroyed or set aflame; glasses and mirrors, even the smallest, were smashed to pieces. It was real vandalism. After the removal of the military cordons (which took place on December 16th), Suk el Turk in particular was a scene of desolation.

Besides shops, many homes, stores, and factories were plundered or damaged. Most of the houses were wholly emptied, and therefore the families who occupied them now find themselves without even personal effects.

The Jewish community, as a body, also suffered a conspicuous part of the damage. In the nine synagogues attacked in Tripoli and in the other minor communities the furnishings, household goods and furniture were

[2] Pages 13–16 of the report, giving the names and ages of widows and orphans. Not included here.

destroyed by fire or damaged; 35 Scrolls of the Law, 2,084 Sacred Books, and 89,086 kg. of silver (sacred ornaments) were plundered.

Those who suffered most were the small merchants, shopmen, and artisans. Nearly all were reduced literally to penury, and they are still inactive awaiting rehabilitation.

Appendix C contains a statistical summary of the claims lodged directly with the Police by the interested parties, a copy of which was submitted to the Jewish community. Appendix D gives a classification of 813 claims for plunder and damage to shops, stores, factories, etc. (excluding homes).[3]

Up to December 31, 1945, the claims reached the number of 1,435 for a sum of 268,231,752 = Military Authority Lire (Official exchange rate M. A. L. 480 = L1).

There is reason to believe that other damage inflicted, especially in the minor communities of Tripolitania, has not been brought to the notice of the Police or of the Jewish community and it may therefore be reasonably assumed that the amount of the damage inflicted on the Jews of Tripolitania is about 300 million M. A. L. and this without bringing into account the indirect damage caused by the idleness forced upon many shopkeepers, factory owners, or ordinary shop clerks, who until now have been unable to resume their work.

CZA (Jerusalem) S 25/5219,
"Anti-Jewish Riots in Tripolitania," pp. 1–6.[4]

[3] Pages 17–18 of the report. These appendices are reproduced in reverse order (i.e., D, C) in Renzo de Felice, *Jews in an Arab Land: Libya, 1835–1970,* trans. Judith Roumani (Austin, 1985), pp. 367–68, Table N-7 and 8.

[4] Sec. 2 of this report is also published in de Felice, *Jews in an Arab Land,* pp. 193–94, using a copy in CZA (Jerusalem) S 25/6457.

SYRIAN JEWISH SPOKESMEN APPEAR BEFORE THE ANGLO-AMERICAN COMMITTEE OF INQUIRY ON PALESTINE

(1946)

In Damascus . . . the government chose three Jews to testify as to political and economic conditions of Jewry in Syria. . . . The government allotted two hours, divided into twenty-minute periods, for the presentation of the testimony by interested groups. These groups included Moslem club-women, Moslem political leaders, Moslem merchants, Moslem journalists, and the Jews.

The committee of three chosen Jews appeared. Only one spoke. There had been testimony in Jerusalem before us by Oriental Jews, charging that Jews in the Oriental countries were given only second-class citizenship. Our subcommittee expected the Jewish spokesman they now heard on the scene to need far more than twenty minutes to tell his story. Instead, he used forty-five seconds of his allotted time. He raced through a one-sentence written statement in which he said that the Jews of Syria were happy and not discriminated against; that their situation was excellent under the present Syrian government; and that they had absolutely nothing whatsoever to do with Zionism.

The three presented a picture of terrified men, McDonald told me.[1] Judge Hutcheson,[2] surprised at the brevity of this presentation, asked, "You have nothing else to add?" The Jewish spokesman shook his head. "Very well," said the Judge, nodding his head, and with the dismissal, the three hurried to their seats in the rear of the room amid murmurs of sly amusement from the Moslem audience, which said, as clearly as words, "They knew what was best for them."

Bartley C. Crum, *Behind the Silken Curtain: A Personal Account of Anglo-American Diplomacy in Palestine and the Middle East* (New York, 1947), p. 239.

[1] Dr. James G. McDonald, one of the six American members of the committee.

[2] Judge Joseph C. Hutcheson, Jr., chairman of the American contingent of the committee.

THE MOOD OF NORTH AFRICAN JEWRY IN 1947

To: Shertok
Dr. Sneh
Sasson
Epstein
Linton
From: Fischer. Paris, the 28th August 1947

Report on the situation of North African Jews
made by Mr. Paul Ghez, a Tunisian lawyer, member
of the Conseil général de Tunisie, representative of the Joint in Tunisia

Mr. Ghez is in touch with our friends in Tunisia, and he was asked by them to see me in Paris.

The following are the main points of what he told me:

Under the German occupation the Tunisian Jews were abandoned by all, Arabs and French. They have not forgiven to the French the way they were left alone to face the Germans and their cruel demands. On the other hand, the Jews notice now the tendency of the French to appease the nationalist movements led, more or less openly, by the Arab League. The Jews are afraid of either a gradual departure of the French, which will leave them under Arab domination, or a Franco-Arab conflict who [sic] would degenerate into a massacre of the Jews.

However, the Arabs, moderates and intellectuals, are not making any anti-Semitic propaganda at present and excesses which are taking place are only being caused by the mob.

In Algiers there is also a grudge of the Jewish population towards the French. The Jews don't forget that Jewish rights were only reluctantly restored after the liberation.

Circumstances during the last year have awakened among all African Jews a mystic trend to Zionism and simultaneously have brought about a change into their character which has become aggressive and violent.

The young Jews who are not Zionists become communists.

In Tripolitania, the situation is much worse than in North Africa. There the Jews are living in constant fear, and 100 percent of the population wants to go to Palestine.

They try to reach Tunisia where they hope to find organizations which will bring them to Palestine. A month ago, 300 young people had already crossed the border. Today, they are already 500.

As soon as the British authorities received knowledge of this exodus, they asked the French to close the frontier and to return to Tripolitania the Jews who had already escaped. The French authorities promised to control the frontier, but they refused to send back the Jews already in Tunisia. The frontier is now severely controlled by all sides, and cases have been reported where Jews trying to cross the border have been killed by sentries.

A group of 500 Jews is reported to have been halted at the frontier and sent back to Tripolitania.

These Tripolitanian Jews are a serious problem to the Tunisian French community and one of the reasons of the trip to Paris of Mr. Ghez was to get in touch with the Joint American Distribution Committee here. Jewish departures from North Africa to Palestine are much irritating to the Moslems, not only because these Jews go to Palestine, but also because the French are not granting any exit visas to Moslems who want to go to Egypt or Syria.

Mr. Ghez told me about preparation being made for further departure from North Africa—in particular he told me about preparations made by representatives of the Bergson group[1] for sending a ship in autumn—and asked me what his attitude should be toward such departures.

Regarding Zionist activity in Tunisia, Mr. Ghez is of the opinion that spectacular manifestations are dangerous and may endanger the security of the Jews there and force the French to counterattack Zionist activity, whereas the French up till now maintained a friendly or a natural attitude.

The fear expressed by Mr. Ghez seems entirely justified, and there is little doubt that revisionist and bergsonist zeal may do much harm in North Africa.

By the way, there seems to be little difference between the activities of the two organizations.

Mr. Ghez complained that the only Jewish newspaper in Tunisia, the "Gazette d'Israël," is in revisionist hands.

So far the report made by Mr. Ghez. There is little doubt that the temperament of North African Jews offers a favorite field to extremist propaganda. It seems therefore that reinforcement of organized moderate activity is an imperative necessity.

CZA (Jerusalem) Z 4/10,310.

[1] The group in the United States led by Irgun member Hillel Kook (alias Peter Bergson).

THE PLIGHT OF THE JEWS IN BAHRAIN FOLLOWING THE PALESTINE PARTITION VOTE (1947)

Copy

BY REGISTERED AIR MAIL

The Secretary,
Jewish Agency for Palestine
Immigration Department,
Jerusalem.

13th December, 1947
Bahrain,
Persian Gulf.

THROUGH:
Mr. Nathan Sacks,
303 Scott Avenue
Syracuse, New York

Dear Sir:

I refer to my recent letters concerning our application for immigration visas and to which I have had no replies from your good-selves. It is quite probable that letters from and to Palestine are being held by adjoining Arab States while in transit, and in view of this I have thought it best to direct all letters to you through my friend in America at this above mentioned address. *It is accordingly requested that you will kindly follow the same method,* i.e., to send *all letter to me to my friend in America at his address as given above.* Requests have been made by me to my friend and he will forward me all.

It is with heavy heart that I have to report the crimes that have been committed against the Jewish Community this week in Bahrain. There have been atrocities of the worst nature committed against us and out of thirty-nine houses only nine remain safe. Houses and shops have been looted completely, synagogue destroyed, scrolls burnt, furniture were looted and destroyed. Women very cruel acts [sic] and unwanted aggression against us, casulities [sic] inflicted some fatal. Some of us who owned houses or shops and were well-to-do now find ourselves quite poor and have to beg for shelter and food. We find ourselves helpless in spirit, broken in hearts, not knowing when the tragic and barberous [sic] atrocities will be repeated. Would the nightmare come once again? They accuse us that we have remitted funds to the Zionist organizations in Palestine, which is false. They wish to reason for their barberous [sic] acts, they have no true reason. Great and real tribute must be paid to the Ruling family and the British Advisor to the Bahrain Government who have shown more than their sympathies. The adviser himself was in action against the criminals and has risked his live [sic] many a time. He is deserving of praise and sincere gratefulness, otherwise the whole Jewish community would have been slaughtered. However, the damage that was done was terrific, nay unrepairable. Our souls are like boats lost in heavy storm, boats that may sink any moment. What shall I relate? The story of an old man who was deaf? He was beaten up in the market after they had succeeded in capturing him he fled from them but they followed him and repeated their crimes. He was stoned, he had blood all over his face and sholder [sic], when he escaped they followed him and repeated the show. Miracally [sic] he escaped into a bank and there he fainted and was taken to a hospital where he stayed for two days for treatment. When he came back to his house he found his house empty, doors broken, windows removed. His family scattered in four houses. O' I am not a writer, I cannot describe the misfortune. I want to say that our future is lost. I do not mean that we were hoping on a bright future in Bahrain, yet things were not bad till recently. I want to say that we are hopeless, we are lost. Had it not been for the government of Bahrain I think that every Jew would have committed suicide [sic].

In this bad hour when we are gathering in grief in a dark room and gloomy, a room which windows we cannot open for fear that our house would be filled with stones, in this hour when we are in dispair [sic] and disappointment, we beg you to extend us your hands. We appeal to you to help us in this time of danger we beg you to consider our case. We have contacted you seven years ago when we were living peacefully. Now we are contacting you when our very security is endangered. The time for your help has come, it cannot be postponed if we are to live. Consider that we have applied to you in 1941 and you have given us hopes. On your hopes we have lived. *We will not live idly in Palestine.*

You are kindly reminded again not to send letters direct to me but care of my friend in America. If I receive letters directly from you I will be in danger perhaps. If you will send certificates please send them in *registered airmail.* Will nine certificates upset your immigration plans? We beg you. We request you.

Yours faithfully,
Ezra H. Zeloof

CZA (Jerusalem) S 25/5291.

REPORT OF THE COMMISSION OF ENQUIRY INTO THE ANTI-JEWISH RIOTS IN ADEN
(DECEMBER 1947)

I. Introduction.[1]

13. Aden consists of a group of steep volcanic rocks rising to a considerable height, almost surrounded by the sea, and joined at the desert mainland by a sandy isthmus. It is roughly divided into three areas (See Map, Appendix 3):—

14. Steamer Point and Tawahi where are the main harbor, Government House, Secretariat, Royal Air Force Officers' Mess and Quarters, and a number of better-class shops behind which is a thickly populated area.

15. Maala on the sea level where there are wharves, an oil area, some business premises, and a number of coolie lines.

16. Crater a thickly populated area where there are business houses, a bazaar, a Jewish Quarter, Armed Police barracks, and the gaol.

17. Steamer Point and Tawahi are connected with Maala by a road running between the rocks and the sea.

18. Crater is separated from Maala and Steamer Point by high, steep rocks and is reached by a pass known as the Main Pass over the rocks and by a tunnel cut through the rocks.

19. Maala is about three miles from Steamer Point, and Crater is about two miles from Maala.

20. Sheikh Othman is a thickly populated Arab town some six miles inland from Maala. It is reached by roads from Maala and Crater which join and cross the isthmus.

21. The Jewish Quarter in Crater consists of rectangular streets with a number of passageways used for sanitary purposes. There were about 226 houses, some of which adjoined houses occupied by Arabs and Indians. It forms part of the area known as Section A.

22. The majority of the houses are three-storied with a door opening onto the street, the residential parts being on the upper floors: the roofs are flat. Inside they are a labyrinth of rooms, passages, and stairways. The majority of windows have no glass but are protected by wooden shutters.

[1] The Introduction is preceded by twelve paragraphs describing the commission and how it gathered the information.

23. Next to the Jewish section in Crater is the bazaar area, where are a number of small lock-up shops: some sixty-four of these intermixed with others are owned by Jews.

24. The Jewish Quarter at Sheikh Othman is at one end of the town.

25. The population of Aden and Sheikh Othman is about 78,400, of which details are given in Appendix 2. It includes a number of Yemeni coolies who are not permanently resident. They are employed as casual labor and live either in coolie lines or in caves in the rocks. They have a low standard of life, are illiterate, fanatical, and, when excited, may be savage.

26. There are also in Aden a number of Yemeni Jews who are not permanently resident and who came within the last few years in the hope of making their way to Palestine. They are now practically all in a Hashed Camp,[2] which is situated in the desert about a mile and a half from Sheikh Othman. Before the disturbances the majority of these Jews, about 2,400, were in that Camp, supported by Jewish organizations, but there were some 600 or 700 in Crater and about 450 in Sheikh Othman who were helped by local Jews.

27. At the time of the disturbances there were in Aden, in addition to the Royal Air Force, a small number of Royal Artillery personnel, the majority of whom were proceeding to Palestine, and the Aden Protectorate Levies, a force recruited in the Protectorate, having British and Arab officers. There Levies were approximately 1,800 strong and consisted of two mobile wings, both in Aden in three different Lines.

28. The Police Force is divided into the Civil police and the Armed police who are armed with lathis,[3] tear smoke guns, rifles, and Lewis guns. At the time of the disturbances the Civil police numbered 350. The Armed police were 250 strong, of whom about 160 were available in the Colony, the others being on leave or detachment.

II. Events leading up to and the immediate cause of the civil disturbances in Aden which started at Crater on the 2nd December 1947 and subsequently elsewhere in the Colony, more particularly in Sheikh Othman, Tawahi, and Maala.

29. Since the end of the War in Aden as in many other places there has been a tendency for some sections of the population to become less law abiding. This is probably due to the general disturbances caused by the War, to the controls imposed which encouraged smuggling, and to increased

[2] Concerning this camp for Jewish refugees from Yemen, see pp. 156, 500.
[3] Long sticks used as whips.

prices leading to a decrease in the purchasing power of money. It is suggested that this tendency may have been encouraged by a successful strike of transport workers organized in January 1947 to protest against the licensing of a foreign (non-Aden) bus company during which there was some violence.

30. Owing to broadcasting and the prevalence of loudspeakers in cafes, many of the population who are illiterate have begun to take interest in outside affairs—in the Arab world, in India, in Egypt, and in particular in events in and connected with Palestine.

31. The arrival of Jews from outside Aden may have caused some fears, no doubt groundless, among local Arab laborers, that the Jews might compete with them, and I was informed that there had been some rumors as to the activities of these Jews.

32. The Commissioner of Police stated:—

"Since I arrived in Aden there has been a steady growing antagonism between Jews and Arabs. Not strong when I first arrived but shown by many petty assaults and by children throwing stones at each other.

"There was distinct worsening in 1947. I think undoubtedly influence of events in Palestine reflected in Aden. We had cases of Arab lorries being driven at Jews walking in the desert. One case a Jew was killed and an Arab driver was arrested and convicted of causing death by rash and negligent act."

33. The announcement by U.N.O. of the decision to partition Palestine on November 30th resulted in a number of young Aden-born Arabs deciding to form a committee to organize a three-day strike in Aden as in other countries.

34. It was arranged that pickets should be placed by the organizers of the strike to prevent any interference with non-Moslems and to prevent disorder.

35. The coolie wharf laborers declared their intention of joining the strike.

36. On the morning of the 2nd December at about 6 A.M. tom-tom men in Crater announced that there would be a three-day strike operating from that morning. This was accompanied by an announcement asking people to refrain from interfering with the Jews and other non-Moslems and to be orderly.

37. At about 8.20 A.M. a number of Arab schoolboys and youths gathered in Crater, Section B, and proceeded to Esplanade Road alongside the Jewish Quarter. This started as a small procession but increased as it

progressed. When the procession was passing a house in Esplanade Road occupied by Jews, two bottles were thrown from the roof, one of them striking Chief Inspector Mohammad Khan. Stones were thrown at the house in retaliation. The Assistant Superintendent of Police, Mr. Bruce, and the Chief Inspector entered the house, and a Jew was found with a bottle in his hand. The crowd was dispersed.

38. Later attempts were made to persuade Moslems working for non-Moslem firms to cease work, and stones were thrown at five Jewish schoolboys, none of whom were injured.

39. A little later Beihani, a blind preacher, appeared and told the crowd that they were doing wrong and that the strike did not mean that they should act in such a manner. With difficulty the crowd was dispersed and nothing happened.

40. Meanwhile the strike was general. Coolies did not work and Arab shops were shut.

41. At 11 A.M. the Commissioner of Police felt that it would be wise to seek the assistance of leading Arabs in maintaining order and to warn them of the consequences of disorder. At Crater police station he met Sheikh Abdul Rehman Zubeidi, Mr. M. A. Luqman, and Ahmed Yehia Yafai—unfortunately Khan Bahadur Ihsanullah and Sheikh Abdullah could not attend. These gentlemen told the Commissioner of Police that they did not anticipate violence or disorder. They promised to assist by sending young men round to advise people not to form crowds and to conduct themselves decently.

42. At the same time Mr. Swain, Senior Superintendent of Police, interviewed at Tawahi five Arab strike leaders, who had arrived from Crater to enforce the strike and told them that whilst he was unable to prevent their requesting shopkeepers to close, he would prevent them forcing them to close.

43. In the afternoon there was a rumor that Amir Ali, son of the late Sultan, would speak from the palace in Crater and a crowd gathered outside. This crowd was orderly. At about 6:15 P.M. a large crowd marched from Eidrus Road and made its way to the palace headed by a banner inscribed "Long live Palestine" and there were similar shouts.

44. Meanwhile a meeting of Arab notables, convened to discuss the question of collecting money for Palestine, was held inside the palace. I was informed by one of them, Sheikh Khalid Abdul Latif, that when they saw the crowd outside they decided to drop the strike and that one day had been enough, and that Beihani, a blind preacher, then addressed the crowd, telling

them there should be no more strike and that they should go to their homes. Unfortunately no other steps seem to have been taken to make this decision more widely known.

45. The crowd, headed by the banner, moved in the direction of the Saila and the Jewish schools and shortly there was serious disorder.

46. In Sheikh Othman the strike was effective and on the 2nd December the shops were closed and there was no transport—otherwise the day was normal and without incident.

47. In Steamer Point and Tawahi police patrols were out during the day but there were no incidents.

48. The immediate cause of the disturbances was anti-Jewish feeling engendered by events outside Aden but, as will be seen later, other factors affected their course.

III. Question whether Government had any Grounds to apprehend the Outbreak and, if so, what Measures were adopted to meet it.

49. Mr. Muchmore, the Acting Chief Secretary at the time of the disturbances, informed me that he had no reason to anticipate anything with which the police could not deal and Air Vice Marshal Lydford, the Air Officer Commanding, agreed that before the disturbances there was no particular reason to anticipate trouble.

50. The Commissioner of Police stated:

"I did not think violence would come on the decision to partition Palestine. I thought it would come as result of implementation.

"I spoke to Chief Secretary after announcement that strike would be held and expressed my apprehension of disorder but hoped would be peaceful.

"We had no indication there would be grave situation particularly after assurances I had had."

51. Mr. Banin, speaking on behalf of the Jewish community stated, "We never expected such things to happen—we all the time living friendly with the Arabs."

52. There was no doubt an atmosphere of some political tension due to events outside Aden, and casual Yemeni coolie labor was a potential threat to security, but I do not think that the local Government had any grounds to apprehend the outbreak as it occurred.

53. No particular measures were adopted to meet the outbreak before it occurred.

54. In July 1947, an Internal Security Scheme had been drawn up by the Air Officer Commanding in collaboration with the Civil Government, the object of which, inter alia, was to provide for forces to come to the aid of the civil power. Within two months of the disturbances a practice of some part of the Scheme had been carried out.

IV. Progress of the Disturbances and the main incidents which occurred therein.

55. As there was no direct connection between the events in the three main areas in which there were disturbances I deal with those areas separately.

Crater—2nd December

56. The crowd which left the Sultan's palace about 6 P.M. moved toward the bazaar area and, when in the neighborhood of the Jewish schools became disorderly. There was stoning of the Jewish Quarter by the Arabs, and bottles were thrown by the Jews. Attempts were made to disperse the crowd with tear gas, but these were not successful.

57. About this time an excited Arab reported to Mr. Bruce that the Jews had killed an Arab in Street No. 2 in the Jewish Quarter. Mr. Bruce went to the spot and found an Arab with, what he described as, an appalling wound in his head. There is no evidence to show how this was inflicted, but it is possible that it was caused by one of the stones or bottles which were flying about. Mr. Bruce had the man taken to hospital. In racial disturbances rumors that member of one party has been killed by members of the other party are common, and this episode may have further excited the Arab crowd.

58. Another attempt was made to disperse the crowd by the use of tear gas, which had some effect, and several persons were arrested for stone throwing.

59. The Deputy Commissioner of Police by telephone informed the Commissioner of Police that a serious position had developed and that a large Arab mob was throwing stones at the Jewish Quarter and that the Jews were retaliating.

60. The Commissioner of Police telephoned to the Governor and to the Air Officer Commanding asking that the first phase of the Security Scheme might be put into operation, i.e., that troops might be at half an hour's readiness to move and the Commissioner of Police accompanied by Mr. Swain, Senior Superintendent of Police, went to the Crater and the Commissioner of Police described to me the condition of affairs which he found as follows—

"We arrived there about 6:45 P.M. and found a state of complete disorder. Police had used tear smoke and had cleared Arab mobs from Saila Road, but mobs had congregated in all the roads and bazaars near border of Jewish Quarter. Several cars owned by Jews were burning and the Jewish girls' school had been set fire to.

"Police patrols round quarter were being stoned."

61. On their arrival at the Crater police station the fire of the Jewish girls' school was reported and Mr. Swain obtained permission to take the fire tender to the fire. On the way the tender was stoned and the glass of the wind-screen and lamps was broken and Mr. Swain was hit and sustained a broken arm and a damaged finger. The fire was extinguished with difficulty as two hoses were cut and the Chief Inspector, Armed police, and two riflemen had to protect the party.

62. Mr. Swain sent the fire tender back by way of the Cloth Bazaar to the police station and himself, with the Chief Inspector of the Armed police and the Armed policemen walked behind. On the way they were met by Arabs, who said there was looting in shops between the Cloth Bazaar and the Bohra Bazaar. Mr. Swain, the Chief Inspector of the Armed police, and a party trapped nine looters in a shop and, after a brief struggle, arrested them and took them to the police station. Mr. Swain described them as being of the "coolie type."

63. Mr. Swain reported to the Commissioner of Police and then went to hospital which he reached at about 8:50 P.M. He was detained there for eight days. It is a matter of regret that the services of such an experienced officer should have been lost at this time.

64. Until the arrival of the Commissioner of Police rifle fire had not been used. He directed that it should be used under the supervision of the Deputy Commissioner of Police and Mr. Bruce and until midnight twenty-four rounds were expended.

65. At this time the police force in Crater consisted of 60 Civil police and 100 Armed police. At 9.15 P.M. the Commissioner of Police decided that the situation was out of police control, and he accordingly telephoned to the Governor and advised him that the time had come for military assistance. Shortly after the governor informed him by telephone that the Air Officer Commanding had ordered a column of Aden Protectorate levies to proceed to Crater and that he, the Commissioner of Police, should report personally at once to Security Headquarters at Air Headquarters. By this time the Governor had asked the Air Officer Commanding to take over responsibility for the maintenance of order and security.

66. It would appear that Mr. Goepel, the District Commissioner, was not consulted before the decision to call for military assistance was taken.

67. At 9:45 P.M. a squadron of Levies under the Command of F/Lt. Heaseman arrived and pickets were sent out.

68. Colonel Jones, commanding the Aden Protectorate Levies, was appointed Military Commander and visited Crater between 10 and 11 P.M., where he found that things had quietened but there were some fires smoldering. He stated that the squadron had not gone into action but was doing picket duty at various crossroads. He took exception to this as they were not policemen and had them withdrawn at once and held as a reserve at the police station.

69. The night was quiet but there were fires at the Jewish schools and two other buildings and a number of motor cars were also on fire. The police, with the most effective assistance of the Service fire brigades, fought these fires all night and succeeded in getting them under control.

3rd December

70. The Deputy Commissioner of Police, Colonel Maclean, who was not available to give evidence, made a report, a copy of which was made available to the representatives of all parties interested. In that report he states that at about 7 A.M. patrols reported that trouble had started again and that he contacted the District Commissioner and asked him to report to the police station in order to accompany the squadron of the Levies and that the District Commissioner did so and that the squadron left at about 8 A.M.

71. The District Commissioner, Mr. Goepel, and F/Lt. Heaseman were also not available to give evidence. Mr. Goepel furnished a report, with page 2 of which he states in a covering letter, F/Lt. Heaseman is in complete agreement. This report was also made available to the representatives of all interested parties.

72. In these circumstances I set out Mr. Goepel's report dealing with these incidents:—

Page 1:

"On Wednesday I went first to the Township office and about 9 A.M. received a call to go at once to Crater police station. I left my car in the Township garage and went in a police car.

"A fire started in Street 2 (all references are to Section A) was still burning and I was told that crowds were interfering with the firemen and it was necessary to disperse them. I enquired about the use of tear smoke and was informed that it had been tried and the situation had got beyond that."

Page 2:

"I accordingly went with F/Lt. Heaseman and about thirty Levies to clear the crowd from the fire engine. The men were told to load with one round of ammunition and not to fire without orders.

"Passing down Street 2, from North to South, not far from house N. 160A, we were subject to a heavy shower of bottles and fire was returned to drive the Jews from the housetops. I may mention that I was saved from injury by a police helmet which I had borrowed, but there was a persistent rumor in the town for some days that I had been injured.

"Continuing down the street another attack with bottles was made from house No. 160A, and fire was again used to drive the Jews from the housetops. There was no indication that any shots had been effective as the assailants withdrew behind parapets as soon as aim was taken. I heard no screams or other indication of wounding, though of course there was a great deal of clamor and vituperation.

"Proceeding South down Street 2 we cleared a crowd from the fire engine and let them get on with their duties. Police whistles were then heard and cries that were fires in Streets 3 and 4 and we returned in a North Westerly direction. In several places we found that beds had been piled against doorways soaked in oil (either petrol or kerosene) and set alight; in other places mats had been similarly used (the beds are straw plait over a wooden frame and are always left in the streets for use at night). There must have been eight or ten such fires which we put out by pulling away the burning materials, but in several other cases buildings were alight. Eventually, in response to appeals for help, we reached Jaffran Road, opposite the Greek Bakery, where there was a fire well alight which we could not control without any apparatus. Goods were being removed from this house and moved to safe custody. While we were here I saw a man carrying a long pole with a wrapper of sacking on it, which at first I took to be some kind of banner, and considered whether we should try to grab him as likely to be a disturbing influence. He was however well among the crowd, and I thought it inadvisable to attempt to arrest him. In any event the persons under Heaseman's command were soldiers, not policemen. Suddenly I noticed that he had got to a house beyond us, the 'banner' was a sack cloth soaked in petrol which he set alight and pushed into a house. Heaseman drew his pistol but could not have shot him except endangering the crowd into whom he fled and got away.

"By now we could see that substantial fires had broken out in Esplanade, but so long as there was a large hostile crowd in the Square near the Greek Bakery I thought it advisable to withdraw, but eventually they melted away and we proceeded to Street No. 4.

"There is on the West side of Street No. 4 by Street No. 13 a large three-storied stone house flanked by a single-story white-washed house. On the roof of the white-washed house a dozen or more Arabs were throwing stones at the large house, undoubtedly Jewish, and the Jews were responding with stones and bottles from above. A few shots from us drove the Arabs away from the street side of the house but they continued attacking the house. There was a large crowd in Street No. 4, to the South of Street No. 13, and I thought it advisable to remove these before undertaking further action. I therefore advanced to them and read the Riot Act commanding them to go home and keep the peace. This was taken up by Arabs in the crowd near me and shouted out very loudly and was well understood by those present. I may mention that the crowd included many children and was observant rather than hostile, though there had been a little stone-throwing from them. We then went South for about thirty yards, clearing the street completely, and retired quickly to the single-story house where the battle with the Jews was still going on violently. The street being fairly clear F/Lt. Heaseman then sent half a dozen men up on to the roof of the single-story building and cleared it.

"For the whole of this period I had not seen one person shot or otherwise injured by the party under F/Lt. Heaseman's command, nor had we sustained any casualities, but as the situation was obviously completely out of hand and I had given what warning I could to the civil population, I thought it advisable to return to the police station.

"We were returning Northwards when we heard single revolver shots from the Jewish Quarter and were warned that sniping was going on. There was no point in trailing out coat through this area so returned to Street No. 2 or 3 and in the meantime heard armored cars passing through the streets firing. We eventually returned to the police station without further incident.

"At the police station I was informed that the military had taken over control and that a state of emergency was being proclaimed with curfew from 12 noon.

"Colonel Maclean provided me with an escort to the Township office where I picked up my car and drove it home, and as I was passing the Treasury there was a small knot of Arabs who recognized me and cheered. I mention this to show that there was no sign of any anti-Government feeling."

73. It will be noticed that there is some discrepancy in the times between the report of the Deputy Commissioner of Police and that of the District Commissioner, but this would not appear to be important.

74. In a statement submitted to me by Mr. Banin, Chairman of the Jewish Emergency Committee, it is stated in paragraph 6:—

"At about 9 A.M. the District Commissioner and a British Officer with a number of Aden Protectorate Levies toured the streets, but took no apparent steps to stop the mobs and thereby gave the mobs encouragement to increase their attacks."

75. Two Jewish witnesses stated that they were in danger from fire and that they called to Mr. Goepel but he did not assist them.

76. At about 9 A.M. Wing Commander Pocock, Aden Protectorate Levies, arrived to assume the duties of Military Commander of the area, bringing with him another squadron numbering about 120 Levies. He ordered this squadron to be deployed. The flight which had gone out with Mr. Goepel had returned and, with two other flights of the original squadron, constituted a reserve.

77. Number 8 Squadron was ordered to deploy on Esplanade Road. Before they went out Wing Commander Pocock told the Squadron Commander to endeavor to disperse mobs by firing above their heads—any fire-raisers to be shot at.

78. An excellent series of photographs of events in Esplanade Road were taken and produced by Mr. Pratley of the Arabian Trading Company. This witness stated that the Levies were firing over the heads of the crowd and did not move the crowd.

79. There is considerable criticism of the conduct of the Levies at this time. It is suggested that possibly owing to the small number of British officers the Levies were operating in small parties, were firing indiscriminately, and were not taking active measures against looters.

80. At 10 o'clock Colonel Jones was in the area and at about this time Sheikh Khalid Abdul Latif, Mr. Luqman, and some eight or ten Notables made their way with difficulty to the Police Headquarters. They informed Colonel Jones that it was their intention to go round and quieten the people. They obtained his permission and went to the Cloth Bazaar. Sheikh Khalid Abdul Latif told me that the people were Arabs, but he could not recognize them. They were coolies and inland people, and they did not know the notables and would not listen to them.

81. Colonel Jones then went to see the Air Officer Commanding. He pressed for a curfew, which was eventually agreed to, and he obtained instructions to use automatic weapons. These latter were necessary in order that the armored cars might be used. He then ordered an armored car to go to Crater and take weapons for the three armored cars already there.

82. At about eleven o'clock Mr. Duncan, Senior Superintendent, C.I.D., going from Tawahi to Crater, found a large crowd of coolies rolling stones onto the roadway of the Pass, and ordered two or three rounds of rifle fire to be aimed at the steep cliffs behind these people. This had a good effect. He then had the boulders cleared and proceeded to the top of the Pass, where he spoke to a small guard of Armed police and warned them not to allow coolies through the Pass to the Crater and to report by telephone signs of any large crowd reassembling in the Pass. He later reported this to Colonel Jones, who said he would guard the Pass with a flight of Levies.

83. Later in the day Mr. Duncan found a large crowd of about 300 coolies, assembled near the pointsman's box in the Pass, and the Police Inspector attempting to get them down the hill. Mr. Duncan found the European officer in command of the Levies, who had arrived at the Pass, and asked him to assist in dispersing this crowd. This officer said he was unable to help as he had instructions to hold the Pass only to prevent its being blocked by stones. Mr. Duncan, with Inspector Patel and the Civil and Armed police, then dispersed the crowd, finding it necessary to use one round of rifle fire as a warning and one round fired low. Two men were injured and were sent to hospital in a truck. Before leaving, Mr. Duncan

instructed Inspector Patel to suspend entirely all foot and nonservice vehicular traffic through the Pass.

84. Reports were received that the fire brigades were being sniped from the top of buildings in the Jewish area. One building in particular, i.e., the Piccadilly Ice Cream Bar in Esplanade Road, was pointed out.

85. Wing Commander Pocock stated that he observed looting on an excessive scale and inquired from the Deputy Commissioner of Police if looters could be shot. The Deputy Commissioner confirmed this, and Wing Commander Pocock passed the order to his Squadron Commanders. Wing Commander Pocock stated that when opening fire it was deliberately kept low and that casualties were observed among the looters. At that time Wing Commander Pocock had three squadrons and three armored cars.

86. Wing Commander Pocock was informed that a curfew would be imposed, and he was given a typewritten notice proclaiming it. On the first day the population were informed by the police tom-tom man, by a notice on a blackboard on a car, and by notices which were circulated. Later, loudspeaker vans and the air raid siren were used for this purpose. It was originally intended that the curfew should be imposed as from noon, but owing to the difficulty of making it known, it was postponed first to one o'clock and later until two o'clock. The curfew was difficult to enforce, and I was informed by several witnesses that they had not heard of it on the first day.

87. Looting was observed on the Jewish side of Zaffaran Road and a section was placed in position under a British officer. Hits were observed on the legs of the looters. At 12:30 P.M. a sniper was said to be observed in a house above the Star Pharmacy. Wing Commander Pocock's account of this incident is as follows:—

"12:30 P.M. sniper observed by me and Superintendent Bruce in house overlooking police station, Street No. 4, Star Pharmacy. I ordered an A.F.V.-armored car to fire one short burst at window where seen. I saw him but difficult to observe as only about nine-inch gap—could not form any opinion as to his nationality. Later in day we saw him in other positions."

88. Mr. Bruce dealing with this incident stated:—

"On one other occasion from a house in Street No. 4 in Saila Road I heard a crack like a small-caliber weapon which might or might not have come from that house. I heard no bullet. This house was the subject of reports by Levies that sniping coming and Levies opened fire on one window with a Bren gun. Apart from those incidents I have no reason to believe there was any sniping."

89. Fires broke out in the Cloth Bazaar, and looting was prevalent. Attempts were made to enforce the curfew, but this was difficult owing to looters who included women and children.

90. The Officer Commanding No. 8 Squadron reported that snipers in the Esplanade Road area had increased and he assumed that they were equipped with pistols or a carbine. Wing Commander Pocock decided at this stage that searching houses for snipers was out of the question as he could not cordon off the blocks effectively.

91. During the day Armed police patrols were operating against looters in the bazaar area, and a loot store was established at Headquarters to which anything found could be taken.

92. About 6 P.M. Colonel Jones visited the area and found the curfew effective. He decided to send out a special anti-looting patrol. For this he collected nine British technical N.C.O's from the Levies and sent them under a British officer to the bazaar area, where they arrested ten looters. This party was only available when not engaged in their normal duties.

93. During the day the Air Officer Commanding had felt it necessary to inquire if any Naval vessels were in the vicinity and had been informed that the destroyers Contest and Cockade were due in Aden the following morning. He requested that they should be told to increase speed. At 7 P.M. he also requested that two companies of British troops should be flown to Aden.

94. Mr. Banin stated that later in the evening houses near his were set on fire and he went on to say:

"Could not open windows—they were shooting direct to our houses—by that time uncontrolled fire. We all in my house hiding in lavatory.

"I think shots came from Levies' corner No. 1 Street and Saila Road.

"Fires spreading rapidly.

"We made bridge from house 57 to house 58. We decided to leave house 58, and when we tried to leave, my father-in-law, climbing to house 59, was shot dead by Levies—could not see them but fire came from direction of Levy picket at corner of street.

"There were no Arab houses opposite.

"Where my father-in-law shot we broke a hole in wall to get through instead of climbing.

"There were about a hundred people in my house and we made a bridge and got to Zenzen house, Street No. 2.

"We got ambulance two hours later and took my father-in-law to hospital. Three Royal Air Force police came and helped me. They very kind to us. I remained in hospital until Friday afternoon. Too dangerous to go down. They advised me to remain."

4th December

95. The destroyers Contest and Cockade arrived at 3 A.M. and two landing parties of approximately forty ratings each were sent ashore. One

of them, under the Resident Naval Officer, Commander Richardson, was sent to Crater and arrived at about 6:30 A.M. Later in the day the party was reinforced, making, in addition to Commander Richardson, a force of three officers and approximately 100 men.

96. Commander Richardson stated:—

"When I arrived Crater crowd milling, curfew attempted to be enforced. Streets not cleared.

"Levies in patrols going up and down streets—firing shots in the air, driving people into their houses.

"Saw signs of looting. Bands broken up and several loads of looters brought into police station.

"When I arrived Levies appeared to be doing their job."

97. The Naval party was split into sections which were first shown by the Levies where to patrol but, after about an hour, the Levies were withdrawn and the naval parties continued by themselves.

98. Commander Richardson's orders to the patrols and sentries were—"Shoot to kill looters when caught in the act."

99. About 9 A.M. Dr. Ferozuddin went with an ambulance into the Jewish Quarter to attend a man who had been shot. While the doctor was standing by the ambulance, he was shot and killed. He was reported to have been shot by snipers from a roof, but one of the eyewitnesses before me stated:—

"A bullet hit the doctor on the forehead and he fell to the ground. The bullet came from soldiers who were in the lane. It is a long lane. I saw a man fire two shots, not one."

100. Another witness stated:—

"I heard a burst of shots—I could not see who was firing them."

101. During the morning barricades consisting of barbed wire knife-rests were set up round the Jewish Quarter. Colonel Jones expressed the view that it would not have been useful to set them up earlier owing to their being some Arabs in the Jewish Quarter. When set up, some of these barricades were manned by Levy sentries and some by Naval personnel.

102. Colonel Jones visited the area at 10 A.M. and after consultation with the Deputy Commissioner of Police decided that the curfew should not be lifted until 6 A.M. the following morning.

103. By 11 A.M. the area was reasonably quiet, but there was still some looting.

104. In the afternoon an attempt was made by Wing Commander Pocock and a leading Jew named Armando to rescue some Jews who were in danger from fire. Wing Commander Pocock stated that he called some Levies from a nearby picket on the barricades and formed a cordon and that about twelve people came out of the house. As they came into the cordon there was a burst of fire, and a girl and a man within two feet of him were shot dead. He stated:—

"My reaction was to assess the shots had come from above and behind me. I made an immediate check of my Levies manning the barriers covering these streets and confirmed that they had not fired."

105. It was stated that later in the day a British officer of the Levies visited the spot with a Naval Officer, who was experienced in ballistics, and the Naval Officer gave his opinion that the wounds inflicted on the dead Jews were made by bullets of the homemade or dum-dum type.

106. Some Jews who were in the house gave evidence that after Wing Commander Pocock left two more people, a child in his nurse's arms and a man were shot and killed, and that the nurse was wounded, on the staircase inside the house. The house has a narrow door opening directly upon a straight staircase. . . . they must have been shot from a spot in the roadway in front of the door. One Jewish witness stated definitely before me that the shots were fired by the Levies.

107. At about 2 P.M. a Levy who was a member of a patrol which was looking for snipers from a rooftop was shot and killed, and an Arab boy who was also on the roof was hit.

108. During the afternoon Mr. Bruce complained to Wing Commander Pocock of the conduct of the Levies and told him that he did not consider they were doing the job for which they were called out. There was a discussion with the Senior Air Staff Officer as to whether the Levies should now be withdrawn and the Senior Air Staff Officer communicated with the Air Officer Commanding. Wing Commander Pocock communicated with Colonel Jones, and in his evidence Colonel Jones stated:—

"At four o'clock Military Commander Crater telephoned—he had had conversation with the Senior Air Staff Officer and Bruce. He said he proposed to withdraw Levies and replace with Armed police and Navy. I said no. I did not consider enough police and Navy to take over. He asked if we could withdraw the ammunition from the Levies. I said coming down. If he wanted to withdraw it he could do so.

"I then spoke to Air Officer Commanding.

"I arrived Crater at 4:30 P.M. I toured whole area and spoke to all the squadrons—two had had their ammunition taken away. I had it restored to them. I told them suggested [sic] not doing job as they should. I said I knew probably getting tired. I had been promised reinforcements next day—they would have to be on duty for another twelve hours at least. They must be efficient and carry out their orders. Murmur of approval from all concerned. Arab officers could not understand what gone wrong and who making complaints."

109. Later Colonel Jones ordered that patrols going out should be issued with ammunition which should be collected when they came in.

110. Colonel Jones himself then took over command of the area from Wing Commander Pocock.

111. Looting continued but the night was quiet.

5th December

112. Attempts were made to bury the dead and gangs of prisoners were employed, but the Arabs refused to bury the Jewish dead.

113. Six tons of flour were distributed to the Jews, and the Civil authorities were able to take over again the feeding of the Civil Hospital.

114. At noon the curfew was lifted and the Main Pass opened.

115. H.M.S. Challenger arrived and a landing party of twenty was sent ashore.

116. A detachment of the North Staffordshire Regiment which had arrived by air in the early morning marched in at about 1:30 P.M. and the Levies were gradually withdrawn.

6th December

117. Curfew was lifted from 6 A.M. to 6 P.M.

118. Parties of the North Staffordshires searched for snipers but did not find any.

119. With the assistance of Father Edmund, who throughout had done all he could to help, a party of young Jews was organized to bury their dead.

120. During the morning the Governor and the Air Officer Commanding visited the area.

121. Thereafter the situation gradually came under control.

122. On the 7th more food was taken to the Jews and on the 8th the Levies began the task of evacuating 600 Yemeni Jews to Hashed Camp.

Those to go were selected by the Jews themselves and taken in lorries. This operation was carried out successfully and without incident.

123. By the 14th all troops had been removed from the area except one platoon of the North Staffordshire Regiment which remained at the Armed Police barracks.

124. H.M.S. Challenger left on the 14th and the two destroyers the following day and on the 16th the Air Officer Commanding handed back responsibility for security for the Governor.

125. In the early stages of the disturbances there was stone throwing by the Arabs and bottle throwing by the Jews. I do not think that either party could be stated to have started this as it occurred at different places and at different times.

126. I think, however, a number of Jews threw bottles, no doubt ill advisedly, because they were frightened and sought to protect themselves.

127. I am satisfied that there was much looting and fire-raising and that looters were in many instances fanatical in their eagerness to loot.

128. There were some savage attacks by Arabs upon Jews but, on the other hand, there were many instances of Arabs and Indians sheltering and otherwise befriending their Jewish neighbors. These were gratefully acknowledged by Mr. Banin and Mr. Bentwich on behalf of the Jewish community.

129. I deal with firing and sniping in a later part of this report.

Sheikh Othman—3rd December

130. Some people began to open shops, but boys led by two young men intimidated them to close.

131. In the morning the police dealt with some minor disorders, but by 1 P.M. a Jew had been killed by a heavy stone, other Jews had been wounded, and looting had begun. Mr. Conway, the Assistant Superintendent of Police, therefore telephoned to Lake Lines and asked for the assistance of the Levies. The strength of the police was sixty-two scattered through the division with an effective reserve of ten or twelve. At 1:30 P.M. F/Lt. Rudd and a party of ninety-three Levies arrived.

132. There were some minor disorders, and a party of Levies was posted to protect some 450 poor Jews, not permanently resident in Sheikh Othman, who were encamped in a compound. Parties of Levies were able

to disperse crowds which were attacking Jewish houses and to evacuate some old Jews and children.

133. The senior Arab officer of the Levies addressed the crowd and for a time his words appear to have had a good effect but disturbances at various places continued and at 3:30 P.M. Lt.-Col. Kiegan, Commanding the Levies at Lake Lines, arrived and after discussion it was decided to evacuate all Jews to Hashed Camp and that a party of Levies would remain to protect Jewish property.

134. F.Lt. Rudd started to collect the Jews and warned them that they must be ready to start and that they could only take with them what they could carry.

135. At about four o'clock the police requested rifle fire to be opened on the crowd and five men were ordered to fire two rounds each. This was followed by a charge which dispersed the crowd. There were no casualties, and the police were able to make some arrests.

136. The evacuation of the Jews in the compound was begun, and they were warned that they must be ready to leave at 4:45 P.M. and that those who were not ready would have to stay behind at their own risk.

137. The Jews were assembled and the procedure was repeated in other Jewish sections, but the Jews there had houses and more property and it was difficult to persuade them to move.

138. Eventually the party moved off but some Jews were seen standing at their doors who did not join it and some fell out.

139. Orders were received that the Levies should be used for escorting the Jews to Hashed and guarding them there and would not be available to guard Jewish property.

140. The party proceeded to Hashed Camp at 5:30 P.M., a police Inspector going with them. They were followed by the crowd, and there was some stoning. The senior Arab officer addressed the crowd, and it was necessary to use fire to protect the Jews but there were no casualties.

141. The party arrived at Hashed Camp about 6:10 P.M.

142. After the departure of the Jews, escorted by the Levies, Mr. Conway took an Inspector and ten constables to see if it was possible to save any Jewish property, but most of it had already been looted and it was nearly dark. He found one Jewish family trying to get an iron safe out of a wall. He took them and the safe to the police station.

143. About 6:30 P.M. there was a large fire which was brought under control by the police.

144. At 7:30 P.M. a message was received saying some Jews in a distillery in the desert, who had been overlooked, were going to be attacked. Mr. Conway left at once with some Armed police and collected nineteen Jews and took them to the police station.

145. At about 8:30 P.M. a flight of Levies arrived and were taken to a section where buildings were still being attacked. The rioters were ordered to disperse but some did not do so. Several bursts were fired from a Bren gun. These cleared the street.

146. Two dead Jews were found in the street who could presumably have left with the party for Hashed Camp had they wished.

147. The Bren gunfire had had a good effect and cleared the town.

148. At ten o'clock night patrols were sent out. One Jew was found with serious head injuries and during the night other Jews were found and a number came to the police station. They were taken in lorries to Hashed Camp, in all about a hundred.

149. The total number of Jews evacuated was about 750.

4th December.

150. There was still some rioting, and buildings were searched and an old Jewess was found and sent to Hashed Camp.

151. Mr. Conway and F/Lt. Jones of the Levies visited the distillery, which had been set on fire and was being looted.

152. In the afternoon more rioters were arrested, but thereafter events became quieter.

Steamer Point and Tawahi—3rd December

153. Mr. Duncan, Senior Superintendent, C.I.D., took over command of this area at 7:50 A.M. vice Mr. Swain. The police force available was a Chief Inspector, two Sub-Inspectors, twelve Armed, and twelve Civil police. Mr. Duncan was informed by Inspector Salole that the night had been quiet.

. . . .

157. Until 4:30 P.M. the situation was fairly normal, but small crowds were being moved along by the police and shortly after that hour a mob of

coal coolies from Hedjuff attempted to force their way past the block by a pumping station.

158. Mr. Duncan went to the scene with six Armed police and found the guard falling back slowly before 200 or 300 coolies.

159. The crowd was warned to disperse but remained firm, and a few commenced to climb along the hillside. They were warned again, and one round was fired over those on the hillside and one round was fired directly on the main crowd. One man was injured. The firing was followed by an advance which had the effect of breaking up the crowd.

160. Mr. Duncan pushed on to the coolie lines at Hedjuff, where he tried to find the head coolies and have them warned that attempts to come to Tawahi would be resisted.

161. He returned to the police station at 6 P.M. and found that an attempt had been made to set fire to a Jewish go-down. The police had dealt with this. At 6:20 P.M. a small Jewish shop was broken into and looted.

162. The same Jewish go-down was again set on fire. When Mr. Duncan arrived, he found the crowd obstructive. He had with him an Inspector and five Armed police. They attempted to force the crowd back to make room for the fire pump and hoses. At the same time showers of stones and bottles, mainly from the roofs of the buildings on the opposite side of the street, fell upon them and this encouraged the crowd. The crowd was warned and three rounds were fired. The area was cleared and the fire got under control, but further looting was reported. Two or three rounds were fired at escaping looters.

163. Unfortunately two innocent men who were working near the market were shot, one was killed and the other wounded, and an Arab youth in a house behind the market was also killed, presumably by this firing.

164. At about 7 P.M. two Armed police who had been let on duty to guard a looted shop were rushed and the shop again broken open. On disentangling themselves, they fired independently on the looters and were then withdrawn. Until 9 P.M. four attempts to set fire to Jewish premises and three attempts to loot Jewish premises were made and on eight occasions persons were fired on. There had, however, been fair control and the Crescent had been kept free from extensive looting or serious fire.

165. At 9:20 P.M. an alarm was raised in an Arab area. Mr. Duncan proceeded there with an Inspector and found crowds rushing about. The light was bad, but he saw a person being attacked by a crowd of people at the mouth of a small lane and there were other crowds stoning and beating

objects on the ground. As he ran to the first crowd he saw the dead body of a Jew, and as the crowd split up and ran away, he found another Jew badly injured who died at once. With the police available he cleared the area and searched the lanes. He discovered in all five dead Jews.

166. At about 9:30 P.M. three Jews and one Arab, who said he had been mistaken for a Jew and had been beaten, were rescued.

167. Mr. Duncan was then joined by the Commissioner of Police, and they searched the area for persons with blood-stained garments or weapons.

4th December

168. At 1:30 A.M. Mr. Duncan again returned to the scene of the murder and searched the house which he was informed had been occupied by these and other Jews. On searching the house two Jews were found alive and uninjured hidden on the roof, and they were taken to the police station. They were too terrified to give any details as to what had happened.

169. At about 2 A.M. a Jewish girl aged 17 years, who stated that she had been in the house at the time of the attack but had not been injured or interfered with, was brought to the police station by two Arabs.

170. At 5 A.M. Mr. Duncan received information that an attack was planned on a house containing four Jews. He went there with a party of police and found a crowd. He removed the Jews and took them to the police station. There was strong anti-Jewish feeling shown by the crowd which followed them to the police station.

171. The police had not been aware that there were any Jews remaining in the bazaar area. On the 3rd December inquiries had been made, and it was understood that the Jews were found there.

172. During the morning attempts were made to set fire to premises in the Crescent.

173. At 11 A.M. S/Ldr. Kirkly informed Mr. Duncan that he was the Military Area Commander and Mr. Duncan asked him for transport to remove the Jews from Mr. Hatooka's house and they were taken to Hashed Camp.

174. At noon S/Ldr. Kirkly and Mr. Duncan patrolled the whole area and S/Ldr. Kirkly informed Mr. Duncan that Naval ratings were in the Naval premises and that Levies were encamping on the football ground and could be called upon. There was also an R.A.F. unit standing by.

175. In the early afternoon there were determined attempts to loot and fire premises, and at 3:30 P.M. Mr. Duncan had a conference with S/Ldr. Kirkly and pointed out to him:—

a. that the Armed police detachment had not been relieved for over 48 hours and was almost continually on duty for about 70 hours;

b. that Tawahi Civil police had also had little or no rest for two days and nights;

c. that he himself was getting exhausted with no European officer to replace him, and that he anticipated more attempts at fire-raising and looting at dusk, with a view to asking for a curfew by six o'clock and for some military pickets at certain points.

. . . .

177. About 9:45 P.M. the streets throughout the area were almost completely cleared, and the pickets had taken up their positions. There were some police patrols until midnight when they were drawn in and all the police allowed to rest.

178. There was some rifle fire during the night.

. . . .

184. The area gradually quietened down, and Mr. Duncan handed over to Mr. Swain on the 11th.

V. Steps taken to deal with the disturbances and their adequacy, and the conduct of the forces employed.

Crater

185. When first asked to assist the Civil Power and later when asked to take over responsibility for security, the Air Officer Commanding considered that the only force that he had available to go to this area was one drawn from the Levies, and a squadron was sent without delay and subsequently other squadrons were sent.

186. This first step taken was adequate in that adequate numbers were sent to Crater, but it proved to be inadequate in that the force sent failed to prevent some loss of life and much damage to property, and had to be reinforced by the Royal Navy and the North Staffordshire Regiment. The force thus obtained was adequate to restore order.

187. On the morning of the 3rd December disturbances began again and a party of Levies under F/L. Heaseman, accompanied by the District Commissioner, went out.

188. As I have already stated these officers were not available to give evidence and I have therefore set out their report, insofar as it affects this episode, in full (see paragraph 72).

189. I cannot but feel that if a more determined effort had been made at this time the situation might have been held, and that the attempt which was made, if it did not actually encourage the rioters, seems to have done little to discourage them.

190. From that time there has been criticism of the conduct of the Levies. That criticism is mainly under two heads:—

a. The Levies were not active in the suppression of looting and fire-raising.

b. There was much uncontrolled or improperly controlled use of rifle and Bren gunfire resulting in the killing and wounding of many innocent persons, the majority of whom were Jews, and also resulting in some damage to property.

191. Several witnesses, in particular Mr. Duncan and Mr. Besse, a merchant living in Crater, gave evidence that the Levies were not active in the suppression of looting and appeared to be sympathetic to looters, and Father Edmund stated:—

"From what I could see, in my opinion, A.P.L. (Levies) being Arabs did not like to shoot their own people."

192. There was undoubtedly much firing, thousands of rounds being expended for which the following would appear to be the main causes, i.e., the suspected presence of snipers, the curfew, and the conduct of individual Levies. I will deal with these separately.

Snipers

193. Throughout the disturbances there were reports that sniping was coming from certain houses, mainly Jewish, and from certain directions.

194. No sniper was caught, and when it became possible to search the suspected houses, no used cartridges or other traces of a sniper were found. In my opinion, the evidence that snipers had actually been seen was not convincing.

195. The leader of the Jewish community stated that he knew of no sniping from Jewish houses and could not believe the Jews would snipe at people helping them, e.g., a good deal of supposed sniping was at the fire squads.

196. There was said to have been sniping on the police station which was used as Headquarters from the house described as the Star Pharmacy, but there were no bullet marks to be seen on the police station when I visited it.

197. Dr. Ferozuddin, the Indian doctor who was shot and killed in the street, and the Jews whom Wing Commander Pocock was trying to take from a burning house and who were shot and killed, were reported to have been shot by snipers, but there was before me direct evidence that both the doctor and the Jews were shot and killed by the Levies.

198. There was evidence that a supposed sniper's ammunition dump was heard to explode during the night. In this connection it may be remembered that a Levy was convicted by Court Martial of losing a box of ammunition, but there is no evidence to connect these events.

199. In view of the evidence I do not feel that I can say that there was no sniping, but I certainly think that many of the shots which were attributed to snipers were stray shots, of which I am satisfied there were a very great number.

200. Whether there were or were not snipers, counteraction was taken by firing through wooden shutters into rooms and at persons on roofs. In particular, when sniping was thought to have come toward Headquarters from the Star Pharmacy, a burst of Bren gunfire was put through the shutters of that house. Fortunately the inmates had taken refuge in the kitchen and bathroom and no one was hit, but the damage to the room and its contents is still plain to see.

201. I consider that there was no justification for this promiscuous use of rifle and Bren gunfire against suspected snipers.

202. There was evidence that some Levies were inclined to wander away and Mr. Bentwich suggested that might explain some of the sniping, but this is only a suggestion.

Curfew

203. The notice that a curfew would be imposed was in the following terms:—

"His Excellency the Governor of Aden has declared state of emergency in Aden and has authorized A.O.C. to declare curfew in Crater.

"The curfew will be from 12 noon 3.12.47 to 12 noon 4.12.47.

"All persons are warned to not come out from their house during the above period and will be shot if they are seen."

204. Colonel Jones stated:—

"I issued no orders for the way the curfew was to be enforced. I simply said there was to be a curfew imposed by noon."

Later he said:—

"I am satisfied that on first day curfew was understood. There was no shooting at actual curfew breakers until next morning.

"I took the view that it was right and proper to shoot a curfew breaker merely because he was a curfew breaker. Those were my orders.

"If you can catch him you arrest him, if you can't catch him you shoot at him. That principle followed.

"We arrested 150 or more."

and he added:—

"The officer on the spot must decide what to do e.g. (if) people run out of burning house."

205. Commander Richardson stated that his orders to patrols and sentries were "Shoot to kill looters when caught in the act," and he added that the sailors were able to deal with curfew breakers by occasional shots in the air, yelling, and waving people into their houses.

206. It is no doubt wise and proper to give warning that when there is a state of lawlessness, persons breaking curfew may find themselves in danger, but I cannot but feel that the curfew notice as issued may have encouraged the Levies, and possibly other troops, to think that they were justified in shooting at any person they saw regardless of what that person was doing.

207. It may be added that there was evidence that on the first day some people did not know that a curfew had been imposed.

Individual Levies

208. There can be no doubt from the evidence that many Levies were firing indiscriminately and some became, as was described by Father Edmund, "trigger happy."

209. Mr. W. G. Chapman, a police officer who was temporarily seconded from Etritrea, held inquiries into the deaths of a number of Jews. From these it appears that, according to the evidence of Jewish witnesses, thirty-one Jews, men, women, and children, were shot and killed in Crater, either inside houses, on the roofs, or in the streets. In some cases the Jews stated that the shots were fired by the Levies or from armored cars. In others they stated that they did not know who fired the shots. I do not think it can be suggested that these persons who were killed were doing anything unlawful, except possibly in some instances, breaking curfew.

210. By the afternoon of the 4th December the officers in Crater, Wing Commander Pocock and Mr. Bruce, had become uneasy as to the conduct of the Levies, particularly as to their indiscriminate use of fire, and their withdrawal was discussed. (See paragraph 108.)

211. It will be appreciated that among the large number of Levies engaged in Crater many may well have been performing a most difficult and unpleasant duty to the best of their ability, but I think it is clear that some were sympathetic to looters and fire-raisers and did little to discourage them, and I am satisfied that there was much uncontrolled or improperly controlled use of rifle and Bren gunfire resulting in a number of innocent persons being killed or wounded and some property being damaged.

212. There was an allegation that some Levies demanded money from Jews. The actual Levies concerned were not before me and I feel that it would not be right that I should express any opinion about this alleged episode.

213. Nine Levies were Court-Martialed for looting. Five were sentenced to one year's imprisonment. I was informed that there was one case of British troops entering a house and removing goods. When this incident came to the knowledge of their Commanding Officer, he at once dealt with it, and the goods were returned.

214. With the exception of one witness who stated that he saw the Armed police looting, there was no criticism of the police. They took the first shock of the disturbances and did not hesitate to engage the mobs on the evening of the 2nd December and thereafter continued anti-looting patrols.

215. The police officers, particularly Mr. Bruce, working with and presumably under the Military Commander, when they felt called upon to criticize the conduct of the Levies, were placed in a difficult and anomalous position.

216. Throughout, the police and service fire squads worked under difficult and dangerous conditions and much credit is due to them.

217. The staff of the Electricity Department, headed by Mr. Brady, also deserve credit for the good work they did.

218. The Medical Authorities worked continuously, tending the wounded in hospital, and it is indeed sad that one of their number who went out should have been killed.

Sheikh Othman

219. I consider that the conduct of all ranks of the police under Mr. Conway and of the Levies under F/Lt. Rudd was most praiseworthy. They performed a difficult task efficiently with a minimum use of fire.

220. As far as is known, with one exception, the Jews who lost their lives did so because they did not carry out the instructions issued to them.

221. I am satisfied that Mr. Conway and F/Lt. Rudd did their best to protect Jewish property, but they had not sufficient forces to enable them to do so in addition to evacuating the Jews.

Steamer Point and Tawahi

222. In this important area Mr. Duncan and the Inspectors and men of the small police force under him received no military support until 11 A.M. on the 4th December and I consider that great credit is due to them. I think that they were able to hold the situation as they did largely owing to their appreciation of the necessity of controlling the movements of the element among the coolies, which was likely to cause trouble.

223. That some Jews were killed was due to the fact that their presence in the area where they were was not known to the police. Those who had moved to the house of Mr. Hatooka were safely evacuated.

224. The death of three Arabs—a man, a youth, and a woman who were shot — was due to unfortunate accidents. They were all some distance from the spot where the shooting took place and the shots were not aimed at them.

225. In the three areas the police and troops arrested 511 persons, of whom 263 were Yemenis. These persons were mostly arrested for looting. The majority were prosecuted and almost all were convicted. The others were deported. These figures do not agree with those given by the Commissioner of Police in the record as they have been revised.

VI. Effect of the disturbances on the local community, including casualties and damage to property, and the adequacy of the relief measures.

226. The disturbances have completely disorganized the lives of the majority of the Jews in Crater. A number have lost for the time being businesses, owing to the premises having been burnt or their stocks destroyed or looted, and others who were employed by them are unemployed.

227. Many have had their houses burnt and the schools are too badly damaged to be used.

228. The Jews of Sheikh Othman are still in Hashed Camp, many of them having lost practically all they possessed.

Casualties

229. The casualties were officially reported to me as follows:—

	Arabs	Jews	Unidentified (presumed Jews)	Indians
Killed	38 (incl. 1 Levy)	76	6	2
Wounded	87 (incl. 1 Armed policeman)	76	—	1

230. Many others (Arabs) are known to have been wounded but treated at home or elsewhere and no reports made to Police or Medical Authorities.

231. These figures include one Indian Medical Officer and one Levy who were killed and one British and one Indian Police Officer who were wounded.

232. I was informed by Mr. Banin that of 170 Jewish shops existing in Aden before the disturbances 106 were totally looted and 8 were partially looted and that in Crater 9 houses were burned before the imposition of the curfew and 21 were burned after the imposition of the curfew. In addition, the Jewish schools were burned. A number of Jewish-owned motor cars were also burned.

233. In Steamer Point 8 premises were damaged by fire.

234. In Sheikh Othman:—
12 houses were burned and looted.
61 houses were damaged and looted.
5 shops were burned and looted.
10 shops were damaged and looted.
26 huts were burned and looted.
40 huts were damaged and looted.
1 synagogue was burned and looted.
1 small school was burned and looted.
1 Jewish-owned car was burned.
1 Jewish-owned distillery in the desert was looted and burned.

235. Mr. Bechgaard, Crown Counsel, is inquiring into the actual amount of financial damage caused.

236. Bullets did much damage to the electric light installation both inside and outside houses in Crater.

Adequacy of relief measures adopted.

237. During the actual disturbances some food was issued to the Jews in Crater and since the disturbances Government has made weekly issues of rations to those Jews on the scale originally considered enough for about 4,000 people, but four weeks ago slightly reduced.

238. At present they are receiving meat on hoof, sweet oil, potatoes, green vegetables and fruit, flour, sugar, rice and tinned milk (for children and sick), and a small quantity of soap.

239. The Public Works Department is helping to get the area clean, and the Medical Department and Education Department are giving what assistance they can.

240. The housing difficulty in Crater is acute as, before the disturbances, the area was overcrowded and a number of houses have been destroyed.

241. The Jews who were removed to Hashed Camp are being fed by Jewish organizations, but Government is making a monthly grant toward the cost of their food and also provided a capital sum for the construction of shelters.

. . . .

253. The continued presence of the Jews in Hashed Camp and the guarding of that Camp must be a source of anxiety to the Government, but I am not in a position to make any recommendations regarding them or their future.

254. If disturbances occur again, the actual measures to be taken must depend upon the course the disturbances take.

255. The necessity for taking early action cannot be overemphasized. If possible the security forces should be ahead of the rioters and their arrival should not be delayed until after the disorders have begun.

. . . .

HARRY TRUSTED,
Commissioner.

G. O. TRUSTRAM,
Secretary.
Aden,
7th April 1948

Colonial Office, *Report on the Commission of Enquiry into Disturbances in Aden in December, 1947*. Colonial No. 233 (London, 1948), pp. 4–28.

A REPRESENTATIVE OF BRITISH JEWRY REPORTS ON THE ECONOMIC SITUATION OF ADENI JEWS FOLLOWING THE RIOTS
(1948)

CENTRAL BRITISH FUND FOR JEWISH RELIEF AND REHABILITATION

REPORT ON THE ECONOMIC SITUATION OF THE JEWS OF ADEN

I was in Aden for seven weeks as Counsel for the 650 or so claimants who were claiming compensation for damage suffered in the riots. That number probably represents about half the heads of families, and in the course of acting for them I obtained a thorough knowledge of the financial position, methods of business, and the way of life of the Jews of Aden in a way one could not normally have done in less than a good many years.

The colony of Aden consists of three main places, Steamer Point, where the European Community and the Government offices are mainly situated and where there are also some of the largest Jewish shops; Crater, where there is a Jewish Quarter and the Bazaar area; and Sheikh Othman, which is something in the nature of a large Arab village in the desert. The Jewish population of Aden consists firstly of the Adenites whose families have been resident for at least 1,000 years and some recent Yemenite immigrants. In Crater and Steamer Point the Jews are almost entirely shopkeepers and their employees. In Sheikh Othman the Adenites as well as the Yemenites were mainly artisans, that is to say Goldsmiths, Silversmiths, Weavers, Carders, and so forth. Near Sheikh Othman there is also a camp for Yemenites on their way to Palestine. As a result of the stoppage of immigrants into Palestine, the number of inhabitants of the camp has largely increased, and as a result of the riots practically the whole Jewish population of Sheikh Othman was moved to Hashid. The present position is that in Crater are some 5,000 Jews almost entirely Adenites, and in Hashid Camp is a separate community of just over 4,000, almost entirely consisting of Yemenite immigrants more or less penniless, and possessing nothing but scanty clothing. Crater is administered very badly as one community, the leader of which is Mr. Selim M. Banin, but it possesses nobody capable of leadership, and the community has not learned to help itself or one another. Hashid Camp is administered by that remarkable woman, Dr. Olga Feinberg, as quite a separate community.

Crater

Of the people in Crater very few escaped damage in the riots, and a large number lost everything. Apart from four or five of the wealthier individuals no one had any money in the bank or in a stock or share in a

Company, and whatever they possessed was in the form of stock in their shops, household goods, and buildings if they owned them, and it was possible, therefore, for a man wealthy by local standards to find himself possessed of nothing but a nightshirt if his house and shop were burned down. The overcrowding in the remaining buildings is appalling. I am thinking, for example, of a flat of six rooms occupied by two brothers who are the managers of two of the largest Jewish concerns in Aden. That floor is occupied by forty-five people. Immediately after the riots 5,000 persons were issued with free rations by the Government, and the number for the last two months has been stationary at 3,500. The rations are not really adequate, but apart from food it is to be noted that their position as a whole is getting very difficult. Those who have lost the stocks of their shops have nothing to buy any stocks with, and one by one they are tempted by Arab neighbors to part with the walls of their houses or the leases of their empty shops for a song. In addition, trade locally is bad. The riots have given a great sense of insecurity to all the local communities; no one imports goods if he can avoid it. A new feature is an Arab boycott of the Jewish shops, which is a very material factor in the situation. The result is that in the Jewish Quarter you will every day see a large part of the population lounging in the streets for want of something to do. Those whose businesses have been looted have no occupation, and the same applies to their employees and to a very large number of other Jews who have hitherto earned their living in various ways by supplying the needs of the Jewish community.

The moral of all this is that whatever money is sent to the Jews of Aden from abroad is needed now and not later. I estimate the material damage to the Jews of Crater and Sheikh Othman at about Pd.Sterling 1 million. I should be reasonably satisfied if the compensation amounts to half a million, and I do not think it is likely to be less than 1/4 million, but it is obviously bound to take at least three months from now until everything is received except small advances to small claimants who could be started in trade thereby.

Sheikh Othman

This place is now denuded of Jews, who are all in Hashid Camp.

Hashid Camp

I need only say of the occupants of the Hashid Camp that before the riots they had very little in the way of possessions, and the present number swelled by the riots has substantially nothing. None of them have any occupation whatsoever. They dare not go to Sheikh Othman in search of work. They would have difficulty in the present circumstances of the Jewish community in obtaining work in Crater or Steamer Point, and it is a journey from Hashid of some thirteen miles to either place, the cost of which they can ill afford, especially as if they leave Hashid their free rations are gone.

When I left Aden about the 8th April, the community was very much disturbed with the slowness with which their friends and well-wishers in England and America were acting. They knew that sums had been generously voted by the Central British Fund and the Joint and this increased their sense of irritation at the delay. The following figures were given to me by one of the few reliable persons in the place when I left. The receipts from abroad up to date in Crater were as follows:

Pd.Stg. 1,150	from Asmara
600	from the Aden Jewish Community in Palestine
500	from the Vaad Hazala, Palestine
Pd.Stg. 2,250.	

In addition, the following sums had been received and by consent shared equally with Hashid:

Pd.Stg. 500	from the Vaad Leumi.
1,000	from the Central British Fund.
250	from South Africa.
25	from boys in Jerusalem.
Pd.Stg. 1,775.	half of which, as I say, went to Hashid.

Not a penny in cash had been received from the Joint. Mr. Vitellis visited Aden in January and promised to help. The Joint decided not without reason that they must send their administrator to supervise the distribution on the spot, and it was understood when I left that he had still not obtained a visa, though attempts were made by the Jews of Aden to help in that direction. I have been told by Mr. Stephany since I returned that he has now heard from Dr. Schwartz that the visa has been granted and the administrator is on his way from Palestine, and I am glad to hear it. I also understand that the Central British Fund, about the 27th March, sent Pd.Sterling 3,500 intended for relief in Aden generally, to Dr. Olga Feinberg at Hashid Camp. Hashid Camp is, of course, administered on funds received from the Joint.

Crater, apart from what I have said, receives nothing. The relations between Hashid Camp and Crater are such that neither body trusts the other, the former community consists substantially of penniless Yemenite refugees, the latter community consists of Adenite shopkeepers. I do not think that any of this Pd.Sterling 3,500 will find its way out of Hashid and into Crater unless strenuous steps are taken in that direction, certainly so far as I know, nothing had been heard of it in Crater when I left.

In the above remarks I have been endeavoring to make clear not so much that the sum voted to Aden should be increased—that is a matter for others to decide—but that every step should be taken to ensure that the money arrives now and not later, when I hope it will not be so much needed. . . . The two Jewish elementary schools that existed before the riots, and have been more or less destroyed, were most unsatisfactory. None of the Jewish teachers were fit for their posts because of the low standard of education in the community. It is doubtful whether there are in the whole of Aden more than six natives of any community who have passed matriculation. Certainly not amongst the Jews. In the long run the restoration and improvement of the schools and the raising of the standard of education are the greatest need for the community, but at present their need is for work . . . but it is not much use talking of education to the Jews of Aden in their present state of need.

27.4.1948 by Mr. A. S. Diamond.

AJDC (Jerusalem) 322A.7.

A REVIEW OF ATTITUDES IN THE EGYPTIAN PRESS TOWARD THE COUNTRY'S JEWISH COMMUNITY IN LATE 1947

THE FOREIGN SERVICE
OF THE
UNITED STATES OF AMERICA

American Embassy
Cairo, Egypt, December 20, 1947

No. 3107
RESTRICTED

Subject: Egyptian Opinion on Role of Local Jews in Regard to Palestine

The Honorable
The Secretary of State,
Washington, D.C.

Sir:

I have the honor to refer to my airgram A-535 of October 15, 1947, concerning a statement by two prominent Egyptian Jews voicing opposition to Zionism[1] and to report an increasing volume of press and radio discussion here as to the position and role of the Jews in Egypt in regard to Palestine. Comment has ranged from plans for tolerance in two pro-government papers, *Al-Assas* and *Akhbār al-Yom*, which said that the Jews in Egypt are entitled to the same rights and protection afforded other citizens of this country, to the thinly veiled attacks and threats in the extremist Moslem Brotherhood's paper, *al-Ikhwān al-Muslimūn*. Most of the comment in papers between these extremes has, however, been quite critical of the role of the local Jewish inhabitants.

For the past several months, *al-Ikhwān al-Muslimūn* has been devoting a considerable amount of space to vituperative comment about the position of Egypt's Jews on the Palestine question. The themes developed by *al-Ikhwān* concern Zionist propaganda among the Egyptian Jews and demands by the Brotherhood that they contribute money to the Arab cause, meanwhile warning them of dire consequences if they aid the Zionists. The newspaper wrote on October 19, 1947, that "Zionists in Egypt spare no effort in spreading Zionist propaganda among the Egyptian Jews using the following media: newspapers and pamphlets, social clubs, meetings, sports clubs, and inducing the Jews to immigrate to Palestine by facilitating immigration." The paper listed the leaders of the Zionist movement in Egypt as "[Henri] Haim, the Director of the Société Orientale de Publicité, Togo Mizrahi, the film producer, [Lt.] Colonel [Clement N.] Ades, formerly of the British Intelligence in Egypt, and Clement Circurel, nephew of [the]

[1] Joseph and René Cattaoui. See below.

proprietor of the famous shop which bears that name." the zionists, it alleged, succeeded in recruiting the help of the Société Orientale de Publicité in publicizing Zionism. As this corporation controls only French and English language papers, the Zionists considered publishing an Arabic daily, *al-Shams* (The Sun), but this plan did not materialize, due to "the opposition of some Jews who were afraid of Egyptian public opinion."[2] *Al-Ikhwān* then said that Zionists had been able to "induce" officials of the passport department to give clearance to Jews desiring to enter Palestine.

A demand that the Arab League compel the Jewish residents of Arab territory to contribute money to the Arab armies appeared in *al-Ikhwān* on December 2. The paper charged that it had learned from "most reliable sources that Mr. Silverman, a senior official of the Jewish Agency, made a speech recently at Tel Aviv in which he stated that the Jews of Egypt had donated L.E. 10,000,000 to the new Jewish State." The Brotherhood's leader, Ḥassan al-Banna, appealed a few days previously to the Jewish citizens of Egypt asking them to prove their loyalty to the country by opposing Zionism. "We did not expect that they would do exactly the opposite thing and give their money, Egypt's money, to the Zionists," it said. *Al-Ikhwān* published a manifesto purportedly issued by al-Azhar students addressed to the Jews of Egypt on December 10, 1947, asking the Jews of Egypt to contribute "freely to save Palestine." The manifesto reminded Egyptian Jews of their declarations disapproving of Zionism and asked to prove their statements by sending money to the Arab League. Jews were warned against cooperating with Zionists or aiding Zionists who enter Egypt illegally. "If you follow this advice, your lives and property will be protected, and if you do not take our advice you will not be entitled to protection." However, the same issue carried another manifesto by the same group, stating the "sons of Israel were kicked out of Egypt by the Pharaohs, but the Zionists continue to dream about their lost empire." Egyptian Jews were asked to give money not only to save Palestine, but also Egypt from Zionism.

Al-Kutla, the morning daily controlled by Makram Ebeid Pasha, Coptic leader of the Wafdist Bloc, took up the questions of sympathy and aid for Zionism among Jews in Egypt in its December 6 issue. Commenting on a denial issued by Yussuf Bey Cattaoui and Deputy René Bey Cattaoui that Egyptian Jews had sent L.E. 2 million to aid the Zionists in Palestine, the paper said, with fine disregard for their statement in *al-Ahrām* on October 14, 1947 (reported in my airgram A-535 of October 15, 1947), declaring that the Jews of Egypt are opposed to Zionism, "These two Jewish gentlemen denied the report but said nothing in condemnation of Zionism. Is it too much to expect the Jews of Egypt to express their sympathy with the Arabs?"

[2] This Jewish paper, founded in 1934, attempted to be both pro-Zionist and pro-Egyptian. See Victor Nachmias, "El Shams—A Jewish Newspaper in Egypt, 1934–1948," *Peʿamim* 16 (1983): 128–41 [Heb.].

The question of financial aid for the Zionists was also discussed during the period by *Sawṭ al-Umma*, pro-Wafdist paper, by *Akhīr Sāᶜa,* a pro-government weekly, and by *al-Ṣabāḥ*, an independent weekly. The reported formation of a committee comprising Jewish financiers in Egypt who sympathize with Zionism was described by *Sawṭ al-Umma* in its October 25 issue. The committee, according to this story, was busy collecting one pound from every Jew in Egypt as a contribution to the Zionist cause in Palestine. The paper said that it refrained from publishing the names at the time in the hope that the individuals might adopt "a more decent attitude" and that, in the meantime, it was drawing the government's attention to "these destructive movements."

Akhīr Sāᶜa declared on December 10, 1947, that the Jews of Lebanon had contributed L.E. 10,000 and those of Iraq L.E. 500,000 for the Arab cause. "We have great admiration for these Iraqi and Lebanese Jews," the paper said, "but our feeling towards the Jews of Egypt is one of suspicion. The Chief Rabbi said that Egypt's Jews were true Egyptians and Zaki al-Oreibi Bey, the Jewish lawyer, declared at the court room that the Jews of Egypt abhorred partition, but we are still suspicious and so is the rest of Egypt." *Akhīr Sāᶜa* posed the argument since the Egyptian Jews share the rights, they must also share the responsibilities of the Egyptians. Disapproval of partition is not enough. "They must contribute money because money is the only weapon with which they know how to fight." *Al-Ṣabāḥ* on the same day wrote that the Arabs have documents which clearly prove that the Zionists of Egypt send six million pounds every year to the Zionists of Palestine. The names of contributors were said to be known and would be published in due course.

In mid-December, *Miṣr al-Fatāt*, organ of the Young Egypt group, demanded that Jewish residents of this country be arrested and their property confiscated since Egypt is in "a state of war with the Zionists" and since it alleged there are Zionists among Jews in Egypt. No other cause or reason of this extreme recommendation was given. About the same time *al-Kutla* said that Jews residing in Egypt should be registered and disarmed by the police.

In contrast to the foregoing attacks, both *al-Assas,* which is regarded as the mouthpiece of Prime Minister Nokrashy Pasha, and *Akhbār al-Yom,* an important pro-government and pro-Palace weekly, defended Egypt's Jews. *Akhbār al-Yom* on November 29 said the Government would protect Jewish life and property in Egypt and that it would deal very severely with any person who agitates against Egyptian Jews. "We must," it said, "differentiate between Jews and Zionists." *Al-Assas* in an important article on December 12 criticized the way in which it said some newspapers are attempting to put the Egyptian Jews in an awkward position. Giving wide publicity to the report that the Jews of Iraq had contributed half a million pounds for the defense of Palestine was, it said, "grossly unfair to the Jews of Egypt who constitute a minority and who are entitled to the full protection of the government and a courteous treatment at the hands of the majority." *Al-Assas* continued that whether or not the Jews of Egypt are Zionists, the Egyptians cannot punish people for the "possible feelings which they may be hiding inside themselves. . . . So long as the Jews of Egypt do not say or do anything in support of Zionism, they must in no way be molested, embarrassed, or annoyed."

Continuing with probably the most reasonable comment on the Zionist question which has appeared in the local Arabic press for some time, *al-Assas*, over the signature of Ibrahim Abdel Kader el-Mazni, said that "it is at once illogical and unfair to expect a Jew to help fight another Jew who is trying to establish a national home to which he can immigrate if he had to. Every Jew is in favor of a Jewish State. This is only natural and it is absurd to imagine that the Jews in Egypt or in other Arab States are against the establishment of a Jewish State. It is therefore wrong to embarrass the Jews in the way they have been embarrassed lately by the Arabic newspapers. So long as they abide by the law and do not say or do anything that hurts our feelings one should have nothing against them. No decent Arab who has pure Arab blood in his veins should ask the Jews to contribute money in aid of the Palestine Arabs. In our opinion, Egypt is a civilized country, and our civilization is the oldest in the world. Our traditions and religion should deter us from embarrassing the Jews by demanding that they should contribute money for the Arab cause."

Al-Ikhwān al-Muslimūn lost little time in criticizing this stand by *al-Assas*. Referring to Ibrahim el-Mazni as "the advocate of the Jews," the Moslem Brotherhood paper on December 14 said it was only asking Egypt's Jews to prove their loyalty by contributing money and not by fighting to save Palestine. Since it was asking the same of Egypt's Moslems and Christians, *al-Ikhwān* could not see why such a request should embarrass the Jews. Replying to *al-Assas'* argument that Egypt's traditions should prevent her from making demands on the Jews, Sheikh Ḥassan al-Banna's paper proclaimed that, "We have great traditions, but there is nothing in our religion that says that we should protect the Jews and forfeit our liberty and dignity. The writer of *al-Assas'* article says that he is not in the pay of the Jews. Ha, Ha, Ha! His words sound very much like the jingling of Jewish gold."

The Grand Rabbi of Egypt, Haim Nahoum Effendi, in a probable attempt to capitalize on the relatively small degree of existing sentiment favoring tolerance, declared in a broadcast in Arabic from Cairo on December 3 to the Egyptian Israelite community that the Jews of Egypt are part of the Egyptian nation, protected by the King and Government, and that, consequently, the Jewish community will model its attitude on that of the Egyptian nation. The Grand Rabbi was reported to have said, "I ordered religious services to be held, and instructed the members of our community to cooperate fully with their Egyptian brothers in these critical times." In this connection it may be of interest to recall the Grand Rabbi's statement last year that the Jewish community in Egypt lives in entire harmony with other elements of the population and feels perfectly secure under the protection of the King and his Government, which was reported in my dispatch no. 1976 of November 13, 1946. The Grand Rabbi added at that time that neither in Egyptian law nor its administration is there any tendency to discriminate on religious or racial grounds.

Underlining the as yet uncertain and insecure position of the Jews in the Middle East, however, the Palestine Government radio station at Sharq al-Adna, located about 12 miles from Jerusalem, broadcast in Arabic on December 7 that the situation of the autochthon Jews in the Near East was still a matter of doubt. "In spite of statements and declarations in which they denounce Zionism, the Arab League countries may ask them yet to define their attitude once and for all toward Zionism."

Respectfully yours,
For the Ambassador:

Jefferson Patterson
Counselor of Embassy

National Archives (Washington)
RG 59 867N.01/12-2047.

WORSENING MUSLIM-JEWISH RELATIONS IN ALGERIA
(1948)

Association D'Etude
D'Aide & D'Assistance

Algiers, January 22, 1948
II rue Bab-El-Oued

Committee for Refugee Aid.
Dr. I Schwarzbart
World Jewish Congress
1834 Broadway
New York

Dear Doctor and Friend:

I have made it my duty to respond to your friendly letter of January 6th.

Judeo-Arab Relations in Algeria.—Let us say right away that the recent events in Palestine have caused profound trouble in these relations and the fault lies with Algerian Zionist extremists who, having violated the tacit agreement which exists between us and the Arabs of Algeria, an agreement according to which neither of us is to take up the Palestine question except with the greatest reserve, have not hesitated for several years now to hold more and more Zionist gatherings, to appeal for international Jewish solidarity in the Jewish papers, and to collect significant sums for the two Kerens.[1] Thus, for example, the number-three Algerian Jewish newspaper, *L'Appel* of Dr. Edouard Ghanassia, displays on every front page a young Irgunist, submachine gun ready, opposing. . . .[2]

The Arabs consider this picture to be a provocation with respect to them and have pointed it out to the French Government in Paris and to the authorities in Algiers.

Emissaries from clandestine Jewish organizations have been traversing North Africa from the heart of Tunisia to Morocco, preaching the exodus to Jews of modest or unfortunate circumstances, saying: "Go to Algiers where boats are ready to take you to Palestine, and you will have nothing to worry about."

These unfortunates do not hesitate to respond to this command, and the city of Algiers has seen, as a result, an influx of thousands of poor people—women, old people, children, people without the means of existence having sold everything, sick people many of whom have contagious diseases (tuberculosis, trachoma, ringworm, etc.). The Jewish Community

[1] Keren Hayesod and Keren Kayemeth.
[2] The ellipses are in the original.

has had a difficult time in housing, maintaining, and clothing them over these long months—even with the aid of the A.J.G.[3]

Attempts at clandestine embarkations have failed lamentably, and this, under the eyes of the anxious French authorities and above all the Muslims, who misinformed, do not hesitate to accuse North African Jewry of sending money, arms, and men to the Zionists—in a word, of complicity with the fighting going on lately in Palestine.

A serious movement is stirring the Muslim masses in North Africa (we have 12 million Arabs as opposed to barely half a million Jews). The Religious Chief of the Ulema, Si Taieb el Okby, a personal friend of this writer, has addressed a protest to the leaders of the Arab League, a copy of which is attached.[4] M. Elie Gozlan,[5] though ill in Paris, was obliged to return promptly to Algeria to calm tempers and attend to the situation.

This state of affairs has ameliorated slightly, but what prudence the Jews must show in dealing with the Palestinian affair!

The article by M. André Chouraqui[6] which appeared in *Vendredi Soir* is noteworthy. It is full of objective truth, but no one has any illusions, a deep malaise reigns in North Africa. Separatist ideas are making headway; and if one speaks of an exodus, it is necessary to specify that there is anxiety in many hearts. Many Europeans and a good number of Jews are thinking about returning to the Metropole or about becoming expatriates.[7] And who can give assurance that security is certain in any part of the world?

Elie Gozlan
President of the Federation of Jewish
Societies of Algeria (Editor in Chief of
"Bulletin")

CZA (Jerusalem) S 25/5217.

[3] The writer must be referring to the American Jewish Joint Distribution Committee.

[4] I could not find the copy of the Shaykh al-ᶜUqbī's protest in the file.

[5] The writer is referring to himself in the third person.

[6] André Chouraqui (b. 1917), a legal scholar, historian, and litterateur, was and continues to be an eloquent advocate of Arab-Jewish rapprochement. He was one of the few North African Jewish intellectuals to settle in Israel, where he became an important public figure. See David Corcos, "Chouraqui, André ," *EJ* 5: 504.

[7] Again, the ellipses are in the original.

Allied Jewish servicemen at an Oneg Shabbat sponsored by the Jewish community of Cairo during World War II. (Photo Collection on Egypt, Folder: Cairo 1. Courtesy of YIVO Institute for Jewish Research, New York.)

The Chief Rabbi of Tripoli, bestowing a blessing upon Brigadier Lush, the first British military governor, and the officers of the Palestinian Brigade in the main synagogue, Tripoli, 1943. (Renzo de Felice, *Jews in an Arab Land: Libya, 1835–1970,* trans., Judith Roumani. University of Texas Press: Austin, 1985.)

Welcoming the British forces at the entrance of the Ḥara of Tripoli, 1943. (Renzo de Felice, *Jews in an Arab Land: Libya, 1835–1970,* trans., Judith Roumani. University of Texas Press: Austin, 1985.)

José Aboulker, leader of the uprising that paralyzed communications and captured strategic points in Algiers on the eve of the Allied landing, November 7–8, 1942. (Gitta Amipaz-Silber, *La Résistance Juive en Algérie, 1940–1942.* Rubin Mass: Jerusalem, 1986.)

Members of the Resistance group led by José Aboulker, receiving the Cross of Liberation in Algiers, 1947. (Aboulker is no. 2 in the picture and his cousin Roger Carcassonne is no. 1.) (Gitta Amipaz-Silber, *La Résistance Juive en Algérie, 1940–1942*. Rubin Mass: Jerusalem, 1986.)

Libyan Jewish survivors of Nazi concentration camps in Europe, on their way home via Italy. (Renzo de Felice, *Jews in an Arab Land: Libya, 1835–1970,* trans., Judith Roumani. University of Texas Press: Austin, 1985.)

Maḥane Ge'ūla (Camp Redemption) for Yemenite Jews on their way to Israel; Hashid, Aden Protectorate, late 1940s. (Yosef Ṣadoq, *Be-Saʿarōt Tēmān: Megillat "Marvad ha-Qesamīm".* Am Oved: Tel Aviv, 1956.)

Yemenite Jews on their way to Israel in "Operation 'On Wings of Eagles'," 1948–1949. (Shlomo Barer, *The Magic Carpet*. Harper & Row: New York, 1952; with permission.)

Wealthy Jewish merchant, Shafīq ᶜAdes, accused of having supplied scrap metal to Israel, being led to his trial in Basra, Iraq, summer 1948. (He was condemned and hanged in front of his home.) (Yosef Meir [Yehoshafat], *Beyond the Desert: Underground Activities in Iraq, 1941–1951*. The Ministry of Defense Publishing House: Tel Aviv, 1973.)

Crowds of Jews outside the Mas^c^uda Shem Tov Synagogue in Baghdad, waiting to register for ^c^aliya to Israel, 1950. (Shlomo Hillel, *Rū'aḥ Qādīm: Be-Shelīḥūt Maḥtartīt le-Arṣōt ^c^Arav.* Edanim Publishers: Jerusalem, 1985.)

General Muḥammad Najīb, just two months after coming to power, making an unprecedented appearance for an Egyptian head of state at Cairo's Great Synagogue on Yom Kippur, 1952. (*Juifs d'Egypte: Images et Textes.* Editions du Scribe: Paris, 1984.)

THE INTERNAL CONFLICT OF A LEADING EGYPTIAN JEWISH BUSINESSMAN AT THE TIME OF THE FIRST ARAB-ISRAELI WAR (1948)

. . . When war was declared between the Arab countries and the State of Israel, I found myself at the meeting in Paris with this banker. Instead of returning to Egypt, I waited in France for events to unfold.

Egypt had sequestered the property of the greater part of the Jewish population, and numerous individuals were sent to concentration camps for long periods. The official circles knew of my Jewish and Zionist activity, and my name was found, naturally, to be among those persons who were targeted. However, I was spared.

I learned later that it was Nuqrāshī Pasha, then Prime Minister, who had himself crossed my name off these lists. I was, therefore, not bothered at all during this period, because Nuqrāshī Pasha had always had, as I have just said, a friendly attitude, appreciating the services that I had rendered the country.

I received regular reports in Paris on the activity of the bank and of the subcompanies that I had created.[1]

After a few months' stay in France, the president of the board of directors of the bank, ʿAbd al-Raḥmān al-Biyālī Bey, came to find me and invited me to come back to Egypt, assuring me that I would not be subject to any vexation.

For my part, I had wanted at this moment to chuck everything and move to Israel. I had met in Paris and Geneva with numerous Israeli personalities, all of whom encouraged me to come to Israel, knowing my feelings and all that I had done during the war for the institutions and for Jewish soldiers.[2] One of these personalities, the most important, said to me one day at the Geneva airport where I ran into him: "Don't hesitate to come to our home—or rather, to your home—the future of the Jews in the Arab lands is not certain. In Israel, all the posts are vacant. We need people like you. You could choose whatever branch of activity you would want, and you would succeed in Israel, just as you did in Egypt."

I was shaken by these words, all the more so because my own personal feelings were pushing me to follow this advice. I remembered the words that the Israeli journalist had said of me: "Īsh she-nōlad Ṣiyyōnī." Could "a

[1] Politi was the head of a syndicate that took over the Commercial Bank of Egypt. See E. I. Politi, *L'Egypte de 1914 à "Suez"* (Paris, 1965), p. 159.

[2] As president of the B'nai B'rith Lodge of Alexandria during World War II, Politi oversaw all Jewish communal works, including the Cuisine Populaire (a soup kitchen), the Jewish Club for Servicemen, and the Hatikva Club for Palestinian soldiers. See ibid., pp. 197–98, passim.

man who was born a Zionist" at the very moment when the millennial dream was being realized, at the very moment when the Promised Land was becoming "Our Land," could he keep out of the way of this historic movement which was going to mark the twentieth century by an act of supreme justice? I did not think so. I knew that my duty was to go without delay, and I failed in my most elementary duty. Torn between my personal sentiments and what I believed to be my duty toward those interests that had been confided in me, I lived a Corneillian drama during those weeks, not knowing what decision to make.

The arrival of the bank president in Paris tipped the balance in favor of my return to Egypt. Thus I went back to Cairo where I was wonderfully received at the airport by my colleagues and my Egyptian friends.

Work, with its habitual rhythm, brought me back into an atmosphere that was the tangible proof of the general appreciation for what I had accomplished up to that time.[3]

E. I. Politi, *L'Egypte de 1914 à "Suez"*
(Paris, 1965), pp. 240–42.

[3] Politi remained in Egypt until 1956, when his citizenship was revoked, his assets were sequestered, and he was expelled from the country. See ibid., pp. 276–79.

THE MOROCCAN SULTAN APPEALS FOR CALM AMONG HIS MUSLIM AND JEWISH SUBJECTS AT THE OUTBREAK OF THE FIRST ARAB-ISRAELI WAR
(1948)

To Our Noble People:

By virtue of the mission with which Almighty God has entrusted us to look after your interests, we address to you this message so that you might observe and respect its terms. Several days ago, war erupted in the Holy land of Palestine after the Arabs had despaired of convincing the Zionists to renounce the idea of taking possession of this land and expelling the inhabitants. The League of Arab States, therefore, found themselves obliged to enter the territory of Holy Palestine in order to defend its inhabitants and to thwart Zionism's unjustified aggression.

As for us, in declaring that we are in complete accord of heart and mind with the Arab sovereigns and the leaders of their governments as we have declared to them, we approve entirely the terms of their declaration making known that the Arabs harbor no evil design with regard to the Jews and do not consider them as enemies. Rather, their only goal is to defend the first Qibla[1] of Islam and to reestablish peace and justice in the Holy Land while preserving for the Jews the status that has always been accorded them since the Muslim conquest. This is why we enjoin our Muslim subjects not to let themselves be incited by the undertaking of the Jews against their brother Arabs in Palestine to commit any act whatsoever that might disturb public order and safety. They must know that the Moroccan Israelites[2] who have lived for centuries in this country which has protected them, where they have found the best welcome, and where they have shown their complete devotion to the Moroccan throne are different from the rootless Jews who have turned from the four corners of the earth toward Palestine, which they want to seize unjustly and arbitrarily.

We likewise enjoin our Israelite subjects not to lose sight of the fact that they are Moroccans living under our aegis and that they have found in us under various circumstances the best defender of their interests and of their rights. They should, therefore, refrain from any act that is liable to support the Zionist aggression or show their solidarity with it; because in doing so they would be violating their particular rights as well as their Moroccan nationality.

[1] The *qibla* is the direction of prayer in Islam. When Muḥammad emigrated to Medina in 622, he originally had Muslims pray in the direction of Jerusalem. See Norman A. Stillman, *The Jews of Arab Lands: A History and Source Book* (Philadelphia, 1979), p. 11.

[2] Ar., *Isrā'īliyyūn* and Fr., *Israélites* were traditionally more positive terms than their synonyms *Yahūd* and *Juifs*. Hence, Muḥammad V used the former when referring to Moroccan Jewry.

We are certain that all of you, Moroccans, without exception, will respond to our appeal and do what we expect of you so that public order might be respected and maintained in our beloved homeland. May God take care of our destinies and yours. He is the best Master and the best Support.

"Proclamation de Sa Majesté le Sultan"
(Rabat, May 23, 1948), in André Chouraqui,
La condition juridique de l'Israélite marocain
(Paris, 1950), p. 221, Annexes.

EXTRACTS FROM BRITISH EMBASSY REPORTS ON ATTACKS ON JEWS AND FOREIGNERS IN EGYPT DURING THE FIRST ARAB-ISRAELI WAR

(1948)

IMPORTANT.
CONFIDENTIAL.

Addressed to Foreign Office telegram No. 1075 of July 19th repeated for information to Amman, Bagdad, Beirut, Damascus, Jedda, and Jerusalem.

Air raid on Cairo.

There was an air raid alert on the evening of July 17th. Heavy A. A. fire was heard but no bombs were dropped and it is doubtful if any aircraft were actually over Cairo.

On July 16th violent anti-Jewish speeches were delivered by members of "Ikhwan El Muslimeen"[1] after Friday prayers, and "Ikhwan" were evidently doing their best to incite the population against the Jews as a whole "Not only the Zionists" as being responsible for previous bombing of Cairo.[2] It was thus not surprising that during and after the alert attacks were made in various parts of Cairo on individual Jews and also on a number of Christian foreigners. Three Egyptian Jews and two others, probably Egyptian Jews, are known to have been killed. Two Frenchmen and several Greeks, Italians, Yugoslavs, and Americans were injured, the Frenchmen seriously.

. . . .

Coincidence of Palestine situation with Ramadan[3] makes the ground particularly fruitful for incitement to fanaticism, and it would not take much to provoke large-scale mob attacks on Christians and Jews alike.

23rd July, 1948.

The state of tension in Cairo which followed the air raid reported . . . in my[4] telegram No. 116 . . . mounted higher as the result of air raid alarms on 17th and 19th July. On the latter occasion the alarm sounded some twenty minutes after a violent explosion had seriously damaged two Jewish department stores in the center of Cairo and done extensive damage to other commercial premises in the vicinity. During this period groups of students and the riffraff of Cairo indulged in Jew-baiting and assaults on a considerable number of foreigners, including British, causing deaths and injuries. In addition, an orgy of looting followed the explosion on the night of 19th July. Even a number of fair-skinned Egyptians have not escaped molestation in

[1] Ar., *al-Ikhwān al-Muslimūn,* the Muslim Brethren (Muslim Brotherhood).

[2] On July 15, the Israeli air force bombed Cairo and Alexandria in retaliation for Egyptian bombings of Tel Aviv.

[3] The Muslim holy month of daytime fasting fell that year between July 8 and August 6.

[4] Sir Ronald Campbell, the British ambassador.

the streets by students and others who have mistaken them for Jews. I have made strong representations to the Minister for Foreign Affairs about the attacks on British subjects, and I have protested to the Prime Minister against the suppression by the censorship of a statement which I caused to be distributed to the press on the subject of my interview with Khashaba Pasha.[5] My Oriental counselor had an interview with the Under Secretary of State for Interior on 21st July and obtained an assurance that every effort would be made to suppress further disorders of this kind and to ensure the security of British subjects and other foreigners. Although it is fairly obvious that the explosion outside the Cicurel store[6] on 19th July must have been caused by a bomb or mine placed on the spot, the Egyptian Prime Minister has publicly ascribed it to the dropping of an aerial torpedo from a Jewish aircraft. It is not yet known, however, whether he intends to register this incident as a violation of the cease-fire arrangement which entered into force on the previous day. At all events, the censorship has prevented the publication of any reports deviating from the supposition that an aerial torpedo dropped by an aircraft caused the explosion.

31st July, 1948.

There was an air raid alarm in Alexandria on 25th July, but no bombs were dropped and no serious incidents have been reported in connection therewith. It is reported by S. S. R. that members of the Moslem Brethren Society were distributing pamphlets in Cairo on 22nd and 23rd July exhorting the public to boycott Jews and generally to make life unbearable for them.

In accordance with a newly issued military proclamation, Jewish families living in the immediate vicinity of Abdin Palace,[7] army establishments, the Arab League headquarters, etc., have been given three days' notice to quit their dwellings. This measure, if strictly enforced, will cause hardship to those evicted owing to the impossibility of finding other accommodations at short notice and at prices within their means. Only one British family is involved, and the Acting British Consul-General has taken up their case with the Governorate.

. . . On 28th July an explosion occurred in the drapery store of Messrs. David Ades and Son,[8] Cairo, doing minor damage and causing only slight casualties. According to the press, a disgruntled ex-employee of the firm, stated to be a Jew, has been arrested on suspicion of being responsible for this incident, but the truth is not yet known. The police succeeded in maintaining order in the street on this occasion.

PRO (London)
FO 371/69259 and 69182.

[5] Aḥmad Muḥammad Khashaba, the minister of justice.
[6] One of Cairo's largest department stores owned by Jews.
[7] The royal residence.
[8] Another major Jewish-owned business.

THE WORLD JEWISH CONGRESS LOBBIES WITH THE BRITISH COLONIAL OFFICE TO ALLOW YEMENITE JEWISH REFUGEES ENTRY INTO ADEN ON THEIR WAY TO ISRAEL
(1949)

Copy

ALE/MAK 8th March, 1949

The Under Secretary of State
Colonial Office
Church House
Gt. Smith Street, S.W. 1.

Sir,

I am directed to refer to reports which have reached us and to statements which have been published in the British press, to the effect that the Government of Aden has requested the Imam of the Yemen to prevent the exit of Jews from the Yemen and their entry into the Aden Protectorate.

You will no doubt be aware that the Jews in the Yemen have for long suffered grave disabilities and have been the victims of racial discrimination, humiliation, and attack, in which the Government of the Yemen has actively participated. The situation of the Yemenite Jews has very seriously deteriorated since last December, by reason of the revival of ritual murder accusations against Jews. In consequence, many rabbis and prominent Jews have been imprisoned and held as hostages. As a result of this, the Jewish population has been in a state of fear and insecurity in face of Arab incitement against them.

This state of fear and insecurity and the long-standing hostility of the Yemenite Government has caused the Jews to seek safety in the State of Israel, and there is a general anxiety on the part of the Jewish population to leave the Yemen, and in this purpose they are supported by the World Jewish Congress and other Jewish authorities. Before they can reach Israel they are obliged to pass through and temporarily to remain in Aden until the transport facilities to Israel can be arranged. Their stay in Aden is of very short duration.

If it is true that the Government of Aden has requested the Yemenite Government to prevent the exit of Jews—and it is reported to us that part of the request is to strengthen the Yemenite guards at the frontier between the Yemen and Aden—the World Jewish Congress is bound to regard this as an act of grave inhumanity and injustice against people who are fleeing from danger and who are seeking asylum from persecution.

I am directed to call your attention to Article 14 of the Universal Declaration of Human Rights recently adopted unanimously by the General Assembly of the United Nations. This Article specifically guarantees as a human right and fundamental freedom that "everyone has the right to seek and enjoy in other countries asylum from persecution." It is pertinent to emphasize that the words "to enjoy" were inserted in this Article on the proposal of the British Government.

The Executive of the World Jewish Congress feels sure that H. M. government cannot approve of any measure which prevents human beings seeking and obtaining safety from persecution and that they will, therefore, make the fullest and most urgent inquiry of the Government of Aden into the circumstances which are the subject of the reports referred to. Should these reports prove to be accurate, it is hoped that H. M. Government will take steps to nullify the effect of the request stated to have been made by the Government of Aden to the Imam of the Yemen and will afford every facility for Yemenite Jews to obtain temporary refuge in the Protectorate until they can be transferred to their ultimate destination in Israel.

I enclose herewith copy of the report published in the Manchester Guardian yesterday, March 7th, and by Reuters News Agency on March 6th.[1]

I shall be glad to have a very early opportunity of discussing this matter with you.

Yours faithfully,

A. L. Easterman
Political Secretary.

PRO (London)
FO 371/75259.

[1] One of these reports is given in the following text.

A BRITISH PRESS REPORT ON THE CONTINUED ARRIVAL OF YEMENITE JEWISH REFUGEES IN ADEN AND THE ATTEMPT BY THE AUTHORITIES THERE TO STAUNCH THE FLOW

(1949)

Copy

From the *Manchester Guardian*, March 7.

Jews Still Arriving in Aden.

From Yemen to Palestine.

Aden, March 6.

The first of 860 military-aged Yemenite Jews, granted permission to leave for Israel, flew from here today soon after the Aden Government had asked the Yemen to stop the trek of Jews into the Protectorate. Yemenite Jews are said to be arriving in Aden at the rate of 100 a month in an attempt to reach Israel, and the British authorities fear that if more come in there will be a repetition of the 1947 pogroms.

Jewish sources said that emaciated Jews arriving here all tell the same story of a ninety-mile trek to avoid capture and imprisonment in the Yemen. They say that rabbis and prominent members of the Jewish Community in the Yemen are imprisoned in chains.[1]

Over 4,000 Jews have been flown out of Aden since the December pogroms here, and it is understood that the remaining 3,124 have asked the American Joint Distribution Committee to continue the "airlift" until they have all reached Israel.—Reuter.

PRO (London)
FO 371/75259.

[1] The Reuters report (which has been omitted here) adds that "45 rabbis and other prominent Jews [were being] held hostage for the alleged murder of two girls."

A REPORT ON THE JOINT DISTRIBUTION COMMITTEE'S EFFORTS TO ASSIST YEMENITE AND ADENI JEWS TO EMIGRATE TO ISRAEL

(1949)

AMERICAN JEWISH JOINT DISTRIBUTION COMMITTEE

Office for
AJD—Paris (o.n.m.)
Mr. Joseph

Tel Aviv, May 16th, 1949

Mr. M. Stephany[1]
Woburn House
Upper Woburn Place
London, W.C.1

Dear Mr. Stephany,

Aden Community

In a few days I hope to send you a report about the activities of the emergency hospital for the first four months of 1949.

. . . .

I had previously advised you that over 2,200 of 2,640 Adenites had registered for emigration to Israel. You will also recall that early March, I visited Aden with the express purpose of urging the Adenites to postpone their emigration to Israel for a few months because I was convinced that the Adenites "cannot take it" under the present conditions. I was unsuccessful in this part of my mission, but I was right in my prognosis. About 1,000 of the 2,200 who had registered for emigration have arrived in Israel. Most of these 1,000 were Adenites for whom the JDC paid the full cost of transportation and therefore may be considered as the poorer element who had nothing to lose by leaving Aden. Most of the other 1,200 who had registered for emigration asked for a stay of two or three months in order to enable them to dispose their property at more reasonable prices than are being offered at the present. There also is some propaganda by our friend, Salīm Banin,[2] who more than anyone else urged immediate emigration and who now is urging the people not to emigrate. The JDC complied with the request and decided to discontinue the shuttle service for two or three months and has agreed, in principle, to renew the emigration in about two or three months of those who decide to emigrate. Of the 1,200 who registered and who have not emigrated, about 300 will pay their own fare and the JDC will have to pay full or part for the other 900. Another reason which made it difficult for some of those who registered to emigrate was the Government of Aden's decision that those who had received loans must repay these loans or furnish

[1] An official of the Central British Fund for Jewish Relief and Rehabilitation.
[2] The head of the Adeni Jewish community.

additional security, as a condition for granting exit visas. I consider this attitude of the Aden Government most unfair and unjustified. I hope that you and your colleagues will be able to make some representations to the Government about this question.

I know that you are also interested in the question of the Yemenite Jews. In the course of my visit to Aden in early March, the Governor refused to entertain the proposal that the JDC should not be compelled to dismantle the Hashed Camp and the JDC also should be allowed to open a transient camp on the border of the Western Protectorate and the Yemen. The governor insisted that he had agreed to the emigration of the Yemenites on condition that the Camp will be liquidated since the existence of the camp was an encouragement for additional Yemenite Jews to infiltrate into the Crater.[3] The Governor also admitted to having requested the Imam to enforce the existing legislation forbidding the departure of the Jews from the Yemen and that he would ask the Legislative Council in Aden to approve new legislation which would make it more difficult for Yemenites and particularly Yemenite Jews, to infiltrate into the Crater.

We moved about 6,200 Yemenites. This number includes over 500 who infiltrated during 1949. There are still about 150 Yemenites in the Crater, nearly all of them aged, sick, and incapacitated and their families who cannot, at least, for the present, emigrate to Israel.

The Aden Government now has advised the J. E. C.[4] in Aden that it would be prepared to lift the restrictions imposed with regard to the admission of Jews from the Yemen to the Crater if the Jewish organizations (JDC) would agree to reopen the Hashed Camp, maintain and house the new arrivals, and also undertake that the new arrivals would be emigrated to Israel within a reasonable time. . . . The AJDC now is considering this proposal. Personally, I believe that it would be most difficult, if at all possible, to get the necessary staff which would be required for the Hashed Camp if it were to be reopened. I also consider that it would be better if we would house the Yemenite Jews who would arrive in the Crater where there is now sufficient accommodation. The Aden Government, however, appears adamant about allowing the Yemenite Jews to go into the Crater. The best solution would be if the Imam would grant entrance visas to JDC representatives who could study the question in greater detail on the spot and perhaps also take up the question of the orderly emigration direct from the Yemen to Israel. The possibilities of such visas being granted are very remote. According to Dr. Cochrane, the Aden Government is doing its utmost to prevent such visas from being granted.

. . . .

AJDC (Jerusalem) Aden, Box 322A.2.

[3] The Jewish Quarter was located in Crater.

[4] The Jewish Emergency Committee was a local group chaired by Salīm Banin to aid victims of the 1947 riots as well as refugees from Yemen. A copy of the governor's letter of May 5, 1949, to the JEC is included in AJDC (Jerusalem) Box 322A.2.

A SUMMARY OF THE IRAQI PARLIAMENTARY DEBATE OF A BILL ALLOWING JEWS TO RENOUNCE THEIR CITIZENSHIP, WITH THE COMMENTARY OF THE BRITISH AMBASSADOR TO BAGHDAD

(1950)

RESTRICTED

BRITISH EMBASSY,
Bagdad.
21st March, 1950

No. 67
(1571/17/50)

The Right Honourable
Ernest Bevin, M. P.,
etc., etc., etc.

Sir:

The debate in the Iraqi Senate on March 4th on the Draft Law supplementary to the Ordinance for Cancellation of Iraqi Nationality produced two speeches of some pathos from the aged Jewish Senator, Sayyid Ezra Menahem Daniel. Senator Ezra said: "Doubtless the Government has brought forward this Bill with reluctance, in view of the painful condition in which Iraqi Jews find themselves today and in order to reduce the disturbances caused by illegal emigration. This Bill deals with only one aspect of the Jewish question in Iraq. What can be done to reassure the Jews who do not wish to leave their homeland for good and who are loyal and law-abiding citizens? These are now deprived of their constitutional and legal rights as a result of administrative measures placing exceptional restrictions on them alone of all Iraqi nationals. They have been discriminated against, and their liberties, actions, education, and means of livelihood have been handicapped. Does not the Government consider it to be its duty to reassure this large section of loyal citizens by removing those extraordinary restrictions in order to restore to Iraqi Jews their sense of security, confidence, and stability? The Jews have lived in Iraq for 3,500 years. That is why they are reluctant to emigrate unless they are really obliged to do so. History will reveal the real reason for this emigration and will show that Iraqi Jews have nothing to do with the unhappy conditions of which their fellow citizens complain."

Later in the debate Senator Ezra spoke again saying that he did not know what the Jew could do in Iraq after he had submitted to the exceptional conditions of the past two years. He had not been admitted to the Higher Colleges and was not allowed to study at his own expense abroad. Work was denied to him and he suffered restrictions in business. But for these severe handicaps, Iraqi Jews would not have gone so far as to attempt large-scale flight from the country. The Senator added that if the Government wanted to reassure the Jews and induce them to resume their ordinary avocations it should remove these handicaps and encourage them to work.

The Minister of the Interior, Sayyid Ṣāliḥ Jabr, in reply, said that the Government was sympathetic with loyal citizens who did not put themselves in an attitude of opposition to the national interest. A not inconsiderable section of Jewish nationals, however, had committed acts which were not consistent with the country's interests and were in fact a disservice to the nation. Their motives might have been political and religious. The Minister continued that the Government felt that it was not in the national interest to prevent the emigration of these people to any destination they might choose. Those who had made up their minds to leave the country for good would do the country harm if they remained. As to the remaining Jewish nationals, the Government considered them as Iraqis equal with Muslim and Christian Iraqis so long as they obeyed the law and acted in accordance with the national interest. The constitution was a guarantee of this.

The remainder of the speeches were of little interest. Muzāḥim al-Pachāchī asserted that those Jews who left the country under the new law would be young men who would constitute a Fifth Column. He referred with approval to an article by Mr. Edwin Samuel in the American periodical "The Middle East" in which he had suggested that it was in the interests of both Jews and Arabs to set up a United Nations Committee to arrange an exchange of population and to liquidate their properties in the interests of both parties. He thought that the Jews would continue to smuggle their property while the Palestine Arabs were not able to smuggle theirs, since it had been frozen. Senator Muṣṭafā al-ᶜUmarī urged caution and a closer study of the Bill. He said that the cancellation of Iraqi nationality should take place on a family and not on an individual basis. If a Jew wished to emigrate, his whole family should go with him. He also inquired why the Iraqi Government had not frozen Jewish property in the same way as Arab property in Israel had been frozen.

The Prime Minister wound up by saying that when his Government had taken office it had found widespread complaints against the economic paralysis caused by thousands of people selling their movable and immovable property by auction. This situation had required a compromise solution. It had become evident that those who were selling their property were attempting to flee the country. The government had seen no point in forcing these people to stay. Those who wished to stay could stay, but those who wished to go should certainly go. This was the compromise solution that the government had reached. The Bill was then put to the vote and passed.

It may be worthwhile to attempt to provide a more convincing answer to Senator Ezra's questions than did the Minister of Interior. As I have already reported, the Prime Minister has told me that there are now no administrative restrictions applied to Jews which do not apply to all other Iraqi citizens. I have no reason to believe that this is untrue. Nevertheless, discrimination against Jews is applied in practice. In the Southern States of America, it is said to be difficult for a negro to obtain his rights against a White American in the Courts or to send his son to study alongside his white fellow citizen in higher colleges. An Iraqi Jew today suffers similar disabilities, which extend to many aspects of his life. Most educated Iraqis deplore this state of affairs, and the Iraqi governing class is increasingly perturbed by the stagnation which has been caused in the markets by the uncertainty with which the Jews regard their economic future. Governments in Iraq, however, are too weak to lead public opinion in a matter of this kind, and any direct attempts on their part to improve the position of Jews are immediately the object of Nationalist attack. I think the Iraqi Government sincerely hoped that the departure of the Jewish malcontents under this new Ordinance would improve the atmosphere and facilitate good treatment for those who remained. Like many well-intentioned Iraqi measures its effects have been different from those intended. It has resulted in an increase in attacks by the Nationalist press on the Iraqi-Jewish community as such. It has produced a still greater stagnation in the markets, while as far as I am aware for the reasons which I have given in my dispatch No. 66 of the 21st March, no Jew has yet come forward to take advantage of the possibility of legal emigration which it provides.

I have the honor to be,
With the highest respect,
Sir,
Your most obedient,
humble Servant,

HENRY B. MACK

PRO (London)
FO 371/75183.

THE IRAQI LAW PERMITTING JEWS TO EMIGRATE WITH THE FORFEITURE OF NATIONALITY
(1950)

Article 1

The Council of Ministers is empowered to divest any Iraqi Jew who, of his own free will and choice, desires to leave Iraq for good of his Iraqi nationality after he has signed a special form in the presence of an official appointed by the Minister of the Interior.

Article 2

Any Iraqi Jew who leaves Iraq or tries to leave Iraq illegally will forfeit his Iraqi nationality by decision of the Council of Ministers.

Article 3

Any Iraqi Jew who has already left Iraq illegally will be considered to have left Iraq for good if he does not return within a period of two months from the date of the putting into operation of this law, and he will lose his Iraqi nationality at the end of that period.

Article 4

The Minister of the Interior must order the deportation of anyone who has lost Iraqi nationality under Articles 1 and 2 unless the Minister is convinced by sufficient reasons that his temporary stay in Iraq is necessary for judicial or legal reasons, or to safeguard someone else's officially testified rights.

Article 5

This law will remain in force for a period of one year from the date of its coming into effect and may be canceled at any time during that period by a Royal Iradah[1] published in the *Official Gazette*.

Article 6

This law comes into force from the date of its publication in the *Official Gazette*.

Article 7

The Minister of the Interior will execute this law.

[1] Ar., *irāda* (decree).

Supporting Arguments

It has been noticed that some Iraqi Jews are attempting by every illegal means to leave Iraq for good and that others have already left Iraq illegally. As the presence of subjects of this description forced to stay in the country and obliged to keep their Iraqi nationality would inevitably lead to results affecting public security and give rise to social and economic problems, it has been found advisable not to prevent those wishing to do so from leaving Iraq for good, forfeiting their Iraqi nationality. This law has been promulgated to this end.

Law No. 1 of 1950 (Annexure to the Ordinance for the Cancellation of Iraqi Nationality, Law No. 62 of 1933), passed by the Iraqi Chamber of Deputies on March 2, 1950, and by the Iraqi Senate on March 4, 1950. Text included in PRO (London) FO 371/82478 and published in Shiblak, *The Lure of Zion: The Case of the Iraqi Jews* (London, 1986), pp. 131–32, App. 1.

THE ZIONIST UNDERGROUND IN IRAQ APPEALS TO THE JEWS TO REGISTER FOR EMIGRATION
(1950)

Saturday, April 8, 1950, 4 P.M.

A Call to the Jewish Community

O Children of Zion Residents of Babylon, Save Yourselves

For the second time in the history of this diaspora, after 2,488 years, we are hearing the echo of the historic prophecy of our prophets which brings us good tidings and warns us to leave quickly.

The Movement[1] in its previous announcements to the Jewish Community requested that Jews refrain from registering to renounce their citizenship. This was a fundamental part of our general plan. The Jews stood by us admirably.

Today, we are standing before a new threshold and a great turning point in the history of this diaspora.

The hour has arrived when all of the Jews together must quickly register because this is the most important stage of our program.

Today, we have decided that we must leave this hell of exile. It is incumbent upon all of us to enter upon this practical stage and to go and register.

The movement calls upon all Jews, whatever their class, to avail themselves of this decisive opportunity.

You men and women of Israel! You are the backbone of your people and its main support. Do not let the torch be extinguished in the darkness of exile.

O Ḥāvēr,[2] know that at this hour you are in the vanguard. You must guide the Jews and urge them to emigrate wherever possible.

O Jews, Israel is calling to you—"Get out of Babylon!"

"Nidā' ila 'l-Yahūd,"
Ar. text in Yosef (Yehoshafat) Meir, *Beyond the Desert: Underground Activities in Iraq, 1941–1951,* (Tel Aviv, 1973), p. 240 [Heb.], App.

[1] That is, the underground Zionist organization.

[2] The Hebrew word for "comrade" or "member," designating members of the Movement.

THE PROGRESS OF JEWISH EMIGRATION FROM IRAQ TWO MONTHS BEFORE THE EXPIRATION OF THE LAW PERMITTING IT
(1951)

CONFIDENTIAL

British Embassy,
BAGHDAD

(1572/5/51)

18th January, 1951

Dear Geoffrey,

Please refer to my letter No. 1571/160/50 on the 20th December about Iraqi Jews.

The Iraqi Ministry of the Interior has informed us that up to the 13th January a total of 85,893 Iraqi Jews had registered for migration to Israel. Of these, 35,766 had been deprived of their nationality by the Council of Ministers, and 23,345 had been flown to Israel. There are thus some 62,000 Jews in Iraq awaiting transportation to Israel and about 12,000 of these have been deprived of Iraqi nationality.

I am sending copies of this letter to the Chanceries at Tel Aviv, Amman, Washington, and the British Middle East Office at Cairo.

Yours ever,

(H. Beeley)

G.W. Furlonge, Esq., C.M.G., O.B.E.,
Foreign Office
LONDON S.W. 1.

PRO (London)
FO 371/91689.

THE IRAQI GOVERNMENT URGES THAT JEWISH EMIGRATION BE SPEEDED UP OR IT WILL TAKE DRASTIC MEASURES OF ITS OWN
(1951)

Cypher/OTP *FOREIGN OFFICE AND WHITEHALL DISTRIBUTION*

FROM BAGHDAD TO FOREIGN OFFICE

Sir H. Mack D. 12.04 P.M. 25th January 1951
No. 59
24th January, 1951. R.12.41 P.M. 25th January, 1951.
CONFIDENTIAL

Addressed to Foreign Office telegram no. 59 of 24th January.

Repeated for information to Tel Aviv
and Saving to British Middle East Office (Cairo)
Washington

Iraqi Jews.

The Acting Prime Minister and Acting Minister for Foreign Affairs expressed again today the anxiety of the Iraqi Government about the situation which would exist when the law authorizing emigration expires in March, leaving about 50,000 Iraqi Jews as stateless persons in Iraq. They feared that these would become a danger to the country and would themselves be in danger from the Iraqi people. They begged for our help and asserted that unless a solution were found the Iraqi Government would be compelled to drive them over the frontier to Kuwait or elsewhere.

2. I repeated that His Majesty's Government could accept no responsibility. The Iraqi Government had passed the law without consulting us. Our only concern was humanitarian. For Kuwait or Cyprus to take these people temporarily was out of the question and I understand that Jordan had refused their passage. The only solution therefore was for the Israeli Government to permit an increase of intake. If this was unobtainable they might be put in camps in Iraq administered by some international Jewish body. (Please see Tel Aviv telegram No. 515 of the 7th November 1950 paragraph 4.)

. . . .

4. The Iraqis are in earnest about this. Their real fear is of a general war which would find them with a large number of stateless and disloyal persons, many of them without means of support within their border. They are also genuinely afraid of a popular outburst against the Jews similar to that of May 1941.

PRO (London)
FO 371/91689.

THE CHALLENGE OF MOROCCAN INDEPENDENCE AS VIEWED BY A MOROCCAN JEWISH INTELLECTUAL (1958)

The Test

The Jews of Morocco are in the limelight today. The condition of the Jews in a given country always has a certain international dimension. It is a kind of sociological test and a touchstone of evolutionary developments. After having been ignored for a long time, the Jews of this country find themselves under the scrutiny of observers throughout the world. An experiment is in the process of being made in Morocco whose results are being awaited by all the world. The Jews here have lived for approximately two years in a fully Arab and Muslim state—a transcendent experience, charged with portents and possibilities yet to be realized. Has it been conclusive?

The question posed, the prophecies and conjectures take their course. From almost all sides people have begun writing about Moroccan Jews and their problems. . . . They speak of the iron curtain that has fallen over the 200,000 Jews of this country. They foresee Draconian solutions such as a mass exodus of Moroccan Jewry for which the funds are in the process of being collected. There is in all of this a clear interpolation of the Middle East situation into the Moroccan reality whose inner givens, marginal character, and "specificity" are misjudged. Is this to say that the Jews in the Sharifan Empire have found an airtight and lasting paradise? The truth is more complex. Morocco is in the process of becoming and the condition of the Jews is a function of variables, of coefficients, of subtle factors, to which the future, political orientation, the performance of the parties now in an outright test of strength, the economic future, that of the cultural system, the diplomatic role that will be assigned to the country, all will remain intimately linked.

It has been my lot to live this reality for months now. . . . My reflections here can be considered as conveying a view "from within."

Premises

In the quest for the Moroccan truths, a prefatory question imposes itself: What have the Jews done for the new Morocco? Before asking ourselves about our chances, it would be fitting to know our qualifications. What was—what is—the participation of the Jews in the building of the body politic of this country? Put another way, what does Morocco represent for the Jews?

Sartre saw in liberty an attitude in the face of a given. We do not choose the given which is imposed on us from without, but we choose our attitude toward it. . . . I greatly fear that the participation of Moroccan Jews in the act of independence strangely approaches this Sartrian liberty and responsibility. This independence was made without them, almost without their knowing, occasionally even against their will, at the least against their secret wish. Something passively given and passively received. However, these events which they did not choose, which—properly speaking—they underwent, they can today naught but "assume" them. It is necessary, therefore, to assume independence by choosing retrospectively an ad hoc attitude.

The evolution of the Jews in Morocco has followed a somewhat dialectic cycle: Moroccanization, demoroccanization, remoroccanization. Thesis, antithesis, synthesis. In this completely Hegelian dialectic, the first two phases have been completed. The third is the present now being lived and which is unrolling before our eyes. Moroccanized for centuries, the Jews in the Sharifan Empire underwent during the Protectorate a process—often involuntary—of demoroccanization which coincided with the general phenomenon of depersonalization observed in all colonialized societies. As a result of the fact of independence, they find themselves today facing the necessity for a remoroccanization which supposes a rather dramatic reconversion and which is the problem of the hour for all those who have opted to remain in the country.

. . . .

Independence has been for the Jews of this country the opportunity for the "politization" that till then had been denied them. . . .

The horizons have been widening in the face of ambitions. . . . The future has been opening up before all those who under the old regime were too obscure or too young. In the absence of nationalist credentials, a past unstained by any "collaborationism" sufficed. That was, in the main, the premium accorded neutrality and silence. The degree holders, who in Europe would have exhausted themselves in a vain competition for subordinate posts in any administration whatsoever, could breeze up to the pinnacles of state. The national poverty of cadres will be one of the opportunities—and not the least—offered to Moroccan Jewry.

. . . .

The Sovereign, Divine Providence

It must be understood that the future of Moroccan Judaism is a function of a series of givens, most of which are beyond our Muslim fellow citizens themselves. The will of the present leaders is clearly for a harmonious coexistence, for a common effort, for national progress—something unthinkable today without the Jews. They want neither our departure, nor our banishment. After that of the Europeans, our departure would be the consummation of the disaster. Morocco's international good name would, furthermore, be compromised by anti-Jewish measures, which the country's adversaries would not fail to highlight (not to mention the opportunity that would thereby be offered to the opposition to rise up against such undemocratic practices). One ought not to suspect a priori, therefore, the egalitarian declarations, tirelessly repeated by the political leaders, whatever their party. One ought not to doubt even less the proclamations to their effect made by the Sovereign, who remains the essential given at the present juncture, who is the primordial factor of stability, the best guarantee of our liberties and our rights, and, in a word, a veritable providence for Moroccan Jewry. For the Jews of Morocco, Providence is called today Muḥammed V. The affection that the Jewish population of this country bears for him is unanimous in its depth and in its sincerity. Never, since the Antonines and certain princes of the Sasanian dynasty, has there been seen such a movement of veneration for the head of the state where the Jews were living. Never in the synagogues, also, did the prayer for the kings better correspond to the true thoughts of the faithful.

However, there is an evolution that by definition escapes human whims—a sociological evolution, a political evolution. . . . It is an evolution that can be an advance or a regression. . . . Beyond the wishes and the desires, beyond the promises and the proclamations, beyond the signs and the symbols, it is this evolution that dominates our horizons and it is in accordance with its definitive orientation that our survival in this country will depend in the final analysis.

The Crossroads

First, the sociological evolution. Will Morocco continue upon this ascendant, Western, progressive course, which the French presence marked out for it, and which its geographical position, the present formation of its elites, and its natural vocation urgently enjoin it? Will it be secular and liberal as is often promised? Or, on the contrary, will it turn back to the Orient and the call of atavistic conscience? Will it henceforth seek in the Nile or the Euphrates Valley inspirations that it had been accustomed to finding elsewhere?

. . . .

At their hour of choice, Moroccan Jews await this decisive choice of Morocco.

Carlos de Nesry, *Les Israélites marocains à l'heure du choix* (Tangier, 1958), pp. 72–83.

A SELECTION OF REFORMS PROPOSED AT THE SIXTH CONGRESS OF THE COUNCIL OF MOROCCAN JEWISH COMMUNITIES
(3–4 MARCH 1952)

. . . .

No. 5 *Primary Instruction*

Considering that instruction in the primary grades is the foundational instruction, the efforts of which can be felt throughout all later studies, the Congress recommends that all of the Alliance's attention be brought to bear upon this situation and that all efforts be employed to further ameliorate the instruction in the lower grade.

. . . .

No. 7 *Reorganization, Unification, and Inspection of Hebrew Instruction*

The Congress declares that Hebrew instruction is being done without a program by personnel that is frequently incompetent. It expresses the wish to see created by the Council of Communities of commission by representatives of the various organs that are interested in the teaching of Hebrew in order to establish a unified program whose application will be controlled.

No. 8 *Arabic Instruction*

The Congress of the Communities expresses the wish regarding the introduction into the Jewish schools of a program of Arabic instruction in the primary cycle, and it relies upon the Alliance Israélite and its Delegate to Morocco with a view that this program will be put into effect in the shortest time possible.

No. 9 *Examinations*

The dates of examinations occasionally fall on Saturdays. Steps were taken at the highest level early enough so that these examinations would not be held on the Jewish holidays and Sabbaths. The office of Public Education has given a certain measure of satisfaction in avoiding the holidays. However, there are many students who do not show up because of Saturdays. It is, therefore, necessary to ask the office of Public Education to kindly see to it that the examinations do not take place on Saturdays either.

. . . .

No. 11 *Emancipation of the Jewish Woman*[1]

Considering that Moroccan Jewry as a whole cannot attain its full maturity as long as the Jewish woman is not emancipated, the Congress

[1]Concerning the progressive improvement in the status of Moroccan Jewish women under the protectorate, see Doris Bensimon-Donath, *L'Evolution de la femme israélite à Fès*. Travaux et Mémoires, No. 25, La Pensée Universitaire (Aix-en-Provence, 1962); and idem, *Evolution du Judaïsme marocain sous le Protectorat français, 1912–1956* (Paris and the Hague, 1968), pp. 69–71.

demands, not only that there be developed to the maximum the action taken by the Annual Rabbinical Council dealing with the unification and evolution of Mosaic Law in Morocco and to which it renders homage, but also that the Council together with the Inspector of Jewish Institutions and Rabbinical High Court undertake henceforth the work of codifying personal and inheritance law. It entrusts the council to carry out this task by those means that appear most opportune and appropriate to it.

No. 12 *Liaison with the Joint*[2]

The Congress of Moroccan Jewish Communities meeting this 4th day of March 1952 pays its warm respect to the work accomplished by the Joint in Morocco and to the understanding which has been shown by its director, Mr. Bein, and his colleagues. The Congress requests of Mr. Bein that he should be so kind as to immediately come together with the Council of Communities, the representative body of all Jewish communities in Morocco, with a view toward a judicious distribution of all new subventions and to communicate to the Council, for the sake of information, the allocations presently being distributed to the various communities.

. . . .

No. 14 *Abandoned Children*

The Congress of Communities charges the Council to make contact with the Office of Health in order to obtain the following:

1. That it be represented on the Commission for Abandoned Children
2. That the aid allocated under this heading be more significant

No. 15 *Jewish Pavilions in the Hospitals*

The Congress draws the attention of the Committees of Communities and notably those of Sefrou and the region to the necessity of assuring from now on that in the hospitals presently under construction special pavilions will be reserved for the Jewish sick and that kashrut will observed there.

No. 16 *Mohalim*[3]

"Eight days after their birth, male children are circumcised. Circumcision is the sign of belonging to the descendents of Abraham."

This first stage of life which consecrates the newborn has always preserved, here in Morocco, the character of a religious ceremony in which prayer plays an essential role. There is, to be sure, the observance rites and precepts, but one ought not to see in these practices only the religious aspect. There is also the matter of hygiene which the law does not set aside. Unfortunately, the mohalim have no idea, no notion of hygiene, and it is desirable that this question of great importance for the health of our children be resolved this year.

[2] I.e., the American Jewish Joint Distribution Committee.
[3] Heb., *mōhalīm* (sing. *mōhēl*) (ritual circumcisors).

Dangers

1. Danger of suction,[4] possible contamination from the mouth to the wound, which might later cause tuberculosis or syphilis;
2. Danger due to ignorance: hemorrhaging caused by cutting a major section of the foreskin;
3. Danger of contagion: hands, instruments; *dressings* not sterilized.

Immediate Solution

1. A medical examination for all present mohalim and elimination of those suspect;
2. Prohibition against suction;[5]
3. A course on aseptic methods in the centers of the Bureau of Health Education;
4. An annual blood test;
5. An obligation to sterilize instruments at a Health Office center;
6. That the authorization to practice be henceforth given by the Rabbinical High Court and the Council of Communities after consultation with a physician.

Wishes

1. Strict Regulation of the profession.
2. Training of mohalim and internships in the hospitals.

No. 17 *Begging*

The Congress of Communities, moved by the disquieting developments, the incidences of which it is unnecessary to underline, as much from the point of view of health and public hygiene as from that of morality, immediately requests the government to incline itself to this unfortunate part of the Jewish population and bring it the necessary support by intensifying its aid in the social domain (housing, nurseries, welfare of all kinds). And it engages the Committee of Casablanca to establish a precise plan for combating beggary, which will have the full backing of the Council.

No. 18 *Recommendation*

The Congress of Communities recommends to the Committees to think from now on about a unified appeal within each community. To this end, it would be most desirable that each Jew contribute according to his means to the coffer of his Community's committee.

. . . .

[4] Suction by the mouth (Heb., *meṣīṣa*) is the stage in the operation following the cutting of the foreskin and the tearing of mucous membrane. In premodern times it was considered a form of disinfection. See Leonard V. Snowman, "Circumcision," EJ 5: 572.

[5] The French Consistoire abolished suction in 1843. Most Western *mōhalīm* now use a swab or a glass tube to perform this part of the operation. Ibid.

No. 31 *Unleavened Bread*

Until various measures are sanctioned, such as the creation of a new company, either affiliated or not with the communities, or an accord with other manufacturers that will induce them to manufacture unleavened bread, it would be desirable that the production of unleavened bread, which is comparable to that of bread, be controlled in a regular and permanent fashion.

No. 32 *Rights of Serara*[6]

The Congress requests the Inspector of Jewish Institutions to kindly ask the Justices of the *Serara* Court to inform him of the latest decision rendered by the Court on the subject of the *serara* of the *shehita*[7] of Fez.

No. 33 *Tax on Wine*

The Congress unanimously expresses the wish that the tax on wine be raised from 3 to 5 francs per liter.

No. 34 *Tax on Mahya*[8]

The Congress hopes:

1. That the tax on *mahya* be unified and raised to 10 francs per liter.
2. That the Council get in touch with the commercial distilleries[9] producing *mahya* in order that they might collect the tax and turn it over directly to the Committees of the cities to which their products are destined.

In the case of difficulty, it will be the right of the Council to bring in the Customs Service.

Conseil des Communautés Israélites du Maroc,
Congrés 1952: Motions
(Rabat, 1952), in mimeograph.

[6] *Serāra,* a Hebrew word meaning "authority," in Morocco indicated the inherited right to hold a communal office held by one's forefathers. See Haïm Zafrani, *Etudes et recherches sur la vie intellectuelle juive au Maroc de la fin du 15e au debut du 20e siècle I: Pensée juridique et environnement social, economique et religieux* (Paris, 1972), pp. 124–27.

[7] Heb., *sheḥīṭa* (ritual slaughtering).

[8] *Maḥya* is a highly potent eau-de-vie (the Arabic name is the literal equivalent of the French) usually made from figs, but also from raisins or dates, flavored with fennel or anise. It was not only the most popular fermented beverage, but it held a special place in Moroccan Jewish social life. Concerning the consumption of *maḥya* by Moroccan Jews, see J. Mathieu, R. Baron, and J. Lummau, "Etudes de l'alimentation au Mellah de Rabat," *Bulletin de l'Institut d'Hygiene du Maroc* 3–4 (1938): 118.

[9] Much of the *maḥya* drunk by Moroccan Jews was produced at home.

THE QUESTION OF THE JEWISH MINORITY IN THE FLN PLATFORM OF THE SOUMMAM CONGRESS[1]
(AUGUST 1956)

The fundamental principle admitted by universal morality favors the birth in Jewish opinion of a hope for the maintenance of peaceful millenary coexistence.

At first the Jewish minority was particularly sensitive to the campaign of demoralization. The representatives of their community at the World Jewish Congress in London proclaimed their attachment to French citizenship, putting themselves above their Muslim countrymen.

However, the unleashing of anti-Semitic hate that followed the colonialist-fascist demonstrations has provoked a profound uneasiness which has given way to a healthy reaction of self-defense.

The first reflex was to preserve themselves from the danger of being caught in the cross fire. It manifested itself in the condemnation of Jews who were members of the "8th of November" and the Poujadist movement,[2] whose too showy activities could engender vindictive discontent against the entire community.

The Algerian Resistance's unswerving correctness, reserving all its blows for colonialism, appeared to the most anxious as the chivalrous quality of the noble wrath of the weak against the tyrants.

Intellectuals, students, merchants took the initiative to rouse a movement of opinion for disassociating themselves from the rich colons and the anti-Semites.

The former do not have a short memory. They have not forgotten the infamous memory of Vichy Regime. During four years, 185 laws, decrees, or ordinances deprived them of their rights, drove them out of positions and out of the universities, despoiled them of their properties and their businesses, stripped them of their jewelry.

Their coreligionists in France were slapped with a collective fine of 1 billion francs. They were rounded up, arrested, interned in the camp at

[1] For ten days, beginning on August 20, 1956, the FLN held its first congress in the Soummam Valley in Kabylia, where it hammered out a political platform and created an executive body, the CCE. See David C. Gordon, *The Passing of French Algeria* (London, New York, and Toronto, 1966), p. 66; and Charles-Henri Favrod, *Le F.L.N. et l'Algérie* (Paris, 1962), pp. 144–48.

[2] The Poujadists were members of an ultra-right-wing group of colons that were active in the 1950s.

Drancy[3] and sent in freight cars to Poland, where many perished in the crematory ovens.

In the wake of the liberation of France, the Jewish community rapidly regained its rights and possessions thanks to the support of elected Muslim officials, despite the hostility of the Pétainist administration.[4] Will it have the naiveté to believe that the victory of the ultra-colonialists, who are precisely the same ones who formerly persecuted them, will not bring back the same misfortune?

The Algerians of Jewish extraction have still not overcome their pangs of conscience nor chosen which side to join.

Let us hope that they will follow in great numbers the path of those who have responded to the call of the generous Fatherland, who have given their affection to the Revolution by already claiming with pride their Algerian nationality.

Despite the silence of the Chief Rabbi of Algiers, in contrast to the encouraging attitude of the Archbishop who courageously and publicly stands against the current and condemns colonialist injustice,[5] the vast majority of Algerians have refrained from considering the Jewish community as having definitively gone over to the enemy camp.

The FLN has nipped in the bud numerous provocations prepared by the specialists of the Government General. Outside of individual chastisement inflicted upon policemen and counter-terrorists responsible for crimes against the innocent population, Algeria has been preserved from any pogrom. The boycotting of Jewish merchants, which had to follow the boycotting of Mzabis,[6] was checked before it even exploded.

That is why the Arab-Israeli conflict did not have grave repercussions in Algeria, which would have gratified the enemies of the Algerian people.

Without drawing from the history of this country upon the proofs of religious tolerance, of collaboration in the highest posts of the East, and of sincere coexistence, the Algerian revolution has shown by its acts that it deserves the confidence of the Jewish minority that, for its part, it will guarantee them well-being in independent Algeria.

Indeed, the disappearance of the colonial regime, which availed itself of the Jewish minority as a buffer to mitigate the anti-imperialist shocks, does not necessarily mean it will be pauperized.

It is an absurd hypothesis to imagine that "Algeria would be nothing without France."

[3] Through this camp in a small town near Paris, over 61,000 French Jews were sent to Nazi death camps. See Zosa Szajkowski, *Analytical Franco-Jewish Gazetteer 1939–1945* (New York, 1966), p. 262; and Shaul Esh, "Drancy," *EJ* 6: 207–8.

[4] Such support was almost nonexistent. See Part One, pp. 127–129.

[5] The reference here is to Mgr. Léon-Etienne Duval, who opted to remain in Algeria after the French withdrawal and became an Algerian citizen.

[6] The Mzabis are the Kharijite Berber Muslims from the south of the country. They formed a separate community from the other Muslims.

The economic prosperity of the emancipated peoples is evident. The more important national revenue will assure all Algerians of a more comfortable life.

Yves Courriére, *Le temps des léopards.*
La Guerre d'Algérie II (Paris, 1969), pp. 598–600,
Annexe 1; also A. R. Abdel-Kader, *Le conflit
judéo-arabe: Juifs et Arabes face à l'avenir*
(Paris, 1961), pp. 387–88, Annexe.

AN APPEAL BY THE FLN FOR THE SUPPORT OF ALGERIAN JEWRY

(1959)

Jewish Algerians!

The colonialist policy, always racist, occasionally anti-Semitic, compelled to "justify" in the eyes of the world the unjustifiable war it is waging against the Algerian people, dares to pretend that today in refusing us our most sacred rights, it is defending yours. Forgetting that it frequently persecuted you, neglecting the fact that thousands of Jews (those for example who stagnated in the "Drabs"[1]) were exploited and humiliated, it makes the pretense of linking your lot with that of the European minority that cannot conceive of their relations with the Algerians except as the relations of masters to slaves. Thus it hopes to associate you with a cause that is not yours and make you participate in the safeguarding of privileges that have nothing to do with the legitimate rights demanded by our revolution for ALL ALGERIANS without discrimination.

Numerous individuals among you have joined the struggle of the Algerian people: deserters from the colonialist army, striking merchants, doctors caring for the underground freedom fighters, lawyers defending the patriots. . . .

Those among you who have become the zealous lackeys of the colonialist regime and its army have been irrevocably excluded from the national community: their misdeeds and their crimes classify them without any equivocation among the traitors. It is not to them that we are addressing ourselves.

Neither is it to those who have thought it well to join their voice to the choir of all the accomplices in the great enterprise of dividing and hoodwinking the Algerian people. This is the case, for example, with the inauguration several months ago of a "GRAND RABBI of France and Algeria": it has to do there with a reform of integrationist inspiration, the need for which was no longer imperative from the religious point of view and which seemed a significant contrast if one takes into consideration the courageous and realistic attitude of the archbishop of Algiers.[2]

We do not address ourselves either to all of you who, without having received any mandate, consider yourselves qualified to speak in the name of the Jewish community of Algeria. Such is the case, for example, of a certain Alexandre Reiter, secretary of the "Zionist Organization of France," whose ramblings[3] testify to such mental confusion and such exceptional ignorance of history that we would not even know how to undertake refuting them.

[1] A slang term for the prison camps.

[2] The reference here is to Mgr. Duval, concerning whom see p. 538, n. 5.

[3] "Libre Opinions," *Le Monde* (October 9, 1959)—footnote to the text.

We address ourselves to all those who, without having disavowed their origins, have not surmounted their troubled conscience. We address ourselves to all our Jewish compatriots—and they are numerous—who wish to be Algerians but who have always remained on the sidelines of their people's struggle, and we say to them:

You are an integral part of the Algerian people. It is not a question for you of choosing between France and Algeria, but of becoming effective citizens of your true country. Either you wish to fully exercise in this country, whose future will be that which all of its children TOGETHER will make of it, the rights that no one would ever put into question again; or you accept to live under the reign of contempt and to content yourselves with a citizenship granted by your oppressors in a context which is the very negation of the most elementary rights of the human being.

These are the terms of the choice.

The supposed economic option, the bet upon a supposedly prosperous future, is no longer an issue. The ideal for which so many Algerian patriots have already fallen is not to be measured in the same terms as such and such material facilities of the colonialist regime that we will have to transform somewhat.

It is to an act of faith that we are inviting you, a true act of faith, beyond all the calculations: faith in your people, faith in your country, faith in yourselves.

Algerian Jews!

Hundreds of thousands of your countrymen have died and more than a million suffer in the prisons and colonialist concentration camps in order to regain for Algeria its liberty, and for all Algerians without distinction, their dignity.

At the moment when your battle is entering into a decisive phase, we wait for you to affirm, as Algerians, your adherence to the ideal of independence and, hence, for you, in order to dispel any equivocation that risks compromising our future relations, to take a GREATER and more ACTIVE part in your people's struggle, so that tomorrow there will live EQUALITY FOR ALL the Algerian Democratic and Socialist Republic.

Front for the National Liberation
Federation in France
Paris, 25 November 1959

FLN Documents à l'adresse du Peuple Français,
Les Juifs d'Algérie dans le combat pour l'Indépendance Nationale (n.p., n.d.), pp. 37–40.

AN ALGERIAN JEWISH INTELLECTUAL REFLECTS UPON MUSLIM-JEWISH RELATIONS AT A TIME OF RISING TENSIONS (1957)

Yesterday

During the period between the two wars, the relations between Jews and Muslims progressively altered. One can assign several causes to this unfortunate evolution.

One is the acceleration, among the Jews, of the process of assimilation which has overtaken successive strata of a numerous and often wretched proletariat. It is highlighted by the profusion of academic successes, by the ever-increasing accession to liberal careers, by the definitive emancipation from consistorial prohibitions of a political order, but also, alas, by the forgetting of the Arabic language and the historical bonds that linked Judaism and Islam here.

To be sure, relations especially business ones, remain intimate and cordial, but the traditional friendships between families have become somewhat loosened.

A second cause was, since 1929, at the call of the Mufti of Jerusalem, the hostility of Arabs to Zionist expansion.

A third cause was the intensification of Hitlerian propaganda which, without finding among the Muslims a very receptive audience, did not fail to produce some impression upon some among them.

However, of all these factors, none was decisive, and they would not have troubled the atmosphere were it not for the official solicitude of interested circles. The disorders were, if not provoked, at least encouraged by the upper-level administration and by colonialist circles.

If, since the denouement of the Dreyfus Affair, the hostility of the European masses has ceased to manifest itself in the public forum, it has survived in the penumbra of the bureaus of the central administration. The doctrine of these bureaus has frequently been indecisive and unstable on other levels, but, thanks to the gods! they have known how to show themselves capable of some continuity of views by making the virulent or larval anti-Semitism one of the constants of their political strategy.

As for the colons, the reason for their anti-Semitism has to be sought in the continuous augmentation in value of Algerian land which too often incited the enriched rural folk to abandon the democratic army, of which they were by tradition the stubborn soldiers, for the now-and-then factious phalanxes of political reaction.[1]

[1] After the troubles at Constantine, where the police and the army had adopted a pure contemplative attitude, an inquiry was entrusted to a notoriously anti-Semitic

There was between their circle and the bureaus of the upper administration complicity—tacit, one would like to believe—in spite of the presence of clear-sighted and generous governors, to divert against the Jews the rather sudden swell of Muslim demands.

Berbers and Arabs had acquired in effect several years ago a political maturity which was translated into an unexpected energy in the expression of their aspirations.

What better outlet to offer these boiling waters than a demonstration for which the Jews would pay the price? That which the European anti-Semites would no longer dare to undertake, what an irresistible temptation to entrust it to the care of the Moors!

An engraving of the period appeared in "L'Oeuvre" (August 2, 1938) to serve as an illustration for an article by the fastidious writer and intrepid republican Jean Mélia.[2] It represented a garroted Jew and a European wearing a colonial helmet designating the victim of the fury of a Muslim armed with a *boussaadi*.[3]

This engraving has only a metaphoric value; nothing armed, in the proper sense of the term, the fanaticized hordes that engaged in the massacres of Constantine on August 5, 1934.[4] However, the incitement was coming from colonialist circles. The highest Muslim personalities bore witness to this fact.

When the tragedy suddenly happened, the anti-Semitic colons, the chiefs of the trusts in competition with the Jews, could barely restrain a sigh of joy, as I have taken occasion to relate elsewhere.[5]

But the Jews got wind of the ruse. Furthermore, after reacting in accordance with the dictates of dignity, they undertook to fill in open gaps. The operation was all the more easy since it simply had to do with the dissipation of the cloud of suspicions not of long standing. Artificial enmity, we have said, is virtual friendship.[6] Furthermore, when there appeared in "La Dépêche Algérienne," the great conservative daily, an article entitled "Who Opposes the Granting of Political Rights to the Natives? Jews and Freemasons," the riposte arrived, published in the same newspaper by a group of Jews proposing a fraternally liberal program in favor of the Muslims. The same group established with progressive Muslim circles and with Catholics of the republican left close relations, the sincerity of which was

---

functionary. His conclusions were of such a clear objectivity that he was disavowed by both the military and the civil authority. (Benichou's note.)

[2] Mélia was an unusually liberal colon, who, in his books *La France et l'Algérie* (Paris, 1919) and *Le triste sort des indigènes musulmans d'Algérie* (Paris, 1935), argued for the complete integration of the native Muslims.

[3] An Arab dagger.

[4] See Part One, p. 100.

[5] See *Le Monde Juif* (September 1950), p. 11.

[6] Ibid.

successfully tested at the time of a suggestive action brought against a Muslim religious leader and leading orator.[7]

In return, during the somber hours of Vichy despotism, the Muslims maintained an attitude of perfect correctness toward the Jews and greeted with contempt the solicitations that were made to them to bully the Jewish population.

So much for the past. It requires a certain dose of voluntary blindness to find in it the trace of a hereditary enmity, as one likes to say, between the Jews and the Muslims of Algeria.[8]

Today

Where are we today?

On the side of the Europeans, the horizon is, for the Jews, considerably clarified. In the Department of Algiers, the most conservative newspapers, such as "L'Echo d'Alger," adopted for their side an attitude of ceremonious and stiff correctness. The Jews' preponderant part in the Resistance and notably in the conspiracy of November 8 which paved the way for the liberation of the country,[9] the fear of seeing the Jews make common cause too openly with the Muslim nationalists, the demonstration made many a time that anti-Semitism is the best precursor of communism,[10] these were, without a doubt, the principal reasons for this sudden turnaround. They silence the petty jealousies provoked by the important place taken by the Jews in the luxury trade and in the liberal professions. They also restrain the impatience of genteel folk with blunders of nouveau riche Jews who scarcely yield in self-admiration to the parvenus of other faiths.

As to Jewish-Muslim relations, let us try to make the point:

They have, evidently, changed. The Muslims themselves are very divided. . . .

[7] Ibid.

[8] This is the place to reproduce some of the words of the declaration that M. Ghlamallah, Shaykh of the Zawiya (lodge of a sufi brotherhood), finance deputy, and Council General of Tiaret, published on the day after the disorders of Constantine: "The Muslim frequents the Jew much more than any other element of this country, even his own coreligionists. The Muslim buys from the Jew, consults him concerning his business affairs, pours out his heart to him concerning all of the misfortunes that have happened to him, asks his advice, etc. . . ." See *Echo d'Alger* (August 11, 1934). (Bénichou's note.)

[9] Concerning the role played by Jewish youth in the insurrection that helped pave the way for the Allied landing in North Africa, see Michel Ansky, *Les Juifs d'Algérie du Décret Crémieux à la libération* (Paris, 1950), pp. 199–221, and Part One, pp. 134–135.

[10] Sidi-bel-Abbes, formerly a bastion of the anti-Semitic leagues, today has a communist mayor. (Benichou's note.)

Regarding the Jews, the attitude of the Muslims has been marked by a certain stiffness. For this change, there is no other serious reason than the events in Palestine. The turn taken by the first battles was felt illogically enough by many of the Arabs of Algeria as a sort of personal humiliation. Inflamed speeches were addressed to chosen congregations exhorting them to support the policy of the Arab League, whose machinations one can scarcely surmise.

Words ordering a boycott circulated and were temporarily followed; then, the effervescence became progressively calmed.

One can see that when an accord will be reached in the Middle East, a return of confidence will preside here in the relations between the two autochthonous populations: the Jewish and the Muslim. My conviction is that, through secret meetings marked by a certain degree of concession, they would have even been able to concur upon the conclusion of such accords were it not for the spectacle of their collaborating and proclaiming their secular entente. Algerian history bears proof that these peoples who consider themselves descended from the same patriarch are not necessarily called to play the role of fraternal enemies.

However, in order for this appeasement whose fruitfulness would extend to the solution of other Algerian problems to survive permanently, there must be propitious conditions in the economic and social order.

Economically, the seeds of discord are barely perceptible. Here, more or less, is how the juncture appears:

The Muslims are becoming more and more numerous in the cities; their number and their proportion follow a precipitous geometric progression by reason of an extremely high birth rate.

The Muslim population is adapting rapidly to urban activities, notably in business. If we limit our inquiry to Algiers, we observe a very curious phenomenon: Arabs and Kabyles are progressively taking the place of the Jewish merchants in the old city. The latter, pushed on the one hand by this migration, aspiring on the other to the new city, are swarming in their turn into the new quarter. This double transfer is inscribed on the ground with the same fatal regularity as the progress of a frontal moraine. Each one finds it to his benefit.

Several branches of the wholesale trade have been held back by the Muslims; no one complains about it, because there is room for everyone.

Finally, many young people of the koranic persuasion are preparing for liberal careers, but there will have to be many more of them over a long period of time in order to be able to even mention the word "competition."

The political field is even more chequered. Those among the Muslim leaders who wear the label of independents—and for whom this title is not always pure derision, in spite of what one may think of it, are the most frequently devoted to the cause of French Algeria. Between the Jews and them, no occasion, on the regional level at least, for heated polemics.

With the autonomist parties, the situation is different. To the extent that their leaders wish to set aside the supercilious attitude they have observed ever since the recent events in the Middle East, they let it be understood that it is as much the right of the ancient Jewish inhabitants of the country as it is theirs to join the champions of its independence.[11] However, the message of this sort is of a Sibylline brevity. The only mass contacts between the Jews and Muslims take place in the midst of Communist demonstrations. . . . It is natural that the Jews who belong to this party or approve of its teachings give their support to the devotees of autonomy. One would not know, however, how to exact a similar assent from the Jews taken as a whole without abuse. To begin with, let us point out in passing that they do not have an officially competent body that can speak in their name and engage in undertaking on their behalf, excepting their religious bodies,[12] which jealously confine themselves within their religious jurisdictions and have long ago cast off any political ambition.[13]

Furthermore, as French citizens by sentiment as well as by statute, they must continually ask themselves regarding the consequence of their choice. They must examine whether their attitude is not of a nature to cause their motherland an unjust prejudice and whether the will does not derive from civic devotion that the heart accords to the religion of the past.

The answer to these questions, the appeasement of these scruples, depends upon the conscience of each one, and no party has the right to dictate its oracles to him.

This firm declaration puts us sufficiently at ease to note the usefulness of such publications as "Consciences Algériennes" in which intellectuals apprehensive of betraying their calling, study, with an intensity that—according to the authors—is devoid of any formal adherence to a simple sympathy, the aspirations of the members of the young Muslim generation.

This declaration also authorizes us to recall the principle by which our attitude and our action have always been inspired in the past and which one may find formulated in the "Bulletin de la Fédération des Sociétés juives d'Algérie" of January 1944: "As high as the leaders responsible for the destiny of France would like to raise up the latter (the Muslim population) . . . so great will be the satisfaction of the inhabitants of Jewish origin in our country."

The character of Algeria's Jewish community should—we believe—remain thus.

A weak minority not having in any case power to dispose, it is perhaps not fitting for it to propose; but it is much less becoming for it to oppose.

There is among us a feeling of pity, if it is not anger, when people point out to us that some Jews of France or some Jews of Algeria are agitating in

[11] See the FLN appeal for Jewish support translated previously, pp. 540–541.
[12] The consistories.
[13] Actually, the consistories were forbidden by law from engaging in politics.

Paris, are making thoughtless proposals concerning the Muslims here at home and are claiming to be showing us from the balconies of the capital the height of our duty.

Such are, from the Jewish side, the postulates of an unclouded entente. For their part, the Muslims will have to make an effort to take no advice but their own in their relations with the Jews and not to draw inspiration any longer from the slogans emanating from the Middle East, even as the Jews here, whatever the steadfastness of their sentimental ties to the State of Israel may be, would not tolerate receiving the like from there regarding their political choice or their line of conduct.

Raymond Bénichou, *Ecrits juifs*
(Algiers, 1957), pp. 188–96.

A PRESIDENTIAL DECREE DISSOLVING THE JEWISH COMMUNITY COUNCIL IN TUNISIA (1958)

Law No. 58–78 of 11 July 1958 (23 Dhu 'l-Hijja 1377), regarding the governance of the Jewish sect.

We, Habib Bourguiba, President of the Tunisian Republic,

Having considered the decree of 15 September 1888 (9 Muharram 1306), regarding associations;

Having considered the decree of 13 March 1947 (20 Rabiᶜa II 1366), regarding the reorganization of the Council of the Jewish Community of Tunis;

Having considered the decree instituting the Jewish Funds for Aid and Charity;

Considering that there is cause to reform the governance of the Jewish religious community with the view of adapting it to the imperatives proceeding from independence and to the profound reforms brought about in the institutions of the country;

Considering that the present structures together with the areas of competence of the bodies charged with the management of the Jewish religious community no longer correspond to the new statute of the State which guarantees to all citizens without distinction equality of rights and obligations;

Considering that there is cause to put an end without delay to the functions of the directors of the existing bodies and to assure provisionally the management of the Jewish religious community;

Having taken into account the opinions of the Secretaries of State for the Presidency, of Justice, of the Interior, and of Finance.

We promulgate the law whose text follows:

. . . .

Art. 17—The Council of the Jewish Community of Tunis is dissolved.

Its patrimony as well as its spheres of competence are devolved without need of sanction upon a provisory Commission for the management of the Jewish Religious Community of the Region of Tunis, composed of eight members designated by order of the Secretary of State for the Presidency.

The Commission is further charged with the constituting of the Religious Association of Tunis and to prepare, with the concurrence of the governor of greater Tunis, the elections of the Administrative Council of the said Association.

Art. 18.—Also dissolved are all the Welfare Funds of the Jewish Religious Community throughout the entire territory of the Republic. The interests that they administer are entrusted to provisory committees for the administration of the Jewish Religious Community designated by the governors concerned.

The mission of each committee will come to an end with the installation of the Administrative Council of the local Religious Association.

The taxes instituted for the benefit of the abovementioned Funds will be collected for the benefit of the provisional committee and the Religious Associations that will succeed them.

Art. 19.—The present law will be published in the *Official Journal of the Tunisian Republic* and executed as law of the State.

Enacted in Tunis, 11 July 1958
(23 Dhu 'l-Hijja 1377)

The President of the Tunisian Republic,
Habib Bourguiba.

Journal Officiel de la République Tunisienne Lois et Règlements (Vendredi 11 Juillet 1958), in Charles Haddad de Paz, *Juifs et Arabes au Pays de Bourguiba* (Aix-en-Provence, 1977), pp. 283–84.

AN EYEWITNESS ACCOUNT OF THE ANTI-JEWISH RIOTS IN TUNIS AT THE OUTBREAK OF THE SIX-DAY WAR (1967)

This is a first report on the events of June 5th as they affected Tunisia written by an eyewitness. This report is not intended for publication but only for information:

The outbreak of hostilities in the Middle East on 5 June saw a major outburst of anti-Jewish demonstrations in Tunis. Shortly before noon a crowd arrived at the British Embassy and in short order the entire building was sacked and the library on the ground floor completely burned out. As the afternoon wore on, the crowd grew larger and different bands attacked the American library, the offices of TWA, and the American Embassy. . . . But by far the heaviest damage was done to Jewish retail establishments throughout the city. The gangs came prepared with gasoline as well as heavy metal cutters with which to open iron shutters. Jewish shops were systematically looted and burned. Over 100 shops were affected, this representing the major part of the shops that were in existence. Little attempt was made by the police to stop the looting and pillage. In most instances police calmly continued to direct traffic while the mobs were running riot in their immediate vicinity. Cars belonging to Jews were identified by the mobs, turned over, and set ablaze. During the course of the afternoon the mobs penetrated into the main synagogue, pulled out some 40 Torah Scrolls, urinated on them, and set them ablaze. Memorial plaques were ripped off the walls and the benches set on fire with gasoline. A number of smaller synagogues around town were similarly dealt with. The Tunis Community flour distribution center was completely destroyed and the book distribution center as well. During the course of the afternoon a group of 30 arrived at the JDC offices, threw gasoline under the door, and set it ablaze. They did not get inside, and the office staff extinguished the fire after they had left.

By 1:30 P.M. Tunis looked like it had been bombed. Smoke was pouring out of scores of Jewish establishments, and the mobs continued to dominate the streets. Tunisian troops, who are quartered in barracks within ten minutes of the center of the city, did not arrive until four in the afternoon and then quickly drove the mobs off the streets. The mobs consisted mostly of youngsters between fourteen and twenty years of age, but I saw as well a considerable number of young men in their twenties who were haranguing and leading them on.

There is no question in the mind of anyone that these demonstrations were organized. The Tunisian Government talks about Algerian troublemakers, but it is likely that certain activist members of the Destourian party were involved as well. The mobs came prepared with gasoline. The pillaging was systematic, and what is more significant, no one at all was hurt during the course of a five hour riot of major proportions. An eyewitness reported seeing a Jew who had lost his nerve as his establishment was being pillaged, begging the mob not to hurt him. He was told that no one had any intention of hurting him, he was simply to go home! The police reacted feebly when they reacted at all, and it took five hours to get troops into the city.

These demonstrations were stopped when President Bourguiba addressed the country over the radio and television later in the afternoon. He is reported to have wept, but in any case, he roundly denounced the rioters and insisted that they cease immediately. It is probable that a major tragedy for the Jews living in the small towns in the interior of the country was averted as a result of the stand Bourguiba took. No attacks on Jews in the South were made during the week of hostilities except in one small town where stones were thrown. Bourguiba found himself in a very difficult position in the weeks that ensued. Although the troops were withdrawn from the Jewish sections of the town within a few days, they remained in the nerve centers of the city for several weeks. Armored cars were placed at several points and the radio-broadcasting station as well as other crucial locations were completely surrounded by armed troops. Despite the fact that a contingent of troops was sent to the "front" (incidentally, reaching the Libyan border after a leisurely three-day voyage just in time to turn right around at the end of hostilities), cries of "Bourguiba yahoud" (Jew Bourguiba) were heard in the streets. There was considerable question regarding the stability of the government for a few weeks, but by now the situation seems well in hand.

On Tuesday morning the Tunis Jewish Community Council was convoked to the steps of the gutted main synagogue and four government ministers came to express their regrets and promised that the rioters would be punished and restitution made for all damages. Since then the government has repaired all store fronts and has repainted the outside of the synagogue and all visible evidence of the riots has been removed. Although a commission has been created to reimburse spoliated Jewish businessmen, no one has received anything as yet, as it is likely that no one ever will. A goodly number of the rioters, however, have received prison sentences.

The immediate result of the riots was a heavy exodus of Jews from Tunisia to France. Our best estimates indicate that within the month following the riots, some 2,500 people left. Many of those were women and childen sent ahead. By now some of these have returned, presumably to prepare for definite departure. Passports continue to be issued in Tunis, although in the interior great difficulties are encountered, as heretofore.

As for those who did not leave immediately following the riots, a large proportion say that they will be leaving in the months that come. This tendency is particularly evident in the different community institutions, which have already lost considerable personnel and will continue to do so. The total destruction of the Bokobza Boukha[1] and Kosher Wine Factory will create a heavy loss of community income, and major reductions in revenue from meat taxes are expected as well.

It is the unanimous opinion of Jews one talks to that if there was any doubt about the question previously, it is quite clear now that there is no future for them in Tunisia. Although it is impossible to make firm predictions, many people feel that of the roughly 23,000 Jews who were in Tunisia in early June, at least 5,000 to 6,000 will have left the country by the end of the year.

AJDC (Jerusalem) 245A.13, confidential memo from Henri Elfen (Geneva) to members of the Standing Conference of European Jewish Community Services, August 16, 1968.

[1] Boukha is the Tunisian Jewish eau-de-vie. The Bokobza company mentioned here is now one of the leading producers of kosher wine in France.

A REPORT ON EGYPTIAN JEWRY IN THE AFTERMATH OF THE SIX-DAY WAR BY A REPRESENTATIVE OF THE WORLD COUNCIL OF CHURCHES
(NOVEMBER 1967)

CONFIDENTIAL

Jewish Minority in the War

1. As is well known, during the first days of the Arab-Israel war in June 1967, almost all male Jews in the UAR aged 16 upwards were interned, including even [those] who had converted to Christianity or Islam.[1] Conditions in the prisons were at first extremely bad, and there was much maltreatment, but following a visit from an official of the Ministry of the Interior, conditions were substantially improved later.

2. Family members were left free. Eventually, through intervention of the ICRC,[2] internees were able to sign documents enabling their families to draw on their bank accounts. Most of the businesses and property of interned Jews were sequestrated.

3. Eventually correspondence was permitted between internees and their families, on ICRC forms for stateless Jews, and on Red Crescent forms for Egyptian nationals. Families were also eventually permitted to send food parcels to the internees through the same channels.

4. No independent agency has been allowed to visit the internees. Efforts of the ICRC to this end have failed.

5. The internees came under three different categories of civil status—Egyptian nationals, stateless, and of foreign nationality. Those of foreign nationality (a small minority) were deported from the UAR after a few days, when they established their nationality.

6. Through the intervention of the Spanish Embassy, invoking a law of the Spanish Republic which enabled Jews of former Spanish origin to reclaim Spanish Nationality, Spanish passports have been provided for a considerable number of both stateless and Egyptian nationality Jews, who had, through their families, indicated their wish to leave the UAR.[3] As this was tantamount to a change of nationality without the consent of the UAR authorities, under Egyptian law such persons were liable to deportation, and in fact were escorted direct from prison to the airport or port of Alexandria. Family of these Jews have been able to accompany the men or, if they preferred, to remain in the UAR to clear up business and personal matters,

[1] Concerning Jewish conversions in Egypt, see pp. 21, 154, 245–249.

[2] The International Committee of the Red Cross.

[3] On the efforts of the Spanish ambassador in Cairo on behalf of the Jews, see AJDC (Jerusalem) 245A.13–14.

and follow them later. This procedure has been carried on with the tacit consent of the UAR authorities, and has been handled, on behalf of the Jewish community, by one of the officials of the community who was not interned, and is known to have the confidence of authorities in the Ministry of the Interior.

7. About twenty Jews have also been released from internment and allowed to remain in the UAR. The reason for these releases is not known, except that they include most of the Jews who had been converted to Christianity or Islam.

8. As of 7 November 1967, there remained in internment 125 Jews from the Sephardic and Ashkenazi communities, of whom 44 were Egyptian nationals and 81 stateless, and also between 120 and 140 Caraite Jews (numbers of nationals and stateless not known).

9. Of the 125 Sephardi and Ashkenazi Jews remaining in internment, over 80 have indicated that they wish to leave the UAR and are expected to be able to do so before the end of 1967. Of the Caraite Jews, only about 10 wish to leave and will be able to do so.

10. Departures are arranged in small numbers at a time, to avoid publicity, and it is regarded as important that there should be no publicity about groups of Jews leaving the UAR. It is also important, for the sake of those who remain, that Jews who have left the UAR should not comment on any hardships they have suffered, nor discuss the procedures which enabled them to depart.

11. Most of the Caraite Jews apparently wish to remain in the UAR. At present there seems no prospect of their being released from internment, and whilst the process of securing the release of those who do wish to leave is functioning more or less smoothly, it is judged better not to press the issue of the others, in case it jeopardizes the whole situation.

12. On behalf of the World Council of Churches, representations were made to the UAR Government on November 7th 1967, through the Ministry of Foreign Affairs (Director of the Department of International Organisations and Treaties), regarding the continued detention of Jews in internment. It is understood that these representations were conveyed to all sections of the Government concerned with the matter, but it was thought better not to press for a formal answer. The representative of the Ministry of Foreign Affairs indicated his understanding that the World Council of Churches was properly concerned with the situation of the interned Jews, both because of its general humanitarian concern, and because of the authority under which it operates in the UAR, on behalf of "nationals of any faith who are desirous to emigrate." It should be possible to make further representations on behalf of any remaining detainees, when those who wish to leave the country have been released.

13. An impression, gained from various sources, is that the Ministry of Foreign Affairs is embarrassed by the whole situation; that the Ministry of the Interior wished all Jews to leave the country and therefore facilitates the

release of detainees for departure; but that the Army may regard the detainees as potential bargaining counters in relation to war prisoners, and would resist any proposals for their general release.[4]

14. The report by Mr. Nils Gussing, Special Representative of the General Secretary of the United Nations, that the UAR Government had stated that "the Stateless Jews were under the mandate of the UNHCR,[5] who has an office in Cairo," has subsequently been denied by the UAR Government, and the UNHCR representative has not been able to intervene on behalf of stateless Jews. (A very few Jews are registered as under UNHCR mandate, and the UNHCR office has continued to deal with these cases, but not if, or while, they were interned.)

15. The Jewish community in the UAR is incurring considerable expenses in securing the release of internees, paying air fares when necessary, and supporting destitute families of internees. A figure of Pd. Egyptian 4,000 per month was mentioned. The available funds may soon be exhausted, and although the community owns various properties in Cairo and Alexandria, the authorities do not permit their realization.

16. It is understood that expenses incurred by the Spanish Embassy in Cairo on behalf of Jews are being refunded by the Jewish community in Madrid.

17. Arrangements should be made with Olympic Airways to give tickets on credit, in the same way and through the same agency as with certain shipping lines. As advance notice cannot be given of departures, arrangements should be made to meet the regular Olympic flights at Athens airport, as is done with the regular boat arrivals at Piraeus. Telephonic advice could then be passed on to Rome or Paris, for cases destined for those cities.

18. About eighty Jews are in the Sephardic Old Age Home in Cairo and Alexandria. As there may soon be no community to support them, it is judged necessary for them to leave the country as soon as possible. The Jewish agencies have been urged to make advance arrangements for their reception, and the community in the UAR will endeavor not to send them out, except in emergency, without having had advance notice that such arrangements have been made.

19. Reports on various individual cases requiring special consideration or action have been submitted to the appropriate agencies.

20. At present insoluble problem is what to do with community buildings—synagogues, schools, etc. These are mainly under guard, their contents, including religious objects, cannot be removed, and the community is prevented from disposing of the properties.

21. Jews eventually remaining in the UAR, mainly Caraites, will remain a source of anxiety. They are likely to face increased difficulties, their position will remain insecure, and it appears that there is no remaining community

[4] Israel had taken nearly 6,000 Arab prisoners during the Six-Day War.

[5] United Nations Human Rights Commission.

organization to support them. It would seem much better for them to leave the country, and advice has been given to this effect.

D. WALLACE BELL
Representative in Greece
World Council of Churches

Athens, 25 November 1967

AJDC (Jerusalem) 254A.12.

BIBLIOGRAPHY

BIBLIOGRAPHY

ABBREVIATIONS OF JOURNALS AND ENCYCLOPEDIAS

AESC	*Annales: Economies, Sociétés, Civilisations*
AJYB	*American Jewish Yearbook*
AM	*Archives Marocaines*
AR	*Alliance Review*
BAIU	*Bulletin de l'Alliance Israélite Universelle*
EI[1]	*Encyclopaedia of Islam,* first edition
EI[2]	*Encyclopaedia of Islam,* new edition
EJ	*Encyclopaedia Judaica,* new English edition
EZI	*Encyclopedia of Zionism and Israel*
Hamenora	Hamenora. Organe Périodique des Béné Bérith du District d'Orient No. XI. Istanbul
Hamizrah Hehadash	Hamizrah Hehadash. The New East: Quarterly of the Israel Oriental Society [Hebrew]
IJMES	*International Journal of Middle East Studies*
Information Juive	*Information Juive. Organe Bi-Mensuel du Comité Algérien d'Etudes Sociales, Alger-Paris* [Mensuel de Liason et d'Information, since April 1963]
Israel's Messenger	*Israel's Messenger. The International Jewish Monthly* (Shanghai)
The Jewish Advocate	*The Jewish Advocate. The Organ of Indian Jewry* (Bombay)
JJS	*Journal of Jewish Studies*
JMH	*Journal of Modern History*
JSS	*Jewish Social Studies*
Judaism	*Judaism. A Quarterly Journal*
MEJ	*The Middle East Journal*
MES	*Middle Eastern Studies*
MGWJ	*Monatsschrift für die Geschichte und Wissenschaft des Judentums*
Michael	*Michael. On the History of the Jews in the Diaspora* [Hebrew, French, and English]
Midstream	*Midstream. A Quarterly Jewish Review*
Mi-Qedem umi-Yam	*Mi-Qedem umi-Yam. Studies in the Jewry of Islamic Countries* [Hebrew]
Les Nouveaux Cahiers	*Les Nouveaux Cahiers. Revue d'Etudes et de Libres Debats Publiée sous les Auspices de l'Alliance Israélite Universelle*

Paix et Droit	*Paix et Droit. Organe de l'Alliance Israélite Universelle*
Peᶜamim	*Peᶜamim. Studies in the Cultural Heritage of Oriental Jewry* [Hebrew]
REI	*Revue des Etudes Islamiques*
REJ	*Revue des Etudes Juives*
RFHOM	*Revue Française d'Histoire d'Outre-Mer*
RHDGM	*Revue d'Histoire de la Deuxième Guerre Mondiale*
RHM	*Revue d'Histoire Maghrebine*
RMM	*Revue du Monde Musulmane*
ROMM	*Revue de l'Occident Musulman et de la Méditerranée*
The Scribe	*The Scribe. Journal of Babylonian Jewry*
Sefunot	*Sefunot. Annual for Research on the Jewish Communities in the East* [Hebrew]
Shorter EI	*Shorter Encyclopaedia of Islam*
Studies in Zionism	*Studies in Zionism. An International Journal of Social, Political and Intellectual History*
WI	*Die Welt des Islams*

MIDDLE EASTERN AND NORTH AFRICAN NEWSPAPERS AND PERIODICALS

Algeria
*Information Juive**

Egypt
al-Ahrām
*L'Aurore**
La Bourse Egyptienne
L'Egypte Nouvelle
*Israël**
al-Muqaṭṭam
Le Progrès Egyptienne
Les Pyramides
*La Tribune Juive**

Iraq
al-Hidāya
*al-Miṣbāḥ**
The Times of Mesopotamia
*Yeshurun**

Israel and Mandatory Palestine
al-Difāʿ
Falasṭīn
*Hed ha-Mizraḥ**
*Haaretz**

Libya
*Deghel Sion**
*Haienu**
*Qol ha-Moreh**
Tripoli Times

Lebanon
*al-ʿAlam al-Isrāʾīlī**
al-Bayraq
Le Jour
al-Nahār
L'Orient
Ṣawt al-Aḥrār

Morocco
L'Action du Peuple
*L'Avenir Illustré**
*Mebasser Tob**
*Or ha-Maʿarav (La Lumière du Maroc)**
*L'Union Marocaine**

Syria
al-Ayyām
Les Echos de Syrie
al-Inshāʾ

Tunisia
La Dépêche Tunisienne
*L'Egalité**
*La Gazette d'Israël**
*Le Reveil Juif**
La Tunisie Française
*La Voix de Sion**
*La Voix Juive**

OTHER NEWSPAPERS AND PERIODICALS

*L'Arche** (Paris)
*Information Juive** (Paris)
*Israel** (Rome)
*Jewish Monthly** (Washington, D.C.)
*Ha-Magid** (Lyck)
*Ha-Meliz** (Warsaw)
Le Monde (Paris)
*Le Monde Juif** (Paris)
New York Times (New York)
*Ha-Sefira** (Warsaw)

*An asterisk indicates a Jewish publication.

ARCHIVAL SOURCES

Alliance Israélite Universelle Archives, Paris (AIU):

Algérie II.C.10
Egypte I.B.7
Egypte I.C.15
Egypte I.C.27
Egypte I.D.3
Egypte I.G.5
France XII.F.22
France XIII.F.24
Irak I.C.1
Irak I.C.2
Irak I.C.3
Irak I.C.4
Irak I.C.5
Irak I.C.7
Irak I.C.8
Liban I.B.3
Liban I.C.1
Liban I.C.2
Liban I.C.3
Liban I.C.4
Liban I.G.2
Liban I.G.3
Liban I.G.4
Liban I.G.5
Lybie I.C.1
Lybie I.C.14
Lybie I.C.16
Lybie I.C.20
Lybie I.G.2
Lybie-Tripoli I.C.18–19
Maroc I.G.1
Maroc II.C.9
Maroc III.C.10
Maroc IV.C.11
Maroc XXV.E.396
Maroc XLVIII.E.743
Petits Pays Divers:
Aden 1–4
Syrie I.B.1–8
Syrie I.G.1
Syrie I.G.2
Syrie XI.E.94
Tunisie II.C.5
Tunisie II.C.6

American Joint Distribution Committee, Jerusalem (AJDC):

241A.9
242A.1
242A.16
245A.7, 10–14, 16
250A.1, 3–5, 9, 12–13, 24–25, 49
250B.51
250C.1
251A.14, 26, 30
251B.4
253B.16
306A.3
306B.3 and 8
307A.10–16
307B.1–28
307C.2–4
308A.1–6
308B.1
310B.27
321A.67
321B.14
321B.23
322A.1–3, 7–8, 12–13
322B.1, 3, 5, 8–9
339B.17
347B.8
382A.19–20
405B.43 and 48–51
419A.6–9, 15
419B.7
420A.18
422B.2–4
489A.47

Central Zionist Archives, Jerusalem (CZA):

A 192/159
F 21/1
KKL 5/414
KKL 5/481
KKL 5/614
KKL 5/1143
S 2/492
S 2/493
S 2/578

Central Zionist Archives,
Jerusalem (CZA): (*continued*)
S 2/579
S 2/628
S 2/657
S 2/691
S 2/692
S 2/777
S 5/455
S 5/492
S 5/795
S 5/796
S 5/1397
S 5/1398
S 5/2204
S 5/2249
S 6/1791
S 6/1983
S 6/1984
S 6/2297
S 6/4582
S 25/2435
S 25/3498
S 25/4971
S 25/5217
S 25/5219
S 25/5291
S 25/6457
S 25/9736
S 32/120
S 32/121
S 32/122
S 32/123
S 32/124
S 32/952
S 32/1068
S 32/1069
S 32/1501
Z 1/279
Z 1/308
Z 1/311
Z 1/313
Z 1/316
Z 1/321
Z 1/336
Z 1/343
Z 1/350
Z 1/359
Z 2/309
Z 2/511
Z 2/635
Z 3/751
Z 3/752
Z 3/979
Z 3/981
Z 3/982
Z 4/10,221
Z 4/10,310
Z 4/272
Z 4/1620
Z 4/2011A
Z 4/2101
Z 4/2149
Z 4/2332
Z 4/2470
Z 4/2624
Z 4/2669
Z 4/3260
Z 4/3262
Z/H.VIII.43

National Archives (Washington, D.C.):
RG 59 740.0011/European War 1939/11281
740.0011 European War 1939/16890
RG 59 763.72119/————
RG 59 867N.01/12–2047
RG 59 890G.4016 Jews/12
RG 59 980G.4016 Jews/12
RG 226 Records of the Office of Strategic Service, 21554
RG 226 OSS Report L45124 Iraq

Public Records Office, London (PRO):
FO 78/368
FO 195/204, f. 2231a–b
FO 195/624
FO 141/779/9065
FO 371/5333
FO 371/7745
FO 371/13150
FO 371/20814
FO 371/27116
FO 371/31576
FO 371/45395
FO 371/69182
FO 371/69211

Public Records Office, London (PRO):
(*continued*)
FO 371/69259
FO 371/69259/2410
FO 371/75128
FO 371/75152
FO 371/75183
FO 371/75183.110994
FO 371/75197
FO 371/75259
FO 371/82477
FO 371/82478
FO 371/91689
FO 371/91689.111074
FO 371/91690
FO 371/91691
FO 371/91693
FO 371/108605
FO 371/119528
FO 406/74
FO 624/29/374
FO 624/34
FO 624/38/502
FO 624/165

Abdel-Kader, A. R. *Le conflit judéo-arabe: Juifs et Arabes face à l'avenir.* Paris, 1961.
Abdo, Ali Ibrahim, and Kasmieh, Khairieh. *Jews of the Arab Countries.* Palestine Monographs, no. 82. Beirut, 1971.
Abitbol, Michel, ed. *Communautés juives des marges sahariennes du Maghreb.* Jerusalem, 1982.
———, ed. *Judaïsme d'Afrique du Nord aux XIXe–XXe siècles.* Jerusalem, 1980.
———. *Les Juifs d'Afrique du Nord sous Vichy.* Paris, 1983. (An English translation has just appeared.)
———. "The Encounter between French Jewry and the Jews of North Africa: Analysis of a Discourse (1830–1914)," in *The Jews in Modern France.* Edited by Frances Malino and Bernard Wasserstein. Hanover and London, 1985.
———. "Waiting for Vichy: Europeans and Jews in North Africa on the Eve of World War II," *Yad Vashem Studies* 14 (1981).
———. "Zionist Activity in the Maghreb," *The Jerusalem Quarterly* 21 (Fall 1981).
Aboulker, José. "La part de la Résistance française dans les événements de l'Afrique du Nord," *Les Cahiers Français,* no. 47 (August 1943).
Aboulker, Marcel. *Alger et ses complots.* Paris, 1945.
Abrahami, Itzhak. "The Jewish Communities of Tunisia during the Nazi Conquest," *Peʿamim* 28 (1986) [Hebrew].
Abramski-Bligh, Irit. "The Jews of Syria and Lebanon under Vichy Rule," *Peʿamim* 28 (1986) [Hebrew].
Abulafia, Isaac. *Penē Yiṣḥāq.* Vol. 1. Aleppo, 1870/71.
Ageron, Charles-Robert. "Contribution à l'étude de la propagande allemande au Maghreb pendant la Deuxième Guerre Mondiale," *Revue d'Histoire Maghrebine* (January 1977).
———. *"L'Algérie algérienne" de Napoléon III à de Gaulle.* Paris, 1980.
———. "Les populations du Maghreb face à la propagande allemande," *RHDGM* 29, no. 114 (April 1979).
———. "Une émeute anti-juive à Constantine (août 1934)," *ROMM* nos. 13–14 (ler semestre 1973) = *Mélanges Le Tourneau,* vol. 1.
Ahmad, Feroz. "Unionist Relations with the Greek, Armenian, and Jewish Communities of the Ottoman Empire, 1908–1914," in *Christians and Jews in the Ottoman Empire.* Vol. 1. Edited by Benjamin Braude and Bernard Lewis. New York and London, 1982.
Aḥmad b. Abī al-Diyāf. *Itḥāf Ahl al-Zamān bi-Akhbār Mulūk Tūnis wa-ʿAhd al-Amān.* Vol. 4. Tunis, 1963.
Albo, Michel Meyer. "Militants juifs pour l'indépendance du Maroc," *Nouveaux Cahiers* no. 70 (Autumn 1982).
Alluf, Nathan. *Bahrain—A Community That Was.* Tel Aviv, 1979 [Hebrew].
Anderson, Lisa. *The State and Social Transformation in Tunisia and Libya, 1930–1980.* Princeton, N.J., 1986.
Annuaire des Juifs d'Egypte et du Proche-Orient. 1942, 5702–5703. Cairo, 1942.
Anon. "Informations: Irak: Répercussion des événements de Palestine," *Paix et Droit* 16, no. 8 (October 1936).
———. "Informations 6. Etat d'Alep. Les israélites et le conseil fédéral," *Paix et Droit* 3, no. 10 (December 1923).

———. "Iraq: L'autonomie de l'Iraq," *Paix et Droit* 11, no. 9 (November 1931).
———. "Maroc: les troubles antisémites," *Afrique Française* 43, no. 11 (November 1933).
———. "La répercussion des événements de Palestine en Syrie," *Paix et Droit* 16, no. 5 (May 1936).
———. "L'exode des juifs de Fez vers la Palestine," *Paix et Droit* 3, no. 1 (January 1923).
———. "Unrest in the North-West African Territories under French Rule (1927–37)," in *Survey of International Affairs 1937*. Vol. 1. Edited by Arnold J. Toynbee. London, 1938.
Ansky, Michel. *Les Juifs d'Algérie du Décret Crémieux à la Libération*. Paris, 1950.
Arberry, A. J., ed. *Religion in the Middle East: Three Religions in Concord and Conflict, I: Judaism and Christianity.* Cambridge, 1969.
Arendt, Hannah. "Why the Crémieux Decree Was Abrogated," *Contemporary Jewish Record* 6, no. 2 (April 1943).
Artom, E. S. "L'importanza dell' elemento ebraico nella popolazione della Tripotalitania," in *Atti del primo congresso di studi coloniali di Firenze (8–12 aprile 1931).* Florence, 1931.
Ashkenzi, Tuvia B. *Yehūdē ᶜIrāq taḥat ha-Shiltōn hā-ᶜAravī: 1914–1960. Parashat Me'ōraᶜōt Bagdād ba-Rishōn veha-Shenī be-Yūnī 1941.* Jerusalem, 1960.
ᶜAṭiyya, Nissim, ed. *Minḥat Yehūda.* Aleppo, 1924.
Attal, Robert. "Le Consistoire de France et les Juifs d'Algérie: Lettre pastorale du Rabbin Isidor (1873)," *Michael* 5 (1978).
———, compiler. *Les élections au Conseil de la Communauté Israélite à Tunis du 24 April 1955: Prospectus, extraits du Presse, diverses.* Ben-Zvi Institute XIV Jc 1742.
———. Les Juifs d'Afrique du Nord: Bibliographie. Jerusalem, 1973.
———. "Les traductions en judéo-arabe tunisien des oeuvres d'Abraham Mapu," *REJ* 134 (1975).
———. *Périodiques juifs d'Afrique du Nord.* Jerusalem, 1980.
———. "The First Jewish Newspaper in the Maghreb—L'Israélite Algérien, 1870," *Peᶜamim* no. 17 (1983) [Hebrew].
———, and Sitbon, Claude, eds. *Regards sur les Juifs de Tunisie.* Paris, 1979.
———, and Tobi, Yosef. "Oriental and North African Jewry: An Annotated Bibliography, 1974–1976," *Sefunot* n.s. 1 (1980).
Avishur, Yitzhak, ed. *Studies on History and Culture of Iraqi Jewry.* Vol. 2. Or Yehuda, 1982 [Hebrew].
Ayoun, Richard, and Cohen, Bernard. *Les juifs d'Algérie: 2000 ans d'histoire*. Paris, 1982.
al-ᶜAzzāwī, ᶜAbbās. *Ta'rīkh al-ᶜIrāq bayn Iḥtilālayn*. Vol. 8. Baghdad, 1956.
Baer, Gabriel. "Urbanization in Egypt, 1820–1907," in *Beginnings of Modernization in the Middle East: The Nineteenth Century.* Edited by William R. Polk and Richard L. Chambers. Chicago, 1968.
Bahloul, Joëlle. *Le culte de la Table Dressée: Rites et traditions de la table juive algérienne*. Paris, 1983.
Bar-Asher, Shalom, and Maman, Aharon, eds. *Yehūdē Ṣefōn Afrīqa ve-Ereṣ Yisrā'ēl: Mi-ᶜAliyyat R. Ḥayyim b. ᶜAṭṭār ᶜAd Yāmēnū (1741–1981).* Jerusalem, 1981.
Barad, Shlomo. *Le mouvement sioniste en Tunisie*. Tel Aviv, 1980 [Hebrew].
Barer, Shlomo. *The Magic Carpet*. New York, 1952.

Barnai, Jacob. "ha-ᶜĒda ha-Maᶜarāvīt bīrūshālāyīm ba-Mē'a ha-19," in *Yehūdē Ṣefōn Afrīqa ve-Ereṣ Yisrā'ēl*. Edited by Shalom Bar-Asher and Aharon Maman. Jerusalem, 1981.
Bat Ye'or (pseud.). *Le dhimmi: Profil de l'opprimé en Orient et en Afrique du nord depuis la conquête arabe*. Paris, 1980.
Batatu, Hanna. *The Old Social Classes and the Revolutionary Movements of Iraq: A Study of Iraq's Old Landed and Commercial Classes and of Its Communists, Baᶜthists, and Free Officers*. Princeton, N.J., 1978.
Bell, Gertrude Lowthian. *Amurath to Amurath*. London, 1911.
Ben Cheneb, Mohammed. *Proverbes arabes de l'Algérie et du Maghreb*. Vol. 3. Paris, 1907.
Ben Ḥayyim, Ephraim. "ha-Haᶜpāla mi-Ṣefōn Afrīqa: Shalōsh hā-Oniyyōt, 1947," in *Shorāshīm ba-Mizraḥ*. Edited by Itshak Avrahami. Tel Aviv, 1986.
Ben-Jacob, Abraham. *A History of the Jews in Iraq: From the End of the Gaonic Period (1038 C.E.) to the Present Time*. Jerusalem, 1965 [Hebrew].
———. *Babylonian Jewry in Diaspora*. Jerusalem, 1985 [Hebrew].
Ben Nāyīm, Joseph. *Malkhē Rabbānān*. Jerusalem, 1931.
Ben Simeon, Raphael Aaron. *Nehar Miṣrayim*. Alexandria, 1907/8.
———. *Ṭūv Miṣrayim*. Jerusalem, 1907/8.
———. *U-Me-Ṣūr Devash*. Jerusalem, 1914/15.
Benaïm, Samuel Yosseff. *Le pèlerinages juif des lieux saints au Maroc: étude de tous les tsadiquimes dont les tombeaux sont éparpillés dans tout le Maroc*. Casablanca, 1980.
Bénichou, Raymond. *Ecrits juifs*. Algiers, 1957.
Bensimon-Donath, Doris. *Evolution du Judaïsme marocain sous le Protectorat français, 1912–1956*. Paris and the Hague, 1956.
———. *Immigrants d'Afrique du Nord en Israël: évolution et adaptation*. Paris, 1970.
———. *L'Evolution de la femme israélite à Fès*. Travaux et Mémoires, No. 25, La Pensée Universitaire. Aix-en-Provence, 1962.
———. *L'Integration des Juifs nord-africains en France*. Paris and the Hague, 1977.
Berger, Peter L. *Pyramids of Sacrifice: Political Ethics and Social Change*. New York, 1974.
Berl, Alfred. "L'enquête ministérielle en Algérie," *Paix et Droit* 15, no. 3 (March 1935).
Berque, Jacques. *Egypt Imperialism and Revolution*. Translated by Jean Stewart. London, 1972.
Blanc, Haim. *Communal Dialects in Baghdad*. Harvard Middle East Monograph Series, vol. 10. Cambridge, Mass., 1964.
Bondy, Ruth. *The Emissary: A Life of Enzo Sereni*. Translated by Shlomo Katz. Boston and Toronto, 1977.
Borgel, Robert. *Etoile jaune et croix gammée*. Tunis, 1944.
Brace, Richard, and Brace, Joan. *Ordeal in Algeria*. Princeton, N.J., 1960.
Braude, Benjamin, and Lewis, Bernard, eds. *Christians and Jews in the Ottoman Empire*. 2 vols. New York, 1982.
Briggs, Lloyd Cabot, and Guède, Norina Lami. *No More For Ever: A Saharan Jewish Town*. Papers of the Peabody Museum of Archaeology and Ethnology, Harvard University, vol. 55, no. 1. Cambridge, Mass., 1964.
Brignon, Jean, et al. *Histoire du Maroc*. Casablanca, 1967.
Cabasso, Gilbert, et al. *Juifs d'Egypte: Images et textes*. Paris, 1984.

Candler, Edmund. *The Long Road to Baghdad*. Vol. 2. London, New York, Toronto, and Melbourne, 1919.
Carlebach, Esriel. *Exotische Juden: Berichte und Studien*. Berlin, 1932.
Carpi, L. "La condizione giuridica degli ebrei nel Regno Unito di Libia." *Revista di studi politici internazionali* 1–3 (1963).
Chabry, Laurent, and Chabry, Annie. *Politique et minorités au Proche-Orient: les raisons d'une explosion*. Paris, 1984.
Chalom, Jacques. *Les Israélites de Tunisie, leur condition civile et politique*. Paris, 1908.
Chemla, Saül. *Le Judaïsme tunisien se meurt, un cri d'alarme*. Tunis, 1939.
Chetrit, Joseph. "Mūdāᶜūt Ḥadasha le-Anōmāliyūt ule-Lāshōn—Niṣṣānēhā shel Tenūᶜat Haskāla ᶜIvrīt be-Marōqō be-Sōf ha-Mē'a ha-19," *Mi-Qedem umi-Yam* 2 (1986).
Chouraqui, André N. *Between East and West: A History of the Jews in North Africa*. Translated by Michael M. Bernet. New York, 1973.
Chouraqui, André. *Cent ans d'histoire: l'Alliance Israélite Universelle et la renaissance juive contemporaine, 1860–1960*. Paris, 1965.
Chouraqui, André. *La condition juridique de l'Israélite marocain*. Paris, 1950.
Cohen, Amnon, and Baer, Gabriel, eds. *Egypt and Palestine: A Millennium of Association (868–1948)*. Jerusalem and New York, 1984.
Cohen, David. "Lyautey et le Sionisme, 1915–1925," *RFHOM* 67, nos. 248–249 (1980).
Cohen, Eliahou. *L'influence intellectuelle et sociale des écoles de l'Alliance Israélite sur les Israélites du Proche-Orient*. Unpublished doctoral dissertation, Université de Paris, 1962.
Cohen, Hayyim J. *ha-Peᶜīlūt ha-Ṣiyyonit be-ᶜIrāq*. Jerusalem, 1969.
———. *Meqōrōt le-Tōledōt ha-Yehūdīm be-Arṣōt ha-Mizraḥ ha-Tīkhōn be-Yamēnū*. Jerusalem, 5732.
———. "Tē'ōsōfīm Yehūdīm be-Baṣra—Sīmpṭōm le-Ma'avaq Dōr hā-Haskāla," *Hamizrah Hehadash* 15 (1965).
———. *The Jews of the Middle East, 1860–1972*. New York, Toronto, and Jerusalem, 1973.
———, and Yehuda, Zvi, eds. *Asian and African Jews in the Middle East, 1860–1971: Annotated Bibliography*. Jerusalem, 1976.
Cohen, Marcel. *Le parler arabe des Juifs d'Alger*. Paris, 1912.
Ha-Cohen, Mordecaï. *Higgid Mordecaï: Histoire de la Libye et de ses Juifs, lieux d'habitations et coutumes*. Edited by Harvey Goldberg. Jerusalem, 1978 [Hebrew].
Ha-Cohen, Mordekhai. *The Book of Mordechai: A Study of the Jews of Libya. Selections from the Highid Mordekhai of Mordechai Hakohen*. Edited and translated, with introduction and commentaries, by Harvey E. Goldberg. Philadelphia, 1980.
Cohen, Naomi W. *Not Free to Desist: The American Jewish Committee, 1906–1966*. Philadelphia, 1972.
Coke, Richard. *Baghdad: The City of Peace*. London, 1927.
———. *The Heart of the Middle East*. New York, 1926.
Colombe, Marcel. *L'évolution de l'Egypte, 1924–1950*. Islam d'Hier et d'Aujourd'hui. Vol. 9. Paris, 1951.
Comunità Israelitica Bengasi. *Norme per le comunità Israeliche della Libia*. Benghazi, 1929.

Confer, Vincent. *France and Algeria: The Problem of Civil and Political Reform, 1870–1920*. Syracuse, N.Y., 1966.
Conseil des Communautés Israélites du Maroc, *Congrès 1952: Motions* (Rabat, 1952), in mimeograph.
Courrière, Yves. *Le temps des léopards*. La Guerre d'Algérie. Vol. 2. Paris, 1969.
Crum, Bartley C. *Behind the Silken Curtain: A Personal Account of Anglo-American Diplomacy in Palestine and the Middle East*. New York, 1947.
Danan, Yves Maxime. *La vie politique à Alger de 1940 à 1944*. Bibliothèque de Droit Public, tome 3. Paris, 1963.
Darmon, Raoul. *La situation des cultes en Tunisie*. 2nd rev. ed. Paris, 1930.
Davet, Michel-Christian. *La double affaire de Syrie*. Paris, 1967.
David, Philippe. *Un gouvernement arabe à Damas: le congrès syrien*. Paris, 1923.
Dawn, C. Ernest. *From Ottomanism to Arabism: Essays on the Origins of Arab Nationalism*. Urbana, Chicago, and London, 1973.
Dayyan, Isaac. "Tōrat Yisrā'ēl ve-ᶜAm Yisrā'ēl." In *Minḥat Yehuda*. Edited by Nissim ᶜAṭiyya. Aleppo, 1924.
de Chair, Somerset. *The Golden Carpet*. London, 1944.
De Felice, Renzo. *Jews in an Arab Land: Libya, 1835—1970*. Translated by Judith Roumani. Austin, 1985.
De Marco, Roland R. *The Italianization of African Natives: Government Native Education in the Italian Colonies, 1890–1937*. New York, 1943.
Deshen, Shlomo, and Zenner, Walter P., eds. *Jewish Societies in the Middle East: Community, Culture and Authority*. Washington, D.C., 1982.
Dinaburg, Benzion. "'Modern Times' in Jewish History," *Zion* 13–14 (1948–1949) [Hebrew].
Druyan, Nitza. *Without a Magic Carpet: Yemenite Settlement in Eretz Israel (1881–1914)*. Jerusalem, 1981 [Hebrew].
Durieu, Louis (pseud. of Eugène Blum). *Les Juifs algériens (1870–1901)*. Paris, 1902.
Dwek, Jacob Saul. *Derekh Emūna*. Aleppo, 1913/14.
Eickelman, Dale F. "Religion and Trade in Western Morocco," *Research in Economic Anthropology* 5 (1983).
Eisenbeth, Maurice. *Les Juifs de l'Afrique du Nord: Démographie & onomastique*. Algiers, 1936.
———. *Pages vécues: 1940–43*. Algiers, 1945.
El-Ad, Avri. *Decline of Honor*. With James Creech. Chicago, 1976.
El-Baz, Camille. *Sarah ou moeurs et coutumes juives de Constantine (Algérie)*. Nice, 1971.
El Fayache, Uthman. "L'origine de la question de Palestine," *L'Action du Peuple* (November 17, 1933): 2.
El Kholti, Mohammed. "Les Israélites et nous . . .", *L'Action du Peuple* (August 18, 1933): 3.
———. "Les Sionistes au Maroc sur la défensive," *L'Action du Peuple* (April 27, 1934): 1.
Eliav, Mordechai. "Relations between Ashkenazim and Sephardim in Eretz-Israel in the 19th Century," *Peᶜamim* no. 11 (1982) [Hebrew].
Elmaleh, Abraham. *ha-Yehūdīm be-Dammaseq u-Maṣṣāvām ha-Kalkalī veha-Tarbūtī*. Jaffa, 1911/12.
———. *In Memoriam: Hommage à Joseph David Farhi*. Jerusalem, 1948.
Encyclopaedia of Islam. 1st ed., 4 vols and *Supplement*, 1913–42. New ed., 5 vols. published as of 1986. Leiden, 1960–.

Encyclopaedia Judaica. 16 volumes and yearbooks. Jerusalem, 1971–1974.
Evans, Trefor E., ed. *The Killearn Diaries, 1934–1946: The Diplomatic and Personal Record of Lord Killearn (Sir Miles Lampson) High Commissioner and Ambassador to Egypt*. London, 1972.
Faraj, Murād. *Maqālāt Murād*. Cairo, 1912.
Fargeon, Maurice. *Les Juifs en Egypte depuis les origines jusqu'à ce jour: histoire générale suivie d'un aperçu documentaire*. Cairo, 1938.
———. *Médecins et avocats juifs au service de l'Egypte, avec une preface par Israël Wolfenson: histoire générale depuis l'antiquité jusqu'à nos jours suivie d'un recueil de biographies des principaux médecins et avocats juifs d'Egypte contemporains*. Cairo, 1939.
Farhi, J. "Aperçu général sur la communauté de Damas," *Hamenora* 2, nos. 7–8 (July–August 1924).
Favrod, Charles-Henri. *Le F.L.N. et l'Algérie*. Paris, 1962.
Fitoussi, Elie, and Benazet, Aristide. *L'état tunisien et le Protectorat français: histoire et organisation (1525 à 1931)*. 2 vols. Paris, 1931.
Flamand, Pierre. *Diaspora en terre d'Islam: Les communautés israélites du sud marocain: Essai de description et d'analyse de la vie juive en milieu berbère*. Casablanca, 1959.
Foreign Relations of the United States: Diplomatic Papers 1943. Vol. 2: *Europe*. Washington, D.C., 1964.
Franco, Marcel. *Essai sur l'histoire des israélites de l'Empire Ottoman depuis les origines jusqu'à nos jours*. Paris, 1897.
Friedlander, Saul. *L'anti-semitisme nazi: histoire d'une psychose collective*. Paris, 1971.
Friedman, Elizabeth Deborah. *The Jews of Batna, Algeria: A Study of Identity and Colonialism*. Unpublished doctoral dissertation, City University of New York, 1977.
Front de Libération National. *Les Juifs d'Algérie dans le combat pour l'indépendance nationale*. FLN Documents à l'adresse du Peuple Français. n.d., n.p.
Funk, Arthur Layton. *The Politics of TORCH: The Allied Landings and the Algiers Putsch, 1942*. Lawrence, Manhattan, and Wichita, 1974.
Gagege, Claude. *Les Juifs de Tunisie et la colonisation française (jusqu'à la première guerre mondiale)*. Unpublished doctoral dissertation, Université de Paris, 1973.
Galanté, Avram. *Histoire des Juifs de Turquie*. Vol. 5. Istanbul, 1985.
Gamlieli (Shukr), Nissim Benjamin. *Tēmān ū-Maḥane "Ge'ūla": (Qōrōt ha-Yehūdīm be-Tēmān, ba-Derākhīm, be-ᶜAden, ūve-Maḥane ha-Pelīṭīm)*. Tel Aviv, 1962.
Gaon, M. D. *Yehūdē ha-Mizraḥ be-Ereṣ Yisrā'ēl*. Vol. 2. Jerusalem, 1937.
Gaudefroy-Demombynes, Roger. *L'oeuvre française en matière d'enseignement au Maroc*. Paris, 1928.
Geertz, Clifford, Geertz, Hildred, and Rosen, Lawrence. *Meaning and Order in Moroccan Society: Three Essays in Cultural Analysis*. Cambridge, 1979.
Gelber, Yoav. *Tōldōt ha-Hitnaddevūt, vol. 3: Nōs'ē ha-Degel*. Jerusalem, 1983.
Gelblum, Aryeh. "ᶜAliyyat Tēmān ū-Vᶜāyat Afrīqa," *Haaretz* (April 22, 1949).
Gendzier, Irene L. *The Practical Visions of Yaᶜqub Sanuᶜ*. Harvard Middle Eastern Monographs, vol. 15. Cambridge, Mass., 1966.
Gershoni, Israel, and Jankowski, James P. *Egypt, Islam, and the Arabs: The Search for Egyptian Nationhood, 1900–1930*. New York and Oxford, 1986.
Ghanīma, Yūsuf Rizq Allāh. *Nuzhat al-Mushtāq fī Ta'rīkh Yahūd al-ᶜIrāq*. Baghdad, 1924.

Ghez, Paul. *Six mois sous la botte*. Tunis, 1943.
Ghunaym, Aḥmad Muḥammad, and Abū Kaff, Aḥmad. *Al-Yahūd wa 'l-Ḥaraka al-Ṣahyūniyya fī Miṣr*. Cairo, 1969.
al-Ghūrī, Emil. *Filasṭīn ᶜabra Sittīn ᶜĀm: 1922–1937*. Vol. 2. Beirut, 1973.
Gibb, H.A.R. "The Islamic Congress at Jerusalem in December 1931," in *Survey of International Affairs*. Edited by Arnold J. Toynbee. London, 1931.
Gil, B. "The Selectivity of the North African Aliyah," *AR* 10, no. 29 (February 1955).
Golan, Aviezer. *Operation Susannah. As Told to Aviezer Golan by Marcelle Ninio, Victor Levy, Robert Dassa and Philip Natanson*. New York, 1978.
Golb, Norman. *Spertus College of Judaica Yemenite Manuscripts: An Illustrated Catalogue*. Chicago, 1972.
Goldberg, Harvey E. *Cave Dwellers and Citrus Growers: A Jewish Community in Libya and Israel*. Cambridge, 1972.
———. "Rites and Riots: The Tripolitanian Pogrom of 1945," *Plural Societies* 8, no. 1 (Spring 1977).
———. "The Jewish Community of Tripoli in Relation to Italian Jewry and Italians in Tripoli," in *Les relations intercommunautaires juives en méditerranée occidentale, xiiiᵉ-xxᵉ siècles*. Edited by J.-L. Miège. Paris, 1984.
———, and Rosen, Rachel. "The Itinerant Jewish Peddlers in Tripolitania at the End of the Ottoman Period and under Italian Rule," in *Communautés juives des marges sahariennes du Maghreb*. Edited by M. Abitbol. Jerusalem, 1982.
Goldscheider, Calvin, and Zuckerman, Alan S. *The Transformation of the Jews*. Chicago and London, 1984.
Goldstein, Daniel. *Libération ou Annexion aux chemins croisés de l'histoire tunisienne (1914–1922)*. Tunis, 1978.
Gordon, David C. *The Passing of French Algeria*. London, New York, and Toronto, 1966.
Gosset, Renée Pierre. *Algiers 1941–1943: A Temporary Expedient*. Translated by Nancy Hecksher. London, 1945.
Gottesman, Lois. *Israel in Egypt: The Jewish Community of Egypt, 1922–1957*. Unpublished master's thesis, Princeton University, 1982.
Goutalier, Régine. "Les Juifs et l'O.A.S. en Oranie," *Les relations entre Juifs et Musulmans en Afrique du Nord, XIXᵉ-XXᵉ siècles*. Paris, 1980.
Govrin, Nurit. "The Encounter of Exiles from Eretz Israel with Egypt and Egyptian Jewry during the First World War," *Peᶜamim* 25 (1985) [Hebrew].
Grinker, Yehuda. *ᶜAliyyātām shel Yehūdē hā-Aṭlas*. Tel Aviv, 1973.
Grobba, Fritz. *Männer und Mächte im Orient. 25 Jahre diplomatischer Tätigkeit im Orient*. Göttingen, 1967.
Haddad, Heskel M. *Flight from Babylon: Iraq, Iran, Israel, America*. As told to Phyllis I. Rosenteur. New York, 1986.
Haddad, Robert M. *Syrian Christians in Muslim Society: An Interpretation*. Princeton, N.J., 1970.
Haddad de Paz, Charles. *Juifs et Arabes au pays de Bourguiba*. Aix-en-Provence, 1977.
Haim, Sylvia G., ed. *Arab Nationalism: An Anthology*. Berkeley and Los Angeles, 1962.
———. "Aspects of Jewish Life in Baghdad under the Monarchy," *Middle Eastern Studies* 12, no. 2 (May 1976).

Halstead, John P. *Rebirth of a Nation: The Origins and Rise of Moroccan Nationalism, 1912–1944*. Harvard Middle Eastern Monographs, vol. XVIII. Cambridge, Mass., 1967.

al-Ḥasanī, ᶜAbd al-Razzāq. *al-Asrār al-Khafiyya fī Ḥarakat al-Sana 1941 al-Taḥarruriyya*. 2nd rev. ed. Sidon, 1964.

———. *Ta'rīkh al-Wizārāt al-ᶜIrāqiyya*. 10 vols. 2nd ed. Sidon, 1953–1960.

Hasin, Eliyahu, and Horowitz, Dan. *The Affair*. Tel Aviv, 1961 [Hebrew].

Hayyim, Abraham. "Teᶜūdōt lifᶜīlūt Ṣiyyōnīt ve-Ḥevrātīt be-Qehillōt Sūreya ū-Lvanōn bēn Shettē Milḥamōt ᶜŌlām," in *Hāgūt ᶜIvrīt be-Arṣōt ha-Islām*. Edited by Menahem Zohori et al. Jerusalem, 1981.

Ḥazzan, Elijah. *Nevē Shālōm*. Alexandria, 1893/94.

———. *Ta ᶜalūmōt Lev*. Vol. 3. Alexandria, 1902/3.

———. *Zikhrōn Yerūshālayim*. Livorno, 1874.

Herzl, Theodor. *The Complete Diaries of Theodor Herzl*. Vols. 2-3. Edited by Raphael Patai. Translated by Harry Zohn. New York and London, 1960.

Hillel, Shlomo. *Operation Babylon*. Translated by Ina Friedman. New York, 1987.

Hirschberg, H. Z. [J. W.]. *A History of the Jews in North Africa*. Vol. 2. Edited by Eliezer Bashan and Robert Attal. Leiden, 1981.

———. *Mē-Ereṣ Mevo' ha-Shemesh: ᶜĪm Yehūdē Afrīqa ha-Ṣefonīt be-Arṣōtēhem*. Jerusalem, 1957.

———. "The Oriental Jewish Communities," in *Religion in the Middle East: Three Religions in Concord and Conflict*. Vol. 1. Edited by A. J. Arberry. Cambridge, 1969.

———, ed. *Zakhor le-Avraham: Mélanges Abraham Elmaleh*. Jerusalem, 1972.

Hirszowicz, Lukasz. *The Third Reich and the Arab East*. London and Toronto, 1966.

Hodgson, Marshall G. S. *The Venture of Islam: Conscience and History in a World Civilization*. Vol. 3. *The Gunpowder Empires and Modern Times*. Chicago, 1974.

Horne, Alistair. *A Savage War of Peace: Algeria 1954–1962*. New York, 1977.

Howe, Irving. *World of Our Fathers*. New York, 1976.

Husry, Khaldun S. "The Assyrian Affair of 1933," *IJMES* 5, Nos. 2–3 (April and June 1974), 2 pts.

Hyamson, Albert M. *The Sephardim of England: A History of the Spanish and Portuguese Jewish Community, 1492–1951*. London, 1951.

Ibn al-Khōja, Muḥammad al-Ḥabīb. *Yahūd al-Maghrib al-ᶜArabī*. Cairo, 1973.

Ilan, Zvi. "'Heḥalutz' in Syria and Attempts to Settle the Ḥoran, 1928–1936," *Peᶜamim* no. 14 (1982) [Hebrew].

Jankowski, James. "Egyptian Responses to the Palestine Problem in the Interwar Period," *IJMES* 12, no. 1 (August 1980).

———. "Zionism and the Jews in Egyptian Nationalist Opinion," in *Egypt and Palestine: A Millennium of Association (868–1948)*. Edited by Amnon Cohen and Gabriel Baer. Jerusalem and New York, 1984.

———. *Egypt's Young Rebels—"Young Egypt": 1933–1952*. Hoover Institution Publications, 145. Stanford, 1975.

———. *The Young Egypt Party and Egyptian Nationalism 1933–1945*. Unpublished doctoral dissertation, University of Michigan, 1967.

Joseph, John. *The Nestorians and their Muslim Neighbors: A Study of Western Influences on their Relations*. Princeton, N.J., 1961.

Julien, Charles-André. *L'Afrique du Nord en marche: Nationalismes musulmans et souveraineté française*. 3rd ed. Paris, 1957.

al-Jundī, Sāmī. *al-Ba^cth*. Beirut, 1969.
Kaddache, Mahfoud. *Histoire du nationalisme algérien: question nationale et politique algérienne, 1919–1951*. 2nd ed. 2 vols. Algiers, 1981.
———. "L'opinion politique musulmane en Algérie et l'administration française (1939–1942)," *RHDGM* 29, no. 114 (April 1979).
Kahalon, Yehuda. "ha-Ma'avāq ^cal demūtāh hā-Rūḥānīt shel hā-^cĒda ha-Yehūdīt be-Lūv ba-Mē'a ha-19 ūvā-^cĀsōr hā-Rishōn shel ha-Mē'a ha-^cEsrīm," in *Zakhor Le-Abraham: Mélanges Abraham Elmaleh à l'occasion du cinquième anniversaire de sa mort (21 Adar II 5727)*. Edited by H. Z. Hirschberg. Jerusalem, 1972.
Kattan, Naim. *Farewell, Babylon*. Translated by Sheila Fischman. Toronto, 1976.
Katz, Jacob. *Out of the Ghetto: The Social Background of Jewish Emancipation, 1770–1870*. New York, 1978.
Katzir, Yael. "Preservation of Jewish Ethnic Identity in Yemen: Segregation and Integration as Boundary Maintenance Mechanisms." *Comparative Studies in Society and History* 24 (1982).
Kedourie, Elie. *Arabic Political Memoirs and Other Studies*. London, 1974.
———. *England and the Middle East: The Destruction of the Ottoman Empire, 1914–1921*. London, 1956.
———. *The Chatham House Version and Other Middle-Eastern Studies*. London, 1970.
Kewenig, Wilhelm. *Die Koexistenz der Religionsgemeinschaften im Libanon*. Berlin, 1965.
Khaddouri, Majid. *Independent Iraq, 1932–1958: A Study in Iraqi Politics*. 2nd ed. London, New York, and Karachi, 1960.
Khazoum, Eliahu. "An Arab View of the Jews of Iraq." *Middle East Review* 9, no. 2 (Winter 1976–77).
Khūrī, Ya^cqūb. *al-Yahūd fī 'l-Buldān al-^cArabiyya*. Beirut, 1970.
Kisch, Lt.-Colonel F. H. *Palestine Diary*. London, 1938; repr. New York, 1974.
Kohn, H. "The Jews in Syria," *The New Judaea* 3, no. 20 (June 17, 1927).
Krämer, Gudrun. *Minderheit, Millet, Nation? Die Juden in Ägypten 1914–1952*. Studien zum Minderheiten Problem im Islam 7. Wiesbaden, 1982. (A revised English version has just appeared.)
———. "'Radical' Nationalists, Fundamentalists, and Jews in Egypt or, Who Is a Real Egyptian?" in *Islam, Nationalism, and Radicalism in Egypt and the Sudan*. Edited by Gabriel R. Warburg and Uri Kupferschmidt. New York, 1983.
Kraus, Samuel. *^cĪr Bērūt ve-Qōrōt ha-Yehudim be-Tokhāh*. Jerusalem, 5662.
Landau, Jacob M. "Abu Naḍḍara, An Egyptian Jewish Nationalist," *JJS* 3 (1952).
———. "Bittersweet Nostalgia: Memoirs of Jewish Emigrants from the Arab Countries (Review Article)." *MEJ* 35, no. 2 (Spring 1981).
———. *Jews in Nineteenth-Century Egypt*. New York and London, 1969.
———. "'Language Competition' in Jewish Education in Modern Egypt." *Bar-Ilan: Annual of Bar-Ilan University. Studies in Judaica and the Humanities*. Vols. 4–5. Ramat Gan and Jerusalem, 1967 [Hebrew].
Landshut, Siegfried. *Jewish Communities in the Muslim Countries of the Middle East*. London, 1950.
Laniado, Ezra. *The Jews of Mosul from Samarian Exile (Galuth) to "Operation Ezra and Nehemia"*. Tirat Carmel, 1981 [Hebrew].
Laroui, Abdallah. *Les origines sociales et culturelles du nationalisme marocain (1830–1912)*. Paris, 1980.

Laskier, Michael M. "A Document on Anglo-Jewry's Intervention on Behalf of Egyptian Jews on Trial for Espionage and Sabotage; December 1954," *Michael* 10 (1986).
———. "Aspects of the Activities of the Alliance Israélite Universelle in the Jewish Communities of the Middle East and North Africa: 1860–1918," *Modern Judaism* 3, no. 2 (May 1986).
———. "From War to War: The Jews of Egypt from 1948 to 1970," *Studies in Zionism* 7, no. 1 (1986).
———. "ha-Yehūdīm bi-Ṣfōn Afrīqa bi-Tqūfat Milḥemet ha-ᶜŌlām ha-Sheniya (1939–1943)," *Yalqut Moreshet* 40 (1986).
———. "Hebbēṭīm Pōlītiyyīm ve-ᶜIrgūniyyīm shel hā-ᶜAliyya mi-Marōqō ba-Shānīm 1949–1956," *ha-Ṣiyyōnūt* 12 (1987).
———. "S. D. Lévy and Moïse Nahon, Two Sephardic Intellectuals in Modern Moroccan History," *Michael* 9 (1985).
———. *The Alliance Israélite Universelle and the Jewish Communities of Morocco: 1862–1962.* Albany, N.Y., 1983.
———. "The Evolution of Zionist Activity in the Jewish Communities of Morocco, Tunisia and Algeria: 1897–1947," *Studies in Zionism,* no. 8 (Autumn 1983).
———. "The Instability of Moroccan Jewry and the Moroccan Press in the First Decade after Independence," *Jewish History* 1, no. 1 (Spring 1986).
———. "The Jewish Agency and the Jews of Morocco and Tunisia," *Proceedings of the Ninth World Congress of Jewish Studies, Division B.* Vol. 3. Jerusalem 1986.
———. "The Jews of Morocco and the Alliance Israélite Universelle: Selected Documents," in *East and Maghreb.* Vol. 3. Edited by S. Schwarzfuchs. Ramat Gan, 1981.
———. "Yom Ṭōv Dāvīd Ṣemaḥ v-Īhūdē Marōqō: 1913–1940 (Nittuaḥ ve-Tīᶜūd)," *Mi-Qedem ūmi-Yam* 2 (1986).
———. "Zionism and the Jewish Communities of Morocco: 1956–1962," *Studies in Zionism* 6, no. 1 (1985).
Lazare, Lucien. "L'Alliance Israélite Universelle en Palestine à l'époque de la révolution des 'Jeunes Turcs' et sa mission en Orient du 29 octobre 1908 au 19 janvier 1909," *REJ* 138, fasc. 3–4 (1979).
Le Glay, Maurice. "Musulmans et Juifs marocains: Etude de moeurs et de l'état des esprits à l'occasion du mouvement antisémite d'Allemagne," *Afrique Française* 43, no. 11 (November 1933).
Lehrmann, Hal. "L'El-Wifaq chez les Juifs marocains: 'entente cordiale' ou collaboration," *L'Arche* (August–September and October).
———. "Report from Morocco," *Midstream* 4, no. 3 (Summer 1958).
Le Tourneau, Roger. *Evolution politique de l'Afrique du Nord musulmane, 1920–1961.* Paris, 1962.
Levy, Joseph. "Témoignage d'un militant juif marocain," *Juifs du Maroc: Identité et dialogue.* Actes du Colloque International sur la Communauté Juive Marocaine. Paris, 1980.
Levy, Joseph M. "Moslem Threatens Jews in Palestine," *New York Times* (December 14, 1931).
Levy, Suzanne. "Jews, Arabs and Europeans in Tunisia in the Writings of Albert Memmi," *Peᶜamim,* no. 4 (1980) [Hebrew].
Lipschits, Isaac. *La politique de la France au Levant, 1939–1941.* Paris and Amsterdam, 1963.

Longrigg, Stephen Hemsley. *ᶜIraq, 1900 to 1950: A Political, Social, and Economic History.* London, New York, and Toronto, 1953.

———. *Syria and Lebanon under French Mandate.* London, New York, and Toronto, 1958.

Luks, Harold Paul. "Iraqi Jews during World War II," *The Wiener Library Bulletin* 30 n.s. nos. 43/44 (1977).

Malek, Yusuf. *The British Betrayal of the Assyrians.* Chicago, 1935.

Malka, Victor. *La mémoire brissée des Juifs du Maroc.* Paris, 1978.

Mandel, Neville J. *The Arabs and Zionism before World War I.* Berkeley and Los Angeles, 1976.

Maoz, Moshe, ed. *Meqōrōt le-Tōldōt Yehūdē Sūreya ve-Ereṣ Yisrā'ēl ba-Mē'a ha-19.* Tel Aviv, 1967.

———. *Modern Syria: Political and Social Changes in the Process of Creating a National Community.* Tel Aviv, 1974 [Hebrew].

Marrus, Michael R., and Paxton, Robert O. *Vichy France and the Jews.* New York, 1981.

Martin, Claude. *Les Israélites algériens.* Paris, 1936.

Martin, Edward Trueblood. *I Flew Them Home: A Pilot's Story of the Yemenite Airlift.* New York, 1958.

Marty, P. "Les institutions israélites au Maroc," *REI* (1930).

Mayer, Thomas. *Egypt and the Palestine Question, 1936–1945.* Islamkundliche Untersuchungen, Band 77. Berlin, 1983.

Meir, Yosef (Yehoshafat). *Beyond the Desert: Underground Activities in Iraq, 1941–1951.* Tel Aviv, 1973 [Hebrew].

Mejcher, Helmut. "North Africa in the Strategy and Politics of the Axis Powers 1936–1943," *Cahiers de Tunisie* 29, nos. 117–118 (3ᵉ et 4ᵉ trimestres 1981).

Memmi, Albert. *The Pillar of Salt.* Translated by Edouard Roditi. New York, 1955.

Meyer, Michael A. "Where Does the Modern Period of Jewish History Begin?" *Judaism* 24, no. 3 (Summer 1975).

Middleton, Drew. "Giraud's Reforms Getting Under Way," *New York Times* (January 16, 1943).

Miège, J.-L., ed. *Les relations intercommunautaires juives en méditerranée occidentale, XIIIᵉ-XXᵉ siècles.* Paris, 1984.

Milano, Attilio. *Storia degli ebrei italiani nel Levante.* Florence, 1949.

Miller, Ellen Clare. *Eastern Sketches: Notes of Scenery, Schools, and Tent Life in Syria and Palestine.* Reprint. New York, 1977.

Mizrahi, Maurice. *L'Egypte et ses Juifs: le temps révolu, XIXe et XXe siècle.* Geneva, 1977.

Moine, André. *La déportation et la résistance en Afrique du Nord (1939–1944).* Paris, 1972.

Moreh, Shmuel. *Arabic Works by Jewish Writers, 1863–1973.* Jerusalem, 1973.

Mosenson, Moshe. *Letters from the Desert.* Translated by Hilda Auerbach. New York, 1945.

Muhsin, Khalid Abid. *The Political Career of Muhammad Jaᶜfar Abu al-Timman (1908–1937): A Study in Modern Iraqi History.* Unpublished doctoral dissertation, School of Oriental and African Studies, University of London, 1983.

Murphy, Robert. *Diplomat among Warriors.* Garden City, N.Y., 1964.

Naḥum, Y. L., and Tobi, Y. "R. Yosef Shemen's Pamphlet *Ḥayei haTemanim* (On the Distress of Yemenite Jewry in the Twentieth Century)," in *The Jews of Yemen:*

Studies and Researches. Edited by Yisrael Yeshaᶜyahu and Yosef Tobi. Jerusalem, 1975 [Hebrew].
Naṣṣār, Sihām. *al-Yahūd al-Miṣriyyūn bayn al-Miṣriyya wa 'l-Ṣahyūniyya*. Beirut, 1980.
Nataf, Félix. *Juif maghrebin: Une vie au Maghreb (racontée à ma fille)*. Paris, 1978.
Nesry, Carlos de. *Le Juif de Tanger et le Maroc*. Tangier, 1956.
———. Les Israélites marocains à l'heure du choix. Tangier, 1958.
Nini, Yehuda. *Mi-Mizraḥ umi-Yam: Yehūdē Miṣrayim, Ḥayyē Yōm Yōm ve-Hishtaqfūtām be-Sifrūt ha-Shūt, 5642–5674*. Tel Aviv, 1979/80.
———. *Yemen and Zion: The Jews of Yemen, 1800–1914. A Political and Social Study of Their Emigration to Palestine*. Jerusalem, 1982 [Hebrew].
Obermeyer, Jacob. *Modernes Judentum im Morgen- und Abendland*. Vienna and Leipzig, 1908.
Ovadia, David. *Fās ve-Ḥakhāmēhā: Krōnīqōt Meqōriyyōt*. Vol. 1. Jerusalem, 1978/79.
———. *The Community of Sefrou*. 3 vols. Jerusalem, 1974–75 [Hebrew].
Ovadia, Yehoshuᶜa Shimᶜon Ḥayyim. *Sēfer Torah va-Ḥayyim*. Jerusalem, 1971/72.
Peres, Yoḥanan. *Yaḥasē ᶜEdōt be-Yisrā'ēl*. Tel Aviv, 1977.
Peretz, Don. *Egyptian Jews Today*. Unpublished report for the American Jewish Committee. New York, January 1956.
———. *Jews in Egypt, Syria, Lebanon and Iraq, July 1957*. Unpublished report for the American Jewish Committee. N.p., n.d.
———. *Report on Middle East Trip, November–December 1957*. Unpublished report for the American Jewish Committee. New York, January 1958.
Pernot, Maurice. *Rapport sur un voyage d'étude à Constantinople en Egypt et en Turquie d'Asie (Janvier–Août 1912)*. Paris, n.d.
Philby, H. St. J. B. *Arabian Highlands*. Ithaca, N.Y., 1952.
Politi, E. I. *L'Egypte de 1914 à "Suez"*. Paris, 1965.
Polk, William R., and Chambers, Richard L., eds. *Beginnings of Modernization in the Middle East: The Nineteenth Century*. Chicago, 1968.
Porath, Y. *The Emergence of the Palestinian-Arab National Movement 1918–1929*. London, 1974.
———. *The Palestinian Arab National Movement: From Riots to Rebellion. Vol. II: 1929–1939*. London, 1977.
Protokol des I. Zionistenkongresses in Basel vom 29. bis 31. August 1897. Neu Herausgegeben. Prague, 1911.
Rabinovich, Itamar. "Germany and the Syrian Political Scene in the Late 1930's," in *Germany and the Middle East, 1835–1939*. Edited by Jehuda L. Wallach. Tel Aviv, 1975.
Rainero, Romain. "La politique fasciste à l'égard de l'Afrique du Nord: l'épée de l'Islam et la revendication sur la Tunisie," *RFHOM* 64, no. 237 (1977).
Ratzaby, Yehuda. *The Yemenite Jews: Literature and Studies. Bibliography 1935–1975*. Supplement to *Kirjath Sepher*, vol. 50. Jerusalem, 1976.
Rejwan, Nissim. "Life among the Muslims: A Memoir." *Present Tense* 9, no. 1 (Autumn 1981).
———. *The Jews of Iraq: 3000 Years of History and Culture*. London, 1985.
Resner, Lawrence. *Eternal Stranger: The Plight of the Modern Jew from Baghdad to Casablanca*. Garden City, N.Y., 1951.
Ricard, Robert. "Notes sur l'émigration des Israélites marocains en Amérique espagnole et au Brésil," *Revue Africaine* 88 (1944).
Richter, Julius. *A History of Protestant Missions in the Near East*. Reprint. New York, 1970.

Rihani, Ameen. *Arabian Peak and Desert*. Boston and New York, 1930.
Rihbany, Abraham Mitrie. *A Far Journey*. Boston and New York, 1914.
Rivlin, Eliᶜezer, and Rivlin, Yosef Yo'el. *Le-Qōrōt ha-Yehūdīm be-Dammeseq ba-Mē'a ha-Rivīʿīt la-Elef ha-Shishī*. Jerusalem, 5687.
Robinson, Nehemiah. *The Arab Countries of the Near East and Their Jewish Communities*. Unpublished report of the Institute of Jewish Affairs, World Jewish Congress. New York, 1951.
Rodrique, Aron. *French Jews, Turkish Jews: The Alliance Israélite Universelle in Turkey, 1860–1914*. Unpublished doctoral dissertation, Harvard University, 1985.
Rose, Norman Anthony. "The Arab Rulers and Palestine, 1939: The British Reaction," *JMH* 44, no. 2 (June 1972).
Rosen, Lawrence. "A Moroccan Jewish Community during the Middle Eastern Crisis," *The American Scholar* 37 (1968).
———. Muslim-Jewish Relations in a Moroccan City," *IJMES* 3, no. 4 (October 1972).
Rosenstock, Morton. "Economic and Social Conditions among the Jews of Algeria, 1790–1848," *Historia Judaica* 18, pt. 1 (April 1956).
———. "The Establishment of the Consistorial System in Algeria," *JSS* 18, no. 1 (January 1956).
Roumani, Maurice M. "Zionism and Social Change in Libya at the Turn of the Century," *Studies in Zionism* 8, no. 1 (1987).
Rubin, Barry. *The Arab States and the Palestine Conflict*. Syracuse, N.Y., 1981.
Rubinstein, Elyakim. "'The Protocols of the Elders of Zion' in the Arab Jewish Conflicts in Palestine in the Twenties," *Hamizraḥ Heḥadash* 26, nos. 1–2 (1976) [Hebrew].
Ruppin, Arthur. *Soziologie der Juden*. 2 vols. Berlin, 1930–31.
Sabille, Jacques. *Les Juifs de Tunisie sous Vichy et l'occupation*. Paris, 1954.
Ṣadoq, Joseph. *Be-Saᶜarōt Tēmān: Megillat "Marvad ha-Qesāmīm"*. Tel Aviv, 1956.
Safran, Nadav. *Egypt in Search of Political Community*. Harvard Middle Eastern Studies 5. Cambridge, Mass., 1961.
Salīm, Muḥammad ᶜAbd al-Ra'ūf. *Ta'rīkh al-Ḥaraka al-Ṣahyūniyya al-Ḥadītha, 1897–1918*. Vol. 2. Cairo, 1974.
Samuel, Sydney Montagu. *Jewish Life in the East*. London, 1881.
Sassoon, David Sulayman. *Massaᶜ Bavel*. Jerusalem, 1954/55.
Sawdayee, Max. *All Waiting to Be Hanged: Iraq Post-Six-Day War Diary*. Edited by S. Benjamin. Tel Aviv, 1974.
Schanzer, Carlo. "Italian Colonial Policy in Northern Africa," *Foreign Affairs* 2, no. 3 (March 1924).
Schechtman, Joseph B. *On Wings of Eagles: The Plight, Exodus, and Homecoming of Oriental Jewry*. New York and London, 1961.
———. *Population Transfers in Asia*. New York, 1949.
Schröder, Bernd Philipp. *Deutschland und der Mittlere Osten im Zweiten Weltkrieg*. Studien und Dokumente zur Geschichte des Zweiten Weltkriegs, Bd. 16. Frankfurt and Zurich, 1975.
Schulmann, Zede. *Autobiographie: l'histoire de ma collection*. Chatillon-sous-Bagneux, 1980.
Schur, Wolf. "Mikhtevē Massāᶜ: Massāᶜ mi-Yam el Yam," *Magid-Mischne* 1, nos. 3–25 (January 8-June 25, 1879).

Schwarzfuchs, Simon, ed. *"L'Alliance" dans les communautés du bassin méditerranéen à la fin du 19ème siècle et son influence sur la situation sociale et culturelle. Actes du deuxième Congrès international de recherche du patrimoine des Juifs Sephardes et d'Orient 1985.* Jerusalem, 1987.
———. "Colonialisme français et colonialisme juif en Algérie (1830–1845)," *Judaïsme d'Afrique du Nord aux XIXe-XXe siècles.* Edited by Michel Abitbol. Jerusalem, 1980.
———. *Les Juifs d'Algérie et la France (1830–1855).* Jerusalem, 1981.
Seager, B. W. "The Yemen," *Royal Central Asian Journal* 42, Parts 3–4 (July–October, 1955).
Segev, Samuel. *Operation "Yakhin": The Secret Immigration of Moroccan Jews to Israel.* Tel Aviv, 1984 [Hebrew].
Segrè, Claudia G. *Fourth Shore: The Italian Colonization of Libya.* Chicago and London, 1974.
Sellon, Duley Marie Schueler. *French Influence on North African Evolués: The Problem of Cultural Identity.* Unpublished doctoral dissertation, University of Michigan, 1979.
Sémach, Yomtob D. *Une mission de l'Alliance au Yémen.* Paris, 1910?.
Sémach, Y. D. *A travers les communautés israélites d'Orient.* Paris, 1931.
———. "L'avenir des israélites marocains," *Paix et Droit* 7, no. 6 (June 1927), and ibid. 8, no. 6 (June 1928).
———. "Le recensement de 1936 au Maroc," *Paix et Droit* 19, no. 6 (June 1939).
Serfaty, A.B.M. *The Jews of Gibraltar under British Rule.* Gibraltar, 1953.
Shamir, Shimon. "The Influence of German National-Socialism on Radical Movements in Egypt," in *Germany and the Middle East.* Edited by Jehuda L. Wallach. Tel Aviv, 1975.
———, ed. *The Jews of Egypt: A Mediterranean Society in Modern Times.* Boulder, Colo., and London, 1987.
Shā'ul, Anwār. *Qiṣṣat Ḥayātī fī Wādi 'l-Rāfidayn.* Jerusalem, 1980.
Shawkat, Sāmī. *Hādhihi Ahdāfunā. Man Āmana bihā fa-Huwa Minnā: Majmū^{c}at Muḥāḍarāt wa-Maqālāt wa-Aḥadīth Qawmiyya.* Baghdad, 1939.
Shiblak, Abbas. *The Lure of Zion: The Case of the Iraqi Jews.* London, 1986.
Shiloah, Amnon, Cohen, Erik, and Ben-Ami, Issachar. *Jewish Communities from Central, Southern and Eastern Asia in Israel: A Compilation of Data.* Jerusalem, 1976 [Hebrew].
Shina, Shlomo, Elazar, Jacob, and Nahtomi, Emmanuel. *Perāqīm be-Tōldōt ha-Maḥteret.* Tel Aviv, 1970.
Shinar, Pessah. "Réflections sur la symbiose judéo-ibadite en Afrique du Nord," in *Communautés juives des marges sahariennes du Maghreb.* Edited by Michel Abitbol. Jerusalem, 1982.
Shochat, Azriel. *Beginnings of the Haskalah among German Jewry.* Jerusalem, 1960 [Hebrew].
Shokeid, Moshe, and Deshen, Shlomo. *Distant Relations: Ethnicity and Politics among Arabs and North African Jews in Israel.* New York, 1982.
———. *Dōr ha-Temūra* [The Generation of Transition: Continuity and Change among North African Immigrants in Israel]. Jerusalem, 1977.
Shorter Encyclopaedia of Islam. Edited by H.A.R. Gibb and J. H. Kramers. Leiden, 1965.
Silver, M. "Les Juifs de Kamechlié," *Paix et Droit* 14, no. 4 (April 1934).

Simon, Rachel. "The Jews of Libya on the Verge of Holocaust," *Peʿamim* 28 (1986) [Hebrew].
Simon, Reeva S. *Iraq between the Two World Wars: The Creation and Implementation of a Nationalist Ideology.* New York, 1986.
Slouschz, Nahum. "La colonie des Maghrabim en Palestine, ses origines et son état actuel," *AM* 2 (1904).
———. "Les Maghrabim à Jérusalem," *RMM* 6 (1908).
———. *Travels in North Africa.* Philadelphia, 1927.
Sluglett, Peter. *Britain in Iraq, 1914–1932.* Oxford, 1976.
Smooha, Sammy. *Israel: Pluralism and Conflict.* London, 1978.
Souriau, Christiane. "Mutations culturelles et presse maghrébine (VII)," *Annuaire de l'Afrique du Nord* 6 (1967).
Stafford, Lt.-Col. R. S. *The Tragedy of the Assyrians.* London, 1935.
Stark, Freya. *Dust in the Lion's Paw: Autobiography 1939–1946.* New York, 1961.
Stenographisches Protokol der Verhandlungen des II. Zionisten-Congresses gehalten zu Basel vom 28. bis 31. August 1898. Vienna, 1898.
Stillman, Norman A. "Antisemitism in the Contemporary Arab World," in *Antisemitism in the Contemporary World.* Edited by Michael Curtis. Boulder, Colo. and London, 1986.
———. "Fading Shadows of the Past: Jews in the Islamic World, in *Survey of Jewish Affairs 1989.* Edited by William Frankel. Oxford, 1989.
———. "Muslims and Jews in Morocco: Perceptions, Images, Stereotypes," in *Proceedings of the Seminar on Muslim-Jewish Relations in North Africa.* New York, 1975.
———. *The Jews of Arab Lands: A History and Source Book.* Philadelphia, 1979.
———. "The Response of the Jews of the Arab World to Antisemitism in the Modern Era," in *Living with Antisemitism: Modern Jewish Responses.* Edited by Jehuda Reinharz. Hanover and London, 1987.
———. "The Sefrou Remnant," *Jewish Social Studies* 35, nos. 3–4 (July–October 1973).
Stillman, Yedida K. *From Southern Morocco to Northern Israel: A Study in the Material Culture of Shelomi.* Haifa, 1982 [Hebrew].
———. "Libās," *EI*^{2} 5.
Stuart, Graham H. *The International City of Tangier.* 2nd ed. Stanford, 1955.
al-Sūdānī, Ṣādiq Ḥasan. *al-Nashāṭ al-Ṣahyūnī fi 'l-ʿIrāq, 1914–1952.* Baghdad, 1980.
Ṣūr, Yaron. *Taqriyyōt Augūst 1917—Anōṭōmiya shel Perāʿōt taḥat Shilṭōn Qōlōniyālī.* Master's thesis, Hebrew University, 1981.
Sutton, Joseph A. *Magic Carpet: Aleppo-in-Flatbush. The Story of a Unique Ethnic Jewish Community.* Forward by S. D. Goitein. New York, 1979.
Szajkowski, Zosa. *Analytical Franco-Jewish Gazetteer 1939–1945 with an Introduction to Some Problems in Writing the History of the Jews in France during World War II.* New York, 1966.
———. "The Schools of the Alliance Israélite Universelle," *Historia Judaica* 22, pt. 2 (April 1960).
———. "The Struggle for Jewish Emancipation in Algeria after the French Occupation," *Historia Judaica* 18, pt. 1 (April 1956).
Taggar, Yehuda. "The Farhud in the Arabic Writings of Iraqi Statesmen and Writers," *Peʿamim* 8 (1981) [Hebrew].

Taggar, Y. "The Iraqi Reaction to the Partition Plan for Palestine, 1937," in *The Palestinians and the Middle East Conflict.* Edited by Gabriel Ben-Dor. Ramat Gan, 1978.

Taragan, Bension. *Les communautés israélites d'Alexandrie: aperçu historique depuis les temps des Ptolémées jusqu'à nos jours.* Alexandria, 1932.

al-Taymūmī, al-Hādī. *al-Nashāṭ al-Ṣahyūnī bi-Tūnis, bayn 1897 & 1948.* Tunis, 1982. (*See also* under Timoumi, Hedi.)

Tessler, Mark, and Hawkins, Linda L. "The Political Culture of Jews in Tunisia and Morocco," *IJMES* 9, no. 1 (February 1978).

Thabault, Roger. "Le Maroc à l'heure du Vichysme," *Les Nouveaux Cahiers* 43 (Winter 1975–1976).

Tibawi, A. L. *American Interests in Syria; 1800–1901: A Study of Educational, Literary and Religious Work.* Oxford, 1966.

Tibi, Bassam. *Arab Nationalism: A Critical Enquiry.* Edited and translated by Marion Farouk-Sluglett and Peter Sluglett. London and Basingstoke, 1981.

Tillmann, Heinz. *Deutschlands Araberpolitik im Zweiten Weltkrieg.* Schriftenreihe des Instituts für Allegemeine Geschichte an der Martin-Luther-Universität Halle-Wittenberg, Band 2. Berlin, 1965.

Timoumi, Hedi. "Nushū' al-Ḥaraka al-Ṣahyūniyya fī Tūnis (1897–1941)," *Les Cahiers de Tunisie* 26, nos. 3–4 (1978). (*See also* under al-Taymūmī, al-Hādī.)

Tobi, Yosef. "An Epistle from Yemenite Jews to the London Jewish Community," in *The Jews of Yemen: Studies and Researches.* Edited by Yisrael Yeshaᶜyahu and Yosef Tobi. Jerusalem, 1975 [Hebrew].

———. "The Emissaries of the rabbinical Court of Sanᶜa to the Communities of Yemen," *Peᶜamim* no. 14 (1983) [Hebrew].

———. *The Jews of Yemen.* Bibliography of Jewish History, 2. Jerusalem, 1975.

———. *The Jews of Yemen in the 19th Century.* Tel Aviv, 1976 [Hebrew].

———, Barnai, Yaakov, Bar-Asher, Shalom, and Abitbol, Michael. *History of the Jews in the Islamic Countries. Part Two: From the Middle of the Nineteenth to the Middle of the Twentieth Century: Sources.* Jerusalem, 1986 [Hebrew].

Toffler, Alvin. *Future Shock.* New York, 1971.

Twena, Abraham Hayim, ed. *Jewry of Iraq: Dispersion and Liberation.* Ramla, 1981.

———. "The Diary of Abraham Twena," *The Scribe* 12, no. 11 (May–June 1973).

———, ed. *The Pogrom in Baghdad.* Ramla, 1977.

Udovitch, Abraham L., and Valensi, Lucette. "Communautés juives en pays d'Islam: Identité et communication à Djerba," *AESC* 35, nos. 3–4 (1980).

———. *The Last Arab Jews: The Communities of Jerba, Tunisia.* Social Orders, vol. 1. Chur, London, Paris, and New York, 1984.

Uhry, Isaac, ed. *Recueil des lois, décrets, ordonnances, avis du conseil d'état, arrêtés, règlements et circulaires concernant les Israélites (1850–1903),* 3rd ed. (Bordeaux, 1903).

United Restitution Organization, Ltd. *Judenverfolgung in Italien, den italienisch besetzen Gebieten und in Nordafrika.* Frankfurt a.M., 1962.

Vilnay, Zev. "ha-Yehūdīm ha-Maᶜarāviyyīm ke-Ḥalūṣē ha-Yishūv bā-Āreṣ," *Yehūdē Ṣefōn Afrīqa ve-Ereṣ Yisrā'ēl.* Edited by Shalom Bar-Asher and Aharon Maman. Jerusalem, 1981.

Voinot, L. *Pèlerinages judéo-musulmans du Maroc.* Paris, 1948.

Wallach, Jehuda L., ed. *Germany and the Middle East, 1835–1939.* Jahrbuch des Instituts für Deutsche Geschichte, Beiheft 1. Tel-Aviv, 1975.

Weingrod, Alex. *Israel: Group Relations in a New Society.* London, 1965.
———. *Reluctant Pioneers.* Ithaca, N.Y., 1966.
Weinschal, Jacob. *Markō Bārūkh: Nevī Milḥemet ha-Shiḥrūr.* Jerusalem, 1980.
Wild, Stefan. "National Socialism in the Arab Near East between 1933 and 1939," *WI* 25 (1985).
Williams, Bill. *The Making of Manchester Jewry, 1740–1875.* Manchester and New York, 1976.
Woolbert, Robert Gale. "Pan Arabism and the Palestine Problem," *Foreign Affairs* 16 (January 1938).
Woolfson, Marion. *Prophets in Babylon: Jews in the Arab World.* London and Boston, 1980.
Yaari, Avraham. *Shelūḥē Ereṣ Yisrā'ēl: Tōledōt ha-Shelīḥūt mēhā-Āreṣ la-Gōla mē-Ḥurbān Bayit Shēnī ᶜad ha-Mē'a ha-Teshaᶜ ᶜEsreh.* Jerusalem, 1950/51.
Yanait-Ben-Zvi, Rahel. *Be-Shelīḥūt li-Lvanōn ūle-Sūreya (1943).* Tel Aviv, 1979.
Yannai, Moshe, and Ḥaddād, Ephraim, ed. *Shōreshīm be-Yahadūt Tūnīsiya.* Beer Sheba, 1978.
Yehuda, Zvi, ed. *From Babylon to Jerusalem: Studies and Sources on Zionism and Aliya from Iraq.* Tel-Aviv, 1980 [Hebrew].
———. "Factors Which Influenced Zionist Activities in Egypt between 1897–1917," in *Miqqedem Umiyyam: Studies in the Jewry of Islamic Countries.* Edited by J. Barnai, J. Chetrit, et al. Haifa, 1981 [Hebrew].
———. "Ha-Irgūnīm ha-Ṣiyyōniyyīm be-Miṣrayim (1904–1917)," *Shevet ve-ᶜAm* 2nd series, 3 (1978).
———, ed. *Miqrā'ā le-Tōldōt ha-Yehūdīm be-Arṣōt hā-Islām ba-Dōrōt ha-Aḥarōnīm.* Haifa, 1978/79.
———. "On a Jewish Community in Iraq in an Era of Change: The Jewish Community of Hilla," in *Studies on History and Culture of Iraqi Jewry,* Vol. 2. Edited by Yitzhak Avishur. Or Yehuda, 1982 [Hebrew].
———. *Organized Zionism in Morocco: 1900–1948.* 2 vols. Unpublished doctoral dissertation, Hebrew University, Jerusalem, 1981 [Hebrew with English summary].
———. "Qeshārīm Ḥevratiyyīm bēn Yehūdīm li-Mūslimīm be-Bagdād be-Sōf ha-Mē'a ha-19 ᶜal pī Meqōrōt Yehūdiyyīm Meqōmiyyīm," *Ūmma ve-Tōledōtēhā* Part 2. Jerusalem, 1984.
———. "The Place of Aliyah in Moroccan Jewry's Conception of Zionism," *Studies in Zionism* 6, no. 2 (1985).
Yeshaᶜyahu, Yisrael, and Tobi, Yosef eds. *The Jews of Yemen: Studies and Researches.* Jerusalem, 1975 [Hebrew].
Zafrani, Haïm. *Mille ans de vie juive au Maroc: Histoire et culture, religion et magie.* Paris, 1983.
———. *Pédagogie juive en terre d'Islam: l'enseignement traditionnel de l'Hébreu et du Judaïsme au Maroc.* Paris, 1969.
Zawadowski, G. "Index de la presse indigène de Tunisie," *REI* 11 (1937).
Zenati, R. "La question juive: le problème algérien vu par un indigène," *Renseignements Coloniaux,* no. 6 (May–June 1938).
Zenner, Walter P. *Syrian Jewish Identification in Israel.* Unpublished doctoral dissertation, Columbia University, 1965.
Zohar, Zvi. *Halakha u-Modernīzaṣiyya: Darkhē Heᶜanūt Ḥakhmē Miṣrayim le-Etgarē ha-Modernīzaṣiyya, 1822—1882.* Jerusalem, 1982.

———. "Halakhic Responses of Syrian and Egyptian Rabbinical Authorities to Social and Technological Change," *Studies in Contemporary Jewry* 2 (1986).

———. "Quelques réflexions sur l'influence de l'Alliance sur les communautés juives en pays d'Islam et son caractère missionnaire," in *"L'Alliance" dans les communautés du bassin méditerranéen à la fin du 19ème siècle et son influence sur la situation sociale et culturelle.* Edited by Simon Schwarzfuchs. Jerusalem, 1987 [Hebrew].

Zohari, Menahem et al., eds. *Hāgūt ᶜIvrīt be-Arṣōt ha-Islām*. Jerusalem, 1981.

Zuaretz, F., et al. *Yahadūt Lūv.* Tel Aviv, 1960.

INDEX

INDEX

Ben Yahuda organization, 446
Benzakein, Félix, 53
Benzaquen, Léon, 172
Benzion department store, 153
Berber Dahir, 347
Berbers, 144, 207, 216, 218, 219, 302, 347, 538, 543, 545
Bergson group, 468
Berliawsky, Dr. J., 73
Berlin, 84, 118, 136
Bessis, Albert, 321
Bessis, Eugene, 321
Bessis, Victor, 321
bēt dīn (rabbinical court), 15–16, 76, 201, 248, 314, 534
Bevin, Ernest, 522
Bialik, Ḥayyim Nahman, 83, 278
Bible, 236, 237, 247, 252, 278, 279, 290, 326
biblical quotations, 186, 187, 208, 222, 241, 243, 290, 294, 295, 326
Bigart, Jacques, 90(n.68), 200
Biqqūr Ḥōlīm Society, 269
Bismut, Victor, 131
al-Biyālī, ᶜAbd al-Raḥmān, 511
Bizerte, 50, 173
Blackely, Brigadier, 462
blood feud, 218–19
B'nai B'rith (Bene Berith), 109, 135, 263, 308, 326, 511(n.2)
Board of Deputies of British Jews, 46
Bocarra, Guy, 131
Boccara, Jacob, 76
Bogdadly, Charles, 69
Bohbot, David, 72
Bokobza Company, 551
Bonan, Henry, 253
Bonan, Isaac, 253
Bonaparte, Napoleon, 3, 7
Borgel, Moïse, 131, 435–36, 438–39
Borgel, Robert, 131, 132(n.43)
Boulakia, Joseph, 321
Bourguiba, Ḥabīb, 172, 174, 365(n.2), 548–51
La Bourse Egyptienne, 109
Boyd, T. W., 418
Brami, Joseph, 77
Brazil, xviii, 38, 204
Brecher, Zvi Halevi, 36
Britian (British), 5, 7, 8, 13, 14, 19, 20, 41, 47, 48, 49, 51, 52, 55, 56, 57, 75, 86, 87, 89, 93, 94, 95, 100, 102, 103, 104, 110, 112, 113, 114, 116, 117, 118, 119, 122, 123, 127, 130, 131, 135, 137, 138, 141, 142, 144–46, 148, 153, 155, 156, 157, 158, 160, 166, 169, 172, 179, 240, 256, 261–62, 300, 301, 307–308, 311, 316, 324, 339, 342, 343, 362, 366, 371, 381, 385, 392, 393, 421, 431, 438, 443–46, 449, 450–55, 462, 463, 466, 467, 469, 471–503, 504, 515–21, 528, 529, 550
British Military Authority, 144–46, 155, 450–51, 462, 463, 465
British Syrian Mission School, 20
Brown, L. Carl, 13
Brunschvig, Robert, 127, 322(n.4), 323(n.5)
Buenos Aires, 205
Bukharans, 81
Bulgaria, 305
Bulletin de la Fédération des Sociétés juives d'Algérie, 510, 546
Bū Minjal (Boumendjel), Aḥmad, 127
Bureau for the Regulation of Jewish Affairs (Service de Réglementation des Questions Juives), 125, 134, 430
Bureau of Aryanization (Service de l'Aryanisation Economique), 125
burial, 191, 192–93, 209, 216, 224, 232–33, 445, 447, 463, 486
Burla, Yehuda, 82, 275–77

Cadima (Moroccan Zionist Organization), 171, 172, 174
Cairo, 5, 11, 20, 21, 22, 25, 38, 40, 68, 69, 70, 87, 88, 109, 114, 142–43, 147, 150, 152–53, 168, 169, 202, 220–21, 241, 245–46, 305–306, 352, 366, 378–80, 385, 393, 396, 402–403, 504, 507, 512, 515–16, 524, 528, 529, 554
Campbell, Sir Ronald, 153, 515–16
Canada, xviii, 175, 320
Canton, 206
capitulations, 3, 178
Caracas, 205
Carmel society and newspaper, 305
Casablanca, 33, 61, 88, 167, 174, 201, 203, 314–15, 318–19, 535
Casablanca Conference of African States, 174
Castro, Léon, 53, 109
Catholic(s, -ism), 20, 21, 143, 245–49, 370, 419, 543
Catroux, General, 115, 276
Cattan, Victor, 322
Cattaoui, Joseph Aslan, 54
Cattaoui, René, 505
Cattaoui, Yussuf Bey, 505
Caucasus, 49
Central British Fund for Jewish Relief and Rehabilitation, 500, 502, 520(n.1)
CESA. *See* Algerian Jewish Committee for Social Studies

Jaffa, 22, 24, 66, 202, 308
Jebel Gharian. *See* Ghariaan
Jebel Nefussa, 218
Jedda, 515
Jerada, 152
Jerusalem, 7, 10, 19, 22–23, 24, 25, 65, 66, 81, 97, 98, 102, 194, 197, 268, 271, 294, 295, 299, 314, 316, 342, 358, 365, 366, 377, 381, 414, 447, 451, 466, 469, 502, 515
Jewish: anti-Nazi boycott, 109–11, 378; assets confiscated or frozen, 125, 134, 151, 154, 163, 165, 168, 169, 511, 512(n.3), 537, 552, 554; assimilation of French culture, 16–18, 21, 28–29, 60, 71, 90, 123, 137, 139, 186–89, 250–52, 302, 322, 531, 542; assimilation of Italian culture, 30–31, 63, 78–79, 137, 155, 324, 419; attitudes toward Arabic language, 32–33, 179, 303–304, 542; attitudes toward European influence, 18, 22, 44–45, 47, 55, 58, 63–64, 178, 204, 256–58, 302, 467; attitudes toward westernization, 18, 22, 34, 44–45, 47, 63–64, 79, 82–83, 178, 187–89, 250–52, 302; cave dwellers, 207–19; communal council(s), 11, 52, 53, 56, 79, 80, 82, 105, 109, 118, 173, 190–96, 231–35, 257, 263–64, 265, 266, 267, 271, 321, 324, 368, 376, 436, 533–37, 548–49, 551; communal institutions, 16–17, 28, 53, 81, 82, 102, 109, 117, 121, 138, 147, 165, 190–96, 231–35, 263–71, 275–77, 284–87, 308, 314, 318, 325–26, 345–46, 361, 368, 374, 447–49, 475, 477, 504, 511(n.2), 533–36, 548–49, 554; communal organization, 11, 15–17, 30, 56, 81, 108, 123, 131–32, 150, 158, 165, 167, 169, 170–71, 173, 176, 190–96, 202, 225–26, 231–35, 263–71, 318, 324, 368, 374, 410, 415, 435–36, 447–49, 461–65, 480, 500, 533–36, 546, 548–49, 551; communal tensions and strife, 17, 21, 29, 41, 42, 53, 63, 78, 79, 80, 81, 132, 158–59, 167, 186, 217–18, 231–35, 267, 276, 277, 288–90, 335, 386–87; courtiers, 5, 54; crisis of identity, 35, 53, 170, 245–52; cultural transformations, xvii, 25, 28, 36, 82–83, 178, 179, 186, 222–24, 238–39, 243–52, 270–71, 275–93, 302–304, 531, 542; economic transformations, 25, 26, 178, 251, 461, 497, 498, 501, 542, 545; elite, 5, 6, 11, 20, 21, 28, 32, 35, 54, 55, 58, 60, 62, 63, 69, 70, 72, 74, 75, 76, 78–79, 80, 83, 90, 98, 108, 117, 123, 131, 132, 137, 138, 151, 153, 154, 158, 159, 164, 165, 167, 175, 206, 220–21, 222, 232, 233, 234, 250–52, 256–58, 260, 263, 270, 272, 277, 281, 286, 291, 297, 298, 324, 331–33, 337, 338, 363, 390, 392, 402–403, 418, 419, 421, 439, 453, 458, 500, 505; family, 20, 21, 28, 29, 37, 42–43, 80, 119, 167, 175, 177, 186, 199–201, 203, 205, 208, 209, 214, 222, 241, 244, 245, 247, 249, 250–52, 281, 316, 368, 410, 428, 454, 456, 457, 458, 461, 464, 516, 552; generation gap, 28, 41, 42–43, 186, 239, 252; homes described, 201, 207–19, 225, 265, 291, 297–98, 450–51, 454, 464, 471, 483, 501; intellectuals, 62, 77, 80, 82, 86, 132, 170, 251–52, 278–79, 337, 530–32, 542–47; lower class, 4, 5, 51, 79, 86–87, 132, 153, 160, 165, 167, 171, 222, 263, 265–67, 268, 281, 286, 291–93, 332, 418, 419, 421, 449, 487, 520; merchants, 5, 6, 14, 20, 31, 32, 72, 74, 78–79, 86, 103, 110, 119, 169, 203–206, 210, 218, 254–55, 291, 297, 330, 347, 360, 392, 447, 448, 538, 545, 551; middle class, 35, 39, 51, 60, 83, 86, 132, 154, 158, 165, 175, 250–52, 369, 461, 488, 544; migration, xvii-xviii, xix, 37–41, 49, 51, 66–67, 70, 72, 80, 87–88, 138, 148, 155–76, 177, 202–206, 213, 266, 291, 294–96, 314–17, 320, 336, 353, 354, 367–68, 418, 517–29, 553–54; occupations, 5–6, 25, 67, 69, 76, 78, 84, 86, 90, 100, 125–26, 134, 149–50, 153, 157, 169, 175, 176, 198, 203–206, 208–10, 212, 213, 215, 216, 217–18, 220, 222, 245, 251, 254, 261–62, 268, 270–71, 273, 291–92, 297, 316, 322, 330, 355, 360, 361, 367, 368, 383, 390, 406, 419–22, 447, 448, 455, 464, 467, 489, 490, 500, 502, 504–505, 506, 511, 534–36, 540, 542, 544, 551; orphans, 52, 82, 119, 147, 264–65, 266, 268, 295–96, 461, 464, 534; philanthropy, 22–23, 53, 65–66, 67, 71, 80, 83, 86, 108, 111, 155, 164, 165, 191, 194, 202, 220, 263–70, 285–86, 292, 355, 449, 450–51, 499, 500–503, 509–10; pro-French sentiment, 15, 49, 60–61, 71, 123–24, 137, 138, 170, 180, 247, 250–53, 270, 302, 314–19, 352, 371–75, 377, 396, 427–29, 537, 546; quarters, 5, 60, 79, 101, 103, 118, 142, 143–44, 147, 152–53, 154, 167, 197–98, 204, 207–19, 250, 251, 264, 266–67, 270, 285–86, 291, 297–99, 316, 357, 359, 360–62, 373, 376–77, 379, 383, 386, 390, 392, 398, 406–407, 416, 448, 453–56, 458, 462, 471, 472, 473, 476–96, 500, 501; responses to anti-Semitism, 104, 108–12, 123, 175, 351–52, 371–75; 387, 457–59; responses to Arab nationalism, 55, 57, 64, 98–99, 108, 110, 112, 139, 143, 170–71, 175, 180, 256–58, 328, 357–59, 371–75,

386–87, 389, 457–59, 531; scouts, 308, 348, 350, 376; social stress, 37, 41, 42, 52, 132, 153, 227, 264, 265, 328, 357–61, 372–73, 383, 386–87, 392, 461–503, 522–24; social transformations, xvii-xviii, 17–18, 25–26, 27–47, 123, 136–39, 178, 179, 180, 199–252, 467, 542; traditionalist opposition to modernization and westernization, 17, 19, 21, 23, 29, 187–89, 222–24, 243–44, 277, 278–79; underground organizations, 138, 152, 158, 162, 168, 457–59, 527; women, 19, 37, 52, 100, 137, 147, 188, 200, 201, 207, 208, 209, 210, 212, 213, 214, 215, 217, 220–22, 241, 243–44, 251, 252, 265, 266–67, 270–71, 276–77, 281, 286, 289, 292, 294, 296, 298, 299, 307–308, 310, 316, 325, 347, 359, 360, 368, 376, 383, 400, 406, 416, 419, 443, 454, 455, 456, 458, 461, 464, 469, 485, 489, 491, 495, 500, 509, 523–24; youth, 20–21, 28, 37, 38, 39, 42, 52, 68, 71, 72, 79, 82, 83, 88, 100, 108, 109, 115, 124, 126, 134, 137, 138, 139, 147, 155, 158, 166–67, 180, 186, 188, 191, 193, 194–95, 199–201, 203, 204, 205, 210, 212, 215, 218, 219, 220, 222, 232, 236–41, 244, 245–52, 261, 264–70, 275–77, 279, 280–87, 288, 289, 291–93, 296, 304, 308, 310, 316, 325, 326, 330, 337, 338, 347, 348, 350, 358, 376, 392, 416, 430, 441, 447, 448, 450, 454, 456, 458, 461, 464, 467, 474, 488, 491, 495, 509, 519, 523

Jewish Agency, 137, 156, 165, 167, 172, 329, 340, 365, 447, 469, 505

Jewish and Muslim attitudes toward westernization compared, 18, 178, 261

Jewish Chronicle, 369

Jewish Colonial Trust, 72, 74

Jewish law, 27, 36, 43–44, 188, 220–21, 225–26, 244, 534

Jewish Legion, 50

Jewish Literary Society (Jamᶜiyya Adabiyya Isrāʾīliyya), 86, 87, 337

Jewish National Council (Vaᶜad Le'ūmī), 400, 502

Jewish National Fund, 80, 86, 323, 326, 335, 342, 343, 344, 355, 455, 509

The Jewish State, 74, 306, 313

Jewish Territorial Organization, 74, 78

Jewish Youth Association (Damascus), 88–89, 328, 358

Jewish Youth Association of Constantine, 68, 71

Jewish Youth Movement (Beirut), 83

Jews: as cabinet ministers, 17, 54, 55, 172, 173; as consuls, 6, 131; as middlemen, 5–6, 25, 420, 421–22; as stateless persons, 54, 150, 161, 162, 165, 169, 529, 552, 553, 554; in Arab nationalist movements, 53, 170, 540, 546–47; in government service, 15–17, 21, 32, 54, 55, 149, 172, 173, 264, 314–15, 318, 321, 335, 369, 408, 420, 424, 448, 531; in military service, 9 (n.17), 49–50, 52, 62, 63, 100, 122, 123, 124, 137–38, 144, 146, 307, 418, 426, 428, 432, 443–46, 452–56; in modern Arabic cultural life, 33; in parliament, 54, 55, 56, 58, 61, 62, 86, 160, 335, 408, 467, 522, 523; in political life, 28, 53–54, 55, 57, 58, 61, 62, 63, 86, 109, 151, 160, 170, 172, 173, 277, 321, 335, 408, 522, 523, 546; seeking British citizenship, 55, 256–58; seeking French citizenship, 60

jihād, 148

jizya, 9, 50(n.8), 225, 298

Joint Distribution Committee. *See* American Joint Distribution Committee

Joshua, Hezkel, 206

Le Journal du Caire, 109

Judenrat, 131

Judeo-Arabic language, 28, 32, 69, 77, 79, 86, 206, 209, 213, 217, 237, 251, 281–83, 303–304, 318, 335

Le Juge (Zionist newspaper), 68

Juin, General, 134

al-Jundī, Sāmī, 106–107

Jung, Leo, 289

Kadimah (Zionist student association in Vienna), 68

Kadimah Club (Zionist youth organization in Damascus), 82, 275

Kadoorie, Sir Ellis, 341

Kadoorie, Sir Elly Silas, 285(n.3), 286, 292, 341

Kafr al-Zayyat, 40

Kahanoff, M. and Mme., 277

al-Kalīm (Karaite magazine), 166

Kanoui, Joseph, 429

Kant, 36

al-Karāda al-Sharqiyya quarter, 409

Karaites, 152–53, 166, 553, 554–55

al-Karkh, 406, 409, 410, 411, 412

kashrut, 36, 190, 194, 223, 243, 252, 374, 447, 537

Kedourie, Elie, 52

Kefar Yehezkel, 335–36

kenīs, 19, 236–37, 238

Keren Hayesod, 86, 320, 321, 322, 326, 333, 335–36, 353, 354, 355, 509

Mussolini, 116, 121, 419–20
Muṣṭafā Rashīd Pasha, 8
Muthannā Club, 107
Mzab, 29, 175, 538

Naamani, Michael, 354
Naan, 455
Nachmias, Leon, 307
Naguib. *See* Najīb, Muḥammad
Nahḍa (Revival), 33
al-Nahḍa (Iraqi newspaper), 95
al-Naḥḥās, Muṣṭafā, 114
Naḥmad, Ḥayyim, 224
Nahmad, Me'ir, 329–30
Nahum, Halfallah, 78–79, 447–49
Nahum, Ḥayyim, 114, 143, 231, 507–508
al-Nā'ib, Muḥammad Tawfīq, 405, 417
Najīb, Muḥammad, 168
Naquet, Alfred, 77
al-Nāṣirī, 14–15
Nasser. *See* ᶜAbd al-Nāṣir, Jamāl
Nasserism, 174
Nassi, M., 380, 403
Nataf, Albert, 131
Nataf, André, 131
Nataf, Elie, 131
Nataf, Félix, 21
Nataf, Lawyer, 438
National Socialism. *See* Nazi(s, -ism)
nationalism: Algerian, 127–28, 170–71, 537–41, 544, 546–47; Arab, 34, 53, 56, 58, 59, 64, 79, 84, 87, 88, 89, 93, 94–107, 112, 113, 115, 116, 120, 123, 127, 139, 141, 146, 149, 158, 165, 169, 170, 171, 173, 174, 179–80, 259–60, 272–74, 276, 328, 331–33, 345–50, 357–59, 365–66, 369, 371–75, 379–85, 397, 400, 467, 473, 474, 510, 524, 537–41, 544, 546–47; Egyptian, 34, 53–54, 95, 109, 165, 169; Iraqi, 56, 57, 87, 88, 95, 101, 116, 120, 158, 259–60, 331–33, 345–47, 389, 524; Jewish. *See* Zionism; Moroccan, 61, 97, 173, 348–50; North African, 59, 149, 170–75, 365–66, 467, 510; Syrian, 58, 59, 84, 88, 101, 106, 115, 272–74, 276, 328, 371–75, 383; Tunisian, 97, 99, 173, 365
Nazi(s, -sm), xvii, 93–94, 105–12, 116, 121, 125, 130–33, 180, 394, 413–15, 431, 435–42, 443, 444, 453, 454, 467, 542
Naẓmī, ᶜUmar, 159
Near East Transport Company, 157, 161
Nehring, General, 435
Neo-Destour party, 99
Netherlands, 301
Netter, Charles, 24
New York City, 39, 297, 509
Nhais, Saul, 400, 401
Nhaisi, Elia, 78, 79
Nietzche, 106
Nissim, Meshumor Shemuel, 354
Noam School, 286
Noguès, General, 133
Nordau, Max, 77
North Africa, xvii, xviii, 3, 4, 12–18, 20, 23, 24, 34, 38, 41, 44, 46, 47, 51, 65, 66, 71–80, 90, 93, 100, 106, 110–11, 113, 121–36, 137, 141, 166–68, 170–76, 178, 179, 302, 311–24, 363–66, 372, 397, 400, 419–56, 467–69, 509–10, 530–51
North America, 38, 53, 165, 175, 267, 268
numerus clausus, 125–26, 369, 430
al-Nuqrāshī Pasha, 143, 151, 155, 506, 511

OAS (Organisation Armée Secrète), 171, 175
Ohana, Joseph, 170
Hā-ᶜŌlām, 89
Operation Ali Baba, 161, 528
Operation Ezra and Nehemiah, 161, 164, 528
Operation Magic Carpet, 157, 161, 519
Operation on Wings of Eagles, 157, 519
opium, 206
Ōra ve-Simḥa Society, 78
Oran, 16, 40, 203, 429
al-Oreibi, Zaki, 506
Organizational Regulations of the Rabbinate, 10–11
Organizzazione Sionistica della Tripolitania, 80
Or ha-Maᶜarab (Moroccan Judeo-Arabic newspaper), 318, 319
Orthodox churches, 7, 143, 246, 276
Orthodox Judaism, 23, 44, 76, 217, 307
Ottoman Empire, 3, 4, 6–13, 14, 26, 29–30, 31, 46, 47, 48, 49, 52, 55, 56, 65, 79, 82, 85, 105, 178, 179, 183, 212, 216, 217, 218, 219, 225, 227, 229, 230, 231–35, 238, 254–55, 257, 273, 281, 284, 291, 299
Ottoman Zionist Society, 85
Oujda, 61, 152
Oulten, Lieutenant-Colonel, 462
ᶜŌzēr Dallīm Society, 266

al-Pachāchī, Muzaḥim, 523
Pact of ᶜUmar, 225–26
Paix et Droit, 369
Palestine, xviii, 3, 7, 8, 19, 39, 50, 52, 53, 63, 64, 65–67, 70, 80, 81, 87, 88, 89, 93,

Protestant(s, -ism), 8, 19, 20, 35, 246, 292
Protocols of the Elders of Zion, 104–105, 351–52
Provisional Commission for the Oversight of Jewish Religious Matters, 173
Puaux, Gabriel, 115, 396

al-Qādirī, Ṣādiq Pasha, 104
Qafiḥ, Yiḥye, 22, 225
Qamishli, 57, 164
al-Qaṣṣāb, ᶜAbd Allāh, 405, 417
Qayrawan, 50
Qusabat, 144, 145, 461

raᶜāya (subject population), 9
Rabat, 61, 167, 172, 314, 514
Rabbanites, 153
rabbinate: Algerian, 16–17, 29, 127, 186, 429, 538, 540; Egyptian, 43–44, 114, 143, 190, 191, 192, 194, 220–21, 241–42; French, 187–89, 540; Iraqi, 19, 102, 118, 158–59, 243–44, 288–90; Libyan, 79, 123, 207; Moroccan, 73, 74, 75, 79, 199–201, 314, 534; Ottoman, 10–12, 31, 231–35; Syrian, 82–83, 84, 222–24, 263, 267, 268, 272, 273, 277, 278–79; Tunisian, 76, 79, 321, 435–36
rabbinical attitudes toward modernization and westernization, 19, 21, 23, 34–35, 43–44, 45, 79, 82–83, 222–24, 239, 241, 243–44, 277, 278–79, 288–90
rabbinical court. *See bēt dīn*
rabbinical emissaries (*shelūḥē de-rabbānān*), 65, 194
rabbinical literature, 36–37, 43–44, 188, 200, 208–209, 217–18, 220–24, 243–44, 252, 278–79
Rabinowitz, Louis, 443, 445–46
racial laws, 64, 115, 121, 124–26, 134, 137, 419–25, 447, 448
Ra'fat, Ḥamīd, 408, 412–13
Rahmany, A., 392
Rahn, Rudolf, 130, 133
Ramadan, 515
Rashīd ᶜĀlī. *See* al-Gaylānī, Rashīd ᶜĀlī
Rauff, Colonel, 435–36, 438–39, 440
Red Cross. *See* International Red Cross
Reform Judaism, 35, 44
reformers and reform movements, 8, 11–14, 17, 45, 48, 186–89, 227–35
refugees: European Jewish, 108, 142, 143, 167, 320, 367–68, 394; Middle Eastern and North African Jewish, 148, 155–64, 169, 175, 180, 202, 294–96, 454, 517–19; Palestinian Arab, 158, 523
Reifenberg, Adolf, 445
Reiter, Alexandre, 540
religious observance: decline in. *See* secularization
Rescue Youth (Shabāb al-Inqādh), 138
Resistance, 134–35, 433–34, 544
responsa, 43–44, 220–21
Reuters, 518, 519
Reveil Juif (Tunisian Revisionist newspaper), 99, 323
Revisionist Zionism, 99, 323, 392, 468, 509
Revka Nouriel School, 286
Revolutionary Command Council, 168
Riḍā, Rashīd, 45
Rifaᶜat, Ḥasan, 153
Rio de Janeiro, 204
rivalry between European powers, 3, 13, 75, 89
Rivlin, Joseph Joel, 82, 263–73
Rōdefē Ṣedeq Society, 266–67
Rolo, Robert J., 403
Rolo family, 50
Romanelli, Samuel, 5
Romano, Marco, 323
Rome, 302, 425, 554
Rommel, Erwin, 113–14, 129, 180
Roosevelt, Franklin D., 439(n.4)
Rosen, Lawrence, 41
Rosenthal, Joseph, 54
Rothschild, Maurice de, 367
Rothschild family, 22, 273
Ruṣāfa quarter, 406, 411
Russia, 7, 73, 302, 307, 320, 324
Rutba, 418

Saᶜāda, Anṭūn, 106
Saᶜadya Gaon, 237
al-Ṣabāḥ (Egyptian newspaper), 506
al-Ṣabāḥ (Tunisian Jewish newspaper), 77
al-Sabᶜāwī, Yūnis, 116, 118, 412–13, 415–16
al-Sabᶜāwī National Force, 118, 412
Sabbah, Marc, 172
Sabbatay Ṣevi and Sabbatianism, 65
Sabbath desecration, 14, 21, 36, 63, 207(n.2), 223–24, 243, 374, 399, 447, 533
Sacher, Harry, 341
Sacks, Nathan, 469
Saevecke, SS-Hauptsturmführer, 425
Safed, 65, 94, 194, 359
Safi, 73, 312–13

Sahara, 17, 175, 210, 214, 215, 218
al-Saᶜīd, Nūrī, 101–102, 151, 158, 161, 163
Ṣāliḥ, Saᶜdī, 405, 417
Salonika, 227, 329
Samama, Felix, 131
Samuel, Sir Herbert, 326
Sanᶜa, 12, 22, 225–26, 236–39, 297–99
San Remo Conference, 79, 87, 309, 320
Ṣanūᶜ, Jacob, 33, 34
Sarfaty, Vidal, 199
Sasson, Aaron, 86, 334(n.3), 342–44
Sasson, Heskell, 288–90
Sassoon, David, 206
Sassoon, Elias David, 206
Saudi Arabia, 100
Sawṭ al-Umma, 506
schools: agricultural 24, 25; Alliance, 21, 23–25, 28, 30, 31, 33, 34–35, 37, 38, 42, 58, 72, 75, 81, 108, 123–24, 126, 199, 201, 204, 205, 235, 240–42, 244, 250–52, 257(n.1), 269, 270, 276, 277, 280, 283, 284–87, 292–93, 303–304, 308, 347, 368, 376, 392, 396, 533; for girls, 19, 20, 22, 24, 82, 191, 194, 244, 269–70, 285–86, 477; lay, 21, 28, 37, 58, 63, 121, 126, 241, 250–52, 287, 369, 430, 447; military, 253; missionary, 19–21, 25, 35, 58, 179, 245–47, 270, 292; modern Jewish, 16, 21–25, 28, 31, 33, 37, 42, 68, 69, 72, 75, 79, 81–82, 83, 85, 88, 108, 109, 121, 123, 126–27, 138, 147, 148, 165, 169, 173, 199, 204, 205, 238–42, 244, 250–52, 264, 269–70, 274, 275, 280, 283, 284–87, 292–93, 303–304, 308, 334, 342, 346, 347, 368, 376, 392, 396, 419, 430, 445, 449, 452, 475, 477, 497, 498, 502–503, 533, 554; traditional Jewish, 19, 22, 42, 147, 191, 194–95, 197, 211, 212, 236–37, 241, 252, 264, 269–70, 449; university level, 25, 126, 170, 177, 257, 268, 273, 284, 322, 369, 379–80, 385, 445, 522, 524; vocational, 19, 25, 286, 407; Zionist, 69, 79, 81–82, 83, 85, 88, 138, 264, 269–70, 274, 275, 308, 334, 342, 445, 452
Schwartz, Joseph, 22
Schwarzbart, I., 509
Schwarzfuchs, Simon, 17
secularization, 27–29, 30, 35–36, 41, 42, 43, 77, 79, 96, 97, 186–89, 222–24, 243–44, 250–52, 270, 277
ha-Ṣefīra (Hebrew newspaper), 35, 36
Sefrou, 74, 534
Ṣeᶜīrē Benē Yehūda, 334
Selective Immigration (*seleqṣeya*), 167–68, 171
seleqṣeya. See Selective Immigration
Sémach, Yomtob, 81, 235, 236–39, 284–87, 291–93
Sephardi(m), 6, 31, 32, 43, 44, 66, 68, 69, 70, 80, 81, 83, 88, 298, 307(n.4), 310(n.2), 322–23, 325–27, 329–30, 340, 353(n.3), 359, 552, 553, 554
Sephardi Federation, 325, 326, 329–30
serāra, 536
Serfaty, Abner, 74
Serrero, Ḥayyim David, 74
La Settimana Israelitica (Italian Jewish weekly), 78, 79
Sfax, 50, 76, 99, 131, 321, 365
Sfez, Batto, 12
al-Shaᶜab, 328
Shaᶜarē Ṣiyyōn Society, 72–73
Shahbandar, ᶜAbd al-Raḥmān, 273
al-Shams (Egyptian Jewish newspaper), 505
Shanghai, 38, 206
Shanshal, Ṣiddīq, 412
Shavuᶜot, 118, 194, 309, 405, 457
Shawkāt, Sāmī, 116
sheḥīṭa, 190, 207, 217–18, 374, 536
Sheikh Othman, 471, 472, 475, 487–89, 496–97, 500, 501
shekels, 69, 70, 73, 74, 75, 85, 307, 312, 335, 343
Shemtov, Ezekiel Gurgi, 336, 341
Shertock, Moshe, 365, 467
Shevet Aḥīm Society, 266
Shiᶜite(s), 12, 295(n.9), 299
Shina, Salmān, 87, 337–39
Shivat Ṣiyyōn Society, 73
Shulḥan ᶜArūkh, 220–21, 223, 224, 244
Sidi, Maurice, 227, 240, 351
Sidi Azzaz, 122
Sidi-Bel-Abbes, 204, 544(n.10)
Sidon, 83, 197–98, 272, 390–92
Sidqī, Bakr, 413–14
Silberstein, A., 328, 357–59
Silvera, Victor, 133
Simel, 57
al-Sirāḥa (Egyptian daily), 166
Sirte, 445
Sitruk, Moche, 321
ṣlā, 19, 215
Smadja, Albert, 429
Smadja, Edmond, 132
Smadja, Isaac, 132
Smooha (Egyptian philanthropist), 268
social stratification, 5, 11, 51, 60, 132, 139, 154, 160, 165, 167, 179, 229–30, 267, 281, 286, 324, 332, 334, 337, 355, 383, 421, 458, 527
La Société Nouvelle (French review), 77

Young Men's Muslim Association, 96, 98, 142, 381–82
Young Tunisians, 97
Young Turks, 31, 39, 48, 49, 227, 365
Youth Phalanxes (Katā'ib al-Shabāb), 117, 118, 407, 412, 415

Zaghlūl, Saᶜd, 53
Zagury, Yahya, 314–15, 318–19
al-Zahāwī, Khālid (Mutaṣarrif of Baghdad), 407–409, 411–13
al-Zaᶜīm, Ḥusnī, 154
Zaja, David, 273
Zamar, 298
Zangwill, Israel, 74, 75, 78
Zanzur, 144, 461, 462, 463
Zawia, 144, 461, 462, 463
Zaydī(s), 12, 295(n.9), 299
Zeire Zion Society, 307, 310
Zeloof, Ezra H., 470
Zifta, 40
Zion Mule Corps, 50
Zionism, xix, 44, 53, 63, 64, 65–91, 93, 94, 95, 96, 97, 98, 99, 101, 102, 112, 114, 120, 123, 137–39, 141, 142, 143, 145, 146, 148, 150, 151, 156, 158, 160–61, 162, 165, 166, 170, 171, 172, 174, 180, 272, 273, 275–77, 298, 305–55, 382, 383, 386, 389, 455–56, 466, 467–68, 469, 504–13, 527, 540, 547; in Aden, 353–55; in Algeria, 68, 71, 166, 509–10, 547; in Egypt, 67–70, 84, 87, 88, 90, 98–99, 114, 137, 305–10, 322, 504–506, 511–12; in Iraq, 84–87, 90, 98, 120, 137, 138, 158, 160–61, 162, 331–47, 527; in Lebanon, 80, 81, 83–84, 88, 137, 325–27; in Libya, 76, 78–80, 88, 137, 138, 155, 324, 455–56, 467–68; in Morocco, 71, 72–75, 76, 78, 84, 87, 88, 89, 97, 99, 166, 171, 172, 174, 311–19, 348–50, 509; in Syria, 80–84, 90, 137, 138, 273, 275–77, 329–30; in Tunisia, 71, 73, 76–78, 79, 84, 87, 88, 90–91, 97, 99, 137, 166, 320–23, 382, 468, 509
Zionist congresses, 68, 71, 72, 73, 76, 323(n.5), 340
Zīwar Pasha, 54, 95, 307, 308

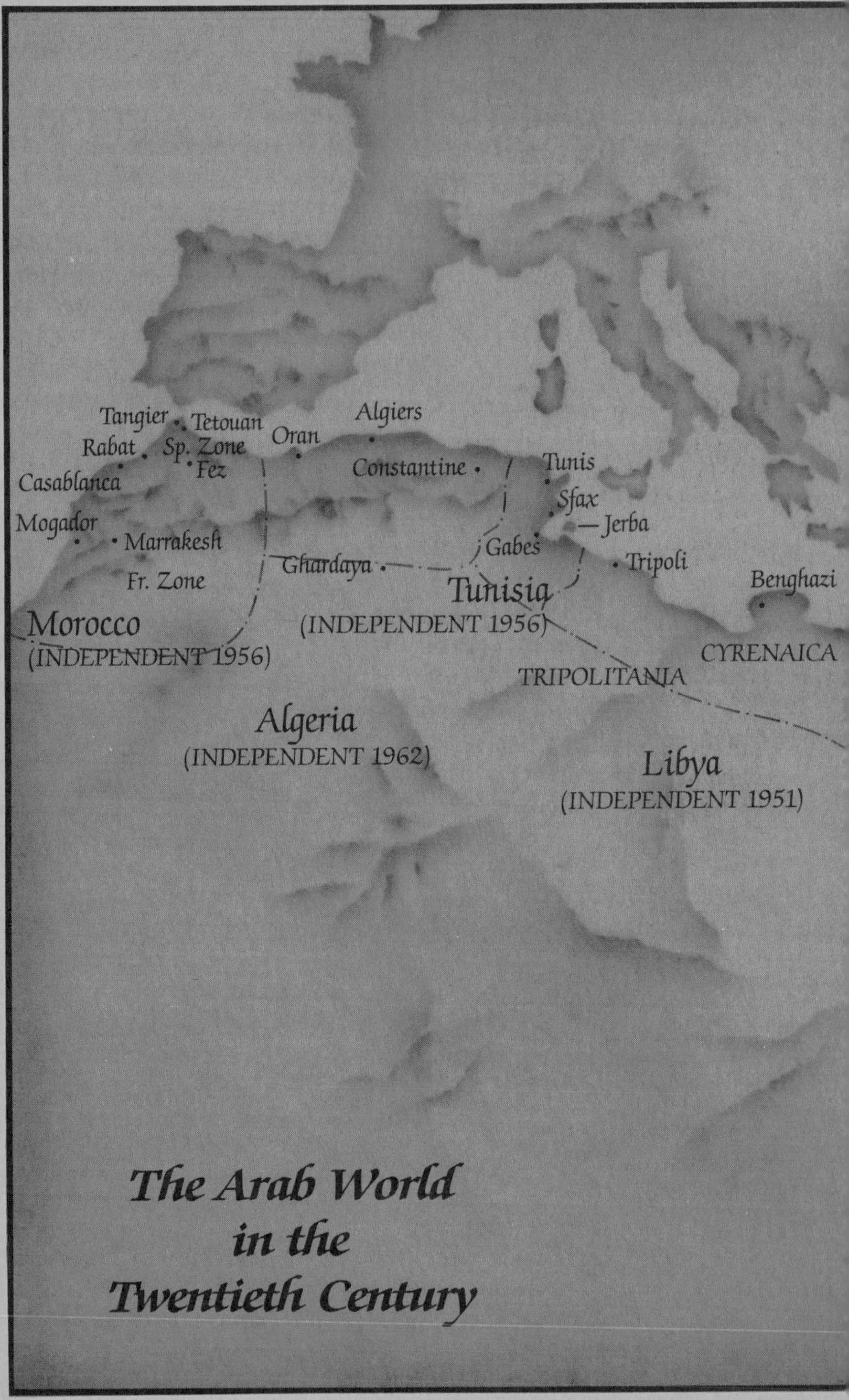
Tangier
Tetouan
Rabat
Sp. Zone
Fez
Casablanca
Oran
Algiers
Constantine
Tunis
Sfax
Jerba
Gabes
Tripoli
Benghazi
Mogador
Marrakesh
Fr. Zone
Ghardaya
Morocco
(INDEPENDENT 1956)
Tunisia
(INDEPENDENT 1956)
CYRENAICA
TRIPOLITANIA
Algeria
(INDEPENDENT 1962)
Libya
(INDEPENDENT 1951)
The Arab World in the Twentieth Century